ALMANACS OF AMERICAN WARS

MIDDLE EAST ALMANAC

U.S. MILITARY ACTION IN THE REGION, 1979 TO THE PRESENT

John C. Fredriksen

Facts On File
An Infobase Learning Company

Middle East Almanac

Facts On File, Inc.
An imprint of Infobase Learning
132 West 31st Street
New York N.Y. 10001

Library of Congress Cataloging-in-Publication Data
Fredriksen, John C.
    Middle East almanac / John C. Fredriksen.
        p. cm.
    Includes bibliographical references and index.
    ISBN 978-0-8160-8094-6 (hc : alk. paper) 1. Middle East—History, Military—20th century—Chronology. 2. Middle East—History, Military—21st century—Chronology. I. Title.
    DS63.15.F77 2011
    956.05021'02—dc22   2010011873

Facts On File books are available at special discounts when purchased in bulk quantities for businesses, associations, institutions, or sales promotions. Please call our Special Sales Department in New York at (212) 967-8800 or (800) 322-8755.

You can find Facts On File on the World Wide Web at http://www.factsonfile.com

Text design by Erika K. Arroyo
Composition by A Good Thing, Inc.
Cover printed by Sheridan Books, Ann Arbor, Mich.
Book printed and bound by Sheridan Books, Ann Arbor, Mich.
Date printed: February 2011

Printed in the United States of America

10 9 8 7 6 5 4 3 2 1

This book is printed on acid-free paper.

# CONTENTS

≋ Introduction

The Middle East region is historically significant in having bequeathed to humanity some of its most important legal, religious, and architectural legacies. From the law code of Hammurabi to the hanging gardens of Babylon, the Persian Empire, and the rise of Islam, all constitute important human achievements that, in one way or another, still resonate in modern times. Yet, while culturally enriching, this same region has an unfortunate legacy of, and tendency toward, extremism and violence. For our purposes, the contemporary crises originated in the seminal year of 1979, when the shah of Iran was overthrown by Islamic populism, while Afghanistan, distant and remote to Western minds, was thrust to the forefront of the cold war through a brutal and protracted Soviet invasion. These occurrences were followed within months by a third and equally deadly event, the Iraqi invasion of Iran, an inconclusive eight-year-struggle that consumed hundreds of thousands of lives. The net result of all these events was that the United States's military presence, heretofore marginal, grew exponentially as its strategic interests in the region were perceived as threatened. This activity varied from clandestine military assistance to the Afghan mujahideen and the restoration of diplomatic ties with Iraq (in concert with military intelligence for fighting Iran), to directly engaging Iranian naval vessels in the Persian Gulf, to open assistance to the governments of Lebanon, Saudi Arabia, and other Middle Eastern states.

The end of the Iran-Iraq struggle in 1988 and the Soviet withdrawal from Afghanistan in 1989 restored some semblance of peace to those nations, but not for long. In the summer of 1990 the Iraqi dictator Saddam Hussein egregiously miscalculated by invading and annexing the oil-rich kingdom of Kuwait, which triggered a massive Western military response headed by the United States, and culminated in the disastrous Gulf War of the following spring. Meanwhile, a major outgrowth of the Afghan conflict was an internecine power struggle raging in its wake, coupled with the rise of the ultraconservative Taliban movement, which ultimately controlled 90 percent of the country by 2000. Worse yet for the United States, a religious-based Saudi dissident named Osama bin Laden began orchestrating a global campaign of terror against its assets in Africa and the Middle East to prompt the removal of American forces from Saudi Arabia. The Taliban regime in Kabul willingly accommodated bin Laden for several years out of religious kinship, even after his dastardly destruction of the World Trade Center in New York City on September 11, 2001. This singular act was a catalyst for U.S. intervention in Central Asia for the first time, which drove the Taliban from power and resulted in an American protectorate until legitimate, stable governance could arise. However, the raw impact of 9/11 stimulated fears of similar attacks by weapons of mass destruction possessed by Saddam Hussein—the same dictator who recklessly invaded Iran in 1980, brutally occupied Kuwait, used poison gas against his own populace, and openly defied UN weapons inspectors for a decade—and induced the United States to preemptively topple him. So, between 2001 and 2009, the United States military found itself locked in its largest overseas combat commitments since World War II, and in regions that had scarcely seen an American footprint. For the Middle East, long a witness to invading armies over the past five millennia, this event is simply the latest thread in a long historical tapestry.

The overall thrust of this book's contents is military, hence subject headings covering aviation, military, and naval occurrences, but these matters are rounded out with relevant entries on politics and diplomacy. Given the close association of Islam to the conduct of state affairs, issues of religious import are also listed under politics, the realm in which these topics are usually addressed. Furthermore, terrorism has experienced widespread proliferation throughout the region and warrants detailed coverage down to individual acts. Also included are 41 biographies of leading personalities, religious figures, and generals, appreciation of whom better contextualizes our understanding of events. Finally, a bibliography of the latest scholarship, carefully subdivided for ease of subject access, is appended. From this assemblage of information, one can readily discern the ebb and flow of events in this strategic region, the terrible rise of modern-day terrorism, and the slow but inexorable pace of American involvement there since 1979. Three decades are but the merest of snapshots in Middle Eastern history, but its context and relevance to contemporary audiences is significant, compelling, and worthy of our attention.

From an American perspective, this book also focuses considerable attention on Operations Enduring Freedom in Afghanistan and Iraqi Freedom, as both remain works in progress. It is surprising how the former endeavor, which proved an almost bloodless military triumph in late 2001, has degenerated into a seemingly intractable guerrilla war with Taliban fanatics. It was not until January 2009, with the inauguration of President Barack Obama, that a complete overhaul of strategy was initiated, which de-emphasizes military action in favor of greater preparation of the Afghan military. Ironically, the United States has enjoyed demonstrably better results in Iraq, which previously appeared engulfed by a violent Sunni-based insurgency that was aided and abetted by the al-Qaeda terrorist network. However, a decisive corner was turned by the "military surge" initiated by President George W. Bush in 2007, coupled with the so-called Sunni awakening that turned many tribesmen against the terrorist movement. It appears that by staying the course the Americans have finally brought viable stability, security, and democracy to that fractious nation, and indigenous security forces can now adequately police it. Such a turn of events appeared unthinkable between 2003 and 2006, which only underscores the old saw that the only predictable thing about the Middle East is its unpredictability!

Finally, the current situation with Iran, while not directly confrontational, certainly merits closer scrutiny within the overall context of regional security. Since 1979, suffice it to say that the mullahs have waged what can only be described as a low-intensity conflict with the United States, including a national hostage situation; a high-profile, failed rescue mission; direct naval conflict in the Persian Gulf; the accidental downing of an Iranian airliner; and a surreptitious proxy war in Iraq by providing Shiite militias and others with modern, shaped ballistic charges and other weapons. Iran also is suspected of similar complicity in neighboring Afghanistan. All these activities resulted in the deaths of several American servicemen and the detainment of others. If the current standoff regarding Iran's uranium enrichment program and the real possibility of nuclear weapons being manufactured is not peacefully resolved, the specter of military intervention cannot be blithely dismissed. This potentially calamitous event could involve military forces from Israel, the United States, or a coalition of concerned Western—and Muslim—powers. The past three decades have certainly transformed Iran from a reliable American ally into an unremitting adversary, while posing a direct challenge to traditionally Sunni Arab states for leadership in the Islamic world. The widespread domestic unrest arising from the hotly contested 2009 presidential election also suggests that the outbreak of political violence is never far from the surface. In sum, Iran is very much connected to the region in terms of history, geography, and religion, and whatever befalls the current regime may very well dictate the fate of neighboring states as well.

The author extends his thanks to editor Owen Lancer for calling this project to his attention. It was arduous and time-consuming to produce but left me with a profound appreciation of this region, its mosaic-like complexity, and the diverse nature of its players. May others find it as informative.

—John C. Fredriksen, Ph.D.

≋ CHRONOLOGY

1979

January
POLITICS: Throughout Afghanistan, security forces controlled by the Khalq faction of the People's Democratic Party of Afghanistan (PDPA) initiate a massive crackdown against dissent. Many Western-educated intellectuals, Chinese-inspired "Maoists," and other members of the country's elite are imprisoned at the concentration camp near Pul-i-Charki, east of Kabul. Hundreds of others, mostly Muslim fundamentalists, are executed and bulldozed into unmarked graves. The Mojaddedis, a leading religious family, loses 96 male members to the firing squad in a matter of hours.

January 6
POLITICS: In Tehran, Iran, Shahpur Bakhtiar is appointed the new prime minister by Mohammad Reza Shah Pahlavi. Despite this new civilian regime, Bakhtiar fails to gains support from religious and secular opposition groups, and the nation is convulsed by political unrest. A crowd of protestors estimated to number 100,000 fills the streets of Qom, a holy city.

In Paris, France, Ayatollah Ruhollah Khomeini calls upon civil servants and government employees not to obey the new civilian administration.

January 7
MILITARY: Afghan resistance spokesmen in Pakistan claim that 5,000 mujahideen are resisting the Soviet-inspired regime in Kabul, Afghanistan.

January 8
POLITICS: Antigovernment rioting in Tehran, Iran, results in at least four deaths.

January 9
DIPLOMACY: In light of mounting instability and violence, the United States advises Mohammad Reza Shah Pahlavi to depart the country for good.

January 16
DIPLOMACY: A rising tide of Islamic extremism forces Mohammad Reza Shah Pahlavi to abdicate after 37 years on the throne. He flees to Egypt, and his departure threatens to roil the entire Persian Gulf region with anti-Western unrest.

January 17
POLITICS: From his exile in Paris, France, Ayatollah Khomeini urges his supporters to continue demonstrating and striking in an attempt to bring down the government of Shahpur Bakhtiar. He also encourages the military to abandon its past allegiance to the deposed shah.

January 19
POLITICS: In Tehran, Iran, nearly 1 million supporters of Ayatollah Khomeini turn out in a massive demonstration against the government. However, Prime Minister Shahpur Bakhtiar refuses to step down because people have fallen under the influence of a "religious personality."

January 20
POLITICS: In Paris, France, Ayatollah Khomeini announces his decision to return to Iran and demands the resignation of the present government. He also warns the military of a "holy war" should it interfere with a coup attempt.

January 25
POLITICS: In Tehran, Iran, Prime Minister Shahpur Bakhtiar offers to resign if Ayatollah Khomeini delays his return and allows the people to decide what type of governance they want. Antigovernment rioting takes 60 lives over the next few days as Khomeini insists that Bakhtiar resign from power before a deal can be negotiated.

January 28
MILITARY: The first mujahideen attacks on Afghan government personnel are reported in the eastern provinces bordering Pakistan.

January 30
DIPLOMACY: In Tehran, Iran, the U.S. embassy orders all dependents and nonessential personnel out of the country. The Iranian government, such as it is, also approves the return of Ayatollah Khomeini, who, in any event, is arriving on his own terms.

February 1
POLITICS: In Tehran, Iran, Ayatollah Khomeini returns to his homeland after 15 years in exile and is greeted by a throng estimated at 3 million people. He declares his intention to establish an Islamic republic to replace the three-week old civilian regime of Prime Minister Shahpur Bakhtiar and threatens to arrest the latter if he does not resign. Bakhtiar, however, refuses to step down and insists he will not allow the country to be run by any force "other then the legitimate authority."

February 2
MILITARY: In Peshawar, Pakistan, large numbers of future Afghan guerrilla fighters begin gathering and organizing for an assault on the communist regime.
POLITICS: In Tehran, Iran, Prime Minister Shahpur Bakhtair offers to form a new government with the support of Ayatollah Khomeini in his cabinet, but the latter still insists that he resign before negotiations can take place.

February 5

POLITICS: In Tehran, Iran, Mehdi Bazargan is appointed the new prime minister of a "provisional government" by Ayatollah Khomeini. This induces Shahpur Bakhtiar, the last prime minister appointed by the shah to threaten to resign from office.

February 6

NAVAL: At the ports of Bandar Abbas and Char Bahar, Iran, 200 Americans and 240 foreign nationals are evacuated by the command ship USS *La Salle*, the destroyers *Blandy, Decatur, Hoel,* and *Kincaid,* and the frigate *Talbot.*

February 8

POLITICS: In Tehran, Iran, an estimated 1 million people demonstrate in the streets and demand the resignation of Prime Minister Shahpur Bakhtiar.

February 9–11

POLITICS: A week of fighting in the streets of Tehran between competing groups of revolutionaries results in the deaths of at least 500 people.

February 11

POLITICS: The Iranian military finally declares its neutrality and orders all troops back to their barracks, whereupon Prime Minister Shahpur Bakhtiar formally resigns.

February 12

MILITARY: Throughout Iran, supporters of Ayatollah Khomeini forcibly subdue the last remaining centers of military resistance to the ayatollah, who appeals for calm in the streets of Tehran.

February 14

DIPLOMACY: In Kabul, Afghanistan, an alleged "Maoist" commando unit kidnaps U.S. ambassador Adolph Dubs, who subsequently dies during a botched rescue attempt directed by Soviet security personnel.

In Tehran, Iran, leftist guerrillas attack the U.S. embassy, taking several Marine guards and Ambassador William Sullivan hostage for two hours. They are ultimately freed by supporters of Ayatollah Khomeini.

POLITICS: In Tehran, Iran, Prime Minister Mehdi Bazargan appoints seven ministers to the new revolutionary government, which is slated to have a distinct "Islamic" character and a mixed economy.

February 15

DIPLOMACY: In Washington, D.C., Acting Secretary of State Christopher Warren issues a strongly worded protest to Soviet ambassador Anatoly Dobrynin over the death of Ambassador

Mohammad Reza Pahlavi, shah of Iran, and his daughter Princess Farah prepare to depart the United States after a visit in 1977. *(Department of Defense)*

Adolph Dubs in Afghanistan. The government accuses Soviet military advisers of directing the action that lead to the ambassador's death.

February 16–20
MILITARY: In Iran, four army generals are executed by revolutionary forces, signaling a violent purge of the shah's former supporters.

February 17
POLITICS: Throughout Iran, oil workers call off their national strike and return to the fields.

February 19
DIPLOMACY: In Kabul, Afghanistan, Foreign Minister Hafizullah Amin rejects diplomatic protests from the United States over the killing of Ambassador Adolph Dubs, dismissing the charges as "completely baseless."

February 22
DIPLOMACY: In Washington, D.C., President Jimmy Carter responds to the death of Ambassador Adolph Dubs with reduced levels of foreign assistance for Afghanistan. Diplomatic staff is also reduced.

February 28
MILITARY: The United States is forced to abandon two electronic eavesdropping stations in northern Iran that had been listening to Soviet radio transmissions.
POLITICS: In Tehran, Iran, Prime Minister Mehdi Bazargan threatens to resign if Ayatollah Khomeini's Revolutionary Council does not stop interfering with his administration.

March 7
POLITICS: In Tehran, Iran, Ayatollah Khomeini goes on record as saying that all women working in government ministries must be clothed according to "religious standards."

March 8
POLITICS: In Tehran, Iran, Prime Minister Mehdi Bazargan, angered by what he considers interference by the Revolutionary Council, tenders his resignation. Ayatollah Khomeini refuses to accept it.

March 8–12
POLITICS: In Tehran, Iran, thousands of women take to the streets to protest Islamic-based restrictions on their rights, especially the mandatory wearing of veils and black cloaks in public.

March 9
AVIATION: Operation Flying Star unfolds as two E-3A AWACS aircraft are dispatched to Saudi Arabia following perceived threats from revolutionary Iran.

March 10
MILITARY: In Herat Province, Afghanistan, armed Muslim fundamentalists, or mujahideen (holy warriors), commence a protracted insurrection against the communist regime in Kabul. They are soon joined by the army garrison of Herat, which

links up with insurgents led by Ismail Khan of the religious movement Jamiat-i-Islami Herat is subsequently recaptured by government forces, backed by Soviet warplanes, but by then the rebellion has also spread to Farah, Ghowr, and Badghis Provinces.

March 16

POLITICS: In Iran, summary trials and executions conducted by the Revolutionary Council result in 60 deaths over the past month. Ayatollah Khomeini consequently meets with Prime Minister Mehdi Bazargan and orders a halt to secret trials and political killings. The prime minister has publicly bemoaned the executions as "irreligious, inhumane, and a disgrace."

March 18

MILITARY: Kurdish militants in northeastern Iran rebel against the government in Tehran, Iran, leading to the deaths of more than 100 people. Ayatollah Mahmoud Taleghani, the second-ranking religious leader in the nation, is dispatched there to restore order.

March 21

MILITARY: Afghan resistance fighters stage a serious assault against Afghan army units in the vicinity of Herat, Afghanistan, killing a number of Soviet advisers.

March 23

DIPLOMACY: In Washington, D.C., a government spokesman states that the United States expects the principle of noninterference to be respected as it relates to Afghanistan, especially by the Soviet Union.

March 25

POLITICS: Kurdish groups in northeastern Iran end their rebellion after receiving limited autonomy, the right to teach their language in public schools, and the ability to select their own security forces.

March 27

POLITICS: In Kabul, Afghanistan, Foreign Minister Hafizullah Amin is appointed prime minister; his rise comes at the expense of President Nur Mohammad Taraki. The two men, representing two factions of the Afghan Communist Party, prove unable to coexist in the same administration.

March 28

DIPLOMACY: In Baghdad, Iraq, leaders of various Muslim countries who oppose Egypt's recent detente with Israel gather, but any real splits in Arab unity are avoided.
MILITARY: In Herat, western Afghanistan, Afghan soldiers led by Ismail Khan rise in revolt, killing a number of Soviet advisers. Many other soldiers desert the Afghan army and join the resistance. Simmering resentment against the Communist regime in Kabul begins spreading throughout the countryside.
POLITICS: In Kabul, Afghanistan, Foreign Minister Hafizullah Amin is sworn in as prime minister. Amin, who champions a radical "Pol Pot" revolutionary activism that distances itself from Soviet influence, is placed on a collision course with the more doctrinaire President Nur Mohammad Taraki.

March 30
POLITICS: In Iran, a national referendum intending to legitimize imposition of an Islamic republic passes by 97 percent of the popular vote.

April
POLITICS: Throughout the month, the Muslim insurrection grows in Wardak, Logar Province, and Jalalabad city once religious leaders, convinced that the Kabul regime is bent on destroying the traditional social structure through agrarian reforms, declare a jihad, or holy war, against them. This requires all Muslim males of good faith to pick up arms against infidels in the name of God.

April–May
POLITICS: Throughout Afghanistan, the Khalq government in Kabul orders punitive measures against rebellious villagers. At Mazar-i-Sharif alone, Afghan army troops pack up 1,500 young Tajiks and Hazaras (Shiites) into trucks, haul them over to the banks of the Amu Darya (Oxus) River, bind them, and toss them into the water to drown. Several hundred village elders, suspected of complicity in the rebellion, are removed to the edge of a desert precipice and machine-gunned. Their bodies are left to rot at the bottom of the ravine.

April 1
POLITICS: In Kabul, Afghanistan, a new government is formally initiated with Hafizullah Amin serving as prime minister and secretary of foreign affairs while Shah Wali is appointed deputy prime minister.

April 2
DIPLOMACY: In Washington, D.C., government officials vehemently deny that they are arming or inciting Afghan guerrillas against the Kabul regime. The Soviet Union nonetheless sticks by its accusation.

April 7–13
POLITICS: In Tehran, Iran, the government resumes executing officials associated with the regime of Mohammad Reza Shah Pahlavi. Over the ensuing week, no less than 35 people are shot by firing squad, including former premier Amir Abbas Hoveida. Since February, no fewer than 119 of the shah's former associates have died in this manner.

April 8
MILITARY: In Kabul, Afghanistan, Soviet vice minister of defense Aleksei Yepishev arrives for discussions with President Nur Mohammad Taraki.

April 12
DIPLOMACY: In Washington, D.C., a government spokesman denounces the Iranian government's secret trials and executions for violating "internationally accepted standards of justice."

April 14
AVIATION: In Kabul, Afghanistan, President Nur Mohammad Taraki requests that the Soviets deploy 15 to 20 helicopters to Afghanistan, along with their crews.

April 15

POLITICS: In Tehran, Iran, Foreign Minister Karim Sanjabi resigns from office to protest interference by the Revolutionary Council, accusing it of establishing "a government within a government." The city's religious leader, Ayatollah Mahmoud Taleghani, also leaves town to protest the lack of coordination between competing revolutionary committees and the discord they are sowing nationwide. He also protests the arrest and detention of his daughter, who was accused of engaging in left-wing activities.

April 17

POLITICS: In Tehran, Iran, Ayatollah Khomeini goes on the airwaves and accuses the United States of fomenting disunity in the country through various "agents."

April 30

DIPLOMACY: In Kabul, Afghanistan, President Nur Mohammad Taraki accuses the government of Pakistan of fomenting unrest in the country's eastern provinces.

May 2

TERRORISM: In Tehran, Iran, the Forghan Fighters, an antigovernment guerrilla group, shoots and kills Ayatollah Morteza Motahari, a significant member of the ruling Revolutionary Council.

May 6

POLITICS: In Tehran, Iran, Ayatollah Khomeini decrees that the Islamic Revolution must be protected at any cost, so he authorizes creation of the Army of the Guardians, an armed religious force numbering 6,000 men.

May 7–9

POLITICS: Throughout Iran, politically inspired executions of former associates of Mohammad Reza Shah Pahlavi reach 200.

May 13

POLITICS: In Tehran, Iran, Ayatollah Khomeini, under pressure from his own Justice Ministry, declares that the death penalty is reserved only for those convicted of murder.

TERRORISM: In Iran, Ayatollah Sadegh Khalkhali, leader of the revolutionary court, publicly clamors for the assassination of the former shah and his family members.

May 24

POLITICS: In light of increased tensions between Islamic fundamentalists and Westernized liberals in Iran, Ayatollah Khomeini attacks all secular adversaries, referring to them as enemies of Islam.

May 30–31

MILITARY: In the port city of Khorramshahr, Iran, ethnic Arabs rise in revolt against the government to gain greater autonomy. Around 200 people are killed and 600 taken prisoner after armed Revolutionary Guards storm buildings housing Arab cultural organizations used to stage sit-ins.

June

MILITARY: In an ominous development, the first detachments of Soviet special forces begin arriving at Bagram Air Base, Afghanistan.

June 4

DIPLOMACY: In Tehran, Iran, the government rejects the new U.S. ambassador, Wallace Cutler, on the basis of alleged antirevolutionary activity while serving in Zaire in 1978. The Americans refuse to withdraw his nomination.

June 13

POLITICS: In Kabul, Afghanistan, the government again accuses Pakistan of assisting a rebellion against it.

June 16

MILITARY: Acting on a request from the Kabul regime, the Soviets deploy a detachment of tanks and personnel carriers to guard the government against mounting unrest and maintain firm control of Bagram and Shindand airfields.

June 23

POLITICS: In Kabul, Afghanistan, military authorities round up 300 Hazaras (Shiites) from the capital's bazaar quarter who are then driven to a field adjacent to the Pul-i-Charki concentration camp. There, half are doused with gasoline and set afire; the remainder are buried alive by Soviet bulldozers. This is retribution for an earlier attack by four young Hazaras on a Kabul police station.

June 25

POLITICS: In Kabul, Afghanistan, the government-run radio announces that protests in the capital by Hazaras (Shiites) were put down and a number of them were killed.

July

POLITICS: Mujahideen in the Panjshir Valley northeast of Kabul, Afghanistan, begin coalescing under the leadership of 24-year-old Ahmad Shah Massoud, a member of Jamiat-i-Islami who has returned from a trip to Pakistan.

July 3

POLITICS: In Washington, D.C., President Jimmy Carter counters what is generally perceived as a rising tide of Soviet interference in Afghanistan by signing an executive order authorizing the Central Intelligence Agency to begin covert propaganda operations against the communist regime there. This is the origin of Operation Cyclone, one of the largest and most successful American covert operations of the cold war.

July 7

AVIATION: A Soviet airborne battalion under Lieutenant Colonel A. Lomakin arrives at Bagram Air Base, Afghanistan. So as to not arouse suspicion, they deploy without combat equipment and are dressed as technical specialists and mechanics.

July 16

POLITICS: In Baghdad, Iraq, Vice President Saddam Hussein assumes the presidency following the resignation of President Ahmad Hasan Bakr, allegedly on the grounds of poor health. Hussein also assumes the chairmanship of the Revolutionary Command Council. Thus empowered, he begins rounding up his opponents—real or imagined—in the Baath Party and the army officer corps.

July 19–20

MILITARY: In Kabul, Afghanistan, the regime of President Nur Mohammad Taraki begins to fear for the worse and requests that the Soviet Union deploy two motorized rifle divisions. A day later Taraki asks for an airborne division as well.

July 23

POLITICS: In Tehran, Iran, all radio and TV music is banned by Ayatollah Khomeini, who characterizes them as "no different than opium." These join the list of prohibited practices, such as drinking alcohol and sun bathing, now regarded as remnants of an earlier, "Satanic" regime.

July 28

DIPLOMACY: In Baghdad, Iraq, President Saddam Hussein cancels plans for unification with Syria on the basis that Syria is conspiring to overthrow him.

POLITICS: In Kabul, Afghanistan, the government reshuffles Hafizullah Amin to serve as prime minister and president of the Revolutionary Council while Shah Wali becomes deputy prime minister and foreign minister.

August 2

DIPLOMACY: In Washington, D.C., a government spokesman warns the Soviet Union not to intervene in the Afghan civil war, despite the spiraling violence there.

August 5

MILITARY: In Kabul, Afghanistan, the garrison of the Bala Hissar fortress rebels and a bloody struggle ensues against other Afghan army troops, backed by Soviet jets and helicopter gunships. A curfew is also imposed on the capital.

August 7

POLITICS: In Tehran, Iran, five members of the ruling Revolutionary Council are sentenced to death by a special court for conspiring against the state. An additional 33 individuals receive jail sentences.

August 8

POLITICS: In Baghdad, Iraq, President Saddam Hussein quickly consolidates power by arresting 22 political rivals on grounds of political conspiracy, including five members of the Revolutionary Command Council. The captives are all executed while an additional 35 prisoners are given jail sentences up to 15 years.

In Tehran, Iran, 21 political prisoners are executed by firing squad.

TERRORISM: In Laghman Province, Afghanistan, Afghan army troops make an example of 650 rebellious villagers from the town of Qala-e-Nadjil by tossing them into several trenches, then burying them alive with bulldozers. The operation is directed by Soviet "advisers."

August 12

POLITICS: In Tehran, Iran, 4,000 leftists protesting the closing of the daily newspaper *Ayandegan* are brutally contained by riot police. The demonstration had been called by the secular National Democratic Front, which opposes creeping radical Islamization of the country.

August 14
MILITARY: In Paveh, northwestern Iran, Kurdish guerrillas seeking national autonomy resume fighting against the Iranian government. Combat is also reported in the towns of Mehabad, Sanandaj, and Saqqiz. The fact that the Kurds are also devout Sunni Muslims does not sit well with the Shiite-dominated regime of Ayatollah Khomeini.

August 18
MILITARY: At Paveh, 300 miles west of Tehran, Iran, government forces reportedly crush a Kurdish revolt, killing 18 rebels and wounding 40 over the past three days. The action was directly ordered by Ayatollah Khomeini.

August 19
MILITARY: In Kabul, Afghanistan, Prime Minister Hafizullah Amin finally admits to the presence of 1,600 Soviet advisers throughout the country.

In Tehran, Iran, Ayatollah Khomeini orders a general mobilization to thwart what he deems is a Kurdish uprising.

August 20
POLITICS: In Tehran, Iran, the revolutionary regime shuts down 20 opposition newspapers and places new restrictions on foreign journalists; five Western journalists are expelled from the country.

August 21
MILITARY: Iranian military forces execute 18 Kurdish rebels involved in a recent uprising.

August 27
POLITICS: In Tehran, Iran, Ayatollah Khomeini offers Kurdish rebels a day's oil revenues (about $75 million) if they will accept a truce and stop fighting. A temporary cease-fire is then arranged.

August 28
MILITARY: Twenty rebels are executed by Iranian soldiers in the Kurdish town of Saqqiz for fomenting a recent rebellion there.
POLITICS: In Tehran, Iran, Ayatollah Khomeini rejects his own cease-fire agreement with Kurdish rebels, insisting that they be crushed.

September 6
MILITARY: In Sardasht, Iran, government forces cap a three-week campaign against Kurdish guerrillas by seizing their final stronghold. An estimated 10,000 fighters fled the city beforehand and either took to the nearby hills or relocated to Iraq.

September 10
POLITICS: In Tehran, Iran, Ayatollah Mahmoud Taleghani, an important voice for moderation, dies from natural causes. He was also the city's prayer leader.

September 10–14

DIPLOMACY: Afghan president Nur Mohammad Taraki, returning from a conference of nonaligned states in Havana, Cuba, stops in Moscow, Soviet Union, for talks with Soviet general secretary Leonid Brezhnev. Back in Afghanistan, this visit convinces Prime Minister Hafizullah Amin that his rival is conspiring with the Soviets to eliminate him. An astute insider, Amin controls the secret police, employs an independent network of informers, and has cleverly prevented cabinet members from establishing their own power bases. He intends to strike first.

September 14

MILITARY: Three senior military figures closely identified with President Nur Mohammad Taraki—Sayyed Muhammad Gulabzoy, Muhammad Aslam Watanjar, and Sherjan Mazdoryar—seek refuge in the Soviet embassy in Kabul, Afghanistan.

POLITICS: In Kabul, Afghanistan, Soviet ambassador Alexander Puzanov brings Hafizullah Amin and Nur Mohammad Taraki into a conference to reconcile their differences. Instead, fighting breaks out between the two factions and Taraki is fatally shot. Amin is promoted to secretary-general of the PDPA and chairman of the Revolutionary Council, although the decision is not announced for several days.

The Hazajarat region of central Afghanistan, dominated by Shiites, rises in rebellion against the communist regime in Kabul, and the rebels seek greater religious guidance by establishing a shura, or revolutionary Islamic Council. Sunni-dominated areas of the country also rise in revolt, especially Ghazni Province.

September 15

POLITICS: In Kabul, Afghanistan, the government sacks Interior Minister Mohammad Aslam Watanjar and Frontier Minister Sherjan Mazdoryar; gunfire erupts in the streets following the announcement.

September 16

POLITICS: In Kabul, Afghanistan, Hafizullah Amin's accession to the presidency is finally announced to the public. Former president Nur Mohammad Taraki's absence is attributed to an "unspecified illness." Faqr Muhd Faqir and Sahibjan Sahri are appointed as interior and frontier minister, respectively.

September 23

POLITICS: In Kabul, Afghanistan, President Hafizullah Amin assures his fellow Afghans that Nur Mohammad Taraki is alive but "definitely sick."

October 8

MILITARY: Afghan government forces commence a major offensive to regain control of the strategic province of Paktia along Pakistan's northwestern frontier. However, mujahideen forces bloodily repel the army and remain in control of the vital Gardez-to-Khost highway.

POLITICS: In Kabul, Afghanistan, the government announces that death sentences on former defense and planning ministers Abdul Qadir and Sultan Ali Keshtmand have been commuted to 15 years in prison.

October 9

POLITICS: In Kabul, Afghanistan, President Hafizullah Amin, seeking to placate the populace, publishes a list of 12,000 people known to have been killed by the previous regime. According to government figures, these people were shot between April 27, 1978, and September 14, 1979. Radio Kabul also announces that former president Nur Mohammad Taraki has died—three weeks after the fact.

October 10

MILITARY: In Moscow, Soviet Union, the government realizes that the Khalq regime in Kabul, Afghanistan, has alienated the population and that the situation in the countryside is violently spiraling out of control. Planning commences in the Kremlin to restore stability through an invasion and occupation of Afghanistan.

October 14–16

MILITARY: Near Kabul, Afghanistan, Afghan army troops garrisoned at the Rishkhur barrack mutiny, only to be crushed by massed government forces two days later.

October 16

AVIATION: Units of the Red Air Force begin arriving at Shindand Air Base, Afghanistan.

October 22

DIPLOMACY: Former shah of Iran Mohammad Reza Pahlavi arrives in New York from Mexico for treatment of cancer and gallstones. The Carter administration decided to admit the ailing monarch, whom former secretary of state Henry Kissinger has hailed as a loyal friend of the United States, for humanitarian reasons. Iranian foreign minister Ibrahim Yazdi assures the Americans that their embassy in Tehran, Iran, will be protected.

November

POLITICS: In Kabul, Afghanistan, the increasingly paranoid Hafizullah Amin demands the withdrawal of Soviet ambassador Alexander Puzanov, despite professed "bonds of friendship" between their two nations.

November 1

POLITICS: In Tehran, Iran, Ayatollah Khomeini exhorts students to observe the anniversary of student protests of November 4, 1978, by attacking the United States and forcing it to turn over the shah. This broadcast apparently incites a takeover of the U.S. embassy.

November 4

TERRORISM: In Tehran, Iran, 500 militants storm the U.S. embassy, seizing 65 hostages while another three are held at the Foreign Ministry. Among them are Colonel Charles W. Scott and Master Sergeant Regis Ragan of the U.S. Military Assistance Advisory Group, who are held for the next 444 days. The U.S. Marine security detachment, numbering 13 men, is also taken. The radicals warn they will hold the Americans until the deposed shah, then receiving medical treatment in the United States, is forcibly returned to face trial. President Jimmy Carter, however, seeks a peaceful, diplomatic end to the crisis.

November 5

DIPLOMACY: In Washington, D.C., the State Department refuses an Iranian demand that deposed shah Mohammad Reza Pahlavi be forcibly extradited back to his home land.

November 6

POLITICS: In Tehran, Iran, Prime Minister Mehdi Bazargan resigns from office after many of Ayatollah Khomeini's advisers openly support the takeover of the U.S. embassy.

November 7

DIPLOMACY: In an attempt to end the hostage crisis peacefully, the Carter administration dispatches emissaries known for their sympathy toward the Iranian Revolution, but Ayatollah Khomeini refuses them an audience.

November 8

DIPLOMACY: In Tehran, Iran, the Canadian embassy secretly grants five American embassy workers sanctuary.

November 9

MILITARY: Around Kabul, Afghanistan, mujahideen fighters report ambushing and killing an estimated 200 Afghan army soldiers.

November 10

DIPLOMACY: To preclude any chance of violence between American and Iranian demonstrators, President Jimmy Carter orders the deportation of any Iranian students residing in the country illegally.

November 12

DIPLOMACY: In Washington, D.C., President Jimmy Carter suspends all Iranian oil imports.

November 14

DIPLOMACY: The U.S. government freezes all Iranian assets in American banks and blocks Iran from convening a UN Security Council meeting until all hostages have been freed.

November 18

DIPLOMACY: In Tehran, Iran, Ayatollah Khomeini declares that some of the captured embassy personnel will be tried for espionage.

November 19

DIPLOMACY: In an attempt to sow discord, radicals in Tehran, Iran, release two African-American Marines and a woman from captivity.

November 20

DIPLOMACY: In Tehran, Iran, radicals release six more African-American marines and four more women. This leaves 50 at the U.S. embassy and three at the Foreign Ministry.

In Washington, D.C., the government warns Iran that it might resort to taking military action if the hostages are not released immediately.

NAVAL: The U.S. Navy orders a six-vessel task force into the Indian Ocean to join an eight-ship group already deployed in the Indian Ocean.

November 25
DIPLOMACY: In New York City, UN Secretary-General Kurt Waldheim requests an urgent meeting of the Security Council to deal with the Iranian hostage situation.

November 26
DIPLOMACY: In New York City, former shah of Iran Mohammad Reza Pahlavi has successful gallstone surgery.

November 27
DIPLOMACY: In Tehran, Iran, Ayatollah Khomeini attacks plans for a UN Security Council meeting as part of a U.S. plot with a predetermined ending.

November 28
MILITARY: In Kabul, Afghanistan, eyebrows are raised following the arrival of KGB General Victor Paputin, the Soviet minister of the interior. At this time, the Afghan army garrison at Asmar, Konar Province, also rises in revolt.
POLITICS: In Tehran, Iran, Acting Foreign Minister Abolhassan Bani-Sadr, who supported a diplomatic solution to the crisis, is fired in favor of Sadegh Ghotzbzadeh.

An American hostage being paraded before cameras by his Iranian captors *(Hulton/Archive)*

November 29
DIPLOMACY: The Mexican government announces that Mohammad Reza Shah
Pahlavi will not be allowed back into the country.

November 30
DIPLOMACY: In Washington, D.C., the government announces that the shah will
depart once his medical treatment has ended. The government also begins secretly
searching for a host nation to accept the ailing refugee.

December 1
DIPLOMACY: In Tehran, Iran, militants holding the American hostages charge two of
them with being undercover operatives of the Central Intelligence Agency.

December 2
POLITICS: In Tehran, Iran, Ayatollah Khomeini is elected absolute leader for life.

December 2–3
POLITICS: In Kurdistan and Azerbaijan Provinces, Iran, rioting breaks out after a
national plebiscite approves a new Islamic constitution for the nation.

December 4
DIPLOMACY: In New York City, the UN Security Council votes unanimously to
demand that all American hostages be released from Iran.

December 5–13
POLITICS: In Baluchistan Province, Iran, antigovernment rioting ensues and results
in 12 deaths and 80 people injured.

December 6
DIPLOMACY: In Tehran, Iran, another American hostage is charged with carrying a
false Belgium passport.

December 7
AVIATION: At Bagram Air Base, Afghanistan, additional detachments of Soviet spe-
cial forces begin deploying; this installation ultimately serves as a major Red Air
Force facility for the next 10 years.

December 10
DIPLOMACY: In Tehran, Iran, the militants holding American hostages allow a captive U.S. Marine embassy guard to be interviewed on television.

December 11–12
DIPLOMACY: In Europe, U.S. secretary of state Cyrus Vance visits several capitals and
asks America's allies for joint economic sanctions against Iran.

December 15
DIPLOMACY: Ailing former shah Mohammad Reza Pahlavi finally finds refuge in
Panama, deflating militant hopes that he would be returned to Iran for trial.
    In The Hague, Netherlands, the International Court of Justice unanimously
demands that Iran unconditionally release all American hostages in their

possession. They also reject any attempt to link their status to consideration of American activities in Iran since 1953.

December 16
DIPLOMACY: In Tehran, Iran, Foreign Minister Sadegh Ghotzbzadeh claims that the United States has "retreated one step" by making the shah leave the country.

December 21
DIPLOMACY: In Washington, D.C., President Jimmy Carter orders many remaining Iranian diplomats out of the country. He also requests that the UN Security Council approve economic sanctions against Iran.

MILITARY: In Washington, D.C., military analysts declare that the Soviet Union has massed three motorized divisions along the Afghan border while a further 1,500 Soviet troops are garrisoned near the capital of Kabul at Bagram Air Base. Invasion appears imminent.

December 24
MILITARY: Elements of three Soviet motorized divisions begin rolling across the Soviet border into Afghanistan, commencing a protracted, decade-long occupation.

December 24–25
DIPLOMACY: In Tehran, Iran, Ayatollah Khomeini allows two Christian clergymen to visit the American hostages over the Christmas holiday.

December 26
AVIATION: At least 300 transports belonging to the Red Air Force begin airlifting 5,000 Soviet troops into Kabul, Afghanistan, in preparation for a military coup.

MILITARY: In Kabul, Afghanistan, additional Soviet special forces begin landing at Bagram airport north of the capital. The United States characterizes this movement as elevating Soviet involvement in Afghanistan to a "new threshold."

December 27
MILITARY: In Kabul, Afghanistan, Operation Storm-333 unfolds as Soviet KGB OSNAZ and GRU SPETSNAZ units, along with paratroopers from the elite 103rd Guards "Vitebsk" Airborne Division, disguised as Afghan troops, storm the Tajbeg presidential palace. These units kill President Hafizullah Amin of the Khalq faction at a cost of 19 dead and 50 wounded, although they also kill more than 200 members of the president's bodyguard. Amin becomes the third Afghan president to die in a span of 20 months.

December 28
DIPLOMACY: In Moscow General Secretary Leonid Brezhnev issues congratulations to Babrak Karmal on becoming president of Afghanistan and secretary-general of the PDPA. He is a member of the more doctrinaire, Soviet-oriented Parcham faction and has also served as ambassador to Czechoslovakia. Brezhnev also sends President Jimmy Carter a cable, explaining that the Afghans had "invited" the Soviets to intervene.

In Washington, D.C., President Jimmy Carter denounces the Soviet invasion of Afghanistan as "a grave threat to peace." He also warns them of "serious consequences" without specifying details.

MILITARY: Along the northern Afghan border, five Soviet motorized divisions of the Fortieth Army under Marshal Sergei Sokolov, totaling 15,000 men, begin flooding down strategic highways, securing cities and strategic positions along their route.

In Kabul, Afghanistan, TASS radio announces the death of KGB General Victor Paputin, who was apparently killed during the raid on the presidential palace.

POLITICS: In Kabul, Afghanistan, Babrak Karmal arrives and declares himself president of the Revolutionary Council and secretary-general of the PDPA. He also insists that the Soviets are supplying the country with "urgent political, moral, and economic aid, including military aid." He then cobbles together a cabinet consisting mostly of former Parcham members who had been either exiled or imprisoned by the previous Khalq regime. Consequently, Asadullah Sarwari becomes deputy prime minister, Sultan Ali Keshtmand is minister of planning, Muhammad Rafi serves as defense minister, and Shah Muhammad Dost is foreign minister. Four senior military officers, Abdul Qadir, Sherjan Mazdoryar, Sayyed Muhammad Gulabzoy and Muhammad Aslam Watanjar are also invited to join.

December 29

DIPLOMACY: In Washington, D.C., President Jimmy Carter declares that there are 20,000 to 25,000 Soviet troops in Afghanistan. He demands that these be withdrawn immediately lest U.S.-Soviet relations suffer.

December 30

DIPLOMACY: In Moscow, the Communist Party newspaper *Pravda* declares that a "limited contingent" of Soviet troops has entered Afghanistan for the purpose of defending it against a foreign attack.

December 31

DIPLOMACY: In New York City, the UN Security Council votes 11-0 to grant Iran one week to release the American hostages before large-scale economic sanctions are imposed. Secretary-General Kurt Waldheim also departs for Tehran to attempt to secure their release through personal diplomacy.

In Washington, D.C., President Jimmy Carter cables General Secretary Leonid Brezhnev, insisting that he had not relayed the facts surrounding the Afghan occupation accurately to him. Why, he inquires, would President Hafizullah Amin invite the Soviets in only to be murdered by them?

MILITARY: In Kabul, Afghanistan, fighting apparently erupts between Soviet forces and dissident Afghan troops opposing their intervention, but control of the capital is never seriously challenged.

1980

January 1

DIPLOMACY: In Moscow, Soviet Union, the government again justifies its intervention in Afghanistan due to a need to repel "reactionary bands" armed and directed by the United States and China. It also accuses Pakistan of training Afghan resistance leaders and providing their followers with arms.

MILITARY: At Bala Zhar, Afghanistan, widespread fighting erupts after Soviet forces surround and demand that the Afghan Army's 26th Parachute Regiment disarm. An estimated 700 Afghans die in combat while reports of massive defections from the army and the resistance are also becoming prevalent.

POLITICS: In Kabul, Afghanistan, President Babrak Karmal commences the new year by announcing that the Soviets have been invited to deter "aggressive actions of the enemies of Afghanistan."

January 1–3
DIPLOMACY: In Tehran, Iran, UN Secretary-General Kurt Waldheim arrives in a failed attempt to negotiate the release of all American hostages. While present, he is not allowed to visit the Americans or confer with Ayatollah Khomeini, but he does meet with the Revolutionary Council.

January 2
DIPLOMACY: In Washington, D.C., President Jimmy Carter orders the U.S. ambassador to the Soviet Union home for consultations. He also informs the U.S. Senate to delay consideration of a Strategic Arms Limitation Talks (SALT) treaty.

POLITICS: Addressing the people of Afghanistan, President Babrak Karmal again beseeches them to unite and support the Afghan revolution.

January 4
DIPLOMACY: In Washington, D.C., President Jimmy Carter announces punitive measures against the Soviet Union for its invasion of Afghanistan, most noticeably a grain embargo and a cutoff of high-technology sales, along with the curtailment of cultural and economic exchanges.

January 5
DIPLOMACY: In New York City, the UN Security Council takes up the issue of Afghanistan and opens debate.

January 6
DIPLOMACY: The United Nations reports that no fewer than 15,000 Afghan refugees had sought shelter in neighboring Pakistan, bringing the total number there to 402,000.

POLITICS: In Kabul, the new puppet government of Babrak Karmal, consisting of 20 Parcham and six Khalq factional leaders, announces a general amnesty. This sparks massive demonstrations in cities by mothers and sisters, who take to the streets demanding that family members be released from the Pul-i-Charki concentration camp. Karmal, impressed by the emotional outpouring, orders the jail emptied of political prisoners, but only a handful of men appear. It is subsequently learned that 17,000 inmates were officially listed as "missing." Thus the massacres at Pul-i-Charki, which began in October 1979, consumed the lives of 29,000 Afghans.

January 6–9
DIPLOMACY: For the first time since 1949, a U.S. secretary of defense visits the People's Republic of China when Harold Brown arrives for talks with military

officials there. This event would not have been possible without the Soviet invasion of Afghanistan.

January 7
DIPLOMACY: In New York City, a UN Security Council resolution mandating the withdrawal of all "foreign forces" from Afghanistan passes 13-2 but is vetoed by the Soviet Union.

January 8
MILITARY: In Washington, D.C., the government announces that it is selling China a ground station for receiving information from the Landsat Earth Resources Satellite, technology which has potential military applications.

January 9
DIPLOMACY: In New York City, UN Secretary-General Kurt Waldheim informs the Security Council that the Iranian militants holding the American hostages make their decisions independent of the Revolutionary Council.
POLITICS: In Washington, D.C., President Jimmy Carter warns the American public that releasing the American hostages from Iran is a lengthy process that may take several months. He notes that there is no legitimate authority there with whom he can negotiate.

January 10
AVIATION: In Kabul, Afghanistan, large Soviet transport aircraft are reputedly landing at the national airport at the rate of a dozen per day.
MILITARY: A report surfaces in the *New York Times* suggesting that Soviet military units are settling into new bases and staging areas, apparently for an extended occupation of Afghanistan.

January 11
POLITICS: In Kabul, Afghanistan, President Babrak Karmal announces the formation of a new administration that includes members from both the Khalq and Parcham factions of the PDPA.

January 12
DIPLOMACY: In Washington, D.C., the United States offers Pakistan $400 million in military and economic aid over the next two years. Such assistance had been cut off on April 6, 1979, when it was learned that the Pakistanis were producing their own nuclear bomb.

January 13
DIPLOMACY: In Moscow, Soviet Union, General Secretary Leonid Brezhnev counters a rising tide of international condemnation by insisting that the Soviet invasion of Afghanistan was simply the response to an appeal by a friendly government. It was undertaken, he says, solely to thwart rising outside interference by foreign powers.

In New York City, the Soviet Union vetoes a Security Council resolution calling for economic sanctions against Iran, prompting the United States and its allies to continue pressing for their imposition.

January 14

DIPLOMACY: In New York City, Abdul Hakim Tabibi, the Afghan representative to the United Nations, defects to the United States. The UN General Assembly also votes 104 to 18, with 18 abstentions, to condemn the Soviet invasion and demands the immediate withdrawal of all "foreign troops." This resolution will be overwhelmingly passed by the United Nations every year until 1988.

The Iranian government expels all American journalists after they report that 43 people were killed in Tabriz during a spate of antigovernment rioting from January 4 to 6.

January 15

DIPLOMACY: In light of the raging Soviet occupation next door, Pakistani president Zia ul-Haq appeals to the world community for military assistance and support.

January 16

DIPLOMACY: In Islamabad, Pakistan, British foreign secretary Lord Carrington arrives on an official state visit and subsequently visits the border regions in a show of support for the government.

MILITARY: By this date, Western military analysts estimate that 85,000 Soviet troops are in Afghanistan, with many of them deployed in the western part of the country near the Iranian border.

The Chinese government declares it is poised to increase the flow of arms and supplies to the Afghan resistance.

January 17

DIPLOMACY: In Islamabad, Pakistan, an angry President Zia ul-Haq dismisses the American offer of $400 million in aid as "peanuts" and insists the situation demanded a far more serious amount.

January 20

DIPLOMACY: In Washington, D.C., President Jimmy Carter announces that if the 1980 Summer Olympics are held in Moscow, the United States would boycott the games unless Soviet troops withdrew from Afghanistan by February 20.

January 23

DIPLOMACY: In Washington, D.C., President Jimmy Carter, clearly outraged by the Soviet invasion of Afghanistan, introduces the new "Carter Doctrine" for resisting Soviet expansionism and requests $30 million in covert aid for the Afghan resistance. Over the next decade, this program, administered by the Central Intelligence Agency (CIA), will channel thousands of Soviet-made weapons into Afghanistan via Pakistan. More importantly, Carter vows to use "any means necessary"—a euphemism for nuclear weapons—to keep the Russians from seizing Middle Eastern oil fields.

MILITARY: By this date, the Soviets have moved 40,000 combat troops into Afghanistan and have begun occupying the major provincial capitals. However, the growing mujahideen movement still controls the countryside.

January 24
MILITARY: In a major turn of events, the United States announces its willingness to directly sell military equipment to China for the first time in the cold war. This is another result of the Soviet invasion of Afghanistan.

January 25
MILITARY: Zia Khan Nassiri, head of the Afghan Islamic and Revolutionary Party, proclaims a Free Islamic Republic in the provinces of Paktia, Ghazni, and Logar, Afghanistan. He openly appeals for foreign aid to resist the Soviet invasion.
POLITICS: In Tehran, Iran, former foreign minister Abolhassan Bani-Sadr wins a landslide victory for the presidency by garnering 75 percent of the popular vote. As the only public figure to openly criticize the militants who stormed the U.S. Embassy, he vows to try to resolve the ongoing crisis with the United States peacefully.

January 27
DIPLOMACY: In Tehran, Iran, President Abolhassan Bani-Sadr backtracks slightly by placing responsibility for ending the hostage crisis on the United States.
POLITICS: In Peshawar, Pakistan, representatives from six Sunni-dominated resistance groups form an Islamic-based, anti-Soviet alliance.

January 27–29
DIPLOMACY: In Islamabad, Pakistan, delegates from the 36 nations attending the Conference of Islamic Foreign Ministers vote to condemn the Soviet invasion of Afghanistan, while also suspending Moscow's membership. They also condemn the holding of 52 American hostages by Iran.

January 29
DIPLOMACY: In Tehran, Iran, six U.S. embassy aides, who have been hiding in the Canadian embassy for the past three months, depart the country using fake Canadian passports forged by the Central Intelligence Agency (CIA). The small Canadian staff remaining is also withdrawn as a precaution.

February 1
MILITARY: Western analysts estimate that the Soviets have deployed 80,000 troops throughout Afghanistan.
POLITICS: The number of Afghan refugees in camps along the Pakistani border is estimated at 500,000.

February 5
DIPLOMACY: In Europe, the leaders of France and West Germany issue a joint statement demanding the immediate withdrawal of Soviet forces from Afghanistan "without delay."

February 6
POLITICS: In Kabul, Afghanistan, President Babrak Karmal denounces the previous reforms imposed on the population by the Khalq faction. He thereupon declares a "new stage" of revolution, hoping that thousands of disgruntled Afghans can be persuaded to support his regime.

In Tehran, Iran, President Abolhassan Bani-Sadr denounces militants holding the American hostages as "self-centered children." He also accuses them of attempting to behave like "a government within a government." Acting on his cue, the Revolutionary Council orders the state broadcasting system to stop granting the militants automatic airtime for their allegations.

February 7
POLITICS: In Tehran, Iran, Abolhassan Bani-Sadr is named head of the Revolutionary Council.

February 8
DIPLOMACY: In Europe, an allied conference of Afghanistan is scheduled, but the government of France declines to attend since it was not "of a nature to reduce international tension."
MILITARY: In Washington, D.C., President Jimmy Carter requests that Congress renew the draft registration as a show of determination to resist Soviet aggression.

February 9
DIPLOMACY: In Washington, D.C., an administration spokesman criticizes France for "rapid shifts" in its policy respecting the Afghan crisis. Generally, tension is increasing between the United States and its Western allies as the former demands that they sacrifice the recent detente with the Soviet Union by cutting exports.

February 12
MILITARY: In Washington, D.C., President Jimmy Carter underscores his determination to strengthen America's visibility in the Persian Gulf region by ordering a 1,800-marine assault battalion to be deployed there.

February 13
DIPLOMACY: In Washington, D.C., President Jimmy Carter gives his blessing to a "carefully defined" international commission of inquiry regarding the shah's misrule. Previously, he insisted that such a commission could be formed only after the hostages had been released.
MILITARY: In Cairo, Egypt, Defense Minister Kamal Hasan declares that his country will provide some support and training to the Afghan resistance.

February 14
DIPLOMACY: In New York City, the UN Human Rights Commission votes 27 to 8 with 6 abstentions, to condemn the Soviet invasion of Afghanistan as "aggression against human rights."

February 15
MILITARY: Reports surface in U.S. newspapers that the American government has begun supplying the Afghan mujahideen with light weapons to resist the Soviet occupation. This also represents the first covert CIA operation since the Angolan civil war of 1976.

February 16
DIPLOMACY: In Tehran, Iran, President Abolhassan Bani-Sadr takes to the airwaves to announce that his government no longer demands the extradition of the former

shah as a precondition to the release of the American hostages. However, he insists that the United States apologize for its past role in Iran, promise not to interfere in Iranian affairs in the future, and not obstruct any future prosecution of the former shah. However, the militants in physical possession of the hostages insist that only the return of the shah—or a direct order from Ayatollah Khomeini—will gain the captives' release.

February 18
MILITARY: The Soviet government reacts with alarm after learning that many of its soldiers from Central Asia are openly fraternizing with religiously active Afghans. The reserve divisions currently deployed are to be replaced with regular divisions staffed by Russians and other Europeans. By this date, the Soviets have deployed seven motorized divisions and one airborne division, totaling more than 100,000 men.
POLITICS: Throughout Afghanistan, political demonstrations and strikes condemning the Soviet occupation are brutally put down by force.

February 19
DIPLOMACY: The European Economic Community suggests that Afghanistan be declared a neutral country and guarded by the international community once Soviet forces are withdrawn.
POLITICS: In Tehran, Iran, Ayatollah Khomeini appoints President Abolhassan Bani-Sadr to serve as commander in chief of all Iranian armed forces.

February 20
DIPLOMACY: In New York City, UN Secretary-General Kurt Waldheim announces establishment of a commission to investigate allegations of misrule by the former shah. It will consist of five lawyers from Sri Lanka, France, Venezuela, Syria, and Algeria; it was also understood that their presence in Iran would facilitate the release of the American hostages.

February 21
POLITICS: In Kabul, Afghanistan, a mass of demonstrators upset by the Soviet invasion go on strike in the city bazaar, at which point the bulk of commercial interests also go on strike. They are urged on by clandestine anticommunist leaflets that have been widely circulated.

February 22
DIPLOMACY: In Moscow, Soviet general secretary Leonid Brezhnev declares he is willing to withdraw Soviet forces from Afghanistan provided that all outside influence and interference is halted.
POLITICS: The government declares martial law in Kabul, Afghanistan, to deal with anti-Soviet strikers and protesters; 300 people are reported to have been killed in rioting.

February 22–23
AVIATION: The skies above Kabul, Afghanistan, are filled with Soviet MiG fighters and helicopter gunships that menacingly buzz anti-Soviet demonstrators throughout the capital.

February 23
DIPLOMACY: The United Nations dispatches a five-member commission to Tehran, Iran, to investigate the rule of the former shah, Mohammad Reza Pahlavi. It also hopes to prevail on newly elected president Abolhassan Bani-Sadr to arrange the release of the American hostages. However, its hopes are deflated once Ayatollah Khomeini decrees that the hostages can only be released by a new parliament due to be elected in March and convene in April. Previously, Bani-Sadr had assured UN Secretary-General Kurt Waldheim that Khomeini welcomed the commission's work.

MILITARY: In Afghanistan, Afghan army troops close down all traffic along the Kabul-Peshawar highway for the first time.

February 24
DIPLOMACY: In Tehran, Iran, the UN commission tasked with investigating the former shah meets with President Abolhassan Bani-Sadr and Foreign Minister Sadegh Ghotzbzadeh. The commission hopes that a sympathetic hearing of grievances might produce a favorable climate for the release of the American hostages.

February 25
DIPLOMACY: In New York City, the Pakistani resolution condemning the Soviet invasion of Afghanistan is adopted by the UN Human Rights Commission.

POLITICS: In Kabul, Afghanistan, the government is increasingly paralyzed by the closing of commercial premises, protests, and civil strikes over the Soviet occupation.

February 26
DIPLOMACY: In Tehran, Iran, the UN commission takes depositions from five Iranian jurists and 140 invalids who claim to have suffered under the shah's regime. Ali Reza Nobari, governor of Iran's central bank, also produces documents that allege that the shah plundered the equivalent of $7.14 billion.

POLITICS: Throughout Kabul, Afghanistan, mass arrests of Hazaras (Shiites) are reported as underway to break anti-Soviet strike activities.

February 28
DIPLOMACY: In Tehran, Iran, the UN commission interviews 1,500 Iranians who were injured in demonstrations prior to the shah's departure. Meanwhile, commission members also press for a meeting with all the American hostages.

February 28–March 10
MILITARY: In the Konar Valley, Afghanistan, Soviet and Afghan troops commence their first large-scale assault upon mujahideen forces. Through extensive use of napalm and chemical agents, the valley is soon cleared of all its 150,000 inhabitants. Within weeks an additional 38,000 refugees have flocked to camps inside the Pakistani border. The Soviets are impressed by the success of such scorched-earth tactics, which are gradually applied to other regions of the country where insurrections appear intractable.

POLITICS: In Kabul, Afghanistan, state security troops forcibly reopen commercial establishments and force civil servants back to work.

February 29

DIPLOMACY: To prevent the military situation inside and outside Afghanistan from spiraling out of control, Britain formally proposes neutralizing Afghanistan with a Western guarantee in exchange for a Soviet troop withdrawal.

In Tehran, Iran, an aide to Ayatollah Khomeini reports that the UN commission investigating the shah has permission to see all the hostages.

March 3

DIPLOMACY: In Tehran, Iran, the UN commission is denied access to the American hostages after receiving assurances from the government that its members may see them.

POLITICS: In Peshawar, Pakistan, the mujahideen alliance suffers its first setback when the Hezb-i-Islami group under Gulbuddin Hekmatyar withdraws. Nonetheless, a Revolutionary Council is formed by the Hezb-i-Islami under Yunnis Khalis, the Jamiat-i-Islami under Burhanuddin Rabbani, the Harakat-i-Inqilab Islami under Nabi Mohammad, the National Liberation Front under Sibghatullah Mojaddedi, and the National Islamic Front under Sayed Ahmed Gailani.

March 4

MILITARY: In Konar Province, Afghanistan, Afghan resistance leaders admit to defeat and that the only armed forces occupying the Konar Valley at present are either Soviet or Afghan army troops. A spokesman for the Mujahideen Muslim Fighters of Konar and Nurestan accuses the Soviets of employing napalm and poison gas against civilians.

March 5

DIPLOMACY: In Islamabad, Pakistan, Foreign Minister Agha Shahi formally rejects a $400 million aid package from the United States, citing its inadequacy. He insists that Pakistan will base its foreign policy on a close alliance with Islamic and non-aligned nations. Some officials consider the snub an embarrassment to American efforts to shore up influence in the Persian Gulf region.

March 6

DIPLOMACY: In Tehran, Iran, the militants holding the American hostages declare that they are turning them over to the Revolutionary Council in light of the "intolerable pressures" placed on them by governmental authorities.

March 7

MILITARY: In Kabul, Afghanistan, Soviet forces increase their visibility by appearing on the streets of the city for the first time in a show of force. Overhead, the skies are full of Soviet jets and helicopter gunships to underscore exactly who is in charge.

March 8

POLITICS: In Tehran, Iran, a meeting between Foreign Minister Sadegh Ghotzbzadeh and militants holding the American hostages degenerates into a shouting match over whether Ayatollah Khomeini has granted permission for the UN commission to visit them.

March 9

DIPLOMACY: In New York City, the United States raises the issue of poison gas being used by the Soviets in Afghanistan with the UN Human Rights Commission. Meanwhile, the Paris-based International Federation of Human Rights declares that it has positive proof that the Soviets are indeed employing chemical weapons throughout Afghanistan.

MILITARY: Reports surface that the Soviets have sustained 5,000 casualties from combat in Afghanistan, although such numbers cannot be verified by Western sources.

March 10

DIPLOMACY: In Tehran, Iran, Ayatollah Khomeini deflates any notions of the UN commission visiting the American hostages after backing the militants and placing stringent conditions on any exchanges with the captives. At this juncture the five-man commission departs Iran and suspends issuing a report of its investigation.

POLITICS: In Kabul, Afghanistan, Justice Minister Abdurrashid Arian announces the arrest of 42 former associates of the late president Hafizullah Amin.

March 11

MILITARY: In Islamabad, Pakistan, government military sources state that the Soviets and their Afghan allies are continuing to drive down the Konar Valley, Afghanistan, to gain all territory right up to the Pakistani border. However, they maintain that the vast bulk of Afghan resistance fighters have taken to the nearby mountain tops for cover and still control every pass leading into northern Pakistan.

March 13

DIPLOMACY: In Moscow, Soviet Union, Afghan foreign minister Shah Muhammad Dost arrives in what is officially described as a "friendly visit."

March 18–21

DIPLOMACY: In The Hague, Netherlands, the United States appeals to the International Court of Justice to condemn Iran's violation of international law.

March 19

MILITARY: As the snow begins melting across Afghanistan, Soviet and Afghan forces take to the field in greater numbers to do battle with the elusive mujahideen, especially in the country's rugged mountain valleys. Soviet troops, trained in conventional warfare and more or less restricted to paved roads, have trouble evicting the Islamic warriors from their mountainous abodes.

POLITICS: In Peshawar, Pakistan, the mujahideen alliance elects Abdul Rasul Sayyaf as chairman.

March 21

DIPLOMACY: White House Chief of Staff Hamilton Jordan arrives in Panama to ask that the shah not leave the country. Panamanian president Aristides Royo assures the former monarch that his nation will not honor an extradition request since it includes the probability of a death penalty.

March 23

DIPLOMACY: In Panama, Mohammad Reza Pahlavi boards an airliner for Egypt at the behest of Egyptian president Anwar Sadat. His exodus takes place a day before Panamanian authorities were to consider an Iranian request for his extradition.

March 24

DIPLOMACY: After the former shah of Iran arrives in Egypt, Iranian clerics call for a mass demonstration to protest his presence there. This is the sixth country to accept him as a refugee following his departure from Iran on January 16, 1979.

March 26

POLITICS: In Tehran, Iran, the first round of parliamentary voting takes place, but further voting is suspended indefinitely. Previously, Ayatollah Khomeini had authorized the new parliament to make all decisions relative to the disposition of the American hostages.

March 28

DIPLOMACY: In Egypt, the ailing Mohammad Reza Shah Pahlavi successfully has his spleen removed by a team of surgeons headed by Dr. Michael E. DeBakey of Houston, Tex.

POLITICS: Despite the high visibility of Soviet forces throughout Kabul, Afghanistan, thousands of demonstrators take to the street in protest.

March 29

MILITARY: A report surfaces in the *New York Times* that all Afghan resistance in the Konar Valley, Afghanistan, has been wiped out by brutal Soviet tactics. It also reports that at least 1,500 Soviet troops had been killed in fierce fighting and that the Afghan army has been reduced by desertion to only 35,000 men.

March 30

DIPLOMACY: The United States delivers an ultimatum to Iran, insisting that the government take control of the hostages no later than March 31 or face the imposition of new economic sanctions. In return, President Abolhassan Bani-Sadr asks that Carter postpone the deadline by 24 hours; Carter agrees to postpone sanctions for the time being.

April 1

POLITICS: In Tehran, Iran, President Abolhassan Bani-Sadr announces that his government will take control of the hostages if the United States pledges not to make additional threats against Iran.

TERRORISM: In Baghdad, Iraq, Vice Premier Tariq Aziz narrowly survives an assassination attempt. The government responds with a harsh crackdown against Shiite Muslims, especially members of the Al Daawa terrorist organization.

April 4

DIPLOMACY: In Moscow, Soviet Union, the Soviet-Afghan accord to provide military "assistance" is ratified by the Presidium of the Supreme Soviet. This agreement allows the Soviets to maintain the "temporary" presence of a "limited" military force in Afghanistan.

MILITARY: Western military analysts believe that while Soviet forces have occupied and now control Afghanistan's major urban cities, the mujahideen enjoy uncontested mobility in the neighboring countryside.

POLITICS: In Kabul, Afghanistan, the Second Plenary Session of the Afghan Communist Party adopts a new platform that initiates the "second stage of the revolution," which promises to be far less harsh than the first. It is hoped that such moderation will win over the bulk of average Muslims and disarm Islamic traditionalists. This, however, flies in the face of a raging fundamentalist insurgency engulfing the countryside.

April 7

AVIATION: In light of rising tensions between the United States and Iran, all Iranian military personnel currently attending military schools in the United States are ordered out of the country within four days. Several are forced to depart the Air Training Command.

DIPLOMACY: Five months into the hostage crisis, President Jimmy Carter finally orders diplomatic relations with Iran severed and orders a ban on all American exports to that nation. Consequently, all entry visas held by Iranians outside the United States are considered voided.

April 8

DIPLOMACY: In Washington, D.C., the Iranian embassy and five consulates across the country are ordered closed.

April 9

DIPLOMACY: In Washington, D.C., Secretary of State Cyrus Vance runs headlong into congressional opposition after permitting the export of $11.2 million of marine engines to Iraq. The sale was meant as a gesture to open up new diplomatic relations with Baghdad.

The American government appeals to Australia, New Zealand, Canada, Japan, and countries in Western Europe to halt all nonfood exports to Iran and to withdraw their ambassadors in a show of support.

In Egypt, Mohammad Reza Pahlavi is discharged from the hospital and flown by helicopter to the Kubbeh Palace, his temporary residence.

MILITARY: In the Panjshir Valley, Afghanistan, a small force of Soviet soldiers advances, looking to attack local mujahideen units. However, the rebels, badly outgunned, simply melt into the population and wait for the Soviets to withdraw.

April 10

DIPLOMACY: In Europe, several nations reject President Jimmy Carter's demand for the imposition of economic sanctions against Iran and the closure of embassies. Instead, they substitute a conventional demand for the immediate release of the American hostages.

April 11

DIPLOMACY: In Europe, the heads of nine Common Market nations fear that economic sanctions against Iran would alienate moderate factions and allow the

Soviets to increase their influence across Southwest Asia. Moreover, because Europe and Japan are heavily dependent upon imported oil, they are reluctant to provoke the wrath of oil-producing nations in that region.

April 12

DIPLOMACY: In Washington, D.C., the U.S. Olympic Committee announces that it will boycott the upcoming Summer Olympics being held in Moscow, Soviet Union. In many political circles, this act is viewed as another limp-wristed response to Soviet aggression.

April 13

DIPLOMACY: In Washington, D.C., an indignant President Jimmy Carter makes a televised broadcast to Europe and requests that the Western allies impose economic sanctions against Iran in April, and to break off diplomatic relations in May if the hostages are not released. Failing this, he does not rule out military action. The governments of Britain and West Germany are reportedly in favor of sanctions but had been vetoed by France, who did not want to be "stampeded into economic warfare with Iran."

April 17

DIPLOMACY: In Washington, D.C., President Jimmy Carter enacts additional sanctions against Iran by banning all imports, financial transactions, and travel there by Americans. He also declares that all military equipment purchased by the shah will be impounded and sold to other nations.

POLITICS: A *New York Times*/CBS Poll indicates that only 39 percent of the public approve of President Jimmy Carter's handling of the hostage crisis.

April 21

POLITICS: In Kabul, Afghanistan, political protests erupt when the government unveils a new flag that resembles the flag flown by the monarchy before it was overthrown two years previously.

April 22

DIPLOMACY: Upon further reflection, and unwilling to allow the Atlantic alliance to fragment, the nine-member European Community votes unanimously to impose sanctions against Iran on May 17 unless "decisive" progress has been made toward releasing the American hostages. After that date a total embargo would be enacted, save for medicine and food. The EC countries are also reducing their diplomatic staffs in Tehran and reducing Iranian representation in Europe, while a visa system is being introduced for Iranians along with a ban of military equipment sales.

April 23–24

DIPLOMACY: The governments of Japan and Canada adopt measures identical to Europe's should the American hostages not be released by May 15.

April 24–25

AVIATION: After several months of failed negotiations to secure the American hostages held in Tehran, Iran, President Jimmy Carter authorizes Operation Eagle Claw, a helicopter-borne commando mission to rescue them by force. This consists of a rescue team comprising Delta Force operatives, Rangers, and Special Forces under

Colonel Charles Beckwith. They are conveyed inland in eight RH-53 helicopters launched from the carrier USS *Nimitz* and land at a site named Desert One (Dasht-i-Kavir, or Great Salt Desert), 250 miles southeast of Tehran. At least three helicopters suffer from mechanical malfunctions after encountering a dust storm and abort, at which point Beckwith cancels the attempt. However, the mission comes to grief when an EC-130 transport and a helicopter collide in a sandstorm, killing eight Americans and wounding five. Five of the remaining helicopters are abandoned, along with the dead. Failure here also prompts the rise of the U.S. Central Command (CENTCOM) to better orchestrate military operations in this theater.

April 25

DIPLOMACY: In Tehran, Iran, Ayatollah Khomeini denounces the American rescue mission as "stupid" and warns that any future attempts might endanger the lives of the hostages.

April 25–29

POLITICS: In Kabul, Afghanistan, a demonstration staged by high school and college students is ruthless by contained by Afghan security forces with the loss of several lives. Among the slain is a student named Nahid, who is elevated to the status of shahid, or martyr.

April 26

DIPLOMACY: In Tehran, Iran, the state radio declares that the American hostages have been separated and distributed to other cities throughout the country to prevent any further rescue attempts.

April 27

POLITICS: In Tehran, Iran, a macabre display unfolds as the Iranian government showcases the charred bodies of eight American soldiers and airmen killed in the aborted rescue attempt.

April 28

DIPLOMACY: At the Brooke Army Medical Center, San Antonio, Texas, President Jimmy Carter excoriates the Iranian government for displaying the remains of the eight American soldiers killed in the failed rescue attempt. He insists such behavior violates "all principles of humanity and decency."

POLITICS: Secretary of State Cyrus Vance resigns from office after failing to support President Jimmy Carter's decision to launch the ill-fated rescue attempt to free the American hostages. He maintains that the hostages could be secured through a combination of negotiations coupled with economic and political sanctions.

In Kabul, Afghanistan, students at the Omar Shaheed School for Boys and the Habibia High School begin burning old and new flags to protest the Soviet occupation. After throwing stones at security forces, the latter opens fire, killing 13 students and arresting 200.

April 29

DIPLOMACY: In Washington, D.C., President Jimmy Carter addresses a news conference, warning that the United States will take "whatever steps are necessary" to free the hostages in Tehran, Iran. He also defends the recent rescue attempt by maintaining it had a reasonable chance for success, and, moreover, failing to try would have constituted a bigger moral failure.

POLITICS: In Washington, D.C., Senator Edmund Muskie (D-Maine) is appointed the new secretary of state to replace Cyrus Vance.

April 30

POLITICS: At the University of Kabul, in Afghanistan, protests against the government spread, and security forces open fire, machine-gunning at least 60 people to death.

TERRORISM: In London, United Kingdom, a group of Iranian Arabs seize the Iranian embassy and demand more rights for minorities in Iran.

May

POLITICS: Radio Kabul and the TASS news agency reveal the Kabul regime's proposal for peacefully ending the ongoing crisis. First, open negotiations are to be conducted among the governments of Afghanistan, Iran, and Pakistan. Second, all Afghan refugees are to be returned under a complete amnesty and freed from arrest and prosecution. Third, the United States and the Soviet Union are to issue a joint guarantee not to interfere with the internal affairs of Afghanistan. From a Soviet perspective, all negotiations will remain focused on issues between neighboring countries and have no relation to the nature of the regime in Kabul, which is considered a "purely domestic problem."

May 5

MILITARY: In London, United Kingdom, British commandos successfully storm the Iranian embassy after five Arabic gunmen begin killing hostages. Two hostages and three gunmen are slain.

May 6

DIPLOMACY: Iran returns the remains of eight Americans killed in the failed rescue attempt.

In London, United Kingdom, Prime Minister Margaret Thatcher says the successful raid on the Iranian embassy underscores the fact that nations have a responsibility to look after the safety of all diplomats on their soil.

May 8

POLITICS: In Tehran, Iran, Farrokhrou Parsa, the former education minister under the shah and the only female cabinet member, is executed by firing squad after being accused of embezzling money.

May 14

DIPLOMACY: In Brussels, Belgium, the foreign defense ministers of members of the North Atlantic Treaty Organization (NATO) vote unanimously to condemn the Soviet invasion of Afghanistan. This action marks a distinct shift in attitudes toward the Soviet Union, as Afghanistan was previously regarded as not crucial to the alliance. To that end, they approve ways of improving the alliance's military preparedness with expanded ammunition stockpiles, enhanced defenses against chemical warfare, and improved defenses along the southern flank.

May 18
DIPLOMACY: In Kabul, Afghanistan, Indian Foreign Secretary R. D. Satha arrives to confer with President Babrak Karmal.

In light of the ongoing hostage crisis in Iran, members of the European Economic Community (ECC) vote to cancel all trade contracts with that nation made since November 4, 1979, when the American embassy was seized in Tehran. This falls short of an earlier pledge to cancel all trade save for medicine and food exports.

May 19
DIPLOMACY: In London, United Kingdom, the government breaks with EEC members by limiting the new trade ban with Iran to new contracts only.

May 20
DIPLOMACY: In Washington, D.C., the government criticizes Britain for not keeping an earlier pledge to cancel all economic contracts with Iran.

May 22
DIPLOMACY: In Islamabad, Pakistan, the Conference of Islamic Foreign Ministers again calls for the immediate withdrawal of "foreign forces" from Afghanistan. It

Three RH-53 Sea Stallion helicopters lined up on the flight deck of an aircraft carrier in preparation for Operation Evening Light, a rescue mission to Iran. *(U.S. Navy)*

also establishes a committee to begin consultations to find a solution to the Afghan crisis.

May 24

DIPLOMACY: At The Hague, Netherlands, the International Court of Justice orders Iran to immediately release the hostages and not put them on trial. The court also informs Iran that it is liable for reparations. These rulings enable the United States to approach the UN Security Council to impose new sanctions on Iran for failing to comply. The Iranian government, which has been asked to present its side of the issue, remains silent.

POLITICS: In Kabul, Afghanistan, mass demonstrations against the Soviet occupation are reported.

May 29

DIPLOMACY: In London, United Kingdom, the government further dilutes trade sanctions against Iran, noting they hurt British business far more than they do Iran's.

June 2–5

DIPLOMACY: In Tehran, Iran, an international conference votes to condemn the United States for its interference in Iranian affairs and also lambasts the Soviet Union for invading Afghanistan. Former U.S. attorney general Ramsey Clark violates the ban on travel to Iran in order to attend, although he implores the government to release the hostages and take him prisoner in their place. For his part, Iranian foreign minister Sadegh Ghotzbzadeh states that the hostage situation would be "clarified" if the United States were to acknowledge its interference in Iran over the past 25 years. The final document issued by the conference makes no references to the hostages, despite repeated attempts by Clark to add them.

June 8

MILITARY: A Soviet offensive up the Konar Valley, Afghanistan, claims the life of Maoist leader Abdul Majod Kalakani, whose demise brings an end to the Maoist movement there.

POLITICS: In Kabul, Afghanistan, government radio announces the execution of 10 former supporters of former president Hafizullah Amin.

June 10

POLITICS: In Washington, D.C., President Jimmy Carter declares that he favors taking legal action against Ramsey Clark and nine other individuals who defied a travel ban to Iran.

June 12

MILITARY: In response to Soviet aggression in Afghanistan, the U.S. Senate votes 58–34 to reenact military draft registration. It also approves $13.3 million to help register 4 million young men for possible military service.

June 14

POLITICS: Reports surface in Kabul, Afghanistan, that Communications Minister Mohammad Zarif, Foreign Affairs Minister Sahibjan Sahrai, and Planning Minister

Mohammad Siddiq Alemyar, all formerly associated with former president Hafizullah Amin, have been executed.

June 15
DIPLOMACY: In Kabul, Afghanistan, the government expels the Red Cross International Committee.

June 21
DIPLOMACY: In Moscow, Soviet Union, General Secretary Leonid Brezhnev announces a partial troop withdrawal from Afghanistan.

June 23
DIPLOMACY: In Moscow, Soviet Union, General Secretary Leonid Brezhnev again declares that "interventionists" have suffered a serious defeat in Afghanistan. Consequently, he is withdrawing one division and 108 tanks from that nation.

June 25
MILITARY: In Washington, D.C., the House of Representatives votes 234–168 in favor of renewing draft registration for young men and women, although women would be restricted from combat roles.

June 27
MILITARY: In another belated response to the Soviet invasion of Afghanistan, President Jimmy Carter signs legislation reactivating draft registration for 19- and 20-year old men.

July
DIPLOMACY: This month the United States, West Germany, Norway, Canada, China, Indonesia, Kenya, Zaire, and 50 other nations declare that they are boycotting the Olympic Summer Games slated to be held in Moscow.
POLITICS: In Kabul, Afghanistan, the regime of Babrak Karmal attempts to consolidate its grip on national power by establishing several mass organizations along Soviet lines. Hence youth movements, women's movements, trade unionists, and agricultural laborers are all lumped together under a new National Fatherland Front.

July 2
DIPLOMACY: In Moscow, the Communist Party newspaper *Pravda* reiterates that peace in Afghanistan is possible only after adjoining states halt their incursions and unwarranted political interference there.
POLITICS: In Washington, D.C., President Jimmy Carter urges that young men register for possible military conscription as soon as possible.

July 3
POLITICS: In Tehran, Iran, two men and two women are buried up to their waists and stoned to death for sexual immorality. The presiding judge of the revolutionary court who condemned them casts the first stone.

July 12
DIPLOMACY: In Tehran, Iran, Iranian radicals release U.S. hostage Richard I. Queen after 250 days in captivity because of extreme illness. He is flown to a U.S.

Air Force base in Wiesbaden, West Germany, and is eventually diagnosed with multiple sclerosis. Ayatollah Khomeini approved of Queen's release on humanitarian grounds.

July 14
POLITICS: In Iran, firing squads execute a former general of the shah's army and several members of the Bahai faith convicted of espionage.

July 18
TERRORISM: In Paris, France, armed gunmen raid the home of former Iranian prime minister Shahpur Bakhtiar; two people are killed, three are wounded, and three gunmen are captured.

July 20
POLITICS: In Tehran, Iran, conservative cleric Hojatolislam Hashemi Rafsanjani is named speaker of the Iranian parliament once legislative power passes from the Revolutionary Council following a seven week interval.

July 22
TERRORISM: In Bethesda, Maryland, Ali Akbar Tabatabai, a former press attaché for the shah, is slain by two gunmen posing as U.S. Mail employees. He was a political opponent of the present regime and president of the Iran Freedom Foundation, which was dedicated to a "secular democracy."

July 23
POLITICS: In Washington, D.C., police arrest two African Americans in connection with the murder of Iranian expatriate Ali Akbar Tabatabai. Both are members of an extreme Black Muslim sect.

July 26
POLITICS: In Tehran, Iran, President Abolhassan Bani-Sadr appoints Mostafa Mir-Salim, a 33-year old French-trained engineer, to serve as his prime minister. Although a member of the Islamic Republican Party's central council and chosen as a compromise candidate to placate fundamentalists, Mir-Salim enjoys the reputation of something of an independent.

July 27
DIPLOMACY: In Cairo, Egypt, former shah Mohammad Reza Pahlavi dies from circulatory collapse complicated by lymphatic cancer. The news sparks joyous celebrations in Iran.
POLITICS: In Washington, D.C., nearly 200 Iranian pro-Khomeini protestors are arrested for scuffling with police during an anti-Khomeini demonstration.

July 29
DIPLOMACY: In Cairo, Egypt, the former shah of Iran receives a military funeral, though the only heads of state in attendance are Egyptian president Anwar Sadat, deposed King Constantine of Greece, and former U.S. president Richard M. Nixon. Meanwhile, President Abolhassan Bani-Sadr declares that the shah's passing will have no effect on the status of the 52 American hostages.

August
POLITICS: Several newspapers report that the number of Afghan refugees living in Pakistan now exceeds 1 million.

In Kabul, Afghanistan, the state radio announces that Justice Minister Abdurrashid Arian is assuming the additional post of deputy prime minister.

August 2
DIPLOMACY: In Washington, D.C., charges against 200 Iranians held in custody for riotous behavior are dropped, though their immigration status has not yet been determined.

August 3
DIPLOMACY: In Tehran, Iran, Ayatollah Khomeini declares that a group of nearly 200 Iranian men and women are being held and tortured in American prisons.

August 4
DIPLOMACY: In Tehran, Iran, the Speaker of the Iranian Majlis (Parliament) declares that debate on the fate of the 52 American hostages has been postponed owing to the mistreatment of Iranians being held in the United States.

August 5
DIPLOMACY: In Riyadh, Saudi Arabia, Iraqi president Saddam Hussein meets with the king and foreign minister, apparently seeking their approval for his decision to attack Iran. The Saudi monarchy had abandoned efforts to seek rational discourse with Tehran, which has denounced them as un-Islamic, corrupt, and pawns of the United States. All told, the Gulf Arab states fear Iran's military potential for upending the regional status quo.

POLITICS: A minor controversy grows in the United States after 171 Iranian men held in a federal prison in Otisville, New York, without charges, are released. Twenty Iranian women incarcerated in a federal detention center in New York City are likewise let go. Previously, they had been visited by Muslim and Christian clergymen and pronounced in good condition with no complaints about their treatment.

August 10
POLITICS: In Tehran, Iran, the Islamic Republican Party rejects President Abolhassan Bani-Sadr's choice for prime minister and instead selects Mohammed Ali Rajai, a mathematics teacher without any governmental experience. Rajai wins a secret ballot, 153–24, and Bani-Sadr complains that the nominee was forced on him.

August 28
POLITICS: The human-rights group Amnesty International declares that 1,000 people have been executed by the regime in Tehran, Iran, over the last 18 months and calls for the killings to stop.

September
MILITARY: Soviet and Afghan forces conduct their first offensive operations up the Panjshir Valley, Afghanistan, in an attempt to rid themselves of mujahideen under Ahmad Shah Massoud. Massoud's forces, badly outgunned, simply melt away into the mountains.

September 2
MILITARY: Near Qasr-i-Sherin, Iran, fighting erupts between Iraqi and Iranian forces for control of this disputed section of border territory.

September 4
MILITARY: Iranian artillery forces begin shelling the Iraqi border towns of Khanaqin and Mandali from the disputed Zain al Qaws village; Iraqi sources maintain that the Iranian Air Force also bombed nearby oil facilities. This date is subsequently cited by Baghdad as the beginning of the Iran-Iraq War.

September 6
DIPLOMACY: In a rapid escalation of rhetoric, the Iraqi government threatens to annex 145 square miles of the disputed Zain al Qaws region from Iran, which it maintains was rightfully ceded to it through an unpublished clause in the 1975 Algiers Accord. Iran has one week to cede the territory.

MILITARY: In response to threats by the Iraqi government to annex disputed border territory, the Iranians step up artillery bombardment of settlements near Zain al Qaws village.

September 7
MILITARY: In the latest escalation of violence, the Iraqi government claims to have seized the disputed Zain al Qaws town and vicinity by force.

September 9
DIPLOMACY: In Baghdad, Iraq, the government signs a new diplomatic accord with Algeria.

In Tehran, Iran, Britain shutters its embassy and removes its personnel after deporting numerous Iranian students involved in violent demonstrations a month earlier.

September 10–13
MILITARY: Along the Iranian border, Iraqi forces claim to have seized Saif Saad, along with five border posts and 90 square miles of territory, thereby forcibly settling a long-standing territorial dispute. The lack of a concerted Iranian response does not go unnoticed by Iraqi president Saddam Hussein, who is emboldened to press his claim on the disputed Shatt al Arab waterway.

September 12
DIPLOMACY: In Tehran, Iran, Ayatollah Khomeini outlines conditions for the release of the American hostages, while omitting a demand for a U.S. apology. He insists that the Americans turn over all property of the late shah, unblock all frozen assets, and pledge not to intervene in Iranian affairs.

The Iranian government accuses the governments of Saudi Arabia and Kuwait of signing a secret agreement to raise their daily oil output by 1.8 million barrels and fund Iraqi aggression against them.

September 14
POLITICS: In Paktia Province, Afghanistan minister of tribes and nationalities Faiz Mohammad is murdered while attempting to persuade his tribe to support the

Kabul regime. His death is a blow to government aspirations of convincing disgruntled tribal leaders to lay down their arms.

September 15
MILITARY: Border skirmishing along the Iran-Iraq border drifts downward to the Shatt al Arab region once Iranian artillery begins shelling Iraqi targets.

September 17
DIPLOMACY: In Baghdad, Iraq, President Saddam Hussein addresses the National Assembly and accuses Iranian leaders of violating the 1975 Algiers Accord by financing and fomenting unrest among the Kurdish minority and refusing to relinquish illegally held Iraqi territory. He thereupon tears up a copy of the accord in front of a televised audience, claiming full sovereignty over the Shatt al Arab waterway, which separates the two nations. Consequently, Iranian vessels using the waterway must now fly the Iraqi flag and employ Iraqi pilots for navigation.

September 18
DIPLOMACY: In Tehran, Iran, the government denounces Iraq for unilaterally abrogating the 1975 border agreement between the two governments, especially respecting the Shatt al Arab waterway divided between them.

In Washington, D.C., Deputy Secretary of State Warren Christopher unleashes a thinly veiled threat to Iran by declaring that the United States will "do whatever is necessary, including military action" to keep the Straits of Hormuz open to neutral shipping.

September 19
AVIATION: The Iranian government concedes that it has lost two F-4 Phantom jets to Iraqi antiaircraft fire along its disputed border region with Iraq.
MILITARY: Iraq concludes two weeks of skirmishing along the Iranian border by deploying 10,000 troops in a disputed area that it considers its own. Daggers are being drawn on both sides of the international boundary.

September 20
MILITARY: In Tehran, Iran, President Abolhassan Bani-Sadr fears the worst from Iraq and orders a general mobilization "to defend the integrity of the country."

September 21
MILITARY: Armed clashes are reported all along the 270-mile Iran-Iraq border as both sides appear to be girding for an inevitable conflict between two ancient enemies.
NAVAL: In Baghdad, Iraq, the government media reports that five Iranian gunboats have been sunk in the Persian Gulf.

September 22
AVIATION: The Iraqi Air Force makes a surprise attack against 10 Iranian air bases, inflicting some damage but failing to deliver a knockout blow against the well-equipped and highly professional Iranian Air Force. The failure is attributed to the reluctance of Iraqi pilots to close with their targets or the mediocre Soviet avionics, which prevent accurate targeting. Also, the Iraqis were more concerned with

cratering the airfields than attacking Iranian aircraft in their hardened bunkers, so most survived the onslaught intact.

DIPLOMACY: The commencement of the Iran-Iraq War leads the United States to believe that the Iranian state could be badly fragmented, thereby allowing further Soviet encroachment in the strategic Persian Gulf region. Washington also fears that the onset of war will delay a return of the American hostages held in Tehran.

Western analysts believe that the Iraqi attack was sparked by widespread belief that the once-formidable Iranian military has been gutted by the country's revolution, coupled with President Saddam Hussein's ambition to become leader of the Sunni Arab world by effectively dealing with an ancient enemy. Hussein is clearly banking that the recent turmoil in Iran has played havoc with its formidable military establishment, and that complete victory is probably obtainable within three weeks. To that end, Iraqi goals center upon seizing undisputed control of the Shatt al Arab waterway, the Three Islands in the Strait of Hormuz, and a large chunk of oil-rich Khuzestan Province, which hosts a near-majority Arabic-speaking population. Moreover, Ayatollah Khomeini's calls for revolution among the majority Shiite population in Iraq can also been viewed as a genuine security risk for the Iraqi regime, hence a considerable provocation.

All told, the Iraqi invasion was totally unexpected by Iran, the United States, the Soviet Union, and several Arab countries. The strategic oil-producing Persian Gulf has now become the front line of a no-holds-barred struggle between two fanatical regimes.

MILITARY: An armed showdown between two ancient enemies unfolds as 45,000 Iraqi troops in four divisions cross the Iranian border to seize a number of strategic cities and areas.

In the north, an infantry division advances upon Panjwin in Iranian Kurdistan to preempt a possible enemy advance upon Sulaymaniyah and the Kirkuk oil fields.

In the center-north front, an Iraqi division seizes the garrison town of Qasr-i-Sherin from an Iranian armored brigade, then occupies the strategic height along the Baghdad-Tehran highway. The Iraqis are now situated to threaten the provincial capital at Bakhtaran, held by a depleted Iranian armored division, and present a formidable obstacle to any Iranian drive toward Baghdad, 75 miles distant.

In the south-central front, an Iraqi mountain division advances onto Mehran, captures it, and works its way as far as the foothills of the Zagros Mountains. The road network west of Zagros is now neutralized and cut off at the strategic junction at Dezful; numerous air bases and oil fields are likewise threatened.

In the southern front, the main Iraqi thrust unfolds as three tank divisions and one mechanized infantry division slice into oil-rich Khuzestan Province, Iran, whose population is 40 percent Arab-speaking. The main drive is against the port cities of Khorramshahr and Abadan, possession of which would grant Iraq uncontested control of the Shatt al Arab waterway. Two divisions are also siphoned off to threaten and possibly take Dezful and Ahvaz.

September 23

AVIATION: The Iranian Air Force recovers quickly from its surprise and commences Operation Kaman 99 by launching 100 warplanes at Iraqi oil installations near Kirkuk and Baghdad. Several Iraqi air bases near Iran are also heavily damaged and out of action for several weeks; four Iranian F-5E Tigers are lost in combat. The Iraqi Air Force, meanwhile, pounds Iranian refineries at Abadan, and the government claims that all 152 oil storage tanks were set ablaze; Iranian aircraft manage to down three Iraqi MiG-23s, two Mig-21s, and one Su-20.

DIPLOMACY: In New York City, the UN Security Council urges Iran and Iraq to cease fighting immediately.

September 24

AVIATION: The Iraqi and Iranian air forces continue to pound each other's oil refineries, forcing both nations to temporarily suspend oil sales and removing 2.7 million barrels of oil daily from the world market.

DIPLOMACY: In Washington, D.C., President Jimmy Carter mentions that he is consulting with other maritime powers to assure that the flow of oil through the Strait of Hormuz is uninterrupted.

MILITARY: Iraqi armored forces cut off and surround Abadan, Khuzestan Province, Iran, southeast of Basra, Iraq. The cities of Dezful and Ahvaz are also heavily shelled by artillery.

NAVAL: In the Persian Gulf, the well-equipped Iranian Navy conducts sorties against the Iraqi port of Basra, attacks two oil terminals on the Fao Peninsula, and imposes a blockade of the Shatt al Arab. This movement traps 60 neutral vessels in the contested waters.

September 25

AVIATION: After Iraqi artillery bombards the Iranian oil refinery at Abadan, then the world's largest, a force of 150 Iranian jets lashes back by striking the poorly defended oil facilities in Basra and Zubair, inflicting heavy damage. At the latter facility, 29 people are killed, including two British and four American workers. Flying at low altitude in groups of two or four, the Iranian F-4 Phantom jets have little difficulty evading Iraqi radar and antiaircraft fire.

DIPLOMACY: In Riyadh, Saudi Arabia, King Khalid ibn Abdul Aziz telephones Iraqi president Saddam Hussein to express his "brotherly feelings" toward Iraq and confirm his support in the war against Iran, which he castigates as the "enemy of the Arab nation."

At an Iranian press conference in Rome, Italy, the government accuses the United States of handing blueprints of Tehran's radar network to the Iraqis. Consequently, the Iraqis knew all the "blind spots," and their warplanes have penetrated as far as Tehran without detection.

MILITARY: Iraqi forces continue penetrating deeper into Iran, cutting an important rail line near the port of Khorramshahr and the rest of the country. They also claim to have surrounded and are besieging Dezful and Ahvaz further north.

September 26

POLITICS: Iraq halts all shipments of oil after Iranian warplanes bomb refining facilities. It usually ships 3.3 million barrels per day, but its refineries have been heavily damaged by aerial attacks.

September 27–30

DIPLOMACY: Pakistani president Zia ul-Haq attempts personal diplomacy in Tehran, Iran, and Baghdad, Iraq in a futile attempt to bring the Iran-Iraq War to a halt. His mission is sponsored by the Conference of Islamic States, but neither Ayatollah Khomeini nor President Saddam Hussein is willing to concede anything.

September 28

DIPLOMACY: In Washington, D.C., Deputy Secretary of State Warren Christopher informs Iraq that the United States does not condone its seizure of oil-rich Khuzestan Province, Iran.

In Baghdad, Iraq, President Saddam Hussein declares that all his military objectives have been met and he is ready to negotiate directly with Iranian leaders to settle their differences through third-party arbitration. However, as a precondition, he insists that Iran accept all territorial concessions, especially the Shatt al Arab waterway and three islands in the Persian Gulf, a stance Iran firmly opposes.

In Moscow, Soviet Union, the TASS news agency prints an essay condemning the Iraqi attack on Iran because it undermines the national liberation movement against Zionism and imperialism throughout the Middle East. The Soviets are angry that Saddam Hussein violated a 1972 Friendship and Cooperation Treaty agreement not to employ Soviet weapons offensively, and, moreover, did not consult with them prior to attacking Iran. Consequently, the Soviets are shutting off all channels of weapons and spare parts to Iraq.

MILITARY: An Iraqi armored division is detailed to capture the huge oil complexes at Kharkiya on the east bank of the Tigris River, though its advance is dogged by persistent Iranian ambushes as it approaches the suburbs of Khorramshahr.

NAVAL: In the Persian Gulf, five Iranian patrol boats put marines ashore on the Fao Peninsula, Iraq, destroying oil storage facilities and other equipment.

September 29

DIPLOMACY: In Baghdad, Iraq, the government embraces the UN Security Council's pleas to suspend fighting should Iran agree to a cease-fire.

In Amman, Jordan, King Hussein unsuccessfully tries to persuade visiting Soviet general Igor D. Sergayev, Chief of Staff, Ground Forces, to resume arms shipments to Iraq.

POLITICS: By this date the Iranian refineries at Kermanshah, Shiraz, and Tehran, are operating at less than half their normal capacity, which leads to gasoline shortages for daily use.

September 30

AVIATION: In light of turmoil arising from the Iran-Iraq War, President Jimmy Carter announces his decision to deploy four highly advanced airborne warning and control system E-3A (AWACS) aircraft to Dhahran Air Base, Saudi Arabia, and provide the region with a viable early warning system, which it currently lacks. These are accompanied by two KC-135 tankers and C-141 transport carrying 300 technical support personnel to keep Gulf surveillance possible around the clock.

Two Iranian F-4 Phantom jets bomb the Iraqi Nuclear Research Center at Tuwaithas, 10 miles from Baghdad, Iraq. French personnel at the site report that both reactors are now out of commission. The French originally named the reactors after the Egyptian deities Osiris and Isis, but they were subsequently changed to Tamuz I and Tamuz II after the Mesopotamian God of Plenty.

DIPLOMACY: In Tehran, Iran, Ayatollah Khomeini rejects a truce offer from Iraqi president Saddam Hussein and vows to keep on fighting to the bitter end. His sentiments are echoed by President Abolhassan Bani-Sadr, who declares peace to be impossible so long as Iraqi troops occupy Iranian soil.

In Washington, D.C., the government informs the government of Turkey that it is neutral in the Iran-Iraq War and therefore has no objection if it were to send American-made spare parts to Iran. This is assuming, of course, that the American hostages have been freed.

In Moscow, Soviet Union, General Secretary Leonid Brezhnev calls upon the leaders of Iran and Iraq to quickly negotiate a peace settlement.

MILITARY: Despite their impressive advances on paper, coalescing Iranian defenses halt the Iraqi drives against Dezful, Ahvaz, and Abadan on the outskirts of the cities. Fighting then breaks down to tank, artillery, and infantry duels from static positions.

October

AVIATION: The United States begins supplying Afghan mujahideen loyal to Ahmad Shah Massoud with Soviet-made SA-7 shoulder-launched antiaircraft missiles.

October 1

AVIATION: As the bloody Iran-Iraq War continues, the United States commences Operation Elf One as E-3A AWACS aircraft and KC-135 tankers in Saudi Arabia closely monitor military communications. They remain in place over the next eight years without mishap.

DIPLOMACY: In Islamabad, Pakistan, President Zia al-Haq explains that the reason his diplomatic effort failed was because Iraq sought to negotiate long-standing territorial disputes and Iran flatly refused any talks so as long as Iraqi troops occupied it soil.

In Tehran, Iran, President Abolhassan Bani-Sadr promises that his country will not blockade the Strait of Hormuz. The Iranians know full well that such an act would precipitate a direct military confrontation with the United States.

MILITARY: President Abolhassan Bani-Sadr arrives outside Dezful, Iran, to direct military operations in person. The Iraqis are reluctant to commit large numbers of troops or to storm the area as long as the struggle for Khorramshahr rages.

October 2

DIPLOMACY: In Ankara, Turkey, the government declares it will not send weapons or spare parts to either Iran or Iraq from across its territory. However, seeing that all three nations share borders, the Turks continue doing so quietly and covertly.

October 3

MILITARY: In Khorramshahr, Iran, Iraqi forces are gradually overcoming fierce resistance from the Iranian Gendarmerie, marines, naval cadets, and Pasdaran (Revolutionary Guards) units deployed there. Most of the oil facilities are either in ruins or in flames.

October 4

DIPLOMACY: To counter what was viewed in the Kremlin as a rising tide of American influence in the Persian Gulf, the Soviet ambassador in Tehran offers to supply the government with weapons and spare parts. Prime Minister Mohammad Ali Rajai rejects the offer over the former's intervention into Afghanistan. However, the Soviets do signal to the Syrians and Libyans that they can airlift arms and ammunition to Iran on their own accord.

In Tehran, Iran, Hojatolislam Ali Khamenei, a leading Shiite cleric, accuses Egypt, Saudi Arabia, Jordan, Kuwait, Qatar, Bahrain, and the United Arab Emirates of all clandestinely supplying Iraq with money and weapons.

October 5

DIPLOMACY: In Baghdad, Iraq, former Iranian prime minister Shahpur Bakhtiar arrives to confer with President Saddam Hussein. Apparently, he is to be installed as head of the new "Free Iranian Government" as soon as the city of Ahvaz is captured. However, the two men do not get along well and the city is never captured.

POLITICS: In Tehran, Iran, Prime Minister Mohammad Ali Rajai leaks to the media the fact that Soviet Union has offered to supply Iran with military hardware, but that Ayatollah Khomeini rejected the offer. The Soviets are trying to curry favor with the Communist Tudeh Party, which they felt was positioned to assert great influence in Iran.

The government of Kuwait, fearful of an Iranian-inspired Shiite uprising, mobilizes its army of 14,000 men and requires all foreigners residing there to declare their religious affiliation.

October 5–6

DIPLOMACY: King Hussein of Jordan pays a secret visit to President Saddam Hussein in Baghdad, Iraq, and the following day he authorizes a large convoy of arms, supplies, and food to the Iraqi army.

October 7

AVIATION: Iranian aircraft drop bombs on Iraqi oil installations at Kirkuk and Sulaymaniyeh as Iraqi warplanes attack the Iranian ground satellite station at Assad Abad near Hamadan.

MILITARY: At Khorramshahr, Iran, Iranian forces fire upon foreign vessels anchored in the Shatt al Arab waterway, sinking three ships and setting five on fire. Such actions are undoubtedly calculated to raise the insurance rates on tanker craft moving through the area and discourage them from dealing with Iraq.

The first shipment of East European arms for the Iraqi army docks at Aqaba, Jordan, to be transhipped by truck to Iraq.

NAVAL: Five of the 62 foreign vessels trapped in the Shatt al Arab waterway are attacked by Iranian aircraft and sunk.

October 8

AVIATION: Iraqi forces fire three Soviet-supplied Frog-7 tactical missiles into the Dezful region for the first time, inflicting civilian casualties.

October 9

MILITARY: In Basra, Iraq, captured Iranian military hardware is put on display, including 58 British Chieftain tanks, 34 American M-60s, and 11 M-48s. Many of these were precipitously abandoned by Iranians after getting bogged down in mud and are still in working condition.

October 10–14

DIPLOMACY: The government of Libya declares its support for Iran in its struggle with Iraq.

MILITARY: The Iraqis dispatch a mechanized division to cut off Abadan Island from the east, and it crosses the Karun River 10 miles north of Khorramshahr. The Iranians begin sending parts of an armored division at Ahvaz to help defend the region, but the Iraqis capture at least 10 Chieftain tanks. Within four days, the Iraqi division is across the river in strength, and its pontoon bridge remains intact.

October 11

AVIATION: It is reported that Iran's American-supplied Cobra helicopter gunships are holding up well in combat and extracting a heavy toll on Iraqi armored formations.

MILITARY: On the southern front, Iraqi armored columns lunge across the Karun River, only 10 miles northeast of Khorramshahr, and cut the strategic Ahvaz-Abadan highway. This move also cuts Abadan off from northern and eastern Iran. However, the Iraqis still encounter fanatical resistance from Iran's Revolutionary Guards, who are both steeped in Islamic theology and fiercely loyal to Ayatollah Khomeini.

NAVAL: In light of continuing tensions with Iran and concerns over Saudi Arabian security, the guided missile cruiser USS *Leahy* is ordered to the Persian Gulf to assist Air Force E-3 airborne warning and control system (AWACS) aircraft already there.

October 13

POLITICS: In Tehran, Iran, Ayatollah Khomeini appoints President Abolhassan Bani-Sadr as chairman of a seven-member Supreme Defense Council. This comprises both military and theocratic figures and is tasked with fighting and winning the war. In Iraq, military matters are also managed by the 10-member National Defense Council, headed by President Saddam Hussein, who has ultimate authority over its decisions.

In Kirkuk, Iraq, numerous oil pumps are shut down and sealed as a precaution against future Iranian aerial attacks.

October 14

DIPLOMACY: In Paris, France, President Valéry Giscard d'Estaing announces that the $1.6 billion arms deal with Iraq would continue. This package includes 60 Mirage F-1 jet fighters, tanks, antitank weapons, guided missiles, and patrol boats.

MILITARY: On the Ahvaz-Abadan road outside Abadan, an Iraqi armored column ambushes an Iranian convoy, whereby the Iranians abandon 20 Chieftain tanks that became stuck in the mud while maneuvering.

October 15

NAVAL: Distrusting Iranian assurances, the Pentagon authorizes Operation Persian Gulf, which involves 30 American warships, including two aircraft carriers, six destroyers, and several guided-missile frigates. Another 30 vessels are to be provided by the navies of Britain, France, and Australia.

October 15–November 5

DIPLOMACY: In Kabul, Afghanistan, President Babrak Karmal and several ranking officials depart for Moscow for high-level discussions.

October 16

MILITARY: In the southern sector, the Iranians have lost contact with their garrison at Abadan. However, the island is not completely cut off and a steady trickle of reinforcement arrives to help the defenders on its southern tip. At night Iranian helicopters airlift the wounded back to the mainland.

October 17

DIPLOMACY: In New York City, Iranian prime minister Mohammad Ali Rajai addresses the UN Security Council and blames the United States for instigating the recent Iraqi invasion. Subsequent debate in the Security Council proves inconclusive.

POLITICS: A report surfaces in the *New York Times* that President Jimmy Carter is trying to arrange a spare parts-for-hostages deal with the Iranian government to free the American hostages prior to the upcoming presidential election.

October 18

DIPLOMACY: In Washington, D.C., President Jimmy Carter declares that Iraqi forces have gone beyond their stated goals in Iran and that the United States wishes to see all invading forces withdraw. He does so in an attempt to curry Iranian favor for a possible hostage release.

October 19

DIPLOMACY: In a secret deal made with U.S. presidential candidate Ronald W. Reagan, the Iranian government pledges not to release the American hostages before election day, whereupon Reagan promises to supply Iran with U.S.-made weapons and spare parts.

POLITICS: In Baghdad, Iraq, President Saddam Hussein goes on the airwaves to explain that complete victory has eluded the nation owing to Iran's preponderance of men and equipment. On this, the day before the Muslim holiday of Eid al Adha, he also declares a jihad (holy war) against the Persians, proclaiming them Shiite heretics.

October 20

DIPLOMACY: In another sop to Iran, the State Department declares that Iraq's recent invasion of that country threatens the stability of the Gulf region and that disputed territory should not be seized by force.

October 21

DIPLOMACY: In Baghdad, Iraq, First Deputy Minister Taha Yassin Ramadan declares that his country intends to annex the oil-rich fields of Khuzestan, Iran, before negotiating with Iran over other disputed territories, namely, the entire Shatt al Arab waterway, three islands in the Strait of Hormuz, and the Musian region of Iran.

October 23

DIPLOMACY: In New York City, the U.S. ambassador to the United Nations declares that Iran's territorial integrity is threatened by the Iraqi invasion. Such statements are intended to convey to Tehran America's demonstrated neutrality on the war with Iraq.

October 24

MILITARY: Iraqi forces have fought their way into the port city of Khorramshahr and claim to have finally captured it. However, they prefer to simply bombard their opponents with superior firepower rather than engaging in costly house-to-house fighting. Fighting has cost each side roughly 7,000 casualties, and the Iraqis have also lost roughly 100 tanks in the struggle. Both sides subsequently refer to the city as Khunistan or "City of Blood."

POLITICS: In Tehran, Ayatollah Khomeini appeals to clerics to refrain from interfering with military decision-making

October 26

AVIATION: The Iraqis launch another seven Frog-7 tactical missiles at Dezful, Iran; the Iranian government reports that the attack killed 100 civilians.

October 27

MILITARY: In another warning to Iran, a Marine Corps amphibious expeditionary force of 8,000 men, 30 helicopters, and 50 landing craft passes through the Suez Canal, Egypt, en route to the Gulf region.

October 28

DIPLOMACY: In Washington, D.C., a wistful President Jimmy Carter declares that if the American hostages are freed from Iran, he would release and airlift $300 million to $500 million in spare military parts needed by the Iranian military in its struggle with Iraq.

In Tehran, Iran, General Ali Aslam, the Syrian deputy chief of staff, arrives to confer with Iranian Defense Minister General Javal Fakouri and General Valiollah Fallahi, joint chief of staff. Shortly afterward a small but steady trickle of arms and spare parts begins arriving.

October 31

DIPLOMACY: In Washington, D.C., a Pentagon spokesman announces that the United States owes Iran $500 million worth of military equipment partially paid for by the late shah, including the latest cluster and laser-guided ordnance, and that the materiel could be delivered promptly—after, of course, the American hostages have been released.

MILITARY: Iraqi forces capture Iranian oil minister Mohammad Javar Baquir Tonguyen when he strays too close to the battlefield. When the Iranian government demands his immediate release, citing international law, the Iraqis point to the American hostage situation in Tehran, and he remains a captive.

November 4

DIPLOMACY: In Tehran, Iran, the government announces four additional conditions for releasing the 52 American hostages. They constitute a pledge to stop intervening in Iranian affairs, unfreeze Iranian assets in the United States, drop all financial claims against the United States, and return all the wealth of the late shah Mohammad Reza Pahlavi. The State Department responds by declaring it will take time to study the proposal and questions if it has the legal authority to fulfill the last two demands.

November 7

POLITICS: In Tehran, Iran, former foreign minister Sadegh Ghotzbzadeh is arrested following a television broadcast in which he criticized the ruling Islamic Republican Party.

November 8

MILITARY: The Iranian government claims that its forces have rebuffed an Iraqi attack outside Abadan. The Iraqi media assert that its forces have killed several enemy troops, destroyed several tanks, and sunk two Iranian gunboats in the Shatt al Arab waterway.

November 9

POLITICS: In Baghdad, Iraq, President Saddam Hussein takes to the airwaves to declare that his nation is waging a holy war based on the ideals of the prophet Muhammad. He further declares that the price of gasoline and kerosene will be raised 400 percent while certain commodities such as sugar and electricity are subject to rationing. The Iranian government imposes similar restrictions on wartime commodities.

November 10

MILITARY: The Iraqi government announces the capture of Khorramshahr, Iran; however, 1,500 Iraqi were killed and 4,000 wounded in the battle, a toll President Saddam Hussein had hoped to avoid. By this date it is estimated that the Iraqis occupy 10,000 square miles of Iranian territory along the 735-mile-long international border. Their penetration ranges from 25 miles inland to only six miles.

POLITICS: In Baghdad, Iraq, President Saddam Hussein holds a news conference in which he blames Iran for starting the war on September 4 by shelling Iraqi settlements along the border. He also reiterates his intention to secure complete control of the Shatt al Arab and now insists on freedom of navigation in both the Persian Gulf and the Strait of Hormuz.

In Tehran, Iran, former foreign minister Sadegh Ghotzbzadeh is released from prison upon the orders of Ayatollah Khomeini.

November 12

AVIATION: Iran, to underscore its displeasure with suspected Kuwaiti support for Iraq, launches an air raid on several border outposts.

DIPLOMACY: The government of Algeria agrees to act as an intermediary between Iran and the United States. It also delivers a secret response from the U.S. State Department, accepting the four new conditions but requesting legal clarification on several details.

MILITARY: In the southern sector, Iraqi forces step up their efforts to take the Iranian city of Abadan, but real territorial gains elude them.

November 13

POLITICS: In Kabul, Afghanistan, President Babrak Karmal threatens to expel any PDPA member who fails to uphold the best interests of the party, regardless of prior activities.

November 14–17
MILITARY: Iraqi forces again fail to capture the Iranian town of Susangard, and a stalemate ensues in the Khuzestan region. Unable to advance further, the invaders begin consolidating their gains and are content to simply shell the city and its inhabitants.

November 16
AVIATION: Iran launches another air raid against Kuwaiti outposts to signify its anger over Kuwait's financial support for Iraq.

DIPLOMACY: The government of Kuwait accuses Iran of launching rockets into its border territory with Iraq.

November 16–17
MILITARY: The Iraqi Army claims to have killed 500 Iranians in the struggle for Susangard, in the southwestern sector, but the settlement remains in Iranian hands.

November 20
DIPLOMACY: In New York City, the UN General Assembly passes a resolution demanding the immediate removal of all "foreign troops" from Afghanistan. It passes on a vote of 111 for and 22 against, with 12 abstentions. The fact that the Soviet Union is not mentioned by name demonstrates the unwillingness of many Islamic countries, embroiled in a struggle with Israel, to embarrass their "champion."

MILITARY: In Kabul, Afghanistan, President Babrak Karmal announces a lengthening of service by all military conscripts to offset high desertion levels in the Afghan military. Over intervening months, the military has declined from 80,000 men to only 30,000. By now, many mujahideen groups are operating in the open in many major cities while the capital itself is subject to raids and mortar attacks at night.

November 21
DIPLOMACY: In Kabul, Afghanistan, Foreign Affairs Minister Shah Muhammad Dost denounces the recent UN resolution as interference in its internal affairs.

November 22
DIPLOMACY: In Tehran, Iran, the government denies Kuwaiti allegations that it had launched rockets into border regions next to Iraq. In turn, it accuses Iraq of launching missile strikes against the settlement of Gilan.

November 27
DIPLOMACY: In Tehran, Iran, the militants holding the American hostages declare that they have turned them over to the Iranian government.

November 28–29
NAVAL: A force of combined Iranian air, sea, and commando forces commence Operation Morvarid (Pearl) by successfully attacking oil refineries on the Fao Peninsula and the offshore oil terminal at Mina al Bakr. Moreover, the Iraqis lose five Osa class gunboats and four P-6 patrol craft, representing 80 percent of its naval assets. The damage slashes Iraqi oil exports to 50,000–55,000 barrels a day, down from 3.5 million before the war commenced.

December 5
AVIATION: The Iranian government declares that Iraqi jets had destroyed a major pipeline and that Iranian jets struck back by hitting oil refineries on the Fao Peninsula.

December 6
AVIATION: The Iraqi government claims that Iranian warplanes bombed several targets in Iraqi Kurdistan, whereupon four were shot down.

December 7
AVIATION: Both air forces continue hitting oil-producing targets at Fao, Iraq, and Abadan, Iran, while the 300-mile front seems to have shifted very little over the past few weeks.

December 8
DIPLOMACY: In Tehran, Iran, Majlis Speaker Hojatolislam Hashemi Rafsanjani announces that resolution of the American hostage crisis is close at hand.

December 10
AVIATION: As the Iran-Iraq War rages in full fury, four additional Boeing E-3A AWACS aircraft are deployed to Ramstein Air Base, West Germany, to help monitor military events throughout the Middle East.
MILITARY: In Baghdad, Iraq, President Saddam Hussein announces that he is turning 36 American-built M-60 tanks, captured from Iran, over to the Jordanians.

December 11
POLITICS: The Iraqi government, perhaps sensing that it has bitten off more than it can chew, begins predicting that the present war is likely to last a long time.

December 13–14
DIPLOMACY: In Tehran, Iran, Ahmad Azzi, director of American hostage affairs with the prime minister's office, announces that the U.S. response to Iranian demands has been positive. He subsequently adds that quick action on behalf of the Americans might result in the hostages returning home in time for Christmas.

December 15
MILITARY: In Khuzestan, Iran, intense fighting is reported to have claimed the life of 96 Iranians and 122 Iraqis. The invaders are meeting increasingly stubborn and fanatical resistance in the form of zealous Revolutionary Guards or Pasdaran.

December 17
MILITARY: In Baghdad, Iraq, a government spokesman announces that the Iraqi Army has begun using captured American M-60 tanks, 155mm cannon, and TOW missile launchers, all of which have been captured from Iran. However, Western analysts question whether the poorly trained Iraqis could cope with such sophisticated weapons systems in so little time.

December 18
POLITICS: In Tehran, Iran, a firing squad executes Simon Farzami, Jewish editor of the newspaper *Tehran Journal,* on charges that he was spying for the United States.

December 19

DIPLOMACY: In Tehran, Iran, the government informs the United States that it must deposit $30 billion of Iranian assets in an Algerian bank and guarantee that it will help track down and return the late shah's wealth. The Americans counter that only $8 billion of Iranian assets are frozen and that the government has no knowledge of the shah's possessions. State Department spokesman John H. Trauttner believes, in light of this turn of events, the hostages will probably not be released in time for Christmas.

POLITICS: By this date, Iraq announces that it has halted all pumping activities in its northern oil fields.

December 20

DIPLOMACY: In Tehran, Iran, Prime Minister Mohammed Ali Rajai declares that the main obstacle to hostage negotiations is the return of the late shah's wealth. He also suggests that Washington deposit between $5 billion and $10 billion in an Algerian account, which the Iranians would draw from as the shah's possessions are identified. The State Department considers this a ransom demand and threatens that future negotiations might be halted until after the inauguration of Ronald W. Reagan.

MILITARY: In Tehran, Iran, President Abolhassan Bani-Sadr is under increasing pressure to begin mounting local counteroffensives to regain land lost to Iraq in the early part of the war. Despite the forthcoming rainy season, he reluctantly begins planning to attack along a 450-mile front by retaking Qasr-i-Sherin and Mehran, reducing pockets around Susangard and Ahvaz, and lifting the siege of Abadan.

December 22

DIPLOMACY: In Tehran, Iran, Majlis speaker Hojatolislam Hashemi Rafsanjani warns that unless the United States places $24 billion in Algeria to cover guarantees of frozen Iranian assets and the shah's property, the American hostages may be put on trial as spies.

MILITARY: The Iraqi military, putting its best face forward, announces that its troops have seized one-third of all oil-producing regions within Khuzestan Province, Iran.

December 24

AVIATION: Iraqi warplanes attack and bomb Abadan for the first time since September 22, while other aircraft also raid Kharg Island in the Persian Gulf.

DIPLOMACY: In Washington, D.C., President Jimmy Carter rules out any possibility of paying ransom for the American hostages being held in Iran. President-elect Ronald W. Reagan also refers to the Iranians as "nothing better than criminals and kidnappers."

MILITARY: In the northern sector, an Iraqi infantry division advances and captures the town of Penjwin, Iran, quickly acquiring 300 square miles of Iranian territory. This last action concludes the first phase of the Iran-Iraq War, in which Iraq occupies 4,126 square miles of territory, but the cities of Abadan and Susangard still elude capture.

December 25

DIPLOMACY: In Tehran, Iran, Monsignor Annibale Bugini, the papal nuncio in Iran, holds a Christmas Day service for 26 of the American hostages. The proceedings were also televised.

MILITARY: In Cairo, Egypt, President Anwar Sadat announces that his nation is supplying weapons and other forms of support to the Afghan resistance.

December 26

DIPLOMACY: In Tehran, Iran, the Algerian ambassador claims to have visited all 52 of the American hostages and says they appeared to be in good health. New film footage is also released by the government.

MILITARY: In Baghdad, Iraq, the government announces that its troops have advanced into Iranian Kurdistan, thereby extending the war front along the entire border region.

December 27

DIPLOMACY: In Tehran, Iran, Afghans living in the city attack the Soviet embassy to protest the Soviet invasion and occupation. After the protesters break into the compound and burn a Soviet flag, Iranian police disperse them.

In Tehran, Iran, the government offers a new plan to the United States, insisting that the United States turn over $9 billion in frozen assets while Iran holds the hostages until the rest of the claims are arbitrated over the ensuing year.

POLITICS: In Rome, Italy, former Afghan monarch Mohammed Zahir Shah states that he is praying for the deliverance of Afghanistan in its war for independence from Soviet occupation.

December 28

DIPLOMACY: The Soviet government strongly protests the takeover of its embassy in Tehran, Iran, and demands better security measures, but also notes that the protesters were Afghans, not Iranians.

In Washington, D.C., President-elect Ronald W. Reagan dismisses the new Iranian hostage offer as "ransom" sought by "barbarians" that should not be accepted. The government also announces that it has been making offers to the Iranians, including the return of $6 billion in frozen assets, the seizure of all the shah's known property, and the dismissal of court claims once an international commission has been established to deal with private claims against Iran. These proposals are only valid following the release of all the hostages.

December 30

DIPLOMACY: In Washington, D.C., the Carter administration, eager to end the hostage situation while it still holds office, proposes setting a deadline for resolving the hostage issue. This entails transferring $6 billion to an Algerian bank as the 52 hostages are released to the Algerian ambassador.

December 31

POLITICS: By this date, in addition to waging a bloody war with Iraq, Iran is also saddled with caring for more than 1 million Afghans who have fled the Soviet invasion of their country.

1981

January 2
DIPLOMACY: In New York City, Pakistan's new foreign minister, Shahabzada Yaqub Khan, approaches UN secretary-general Kurt Waldheim to appoint a representative to frame a negotiated settlement to end the Afghan crisis. Thus begins the process of setting up "indirect talks" between Pakistan and Afghanistan, in which a UN special envoy functions as the go-between. However, Afghan representatives are from the Kabul regime only, with none of the armed opposition being privy to discussions.

January 3
DIPLOMACY: In Tehran, Iran, the Algerian intermediaries meet with Iranian government officials to discuss freeing the hostages, but no official response is forthcoming.

January 5
MILITARY: Gathering its strength, Iran launches a counterattack in the Dezful-Susangard area with three understrength armored regiments from the 16th Armored Division. The Iraqis allow the Iranian tanks to advance, unsupported by infantry, as far as Hoveyheh as they mass their own armor in the vicinity of Achmed Abad before counterattacking.

Two Iranian mountain regiments attack out of the Qasr-i-Sherin pocket toward Gilna Garb and drive back Iraqi forces about five miles in mountainous terrain. Several prisoners and some equipment are taken.

Fighting in the Mehran pocket commences and advances toward the upper reaches of the Galal River, where some slight territorial gains are registered.

Iranian mechanized units also attack besieging Iraqi units outside the city of Ahvaz and drive their advanced forces back a few miles. However, the city remains within range of Iraqi artillery and is constantly shelled.

POLITICS: In Tehran, Iran, President Abolhassan Bani-Sadr, putting his best face forward, claims that Iranian forces killed 200 Iraqis and captured 500 near Ahvaz, Iran, with a further 100 killed near Gilan. He makes no mention of Iranian casualties.

January 6
MILITARY: Outside Hoveyheh, Iran, the Iranian 16th Armored Division lurches forward in muddy conditions and stumbles headlong into a killing field prepared for them by the Iraqis. Both sides operate roughly 300 tanks apiece, but the Iraqis had deployed on all three sides of the oncoming enemy, decimating the 1st Brigade, which loses 100 vehicles. This is also the largest tank engagement since the 1973 Arab-Israeli War.

January 7
MILITARY: At Hoveyheh, Iran, the 2nd Iranian Brigade charges forward into Iraqi positions, becomes stuck in a three-sided trap set for them, and suffers heavy losses. Many tanks are trapped in the deep mud and are unable to maneuver normally. Iranian losses are severe before combat ends.

In Tehran, Iran, 500 Iraqi captives, taken outside of Qasr-i-Sherin, are humiliatingly paraded down the city streets.

January 8

MILITARY: At Hoveyheh, Iran, the 3rd Iranian Tank Brigade charges into the three-sided Iraqi trap and is badly battered but nonetheless extricates itself before losses become prohibitive. Many vehicles, however, are either destroyed or simply abandoned.

January 9

DIPLOMACY: In Tehran, Iran, the government raises questions about the total amount of frozen assets it would receive from a deal struck with the United States.
MILITARY: Outside of Hoveyheh, Iran, the Iranian 16th Armored Division pulls back and disengages from combat. Its leaders admit to a loss of 88 tanks while the Iraqis claim to have captured or destroyed 214. Either way, it is a humiliating setback for the Iranian regular army, especially its armored branch. Iraqi losses are about 100 tanks, many of which will be repaired and back in service shortly.
POLITICS: In Tehran, Iran, President Abolhassan Bani-Sadr vows that Iran will continue fighting as long as Iraqi troops are on its soil.

January 10

DIPLOMACY: In Washington, D.C., the government announces that Iran would initially receive $5.5 billion in frozen assets once the hostages have been freed, and that the remaining 70 percent of all assets would probably be transferred a few days later.
MILITARY: The Iraqi military claims to have won a major engagement in the oil-rich province of Khuzestan, Iran, destroying parts of an Iranian armored division.

January 11

DIPLOMACY: In Tehran, Iran, special minister Ahmad Azizi declares that his government has accepted the Algerian proposal that, instead of putting up $24 billion in Algerian banks, the United States would simply guarantee its payment.

January 12

POLITICS: In Nicosia, Cyprus, it is announced that Iraq is raising the price it charges for a barrel of oil by $4. This change will have no effect on the United States, which imports only 1 percent of its oil from that country, but it is expected to affect major importers such as France, Italy, Brazil, Japan, and India.

January 13

MILITARY: Fighting along the Iranian border subsides slightly as Iraqi forces appear to be digging in to defend their territorial gains.
POLITICS: In light of the recent Iranian debacle outside of Hoveyheh, Ayatollah Khomeini goes on the airwaves and urges public criticism of the military, which is demoralizing to soldiers and civilians alike, to cease immediately.

January 14

POLITICS: In Tehran, Iran, the Council of Guardians, a body that approves all legislation passed by the Majlis, approves two bills authorizing arbitration of disputes involving Iranian assets and another nationalizing the shah's wealth.

January 15

MILITARY: In the northern sector, parts of an Iraqi mountain division crosses the border and seizes the Iranian town of Nowdesheh. This is done to establish a viable supply route for Kurdish Democratic Party *peshmerga* (guerrillas) operating against Iran.

POLITICS: In Tehran, Iran, Ayatollah Khomeini lectures the Iranian people and calls on them to stop criticizing President Abolhassan Bani-Sadr's conduct of the war with Iraq. He also accuses the Soviet Union of dispatching military advisers and weapons to the Iraqis.

January 15–16

DIPLOMACY: In Tehran, Iran, Behzad Nabavi, minister of state for executive affairs, insists that all frozen Iranian assets must be placed in Algerian banks no later than January 16, then retracts his statement after the United States declares the time frame is impossible.

In Washington, D.C., President Jimmy Carter orders $900 million worth of gold exchanged with Britain, so that the United States would possess sufficient stocks in the Bank of England for a transfer to Iran.

January 17

POLITICS: Twelve large banks in the United States agree to forgo lawsuits seeking repayment of loans owed by Iran if Iran agrees to pay down a portion of the debt and settle the rest later.

January 18

DIPLOMACY: After three months of intense negotiations, Iran and the United States reach an agreement for releasing the American hostages. This entails placing $8 billion of an estimated $12 billion in frozen Iranian assets into an Algerian escrow account. Only $2.9 billion is released directly to Iran, while $3.7 billion pays off American bank loans with a final $1.4 billion left in escrow until an international claims commission settles all disputes. The Algerian government played a major role as a go-between in the negotiations.

January 20

DIPLOMACY: In Islamabad, Pakistan, the government declares that it will recognize only six mujahideen groups operating from its soil. They are predominately Sunni, which requires Shiite resistance fighters to seek assistance from neighboring Iran.

In Tehran, Iran, radical students release 52 captive American hostages after 444 days of captivity, ending a crisis that brought down the administration of President Jimmy Carter. They are flown to Athens on an Algerian airliner, then transferred to a U.S. Air Force transport for conveyance to a military hospital in Wiesbaden, West Germany, for testing.

POLITICS: In Washington, D.C., Ronald W. Reagan is sworn in as president of the United States. His arrival at the White House will mark a paradigm shift as far as military assistance to the Afghan resistance is concerned.

January 21

POLITICS: Former president Jimmy Carter flies to Wiesbaden, West Germany, as President Ronald W. Reagan's personal representative. He is shocked to hear that the hostages had been tortured with beatings and months of solitary confinement and were also subject to mock firing squads.

January 25
POLITICS: At Stewart International Airport, New York, an Air Force VC-137 nicknamed "Freedom One" lands with the 52 former hostages. They are bused to the nearby U.S. Military Academy to meet with family members.

January 25–30
DIPLOMACY: In Taif, Saudi Arabia, the annual Conference of Islamic States passes a resolution demanding the removal of "foreign" forces from Afghanistan. However, it does not mention the Soviet Union by name, to avoid antagonizing the only superpower championing the group's cause against Israel. Nonetheless, the Afghan delegation is not seated. The five-member Iranian delegation is also absent, having been instructed by Ayatollah Khomeini to boycott the proceedings owing to the presence of Iraqi president Saddam Hussein. Libya is also absent to protest the presence of U.S. AWACS aircraft on Saudi soil.

January 26
DIPLOMACY: In Taif, Saudi Arabia, UN secretary-general Kurt Waldheim appeals to the Conference of Islamic States to mediate an end to the Iran-Iraq conflict.

January 27
POLITICS: In Washington, D.C., the 52 former hostages, with about 400 family members, gather on the South Lawn of the White House to celebrate their freedom. Their motorcade is greeted by thousands of cheering onlookers.

January 30
POLITICS: In New York City, 21 former hostages participate in a ticker-tape parade down Broadway.

February
DIPLOMACY: In New Delhi, India, an international conference of nonaligned nations adopts a resolution calling for the removal of foreign troops from Afghanistan and the imposition of self-determination.

February 1
AVIATION: In a major escalation, France agrees to sell Iraq 60 advanced F-1 Mirage fighter jets.

February 2
MILITARY: The Iranian government claims to have killed more than 200 Iraqis in limited counteroffensives in Iranian Kurdistan and Azerbaijan over the past two days. Iraq, for its part, insists that it has killed 166 Iranians and shot down an F-4 Phantom jet and two helicopters.

February 3
AVIATION: In Baghdad, Iraq, the Foreign Ministry confirms the arrival of the first four French Mirage F-1 fighters. These are far more formidable than the Soviet-supplied MiG aircraft then in use.

DIPLOMACY: Reports begin to surface that Saudi Arabia, and other Gulf states, which greatly resent and fear Iran, have been clandestinely coordinating efforts to send the embattled Iraqi regime money and weapons.

MILITARY: Reports surface in London, United Kingdom, that 100 Soviet-made tanks from eastern Europe have been shipped to Iraq through Saudi Arabia.

February 4

DIPLOMACY: Iran releases Mohi Sobhani, an Iranian-American citizen from Los Angeles, California, who had been charged with spying the previous September.

Swiss authorities also meet with Iranian counterparts relative to the captivity of American journalist Cynthia B. Dwyer, who had been arrested on May 5, 1980, and charged with espionage.

February 9

DIPLOMACY: In Pakistan, Foreign Minister Agha Shahi claims that his proposal to visit both Baghdad and Tehran in the interest of promoting a cease-fire has been well-received by the leaders of eight Islamic nations.

February 10

MILITARY: In Ilam, Iran, Iraqi president Saddam Hussein pays a morale-boosting visit to the troops, who then attack Iranian positions in the nearby hills; they reportedly kill 163 defenders at a cost of 45 of their own.

POLITICS: In Tehran, Iran, a spokesman for the Iranian Government Foundation for War Refugees claims that Iraq's shelling of border settlements has created 2 million refugees within the country, mostly from Khuzestan Province.

February 11

DIPLOMACY: The Iranian government releases freelance writer Cynthia B. Dwyer after holding her for nine months in jails for spying.

February 18

DIPLOMACY: Afghan president Babrak Karmal returns to Moscow, Soviet Union, for additional talks with Soviet leaders.

February 19

DIPLOMACY: In Tehran, Iran, President Abolhassan Bani-Sadr confers with UN special envoy Olof Palme, the former Swedish prime minister, to discuss a way of ending the war. The Iranians appear united in their demand that all Iraqi forces must withdraw from their territory before talks are possible. It was also hoped that the talks would allow the 70 or so foreign vessels trapped in the Shatt al Arab waterway to safely depart.

February 23

DIPLOMACY: The Iranian government closes down all Anglican churches in the country and releases three missionaries held captive under charges of espionage.

February 28

DIPLOMACY: In Tehran, Iran, a high-level Islamic mission arrives, including the presidents of Bangladesh, Gambia, Guinea, and Pakistan, and high-ranking ministers of

Malaysia, Senegal, Turkey, and the PLO. They hope to have discussions with both President Abolhassan Bani-Sadr and Ayatollah Khomeini.

March 1–5
DIPLOMACY: In Tehran, Iran, Ayatollah Khomeini confers with the nine-member team from the Islamic states and urges them to firmly establish who the aggressor was in the present war. The members then draft a proposed cease-fire agreement followed by a return of all forces to their international boundaries, but the Iranian Supreme Defense Council (SDC) rejects it out of hand, insisting the war will continue for as long as Iraqi units are deployed on its territory.

March 3–4
DIPLOMACY: The high-level Islamic peace commission decides to proffer specific cease-fire proposals to both Tehran and Baghdad in the hopes of ending the present conflict. After conferring with Ayatollah Khomeini and President Saddam Hussein, commission members return to Jidda, Saudi Arabia, to await their response.
MILITARY: Mujahideen activity in the Panjshir Valley, Afghanistan, prompts the Soviets to dispatch four battalions of troops into the area to reassert control. No resistance is encountered, and, once the Soviets depart, the resistance units filter back in.

March 4
NAVAL: The Italian government agrees to sell Iraq two Lupo Class frigates, six corvettes, a floating dock, and a Stromboli class support vessel.

March 7
DIPLOMACY: In Baghdad, Iraq, the government declares it will not give up a "single inch" of Iranian territory until Iraqi rights are recognized.

March 9
DIPLOMACY: In Washington, D.C., President Ronald W. Reagan unequivocally declares his willingness to supply the anti-Soviet mujahideen in Afghanistan with arms.

March 11
DIPLOMACY: In Geneva, Switzerland, the UN High Commissioner for Refugees announces that an estimated 2 million Afghans are living in camps throughout Pakistan.
POLITICS: In Tehran, Iran, the ongoing struggle between President Abolhassan Bani-Sadr and fanatical cliques within the Islamic Republican Party intensifies when the Majlis (parliament) votes to restrict his powers.

March 12
AVIATION: The Iraqis bombard Dezful and Ahvaz, Iran, with Soviet-supplied Frog-7 tactical missiles; many civilian casualties are reported.

March 15
DIPLOMACY: In Baghdad, Iraq, General Adnan Khairallah, the Iraqi defense minister, returns from a visit to the Soviet Union and angrily states that not a single bullet has been provided by Moscow since the war with Iran commenced.

POLITICS: In Baghdad, Iraq, President Saddam Hussein offers to arm Iranian political refugees associated with the Mujahideen-i-Khalq, a sign that recent peace discussions have been rejected.

March 17
POLITICS: In Washington, D.C., Senator Alan Cranston claims that Iraq is capable of manufacturing a nuclear weapon by year's end and calls for greater international efforts against proliferation.

March 19
DIPLOMACY: In Washington, D.C., Secretary of State Alexander M. Haig Jr. testifies before the Senate Foreign Relations Committee, noting that Iraq, locked in a huge war with Iran, may be motivated to shift many of its most distasteful policies, raising the possibility of improved relations with the United States.

MILITARY: Near Gilan, Khermanshah Province, Iran, heavy fighting erupts between Iraqi and Iranian forces, and the former claim to have killed 124 of the latter.

March 19–20
MILITARY: Iraqi forces make another failed attempt to seize Susangard, Iran, indicating that they have exhausted their ability to make additional territorial gains. Defeat here also marks a turning point in the conflict as, hereafter, the strategic initiative passes into Iranian hands.

Vice President George Bush welcomes Colonel Thomas E. Schaefer, one of the Americans held hostage by Iran. *(Department of Defense)*

March 22
AVIATION: The Iraqis strike Dezful and Ahvaz, Iran, for a second time with Frog-7 tactical missiles, apparently in frustration for failing to capture it with ground forces.

March 27
DIPLOMACY: In Islamabad, Pakistan, the government insists that the Afghan resistance movement obtain "durable and certain" military assistance in their struggle against the Soviets, but their sanctuary camps along the border should also be strengthened against attack.

March 30–31
DIPLOMACY: In Tehran, Iran, another Islamic peace mission headed by President Ahmed Sekou Toure of Guinea fails to persuade Iran to accept a cease-fire, and flies to Baghdad, Iraq, where talks prove equally unproductive.

March 31
DIPLOMACY: In Cairo, Egypt, President Anwar Sadat admits that he sold 4,000 tons of military supplies and missiles to Iraq, even though the two countries are diplomatically estranged from each other.

April

DIPLOMACY: In New York City, UN secretary-general Kurt Waldheim selects the Peruvian diplomat Javier Pérez de Cuéllar to serve as a special envoy between Pakistan and Afghanistan. He immediately visits Kabul and Islamabad to help launch negotiations between them.

April 2

DIPLOMACY: Members of the failed Islamic peace conference announce that they will dispatch two members back to Baghdad and Tehran for additional discussions relative to a cease-fire.

April 4

AVIATION: In a major air raid, Iranian F-4 Phantom jets strike the main Iraqi air base at Walid, near the Syrian border, damaging or destroying 46 aircraft, including large Tu-22 bombers. Their ability to hit targets 506 miles from their own border indicates Iran's impressive aerial reach. The apparent ease with which the raid was conducted forces the government in Damascus, Syria, to deny Iraq's allegations of having colluded with Iran.

DIPLOMACY: In Tehran Iran, the Islamic Republican Party votes to endorse the overthrow of Iraqi president Saddam Hussein. This comes over the objections of President Abolhassan Bani-Sadr, who sought more moderate ends towards ending the present conflict.

April 6

DIPLOMACY: In Tehran, Iran, President Abolhassan Bani Sadr dismisses the proposals by the recent Islamic peace commission as too vague to be workable.

April 7

DIPLOMACY: The government of Saudi Arabia announces that it is severing diplomatic relations with the "illegal regime" in Afghanistan.

April 15

MILITARY: As Iranian forces continue gathering strength, intense fighting breaks out in the oil-rich province of Khuzestan, Iran.

April 22

POLITICS: In Peshawar, Pakistan, irreconcilable difference between competing mujahideen factions lead to the dismantling of the first alliance of Islamic resistance groups. The schism gives rise to two separate alliances—moderates under Mohammad Nabi Mohammadi, Sibghatullah Mojaddedi, and Ahmad Gailani, and fundamentalists under Gulbuddin Hekmatyar, Yunnis Khalis, and Burhanuddin Rabbani.

April 24

DIPLOMACY: In Washington, D.C., President Ronald W. Reagan lifts the 15-month-old grain embargo against the Soviet Union, calling it unsound to punish American farmers for Soviet aggression.

April 28

POLITICS: Throughout Iraq, President Saddam Hussein's birthday is celebrated as a national holiday, and he is heralded as a towering Arab hero in a war against the hated Persians.

April 30

NAVAL: In the Persian Gulf, an Iranian naval vessel accosts a Kuwaiti survey ship owned by an American firm and escort it back to Bushehr, where it is released on May 18.

May 4–7

DIPLOMACY: In Moscow, Soviet Union, UN secretary-general Kurt Waldheim and special envoy Javier Pérez de Cuéllar arrive for three days of talks over the Afghan crisis.

POLITICS: In Kabul, Afghanistan, Sultan Ali Keshtmand, a Shiite, is appointed as prime minister.

May 9

POLITICS: Western analysts believe that as many as 2 million Afghan refugees are residing in Pakistan. Substantial numbers are also in Iran.

May 11

POLITICS: In Kabul, Afghanistan, Sultan Ali Keshtmand is sworn into office as prime minister.

May 28

TERRORISM: Militants belonging to the Shiite Al Daawa group manage to sabotage an ammunition depot and fuel tanks near Baghdad Airport, Iraq.

May 31

MILITARY: The Iranian government claims to have halted an Iraqi offensive on the city of Dehloran in the Musian sector.

June 1

POLITICS: In Tehran, Iran, a special commission established by Ayatollah Khomeini informs President Abolhassan Bani-Sadr that he violated the constitution by refusing to sign bills passed by the Majlis (parliament). However, no legal action is recommended against Bani-Sadr.

June 5

POLITICS: In Tehran, Iran, President Abolhassan Bani-Sadr vows to remain in office. Nonetheless, he divines that the end is near for his tenure as chief executive—and he prepares to flee the country.

June 7

AVIATION: At Tuwaythat, Iraq, Israeli warplanes drop "smart bombs" on the French-built nuclear reactor/research center outside Baghdad at 6:30 P.M., killing one French technician. The 15 U.S.-supplied F-15 Eagles completed the 1,500-mile round-trip mission by surreptitiously violating Jordanian and Saudi airspace and returned without loss. It was feared that the $275 million facility, constructed by Italy and France, was capable of producing enriched uranium for nuclear weapons.

June 8

DIPLOMACY: In Washington, D.C., an administration spokesman condemns the recent Israeli raid in the strongest possible terms.

POLITICS: In Tehran, Iran, Ayatollah Khomeini verbally attacks President Abolhassan Bani-Sadr, warning that he would remove any politician from office who challenges Islamic authority.

June 9
DIPLOMACY: In Moscow, Soviet Union, the government charges the United States with complicity and "gangsterism" regarding the recent Israeli air raid on Iraqi nuclear facilities. However, the Russians evince little sympathy for their previous client state, an indication of worsening relations between the two.

June 10
DIPLOMACY: In Washington, D.C., President Ronald W. Reagan goes on record to state the recent Israeli air raid against Iraq may have violated a prior agreement with that government respecting arms transfers. Consequently, four F-16s are held up from delivery. On a personal note, Reagan accepts parts of Israeli's reasoning for attacking the site.

MILITARY: In Iran, President Abolhassan Bani-Sadr is dismissed as commander in chief by Ayatollah Khomeini. Islamic fundamentalists are suspicious of Bani-Sadr because of his Western education and training.

June 11
POLITICS: In Kabul, Afghanistan, President Babrak Karmal removes Abdurrashid Arian as deputy prime minister.

Members of the Arab League call upon the United Nations to impose binding sanctions on Israel for its attack on the Iraqi nuclear reactor.

In Tehran, Iran, protesters begin swarming into the streets, calling for the arrest, trial, and execution of President Abolhassan Bani-Sadr. The marchers are mobilized by the extreme organization called the Party of God.

June 13
POLITICS: In Kabul, Afghanistan, the Revolutionary Council elects Nur Ahmad Nur and Abdurrashid Arian as its vice presidents.

In Tehran, Iran, President Abolhassan Bani-Sadr takes the hint and goes into hiding while still holding office.

June 14–15
POLITICS: In Tehran, Iran, Ayatollah Khomeini maintains that President Abolhassan Bani-Sadr is still empowered to carry out his duties, then reverses himself by demanding a public apology for urging people to defy the Islamic clergy.

June 15
MILITARY: Iranian artillery commences a heavy bombardment of Basra, Iraq, and environs. The Iraqis respond in kind by shelling Iranian settlements.

June 18
POLITICS: In Tehran, Iran, it is becoming apparent that President Abolhassan Bani-Sadr is in hiding, so the Majlis begins impeachment proceedings against him. In the streets, 19 people are reported to have been killed and 20 injured in armed clashes between rival groups.

June 19

DIPLOMACY: In New York City, the UN Security Council votes unanimously to condemn the Israeli air raid against Iraqi nuclear facilities. The United States, however, only supports the resolution after Baghdad strips all references to American defense commitments to Israel. This is a major Iraqi concession.

June 20

POLITICS: In Tehran, Iran, the Majlis finds President Abolhassan Bani-Sadr unfit for office and removes him. The Iranian prosecutor general subsequently orders his arrest.

TERRORISM: In Iran, the Mujahideen-i-Khalq declares war on the Islamic government of Iran and begins a bombing campaign throughout the capital.

June 21

MILITARY: General Mustafa Ali Chamran, the Iranian defense minister, is killed while inspecting the front in Khuzestan Province, Iran.

June 22

POLITICS: In Baghdad, Iraq, the speaker of Iraq's parliament calls for oil and financial sanctions against the United States while addressing a gathering of Arab representatives.

June 23

POLITICS: In Tehran, Iran, the government steps up its pressure on fugitive former president Abolhassan Bani-Sadr with a mass arrest of his friends and supporters.

June 24

POLITICS: The Iranian government announces that presidential elections would be held on July 24.

June 27

TERRORISM: In Tehran, Iran, a bomb hidden in a tape recorder explodes in the Abouzar mosque, injuring Hojatolislam Ali Khamenei, a close aide to Ayatollah Khomeini.

June 28

TERRORISM: In Tehran, Iran, a bomb rips through the Islamic Republican Party headquarters, killing Chief Justice Ayatollah Mohammad Beheshti and 73 members of parliament and cabinet officials. Prosecutor General Abdulkarim Musavi Ardebili is appointed the new chief justice by Ayatollah Khomeini. The government blames the United States and left-wing groups in league with Abolhassan Bani-Sadr.

July–August

POLITICS: In Kabul, Afghanistan, President Babrak Karmal determines to reverse the anti-religious tenor of the previous Khalq regime by persuading noncommunist elements to support the National Fatherland Front. He goes so far as to appoint Sayyad Afghani, a respected (Islamic scholar) to head the new Department of Islamic Affairs. The mujahideen alliance makes clear its determination to hunt down and kill anybody supporting the National Fatherland Front.

July 1

POLITICS: In Tehran, Iran, 50 leftists of the Mujahideen-i-Khalq are rounded up and charged with plotting to blow up the Majlis (Parliament). The group had been severely denounced by Ayatollah Khomeini, who blamed it for the June 28 bomb blast that killed 73 members of the Islamic Republican Party. The government also announces that some 80 supporters of former president Abolhassan Bani-Sadr have been executed by firing squad.

July 2

DIPLOMACY: In Washington, D.C., the Supreme Court rules that former president Jimmy Carter and President Ronald W. Reagan possess legal authority to fulfill arrangements made to free the American hostages. Consequently, $2 billion of frozen Iranian assets can now be transferred out of the country.

July 4

POLITICS: A London magazine infers that former Iranian president Abolhassan Bani-Sadr has taken refuge among the Kurds in northwestern Iran.

July 5

POLITICS: In Tehran, Iran, the government announces the execution of 27 more suspected leftist guerrillas.

July 9

POLITICS: In Tehran, Iran, the government executes nine more suspected leftist guerrillas and also orders the Reuter news agency to close its Tehran bureau. Meanwhile, a tape recording made by fugitive president Abolhassan Bani-Sadr is clandestinely circulated and broadcast; it urges the populace to support him against the growing tyranny of the government.

July 12

MILITARY: In Afghanistan, General Fateh Muhammad of the national committee of the National Fatherland Front, is killed by the resistance.

July 13

POLITICS: The Iranian government executes 22 more people for "anti-state" activities and an additional six more for drug or sex offences.

July 15–16

POLITICS: By this date an estimated 200 supporters of former president Abolhassan Bani-Sadr have been shot by firing squads, and members of his former bodyguard are ordered to turn over their weapons. An additional 200 suspected leftists are rounded up, and four of these are put to death.

July 22

MILITARY: At Paghman, Afghanistan, heavy fighting reportedly erupts between Soviet forces and mujahideen fighters. This places the front line only 16 miles from Kabul.

July 23

AVIATION: Over Yerevan, Armenia (Soviet Union), a Red Air Force fighter rams into a large, unidentified transport that was violating national airspace and the intruder crashes. This was apparently an Iranian aircraft used to smuggle in spare parts from Cyprus and Turkey.

July 24

POLITICS: In Tehran, Iran, Prime Minister Mohammed Ali Rajai wins the nation's second presidential election by a larger margin than his highly popular predecessor. In this capacity he appoints General Musa Namju to serve as defense minister while General Valiollah Fallahi held onto his position as acting chief of staff and General Javad Fakour maintained control of the Air Force. Ali Kolahduz was authorized to control the Pasdaran along the battle fronts.

July 29

DIPLOMACY: In Tehran, Iran, a military plane carrying former president Abolhassan Bani-Sadr is hijacked and flown to Turkish airspace. He is granted political asylum in France, but only on the condition that he refrain from political activities. The Iranian government, meanwhile, demands his immediate extradition.

August 3

DIPLOMACY: In France, former president Abolhassan Bani-Sadr says that he is considering moving to Austria or Sweden since France threatened to deport him should he engage in political statements.

August 5

MILITARY: Iranian artillery begins shelling the largely deserted oil port of Fao, Iraq, then bombards Zubari on the Kuwaiti border.

August 6

DIPLOMACY: In Kabul, Afghanistan, Foreign Minister Shah Mohammad Dost confers with UN special envoy Javier Pérez de Cuéllar.

In Tehran, Iran, the government detains a group of 62 French citizens attempting to leave the country and turns back the aircraft sent to retrieve them.

August 7

DIPLOMACY: In Washington, D.C., supporters of former president Abolhassan Bani-Sadr occupy the Iranian Interest Section building for an hour, and one demonstrator is shot while inside. Police take 24 protesters into custody.

August 10–12

DIPLOMACY: The Iranian government releases 57 French citizens whose departure was held up by France's granting of asylum to former president Abolhassan Bani-Sadr. Another group of 5 departs two days later.

August 12

NAVAL: In the Persian Gulf, Iranian naval vessels seize a Danish cargo craft suspected of carrying arms to Iraq, and it is escorted back to Bandar Abbas.

POLITICS: In an attempt to appease religious traditionalists, the regime of President Babrak Karmal lifts government-imposed limits on acreage held by religious and tribal authorities.

August 15

Naval: Three French patrol craft previously sold to Iran depart Cherbourg, France, but one of them is hijacked by Admiral Habibollah and a group of exiled monarchists in Cádiz, Spain. The gunboats eventually are towed to Iran by a merchant vessel.

August 15–31

Military: In the Panjshir Valley, Afghanistan, Soviet and Afghan forces make another sweep intending to rid the area of mujahideen fighters under Ahmad Shah Massoud.

August 17

Politics: In Tehran, Iran, the state radio announces that an additional 23 leftists have been executed by firing squad.

August 19

Aviation: VF-41 F-14 *Tomcats* from the carrier *Nimitz* down two Libyan Su-22 jets over the Gulf of Sidra, 60 miles from the Libyan coast, after they fired on the Americans in international airspace. Previously, Libyan dictator Muammar Qaddafi had proclaimed a "line of death" that American vessels should not cross.

August 22

Politics: In Peshawar, Pakistan, the mujahideen alliance creates a 50-member advisery council.

August 26

Politics: The Iranian government announces that it has executed an additional 26 leftists for anti-state activities.

August 30

Terrorism: In Tehran, Iran, a bomb blast kills President Mohammed Ali Rajai and Prime Minister Mohammad Javad Bahonar in the latter's office. Several others are killed and wounded.

August 31

Politics: In Tehran, Iran, Hojatolislam Hashemi Rafsanjani and Chief Justice Aya-tollah Moussavi Ardebeli are appointed to a presidential committee that will run the nation until a special election can be scheduled.

September

Aviation: Warplanes belonging to the Afghan Air Force (probably flown by Soviet pilots) violate Pakistani airspace for the first time.

Military: In Kabul, Afghanistan, the regime of Babrak Karmal orders the mobiliza-tion of all reservists up to the age of 35. When demonstrations arise to protest the new order, they are dispersed by tanks and riot police.

September 1

Military: Iranian military forces begin crossing the Kharkheh River with a view towards lifting the siege of Abadan. They consist of three divisions of armor, artillery, and mixed infantry/Pasdaran companies. Their initial deployment suggests that they are massing to attack Al Qurnah on the Basra-Baghdad Road.

POLITICS: In Tehran, Iran, Interior Minister Ayatollah Mohammad Reza Mahdavi-Kani temporarily replaces the late Prime Minister Mohammad Javad Bahonar. The Tehran prayer leader Hojatolislam Ali Khamenei is appointed the new chief of the Islamic Republican Party. The government also announces a new presidential election within 50 days.

September 3

MILITARY: In downtown Tehran, Iran, Revolutionary Guards engage in a fierce gun battle with leftists, killing 10.

September 5

TERRORISM: In Tehran, Iran, a bomb blast kills Prosecutor General Hojatolislam Ali Qoddousi and police chief Houshang Dasterdi.

September 6

MILITARY: In the Panjshir Valley, Afghanistan, the Soviets dispatch sizable forces to attack mujahideen units commanded by Ahmad Shah Massoud. He attacks sapper units sent ahead of the column to clear the way for the main forces, inflicting considerable losses. The Soviets advance only 20 miles into the valley, then retire with a loss of about 100 men and several vehicles.

September 9

DIPLOMACY: In New Delhi, India, Afghan foreign minister Shah Mohammad Dost arrives to confer with Prime Minister Indira Gandhi.

September 11

TERRORISM: In East Azerbaijan, Iran, Ayatollah Assadollah Madani is killed by a bomb explosion during prayer services. He was Ayatollah Khomenei's personal representative to that region. Six others are also killed, and the act is attributed to the Mujahideen-i-Khalq

September 17

POLITICS: Iranian government radio announces that an additional 17 leftists have been executed by firing squad.

September 20–21

POLITICS: In Tehran, Iran, the government executes 194 leftists.

September 22

MILITARY: During an interview on American television, Egyptian president Anwar Sadat states that the United States has been buying up Soviet weapons from the Egyptian Army for use by the Afghan resistance.

The first anniversary of the Iran-Iraq war leaves a death toll estimated at 38,000 Iranians and 22,000 Iraqis, with twice as many combatants wounded. However, because Iran possesses a population base three times larger, it can more readily absorb such losses without serious effects on its military.

September 26–28

MILITARY: The Iranians launch several divisions across the Karun River, intending to break the siege of Abadan. The 60,000 Iraqis present are taken by surprise in the flanks and rear and rolled back to the north side of the river. They retreat across a single pontoon bridge, abandoning 200 tanks and other armored vehicles in the process.

September 27

MILITARY: In Tehran, Iran, a seven-hour street battle erupts between the Revolutionary Guards and Mujahideen i Khalq guerrillas; the government reports that several people were killed and 40 wounded.

September 29

AVIATION: Near Tehran, Iran, a plane crash kills Major General Valiollah Fallahi, the acting chief of staff, and two leading military figures. The event is treated as an accident, not sabotage.

MILITARY: Two Iranian infantry divisions, having infiltrated defensive positions at Abadan by crossing the Bahmanshir River, Iran, attack and encircle several Iraqi armored formations. The Iranian government next announces that its forces have broken the siege of Abadan. Iraqi forces had besieged and bombarded it for nearly a year, only to be upended by a surprise Iranian offensive that kills 600 Iraqis, captures 1,500, and completely destroys the Iraqi 10th Armored Brigade. The remaining Iraqi formations near the city are driven off to the western bank of the Karun River. The Iraqis deny any such reverse and say that a retreat to Khorramshahr was only a "tactical withdrawal."

POLITICS: The Iranian government announces that 43 more leftist guerrillas have been executed by firing squad.

TERRORISM: In Tehran, Iran, a grenade takes the life of Hojatolislam Abdulkarim Hashemi Nejad, a member of the Majlis.

September 30

DIPLOMACY: In Tehran, Iran, the government again rejects a truce proposal advanced by Iraqi president Saddam Hussein.

October 1

AVIATION: Iranian warplanes strike at the oil refinery at Umm, Kuwait, as a warning against Kuwait's continuing financial and military assistance for Iraq. Tehran publicly denies the action, but Saudi AWACS aircraft continually track the warplanes to and from bases in Iran.

MILITARY: In Tehran, Iran, Ayatollah Khomeini appoints Major General Ali Zahirnejad as the military's new chief of staff.

POLITICS: In Paris, France, former president Abolhassan Bani-Sadr declares that he is forming a transitional government in exile that will soon replace the fundamentalist government in Tehran, Iran. He also appoints himself to serve as provisional president.

October 2

POLITICS: In Tehran, Iran, Hojatolislam Ali Khamenei is elected president with 95 percent of the popular vote. He is the third chief executive in 21 months and announces that he will keep Ayatollah Mohammad Reza Mahdavi-Kani as prime minister.

October 3–4

POLITICS: Reports surface that the Iranian government has executed 30 guerrillas belonging to the outlawed Mujahideen-i-Khalq, quickly followed by an additional 40. This brings the total amount of executions since the exile of President Abolhassan Bani-Sadr to 1,500.

October 7

POLITICS: In Tehran, Iran, former prime minister Mehdi Bazargan raises eyebrows in the Majlis by condemning the wholesale execution of leftist guerrillas.

October 8

POLITICS: In Tehran, Iran, the Majlis is preparing to expel former prime minister Mehdi Bazargan for his criticism. An additional 26 leftists are also reported to have been executed in Isfahan.

October 11

POLITICS: The Iranian government reports that an additional 82 suspected leftist guerrillas have been executed by firing squad.

October 13

POLITICS: In Tehran, Iran, Hojatolislam Ali Khamenei is sworn in as president, whereupon he vows to eradicate deviationism, liberalism, and American-oriented leftists.

The Iranian government declares that another 22 suspected leftists had gone before the firing squad. Amnesty International, meanwhile, calculates that more than 1,800 people have been shot in Iran since President Abolhassan Bani-Sadr's ouster.

October 17

DIPLOMACY: In the United States, leaders of the Baha'i faith accuse the Iranian government of persecuting its members on account of their traditional friendly relations with the Jews. According to them, Iranian Bahais are losing pensions, state jobs, and rank in the military while their places of worship have also been destroyed.

October 19

POLITICS: In Tehran, Iran, Ali Akbar Velayati replaces Ayatollah Mohammad Reza Mahdavi-Kani as prime minister.

October 24

MILITARY: The port of Khorramshahr, Iran, finally falls to Iraqi units; this is their biggest victory of the entire war in Iran.

October 25

POLITICS: In Tehran, Iran, Ayatollah Moussavi Ardebeli, president of the Supreme Islamic Revolutionary Court, deflates critics by declaring that since June 20 *only* 2,070 political executions have taken place.

October 27

POLITICS: In Tehran, Iran, Foreign Minister Mir Hossein Mousavi succeeds Ayatollah Mohammad Reza Mahdavi-Kani as prime minister. President Hojatolislam Ali Khamenei's first choice, Ali Akbar Velayati, was rejected.

November 9

POLITICS: In Baghdad, Iraq, President Saddam Hussein again calls for a jihad against Iran.

November 10

DIPLOMACY: In Tehran, Iran, Ayatollah Khomeini advances a peace plan for Afghanistan that consists of diplomatic talks among the Soviet Union, Pakistan, and Iran, with representation for all mujahideen resistance groups and a Muslim peace-keeping force once peace has been resumed.

November 13

DIPLOMACY: In New York City, the UN General Assembly votes to condemn the Israeli attack against Iraqi nuclear facilities, with 34 abstentions. Only the United States and Israel vote no.

November 18

DIPLOMACY: In New York City, the UN General Assembly votes 123–16, with 12 abstentions, to condemn the continuing presence of foreign forces in Afghanistan and demands their immediate withdrawal. This is the third consecutive approval.

November 21

AVIATION: In the Konar Valley, Afghanistan, Soviet helicopters begin sowing mines and booby traps from the air. Many of these are deliberately disguised as stones or toys. Such devices are intended to wound and maim people, not kill them, thereby creating a drain on resistance medical resources.

MILITARY: An Iranian offensive recaptures the town of Bustan from Iraqi forces, who are continuing to lose ground.

December 9

MILITARY: After a return to the front lines, President Saddam Hussein concedes that his army has recently lost ground to the Iranians.

December 11

MILITARY: The Iranian government announces that its forces have launched another offensive against Iraqis in Khuzestan Province, in this instance, killing 1,000 of the enemy and capturing another 200. Iraq disputes the claim and says that 500 Iranians have been killed.

TERRORISM: In Shiraz, Iran, a bomb takes the life of Ayatollah Abdol-Hossein Dastgheib and seven companions. Government radio blames the Mujahideen-i-Khalq for the deed; to date, around 1,000 clerics and government officials have been killed since the ousting of former president Abolhassan Bani-Sadr.

December 15

DIPLOMACY: In Moscow, Soviet Union, Afghan president Babrak Karmal arrives for his latest talks with Soviet leaders.

In Baghdad, Iraq, President Saddam Hussein announces that he is willing to end the war with Iran once Tehran recognizes Iraqi borders.

December 16

MILITARY: Iraqi forces claim to have killed 282 Iranians in the Gilna Garb and Sumar regions while Iran claims to have shot down two Iraqi jet fighters.

December 17

MILITARY: The Iraqis claim that their forces have recaptured lost territory in the Gilan area of Iran.

December 23

TERRORISM: In Meshed, Iran, Mojtaba Ozbaki, a Majlis member, and Gholamali Jaafarzadeh, governor of Meshed, are killed by a hand grenade while driving.

December 28

TERRORISM: In Tehran, Iran, Mohammad Taki Behsharat, a Majlis member, is killed by gunfire.

1982

January 5

MILITARY: In the center sector, Iraqi forces disregard harsh winter conditions and launch a two-pronged attack against Gilan Garb on the Baghdad-Tehran Highway, and further south at Naft-e-Shah in the Sumar area. They make modest gains for an admitted loss of 20 men and also capture some quantities of arms and ammunition.

January 6

MILITARY: In Baghdad, Iraq, President Saddam Hussein celebrates Army Day by announcing the formation of a new Special Task Force, which is to focus on commando training and urban warfare, in order to increase the ratio of infantry to armor and afford tanks better protection.

Western analysts believe that 110,000 to 120,000 Soviet combat troops have been deployed to Afghanistan in various combat capacities.

January 12

DIPLOMACY: A report issued by the International Committee of the Red Cross indicates that Iran is holding 28,243 Iraqi prisoners while Iraq is detaining 5,285 Iranians.

January 19

POLITICS: In Paris, France, the Front for the Liberation of Iran is founded by Ali Amini, whose goal is to topple the Islamic regime in Tehran.

January 29

MILITARY: In Amman, Jordan, King Hussein announces that an all-volunteer Yarmuk Brigade is being assembled to fight alongside Iraq and against the Iranians. The

first detachment will arrive in March and basically be used for training purposes
and to guard vital installations.

February
DIPLOMACY: In New York City, Peruvian diplomat Diego Cordovez gains appointment as the UN special envoy tasked with facilitating indirect peace talks between
the governments of Pakistan and Afghanistan.

February 5–8
MILITARY: Iraqis forces, determined to recapture territory lost earlier to the Irani
ans, launch an attack from Sabeh to Bostan; they advance in driving rain and push
back the defenders but cannot overcome Pasdaran units defending the settlement.

February 9
DIPLOMACY: In Paris, France, the government grants an export license to Iraq so
Baghdad can obtain 100 AMX-30 tanks that have been on order since 1980.
TERRORISM: In Tehran, Iran, Pasdaran forces raid a building controlled by the Muja-
hideen-i-Khalq, triggering a huge gun battle. Musa Khaibani, the movement leader,
nine members of the Central Committee, and 11 other members are shot dead.

February 10
POLITICS: In Tehran, Iran, the state radio announces that a security sweep has net-
ted 22 opponents of the government, including the second-in-command of the
Mujahideen-i-Khalq.

February 13–14
MILITARY: Spurred on by orders from President Saddam Hussein, who wants Bostan
for prestige reasons, Iraqi forces shell the town heavily, but a two-day night attack
fails to capture it.

February 20
DIPLOMACY: After the regime in Kabul, Afghanistan rejects Archer K. Blood to serve
as U.S. chargé d'affairs, the State Department announces travel restrictions on all
Afghan diplomats in Washington, D.C.

February 23
TERRORISM: In Tehran, Iran, a bomb explodes outside a Pasdaran barracks, killing
15 people and wounding 60. Government spokesmen indicate that this is the work
of monarchists, not leftists.

March 4
MILITARY: In Baghdad, Iraq, the deputy oil minister concedes that the Iranian military had inflicted considerable damage on Iraqi oil production and storage facilities,
especially at Basra and Kirkuk. However, exports are still relatively high at 900,000
barrels a day.

March 8
DIPLOMACY: In Washington, D.C., Deputy Secretary of State Walter J. Stoessel Jr.,
informs the Senate Foreign Relations Committee that the Soviets have killed at least
3,000 people in Afghanistan using chemical weapons. According to information

received from defectors, the chemicals in question are irritants, incapacitants, nerve agents, mustard gas, and toxic smokes. Stoessel insists this is a violation of the 1925 Geneva Protocol against Gas Warfare. He also declares that an estimated 2 million Afghans have fled to neighboring Pakistan.

March 10
DIPLOMACY: In Washington, D.C., President Ronald W. Reagan declares March 21 to be "Afghanistan Day" in honor of the struggle unfolding there.

March 14
DIPLOMACY: An agreement is reached between Syria and Iran whereby Iranian crude oil is to be refined at Syrian facilities, in exchange for Syrian phosphates.

March 14–15
POLITICS: In Kabul, Afghanistan, the PDPA sponsors a large national conference to advocate national reconciliation. President Babrak Karmal intends to solicit the support of Islamic traditionalists for his regime.

March 19
AVIATION: The Iraqi air force, now partially armed with French-supplied Mirage F-1 fighters, flies several hundred sorties in a failed attempt to assist ground forces fighting in the Dezful-Shush region of Iran.

MILITARY: In the Dezful-Shush region of Khuzestan Province, Iran, the Iranians begin a major offensive called Fatah-al-Mobin (Clear Victory) by massing 100,000 men in seven divisions, mostly lightly armed Revolutionary Guard and Basij militia volunteers. What they lack in training and weapons is counterbalanced by a frightful religiosity and willingness to sacrifice themselves in combat. Overall command of the operation is entrusted to General Sayed Shirazi, the Iranian Army chief of staff. His plan entails a two-pronged attack against the Iraqi Fourth Army Corps, in concert with commando operations behind their lines.

March 20
MILITARY: In Tehran, Iran, Ayatollah Khomeini declares that schoolboys between the ages of 12 and 18 would be allowed to join and fight in the new Basij e-Mustazfin (literally, Mobilization of the Deprived) militia. They are to serve as youthful auxiliary forces of the Revolutionary Guard (Pasdaran).

March 22–29
MILITARY: In the southern sector, Operation Fatah-al-Mobin commences as thousands of fanatical Pasdaran and Basij volunteers attack Iraqi defenses in "human wave" formations. The entrenched defenders are surprised and encircled in a major rout. The Iranians claim to have destroyed two Iraqi armored divisions and one mechanized division; wrecked 320 Iraqi tanks and captured 350 more; and killed 10,000 soldiers, wounded 15,000, and captured 15,450. Iranian losses are put at 4,000 dead, 8,000 wounded, and 6,000 prisoners. Moreover, the Iranians claim to have pushed the front line in this region to with 15 miles of the Iraqi border.

April
POLITICS: In Geneva, Switzerland, Poul Hartling, the UN High Commissioner for Refugees (UNHCR), declares that an estimated 2.5 million Afghans are presently living in Pakistan. The UN mission in Islamabad is also his organization's largest.

April 1

POLITICS: In New York City, the UN World Food Program declares that it will provide an additional $18.5 million in food aid for Afghan refugees in Pakistan.

April 5

AVIATION: Soviet warplanes violate Iranian airspace for the first time by bombing Afghan refugee camps in Baluchistan Province. This occurs even though Iranian support for the mujahideen has been mostly lip service and restricted to small Shiite groups in the Hazarajat.

April 7

DIPLOMACY: King Hussein of Jordan visits President Saddam Hussein in Baghdad, Iraq, to impress upon him how serious the military situation is in the wake of Operation Fatah. He also offers Iraq two of his armored divisions, but Saddam, believing that Western media exaggerated the Iranian threat, declines to accept.

April 8

DIPLOMACY: In a major blow to President Saddam Hussein, Syria announces that it is closing the Iraqi oil pipeline running through its territory. President Hafiz al-Assad says it is in retaliation for Iraq's continuing support of the Muslim Brotherhood and its attempts to overthrow the government. The closure reduces the flow of Iraqi oil to 600,000 barrels a day through the Turkish pipeline, a drop sufficient enough to cause an economic crisis.

In Cairo, a secret Iraqi delegation arrives to ensure a steady flow of weapons from Egypt.

April 10

DIPLOMACY: In Damascus, Syria, the government breaks off diplomatic relations with Iraq, urging the populace to overthrow the regime of President Saddam Hussein. It also closes its oil pipeline to Iraq, forcing Baghdad to place even greater reliance on the Turkish pipeline, then working at full capacity.

POLITICS: In Tehran, Iran, the state media reports that former foreign minister Sadegh Ghotzbzdeh has been arrested and charged with plotting to kill Ayatollah Khomeini and members of the Supreme Defense Council. He was previously one of the ayatollah's closest confidants, and he implicates several dissident military officers and the Ayatollah Kazem Shariet-Madari.

April 12

DIPLOMACY: In Baghdad, Iraq, President Saddam Hussein declares that Iraqi forces would withdraw from Iran if Tehran gave assurances that the conflict would end. No such assurances are given by Tehran.

April 13

AVIATION: Two Iranian naval pilots fly a small aircraft to Oman and request political asylum.

DIPLOMACY: In Tehran, Iran, Major General Ali Zahirnejad, joint chief of staff, declares that despite recent Iranian successes, his country has no intention of invading another country. This statement is apparently for foreign consumption as Ayatollah Khomeini does not wish to spark Western military intervention in the Gulf War.

POLITICS: A split in conservative Shiite ranks appears in Iran when the highly conservative members of the Hojatai Society a religious organization of clerics, indirectly challenge Ayatollah Khomeini by declaring that clergy should be less involved in governance.

April 18

POLITICS: During Armed Forces Day in Tehran, Iran, Ayatollah Khomeini appeals for an end to discord in the military. The regular officer corps is apparently disheartened by the unceasing praise heaped on the Revolutionary Guard (Pasdaran) at their expense.

April 23–28

MILITARY: In Paktia Province, Afghanistan, mujahideen fighters take to the offensive by attacking a Soviet garrison in the town of Khost. This attack is made by the Hezb-i-Islami under Jalaluddin Haqqani, who commands one of the best-equipped resistance groups.

April 29

MILITARY: Along the Dezful-Shush front, the Iranians mass 70,000 troops and 200 tanks for Operation Bait al Muqaddas (the Sacred House) to finally expel Iraqi forces from the region and recapture the port city of Khorramshahr. They are opposed by seven Iraqi divisions in and around the city.

April 30

AVIATION: In support of Operation Bait al Muqaddas, three Iranian transports drop 100 parachutists near the Karun River to cut a critical rail link.

MILITARY: Despite intense aerial bombardments by the Iraqi Air Force, the Iranians grind ahead toward Khorramshahr, seizing an additional 300 square miles. Once again the Pasdaran commit themselves to suicidal "human wave" charge against the Iraqis, forcing the defenders to exhaust their ammunition before the main attack is launched.

May 1

MILITARY: Iranian forces in the vicinity of Khorramshahr establish a bridgehead on the Karun River and begin ferrying forces across near the settlement at Jish Haloub.

May 3–4

MILITARY: At the Dezful-Shush front, Iraqi force scrape together a counterattack and regain some lost ground. In response, the Iranians gird themselves to take the border town of Fakkeh, interdict Iraqi supplies, and divert enemy forces to this area.

May 4

TERRORISM: In Tehran, Iran, a running gun battle erupts between Pasdaran and Mujahideen-i-Khalq members; the government claims to have killed 63 guerrillas.

May 7

MILITARY: As Iranian forces continue gathering strength, they launch a sharp, modest offensive near the southern Iran-Iraq border and claim to seize a 22-mile strip of land.

May 8

MILITARY: Iranian state radio announces that its forces have retaken Hoveizeh and Hamid while the Iraqis admit they have conducted a "tactical withdrawal" in Khuzestan Province, Iran, to reinforce units around Khorramshahr. Meanwhile, Iranian forces have pushed to within 15 miles of that vital port.

May 9

MILITARY: In the Dezful-Shush region, Operation Bait al Muqaddas continues rumbling forward with the destruction of two more Iraqi infantry divisions and the recapture of 166 square miles of Iranian territory north of Khorramshahr. The town of Jofeyr also falls. This latest advance places troops near Shalamache on the Shatt al Arab waterway, only 13 miles southeast of Basra.

May 10

DIPLOMACY: With the tide of war in the Persian Gulf clearing turning against Iraq, various Arab and European diplomats begin fearing that Iran will destabilize the entire region. Moreover, they consider Secretary of State Alexander M. Haig, Jr, as too, fixated upon South America to assist, while the Soviet Union and Syria are judged as supporting Iran.

MILITARY: In Baghdad, Iraq, President Saddam Hussein has growing awareness of the perils facing his forces outside Khorramshahr and orders two divisions to withdraw and form a shorter defensive arc outside the city. The withdrawal is hastily conducted, and around 100 armored vehicles are abandoned. The garrison of the city itself, comprising 35,000 troops, is ordered to turn it into a virtual "Stalingrad" by constructing bunkers and defensive positions, offset by minefields and barbed wire entanglements.

May 11

MILITARY: Throughout the southern sector, Iranian forces continue surging forward, with several units approaching the outskirts of the port city of Khorramshahr.

May 12

MILITARY: Operation Bait al Muqaddas concludes with the successful Iranian capture of Shalamache, astride the Shatt al Arab waterway, which adds 366 square miles of territory recently liberated. Fighting cost each side about 15,000 casualties.

POLITICS: The Soviets, intent on welding northern Afghanistan to its republics in Central Asia, inaugurates a new road and railway bridge over the Amu Darya River that reaches from Termez, Uzbekistan, to Hairatan, Afghanistan. This route will help develop the gas and petroleum region of Sheberghan, with additional pipelines to be laid down in coming months.

May 14

TERRORISM: In Tehran, Iran, the government announces the execution of several more Mujahideen-i-Khalq members and says that the movement for all intents and purposes has been destroyed.

May 16

MILITARY: In the Panjshir Valley, Afghanistan, the Soviets have been goaded into committing a formal offensive through the region, this time involving 12,000 soldiers, 104 helicopters, and 26 aircraft. The mujahideen under Ahmad Shah Massoud were surprised with large contingents of airborne units, 4,200 men in all, were helicoptered in behind them. One unit, however, lands at Rukha and is mauled by resistance fighters until a motorized rifle battalion rescues them. Massoud rearranges his men into smaller units and flees into the hills, ambushing enemy units that approach too near. At length, the Soviets establish major bases at Rukha, Bazarak, and Anava, which give them control over the valley, but the resistance still controls the surrounding high ground.

POLITICS: In Kabul, Afghanistan, a PDPA conference votes to support the ongoing purge of dissidents as well as continuing Soviet-inspired programs for land reform.

May 17

MILITARY: In the Panjshir Valley, Afghanistan, Soviet and Afghan forces continue their third offensive to drive out mujahidden under Ahmad Shah Massoud. This time their tactics involve dropping paratroops and helicopter-borne commandos behind enemy lines, but resistance fighters, who know the ravines and gorges intimately, simply avoid encirclement and await the enemy's departure.

May 21

MILITARY: The second phase of Operation Bait al Muqaddas commences when a fanatical Pasdaran division overruns an Iraqi infantry force at Shalamsha, cutting off the only remaining supply route into Khorramshahr.

May 22

DIPLOMACY: In Washington, D.C., the State Department admits to approaching various Arabic countries to help end the Iran-Iraq War before Iraqi president Saddam Hussein is driven from power and the entire region is destabilized. The officials also maintain that the recent turnaround of events was due largely to the mediocre performance of Iraqi forces.

In Baghdad, Iraq, Saddam Hussein appeals to the Arab League for military assistance in light of Khorramshahr's imminent fall, but no response is forthcoming.

May 22–24

MILITARY: The Iranian port city of Khorramshahr, defended by 35,000 Iraqi troops, is attacked on the outskirts of the city by 70,000 Pasdaran (three divisions), which charge headlong into enemy defenses. Iraqi minefields and trenches fail to halt their onslaught, and, while the bulk of Iraqi regular forces manages to escape on small craft to the west side of Shatt al Arab, around 15,000 soldiers in the poorly trained Popular Army are taken captive along with the city. Victory here triggers mass jubilation throughout Iran; all told, Operation Bait al Muqaddas liberated 2,077 square miles of Iranian soil and seized 25,400 captives.

May 23

MILITARY: The central sector near Qasr-i-Sherin, Iran, is strengthened by the arrival of a Pasdaran division to reinforce the two infantry divisions already there. They are facing men of the Iraqi Second Army Corps, whose lines stretch from Qasr-i-Sherin northward to Mandali.

May 25

DIPLOMACY: In Washington, D.C., administration officials concede that the prospects of an Iranian victory threaten the entire Persian Gulf region. By this time, Iran has recaptured all lost territory and is preparing to make inroads into Iraq itself.

MILITARY: In Baghdad, Iraq, the government media admits the loss of Khorramshahr to the Iranians, which also places them within striking distance of Basra, Iraq's second-largest city and a vital port.

May 26

DIPLOMACY: In Washington, D.C., Secretary of State Alexander M. Haig Jr. declares that the United States will become more involved in attempting to end the Iran-Iraq War before it spills over into adjoining countries. This appears to be a none-too-veiled threat to Iran that the Americans would protect its vital interests throughout the region. The U.S. Commerce Department also announces the approval of the export of six Lockheed L-100 transport planes to Iraq.

May 27

MILITARY: The Iranian government claims that fierce battles are being waged in a mountainous region only 80 miles east of Baghdad; it also admits that Iraqi artillery continues to pound Khorramshahr, in one instance killing 55 Iranians.

May 28

DIPLOMACY: In Pakistan, the International Committee of the Red Cross begins transferring Soviet captives from mujahideen prison camps to a minimum security facility in Switzerland. Eventually, 11 such detainees are transferred before facing repatriation back to the Soviet Union, but one solider, Yury Vaschenko, flees to West Germany and seeks political asylum rather than return home. Two others request asylum in Switzerland and receive it, while the remaining eight are sent back to an uncertain fate.

MILITARY: In the central sector, Iranian forces launch a probing attack against the Iraqis Second Army Corps around the Sumar Mountains near Mandali, Iran, and are repulsed.

May 30

AVIATION: The Iranian oil facilities on Kharg Island in the Persian Gulf are heavily struck by Iraqi aircraft.

MILITARY: The recent spate of Iranian victories at Khorramshahr and elsewhere triggers widespread Shiite uprisings in Karbala, Basra, Hilleh, and Nasiriyah, Iraq. These are brutally suppressed by state security forces.

June 2

DIPLOMACY: In Riyadh, Saudi Arabia, a meeting of Gulf Cooperation Council foreign ministers proposes a possible peace plan involving a cease-fire between Iran and Iraq, the immediate withdrawal back to international boundaries, and a negotiated settlement of outstanding issues.

June 6

DIPLOMACY: In Riyadh, Saudi Arabia, members of the Gulf Cooperation Council advance a peace plan involving a cease-fire, a withdrawal, and negotiations to Iran and Iraq. Iraqi president Saddam Hussein embraces the scheme, but Ayatollah Khomeini fails to respond. Following the Israeli invasion of Lebanon, member nations urge the two countries to stop fighting each other and concentrate on fighting the Jews.

June 8

MILITARY: By this date, Soviet and Afghan army forces have driven mujahideen loyal to Ahmad Shah Massoud out of the Panjshir Valley, Afghanistan. The guerrillas will filter back into the region after they depart.

June 9

DIPLOMACY: In Baghdad, Iraq, during a gathering of the Regional and National Commands of the Arab Baath Socialist Party and the Revolutionary Command Council, the government makes a peace offer to withdraw all troops from Iran within two weeks in order to redirect them against Israel, which had invaded southern Lebanon. In return, Majlis speaker Hojatolislam Hashemi Rafsanjani demands right of passage through Iraq for Iranian forces attacking their common enemy.

June 10

DIPLOMACY: In Baghdad, Iraq, the government announces that it will observe a unilateral cease-fire.

June 11

NAVAL: The Iraqis, having mined the channel between Bandar-e Khomeyni and Bandar Mahshahr, claim that three foreign vessels were sunk or damaged in that region.

Hojatolislam Mohammad Ali Amininejad, head of the Naval Political Section, is assassinated, probably by the Mujahideen-i-Khalq operatives.

June 12

DIPLOMACY: Despite persistent Iranian artillery barrages, the government in Baghdad, Iraq, insists it is observing a unilateral cease-fire and orders its troops to shoot back only in self defense.

In New York City, the UN Security Council passes another resolution calling for an immediate cease-fire between Iran and Iraq, followed by the withdrawal of all forces to international boundaries. The Iranians reject the resolution outright.

June 13

DIPLOMACY: In Tehran, Iran, Ayatollah Khomeini drops his demand for $150 billion in war reparations if the Iraqi people would overthrow the Baathist regime in Baghdad.

June 14

DIPLOMACY: In Baghdad, Iraq, President Saddam Hussein increases the pressure on Iran by warning all international shipping to steer clear of the northern reaches of the Persian Gulf.

MILITARY: It is reported that the first group of Iranian volunteers have been flown to the Bakaa Valley, Lebanon, where they are to help fight the Israelis and assist the militant group Hezbollah.

June 15

DIPLOMACY: In Tel Aviv, Israel, the defense minister publicly declares that the government had been routinely supplying Iran with weapons and spare parts worth $27 million. All shipments abruptly cease after this admission.

June 16

DIPLOMACY: The European Parliament passes a resolution extending recognition to the Afghan mujahideen and acknowledges that they should receive "all necessary aid."

June 16–25

DIPLOMACY: In Geneva, Switzerland, the first direct talks between representatives from Afghanistan and Pakistan are held.

June 20

DIPLOMACY: In Baghdad, Iraq, President Saddam Hussein declares that all Iraqi forces will be withdrawn from Iran within 10 days. This offer is largely moot seeing how recent Iranian offensives have largely driven them back into their own territory anyway. Nor does the offer extend to regions that Iraq had claimed prior to the outbreak of hostilities. Furthermore, he muses how strange it is that the superpowers have made no real effort to stop the war as it rages in one of the most strategic regions of the world.

June 21

DIPLOMACY: In Tehran, Iran, Ayatollah Khomeini declares that the war with Iraq will continue whether Iraqi forces evacuate Iranian soil or not. His stated goal remains toppling President Saddam Hussein from power.

June 24

POLITICS: In Baghdad, Iraq, President Saddam Hussein convenes the ninth Regional Baath Party Congress, whereby he blames recent Iraqi defeats on internal enemies, says he intends to purge the party of weak elements, and stresses the need to replace them by stout-hearted individuals capable of "great courage in adversity." Consequently, the Revolutionary Command Council is halved in size, and many more of Saddam Hussein's allies are appointed to high cabinet positions.

June 26

MILITARY: In the northern sector, Iranian forces holding the town of Mahabad repel a large attack by Kurdish guerrillas of the Patriotic Union of Kurdistan.

June 27

POLITICS: In Tehran, Iran, the government announces that its forces have crushed a military coup attempted by Colonel Azar Dahkam.

The fearsome Soviet Mi-24 Hind-D assault helicopter. Heavily armed and armored, it was the bane of the Afghan resistance until the CIA supplied it with Stinger antiaircraft missiles. (*Department of Defense*)

June 28

POLITICS: In Baghdad, Iraq, President Saddam Hussein seeks to quell unrest among the majority Shia population by inviting five Shiite ministers to join the cabinet. Money is also allocated to rebuild the Holy Shrines at Najaf and Karbala.

June 30

MILITARY: By this date, Iraqi forces have unilaterally evacuated Iranian territory and begin assuming a defensive strategy until the spring of 1988. This enables the Iranians, who enjoy a decided manpower advantage, to regain the tactical initiative on the ground.

July 2

TERRORISM: At Yadz, Iran, a grenade thrown by a suicidal mujahideen member claims the life of Ayatollah Mohammad Sadduqi of the Council of Guardians, and a Majlis deputy, at a prayer meeting.

July 7

TERRORISM: In Tehran, Iran, the government again claims to have eliminated the Mujahideen-i-Khalq as a movement; to date, no less than 4,000 members have been arrested and executed.

July 9

DIPLOMACY: In Tehran, Iran, Majlis speaker Hojatolislam Hashemi Rafsanjani outlines conditions for a cease-fire with Iraq: retention of the 1975 Algerian Accord, repatriation of 100,000 Iraqi citizens expelled by the government, the fixture of war guilt firmly on Iraq, the payment of $100 billion in war damages, and the trial of Saddam Hussein as a war criminal.

July 11

TERRORISM: In Dujayal, Iraq, an unsuccessful assassination attempt is made by agents of the Shiite Al Daawa organization against President Saddam Hussein with machine guns and rocket-propelled grenades. He responds by executing 150 Shiite suspects from the town.

July 12

DIPLOMACY: In New York City, the UN Security Council unanimously passes a Jordanian-inspired resolution calling for an immediate cease-fire in the Persian Gulf followed by the withdrawal of all warring forces to their respective international borders. However, Tehran again rejects the proposal.

MILITARY: In Washington, D.C., an administration spokesman declares that large numbers of Iranian forces have massed along the Iraqi border and that an invasion seems pending.

July 13–20

MILITARY: On the southern front, massed Iranian forces commence Operation Ramadan al Mubarak (Blessed Ramadan) in an attempt to capture the strategic Iraqi port of Basra. The city is ringed with an extensive network of trenches, defensive barriers, and minefields, with interlocking machine-gun and artillery fields of fire, all manned by soldiers of the Third Army Corps. However, by rushing forward five infantry divisions, the Iranians are able to overrun the first lines of defense, placing them 10 miles north of the city. The Iraqis hurriedly counterattack with four divisions, and the total of 130,000 men locked in battle is the largest armed encounter since World War II. Moreover, the Iraqis have an edge in the number of tanks deployed, and their Air Force is extremely active, especially helicopter gunships. Despite heroic sacrifices, Pasdaran "human wave" attacks finally bog down in swampy terrain, and both sides begin marshaling their forces for another contest. The Iranians are further disappointed when the large Arab Shia population does not rise in rebellion as anticipated.

July 14

MILITARY: The Iranian national media announces that its forces have advanced into Iraqi territory and are moving toward Basra. U.S. sources confirm that the Iranians had penetrated six to 12 miles inside of Iraq, which places them only four miles from their objective.

July 18

DIPLOMACY: In Washington, D.C., Senator Henry M. Jackson of the Senate Armed Services Committee states that while the loss of oil from Iran and Iraq would have little impact on the United States, chaos looms if Iran advances into the Persian Gulf region and cuts off oil shipments from Kuwait and other Gulf states.

July 21–24

AVIATION: Warplanes of the Iranian Air Force attack Baghdad, Iraq, damaging several oil facilities. The Iraqi Air Force also attacks several targets in Khuzestan Province, Iran, killing 120 people.

MILITARY: The second phase of Operation Ramadan al Mubarak unfolds as four Iranian divisions, consisting mostly of lightly armed but fanatical Pasdaran and Basij volunteers, commits a two-pronged attack against Iraqi defenses. They penetrate a further five miles, but the defenders, assisted by ample tank, artillery, and air power, grind the lightly armed Iranians to another costly standstill.

POLITICS: In Baghdad, Iraq, the government announces that the Iraqi army has withdrawn from all Iranian territory, except that which was "originally Iraqi." This includes six pockets totaling 373 square miles near Qasr-i-Sherin, Naft-e-Shah, Sumar, Mandali, Mehran, and Musian.

July 23

MILITARY: In Tehran, Iran, the chief of staff, Major General Ali Zahirnejad informs the mullahs of the Supreme Defense Council that he will resign if "unqualified people continue to meddle with the conduct of the war." The military had cautioned against an attack on Basra and is now taking the blame for its failure.

July 24

DIPLOMACY: In Tehran, Iran, government sources declare that they are willing to consider mediation of the current conflict by Algeria.

July 25–26

MILITARY: Outside Basra, Iraqi units counterattack exposed Iranian units on their flanks, driving them back toward their original starting positions. This attack, which the mullahs insisted upon and military authorities warned against, shapes up to be a huge setback for Iran.

July 28

MILITARY: On the southern front, the Iranians make one final attempt to capture the port city of Basra, Iraq, but are thwarted by its dug-in defenders, backed by superior firepower. All the Iranians retain is a 10-mile strip of Iraqi territory from which they can begin shelling the city; their losses are estimated at 20,000, as opposed to Iraq's 7,000 casualties and 1,400 captured.

July 31

MILITARY: Having blunted a major Iranian drive against Basra for the time being, the Iraqi government claims it has killed more than 27,000 enemy troops over the past 18 days.

August 1–3

MILITARY: Outside Basra, the final phase of Operation Ramadan al Mubarak unfolds as exhausted Pasdaran and Basij units hurl themselves against prepared Iraqi positions, only to be cut down by heavy firepower. The costly impasse ends with Iran gaining a toehold on Iraqi territory.

August 2

MILITARY: In Kabul, Afghanistan, President Babrak Karmal attempts to stop the flow of Afghan army deserters by raising the term of compulsory military service for all able-bodied men to three years.

POLITICS: During a meeting between Khalq and Parcham factions in the so-called People's Palace at Kabul, Afghanistan, gunfire breaks out and casualties ensue. Internecine factionalism remains rife.

August 4

DIPLOMACY: Newspapers begin speculating that the United States is willing to reestablish diplomatic relations with Iraq, now that Baghdad has dropped many of its radical policies. Such a move was expected to shore up Iraqi resolve throughout the ongoing struggle with Iran.

MILITARY: To all appearances, the Iran-Iraq War is deadlocked with neither contestant capable of mustering the manpower and materiel to score a knockout blow. Analysts compute that, since September 1980, 80,000 troops on both sides have been killed, 200,000 injured, and 45,000 captured.

August 7

MILITARY: The Iranian government announces that it has captured the town of Qasr-i-Sherin inside its territory, killing 200 Iraqis in the process. It also touts the fact that Iraq has yet to withdraw all its forces from Iranian soil, despite Saddam Hussein's claim.

August 8

MILITARY: On the Zain al Qaws plateau, Iran, a force of 1,000 Pasdaran, armed only with assault rifles and RPG-7 rocket launchers, attacks dug-in Iraqi forces. They are mowed down yet keep advancing, spurred on by shouting and chanting mullahs in the rear. The Iranians finally break, leaving 400 dead on the ground.

August 9
MILITARY: Heavy fighting occurs northeast of Basra, Iraq, with each side claiming to inflict grievous losses on the other.

August 12
NAVAL: In Baghdad, Iraq, President Saddam Hussein declares a "maritime exclusion zone" at the northern end of the Persian Gulf up to 30 miles offshore. This legally enables his aircraft to attack Iranian ports, offshore installations, and, above all, neutral vessels visiting those facilities. These actions cause a temporary drop in Iranian oil exports to 800,000 barrels per day, down from 2 million.

August 16
DIPLOMACY: In Geneva, Switzerland, the first indirect talks between Afghan and Pakistani diplomats begin under UN auspices. Their goal is to hammer out a "peace" agreement that is acceptable to all sides.
POLITICS: In the Hazarjat Region of Afghanistan, civil war erupts between traditionalist Shiites and pro-Khomeini extremists. The latter finally triumphs in 1984.

In Tehran, Iran, the government announces that 70 military officers have been executed for their role in the alleged plot of Sadegh Ghotzbzadeh.

August 18
AVIATION: Iraqi warplanes strike at Iranian oil facilities on Kharg Island in the Persian Gulf, which is seen as a warning to Iran to halt shelling of Basra and Khanaqin.
MILITARY: In Tehran, Iran, Prime Minister Hojatolislam Hossein Musavi announces that the Pasdaran are to be granted their own special ministry. This move triggers an outcry from the Iranian Army, which believes that the Revolutionary Guards are receiving attention and consideration far out of proportion to their military significance.

August 19
MILITARY: The Iranian government boasts that it has killed 50 Iraqi soldiers after damaging an oil terminal at the head of the Persian Gulf. Iraqi president Saddam Hussein warns that foreign vessels using Iranian ports and other facilities are vulnerable to attack from the air.

August 22
POLITICS: In Tehran, Iran, the Islamic Republican Party newspaper *Islamic Republic* accuses the Tudeh (Communist) Party of opposing the war with Iraq on the grounds that it might inspire a counterrevolution.

August 25
AVIATION: Iraqi warplanes attack Iranian oil facilities on Kharg Island in the Persian Gulf.

August 30

TERRORISM: In Baghdad, Iraq, a large explosion kills 30 people and is attributed to the Shiite-dominated Al Daawa organization.

September

MILITARY: As an anti-insurgency measure, Soviet troops begin systematically burning grain stocks and cutting down fruit trees throughout Afghanistan to deprive the mujahideen access to food. This tactic seriously exacerbates an already precarious agricultural condition, and the Kabul regime introduces price controls on wheat to keep it affordable.

September 6

TERRORISM: In Tehran, Iran, a car-bomb explosion kills 20 people and injures more than 100, mostly Pasdaran members. Prime Minister Hojatolislam Hossein Musavi blames the Mujahideen-i-Khalq for the incident, and several members in captivity are executed.

September 11

DIPLOMACY: In Fez, Morocco, Iraqi president Saddam Hussein attends the annual summit conference of the Arab League and officially endorses the peace plan advanced by King Fahd: a cease-fire during the upcoming hajj pilgrimage, a complete evacuation of all Iranian territory by Iraqi forces, and the payment of $70 billion in compensation to Iran by the Gulf states and their Islamic Reconstruction Fund. Tehran, however, rejects the proposal.

September 13

TERRORISM: In Logar Province, Afghanistan, Soviet and Afghan troops round up 105 Afghan old men, women, and children from the village of Pad-Khwab-e Shana, force them into an irrigation ditch, and burn them alive with gasoline. Similar atrocities are being committed across the country after the Soviet military command adopts the tactic as a measure of deterring the local populace from supporting the resistance movement. The mass exodus of women and other traditional crop growers and flour grinders also causes endemic food shortages.

September 16

POLITICS: In Tehran, Iran, former foreign minister Sadegh Ghotzbzadeh is executed for conspiring against the government.

September 26

DIPLOMACY: In Baghdad, Iraq, President Saddam Hussein admits that the Soviet Union has finally and formally resumed arms shipments by honoring contracts signed before September 1980. Such aid includes MiG-25 aircraft, advanced T-72 tanks, Scud-B missiles, and SAM-8 missiles, along with 1,000 military and technical advisers. In return, the Iraqis are expected to release 180 Communist political prisoners.

September 29

MILITARY: Vessels of the Sixth Fleet deliver the 1,200 men of the 32nd Marine Amphibious Unit to Beirut, Lebanon, and joins French, British, Italian, and

Australian troops as part of an international peacekeeping force. The marines are positioned at Beirut International Airport.

October
MILITARY: In Herat Province, Afghanistan, mujahideen under Ismail Khan put up dogged resistance against Soviet forces trying to dislodge them. Violent outbreaks are also recorded this day in Paktia Province and the Kabul suburb of Paghman.

October 1
MILITARY: In the central front, massed Iranian forces commence Operation Muslim ibn Aqil from the Sumar Hills overlooking Mandali. This places a large concentration of Iranian troops only 65 miles northeast of Baghdad, Iraq. Over the next few days a force of 50,000 Revolutionary Guards and Basij volunteers charge heroically forward, only to be decimated by superior Iraqi firepower from entrenched positions. Fighting ceases in another bloody stalemate, but Iran claims to have seized control of the road running north from Mandali to Naft Kaneh.

October 2
MILITARY: In Tehran, Iran, a bomb planted outside a hotel kills 60 people and injures more than 700; the Mujahideen-i-Khalq are blamed for the incident.

October 2–4
MILITARY: Iranian forces continue advancing around Mandali, Iran, until a sudden Iraqi counterattack throws them back to their starting positions. After two more days of inconclusive fighting, the Iranian offensive bogs down and an impasse sets in. The Iraqis then fly journalists over the area to prove that Mandali has not been captured, as the Iranians claim.

October 4
DIPLOMACY: The government of Sudan offers to dispatch volunteers to fight alongside Iraq and against the Iranians.

October 5
DIPLOMACY: In New York City, the UN Security Council unanimously adopts Resolution 522, mandating an immediate end to the Iran-Iraq War and a complete pullback of armed forces to their respective borders. After Iran boycotts the session and rejects the request, the Iraqi delegation is well-poised to characterize its adversary as an opponent of peace. Olaf Palme, former prime minister of Sweden, agrees to serve as a UN mediator and commences his own personal shuttle diplomacy between Baghdad and Tehran. However, once again, the Iranians reject the plan out of hand.

POLITICS: In Baghdad, Iraq, President Saddam Hussein, eager to placate the Shia majority population, declares that Shiite saint Imam Ali's birthday is to be considered a national holiday.

October 5–6
MILITARY: Iranians launch a nighttime assault in the Mandali-Sumar region of the central sector but are again thwarted by superior Iraqi firepower. An Iranian armored unit nearby also fails to support the attack in a timely manner. Moreover,

the offensive does not panic President Saddam Hussein, and he does not shuttle reinforcements there from the southern sector as anticipated.

October 6
AVIATION: The Iraqi government announcers that its jets and helicopter gunships were instrumental in repelling another Iranian offensive near Sumar, killing 2,352 enemy soldiers.

October 7
MILITARY: In the southern sector, Iranian artillery bombards Iraqi oil facilities at Charhar Cheraqh.

October 8
MILITARY: In light of increasing Iranian casualties with little to show for them, Majlis speaker Hojatolislam Hashemi Rafsanjani declares that the new policy is to strike the enemy "with restricted blows." This suggests that Iran's offensive ambitions have been somewhat curtailed.

October 10
MILITARY: In the central front, the Iranians launch additional "human wave" attacks against Iraqi forces dug in around the town of Mandali. The Revolutionary Guards and Basij volunteers fight their way into the town but prove unable to hold it, and they withdraw. For all their recent sacrifice, they managed to liberate only 60 square miles of territory. Moreover, open squabbling is reported between Iranian army commanders and leaders of the Pasdaran as to who is responsible for the failed offensive.

October 14
AVIATION: The Iraqi government again claims that its warplanes attacked Iranian oil facilities at Kharg Island in the Persian Gulf.
MILITARY: In Tehran, Iran, the Pasdaran leadership calls for additional volunteers to replenish its losses. This is considered an unusual move at this stage of the conflict.

October 15
AVIATION: As the air war escalates, the Iraqis claim to have killed 156 Iranians in a single raid while the Iranians claim to have shot down one of the attacking jets.

October 19
POLITICS: A report surfaces that Iran intends to acquire a nuclear power plant and produce uranium from domestic deposits. The bulk of research is to be conducted at the Isfahan Nuclear Technology Center.

October 23
DIPLOMACY: In Tehran, Iran, a delegation from the Islamic Conference Organization meets with Iranian leaders to arrange a cease-fire but departs empty handed.

October 27
AVIATION: The Iraqis pummel Dezful, Iran, with several Scud-B missiles, killing 21 and wounding upwards of 100 civilians.

DIPLOMACY: In Baghdad, Iraq, President Saddam Hussein seeks to improve his international image by announcing that he is willing to end the war with the 1975 Algerian Accord intact. This means that the Shatt al Arab waterway will remain the boundary between Iran and Iraq.

October 30

MILITARY: In the Hindu Kush Mountains, Afghanistan, a Soviet troop and fuel convoy is obliterated by an explosion inside the three-mile long Salang Tunnel linking the highway from Kabul to the Soviet Union. An estimated 700 soldiers and 300 Afghan civilians perish in the ensuing conflagration, which is considered an accident.

October 31

MILITARY: In the central and south-central fronts, massed Iranian forces commence Operation Muharram al Harram (Holy Murram) against the oil-bearing regions of Naft-e-Shah and Tib. Four divisions of Revolutionary Guards and Basij militia redeploy in the middle of the rainy season. They bravely overcome Iraqi tank, jets, and helicopter gunships and score a tactical breakthrough. The Iraqi high command is forced to tap into its last reserves, an army corps south of the capital and two understrength armor brigades guarding the northern oil fields, to finally stop them. Beforehand, the Iranians captured the Bayat oilfield and threatened Mandali after liberating another 330 square miles of territory. To the south they actually penetrated six miles inside of Iraqi territory, which causes a panic in Baghdad. In several political circles, critics of President Saddam Hussein urge him to step down to preempt a major Iranian invasion that might prove unstoppable.

POLITICS: In Tehran, Iran, Ayatollah Khomeini exhorts his troops to even greater sacrifice by insisting that "war can be as holy as prayer when it is fought for the sake of defending Islam."

November

DIPLOMACY: In New York City, the UN General Assembly passes another resolution demanding the immediate removal of "foreign troops" from Afghanistan by a vote of 114 to 21 with 14 abstentions.

November 1

DIPLOMACY: In Baghdad, Iraq, President Saddam Hussein declares at a news conference that the defense treaty with the Soviet Union is not working during the present conflict with Iran. He also suggests that improved relations with Washington might be possible.

November 1–3

MILITARY: Massed Iranian forces launch Operation Muharram al Harram (Holy Muharram) in the central sector near Musian. Their goal is to cut the Baghdad Road between Kut and Al Amarah. Two divisions advance along a 10-mile front and lurch towards the Bayat oilfields. The first strike by "human wave" tactics overwhelms the first line of Iraqi defenses, crosses the Doverich River, and moves adjacent to the Dehloran-Musian road.

November 5–6
MILITARY: In the central sector, the Iranians launch another mass attack against Iraqi troops in the Doverich Valley, forcing their withdrawal after heavy fighting.

November 6
POLITICS: As part of the government crackdown on the Tudeh (Communist) Party, the party newspaper *Mardom* is closed down and hundreds of members are arrested.

November 7–12
MILITARY: Iranian forces near Musian continue advancing into Iraqi territory, taking several border posts and repelling a local counterattack. Thus far the Iranians had advanced five miles in seven days and occupied the Bayat oilfield, which encourages the mullahs on the Supreme Defense Council to demand greater gains.

November 9
MILITARY: In Tehran, Iran, the Majlis formally approves creation of a special Pasdaran Ministry. This is accomplished to partly deprive the army, still not completely trusted by the mullahs, of its absolute authority on the battlefield. Mohsen Rifiqdust is appointed the new Pasdaran minister.

POLITICS: In Baghdad, Iraq, President Saddam Hussein seeks to shore up flagging political support by holding a referendum to see who is more popular in his own country: himself or Ayatollah Khomeini. He accuses the Iranians of continuing the war not because he is in power, but out of an urge to "control all Iraq."

November 13
POLITICS: In Baghdad, Iraq, political theater unfolds as 4 million people march in a carefully orchestrated demonstration in favor of Saddam Hussein.

November 15–16
MILITARY: Iranian forces in the Mandali area launch another five-pronged attack against Iraqi defenders, but the fighting proves inconclusive and peters out. Thereafter, Mandali remains something of a no-man's-land, with Iranian troops on surrounding hills east of the city staring down Iraqi units on hilltops to the west.

November 20
DIPLOMACY: In Washington, D.C., an administration spokesperson denies Iraqi charges that the government had recently sold arms to Iran at a time when there was a firm policy of denying arms to either side.

December
MILITARY: This month the Central Intelligence Agency makes a concerted effort to expand the volume and types of weapons delivered to mujahideen units in Afghanistan. The arsenal includes bazookas, mortars, grenade launchers, mines, and recoilless rifles.

December 10–15
DIPLOMACY: In Kabul, Afghanistan, President Babrak Karmal declares six days of official mourning following the death of Soviet premier Leonid Brezhnev.

December 15
DIPLOMACY: In Washington, D.C., the government gives its final approval to extending $210 million in export credits to Iraq.

December 17–20
DIPLOMACY: In Paris, France, the Russell Tribunal allows Afghan refugees to testify, and they describe torture chambers established in the cellars of the Ministry of the Interior in Kabul, Afghanistan. Some of the witnesses are flown to New York City, where they obtain wide news-media coverage.

December 18
AVIATION: The Iraqis unleash another barrage of Scud-B and Frog-7 missiles at Dezful, Iran, killing 64 civilians and wounding more than 300.

December 19
POLITICS: Universities in Iran are opened for the first time since December 1980.

December 22
POLITICS: In Tehran, Iran, Ayatollah Khomeini, alarmed by the zeal with which the Pasdaran and other security services are pursuing mujahideen and other perceived "enemies of the state," appeals for unauthorized searches and arrests to cease as they are un-Islamic.

1983

January 4
MILITARY: In the Panjshir Valley, Afghanistan mujahideen leader Ahmad Shah Massoud arranges an informal truce with Soviet forces in an attempt to replenish his ammunition supplies and extend his political influence farther north.

POLITICS: In Tehran, Iran, the government announces that fuel rationing, which began in September 1980, is now ended owing to enhanced refining capabilities. The refinery of Kharg Island alone is exporting 2 billion barrels of oil daily.

TERRORISM: In Kabul, Afghanistan, a mujahideen bomb demolishes the Iqbal movie house, known to be frequented by Communist dignitaries. This attack also marks the beginning of urban terrorism by the Afghan resistance.

January 9
DIPLOMACY: In Baghdad, Iraq, Iraqi deputy prime minister Tariq Aziz meets with Iranian Mujahideen-i-Khalq leader Massoud Rajavi, whose left-wing guerrillas were waging their own personal war against the regime in Tehran, Iran.

January 18–31
AVIATION: The Iraqi Air Force begins a sustained bombardment effort over the southern front, losing 117 aircraft to effective Iranian defenses. However, it makes up for its losses by accepting deliveries of Chinese-made MiG-19s and MiG-21s from Egyptian stockpiles and maintains its overall strength at 332 aircraft.

January 19
DIPLOMACY: UN special envoy Diego Cordovez begins personal peace diplomacy with scheduled stops in Geneva, Switzerland, and Tehran.

January 29
POLITICS: In Kabul, Afghanistan, government radio announces the capture of French doctor Philippe Augoyard, who was captured by Afghan forces in the Logar Valley. Hundreds of French doctors and nurses are serving throughout the countryside to tend wounded mujahideen and civilians affected by war.

In Tehran, Iran, government radio criticizes the Soviet Union's apparent shift in favor of Iraq during the present hostilities; a week later, TASS correspondent Oleg Zuinko is expelled from the country.

February 6
MILITARY: In the southern front, massed Iranian forces commence Operation Wa al Fajr (By the Dawn) to retake the Fakkeh region of Khuzestan. Six divisions of Revolutionary Guards and Basij volunteers are massed—more than 100,000 men—and begin a concerted drive against Al Amarah, capital of Misan Province, and along the Basra-Baghdad Highway. However, this is undertaken in the absence of adequate air cover and armored support, and the usual "human wave" attacks by Pasdaran and Basij volunteers are cut down by superior firepower. By day's end, the attack is blunted a few miles within Iraq by six divisions of the Fourth Army Corps under Major General Hisham Sabah Fakhri. All told, the attackers suffer severely at the hands of Iraqi warplanes and helicopter gunships.

February 7
AVIATION: New Iraqi Mirage F-1 fighters are committed to ground-support missions for the first time, flying 129 combat missions against Iranian forces near Fakkeh. Iraqi helicopter gunships also take their toll on the massed, lightly armed formations.
MILITARY: In the southern sector, Operation Wa al Fajr continues as Iranian Pasdaran and Basij formations make repeated assaults against dug-in Iraqi defenders, only to be overwhelmed by heavy firepower.

February 8
DIPLOMACY: In Washington, D.C., a State Department spokesman reiterates that the United States supports the territorial integrity of both Iran and Iraq and is completely in favor of a cease-fire followed by a negotiated settlement.
MILITARY: In the Fakkeh region of Iran, Pasdaran and Basij units continue making "human wave" attacks against entrenched Iraqi forces, suffering staggering losses for little gain. Nonetheless, the government claims to have liberated 120 square miles of its own territory.
POLITICS: In Tehran, Iran, authorities arrest Nuredin Kianouri, secretary-general of the Tudeh (Communist) Party, and charge him with spying for the Soviet Union.

February 9–10
MILITARY: Near Fakkeh, Iran, Operation Wa al Fajr enters a new phase as the Iranians pour in armored units across a mile-long front and attack the frontier post of

Shib. However, they advance without infantry support and a quick counterattack by Iraqi T-72 tanks, striking their flanks, throws the attackers back in disarray. Fighting dies down on the 10th with the Iraqis having won a sharp tactical victory. Western analysts suggest that the Iranians lost 7,000 men to an Iraqi total of 2,000.

February 12
MILITARY: In the northern sector, Iranian units backed by *peshmerga* of the Kurdish Democratic Party attack Iraqi positions near the Dardani-Khan Dam, which supplies 40 percent of Iraq's domestic electricity supply. They claim to fight their way to within six miles of the dam before halting.

February 13
MILITARY: In Baghdad, Iraq, 1,000 Iranian prisoners captured near Fakkeh are mockingly paraded through the city.

February 14
POLITICS: In Tehran, Iran, a deeply disappointed Majlis Speaker Hojatolislam Hashemi Rafsanjani declares that Operation Wa al Fajr will continue.

February 16
DIPLOMACY: In New York City, the UN Human Rights Commission votes 29 to 7, with 5 abstentions, to demand an immediate withdrawal of Soviet troops from Afghanistan.

March 4
POLITICS: In Iran, Ayatollah Khomeini releases 8,300 political prisoners under a broad amnesty program. He is probably motivated by an urgent need to win over the Bazaaris (middle class), and he also promulgates new, regularized procedures for arresting, trying, detaining, and convicting suspects.

March 15
DIPLOMACY: In Oslo, Norway, an international symposium opens, highlighting the experiences of Afghan refugees who had been tortured in cellars of the Ministry of the Interior in Kabul, Afghanistan.

March 21
TERRORISM: In Kabul, Afghanistan, a bomb explodes in a crowded mosque, killing four and injuring seven.

April
DIPLOMACY: In Moscow, Soviet Union, President Zia ul-Haq of Pakistan, then attending funeral services for General Secretary Leonid Brezhnev, is informed by Yuri Andropov, his successor, that the Soviets are willing to withdraw from Afghanistan once Pakistan ceases all aid to the armed resistance.

April 8-22
DIPLOMACY: In Geneva, Switzerland, representatives from Pakistan and Afghanistan begin a second round of UN-sponsored peace talks. The talks end without reaching an agreement.

TERRORISM: At Qara-Bagh, Afghanistan, Soviet forces massacre another group of unarmed civilians suspected of aiding local mujahideen. Far from terrorizing the populace, such acts only encourage young men to seek martyrdom and revenge by joining the resistance.

April 10–17

MILITARY: In the southern front, massed Iranian forces commence Operation Wa al Fajr-1 north of Fakkeh to seize and cut the strategic Basra-Baghdad highway. As they advance, they are mauled by superior Iraqi air power and helicopter gunships, suffering heavy casualties while liberating 60 square miles of territory. Iranian fanaticism on the battlefield has again failed to overcome Iraqi technical superiority in combat arms.

April 18

TERRORISM: In Beirut, Lebanon, the U.S. embassy is destroyed by a bomb blast that kills 61 people, including 17 Americans (of whom three are soldiers and one a marine).

April 20

AVIATION: The Iraqis unleash three more Frog-7 tactical missiles against Dezful, Iran, killing 15 people and wounding more than 105.

DIPLOMACY: The governments of Iraq and Turkey sign an agreement allowing Turkish forces to cross the border in hot pursuit of Kurdish guerrillas.

April 22

AVIATION: Iraqi Frog-7 tactical missiles again slam into Dezful, Iran, inflicting further casualties upon the civilian populace.

DIPLOMACY: In Rome, Italy, former Afghan king Mohammad Zahir Shah informs the French newspaper *Le Monde* that a united front is needed in Afghanistan to coordinate the resistance against Soviet forces. He also offers his services as a rallying point for his nation and a "reconciler" to promote harmony among competing Afghan factions.

April 28

POLITICS: In Baghdad, Iraq, President Saddam Hussein bolsters his personality cult on this, his 46th birthday, with carefully orchestrated exhibitions, demonstrations, and public celebrations extolling his virtues. He does so to forestall any attempt to remove him from power by force.

April 30

AVIATION: In Tehran, Iran, the government announces that Colonel Hush Seddiq is appointed chief of staff of the Iranian Air Force.

POLITICS: Tudeh (Communist) Party general secretary Nuredin Kianouri appears on national television and makes a complete "confession" that he was plotting a coup against the government.

May 4

POLITICS: In light of overt Soviet assistance to Iraq, especially shipments of Frog-7 ballistic missiles, the government in Tehran, Iran, formally outlaws the Tudeh

(Communist) Party and begins rounding up its 1,500 members. Ten military officers with ties to the party will be found guilty of spying for Moscow and executed.

May 10
POLITICS: In Tehran, Iran, Pasdaran leader Mohsen Rezai declares that more than 1,000 Tudeh members are under arrest.

May 13
AVIATION: Iraqi forces unleash two Frog 7 tactical missiles at Andimeshk, north of Dezful, killing 16 people and wounding 120. Two other missiles hit Dezful itself, killing 60 people and wounding more than 300. Iraqi warplanes also bomb Pol Dokhtar, north of Dezful, inflicting civilian casualties.

DIPLOMACY: In Washington, D.C., Secretary of State George P. Shultz and Iraqi foreign minister Tariq Aziz meet for the first time and discuss ways that the United Nations can help end the Iran-Iraq War. Aziz also dwells on the fact that better relations between his country and the United States would be a positive development.

May 14
DIPLOMACY: In Kabul, Afghanistan, the government announces that it will boycott the 1984 summer Olympics in Los Angeles, California.

May 17
DIPLOMACY: At the Khyber Pass, Pakistan, Vice President George H. W. Bush arrives to voice continuing American support for the mujahideen movement.

May 23
MILITARY: An agreement between France and Iraq allows the latter to barter for advanced weapons using oil.

POLITICS: In the holy city of Najaf, Iraq, the government arrests 90 members of the families of Shiite Ayatollah Abdul al-Qasim al-Khoei and Hojatolislam Baqir Hakim, who failed to adequately endorse official polices; six are ultimately executed.

May 25
AVIATION: Iraqi warplanes strike at Baneh, a Kurdish town in the northern sector; civilian casualties are reported.

DIPLOMACY: In Baghdad, Iraq, Foreign Minister Tariq Aziz advocates a special peace accord to halt all shelling of civilian targets, which would be administered by the United Nations, but the Iranian government rejects it.

May 25–29
MILITARY: In northern Iraq, two Turkish commando brigades cross the border and penetrate 20 miles while performing a "cordon and search" operation against *peshmerga* (guerrillas) associated with the Patriotic Union of Kurdistan.

May 28
POLITICS: In Iran, five Air Force officers are arrested and charged with planning a coup by bombing Ayatollah Khomeini's residence at Jamaran.

June 8

DIPLOMACY: In the latest war of words between Moscow and Washington, the Soviets accuse the United States of secretly providing Iran with weapons and spare parts with a view of deliberately prolonging the conflict. This, in turn, provides a convenient pretext for a naval buildup in the Persian Gulf.

June 12

AVIATION: Lieutenant Iraj Fazeli of the Iranian Air Force defects with a F-4 Phantom jet to Turkey; he receives asylum, but the aircraft is sent back to Iran.

June 15–24

DIPLOMACY: In Geneva, Switzerland, foreign ministers from Pakistan and Afghanistan commence a third series of peace talks centering on Soviet troop withdrawals. The talks conclude without any progress.

June 20

POLITICS: Iranian authorities execute Nuredin Kianouri, several other Tudeh leaders, and Captain Bahram Afzali, former head of the Iranian navy.

June 24

DIPLOMACY: A UN special report acknowledges that Iran and Iraq have suffered from damages to civilian sites, but that Iran has clearly suffered the most with cities like Khorramshahr, Abadan, Musian, Dehloran, and Hoveyheh being wholly or partly devastated.

July

TERRORISM: In Rauza, Afghanistan, Soviet troops endure a mujahideen ambush, then go on a rampage in the nearest village, shooting scores of civilians down.

July 1

AVIATION: In light of the ongoing Iran-Iraq War, the Air Force deploys a provisional support squadron at Riyadh Air Base, Saudi Arabia. The oil-rich region of the Persian Gulf remains an area of vital strategic interest to the United States and the West.
DIPLOMACY: In Baghdad, Iraq, Foreign Minister Tariq Aziz declares that attacks against Iranian economic assets will increase.

July 20

DIPLOMACY: In Baghdad, Iraq, Foreign Minister Tariq Aziz declares that large numbers of American weapons are arriving in Iran, though he does not formally accuse the United States of supplying them outright.

July 22–29

MILITARY: In the northern front, massed Iranians commence Operation Wa al Fajr-2 to seize Rawanduz, Iraq, and stir up a rebellion among the neighboring Kurds. Assisted by members of the Kurdish Democratic Party and armed Iraqi Shiites of the resistance group Al Mujahideen, the Iranians manage to capture Mount Karman and the garrison town of Hajj Umran. An Iraqi counterattack, backed by helicopter gunships, is easily repulsed in the rugged terrain. Thus the Iranians not only seize 150 square miles of territory, half of it in Iraq, but they also cut off Iraqi supplies to Iranian Kurdish insurgents.

July 26
MILITARY: In Washington, D.C., the U.S. House of Representatives votes to approve $50 million in covert military assistance to the Afghan resistance.
NAVAL: U.S. government officials warn of the eventual need for naval forces in the Persian Gulf to protect navigation rights.

July 30–31
MILITARY: In the central front, three Iranian divisions commence the Wa al Fajr-3 offensive west of Mehran with a view toward penetrating Iraqi territory in the direction of Kut. The Iraqis try a counterattack by launching two armored brigades at Iranian forces gathering for the assault, but they withdraw in the face of stiff resistance.

July 31
POLITICS: Paul Adair, a U.S. specialist on oil-well safety, inspects damaged Iranian facilities by air and states that the ensuing leaks would probably ruin the Persian Gulf's ecology.

August–January 16, 1984
MILITARY: In Paktia Province, Afghanistan, the 15th Brigade of the Afghan Army under Colonel Sayed Rahman is besieged in Urgun by several thousand mujahideen under Jalaluddin Haqqani and others.

August 1
MILITARY: Operation Wa al Fajr-3 continues as several days of intense combat carries the Iranians six miles into Iraq, despite 150 air raids launched against them daily. The Iraqi town of Doraji and the Badra Dam, along with the Dehloran-Mehran Road, are in their possession.

August 2
MILITARY: In the central sector, President Saddam Hussein and his defense minister personally visit the Iraqi Second Army Corps headquarters to bolster morale.

August 3
MILITARY: By this time the Iranians claim to have killed 6,000 Iraqis, taken 400 captive, and destroyed 13 tanks and other vehicles, along with 30 trucks. They have also liberated 40 square miles of their territory.

August 6–7
MILITARY: Near Mehran, Iran, Iranian forces begin attacking Iraqi positions on the western heights overlooking the city, but few gains are registered.

August 8–10
MILITARY: Near Mehran, Iran, Operation Wa al Fajr-3 winds down as Iranian forces attack Iraqi defenses on heights surrounding three sides of the city, but an impasse settles into the region.

August 12

DIPLOMACY: In Baghdad, Iraq, President Saddam Hussein imposes a Naval Exclusion Zone on the upper part of the Persian Gulf, extending from the Shatt al Arab waterway to Kharg Island. All commercial vessels trespassing in this region are liable to face an aerial attack.

August 13–14

MILITARY: In Kabul, Afghanistan, Abdul Haq of Hezb-i-Islami executes attacks on Radio Kabul, the government television headquarters, and the Bala Hissar fort. The mujahideen are becoming adept at urban warfare, which further emboldens its leaders to do more.

August 19

NAVAL: In Tehran, Iran, the government pledges to safeguard any oil tanker or freighter stopping at either Kharg Island or Bandar Khomeini. To do so, it initiates a convoy system that will operate close to the Iranian coastline, where ships can be covered by land-based aircraft, guns, and missiles.

August 25

MILITARY: In northern Iraq, Turkish forces make a second incursion against Kurdish guerrillas, seizing several hundred prisoners, including many "wanted men." Many of them are then handed over to the Baghdad regime for trial and execution.

August 27

DIPLOMACY: In Geneva, Switzerland, foreign ministers of Afghanistan and Pakistan meet in separate talks with UN peace emissaries.

August 31

TERRORISM: A bomb explodes at Kabul airport, Afghanistan, and is assumed to have been placed there by the mujahideen.

September 8

MILITARY: In Beirut, Lebanon, the frigate USS *Bowen* supplies close support fire to assist marines deployed there as an international peacekeeping force. Its 5-inch guns are trained on Druze militiamen who had been firing on the marines with small arms and mortars.

September 14

AVIATION: A Turkish military aircraft crashes in northern Iraq, and the two-man crew is captured by *peshmerga* of the Socialist Party of Kurdistan. Rather than face another "'cordon and search" operation by Turkish troops, the captives are quietly released.

September 16–19

MILITARY: In the Marvian sector, 25 miles south of Penjwin, Iranian commanders launch an unauthorized attack against Iraqi positions, backed by *peshmerga* of the Kurdish Democratic Party (KDP). They make minor territorial gains over the next three days, capturing some men and equipment. Their success prompts Iraqi aerial attacks against Marvian and Baneh.

September 17
POLITICS: Iraqi president Saddam Hussein informs the Islamic Conference Organization's Peace Committee that he seeks peace and good relations with Iran. He adds that he would welcome any effort by the group to help end the current war.

September 18
MILITARY: In Urgun, Afghanistan, mujahideen fighters overrun the Nek Mohammad Kala fortress with the use of a captured tank, capturing 243 Afghan army prisoners. However, they are unable to storm the nearby town of Urgun, which is well-garrisoned and supplied by air. The siege is further beset by squabbling among the mujahideen, in which several factions refuse to coordinate their efforts with others.

September 19
POLITICS: In Tehran, Iran, Ayatollah Khomeini reacts angrily to France's decision to supply Iraq with five Super Etendard jets and Exocet missiles by threatening to "cut off the hands" of those assisting Iraqi president Saddam Hussein, by reducing their access to Persian Gulf oil.

September 23
AVIATION: In Tehran, Iran, Majlis speaker Hojatolislam Hashemi Rafsanjani warns France not to sell Super Etendard jet fighters and Exocet missiles to Iraq, warning that it would turn France into "Iran's enemy."

October 1
AVIATION: The city of Dezful, Iran, is struck by Iraqi Frog-7 tactical missiles for the 21st time.

October 3
AVIATION: Captain Hamid Zirak-Bash of the Iranian Air Force hijacks a C-130 transport to Dubai, where he is granted political asylum; the plane is returned to Iran.

October 8
AVIATION: The French news services formally acknowledge that the government is supplying Iraq with five Super Etendard jet fighters capable of deploying advanced Exocet antishipping missiles. Despite expressions of fear by the United States and Persian Gulf nations that this move threatens to escalate tensions in the region, France cannot allow Iran to win the war, since Iraq owes it $4 billion to 5 billion.

October 9
MILITARY: The French government, anxious about Iranian threats to close down the Persian Gulf, rushes another 30 Exocet missiles, 100 AMX tanks, and large quantities of antitank and high-explosive bombs to Iraq.

October 15
AVIATION: Five Iranian cities, Marvian, Dezful, Andimeshk, Navahand and Behbehan, are struck by Iraqi Scud-B missiles; in Behbehan, 38 children die when their school is hit.

DIPLOMACY: In Tehran, Iran, the Supreme Defense Council, chaired for the first time by Ayatollah Khomeini, meets to discuss Iraqi threats against Iranian economic assets in the Persian Gulf. It releases a communiqué warning that Iran is prepared to close the Gulf region down to all shipping, coupled with attacks on Western oil interests and the Kirkuk oil fields of Iraq.

October 20–28

MILITARY: In the northern front, Iranian forces commence Operation Wa al Fajr-4 against the Iraqi First Army Corps in the Penjwin region. As before, they are assisted by Kurdish guerrillas and dissident Iraqi Shiite militias. They attack and drive the Iraqis from the towns of Baneh and Marvian, and gradually penetrate 25 miles into Iraq proper. President Saddam Hussein is so alarmed by their progress that he dispatches elite Presidential Guards units from Baghdad, but their counterattack is repulsed. Iran's success here further stokes rebellious sentiment among the Kurdish population throughout the region. The Iraqis, for their part, claim to have killed 5,000 Iranians and their allies; the Iranians claim to have killed or captured 2,800 Iraqis.

October 23

TERRORISM: An explosive-laden truck driven by suicide jihadists explodes in the 24th Marine Amphibious Unit compound at Beirut, Lebanon, killing 241 and wounding 71 men of the 1st Battalion, 8th Marines. This is the highest one-day death toll of marines since World War II. Minutes later, a second truck bomb kills 58 French soldiers of a nearby peacekeeping force. President Ronald W. Reagan consequently reevaluates the marines' role in the peacekeeping mission there.
AVIATION: Transports of the Military Airlift Command convey 239 dead and 95 wounded marines from Beirut, Lebanon, to European and American hospitals for treatment or burial.

October 24

AVIATION: A civilian Iranian pilot defects and states that only 10 of Iran's 31 jet airliners are functional, and that more than 50 pilots and flight engineers have been arrested, grounded, or dismissed for political reasons.

October 28

AVIATION: Five French-built Super Etendard jet fighters arrive in Iraq, which give the Iraqis sufficient range to cover two-thirds of all targets in Iran and a large portion of the Persian Gulf. These aircraft are also equipped to fire the deadly Exocet "fire and forget" missile.

November 4

POLITICS: In Kabul, Afghanistan, the government executes nine people it claims were responsible for exploding a bomb at Kabul airport.

November 6–9

MILITARY: In the northern sector, the third and final phase of Operation Wa al Fajr-4 commences as Iranian and Kurdish elements claim to capture several villages near Penjwin, without actually taking the village itself. The situation was deemed so perilous that parts of the elite Iraqi Presidential Guard were again flown in by helicopter under orders to hold at all cost.

November 8
DIPLOMACY: In New York City, the Iranian UN delegation formally asks the Security Council to assign a Commission of Experts to investigate its charges that Iraq was employing illegal chemical weapons.

November 19
MILITARY: In the northern sector, the Iranians launch a division-size night attack in the vicinity of Penjwin, Iran, claiming to seize 20 villages. The Iraqis deny any such gains have been made.

November 20
AVIATION: In Pakistan, an Afghan Air Force Su-7 fighter bomber lands, and the pilot, originally from Wardak Province, Afghanistan, defects and denounces the Communist regime in Kabul.

November 23
DIPLOMACY: In New York City, the UN General Assembly votes 116 to 20, with 16 abstentions, for an immediate withdrawal of all Soviet troops from Afghanistan.

November 26
DIPLOMACY: In Washington, D.C., President Ronald W. Reagan signs a National Security Decision Directive that facilitates better relations with the regime in Baghdad, Iraq.

November 27
TERRORISM: In Baghdad, Iraq, a truck bomb explodes, killing more than 90 people and wounding many more; the act is attributed to the Al Daawa organization.

November 28
POLITICS: The groups Resistance International and Freedom House secure the first two Soviet defectors in Afghanistan for their transfer to the United States.

December 6
MILITARY: Unsubstantiated reports surface that Soviet forces have withdrawn north of Kabul in the face of heavy losses. Evidence points to the apparent fact that they had completely underestimated the resilience of the Afghan resistance.

December 10
AVIATION: In response to Iranian-supported terrorism in Kuwait, the Iraqis unleash Scud-B missiles at five towns, killing 21 people and wounding 222.
POLITICS: Faced with certain annihilation, Jalal Talabani of the Patriotic Union of Kurdistan signs a cease-fire with Iraqi president Saddam Hussein.
TERRORISM: A spate of bombing damages several embassies in Kuwait, including that of the United States; six people die, and 80 are wounded. The Shiite resistance group Al Daawa is suspected of planting the bombs with Iranian help.

December 22
MILITARY: In London, United Kingdom, the British Defense Sales Organization admits to having sold Iraq 10,000 "protective kits" to minimize the effects of chemical weapons on its troops.

December 27

DIPLOMACY: In Kabul, Afghanistan, the government announces that it will request the departure of 105,000 Soviet troops after receiving international guarantees that all opposition groups stop fighting, and all foreign support they receive has ended.

December 29

MILITARY: A Soviet deserter informs the Western news media that Red Army troop morale in Afghanistan is low and that drug abuse is rising.

1984

January

MILITARY: In Kabul, Afghanistan, high desertion rates in the Afghan national army forces the government to lower the age for compulsory military service to 16. The General Staff is also overhauled, with Major General Mohammad Nazar gaining appointment as the new chief of staff.

January 2

AVIATION: The Iraqi government claims that its jets have sunk five naval vessels in the Persian Gulf, south of Bandar Khomeini.

January 10

AVIATION: Afghan antiaircraft fire scores its first big success by downing three Soviet jets on a single day.

January 16

MILITARY: In Paktia Province, Afghanistan, an Afghan column easily dispenses mujahideen forces surrounding the town of Urgun, breaking the six-month siege.

January 23

DIPLOMACY: In the United States, the State Department adds Iran to the list of nations that support terrorism worldwide. This comes about largely in reaction to the October 23, 1983, bombing of the Marine Corps barracks in Lebanon. Henceforth, the Americans also enact Operation Staunch, intended to discourage the United Kingdom, Israel, Italy, South Korea, Turkey, and West Germany from selling modern arms to the Iranians. It also begins passing highly detailed satellite reconnaissance photos of the Persian Gulf to Saudi Arabia, which in turn hands them off to the regime in Iraq. All this constitutes a marked, anti-Iranian shift in U.S. policy.

January 24

MILITARY: In Kabul, Afghanistan, President Babrak Karmal institutes a major shake-up in his top military brass in which Deputy Defense Minister Major General Khalilullah is sacked in favor of Major General Mohammad Nabi Azami and Chief of Operations General Issa Nuristani is dropped for Major General Ghulam Qadir Miakhel.

January 25

AVIATION: In a thinly veiled warning to Iran, the Iraqi government announces that it has obtained an unspecified number of Soviet-built SS-12 tactical missiles with a range of 500 miles Virtually every Iranian city, save for Mashad, is now under the threat of bombardment.

February

NAVAL: In light of continuing Iranian offensives against Iraq, the U.S. Navy begins preparing to keep the Strait of Hormuz open to navigation, by force if necessary.

POLITICS: In Peshawar, Pakistan, cracks appear in mujahideen unity after Abdul Rasul Sayyaf is accused by Burhanuddin Rabbani and Yunnis Khalis of channeling funds to his own organization inside Afghanistan. Other splits appear after moderate members accuse ultraconservative Gulbuddin Hekmatyar of encouraging his resistance fighters to attack those belonging to other groups. Tension between moderate and conservative factions within the alliance are never far below the surface.

February 3

DIPLOMACY: In Tehran, Iran, Prime Minister Hojatolislam Hossein Musavi warns that if Iraq attacks Iranian cities, the cities of Basra, Khanaqin, and Mandali face similar treatment.

February 7

MILITARY: Rather than lose more men to internecine civil strife, President Ronald W. Reagan orders marine detachments stationed at Beirut, Lebanon, withdrawn.

February 9

NAVAL : Off Lebanon, the destroyers USS *Caron* and *Moosbrugger* fire 400 5-inch rounds against hostile positions along the shore. This is the heaviest American bombardment of the Lebanese civil war.

February 10–11

AVIATION: With the situation in Lebanon spiraling out of control, Navy and Marine helicopters evacuate several hundred American citizens and foreign nationals from Beirut.

February 11

AVIATION: A score of Iraqi Scud-B missiles slam into the town of Dezful, Iran, killing 36 civilians and wounding 140. The Iranians counter by striking at Khanaqin and Mandali.

February 12

MILITARY: For the first time, Iranian artillery subjects Basra, Iraq, to serious, sustained shelling, which unleashes a flood of refugees from the area. Previously, the ayatollah forbade such action in the hopes that the resident Shia population would rise up against the regime. When this failed to materialize, the city and its inhabitants became just another target.

February 14

DIPLOMACY: In Baghdad, Iraq, a government spokesman announces that attacks on civilian settlements are being suspended for seven days. This is in response to a request by Iranian mujahideen leader Massoud Rajavi. It evokes a negative response from President Hojatolislam Ali Khamenei, who declares that all Iraqi cities are subject to attack except the holy cities of Najaf and Karbala, which house Shiite shrines.

The Iraqis also declare that they will sink any vessel, commercial or otherwise, that approaches the Iranian ports of Bandar Khomeini or Bushehr.

NAVAL: In Tehran, Iran, a meeting of the Supreme Defense Council results in a decision to fortify Goat Island in the Strait of Hormuz, which is a distinct threat to freedom of navigation.

February 15
AVIATION: Iranian warplanes bomb a suburb in Baghdad, Iraq, inflicting some civilian casualties.

February 16
MILITARY: In the central theater, massed Iranian forces commence Operation Wa al Fajr-5 near Mehran. Their goal is to strike west toward Baqubah on the Baghdad-Tehran road and possibly threaten the Iraqi capital. The region is defended by 10 divisions of the Iraqi Second Army Corps, roughly 100,000 troops. The operation is actually a diversion to draw Iraqi reserves from the south.

February 18
AVIATION: Iran and Iraq embrace a UN-mediated agreement not to launch aerial attacks against each other's population centers, but Iraqi president Saddam Hussein orders his air force to strike at Iran's port facilities and shipping in the Persian Gulf.

The bombed remains of the U.S. Marine barracks at Beirut International Airport *(Department of Defense)*

February 21–23
MILITARY: In the central sector near Dehloran, Iranian forces unleash Operation Wa al Fajr-6 to gain the Iraqi-held town of Ali al-Gharbi on the Basra-Baghdad highway. The attackers make little headway, but this action is also a diversion for bigger events further south.

February 22
MILITARY: In the southern front, Iranian forces commence Operation Khaibar by massing several divisions of Revolutionary Guards at Hoveizeh and staging carefully orchestrated boat and helicopter raids through the forbading Haur al Hawizeh marshes. Their goal is the capture of Al Qurnah, possession of which would cut the Basra-Baghdad highway. The operation is personally orchestrated by General Ali Jalai, deputy commander of Iranian ground forces. The region is defended by the Iraqi Third Army Corps under Major General Maher Abdul al-Rashid and the Fourth Army Corps under General Hisham Sabah Fakhri.

Farther south, a second group of 20,000 Iranians landed unopposed on Majnoon Island and began erecting defensive positions. This is the site of an enormous, abandoned oil refinery complex.

February 25–27
MILITARY: Operation Khaibar continues as Iranian forces attack the Northern and Western Islands of Majnoon in the Persian Gulf. This is an oil-rich region constructed from artificial islands, the Iraqis fail to muster an adequate defense and both are captured. The Iraqis also make extensive use of mustard gas during this operation.

February 25–March 1
AVIATION: Iraqi warplanes attack seven Iranian naval targets in the Persian Gulf, enacting a new phase of combat called the "Tanker War."

February 27
DIPLOMACY: In Baghdad, Iraq, the government declares that Iran's Kharg Island oil terminal is under siege and subject to aerial attack to discourage foreign vessels from docking there.

February 28
MILITARY: In a communiqué to President Saddam Hussein, General Maher Abdul al-Rashid, commander of the Iraqi Third Army Corps in Basra, boasts of killing thousands of Iranians and turning "what is left of these harmful insects into food for the birds of the wilderness and fish of the marshes." At one point, 3,000 dead Iranians, mostly young men, are bulldozed into a common grave.

February 29
MILITARY: In the southern front, Operation Khaibar enters its final phase as three divisions of Pasdaran volunteers press to within rifle-shot of the Basra-Baghdad highway at Al Qurnah, only to be violently thrown back by an Iraqi counterattack assisted by artillery, warplanes, helicopters—this time armed with chemical bombs and rockets.

March 1–2

MILITARY: Massed Iranian infantry charges headlong into Iraqi positions at Ghuzail, only to be crushed by superior firepower and driven back into the swamps.

March 1–9

MILITARY: In the southern sector, massed Pasdaran forces, numbering 20,000 men, gather their strength for a final lunge at Al Qurnah, Iraq. They attack by pushing two divisions of fanatical Revolutionary Guards, backed by armor and earth-moving machinery, forward. However, they are savaged by Iraqi air power and driven off with heavy loss of life. Operation Khaibar is thought to have involved 300,000 Iranians and 200,000 Iraqi; losses are estimated at 20,000 Iranians and 7,000 Iraqis.

March 4

DIPLOMACY: In Tehran, Iran, Majlis Speaker Hojatolislam Hashemi Rafsanjani accuses Iraq of recently employing chemical weapons that killed 400 soldiers and injured 1,100.

March 5

DIPLOMACY: In Washington, D.C., a State Department spokesman suggests there is a mounting body of evidence collected by the International Committee of the Red Cross to infer the Iraq has utilized outlawed chemical weapons in violation of the 1925 Geneva Protocol. Iran is also criticized for its refusal to end the war through a negotiated settlement.

March 6–12

DIPLOMACY: In Baghdad, Iraq, Defense Minister General Adnan Khairallah accuses the United States of making egregiously false accusations regarding the use of chemical weapons.

MILITARY: In the southern sector, the Iraqis gather their strength together and counterattack on Majnoon Island, meeting fierce resistance from dug-in defenders. After several days of heavy fighting, they are content simply to maintain their toehold on the island.

March 7

DIPLOMACY: A medical team from the Red Cross, having examined several Iranian soldiers, concludes that they have in fact been injured by "substances prohibited by international law."

March 9

MILITARY: In Tehran, Iran, a military communiqué accuses the Iraqis of deploying homemade mustard gas against Iranian forces in the southern marshlands.

March 15

DIPLOMACY: In New York City, the UN Human Rights Commission appoints Austrian professor Felix Ermacora to investigate accusations of Soviet abuses and atrocities in Afghanistan. His report, which is highly critical of the Soviet Union, is approved by the commission.

March 27

AVIATION: In the Persian Gulf, Iraq declares that it employed its Super Etendard fighters and Exocet missiles against two tankers southwest of Kharg Island. This is a particularly lethal attack, and also the first time the duo had been specifically mentioned in an official war communiqué.

NAVAL: In Baghdad, Iraq, President Saddam Hussein ups the international ante by declaring a 1,126-kilometer exclusionary zone in the Persian Gulf, designed to prevent oil tankers from reaching Iran's main oil terminal on Kharg Island. These vessels are now vulnerable to attack from the air, a tactic expected to send insurance rates for such vessels skyrocketing.

March 28

DIPLOMACY: The UN Commission of Experts, having examined and interviewed several Iranian wounded, concludes that Iraq had employed mustard gas on several occasions.

March 30

DIPLOMACY: In New York City, the United Nations appeals to Iran and Iraq to refrain from using chemical weapons in their struggle; however, Iraq is not singled out as the transgressor.

The USS *New Jersey* fires a salvo during a deployment off the coast of Beirut, Lebanon. *(U.S. Navy)*

March 31
DIPLOMACY: In Washington, D.C., the United States government prohibits the export to Iraq of chemicals that might be involved in the production of outlawed weapons.

April 5
DIPLOMACY: In Washington, D.C., President Ronald W. Reagan signs another National Security Decision Directive, this time paving the way for closer cooperation with Iraq on shared electronic intelligence.

April 11
DIPLOMACY: In Kabul, Afghanistan, Third Secretary Richard S. Vandiver of the U.S. embassy is ordered out of the country on grounds of espionage; the American government denies the charge.

April 18
AVIATION: In the Persian Gulf, Iraqi warplanes attack a Panamanian tanker near Kharg Island as the "Tanker War" escalates.

April 22
AVIATION: For the first time, Soviet Tu-16, Tu-22, and Su-24 jet bombers perform high-altitude saturation bombardment of mujahideen positions throughout the Panjshir Valley, Afghanistan.

MILITARY: In the Panjshir Valley, Afghanistan, 20,000 Soviet and Afghan forces, backed by tanks and armored vehicles, launch their fourth concerted offensive to eliminate mujahideen fighters under Ahmad Shah Massoud. Here the assaults are made entirely by helicopter-borne commandos, who are free to operate without cumbersome tanks and armored vehicles. The civilian population is also mercilessly uprooted and relocated while five military bases are established along the valley to control it. Hopelessly outgunned, Massoud abandons the Panjshir Valley for the time being and continues his guerrilla tactics in regions of the northwest.

As the Afghan occupation enters its fourth year, the Soviets begin dramatically shifting their tactics from conventional armored deployments along roads to mobile air assaults by paratroopes, SPETSNAZ units, and other elite troops. They also determine to break the will of the Afghan people by sowing millions of mines disguised as everyday items such as watches, cameras, toys, radios, and tape recorders. These are designed to explode while being handled and to maim rather than kill the victim. Several thousand Afghan children are horribly mutilated in consequence.

April 30
MILITARY: In the Hazrara Valley, Afghanistan, a battalion of the Soviet 682nd Motorized Rifle Regiment is ambushed by mujahideen forces and loses 60 killed before retreating.

May
DIPLOMACY: The European Community foreign ministers release a communiqué appealing to the Soviet Union to contribute positively to UN General Assembly

resolutions regarding an Afghan solution. In sum, Soviet leaders will have to weigh their involvement in Afghanistan against continued good relations with the West.

MILITARY: The respected publication *Jane's Defense Weekly* declares that the Soviets are dropping "liquid fire" bombs and fuel air explosives on mujahideen positions. These weapons produce shock waves capable of killing people at ranges of up to 400 yards. The magazine also asserts such ordnance has been used in Afghanistan since the summer of 1983 as part of a battlefield weapons program.

May 13

AVIATION: The Iranian Air Force, unable to strike at tankers since they do not visit Iraqi ports, begins lashing out at Saudi and Kuwaiti vessels by attacking a tanker near Bahrain. These activities are contributing to escalating increases in shipping insurance.

May 15

DIPLOMACY: In New York City, the Iranian UN representative declares that, while Iran supports freedom of navigation, it will not allow the Persian Gulf to be used against it. In that contingency, it is prepared to shut the Gulf down for everybody.

May 16

NAVAL: In the Persian Gulf, a Saudi supertanker is struck by a missile near the port of Jubail, inside Saudi territorial waters. Hereafter, the United States intends to pass AWACS information onto the Saudi defense forces more quickly.

May 20

DIPLOMACY: In Tunis, the Gulf Cooperation Council persuades the Arab Council that Iranian attacks against Saudi and Kuwaiti vessels outside the declared war zone are acts of aggression.

May 24

AVIATION: In the Persian Gulf, a five-day lull ends after Iraqi aircraft attack two large naval targets near Kharg Island. The Saudi Air Force also begins patrolling its coastline to thwart Iranian attacks against tankers.

DIPLOMACY: Iraq and Jordan agree in principle to construct an oil pipeline from the Kirkuk oilfields to the port of Aqaba. However, the project is dropped in November due to the potential for Israeli sabotage.

June 1

DIPLOMACY: In New York City, the UN Security Council votes 13-0 to adopt a Gulf Cooperation Council-sponsored resolution that condemns Iranian attacks on commercial Saudi and Kuwaiti shipping in the Persian Gulf. It further calls upon all belligerents to respect neutral shipping.

June 3

AVIATION: In the Persian Gulf, Iraqi warplanes attack and sink a Turkish-register tanker off Kharg Island.

June 5

AVIATION: Over the Persian Gulf, Saudi F-15 jet fighters intercept and shoot down two Iranian F-4s that had intruded into their air space. They were guided to the intercept by American AWACS aircraft. The government insists its aircraft only fired after the Iranians ignored a warning to turn back. Iran also reports that 600 people were killed by an Iraqi air raid on the town of Baneh.

MILITARY: Iranian artillery heavily shells Basra, Iraq, inflicting casualties and forcing civilians to flee again.

June 6

AVIATION: The Iraqi Air Force conducts retaliatory air raids by striking Dezful, Masjed Soleyman, and Nahavand.

June 8

DIPLOMACY: In light of skirmishing between Iranian and Saudi aircraft in the Persian Gulf region, President Hojatolislam Ali Khamenei professes no aggression against Saudi Arabia and Kuwait, provided they remain neutral in the ongoing strife.

June 10

AVIATION: In the Persian Gulf, Iranian airplanes strike a Kuwaiti supertanker in the Lower Gulf region, 100 miles off the Qatari coast. This is the first hostile act committed in this distant region.

June 12

DIPLOMACY: In light of ongoing air raids against population centers, the United Nations sponsors another aerial cease-fire between Iran and Iraq. UN monitors are also to be deployed in their respective capitals to observe all breaches.

June 15

DIPLOMACY: In Tehran, Iran, the government proposes extending the aerial cease-fire between the cities to shipping in the Persian Gulf. However, when Iraq insists that it be allowed to repair its own oil-exporting facilities, nothing comes of the suggestion.

June 20

AVIATION: In Washington, D.C., the State Department declares that the Saudi government has established an Air Defense Interception Zone, or Fahd Line, beyond its territorial limits. Thus disposed, Saudi warplanes, aided by U.S. AWACS aircraft and aerial tankers, can engage hostile targets threatening its shipping in the Persian Gulf.

June 24

AVIATION: The latest lull in the "Tanker War" ends after Iraqi jets attack a Greek tanker off Iran's Kharg Island oil-loading terminal; the vessel receives light damage. However, Iran admits that significant damage was inflicted on facilities on the island's western side.

June 27

AVIATION: In the Persian Gulf, Iraqi jets attack a Swiss tanker off Kharg Island, killing eight and wounding three.

June 30

DIPLOMACY: The governments of Iraq and Turkey agree to construct a third pipeline to the Mediterranean coast. Such a project would allow Iraq to regain some economic prosperity without its former oil export routes through the Persian Gulf.

July

DIPLOMACY: UN Secretary-General Javier Pérez de Cuéllar is approached by Soviet Premier Konstantin Chernenko, who informs him that while there is no change in Soviet terms regarding an Afghan political settlement, his country backs the United Nation's negotiating efforts.

POLITICS: In Islamabad, Pakistan, the government announces that an estimated 2.8 million Afghan refugees are residing within its borders.

July 1

AVIATION: The Iraqi government claims that its jet shot down an Iranian F-14 Tomcat fighter in the northern Persian Gulf; Iran denies the charge.

July 5

AVIATION: Responding to the latest attack against Kharg Island, Iranian warplanes attack a Liberian-registered tanker carrying Saudi oil in the Lower Persian Gulf.

July 7

TERRORISM: In Baghdad, Iraq, a suicide car bombing outside an officer's club kills 10 people and injures many more. Authorities accuse Islamic Amal, a Syrian-based resistance group.

July 8

DIPLOMACY: Despite the downing of Iranian F-4 Phantom jets in Saudi airspace, the government in Tehran indicates a desire to mitigate outstanding differences through diplomacy. King Fahd returns the gesture by dispatching a diplomat with a note expressing identical sentiments.

July 22

DIPLOMACY: The United States grants political asylum to four more Soviet deserters.

July 31

POLITICS: In Bonn, West Germany, the Mujahideen-i-Khalq holds a news conference in which Captain Mohammad al Aryafar, who recently defected, describes the Iranian Navy as in a shambles due to purges of the regular officer corps. He also feels that the reason Iraq has not attacked and totally destroyed the Kharg Island facilities is because of pressure from Western nations who need the oil.

August 1

AVIATION: Three Iranians hijack a jet bound from Frankfurt, West Germany, to Paris, forcing it to land in Tehran, Iran. Once there, they demand the release of five Iranians held for conspiring to assassinate an opponent of Ayatollah Khomeini. The hostages are eventually released, but the aircraft is damaged by a bomb.

August 7

DIPLOMACY: In Tehran, Iran, the state media praise a series of unexplained explosions in the Red Sea that had damaged as many as 15 vessels and forced the United States and other nations to dispatch mine-sweeping helicopters and equipment.

August 9

POLITICS: In Tehran, Iran, Ayatollah Khomeini denounces mines in the Red Sea and criticizes the state radio for its favorable commentary on them.

August 12

AVIATION: In the Persian Gulf, Iraqi warplanes strike Iranian oil facilities on Sirri Island, damaging three tankers with Exocet missiles. Because this target lies 490 miles beyond Shuaiba, Iraq's southernmost airbase, the Iranians charge that the sortie could only have been made with inflight refueling—or staging at an airport in an unidentified Gulf state.

August 14

MILITARY: In Tehran, Iran, Defense Minister Colonel Mohammad Salimi is sacked after the Majlis accuses him of mishandling Operation Khaiber and expresses its general dissatisfaction with the conduct of the war. Many on his staff are also accused of mismanagement, inefficiency, and nepotism.

August 21

NAVAL: In Cairo, Egypt, an official says that the mines found in the Red Sea were obviously deployed to damage and frighten vessels, not sink them.

August 27–30

DIPLOMACY: In Geneva, Switzerland, the third round of UN-sponsored peace talks between Pakistan and Afghanistan take place without making any progress.

August 29

AVIATION: An Iranian F-4 Phantom jet defects to an Iraqi air base, and the crew is given political asylum.

September 3

MILITARY: On the Fao Peninsula, Iranian forces launch Operation Karbala by attacking across a second pontoon bridge thrown across the Shatt al Arab waterway. Some minor successes are scored before the offensive bogs down.

September 7

DIPLOMACY: In a sign of growing official contacts, a U.S. undersecretary of state meets with his Iraqi counterpart in Washington, D.C.

September 8

TERRORISM: An Iranian commercial Boeing 727 landing at Bahrain is hijacked by five monarchists, who force the craft to fly to Egypt with 52 passengers.

September 9

TERRORISM: A hijacked Iranian airliner touches down at Baghdad, Iraq, where five Iranian monarchists receive political asylum and the hostages are allowed to depart.

September 22

MILITARY: By this date, the sixth anniversary of the Iran-Iraq War, the number of Iraqi dead is estimated at 100,000 to 120,000 while those of Iran are roughly twice that. However, because the rate of attrition still favors Iran, the Baghdad regime orders 125,000 university students and teachers into the military for the first time, while the draft age is extended to able-bodied males up to 50 years in age.

October 4

POLITICS: In Washington, D.C., Congress passes the Tsongas Resolution, which authorizes the president to provide direct military aid to Afghan resistance fighters. It specifically states that "it should be the policy of the United States to encourage and support the people of Afghanistan to continue their struggle to be free of foreign domination."

October 12

DIPLOMACY: In Washington, D.C., a State Department spokesman announces that the United States is ready and willing to reestablish diplomatic relations with Iraq. President Saddam Hussein expresses similar sentiments in Baghdad.

October 18–23

MILITARY: In the central sector, the Iranians launch Operation Wa al Fajr-7 near Mehran to dislodge Iraqi units posted on the nearby Meymek Heights. After five days of infiltration and hard fighting, some progress is made, but an impasse sets in for the rest of the year.

Afghan resistance fighters return to a village destroyed by Soviet forces. *(Department of Defense)*

October 22

MILITARY: In Tehran, Iran, General Ali Zahirnejad, the joint chief of staff, becomes Ayatollah Khomeini's personal representative on the Supreme Defense Council. His presence is thought to signal a change from relying on mass Pasdaran/Basij "human wave" attacks to more limited objectives in a prolonged contest of attrition.

October 25

MILITARY: In Tehran, Iran, General Esmael Sohrabi becomes the new Iranian joint chief of staff.

POLITICS: In Kabul, Afghanistan, the government reveals plans to send 870 Afghan orphans to the Soviet Union for their education. In this manner the Soviets hope to eliminate the vicious factionalism and infighting prevalent among the current generation of Afghan Communist leaders.

November

POLITICS: Iraqi national elections are held, and not surprisingly, the Baath Party wins 70 percent of seats in the National Assembly. This is seen as confirmation of President Saddam Hussein's popularity and his grip on power.

November 26

DIPLOMACY: Relations between the United States and Iraq, broken in 1967, are formally restored with an exchange of ambassadors. Accordingly, David G. Newton presents his credentials in Baghdad, while Nizar Hamdoun does the same in Washington, D.C. It is unlikely this move could have been possible were it not for the ongoing Iran-Iraq War, but the United States still maintains its neutrality in that conflict.

November 28

MILITARY: Congress appropriates $285 million for clandestine assistance to the Afghan resistance, twice the total provided in 1983.

December 3

MILITARY: In Kabul, Afghanistan, government radio announces that Defense Minister Lieutenant General Abdul Qadir is being replaced by Army Chief of Staff Mohammad Nazar.

December 4

TERRORISM: Over Kuwait, four Arabic-speaking passengers hijack a Pakistan-bound jet and force it to land in Tehran, Iran. Once there, they kill Charles Hegna, an employee of the U.S. Agency for International Development.

December 5

TERRORISM: In Tehran, Iran, hijackers release most of their hostages and promise to blow up the plane if Kuwait does not release 17 men imprisoned for terrorism. They also kill William Stanford, another U.S. AID worker.

December 9

TERRORISM: In Tehran, Iran, security personnel disguised as medical workers overpower the hijackers and release the remaining nine hostages.

December 11
DIPLOMACY: The U.S. government accuses Iran of moving slowly against the hijackers in Tehran, possibly to encourage them.

December 12
TERRORISM: In Tehran, Iran, the government refuses to accede to a U.S. demand that the hijackers, who killed two American passengers, be extradited.

December 14
TERRORISM: In Mazar-i-Sharif, mujahideen leader Abdul Qader (Commander Zabiullah), a leader of the Jamiat resistance forces, is killed by a mine. Jamiat leader Burhanuddin Rabbani blames his death on pro-Soviet "traitors," though it could just as easily have been engineered by another Islamic faction.

December 17
AVIATION: Unsubstantiated reports surface in Western circles that Soviet aerial saturation bombing has killed thousands of Afghan civilians.

December 18
AVIATION: Iranian warplanes clearly demonstrate the relative weakness of Saudi and Kuwaiti aerial defenses by bombing a Kuwaiti-bound freighter in the upper Gulf.
POLITICS: After one of the Red Army defectors returns to the Soviet Union from the United States, he is quickly sentenced to 12 years in prison.

December 20
MILITARY: The French newspaper *VSD* reports that a recent failed coup against Iraqi president Saddam Hussein resulted in the execution of 62 army officers.

1985

January
DIPLOMACY: West German parliamentarian Jurgen Todenhofer, having returned from an inspection tour of Afghanistan, strongly denounces the Soviet Union for the atrocities it is perpetuating on an almost daily basis. According to him, the combination of helicopter gunships strafing villages, "butterfly bombs" designed to injure children, and scorched-earth tactics systematically applied against crops before they can be harvested has produced unbelievable suffering among the Afghan people.
MILITARY: No sooner does the first shipment of Chinese-made ground-to-ground missiles appear in mujahideen hands than they are used to bombard various parts of Kabul, Afghanistan.
POLITICS: A mass influx of refugees from the countryside has increased the population of Kabul, Afghanistan, from half a million to 1.5 million. Shortages and inflation are becoming rampant.

The government of Pakistan estimates that there are 3 million Afghan refugees within its borders with another 2 million residing in Iran. In only five years of Soviet occupation, one-third of Afghanistan's population has fled abroad so that one out of every two refugees in the world is an Afghan.

January 18

MILITARY: In Washington, D.C., Reagan administration officials declare that they are increasing covert military assistance to the Afghan resistance to $280 million. This is in addition to aid also being provided by China, Israel, and Saudi Arabia.

January 26

POLITICS: In Paktia Province, Afghanistan, mujahideen leader Khan Gul is sentenced to death for his anti-government activities.

January 28

MILITARY: In the southern sector, four Iraqi divisions under General Mahir Abd al-Rashid attack Majnoon Island. They storm ashore after a predawn artillery bombardment, then send in tanks while infantry in boats outflank the defenders. In fierce fighting the Iraqis manage to capture and secure the western portion of the island.

January 29

MILITARY: In Afghanistan, Commander Zabiullah, a leader of the Islamist Movement, dies after his jeep strikes a land mine.

January 31

MILITARY: In the central sector, Iraqis forces launch a limited counterattack near Qasr-i-Sherin, but little territory appears to change hands over the next several days.

March

TERRORISM: In Takhar, Kunduz, and Khanabad, Afghanistan, reports surface that Soviet forces have gunned down hundreds of Afghan civilians in reprisal for the deaths of several Soviet advisers. Thousands of inhabitants from these northern regions have begun fleeing to the supposed sanctuary of Pakistan.

March 3

MILITARY: In the southern sector, Iranian and Iraqis artillery begin pounding each other's oil and population centers in preparation for a major offensive action.
POLITICS: In Tehran, Iran, an alliance is announced among the Shiite resistance groups of Nasr, Pasdaran, Guardians of the Islamic Revolution, and the United Front of the Islamic Revolution.

March 4

AVIATION: Iraq breaks the cease-fire in the "War of the Cities" arranged by the United Nations on June 12, 1984, by lobbing missiles at several Iranian cities. These include a steel mill in Ahvaz and an unfinished nuclear power plant in Bushehr.

March 10–11

MILITARY: Iranian artillery commences a heavy bombardment of Basra, Iraq, only 12 miles from the Iranian front lines. This comes in retaliation to Iraqi aerial attacks on civilian targets.

March 11

AVIATION: Iranian warplanes bomb the outskirts of Baghdad, Iraq, for the first time in many months. That evening the Iraqis counter by launching an attack against Tehran.

MILITARY: On the southern sector, massed Iranian forces commence Operation Badr by launching 60,000 Revolutionary Guards and Basij across the Haur al Hawizeh marshland. Their goal is to seize the lower reaches of the Tigris River, cross over, and cut the strategic Basra-Baghdad Highway. Using boats and small craft, the Iranian "human waves" surge ahead and overpower the first line of Iraqi defenses.

March 12
AVIATION: The "War of the Cities" escalates further when massed Iraqi airpower strikes at 16 cities and towns in Iran while the government is threatening to turn Iranian airspace into a war zone.

March 12–14
MILITARY: In the southern sector, continued massed attacks by Pasadran and Basij volunteers push Iraqi defenders back six miles in some places. A group of fighters backed by tanks and other equipment reaches the Tigris River, where three pontoon bridges are constructed.

March 13–16
AVIATION: Iran retaliates for Iraqi attacks on its cities by launching a Soviet-made Scud-B missile against Kirkuk. These weapons, which carry 185-pound warhead and possess a range of 200 miles, have been provided to Iran by Libya.

March 15
AVIATION: Iraqi warplanes launch a heavy air assault against Tehran, Iran, projecting their power 300 miles deep into the Iranian heartland. Because Iraqi F-1 Mirages are equipped with advanced Matra-530 and Magic-1 air-to-air missiles, they enjoy an advantage in dogfighting over most Iranian fighter aircraft.

The Iraqi Air Force is extremely active over the next three days, flying over 250 ground-support sorties as the army advances.

MILITARY: In the southern sector, the Iraqis begin massing for a counterattack by forming a three-sided "killing field" around the Iranian bridgehead. President Saddam Hussein is sufficiently alarmed by developments to commit units of his elite Presidential Guard to combat. Their tanks and helicopter gunships inflict grievous losses on the lightly armed Iranians, who withdraw to their starting positions during the night.

TERRORISM: In Tehran, Iran, Hojatolislam Ali Khamenei survives an assassination attempt that kills the attacker and five bystanders.

March 16
MILITARY: In the southern sector, massed Iraqi armor, infantry, and artillery continue hounding the fleeing Iranians through the Haur al Hawizeh marshes while jets and helicopters attack and destroy pontoon bridges. The Iraqis also employ chemical weapons against the attackers. At length, the Iranian's materiel inferiority forces them to withdraw from the marshlands.

March 17
AVIATION: In Baghdad, Iraq, President Saddam Hussein declares a "Military Exclusion Zone" around Iran, which forces many foreign civilian airlines to cancel flights to that nation rather than face attack.

Military: With the Iranians in full retreat, Iraqi artillery and helicopter gunships continue harassing the survivors. Government radio is quick to proclaim complete and utter victory, having recovered all territory lost in the course of the offensive.

March 18

Diplomacy: In Baghdad, Iraq, King Hussein of Jordan and President Hosni Mubarak of Egypt arrive to congratulate President Saddam Hussein on his most recent victory over Iran. This is also the first visit by an Egyptian head of state to Iraq since 1979.

In Iran, former Iranian prime minister Mehdi Bazargan, now head of the Freedom Party, sends a letter to the UN secretary-general to criticize continuation of the war with Iraq. Thereafter he is harassed by the Iranian secret service.

March 19

Diplomacy: In Damascus, Syria, President Hafiz al-Assad greets the Iranian foreign minister, who is on hand to attend a meeting of delegates from Syria, Libya, Algeria, and South Yemen. One outcome is continuation of the Libyan policy of selling Soviet Scud-B tactical missiles to Iran.

Military: In the southern sector, two divisions of Iranian forces on Majnoon Island come ashore and attack the fringes of the Iraqi Third Army Corps; they are completely repulsed.

March 20

Military: In Washington, D.C., a State Department spokesman announces that Iraqi forces have apparently ejected Iranian forces from the Haur al Hawizeh marshes. This fact, coupled with intelligence that the Iraqi Air Force has bombed six Iranian cities, points to increased pressure on Ayatollah Khomeini to agree to a cease-fire. None is forthcoming.

March 21

Military: In the southern sector, the Iranians again launch an attack on the Iraqi Third Army Corps from Majnoon Island; once again they are repelled by superior firepower.

March 22

Aviation: The "War of the Cities" recommences in earnest as 16 cities on both sides are attacked by warplanes and missiles.

March 31

Aviation: In Tehran, Iran, the government announces that the latest spate of Iraqi air attacks on population centers has killed 1,450 civilians and wounded more than 4,000. This information is released as UN Secretary-General Javier Pérez de Cuéllar is touring the region, sounding out the possibilities of a cease-fire.

April

Politics: In Peshawar, Pakistan, after further wrangling, the seven mujahideen groups announce that they have formed an alliance with a single spokesman, subject to rotation every three months. This arrangement does not completely dampen

ongoing rivalries, but it does allow the resistance to address other nations and bene-
factors with a single voice.

April 1

MILITARY: In Konar Province, Afghanistan, the 1st Company, 334th Detached
SPETSNAZ Group attacks a group of Afghan mujahideen in the villages of Sangam
and Daridam in the Maravar Pass. They drive off resistance fighters only after severe
fighting, with 31 killed and 100 wounded in the process. Afghan losses are unknown
but presumed heavy; hereafter the unit involved acquires the nickname "Maravar
Company."

April 6

DIPLOMACY: The regimes in Iran and Iraq again agree to stop bombing each other's
population centers.

April 23

POLITICS: In an attempt to curry favor with the Afghan populace, President Babrak
Karmal summons a *loya jirga* (assembly) to win support for fighting the Afghan
resistance.

April 26–27

MILITARY: In Badaber, Pakistan, a group of 12 Soviet and 40 Afghan army captives
attempt to break free from the fortress-jail containing them. This was one of the
mujahideen's main training centers, and it was well-stocked with ammunition and
weapons. The captives overpower a handful of guards and break into the armory,
where they are surrounded by resistance fighters and units of the Pakistan Eleventh
Army Corps. Mujahideen leader Burhanuddin Rabbani attempts to negotiate their
surrender, but, after this fails, an artillery bombardment begins. One round touches
off stocks of ammunition that explode, leveling the fortress and killing all the prisoners. Approximately 100 mujahideen and Pakistanis are also killed in the fighting.

May

DIPLOMACY: In Geneva, Switzerland, UN-sponsored "indirect" talks between Pakistan and Afghanistan have settled upon four distinct areas of contention that must
be addressed. First, an agreement of noninterference in each other's affairs; second,
international guarantees behind that agreement; third, the repatriation of all Afghan
refugees living abroad; fourth, an agreement on the eventual withdrawal of all "foreign forces" from Afghanistan. The first three points are resolved by 1986, but the
issue of troop withdrawals remains a sticking point until 1988.

May 10

POLITICS: In Peshawar, Pakistan, resistance leaders reject Abdul Rasul Sayyaf's
attempt to appoint himself to another term as spokesman for the Alliance of Afghan
Mujahideen.

May 16

DIPLOMACY: In New York City, the UN Human Rights Commission releases a special report compiled by Austrian professor Felix Ermacora that excoriates both the

Soviet Union and the regime of Afghan president Babrak Karmal for gross violations of human rights throughout Afghanistan. Ermacora goes on to state that the presence of "foreign" forces in that nation remains the largest single cause for the present "situation" there.

MILITARY: In London, United Kingdom, the International Institute for Strategic Studies declares that the Soviet Union has endured between 20,000 to 25,000 casualties after five years of fighting Afghan insurgents. It also notes that the Afghan national army has dropped in manpower from 90,000 to 40,000 owing to constant desertion. In comparison, the mujahideen is having better luck overcoming political and theological divisions in its ranks, and its combat strength appears to be increasing.

POLITICS: In Peshawar, Pakistan, the seven mujahideen resistance groups fall under increasing American pressure to present a united front, further obtaining greater military aid. However, political and theological friction persists.

May 17

POLITICS: In the middle-class reaches of northern Tehran, Iran, residents take to the street in their cars and stage a massive "traffic jam" to protest the ongoing war. There is some violence between the drivers and the Pasdaran.

May 18

DIPLOMACY: In Tehran, Iran, Saudi foreign minister Prince Saud al Faisal meets with President Hojatolislam Ali Khamenei to discuss improved relations between the neighbors. Differences on the Gulf War cannot be bridged, but both sides aspire for increasing dialogue in the future.

May 20

DIPLOMACY: In Tehran, Iran, Saudi foreign minister Prince Saud al Faisal visit on the eve of Ramadan to seek a cease-fire; nothing comes of his efforts.

May 25

TERRORISM: In Kuwait, a car packed with explosives explodes near Sheikh Sabah al Sabah, the head of state; Iran is immediately suspected of being behind the attack.

May 26

AVIATION: A seven-week pause in the "War of the Cities" is broken after Iraq launches a tactical missile at an Iranian city; the Iranians retaliate by launching several Scud-Bs at Iraq.

May 30

AVIATION: Iraqi president Saddam Hussein, using the failed attack against the Kuwaiti ruler as a pretext, resumes the "War of the Tankers" by striking Iranian oil facilities on Kharg Island.

June 3

AVIATION: Over Tehran, Iran, local surface-to-air batteries claim to have bagged an Iraqi warplane on a bombing mission.

June 4

AVIATION: As if to underscore Iranian aerial impotence, Iraqi aircraft again strike Kharg Island in the Persian Gulf, inflicting some damage.

June 13

AVIATION: Tehran, Iran, sustains its 50th Iraqi air raid since March; 17 other Iranian cities are likewise bombed, with 78 killed and 325 injured.

June 14–15

AVIATION: In Baghdad, Iraq, President Saddam Hussein calls for a 15-day moratorium against bombing civilian targets; Iran responds by lobbing its 12th Scud-B missile at Baghdad.

DIPLOMACY: Iraqi president Saddam Hussein halts air strikes against Iranian targets for two weeks to allow the Iranian people time to pressure their leaders into accepting peace.

MILITARY: In the southern sector, the Iranians launch some commando-style operations in the Haur al Hawizeh marshes. They claim to have reached the River Tigris, killed 250 Iraqis, and withdrawn safely.

June 14–30

TERRORISM: Shiite extremists seize Trans World Airlines Flight 847 midway on a flight between Athens, Greece, and Rome, Italy, and force it to land at Beirut, Lebanon. Navy steelworker second class Robert D. Walker is murdered by the hijackers, but subsequent negotiations eventually free the 39 hostages on June 30.

June 16

MILITARY: In the Panjshir Valley, Afghanistan, Soviet forces attack mujahideen under Ahmad Shah Massoud, who had previously captured the Afghan army garrison at Peshgur. Soviet helicopter gunships catch the group in the open, killing most of the prisoners.

June 17

DIPLOMACY: In Washington, D.C., Soviet and American dignitaries meet for the first time in three years to discuss the Afghanistan crisis and possible solutions.

June 19

MILITARY: In the central sector, the Iranians launch another commando-type operation near Qasr-i-Sherin, claiming to have killed several Iraqis, demolished several bunkers, and destroyed two tanks.

June 20–25

DIPLOMACY: In Geneva, Switzerland, delegates from Pakistan and Afghanistan commence the fourth round of UN-sponsored peace talks and this time substantial agreement exists on "instruments" of noninterference, international guarantees, and repatriation of refugees. However, whereas Pakistan insists on a simultaneous implementation of all issues, Afghanistan wants them implemented consecutively, commencing with noninterference.

June 27

NAVAL: In Tehran, Iran, the government appoints Captain Mohammed Hussein Malek-Zadegan as head of the Iranian Navy. He determines to make it more active in stopping and searching Gulf shipping vessels for contraband.

June 28

MILITARY: In the southern sector, both the Iraqis and the Iranians launch commando-style operations in the vicinity of Majnoon Island; each claims to have killed more than 100 of the enemy.

July

MILITARY: Outside the Panjshir Valley, Afghanistan, mujahideen under Ahmad Shah Massoud capture an Afghan army base at Pashgur, and General Ahmeduddin, a commander of regular forces in central Afghanistan, dies in the fighting.

July 22

NAVAL: After many months of inactivity, three Iraqi Osa-class gunboats depart Khor Abdullah and attack the Iranian Cyrus oilfield, 70 miles offshore, with Styx missiles. They claim to inflict heavy damage on the installation.

July 24

POLITICS: In Tehran, Iran, both President Hojatolislam Ali Khamenei and Majlis Speaker Hojatolislam Hashemi Rafsanjani claims that the nation has regained internal stability with no outbreaks of violence over the past three years.

August 10

AVIATION: Iraqi warplanes strike eight Iranian cities, including Isfahan, the most distant so far in the war.

August 13

DIPLOMACY: In Casablanca, Morocco, the summit of the Arab League convenes and 16 members vote to uphold the 1982 Fez Summit Resolution to condemn Iran for aggression. The session is boycotted by Syria, Libya, Algeria, South Yemen, and Lebanon.

August 15

AVIATION: In the Persian Gulf, Iraqi jets launch three waves of attacks against Iranian oil installations on Kharg Island, this time employing antitank rockets against their targets. Two of three jetties and several docked vessels are hit and put out of commission.

POLITICS: Mujahideen-i-Khalq leader Massoud Rajavi claims that the regime in Tehran, Iran, has executed more than 50,000 people over the past five years. Moreover, 150,000 people still languish in prison.

August 16

POLITICS: In Tehran, Iran, President Hojatolislam Ali Khamenei is easily reelected to his second term with 88 percent of the popular vote, down from 95 percent in his first victory.

August 26
DIPLOMACY: In Geneva, Switzerland, the fifth round of UN-sponsored peace talks between Pakistan and Afghanistan commences, though no breakthrough is reported.

August 28
POLITICS: In Tehran, Iran, the Ministry of Information declares that 494 people have been arrested and charged with terrorism since September 1984, and the government security service has also disbanded 39 terrorist groups.

August 30
DIPLOMACY: In Geneva, Switzerland, UN special envoy Diego Cordovez announces that progress has been made for an Afghan peace plan, but the key stumbling block continues to be the withdrawal of Soviet forces.

September–October
MILITARY: In Paktia Province, Afghanistan, elements of the Afghan Army's 12th and 25th Divisions attack and attempt to capture the mujahideen supply base at Zhawar, less than three miles from the Pakistani border. They encounter heavy resistance and are unable to make much headway despite heavy support from Soviet air units. At one point the resistance counterattacks with two captured T-55 tanks, and the Afghan troops withdraw after 42 days of sustained combat. Victory here greatly bolsters mujahideen morale.

September 4
AVIATION: Outside Kandahar Airport, Afghanistan, a mujahideen Stinger missile brings down a domestic Bakhtar Airlines transport as it takes off, killing all 52 passengers.

September 7
AVIATION: In the Persian Gulf, an Iranian Navy helicopter lands on the deck of an Italian container ship 55 miles out of the Saudi port of Jubail.

September 8
MILITARY: In the northern sector, Iranians launch a carefully planned offensive against Rawandoz in concert with help from guerrillas from the Kurdish Democratic Party. Considerable territory is gained by the time the attack peters out.

September 11
MILITARY: In the southern sector, Iranian forces continue their attempt to encircle Basra by overrunning the southern portion of western Majnoon Island. An Iraqi counterattack with the elite Presidential Guard fails to dislodge them.

September 13
AVIATION: In Washington, D.C., a White House spokesman confirms that Iraq will be allowed to purchase 45 unarmed Defender helicopters from the Bell Textron Corporation, a deal estimated at $250 million. This sale comes despite professed U.S. neutrality in the Iran-Iraq War.

MILITARY: A shipment of 508 TOW antitank missiles, removed from Israeli stocks with U.S. consent, arrives in Tehran, Iran. The following day an American hostage is released in Lebanon.

September 19
AVIATION: In the Persian Gulf, Iraqi warplanes commence another serious strike against oil installations on Kharg Island, which reduces export output by two-thirds. Repairs quickly bring this amount back up to 500,000 barrels per day.

September 20
DIPLOMACY: In light of renewed Iraqi air attacks against Iranian oil assets in the Persian Gulf, President Mohammad Ali Khamenei again threatens to close down the Strait of Hormuz, but no action is taken.

September 23
MILITARY: In Tehran, Iran, the government mounts an impressive military parade in honor of the fifth anniversary of the Gulf War. Several long-absent F-14 Tomcats of the Iranian Air Force, previously grounded by a lack of spare parts, are flown overhead.

September 25
MILITARY: In the central sector, Iranian forces launch a three-hour attack against Iraqis in the Sumar region, claiming to inflict heavy damage and loss of life on them.

October
DIPLOMACY: In New York City, Gulbuddin Hekmatyar attends the autumn session of the United Nations as spokesman for the new mujahideen alliance. The General Assembly again passes a resolution condemning the Soviet occupation of Afghanistan, but Hekmatyar fails to obtain diplomatic recognition for the alliance on a par with the Palestinian Liberation Organization of Yassir Arafat.
MILITARY: In Kunduz Province, Afghanistan, Soviet troops of Tajik descent rise in rebellion against their own government and are brutally put down but loyal forces in a day-long battle. Eighty Tajiks are killed while several military vehicles are destroyed or damaged.

October 14
POLITICS: In Kabul, Afghanistan, the government orchestrates a tribal jirga in which delegates from Pakistan enjoy safe passage to attend. Apparently, the regime of President Babrak Karmal seeks to become leader of the large community of Pashtuns and Baluchis straddling the border with Pakistan in an attempt to destabilize that nation. However, tribal elders want no relations with what they consider a puppet government of the Soviet Union.

October 18
NAVAL: In the Persian Gulf, an Iranian gunboat intending to stop and search a French cargo vessel is intercepted by a French frigate and warned off.

October 23
DIPLOMACY: In Kabul, Afghanistan, Foreign Minister Shah Mohammad Dost states that the withdrawal of Soviet forces from his country can best be achieved through direct negotiations between Pakistan and the Soviet Union.
MILITARY: In Kabul, Afghanistan, the government announces that all Afghan males up to 40 years of age are now subject to three years of military service.

October 29
POLITICS: In Tehran, Iran, the Majlis approves Prime Minister Hojatolislam Hossein Musavi's new cabinet, whereby Colonel Mohammad Hussein Jalali becomes minister of defense. The Assembly of Experts also designates Ayatollah Hossein Ali Montazeri to succeed the ailing Ayatollah Khomeini as the supreme spiritual authority.

November
POLITICS: In Moscow, Soviet Union, government media seeks to reassure a doubtful populace of the correctness of Soviet actions in Afghanistan by publicly celebrating the heroism of Red Army soldiers there.

November 6
AVIATION: The Syrian national airline resumes regular flights to Tehran, Iran.

November 11
NAVAL: A report surfaces in the *Washington Post* suggesting that the Iranians have searched more than 300 vessels in the Persian Gulf to find any Iraqi-bound arms or ammunition. They have also enhanced their ability to strike shipping in the lower Gulf by constructing a helicopter base on an offshore oil platform, only 75 miles from the Qatari coast.

November 13
DIPLOMACY: In New York City, the UN General Assembly approves a Pakistani resolution calling for the immediate removal of all foreign troops from Afghanistan. This sixth recorded vote is 122 to 19 in favor, with 12 abstentions.

November 22
POLITICS: In Kabul, Afghanistan, the political purge of undesirables continues as Abdul Qadir, Ghulam Panjshiri, and Ismail Danesh are sacked from the PDPA politburo.

November 25
AVIATION: A preliminary shipment of American-made Hawk antiaircraft missiles arrives in Iran to help free more American hostages in Lebanon; however, the Iranians reject the weapons, finding them defective.

December
DIPLOMACY: In Geneva, Switzerland, the sixth round of UN-sponsored peace talks between Pakistan and Afghanistan produces no real progress, but the Kabul regime introduces a timetable for the withdrawal of all Soviet forces.

December 5
DIPLOMACY: In Washington, D.C., President Ronald W. Reagan signs a Presidential Finding that retroactively authorizes a supply of weapons to Iran through the shipment of Israeli stocks. This is done strictly with a view toward releasing American hostages in Lebanon.

December 6
POLITICS: In Kabul, Afghanistan, Ghulam Faruq Yaqubi gains appointment as the head of KHAD, the Afghan secret police.

December 13
DIPLOMACY: In Washington, D.C., a government spokesperson announces that the United States is willing to act as guarantor of peace in Afghanistan, contingent upon a Soviet troop withdrawal and suspension of military aid to the Afghan regime.

December 19
DIPLOMACY: In Geneva, Switzerland, negotiators from Pakistan and Afghanistan suspend talks to study a new UN proposal for a timetable pertaining to the removal of all Soviet forces.

December 27
DIPLOMACY: In Washington, D.C., Secretary of State George Shultz declares that while the United States will attempt to block the sale of weapons to Iran, it would not place identical restrictions on weapon sales to Iraq. These sentiments mark a growing shift in policies aimed at indirectly supporting Iraq in its war with Iran.

December 31
DIPLOMACY: At Geneva, Switzerland, the Afghan delegation establishes a tentative table of withdrawal for Soviet forces as part of an overarching peace agreement.

1986

January
DIPLOMACY: In Fez, Morocco, the annual Islamic Conference of Foreign Ministers meets and again reaffirms its complete support for Afghan resistance fighters and the unconditional withdrawal of all foreign forces from that nation.

January 1
AVIATION: In the Persian Gulf, an Iraqi missile strikes a Cypriot tanker near Kharg Island as the "War of the Tankers" continues in earnest.

January 6
MILITARY: In the southern sector, Iraqi forces stage a well-planned and well-coordinated attack on Majnoon Island. Two brigades from the Third Army Corps storm ashore, supported by ample air power, and drive the Iranians into a small corner of the island before the offensive loses steam.

January 7
POLITICS: The Iranian government announces that it is opening three new oil terminals along its southern coast, far beyond the reach of Iraqi aircraft.

January 9
NAVAL: In the Persian Gulf, the Iranian navy stops a German freighter for the first time and inspects it.

January 10
MILITARY: In Tehran, Iran, the Majlis orders that all military conscripts must spend part of their tour of duty in an "operational area." This is to prevent wealthy or influential families from having their sons assigned to garrison duties in the cities and provinces. Moreover, men who violate the three-month grace period for draft registration face an additional 306 months of active duty.
POLITICS: On Majnoon Island, Iraq, General Mahir Abdul al-Rashid of the Third Army Corps takes journalists on a tour of the recent battlefield. The Iranians are holed up in a small corner of the island, but they are constructing additional roads and pontoon bridges to support them.

January 11
DIPLOMACY: In Kabul, Afghanistan, President Babrak Karmal rejects the United States' offer to act as the guarantor of a peace settlement.

January 12
NAVAL: In the Persian Gulf, the Iranian navy stops an American vessel for the first time and inspects it.

January 13
NAVAL: In the Persian Gulf, the Iranian navy stops a British vessel for the first time and inspects it.

January 17
DIPLOMACY: In Washington, D.C., President Ronald W. Reagan signs an order authorizing the Central Intelligence Agency to acquire 4,000 TOW antitank missiles from the Defense Department and sell them to Iran in an attempt to obtain freedom for American hostages in Lebanon. Israeli agents are still required to set up contacts and arrange the transfer, but as of now the Americans are a direct supplier of arms to Iran.

January 29
AVIATION: Iranian warplanes attack the Iraqi garrisons of Rawandoz and Kulak, which stimulates counter-raids from their opponents.

February
POLITICS: In Moscow, Soviet Union, reform-minded General Secretary Mikhail Gorbachev addresses the 27th Soviet Party Congress and announces a phased withdrawal of all forces from Afghanistan as soon as a political solution can be reached

to end all foreign interference in that country. He also characterizes the current struggle as a "bleeding wound."

February 4
POLITICS: In Kandahar Province, Afghanistan, a mujahideen group led by Asmatullah Achakzai Muslim switches sides and endorses the Kabul regime.

February 10
MILITARY: In the southern sector, massed Iranian forces commence Operation Wa al Fajr-8, a two-pronged attack centered 25 miles north of Basra, Iraq, with an additional amphibious thrust aimed at the Fao Peninsula, on the Shatt al Arab waterway, near Kuwait. In hard fighting the Iranian attacks establish bridgeheads at Umm Rasas and Shibam but are repelled. However, the attackers manage to surprise the Iraqi defenses at Fao by crossing the 300-yard-wide Shatt al Arab in boats in a driving rainstorm and catch the bulk of defenders as they slept. The Iranians also capture tons of ammunition and weapons.

February 11
DIPLOMACY: In light of Iranian success on the Fao Peninsula, which places its forces within sight of the Kuwaiti border, Iran radio announces that Kuwait has become its "new neighbor."

MILITARY: In the southern sector, the Iranians make another advance against Basra, Iraq, through the marshlands north of the city. A division of Pasdaran troops attack dug-in Iraqi troops near Al Qurnah, at the junction of the Third and Fourth Army Corps, but are repulsed in three days of intense fighting. This operation is intended as a diversion to assist the forces at Fao.

February 12
DIPLOMACY: In Riyadh, Saudi Arabia, King Fahd apparently telephones Iraqi president Saddam Hussein in reference to the surging Iranian offensive.

MILITARY: In the southern sector, Iraqi units counterattack the Iranian bridgehead at Umm Rasas, driving the defenders back to the Shatt Road and capturing their supply depot.

February 13
MILITARY: The Iranian government declares that 13 of its soldiers have been killed by illegal chemical weapons used by Iraq.

February 14
AVIATION: Over the Fao Peninsula, Iraq, Iraqi warplanes brave heavy antiaircraft fire and missiles, along with Iranian F-14 Tomcat fighters, to attack enemy positions. However, as their attack is launched in bad weather, the effect is minimal, and 55 jets and helicopters are lost in action.

DIPLOMACY: In New York City, the UN Security Council passes Resolution 582, which again calls for a cease-fire between Iran and Iraq, followed by a negotiated resolution to the conflict. This bill passes amidst mounting concern over the Iran-Iraq War and its potential to spread to neighboring states.

MILITARY: The Iraqis finally launch a large and determined counterattack against Iranian forces holding the Fao Peninsula, with three armored columns of the Seventh Army Corps down the side and center of the region, backed by heavy artillery support. They, however, are unable to overcome dug-in Iranian defenders, armed with antitank missiles and armored vehicles of their own, many captured from Iraq. The Iraqis withdraw and dig in with the Iranians having moved their front line within sight of the Kuwaiti border.

On Majnoon Island, the Iranian pocket, having been heavily reinforced, attacks Iraqi positions nearby, only to be savaged by superior firepower, including artillery and helicopter gunships. They retreat to their foothold on the island.

February 15–16

MILITARY: In the central sector, Iranian forces commence Operation Wa al Fajr-9 as a diversionary effort. This pits two Iranian infantry brigades, assisted by *peshmerga* from the Kurdish Democratic Party, against Iraqi defenses in their region of Kurdistan. Their efforts are aided by wintery conditions, which hinder the Iraqi air force in its ground support efforts.

The United States government ships 1,000 TOW antitank missiles to Israel, which, in turn, arranges their transfer to Iran. However, rather than release hostages as agreed, the Iranians insist on receiving Hawk missile spare parts and radars.

February 18–19

MILITARY: Despite bad weather and plucky Iranian defenders, the Iraqi army manages to stabilize its hold on the Fao Peninsula by bringing in additional tanks and artillery to support the infantry. However, it forced to admit that its three-pronged offensive has ground to a halt after seven days of intense fighting.

February 20

AVIATION: Over Ahvaz, Iran, Iraqi warplanes shoot down an Iranian C-130 transport, killing all 40 passengers on board, including eight Majlis deputies, some senior military officers, and Ayatollah Khomeini's personal representatives to the Pasdaran.

POLITICS: In Kabul, Afghanistan, the Revolutionary Council appoints a 74-member commission to draft a new national constitution.

February 21

MILITARY: On the Fao Peninsula, Iraq, Iraqi forces from the Third Army Corps employ chemical weapons against dug-in Iranian defenders, but their effect is largely neutralized by rain and humidity.

POLITICS: In Tehran, Iran, Majlis Speaker Hojatolislam Hashemi Rafsanjani declares that Iran's present military policy is to hold on to the Fao Peninsula, possibly as a prior step to seizing Basra to the north.

February 23

MILITARY: The Iraqis launch an attack upon Iranian lines on the Fao Peninsula and are repulsed with the loss of two battalions. President Saddam Hussein orders units of his elite Republican Guard into action, and the fighting recommences.

February 24

MILITARY: In the northern sector, Operation Wa al Fajr-9 continues in Iraqi Kurdistan and drives to within 14 miles of Sulaymaniyah. This is undertaken to prevent the Iraqi high command from shunting additional troops into the Fao Peninsula region. Within a week of the attack, the Iranians assisted by Kurdish guerrillas, gains 130 square miles of Iraqi territory under their control and at the edge of Darband Khan Lake, whose dam supplies electricity to Baghdad.

The Iranian government claims that no fewer than 1,800 of their troops have been injured or killed by Iraqi chemical weapons, a charge denied by Iraq.

February 25

MILITARY: In Tehran, Iran, Mohammad Ali Rahmani, head of the Basij organizations, calls for older and more experienced men to report to duty. With the Fao offensive then in full swing, Basij units are taking heavy casualties and need to be replenished.

February 26

DIPLOMACY: A UN Commission of Experts, drawn from Austria, Spain, Sweden, and Switzerland, pays a second trip to Iran and confirms that the Iraqis had indeed been employing illegal chemical weapons in combat. The agents identified include mustard gas, cyanide, and nerve agents.

February 28

DIPLOMACY: In Tehran, Iran, Majlis Speaker Hojatolislam Hashemi Rafsanjani makes a thinly veiled threat against the Gulf states, insisting that now they are "neighbors" and Iran looks askance at the oil and other supplies they are clandestinely providing Iraq.

MILITARY: In its closing phases, Operation Wa al Fajr-9 pushes Iranian and Kurdish forces to within 14 miles of Sulaymaniyah and occupies 25 square miles of Iraqi territory. However, it fails to attract Iraqi reinforcements from the southern sector as anticipated.

February 28–April 19

MILITARY: In Paktia Province, Afghanistan, a force of 12,000 Afghan and Soviet troops led by General Nabi Azami attacks a mujahideen stronghold and supply base at Zhawar, less than three miles from the Pakistan border.

March

AVIATION: In Washington, D.C., President Ronald W. Reagan decides to provide Afghan mujahideen forces with advanced Stinger antiaircraft missiles. These are expected to be much more effective against the deadly HIND-D helicopter gunships than the erratic Soviet-made SA-7 missiles presently in their hands.

DIPLOMACY: In Geneva, Switzerland, the UN Human Rights Commission issues a second report relative to conditions in Afghanistan. Once again, it asserts that the only solution to present violations is the immediate withdrawal of foreign forces.

In Washington, D.C., Secretary of State George Shultz reaffirms the United States' commitment to the Afghan resistance.

In New York City, the UN secretary-general accuses Iraq of using mustard gas and nerve agents against Iranian troops, as it had in 1981 and 1984.

March 1–3

DIPLOMACY: In Riyadh, Saudi Arabia, Gulf foreign ministers vote to condemn Iran's recent occupation of the Fao Peninsula and its less-than-subtle threats against their countries. They also praise Iraqi president Saddam Hussein for his willingness to end the war peacefully through negotiations. Henceforth, two brigades of Saudi and Kuwaiti troops are also deployed along their mutual northern border in a sign of defiance to Iran.

MILITARY: In the central sector, no sooner does a 2,500-man Iraqi mountain brigade depart the town of Sitak for the Fao Peninsula than Iranian and Kurdish forces attack and take it. From this new position, the invaders are able to shell Sulaymaniyah for the first time, causing civilian casualties.

March 3

MILITARY: In the southern sector, the Iraqi "western column" drives into the Fao Peninsula's western section, but bogs down prior to reaching the bend in the Khor Abdullah Road opposite Umm Qasr. That evening they manage to repulse several Iranian "human wave" attacks and dig in.

NAVAL: In the Persian Gulf, an Iranian helicopter strikes a Turkish tanker carrying Arab oil with a missile, ostensibly for previous Iraqi attacks on their tankers using the "Sirri shuttle" to circumvent Kharg Island.

March 5

AVIATION: In accordance with the 1986 McCollum Amendment, passed by Congress, the Air Force beings transporting Afghan refugees and patients from the Soviet invasion from Pakistan to the United States.

March 9–10

MILITARY: Iraqi president Saddam Hussein, unwilling to accept a stalemate on the Fao Peninsula, orders a large flanking action against Iranian defenses, but this is repulsed with heavy losses.

March 11

MILITARY: In the southern sector, the Iraqi "central column" slices into the Fao Peninsula, but continual rain and mud bog down their progress. The overall Iraqi advance has been restricted to only four miles in three weeks due to poor weather and fanatical resistance. Worse, Iraqi casualties are between 8,000 to 12,000 to an Iranian loss of 20,000—a favorable ratio to the latter, given their larger manpower pool. The Iranians, for their part, are able to support two infantry divisions on the peninsula and can draw upon an additional five deployed across the Shatt al Arab waterway. However, they lack the tanks and artillery needed to attack Basra to the north or the Kuwait-Basra highway 35 miles to the west.

March 13
AVIATION: Iraqi warplanes strike the Qotar Bridge between Iran and Turkey, which carried a heavy flow of commercial traffic into Iran.

March 17
DIPLOMACY: In Kabul, Afghanistan, the Foreign Ministry rejects a UN report on repeated human-rights violations as "groundless slander and accusations."

March 20
DIPLOMACY: In Islamabad, Pakistan, the government strongly protests an attack against the Khurram refugee camp two days earlier, which resulted in six deaths.

March 21
POLITICS: In Tehran, Iran, Ayatollah Khomeini, on the eve of the Iranian new year, declares 1986 the "Year of Victory."

March 23–24
AVIATION: In the Gulf of Sidra, Libyan antiaircraft batteries fire missiles at navy warplanes belonging to the *Coral Sea* and miss. On the following day Operation Prairie Fire unfolds as six A-6 aircraft from the carrier *America* attack and sink two Libyan patrol boats and a guided missile corvette with Harpoon anti-ship missiles. Freedom of navigation in the Gulf has been deftly underscored.

March 25
AVIATION: Since February 6 of this year, the Iraqi air force has mounted 18,648 sorties against Iranian forces on the Fao Peninsula, a good indication of the serious nature of affairs there. By contrast, only 20,011 missions were launched in all of 1985.

April
MILITARY: In Paktia Province, Afghanistan, Soviet and Afghan army troops launch an offensive that captures the mujahideen base at Jawar after fierce fighting. The Soviets withdraw soon after, and the resistance reoccupies the territory. Hereafter, the guerrillas avoid constructing major bases that can be identified and overrun by concentrated enemy forces at a specific point.

POLITICS: This month Ayatollah Khomeini issues a religious edict, or fatwa, calling on military commanders to achieve a military victory over Iraq no later than March 21, 1987.

April 1
POLITICS: In Tehran, Iran, Ayatollah Khomeini calls for an all-out mobilization of manpower to crush Iraq once and for all. A plan is then announced to impart military training for the 1.6 million civil servants, while accepting up to 20 percent of them into service. The government also toyed with the idea of allowing females

to join the Basij militia, feeling that it would pressure their male relatives to join. Khomeini also establishes an eight-member Supreme Council for War Support to oversee 90 mobilization councils throughout the country, each with assigned manpower quotas.

April 2

MILITARY: Reports surface that the United States is supplying the Afghan resistance with hundreds of advanced Stinger surface-to-air missiles and providing CIA teams to instruct them in their use.

In Paktia Province, Afghanistan, an Afghan army commando unit intending to attack the mujahideen supply base at Jawar accidentally lands by helicopter on Pakistani territory, and its 530 members are captured. A counterattack by resistance fighters on several other landing zones destroys 24 helicopters, and the Afghan 38th Brigade is eliminated as a fighting force.

April 5

TERRORISM: An American sergeant is killed and 60 others wounded when a bomb explodes at a discotheque in West Germany. The American government suspects Libyan agents are behind the blast and prepares to act accordingly.

April 6

TERRORISM: In Kabul, Afghanistan, a car bomb explodes, wounding 22 civilians.

April 11

MILITARY: Soviet and Afghan army forces commence joint operations against mujahideen units in Jawar, Afghanistan.

April 14–15

AVIATION: Operation El Dorado Canyon unfolds as a strike force of 24 F-111F bombers from the Statue of Liberty Squadron, 48th Tactical Fighter Wing, launches from Britain and performs a retaliatory strike against Tripoli, Libya. To get there, these aircraft, lacking overflight permission from Spain and France, fly a 5,500-mile round trip around Continental Europe. Nonetheless, the attackers inflict heavy damage on the Jumahiriya Military Barracks and Benina Military Airfield. The attack is joined by carrier strike craft launched from the *America* and *Saratoga*, including jets from VMFA-314 and 323. One F-111 is lost in action, presumably to a surface-to-air missile.

April 17

MILITARY: In Paktia Province, Afghanistan, Afghan troops and Soviet advisers resume their attack on the mujahideen supply base at Jawar, making little progress until a unit of Hezb-i-Islami withdraws without orders. The remaining mujahideen units follow suit and Jawar is overrun by government forces. However, the base is quickly reoccupied once they withdraw. A total of 530 Afghan commandoes are captured by the resistance, of which 78 officers are tried and executed, including their commander, Colonel Qalander Shah.

April 22

AVIATION: In Bermuda, U.S. and Bermudan law-enforcement agents arrest 10 Americans, Israelis, and West Europeans for attempting to sell spare parts and weapons to Iran.

May 4

AVIATION: In another first, Pakistani jets shoot down an Afghan air force warplane that violated their airspace.

POLITICS: In Kabul, Afghanistan, President Babrak Karmal is pressured to yield his post as secretary-general of the PDPA and is replaced by Mohammad Najib, former head of the Soviet-trained KHAD, or Afghan secret police. This demotion arises over Karmal's apparent failure to mollify long-standing Khalq and Parcham factional infighting within the PDPA. Moreover, Najib declares that existing ties to the Soviet Union will be strengthened. Questions also arise whether or not the change in leadership will impact negotiations on a timetable for a Soviet withdrawal at Geneva. Presently, the Kabul regime had insisted on a four-year timetable while Pakistani representatives are demanding one of six months or less.

May 5

DIPLOMACY: In Geneva, Switzerland, forthcoming rounds of UN-sponsored peace talks between Pakistan and Afghanistan are announced.

May 7

AVIATION: After an absence of several months, Iraqi warplanes return to bomb and damage the Tehran oil refinery.

May 14

AVIATION: Iraqi warplanes attack a stationary troop train at Haft Tappeh, north of Dezful, Iran, killing 77 soldiers.

May 14–17

MILITARY: In the central sector, Iraqi president Saddam Hussein personally orders the commander of the Second Army Corps, General Adin Tawfik, to recapture the Iranian town of Mehran and close a direct invasion route to Baghdad. Four brigades are committed to combat, and within three days they have captured two strategic peaks overlooking their objective. The town falls soon after, along with 100 square miles of Iranian territory. However, they fail to eject Iranian forces from the high ground nearby.

May 15

DIPLOMACY: In Washington, D.C., President Ronald W. Reagan authorizes a secret visit to Iran by American dignitaries with a document outlining future U.S. policy toward that nation. He declares that the United States has no interest in an Iraqi victory over Iran and views the Soviet Union as a long-term threat to regional security.

MILITARY: In the northern sector, Iranian and Kurdish *peshmerga* of the Kurdish Democratic Party attack and carry Mangesh, near Mosul and very close to the strategic Oil Road and the Kirkuk-Turkish oil pipeline.

POLITICS: In Kabul, Afghanistan, Mohammad Najib formally becomes secretary-general of the PDPA while Babrak Karmal serves as head of the Revolutionary Council Presidium, and Sultan Ali Keshtmand functions as prime minister.

May 19

MILITARY: In the northern sector, the Iraqis muster a mountain brigade, some elite Republican Guard detachments, and local auxiliaries in an attempt to retake Mangesh but are repulsed by Iranians and Kurdish *peshmerga*. Thereafter, the Iraqi 11th Division is garrisoned at nearby Zakho to guard the Kirkuk-Turkish oil pipeline, while local Arab farmers are drilled, armed, and organized into a militia.

May 19–23

DIPLOMACY: In Geneva, Switzerland, the seventh round of UN-sponsored peace talks between Pakistan and Afghanistan unfolds with no real progress reported.

May 25–29

DIPLOMACY: In Tehran, Iran, a shipment of 508 TOW missiles and some Hawk missile spare parts arrive by air, along with National Security Advisor Robert McFarlane. However, during his four-day stay he is not allowed to meet with either Majlis speaker Hojatolislam Hashemi Rafsanjani or President Hojatolislam Ali Khamenei. Nor are any hostages released.

May 28

POLITICS: In Kabul, Afghanistan, President Mohammad Najib declares that a new bicameral parliament, based on free and open elections, is to be established.

May 31

MILITARY: In Tehran, Iran, Mohsin Rezai, commander of the Revolutionary Guards, declares that only 2 percent of available manpower has been conscripted for use in the war with Iraq, and it is time to mobilize four times as many in order to crush the Iraqis.

June 9

AVIATION: An Iraqi air raid upon the Iranian Ground Satellite Statio at Assad Abad, Iran, knocks out telexes and dial telephones for several days.

June 16

DIPLOMACY: In Washington, D.C., President Ronald W. Reagan hosts four mujahideen leaders at the White House in their first official visit. Reagan also declares that the United States remains firmly on the side of the resistance and hopes that an end to the war can be negotiated through an immediate Soviet withdrawal.

June 17

POLITICS: In Peshawar, Pakistan, Gulbuddin Hekmatyar and Abdul Rasul Sayyuf criticize the recent meeting of mujahideen leaders in Washington, D.C.

June 20–July 3

MILITARY: In the central sector, five brigades of Iranian Pasdaran forces secretly mass on the high ground around Mehran and commence Operation Karbala-1, which catches the Iraqi defenders off guard and retakes the town. President Saddam Hussein, fearing that Badra or Baquba are the real objectives, shifts badly needed reserve mobile brigades from the southern and central sectors as a precaution.

June 24
AVIATION: In the Persian Gulf, Iraqi aircraft make an aerial reconnaissance of Iran's Sirri oil terminal, inducing the Iranians to hurriedly shift its operations to Larak Island, 120 miles to the east. Because no attack materializes, operations shift back to Sirri by the end of July.

July
POLITICS: In Kabul, Afghanistan, the Soviets help engineer another major shake-up of the PDPA's Central Committee, although Lieutenant General Sayyed Muhammad Gulabzoy, a member of the Khalq faction, retains his appointment as minister of the interior.

July 3–4
DIPLOMACY: In Tehran, Iran, a plane arrives carrying seven tons of U.S. spare parts for Iranian weapons, warplanes, and tanks. The Americans begin pressing for the release of hostages in Lebanon.

July 12
AVIATION: In Baghdad, Iraq, the Baath Party Congress requests President Saddam Hussein to use the Iraqi air force to cripple Iranian oil-exporting capabilities to increase Iran's economic distress.

July 21
MILITARY: Reports surface that hundreds of idealistic young men from across the Arab world are flocking to Pakistan to join the Afghan resistance. One of them is Osama bin Laden, son of a wealthy construction magnate.

July 26
DIPLOMACY: In Beirut, Lebanon, Shiite terrorists release the Reverend Lawrence Jenco, undoubtedly after prodding from Iran.

July 27
AVIATION: Iraqi warplanes attack Arak, in western Iran, killing 70 civilians and wounding others. In return Iran threatens to resume the "War of the Cities."

July 28
DIPLOMACY: At Vladivostok, Soviet Union, General Secretary Mikhail Gorbachev declares that six Soviet regiments are going to be withdrawn from Afghanistan by December. This is the start of a diplomatic offensive designed to convince the world that the Soviet Union is serious about seeking a political settlement to the Afghan crisis. Moreover, the Soviets insist that continuing foreign aid to the Afghan resistance only serves to delay an ultimate Soviet troop withdrawal.

July 30
DIPLOMACY: In Geneva, Switzerland, the seventh round of UN-sponsored peace talks between Pakistan and Afghanistan commences its second phase.

August 2
DIPLOMACY: In Baghdad, Iraq, President Saddam Hussein composes an open letter to the Iranian people, extolling the virtues of peace and inviting their government to join him in a cease-fire.

August 3
DIPLOMACY: In Tehran, Iran, an aircraft arrives with the balance of Hawk missile spare parts that the Iranians had been demanding.

August 8
AVIATION: In the Persian Gulf, Iraqi warplanes damage five of the 11 oil tankers employed by Iran for ferrying oil between Kharg Island and Sirri Island, where the crude was stored for transportation to the mainland.

DIPLOMACY: In Geneva, Switzerland, reports surface that Pakistani and Afghan dignitaries remain far apart in negotiations for a political settlement in Afghanistan, especially regarding terms for a Soviet troop withdrawal. Further talks are therefore suspended without agreement on a date to recommence discussions.

August 12
AVIATION: Over the Persian Gulf, four Iraqi Mirage F-1 jet fighters attack the Sirri oil terminal, 450 miles distant from the nearest Iraqi airfield. They also employ French-made laser-guided bombs for the first time.

August 15
TERRORISM: A car bomb explodes in the holy city of Qom, Iran, killing 13 people and injuring more than 100.

August 18
POLITICS: In the Persian Gulf, Iran's Larak Island oil terminal is operating at full capacity as tankers on the "Sirri shuttle," bringing oil from Kharg Island, continue arriving.

August 19
TERRORISM: In Tehran, Iran, 20 people are killed by a car bomb that explodes in the city's central square; many others are reported injured.

August 23
MILITARY: In northern Afghanistan, Ahmad Shah Massoud configures his forces into a five-province, military-political "front" to advance his cause. His fighters also attack and capture the Afghan army base at Farkhar, Takhar Province, which borders the Soviet Union.

August 25
MILITARY: At Qargah, near Kabul, Afghanistan, mujahideen under Abdul Haq ignite an Afghan army ammunition dump with Chinese-made and -supplied ground-to-ground missiles.

August 28–29
AVIATION: In the Persian Gulf, Iraqi warplanes raid radar installations on Farsi Island, 60 miles south of Kharg Island, which were set up for surveillance and tracking hostile aircraft.

August 29

MILITARY: In Tehran, Iran, Majlis Speaker Hojatolislam Hashemi Rafsanjani boasts that 650,000 Iranians are now massed and prepared to launch a final attack. This statement reflects the greater urgency placed on complete mobilization of population resources.

August 31–September 2

MILITARY: In the central sector, the Iranians launch Operation Karbala-2 in the Haj Omran Valley with three brigades of Pasdaran. Their goal is to retake strategic Mount Marman from the Fifth Iraqi Army Corps, which is accomplished after a successful penetration of eight miles over the next three days.

September

AVIATION: In a major turn of events, the United States begins supplying mujahideen fighters with advanced Stinger antiaircraft missiles. These weapons are capable of bringing down fast flying Soviet jets or heavily armored HIND-D helicopter gunships by dint of their great accuracy. The ensuing loss of men and machines prompts the Red Air Force and its Afghan counterpart to bomb targets from greater altitudes, thereby reducing overall accuracy. This constitutes a major turning point in the ground war as well.

TERRORISM: In Islamabad, Pakistan, assassins kill Captain Vladimir Smolnyar, the Soviet military attaché.

September 1–2

MILITARY: In the southern sector, Iranian frogmen/commandos launch Operation Karbala-3 against the al-Amaya oil platform, located 15 miles south of Fao. This is also the site of an Iraqi radar post for attacking Iranian-bound shipping in the Gulf; it falls quickly, and the nearby al-Bakr oil platform is also set on fire.

September 2

NAVAL: In the Persian Gulf, the Iranian navy stops and inspects a Soviet vessel of the first time, which sparks a heated protest from Moscow.

September 3

POLITICS: In Baghdad, Iraq, President Saddam Hussein declares all ports and oil terminals in Iran within its Naval Exclusion Zone, making them subject to attack.

In Tehran, Iran, the government announces that all colleges will be closed and all 30,000 teachers will be drafted into the military.

September 10

MILITARY: In Tehran, Iran, Majlis speaker Hojatolislam Hashemi Rafsanjani again declares that Iranian mobilization is nearly completed and that a decisive onslaught is at hand. Satellite intelligence provided to Iraq via Saudi Arabia indicates the presence of 650,000 Iranian troops on or near the front lines, especially in the southern sector.

September 16

MILITARY: In the central sector, the Iranians launch a surprise attack on "Hill 270" outside of Mehran, Iran, seizing it and the heights overlooking Badra, Zurbatiya, and Varmahraz after heavy fighting.

September 21
POLITICS: In Tehran, Iran, President Hojatolislam Ali Khamenei revives the idea of pumping oil from the newly seized Majnoon Island complex unless Iraq agrees to pay reparations.

September 22
MILITARY: In Tehran, Iran, the government marks the seventh year of the Iran-Iraq War by staging a large military parade, replete with a detachment of frogmen clad in wet suits and scuba equipment. After a long absence, from Iranian skies, a formation of 12 F-14 Tomcats also flies overhead.

September 23
NAVAL: In the Persian Gulf, an Iranian missile slams into a British vessel; it had been fired by a helicopter operating out of Abu Musa.

October 10
AVIATION: In eastern Afghanistan, Soviet warplanes bomb a French hospital run by doctors and nurses of Medecins du Monde, undoubtedly to deter Westerners from rendering aid and assistance to the mujahideen and general populace.

DIPLOMACY: In Moscow, Soviet Union, the government media announces that it is withdrawing 8,000 men from Afghanistan who are presently there "cooperating in the maintenance of order."

MILITARY: In northern Iraq, Iranian airborne commandoes attack an oil pipeline neat Kirkuk, aided by guerrillas of the Kurdish Democratic Party. The attack succeeds in cutting the pipeline. This is the first air drop by either side in the war. The operation itself is meant to draw Iraqi reserves from the southern sector northward.

October 15
MILITARY: In Kabul, Afghanistan, Western correspondents are invited to observe ceremonies marking the withdrawal of six Soviet regiments back to the homeland. Three of these formations are antiaircraft units, therefore of little use for combating an insurgency. This withdrawal is actually a disguised troop rotation whose token numbers are completely offset by the secret arrival of thousands of additional combat troops estimated by Pakistani military intelligence at 15,000 men.

In Washington, D.C., Defense Secretary Caspar Weinberger characterizes the ballyhooed Soviet troops withdrawal from Afghanistan as a hoax. He asserts that the American are aware that the Soviets had quietly inserted a larger number of combat troops over intervening weeks leading to this staged event.

October 29
DIPLOMACY: In a sign of Saudi willingness to cultivate better relations with Iran, King Fahd dismisses Oil Minister Ahmad Zaki Yamani, who held that position for 24 years, for failing to support a fixed price of $18 per barrel, as favored by Tehran.

MILITARY: A shipment of 500 TOW antitank missiles arrives in Tehran, Iran, to facilitate the release of additional American hostages from Lebanon.

October 31

AVIATION: In light of continuing Soviet violations of Pakistani airspace, Secretary of Defense Caspar Weinberger does not rule out providing Pakistan with Airborne Warning and Control System (AWACS) aircraft to better monitor its borders.

MILITARY: In Washington, D.C., the director of the Defense Intelligence Agency declares that the United States possesses clear and compelling evidence that the recent Soviet troop withdrawal is a sham and that the actual number of troops removed is closer to 2,000.

POLITICS: In Washington, D.C., the State Department asserts that more Pakistanis and Afghans have been killed in the first half of 1986 than in all of the previous year. These deaths are attributed to increased Soviet air attacks, cross-border artillery shelling, and terrorist attacks by Afghan intelligence operatives.

November 3

DIPLOMACY: This month the Lebanese weekly *Al Shitraa* announces that the United States has been supplying the Iranian regime with weapons in a high-level secret operation employing Israel as an intermediary. This was done in the hopes of influencing the release of American hostages being held in Lebanon by Iranian-leaning terrorists. This is the beginning of the Iran-contra affair, which rocks the administration of President Ronald W. Reagan.

November 5

DIPLOMACY: In New York City, the UN General Assembly again passes a resolution calling for the removal of all "foreign" forces from Afghanistan on a vote of 122 to 20, with 11 abstentions. This is the eighth time it has passed. The UN Commission of Human Rights, moreover, declares that the situation throughout Afghanistan is worsening, especially for women and children, while the refugee problem in neighboring Pakistan is also increasing.

A report issued by Amnesty International states that political prisoners in Afghanistan are routinely tortured, usually with Soviet advisers present.

November 11

MILITARY: At Nehrin, Afghanistan, mujahideen under Ahmad Shah Massoud storm into and capture an Afghan army base.

November 13

POLITICS: In Washington, D.C., President Ronald W. Reagan admits that only a small quantity of defensive arms had been supplied to Iran in exchange for the release of American hostages in Lebanon. He also asserts there is no necessary conflict between American and Iranian national interests, especially in the Gulf region.

November 14

AVIATION: In the Persian Gulf, Iraqi Super Etendard jets attack Iranian oil platforms in the offshore Sassan oil field.

November 15

DIPLOMACY: In Baghdad, Iraq, a government spokesman condemns the American practice of clandestinely supplying arms to Iran in exchange for hostages.

November 19
POLITICS: In Washington, D.C., President Ronald W. Reagan pledges that the practice of sending arms to Iran for help with hostages will cease.

November 20
POLITICS: In Kabul, Afghanistan, the 20th plenary session of the PDPA Central Committee forces President Babrak Karmal to yield his post as president and chairman of the Revolutionary Council. He is temporarily succeeded by Haji Moham mad Chamkani and new members are also appointed to the Central Committee.

In Tehran, Iran, Ayatollah Khomeini boasts that the recent flap regarding illegal arms sales by the United States to Iran is "an issue greater than all our victories."

November 21
DIPLOMACY: In Canada, five Soviet defectors receive political asylum.
MILITARY: In Washington, D.C., congressional hearings reveal that Iran paid $21 million for a shipment of 2,008 American-made antitank missiles. Most of the weapons were released from Israeli stockpiles.

November 22
DIPLOMACY: In Washington, D.C., Iraqi ambassador Nizar Hamdoun tells reporters that his government has raised the issue of illegal arms sales to Iran by Israel for several months, and that such activities have harmed efforts to reestablish diplomatic ties with the United States.

November 24
AVIATION: In San Diego, California, a federal judge sentences a Navy veteran and a divorced couple to prison for their role in a plot to smuggle F-14 parts to Iran.

November 25
AVIATION: Iraqi warplanes stage something of a minor coup by striking Iranian oil facilities on Larak Island. Because the round-trip distance of the sortie was 1,560 miles, further than Iraqi warplanes could fly, the Iranians charge that they were secretly refueled at an airbase in Saudi Arabia. Meanwhile, General Hamid Shaban, Iraqi Air Force commander, boasts of inflicting heavy damage upon the installation, which, in truth, was little more than a barren atoll.

The Iraqi air force also mounts 163 sorties across the front, though the Iranians claim to have shot down 10 of the intruders. They also declare that no less than 175 civilians were killed in these actions.

The Iranian air force attacks the Abu Bakoush oil platform in Abu Dhabi waters, then deny it. They subsequently offer the owners compensation.
POLITICS: In Washington, D.C., President Ronald W. Reagan states that he was not in complete control over Iran policy. Henceforth, Secretary of State George Shultz is given control of all dealings with that nation.

November 26
AVIATION: In retaliation for recent air attacks on civilian targets, the Iranians fire a Scud-B missile at Baghdad, Iraq, which kills several people. This is the 19th such

projectile to hit the capital. They also fire a missile at Basra for the first time, which up until now has been hit only by artillery.

December

DIPLOMACY: In Moscow, Soviet Union, President Mohammad Najib confers with General Secretary Mikhail Gorbachev and declares his intention to form a government of national unity. Afghans in exile would be welcome to return.

POLITICS: In Kabul, Afghanistan, Soviet puppets continue tightening their grip on the instrument of governance as Minister of Defense General Abdul Qader is replaced by General Muhammad Rafi and Minister of Foreign Affairs Shah Mohammad Dost yields his position to Abdul Wakil Dost, however, is sent to New York to become Afghanistan's UN representative.

December 3

MILITARY: In Tehran, Iran, 100,000 Pasdaran and Basij troops, accompanied by 2,000 mullahs, fill the large Azadi Stadium and are addressed by Majlis Speaker Hojatolislam Hashemi Rafsanjani. Despite tough talk, there is still no sign of the promised Iranian offensive.

December 8

AVIATION: In Kandahar, Afghanistan, two Soviet MiG jets accidentally bomb the wrong section of the city, killing an estimated 600 people. The air raid was in response to the ambush of a Soviet column near Mahalajat, 27 miles from the city.

December 12

AVIATION: Reports surface that the mujahideen have begun using U.S.-supplied Stinger antiaircraft missiles against Soviet warplanes and helicopter gunships in Afghanistan. Soviets aerial losses rise exponentially.

December 15

POLITICS: In Washington, D.C., a State Department official admits that the United States has shared aerial intelligence with Iraq to assist it during the war against Iran. He repeats that a negotiated settlement is the best possible solution and that an Iraqi defeat would prove disastrous for American interests in the oil-rich Persian Gulf.

December 19

AVIATION: In the Kurrum Tribal Agency, Pakistan, four jets belonging to the Afghan air force attack and bomb a wedding party 10 miles north of Parachinar, killing seven people. The Mangal tribe to which they belong straddles the border between Pakistan and Afghanistan.

December 21

AVIATION: Iraqi warplanes strike the civilian target of Bankaran, killing 80 people and wounding scores more.

December 23

MILITARY: The Afghan national army constructs new military posts at Sherkhana and along the Kabul-Jalalabad highway. In light of the mounting insurgency, commercial traffic is temporarily suspended along this route.

December 24

MILITARY: In the southern sector, massed Iranian forces commence Operation Karbala-4 by striking at Abu Khasib, 10 miles southeast of Basra. Four divisions of lightly armed Revolutionary Guards and frogmen detachments came filtering across the waterway and into the teeth of strongly posted Iraqi troops, and are quickly decimated by superior firepower and air power. Another division attacking Umm Rasas further south is likewise repelled. The Iranians pull back after sustaining an estimated 8,000 casualties to an Iraqi loss of only 3,000. This disaster was personally organized by Majlis speaker Hojatolislam Hashemi Rafsanjani against the advice of many senior military leaders.

POLITICS: In Kabul, Afghanistan, newly elected President Mohammad Najib confers with elders and representatives from Nangarhar, Konar, Paktia, Laghman, and Khost Provinces and urges them to join and support his program of national reconciliation.

December 25

AVIATION: In Saudi Arabia, 60 people die as a Boeing 737 airliner carrying 107 passengers is hijacked and crashes. Iran subsequently denies Iraqi and Jordanian accusations that it instigated the incident.

December 27

MILITARY: Mujahideen belonging to Hezb-i-Islami attack and capture eight Afghan army bases in Konar Province, only eight miles from the Pakistani border. The Soviet garrison at Barikot is now in danger of being isolated.

An Afghan mujahideen demonstrates the position used to fire a hand-held surface-to-air missile, one of the early Stingers provided by the United States to help drive out the Soviets. *(Department of Defense)*

December 28

AVIATION: At Jalalabad airport, Afghanistan, mujahideen rockets destroy two Soviet-built helicopters belonging to the Afghan air force.

MILITARY: In the western city of Herat, Afghanistan, rebel positions manned by Jamiat-i-Islami guerrillas are attacked by 4,000 Afghan troops and 60 Soviet armored vehicles.

December 30

POLITICS: In Kabul, Afghanistan, President Mohammad Najib officially unveils his proposed plan for national reconciliation that will be introduced with a unilateral cease-fire on January 15, 1987. He also announces a general amnesty that will go into effect at that time while a new constitution will enshrine Islam as the official religion of Afghanistan. Thus begins the government's new "national reconciliation" campaign intended to persuade mujahideen and Islamic traditionalists to accept a peaceful solution to the ongoing crisis. The Communist Party hopes to make participation in the government appear more appealing while maintaining complete dominance over national affairs.

1987

January 1

POLITICS: In Moscow, Soviet Union, Secretary-General Mikhail Gorbachev underscores that his primary goals are the withdrawal of Soviet forces from Afghanistan along with a lasting political settlement there.

In Kabul, Afghanistan, President Mohammad Najib formally announces that a unilateral cease-fire will commence on January 15. Western analysts are inclined to believe that this policy is a prelude to an eventual Soviet withdrawal from Afghanistan.

January 2–3

AVIATION: In the Persian Gulf, Iraqi warplanes attack Iranian oil facilities on Kharg Island for two consecutive days.

DIPLOMACY: In Washington, D.C., State Department official Zalmay Khalilzad declares that the Afghan resistance will defeat the Soviet Union and its puppets no matter what they do because of "perseverance and growth in strength."

January 3

POLITICS: In Kabul, Afghanistan, the government reiterates its pledge to guarantee all rebel leaders safe passage to talks concerning national reconciliation.

In Peshawar, Pakistan, the mujahideen leadership rejects the Afghan government's offer of amnesty as a trap.

January 6

DIPLOMACY: In Kabul, Afghanistan, Soviet foreign minister Eduard Shevardnadze and Soviet party secretary for foreign relations Anatoly Dobrynin arrive for talks with the Afghan government regarding national reconciliation and a cease-fire.

In Peshawar, Pakistan, the mujahideen leadership suggests direct talks with the Soviet Union with a view toward facilitating a complete withdrawal from Afghanistan.

January 7

DIPLOMACY: In Kabul, Afghanistan, Soviet foreign minister Eduard Shevardnadze and Party Secretary for Foreign Relations Anatoly Dobrynin return to Moscow after concluding talks with the government of President Mohammad Najib.

MILITARY: In the Gozareh district, Herat Province, Afghanistan, Sayed Ahmad and 1,000 of his fighters lay down their arms as part of the national reconciliation program.

NAVAL: In light of the "War of the Tankers" in the Persian Gulf, the news media report that several commercial vessels are being fitted with a British radar set named "Matilda," which detects incoming missiles strikes.

POLITICS: In Peshawar, Pakistan, mujahideen leaders reject the Afghan government's offer of cease-fire and offer to negotiate directly with the Soviet Union regarding a truce and withdrawal of all foreign forces.

January 8

AVIATION: In the Persian Gulf, an Iranian helicopter fires a missile at a tanker sailing from Kuwait, which strikes but fails to explode.

DIPLOMACY: In Moscow, Soviet Union, no sooner does Foreign Minister Eduard Shevardnadze arrive than rumors of Soviet troop withdrawals begin appearing in the press and other media.

January 9

AVIATION: Iranian forces in the Fish Lake area fire an American-supplied HAWK antiaircraft missile and bring down an Iraqi MiG-25 fighter. Consequently, Iraqi aircraft are conspicuously absent from combat over the next few days.

An Iranian warplane drops bombs on a residential district of Basra, Iraq, the first such attack in many months. A series of Scud-B missile strikes follows over the next few weeks.

MILITARY: In the southern sector, Iran once again masses its manpower resources for Operation Karbala-5, an all-out attempt to capture the strategic port of Basra, Iraq. This evening four Revolutionary Guard divisions infiltrate Iraqi defenses along a 16-mile front and overrun the town of Duaiji at the southern edge of Fish Lake. A flanking maneuver subsequently carries them through the first two Iraqi defense lines and the town of Shalamache also falls as their bridgehead swells to 35,000 men within days.

January 10

MILITARY: In the southern sector, Iraqi armored units counterattack Iranian bridge-heads in the Fish Lake region but are rebuffed by dug-in Iranian defenders.

January 12

AVIATION: Waves of Iraqi aircraft bomb the Iranian cities of Qom, Arak, Boujerd, and Isfahan, inflicting scores of civilian casualties.

MILITARY: A report surfaces in the *New York Times* suggesting that the Reagan administration had clandestinely fed false military information to both Iran and Iraq so that neither side would win.

In the southern sector, events look threatening enough to warrant a personal visit by Iraqi president Saddam Hussein, who also orders up additional units of his

Republican Guard to bolster the Iraqi Third and Seventh Army Corps. The Iranian drive, having penetrated the first two Iraqi lines of defense, has stalled and is being successfully held in place.

POLITICS: In Peshawar, Pakistan, the seven Afghan resistance groups formally coalesce into the new High Council of the Mujahideen Alliance.

January 13

MILITARY: In Tehran, Iran, the Pasdaran Ministry calls upon the male populace to register for military service at local mosques, offices, and factories. They had hoped to induct a further 500,000 men into the "Mohammad Mobilization Corps," but the actual total is less than half that. Nonetheless, mullahs running the country say that a final, massive, human-wave attack would clinch the final victory.

NAVAL: In London, United Kingdom, the chairman of the International Chamber of Shipping demands that the United Nations begin patrolling the Persian Gulf region, noting that the "War of the Tankers" between Iran and Iraq has led to the deaths of more than 100 sailors while 6 million tons of shipping has been destroyed.

January 14

AVIATION: Iraqi warplanes attack the Iranian town of Masjed Saleyman, reportedly killing 30 people and wounding 120 more.

DIPLOMACY: In Washington, D.C., a State Department spokesman denounces Kabul's offer of a unilateral cease-fire as "the worst kind of grandstanding" simply because it dodges the central issue of a Soviet withdrawal and continuing Soviet presence in Afghanistan.

The administration also affirms its determination to adhere to the "Carter Doctrine" to keep neutral commerce flowing in the Persian Gulf.

MILITARY: In the central sector, the Iranians attempt to pin down Iraqi forces and prevent them from assisting the Basra defenses by launching Operation Karbala-6 near Sumar. This attack, delivered mainly by regular Iranian army forces, seizes the sector near Qasr-i-Sherin and liberates 100 square miles of occupied territory from Iraq.

In the southern sector, a force of 3,000 specially equipped Pasdaran troops lands on the east bank of the Shatt al Arab waterway and occupies several small river inlets on the Iraqi flank.

January 15

DIPLOMACY: In Washington, D.C., State Department deputy spokesman Charles Redman insists that the main and unavoidable obstacle to a peace settlement in Afghanistan remains the presence of Soviet military forces. White House press secretary Albert Brashear further notes that only the withdrawal of Soviet troops and self-determination of the Afghan people can assure an end to the present crisis in the region.

In Moscow, Soviet Union, the TASS new agency reports that the recent cease-fire offer by the regime in Kabul, Afghanistan, was aimed at encouraging formation of a coalition government.

MILITARY: On this, the first day of the Afghan government's unilateral cease-fire, mujahideen fighters ambush a Soviet convoy along the Salang highway, killing several soldiers and destroying a number of armored vehicles.

POLITICS: In Kabul, Afghanistan, President Mohammad Najib appears on national television and appeals to mujahideen leaders to accept a national cease-fire. He also announces a general amnesty of army deserters and releases several political prisoners.

January 16

DIPLOMACY: In Washington, D.C., Secretary of State George Shultz declares that agreement on a short timetable for the removal of all Soviet forces from Afghanistan is the missing "ingredient" to an Afghan peace settlement. Should that transpire, he assures that the United States will respond in a positive and timely fashion.

MILITARY: In Kabul, Afghanistan, Western journalists report the sudden appearance of Soviet armored vehicles throughout the city. Speculation arises whether Moscow is concerned over dissident factions in the present regime or a possible coup by supporters of Babrak Karmal.

Heavily armed Soviet troops are reported to have been deployed at Jalalabad airport, Afghanistan.

POLITICS: Despite violations and provocations by the Afghan resistance, the government in Kabul, Afghanistan, insists that it is honoring its cease-fire.

January 16–20

POLITICS: In Peshawar, Pakistan, the mujahideen alliance categorically rejects the cease-fire proposed by the Afghan government. However, during the annual Conference of Islamic states in Kuwait, the alliance delegate is not allowed to occupy the seat first vacated in 1980 following the Soviet invasion.

January 17

DIPLOMACY: In Baghdad, Iraq, Deputy Prime Minister Taha Yassin Ramadan accuses the United States of supplying misleading information that led to a major defeat of the Iraqi army a year earlier. He also castigates Washington for selling arms to Iran.

MILITARY: In Kabul, Afghanistan, Soviet forces continue their show of force, possibly in support of President Mohammad Najib's regime or to thwart a possible coup against him.

In Baghdad, President Saddam Hussein calls an all-day meeting with his military commanders to discuss events in the southern sector.

January 18

MILITARY: In Afghanistan, some Western diplomats assert that Afghans are being trained at the regime's police academy to serve to infiltrate resistance groups and refugee camps in Pakistan.

POLITICS: In Kabul, Afghanistan, the new National Front congress (formerly the National Fatherland Front) has been expanded to include members from the leftist Pakistani Awami National Party of Khan Abdul Wali Khan, the communist Tudeh Party of Iran, and Rajiv Gandhi's Congress Party of India.

In Peshawar, Pakistan, mujahideen leaders declare their intention to both intensify the war against the Kabul regime and also found a government in exile.

January 19

DIPLOMACY: In Islamabad, Pakistan, American and Soviet diplomats arrive for separate discussions with government officials; at issue is the growing intensification of the Afghan war on Pakistani soil.

MILITARY: As the Iranians intensify their offensive in the Basra region, reaching to within seven miles of the city, thousands of refugees flood from the region. Iraq responds by deploying units of the Seventh Army Corps and the elite Presidential Guard, but it stretches reserves so thin that a potential Iranian breakthrough could probably not be contained.

POLITICS: In Kabul, Afghanistan, President Mohammad Najib goes on record as stating that Soviet forces will remain in the country until after all fighting has ended.

January 20–24

DIPLOMACY: In Islamabad, Pakistan, Soviet first deputy foreign minister Anatoly Kovalev meets with Prime Minister Mohammad Khan Junejo, Foreign Minister Sahabzada Yaqub Khan, and Foreign Secretary Abdus Sattar. Kovalev also calls upon President Zia ul-Haq and delivers a letter to him from General Secretary Mikhail Gorbachev.

Concurrently, U.S. undersecretary of state Michael Armacost meets with Pakistani officials about Afghanistan and bilateral relations between them. The Pakistani Foreign Office subsequently declares that the United States has reaffirmed its support for the Afghan resistance and also supports Pakistan's diplomatic efforts to reach an early settlement of the Afghan war on accepted principles.

January 21

DIPLOMACY: In Baghdad, Iraq, President Saddam Hussein composes a "Letter to the Iranian People" and challenges them to question Ayatollah Khomeini's claims of divine sanction. He also notes that Iran's failure to breech Iraq's defenses, despite tremendous sacrifice, clearly illustrates whose side God is on.

MILITARY: With Iraq's 15.4 million people struggling against Iran's 47 million, a three-to-one disadvantage, President Saddam Hussein is forced to call for volunteers between the ages of 14 and 35 years while university students and teachers under 35 are to enroll as officer cadets. Previously, Hussein stated that sending soldiers under 18 to the front was immoral, but even this notion is being revised.

January 22

POLITICS: A report in the *New York Times* suggests that, while the Soviets are quite willing to withdraw their forces from Afghanistan, they will not unless the resistance moderates its stance and accepts a coalition government in Kabul that is acceptable to Moscow. This seems an unlikely proposition.

A party of foreign journalists descends upon Jalalabad, Afghanistan, to view firsthand the damage that has been inflicted by incessant fighting.

January 23

DIPLOMACY: In Islamabad, Pakistan, government officials declare that they will intensify talks with Moscow to reach a negotiated settlement in Afghanistan.

January 24

POLITICS: In Kabul, Afghanistan, the Revolutionary Council declares a general amnesty as part of the overall program of national reconciliation. It is extended to all Afghans who conducted anti-government activities prior to January 15 and also applies to several categories of political prisoners currently held by the government.

A report surfaces in the *New York Times* that Soviet soldiers and civilians living and working in Kabul, Afghanistan, feel unwelcome and that many have been killed while visiting bazaars or back streets of the city.

January 25

AVIATION: In the Persian Gulf, Iraqi warplanes make another long-distance raid by bombing Iranian facilities on Larak Island, damaging an oil-storage tanker.

DIPLOMACY: The Islamic Conference Organization assembles in Kuwait and votes to send its Good Office Committee to visit Iran and discuss a possible cease-fire; the Iranians deny them entry.

MILITARY: In Ahvaz, Iran, the government stages a news conference in which 1,000 prisoners are put on display, including a MiG-25 jet pilot.

POLITICS: According to the U.S. State Department, the regime in Kabul is fabricating accounts of resistance fighters who have surrendered in response to national reconciliation offers. Some Western officials maintain that many mujahideen fighters were actually local militia units ordered to "surrender" on government-controlled media. In at least one instance the "returnees" are the identical party of people who turned themselves in several months previously.

January 26

DIPLOMACY: In Kuwait, UN secretary-general Javier Pérez de Cuéllar addresses the Islamic Conference Organization and calls for the establishment of an international panel to determine precisely what country started the Iran-Iraq War. This is viewed abroad as a concession to the Iranians, who have demanded that Iraq accept the blame.

POLITICS: The *New York Times* reports that foreign journalists remain divided in their reporting as to whether the Soviet invasion has helped or hurt Afghanistan. The discrepancies are divided along Western versus Eastern bloc and nonaligned newspapers.

In Kabul, Afghanistan, the government claims that 186 mujahideen fighters surrendered in Daulatabad, Faryab Province, bringing the total number of "returnees" to 4,000 over the past 10 days.

January 27

MILITARY: Fighting is reported across Afghanistan, despite the recent cease-fire, as the majority of the mujahideen leadership stands squarely against any accommodation with the Communist regime in Kabul.

In Parvan Province, Afghanistan, a 14-member national reconciliation delegation is captured and interned by local resistance fighters.

January 28

DIPLOMACY: In Washington, D.C., Secretary of State George Shultz informs a Senate panel that a possible extension of the Iran-Iraq War into the Persian Gulf region would be detrimental to American strategic interests. Rumor has it that the Americans are increasing the flow of electronic intelligence to the Iraqi military.

January 29
MILITARY: In Kunduz Province, Afghanistan, local mujahideen assassinate a high-ranking government official attempting to promote national reconciliation.

In the southern sector, Iranian forces break the stalemate as Operation Karbala-5 resumes the offensive and breaks through the third Iraqi defensive arc. The Iraqis hastily fall back to new lines and dig in while the Iranians consolidate their gains.

January 30
DIPLOMACY: In Geneva, Switzerland, the next round of UN-sponsored peace talks is suspended for two weeks in order for negotiators to confer with their respective governments.

January 31
AVIATION: In light of the rain of Iraqis bombs falling on Iranian cities, Majlis speaker Hojatolislam Hashemi Rafsanjani urges residents of Tehran to construct air-raid shelters as a "sign of resistance, not fear."

February
AVIATION: Over Pakistan, warplanes of the Afghan air force—most likely flown by Soviet pilots—begin the first of several murderous bombing attacks against Afghan refugee camps. This is more proof of increasing Soviet pressure upon the Pakistani government.

The use of American-supplied Stinger antiaircraft missiles is beginning to turn the tide of the air war in favor of the resistance, which is now downing a Soviet jet or helicopter at an average of one per day. Even now, Soviet aircraft flying out of Bagram airport north of Kabul, Afghanistan, have to climb and bank sharply to avoid being hit.

February 1
AVIATION: Iraqi warplanes strike at Maineh, Iran, allegedly hitting a girls' school and killing 68 students.
DIPLOMACY: The Iranian government releases journalist Gerald F. Seib of the *Wall Street Journal,* who had been accused of being a Zionist spy.
TERRORISM: In Kabul, Afghanistan, a car bomb explodes outside the Indian embassy and the Ministry of State Security; four people die and 15 members of the Indian diplomatic staff are injured. This attack is apparently in response to Indian support for the current regime and its noncritical stance toward Soviet activities there.

February 4
TERRORISM: In Jalalabad, Afghanistan, a car bomb explodes near the local radio and television center, but the ensuing conflagration destroys 50 shops and kills 35 people.

February 5
AVIATION: Basra, Iraq, is struck by another Iranian Scud-B missile; this is the ninth such attack since January.

February 9
AVIATION: In Khost Province, Afghanistan, mujahideen forces shoot down a military transport aircraft, apparently with a U.S.-supplied Stinger missile.

February 10
POLITICS: In Islamabad, Afghanistan, mujahideen officials claim that the transport they shot down a day earlier belonged to the Afghan air force. The regime in Kabul, Afghanistan, counters that it was a civilian aircraft and that 30 people died.

February 12
POLITICS: In Tehran, Iran the ailing Ayatollah Khomeini celebrates the eighth anniversary of the Iranian revolution by explaining that waging war should be seen as a "divine cause" rather than a single offensive action. He reminds the audience of his fatwa of April 1986, which requires the war to be won no later that March 21, 1987.

February 14
DIPLOMACY: In Moscow, Soviet Union, Iranian foreign minister Ali Akbar Velayati arrives for talks. The Soviets clearly relish a mediating role in the conflict and have openly criticized Iraq's tactic of bombing urban centers.

February 16
AVIATION: In Baghdad, Iraq, a government spokesman declares that Iraqi warplanes have flown more than 200 bombing sorties against 35 cities, including 10 strikes directed at Tehran over the past four days, and no fewer than 25 strikes on the holy city of Qom. He admits the war was to try and force the Iranians to the bargaining table.

February 17
DIPLOMACY: In Washington, D.C., Defense Department spokesman Fred Ikle testifies before a joint congressional task force on Afghanistan and condemns the latest Soviet peace offensive as a "thinly disguised attempt at deception" since it completely dodged the issue of a prompt troop withdrawal.

February 18
AVIATION: In Baghdad, Iraq, the government agrees to suspend the latest round of the "War of the Cities" after the Soviet Union pledges to provide it with advanced MiG-27 and MiG-29 aircraft. From January 9 to February 18 of this year, the Iranians suffered considerable devastation, 4,000 deaths, and 12,000 injured. Iraqi deaths to missile attacks and artillery bombardments are far less, around 300 dead and 1,000 injured.

DIPLOMACY: In Moscow, Soviet Union, Afghan prime minister Sultan Ali Keshtmand arrives for talks with Soviet leaders.

POLITICS: The *New York Times* reports that combat activity in Afghanistan has slowed for the winter months, but that neither side appears to be winning the struggle.

February 20
TERRORISM: In Peshawar, Pakistan, a bomb explodes at the office of a mujahideen group, killing 10 people and wounding 62. This is viewed as the work of Afghan

intelligence agents, and it sparks an outbreak of resentment and violence against Afghan refugees, of which four are killed.

February 22–26

MILITARY: In the southern sector, massed Iranian forces resume Operation Karbala-5 from its bridgehead at Shalamache and attempt to overrun the Jasim Canal; some gains are scored, but the attack bogs down in the face of determined defenses. This latest "human wave" assault is called off after four days of fighting. An official Iranian war communiqué declares the operation a great victory when, in fact, little territory changed hands.

February 23

DIPLOMACY: In Moscow, Soviet Union, Pakistani foreign minister Sahabzada Yaqub Khan arrives for talks with Foreign Minister Eduard Shevardnadze on Afghanistan.

February 24

AVIATION: The mujahideen declare that they have destroyed 20 Soviet and Afghan aircraft over the past three weeks, despite the Kabul regime's unilateral cease-fire.

February 25

DIPLOMACY: At a conference, UN special envoy Diego Cordovez declares that progress has been made between Pakistani and Afghan dignitaries, except for the touchy issue of a timetable for the withdrawal of Soviet forces.

In New York City, the United Nations releases a third report on human rights in Afghanistan, noting that "no marked change" has been registered since the announcement of a cease-fire and a general amnesty. It also notes that fighting is on the upswing in many parts of the country, which has resulted in another wave of refugees in Pakistan.

February 26

AVIATION: In the North Waziristan Pakistan tribal agency, Pakistani, Soviet, and Afghan warplanes bomb three border villages near Miranshah, killing 58 people and injuring 190. The formation of 16 jets attack crowded bazaars filled mostly with Afghan refugees.
DIPLOMACY: In Geneva, Switzerland, the 10th round of UN-sponsored peace talks between Pakistan and Afghanistan resume. The main sticking point remains the removal of 120,000 Soviet troops from the region and when.

February 28

DIPLOMACY: In Islamabad, Pakistan, Foreign Minister Yaqub Khan accuses the regime in Kabul, Afghanistan, of trying to derail peace negotiations by attacking Afghan refugees camps.

March–April

POLITICS: In Tyube, Soviet Tajikistan, Muslim preacher Abdullah Saydov is put on trial by Soviet authorities for inciting the local population to side with the Afghan resistance. This incident affords tangible proof that the struggle in Afghanistan is affecting the Uzbek, Tajik, and Turkmen regions of the Soviet Union.

March 1

MILITARY: In the southern sector, President Saddam Hussein orders an Iraqi offensive in the vicinity of Fish Lake to break the impasse around the Basra sector. However, the ensuing operation lacks proper cooperation between infantry and armor elements, and the attempt fails. By the time Operation Karbala-5 ends, Iranian casualties are estimated at 10,000 dead and 20,000 wounded to an Iraqi total of 3,000.

March 2

DIPLOMACY: In a report in the *New York Times,* a Thai official quotes Soviet foreign minister Eduard Shevardnadze as stating that a complete Soviet pullout from Afghanistan could be completed in as little as 22 months.

March 3

DIPLOMACY: In Geneva, Switzerland, the third phase of the seventh round of UN-sponsored indirect peace talks ends inconclusively while heavy fighting rages in Afghanistan.

March 4

AVIATION: At Bagram Air Base, west of Kabul, Afghanistan, a mujahideen Stinger missile brings down a military transport plane.

In northern Iraq, Turkish warplanes bomb the Kurdish villages of Sirac, Era, and Alanish, to destroy *peshmerga* training camps and supply depots. This comes in retaliation for an earlier raid by the Kurdish Workers' Party, which attacked the Turkish frontier town of Sirnak and killed 34 men, women, and children.

DIPLOMACY: The UN High Commissioner for Refugees reports that the influx of Afghan refugees into Pakistan has reached 8,000 per month.

MILITARY: In an audacious move, mujahideen fighters wade across the Amu Darya River and unleash rockets against the town of Panj in Soviet Tajikistan. The Soviet press attempts to stir up national pride against the threat by labeling the attackers *basmachi* (bandits).

In Kunduz Province, Afghanistan, Soviet troops retaliate for attacks on their home soil by conducting a murderous campaign against civilians living along the border. Hundreds of civilians are gunned down while others, having their homes and crops destroyed, commence an overland trek to the perceived safety of Pakistan.

March 4–9

MILITARY: In the northern sector, Iranian forces backed by Kurdish *peshmerga* guerrillas commence Operation Karbala-7 by attacking through the Haj Omran area east of Rawandoz. Revolutionary Guards manage to infiltrate Iraqi defenses along the 8,400-foot-high mountain range, capturing soldiers. A series of sharp counterattacks by the Iraqi Fifth Army Corps fails to dislodge the Iranians, who claim a 12-mile advance.

March 7

NAVAL: In Washington, D.C., President Ronald W. Reagan, anxious to keep the flow of petroleum to the West unimpeded, announces that 11 Kuwaiti tankers will be reflagged with American colors to protect them from Iranian attack. It is not mentioned that both Kuwait and Saudi Arabia had privately threatened to sell off their large holdings of U.S. treasury bonds if the Americans refused to help.

March 10

DIPLOMACY: In Geneva, Switzerland, UN special envoy Diego Cordovez reports that representatives from Pakistan and Afghanistan have reached agreement on three of four diplomatic issues relative to a peace agreement. However, the Afghan government refuses to agree on a timetable for the pullout of all Soviet forces while the nature and composition of a post-Soviet government remains undiscussed. Cordovez states that the difference in a timetable for a pullout has a gap of "less than a year." At length, the stalemated talks are adjourned, though Pakistan, pressured by 323 violations of its airspace in the first three months of 1987, remains firm in its support of the Afghan mujahideen.

MILITARY: In Herat and Kandahar Provinces, Afghanistan, mujahideen fighters enjoy a measure of success by repelling Soviet and Afghan army attacks with significant losses.

March 11

DIPLOMACY: In Geneva, Switzerland, the Afghan delegation to UN-sponsored peace talks suggests that the 120,000 Soviet troops currently garrisoned in Afghanistan could be withdrawn in 18 months. However, the Pakistanis insist on half that period.

March 12

MILITARY: In Kandahar, Afghanistan, mujahideen steal to within point-blank range of Soviet troops at the nearby airport, then unleash a surprise rocket bombardment that inflicts heavy casualties on them. These forces have recently completed operations along the Pakistani border and redeployed from Herat and Shindand to the airport.

POLITICS: In Peshawar, Pakistan, mujahideen leaders state their concerns that Western governments could be duped by Soviet pretensions toward a negotiated settlement, causing them to prematurely withdraw their support.

March 15

AVIATION: A report is issued by Western diplomats that the mujahideen recently shot down three Afghan helicopters over Nangarhar Province. They also attacked Jalalabad airport.

U.S. satellite intelligence reveals that the Iranians have begun installing Chinese-supplied Silkworm anti-shipping missiles on Qeshm Island. The Chinese flatly deny supplying Iran with any such weapons.

MILITARY: In Baghdad, Iraq, President Saddam Hussein warns military and political leaders against possible defeat through sheer attrition—Iran still enjoys significant manpower advantages.

March 18

POLITICS: In Kabul, Afghanistan, the government declares that Afghanistan and the Soviet Union have concluded a 21-million ruble contract ($30 million) to develop the Yateem-Tao natural-gas field. Construction will commence in June and last an estimated 14 months.

March 19

DIPLOMACY: In Washington, D.C., the State Department announces that, appearances to the contrary, the Soviet government has not agreed to a rapid pullout of its forces from Afghanistan. Meanwhile, President Ronald W. Reagan repudiates his previous Iran policy and states he would not order the same actions again. He also denies any knowledge of diverting profits from arms sales to Iran to the Nicaraguan contras.

March 20

MILITARY: In Baghdad, Iraq, the government stages a massive military parade on the Iranian New Year to underscore Iran's inability to score a knockout blow despite extensive loss of life.

POLITICS: In Washington, D.C., President Ronald W. Reagan marks "Afghanistan Day" by declaring that a cease-fire in that country is "meaningless" if not attached to a speedy withdrawal of Soviet forces. Moreover, he insists that it is essential that Western governments continue aiding the Afghan resistance at current levels since its success has driven the Soviets to grope for a political solution to the war.

State Department official Charles Dunbar, the special assistant for Afghanistan, declares that the Soviet invasion of Afghanistan has spawned a new national movement with its own generation of sophisticated and politically savvy leaders.

March 21

DIPLOMACY: At Columbia University, Soviet UN envoy Roland Timerbaev candidly admits that the Soviet invasion of Afghanistan was "a mistake." He subsequently clarifies his position by insisting he spoke strictly as an individual, and not for his government.

MILITARY: On this day of Nowaz, the Iranian new year, a long anticipated mass offensive by Iranian forces fails to materialize. Iraqi president Saddam Hussein is quick to crow about this lack of aggressive action, and public morale in Iraq rose slightly.

March 23

AVIATION: Western diplomatic sources announce that mujahideen fighters have downed three more helicopters near Khost and Kandahar, Afghanistan.

March 24

AVIATION: Warplanes belonging to the Afghan air force bomb a suspected guerrilla stronghold in Pakistan, killing and wounding 105 people.

DIPLOMACY: In Tehran, Iran, the government denies allowing the Soviet Union to establish two electronic intelligence gathering stations on its soil in exchange for 200 Scud-B missiles. Presently, there are more than 300 Soviet technicians repairing armored vehicles at Masjid Suleiman.

March 25

AVIATION: Soviet and Afghan warplanes attack refugee centers at Rabat, along the joint borders of Iran, Afghanistan, and Pakistan. Iranian troops in the area fire back but fail to score any hits. Rabat is considered to be a major avenue of entry into Afghanistan by mujahideen operating from bases in Iran and Pakistan, so the air raid here is not exactly surprising.

DIPLOMACY: The Pakistani government confirms that Soviet or Afghan jets had recently bombed a village within its borders, apparently in an attempt to intimidate Islamabad into granting better terms at peace talks in Geneva, Switzerland. Moreover, such attacks appear to be intensifying as discussions center more upon a timetable for the withdrawal of Soviet troops.

March 26
POLITICS: In a major development, a newspaper in Moscow publishes a letter written by prominent Soviet émigrés that call upon General Secretary Mikhail Gorbachev to withdraw unconditionally from Afghanistan. In response, the letter is highly criticized by *Pravda,* the Communist Party newspaper.

March 31
AVIATION: Pakistani jets intercept and shoot down another Afghan warplane that had violated its air space.

In Kabul, Afghanistan, Western diplomats declare that over the past 10 days the mujahideen have shot down no fewer than 10 Soviet and Afghan aircraft. The majority of these were probably felled by sophisticated Stinger missiles supplied by the United States.

April 1
AVIATION: In Kabul, Afghanistan, the government media announce that Pakistani warplanes have shot down a civilian airliner, killing all 30 passengers.

April 2
MILITARY: The Afghan resistance declares that two large bodies of Soviet and Afghan army troops are in motion toward mujahideen camps located near the Pakistani border.

In Kandahar, Afghanistan, street fighting erupts after local citizens reject food and other supplies given to them by the Soviets. The government reports that 14 of its soldiers died.

April 6
AVIATION: In Washington, D.C., President Ronald W. Reagan declares that the United States will continue supplying Afghan resistance fighters with Stinger anti-aircraft missiles. However, this policy is also causing fears that such advanced weaponry might fall into unfriendly hands.
POLITICS: Western analysts figure that heavy fighting will erupt along the Pakistani border as the Afghan and Soviet governments apply increasing military and psychological pressure to secure better terms at Geneva.

April 6–10
MILITARY: In the southern sector, 35,000 Iranian Pasdaran troops begin draining the water barriers around Basra in order to launch Operation Karbala-8. They intend to seize the Dual Canals defenses and launch several human waves against Iraqi defenses over the next three days; modest gains are scored, but at a cost of 8,000 casualties. In fact, the Iraqis had been tipped off about the offensive beforehand by

dissident elements in the Iranian defense establishment. However, the action was considered serious enough to preclude the Third and Seventh Army Corps from rushing reinforcements to the threatened northern sector.

April 7

MILITARY: Near Khejan, Afghanistan, an avalanche on the highway north of the Salang tunnel apparently destroyed a 70-man Soviet post, along with most of the garrison. The Soviets were subsequently obliged to use artillery to blast the debris blocking the highway.

April 8

MILITARY: Radio Moscow issues a report stating that resistance fighters attacked the town of Panj, Soviet Tajikistan, killing several citizens and setting off numerous fires.

POLITICS: In Tehran, Iran, Majlis Speaker Hojatolislam Hashemi Rafsanjani addresses the nation and assures them that "we will defeat Iraq during the current year." However, the aggressive mullah school of thought driving the war is suffering from a severe psychological setback due to the recent and bloody defeats.

April 9–11

MILITARY: In the northern sector, two divisions of Iranian Pasdaran troops commence Operation Karbala-8 in the Qasr-i-Sherin region. Little territory changes hands, and another impasse ensues; casualties are unknown.

TERRORISM: Outside of Mosul, Iraq, al-Daawa militants attack a motorcade carrying President Saddam Hussein. Six bodyguards are killed, but the president remains unscathed.

April 11

DIPLOMACY: In Washington, D.C., President Ronald W. Reagan challenges the Soviets to establish a firm date for the withdrawal of Soviet forces from Afghanistan—then live up to it. He also urges them to conclude an agreement respecting medium-range nuclear missiles to further increase pressure on them.

April 13

MILITARY: In the northern sector, Jalal Talabani of the Patriotic Union of Kurdistan claims that 2,000 of his fighters attacked the Iraqi garrison at Sulaymaniyah, killing 600 of them, then withdrew. The Iraqis deny such an event even occurred.

April 13–15

MILITARY: In the northern sector, Iranian forces, backed by guerrillas of the Kurdish Democratic Party, launch Operation Karbala-9 to capture the strategic heights of Sulaymaniyah in Iraqi Kurdistan. The Iraqis respond by unleashing chemical weapons against 20 Kurdish villages, inflicting hundreds of casualties, civilian and military alike.

April 15

MILITARY: In Kabul, Afghanistan, government radio announces that the mujahideen launched 13 heavy rockets into Gardez, the capital of Paktia Province.

April 17
AVIATION: Pakistan reports that it downed another Afghan military aircraft violating its airspace.

April 19
POLITICS: In Kabul, Afghanistan, President Mohammad Najib seeks to improve his image among the international community by lauding private-sector investors and declaring that Afghanistan's economy should not be separated from international commercial and capital markets. He also hopes to attract foreign investment.

April 20–27
DIPLOMACY: In Moscow, Soviet Union, Russian and Chinese diplomats engage in a week-long discussion respecting Afghanistan and Kampuchea (Cambodia), apparently without achieving any clear results.

April 21
POLITICS: In Kabul, Afghanistan, the Bakhtar News Agency states that an assassination plot against President Mohammad Najib had been uncovered and implicates the intelligence service of Pakistan. However, Western analysts theorize that any such plot was probably hatched among dissident elements of the PDPA. The fact that Najib has appeared twice in public ringed by Soviet bodyguards suggests that the plot was real.

April 22
DIPLOMACY: In Kabul, Afghanistan, K. F. Katushev, chairman of the Soviet State Committee for Foreign Relations, ends a formal state visit. While present, he endorsed a Soviet-Afghan protocol promoting greater cooperation on 171 projects in Afghanistan. These apparently include 38 private and mixed-sector projects and 121 joint Soviet-Afghan projects slated for the private sector.

April 24
MILITARY: In Kabul, Afghanistan, Western diplomats speculate that a recent rash of Soviet artillery bombardments along the border regions of Kunduz Province, which completely destroyed several villages, is part of a deliberate strategy to depopulate the area near Soviet Tajikistan and preclude any future guerrilla raids from there.

April 26
DIPLOMACY: In Kabul, Afghanistan, a delegation from the Soviet republic of Uzbekistan arrives to promote deeper economic ties between the northernmost Afghan provinces and Soviet Central Asia.

April 27
MILITARY: In Kabul, Afghanistan, the government celebrates the ninth anniversary of the 1978 Communist coup with a large military parade amidst tight security. President Mohammad Najib declares the theme of this year's celebration will be national reconciliation.

In the northern sector, Iranians and Kurdish guerrillas commence Operation Karbala-10 by attacking from Iran's Sardasht area with a view toward overrunning

Mawet and Qala Diza, Iraq. Within days they capture 100 square miles of territory and inflict an estimated 4,000 casualties.

POLITICS: Confusion reigns among various government agencies after Afghan foreign minister Abdul Wakil declares that 35,000 Afghans had embraced national reconciliation while the Kabul *New Times* states the number 44,000. On April 16, the same paper had pegged the number of returnees at 52,000.

April 30

DIPLOMACY: The regimes in Tehran and Damascus announce an annual oil agreement whereby Syria will receive a grant of 1 million tons of Iranian oil and proceeds from the sale of 2 million tons at official OPEC prices.

May

DIPLOMACY: In Kabul, Afghanistan, Indian minister of foreign affairs Narayan Tiwari arrives on an official state visit, in a move calculated to intimidate the government of Pakistan.

Soviet general secretary Mikhail Gorbachev informs the Italian Communist daily *Unita* that the Soviets and Afghans are willing to extend the program of national reconciliation beyond Afghanistan's borders to refugees and emigrants alike—a veiled hint aimed at former king Mohammad Zahir Shah.

May–June

MILITARY: In Afghanistan, deserters from the Afghan army report lowering morale due to American-supplied Stinger missiles that have all but discouraged close air support by Soviet warplanes.

Afghan resistance forces take to the offensive and wage a full-scale battle with Soviet troops around the western city of Herat, Afghanistan.

A sustained Soviet/Afghan army offensive in the southern region of Kandahar, Afghanistan, ends in failure; among the most notable casualties is General Qayum Saddi, chief of the Afghan army political branch. Before departing, Soviet troops bulldoze trees, vineyards, and orchids to deny food for local resistance fighters.

May 1

NAVAL: In the Strait of Hormuz off the Persian Gulf, Iranian vessels stop and search 14 vessels headed for Iraq, detaining one for carrying contraband.

May 2

AVIATION: In Kabul, Afghanistan, the government claims to have downed a Pakistani F-16 fighter that strayed into its air space.

May 4

DIPLOMACY: In Kabul, Afghanistan, foreign minister Abdul Wakil admits to his Indian counterpart, Naragan Tiwari, that guerrilla activity is on the upswing ever since the government announced its unilateral cease-fire. Furthermore, he acknowledges that the mujahideen still control large swaths of countryside and that the government intends to retaliate on a massive scale if this state of affairs persists at the cease-fire's end.

POLITICS: In Kabul, Afghanistan, former president Babrak Karmal is arrested and confined. Officially, he is reported to have left for the Soviet Union to undergo unspecified medical treatment.

May 5
POLITICS: In Kabul, Afghanistan, national radio confirms that former president Babrak Karmal is in the Soviet Union receiving medical treatment.

May 6
MILITARY: In western Afghanistan, the trading city of Herat, with a population of 150,000, is finally occupied by Soviet forces after a period of severe fighting.
NAVAL: In the Persian Gulf the Soviet tanker *Ivan Koroteyev,* leased to Kuwait, strikes an Iranian mine and is damaged.

May 8
DIPLOMACY: In Washington, D.C., State Department official Zalmay Khalilzad declares that the United States will never sacrifice Afghanistan while pursuing other contentious topics with the Soviet Union. He characterizes the struggle there as the most important regional issue between the superpowers and says that only an eventual resolution could improve relations.
POLITICS: In Kabul, Afghanistan, student demonstrations erupt in front of the Interior Ministry for the return of exiled leader Babrak Karmal. It is also suspected that three bombs that exploded in the Microrayon district of the city are the work of Karmal supporters.

May 9
POLITICS: In Kabul, Afghanistan, the party newspaper *New Times* writes that several Afghan delegations recently departed for discussions with Soviet authorities in the republic of Uzbekistan. At issue was how to expand economic ties between Afghanistan's northernmost provinces and the heart of Soviet Central Asia.

May 11
MILITARY: At Miranshah, Pakistan, a group of 63 Afghan soldiers defect after killing their officers and fleeing from a barracks in Kabul, Afghanistan.

May 13
POLITICS: A report in the *New York Times* says that the regime in Kabul, Afghanistan, remains torn by factionalism and the fact that the war against the resistance is stalemated. Reportedly, the Soviet government has tired of the infighting and is seeking a diplomatic way out of the contest.

May 14
NAVAL: In the Persian Gulf, the destroyer USS *Coontz* prepares to engage an Iraqi Mirage F-1 fighter that approaches to within 10 miles, then suddenly turns around.

May 15
AVIATION: In and around Kabul, Afghanistan, Stinger-armed mujahideen fighters have shot down three Afghan army helicopters. Such activity is forcing the government and the Soviets to rely more heavily on flying at night.

DIPLOMACY: In an attempt to attract foreign support and investment, the regime in Kabul, Afghanistan, begins touting its new policies of free-market economics, women's rights, and tolerance for Islam.

POLITICS: Foreign diplomats in Afghanistan postulate that the regime is attempting to expand Soviet influences at home by dispatching thousands of its best students to study in the Soviet Union. They have also accepted Soviet aid in the construction of hospitals, schools, and mosques to advance their influence throughout urban centers.

May 16
MILITARY: In the Charikar region of Parvan Province, Afghanistan, fighting between Soviet and mujahideen forces temporarily closes down the strategic Salang tunnel on the main highway that links Kabul to the Soviet Union.

NAVAL: In the Persian Gulf, the Soviet tanker *Marshal Zhukov,* leased to Kuwait, strikes a mine previously supplied to Iran and suffers damage.

May 17
NAVAL: In the Persian Gulf, 85 miles northeast of Bahrain, the frigate USS *Stark* is struck by a pair of French-made Exocet missiles fired by an Iraqi F-1 Mirage; 37 sailors are killed, and the vessel is badly damaged. The vessel's defensive measures were not operational at the time of the attack, despite the element of danger present. The incoming missile was sighted visually by a lookout, but, because the Phalanx defensive gatling was in manual mode instead of automatic, it failed to respond in time. The Iraqi government also agrees to pay $27.3 million in compensation to the families of the dead sailors.

May 19
DIPLOMACY: The Iraqi government of Saddam Hussein acknowledges responsibility in launching the missile that struck the USS *Stark* but declares it will not alter relations between the two countries; President Ronald W. Reagan announces his decision to fly the American flag over 11 Kuwaiti oil tankers in the Persian Gulf to protect them as the Iraq-Iran War rages. Reagan also places the blame on Iran for refusing to negotiate an end to the conflict.

May 20
DIPLOMACY: The UN High Commissioners for Refugees reports that, to date, 5 million Afghans—nearly half the population—have fled their homeland due to the Soviet invasion and fighting to evict them. Figures indicate that 3 million are presently residing in Pakistan while 2 million are in Iran.

May 2–June 13
MILITARY: In Paktia Province, Afghanistan, a large force of Soviet troops, including airborne soldiers, SPETSNAZ, and Afghan regulars attack a cave complex nicknamed al-Masada ("Lion's Den") near Ali Sher. The defenders, largely under Jalaluddin Haqqani and Mohammad Anwar, include a detachment of 50 Arab fighters under Saudi expatriate Osama bin Laden. They manage to fend off their opponents for a month in difficult terrain, until the Soviets and their allies withdraw. Casualties

are unknown. Bin Laden apparently suffers a foot wound in this encounter, and his contribution to the victory attracts additional followers to his cause.

May 21

DIPLOMACY: General Secretary Mikhail Gorbachev, during an interview with the Italian Communist newspaper *l'Unità,* vaguely suggests that he would favor former king Mohammad Zahir Shah as part of a coalition government following the departure of Soviet forces from Afghanistan.

POLITICS: The *New York Times* prints an editorial by Selig Harrison that suggests that Moscow and Washington should compromise by deemphasizing the roles of Kabul and Islamabad and endorse former king Mohammad Zahir Shah as a neutral figure around whom Afghans could rally.

In Washington, D.C., the U.S. Senate votes 91–5 to require the administration to inform Congress on the situation in the Persian Gulf before reflagging the Kuwaiti tankers. Ironically, other maritime nations that are much more dependant upon oil from Kuwait than the United States display no interest in protecting its tankers.

May 22–late June

DIPLOMACY: Peace talks in Geneva, Switzerland, appear hopeless once the governments of Afghanistan and the Soviet Union reject any notion of power sharing with the Afghan resistance following a Soviet withdrawal.

MILITARY: In Kandahar Province, Afghanistan, the Afghan Army, assisted by Soviet troops, attacks mujahideen forces in the Arghandab district. The resistance fighters are well supplied and dug in, so the Afghan army takes severe losses in trying to expel them from their positions. Within a month they withdraw, after suffering 500 killed and wounded, along with 1,200 defections. Approximately 60 mujahideen are dead.

May 23–29

MILITARY: In Paktia Province, Afghanistan, Soviet and army troops commence a concerted drive to cut mujahideen sources of supply with Pakistan. Fearing that the move will spawn a wave of desertions, they proceed with assistance from Afghan army units. The attempt ultimately fails, and the Soviets withdraw.

May 29

AVIATION: Outside Kabul, Afghanistan, a mujahideen Stinger missile downs a military transport, killing all 12 Afghan pilots flying to nearby Bagram Air Base.

DIPLOMACY: In Washington, D.C., Assistant Defense Secretary Richard Armitage openly declares that the United States "can't stand to see Iraq defeated," which further reveals the anti-Iranian tilt of the American government.

June

AVIATION: Over Kandahar, Afghanistan, a Stinger missile fired by mujahideen fighters brings down a Soviet-built Antonov An-26 airliner, killing all 53 passengers on board. Soviet sources claim this was a civilian aircraft, but the Hezb-i-Islami declares it was a military transport flying food and other supplies to Kabul.

June 1

MILITARY: Intense fighting erupts as mujahideen fighters under Abdul Wahab halt a determined Afghan army offensive, backed by Soviet air power, in Paktia Province, Afghanistan. Wahab and 25 of his men are killed, and 80 are wounded. The rebels claim to have downed two jets and a helicopter while capturing 150 Afghan soldiers.

June 2

POLITICS: In Tehran, Iran, Ayatollah Khomeini dissolves the Islamic Republican Party to end internecine infighting among various factions. Henceforth, the Majlis serves as the only legitimate political arena for factional maneuvering.

June 6

MILITARY: In northwest Pakistan, Afghan army units shell a refugee camp from across the border, killing 20 people and wounding 14.

NAVAL: In Washington, D.C., Defense Secretary Frank Carlucci declares that he does not believe that China is selling Iran Silkworm anti-shipping missiles.

June 7

DIPLOMACY: In Washington, D.C., Secretary of State George Shultz warns Iran that the United States might retaliate militarily if Tehran acquires and deploys Chinese-made Silkworm anti-shipping missiles along the Strait of Hormuz.

June 10

MILITARY: In northern Herat Province, mujahideen fighters seize a key mountain region overlooking the strategic Towraghondi-Herat road. This functions as one of the most important lines of supply for Soviet forces in western Afghanistan.

June 11

AVIATION: An Afghan Antonov An-26 transport makes an emergency landing in the Shahjui district of Kabul, Afghanistan, leading Western diplomats to speculate that its was struck en route by a mujahideen Stinger missile.

MILITARY: In Washington, D.C., President Ronald W. Reagan abandons plans to sell Saudi Arabia 1,600 Maverick guided missiles after Congress makes clear its intention to vote down the plan.

June 12

AVIATION: In Kabul, Afghanistan, government radio announces that Stinger-armed mujahideen fighters recently downed a civilian transport, killing 53 people.

June 14

AVIATION: According to Western diplomats in Afghanistan, mujahideen apparently downed another An-26 military transport near Mazar-i-Sharif, killing 43 passengers.

NAVAL: In Washington, D.C., the House of Representatives releases a committee report that says negligence was behind the *Stark* disaster, declaring that the Iraqi jet had not been warned off in a timely fashion, and the alarm designed to detect incoming missiles at a safe distance had been turned off because it had been producing false alarms.

June 15

MILITARY: In Afghanistan, Defense Minister Major General Muhammad Rafi tours the Kandahar region following the apparent defeat of a combined Soviet-Afghan attempt to clean out mujahideen fighters operating there. This three-week endeavor resulted in high desertion rates and nearly 1,000 casualties, according to Western diplomatic sources. Many of those killed were teenagers forcibly conscripted from schools and colleges in Kabul.

June 16–23

DIPLOMACY: In Washington, D.C., President Ronald W. Reagan welcomes Burhan-uddin Rabbani and a delegation from the mujahideen alliance to the White House. However, this move occasions unfavorable commentary criticism from Gulbud-din Hekmatyar and causes additional strains between conservative and moderates within the alliance. Rabbani is subsequently received in Paris, France, by Prime Minister Jacques Chirac, who assures him of France's continuing support for the Afghan resistance.

June 19

NAVAL: In Washington, D.C., the Navy Department declares that Captain Glenn Brindel and two other deck officers of the USS *Stark* are being relieved of duty over "lack of confidence in their performance."

In the Persian Gulf, tension rises again after a Soviet-registered tanker used by Kuwait strikes a mine off its coastline and is damaged. Iran is immediately suspected of laying the mines in the channel leading to the Mina Ahmadi oil terminal, and it takes U.S. and Saudi naval units an entire month to sweep the region clear.

June 20

AVIATION: Iraqi warplanes break the month-long lull in the tanker wars by attacking a tanker carrying Iranian oil in the Persian Gulf.

June 24

MILITARY: Reports surface that intense combat activity in the vicinity of Kandahar, Afghanistan, resulted in the deaths of hundreds of soldiers and civilians.

June 26

MILITARY: In the Pagham Mountains, nine miles west of Kabul, Afghanistan, Soviet troops arrive to reinforce Afghan army troops in a major engagement against muja-hideen fighters.

June 30

MILITARY: In Kandahar, Afghanistan, Soviet forces bulldoze the residences of suspected mujahideen supporters along a 14-mile stretch of road to the airport to achieve a clear field of fire. Reportedly, the city's prewar population of nearly 200,000 has dwindled to only 40,000.

July

MILITARY: In northwestern Afghanistan, mujahideen under Ahmad Shah Massoud capture the Afghan army base at Kafalgan.

POLITICS: In Kabul, Afghanistan, the government releases the draft of a new constitution for the country. No mention of Marx or Communism appears, but the president holds considerable power. Using the facade of Islamic terminology, the documents maintain that religion will not be used to "provoke hatred" among Afghanistan's citizens.

TERRORISM: This month a wave of explosions rocks the cities of Karachi, Peshawar, Mardan, and Rawalpindi, Pakistan, killing more than 200 people and injuring hundreds more. Afghan intelligence agents are suspected to have planted the charges in an attempt to intimidate resistance leaders and the Pakistani government.

July 7

AVIATION: The *New York Times* quotes a State Department report that states Stinger-equipped mujahideen fighters have been shooting down Soviet and Afghan aircraft and helicopters at the rate of at least one per day.

At the border village of Gadai, Pakistan, Soviet and Afghan warplanes drop bombs, killing and injuring several Pakistanis.

MILITARY: In Washington, D.C., a State Department official crows about the willingness of Afghan mujahideen to engage in hand-to-hand combat with elite Soviet SPETSNAZ forces. He declares that heavy Soviet casualties in Paktia and Kandahar Provinces are the consequence. It is further noted that improved air defenses on the part of the resistance are forcing Soviet jets to drop bombs from higher altitudes, thereby compromising their accuracy. The heretofore formidable helicopter gunships employed by the Soviets are also vulnerable to Stinger missiles at high altitude and 12.7mm heavy machine-gun fire at low altitude, so their combat effectiveness has also been diminished.

July 14

AVIATION: In the Persian Gulf, Iraqi warplanes attack Farsi Island in the upper Gulf region. Iranian speedboats deployed there, manned by Revolutionary Guards, have been attacking ships sailing to Kuwait and Saudi Arabia.

MILITARY: West of Kabul, Afghanistan, Soviet and Afghan army forces withdraw from the mountainous Pagham-Maidan region after several weeks of trying to eradicate mujahideen fighters operating there. It is speculated that improved rebel antiaircraft capabilities severely limited the impact of Red Air Force bombing.

TERRORISM: In Karachi, Pakistan, two car bombs explode on the streets, killing 72 people and wounding 250. Government authorities quickly blame Afghan intelligence operatives.

July 15

DIPLOMACY: In Washington, D.C., Najibullah Lafraie of Jamiat-i-Islami challenges the Soviet Union to demonstrate its commitment to peace by withdrawing its force from Afghanistan without conditions or delays. Moreover, he asserts that the Soviet military is using his country as a testing ground for its newest weapons and intends to use his country as a springboard for further aggression. Lafraie concludes by declaring that 70 percent of Afghanistan lies in ruins and 5 million Afghans are living as refugees in Pakistan and Iran.

July 16

DIPLOMACY: In a joint statement, the U.S. State Department and President Zia ul-Haq of Pakistan blame the recent car bombs in Karachi on Afghan agents.

July 17

DIPLOMACY: The French government severs diplomatic relations with Iran after pursuing terrorist suspects involved in bombing attacks in France to the Iranian embassy in Paris.

MILITARY: According to Kabul Radio, mujahideen rockets have recently struck Gardez, the capital of Paktia Province, Afghanistan.

July 18

POLITICS: In Kabul, Afghanistan, the Bakhtar News Agency reports that the Soviet Union has invested the equivalent of $1.1 billion in project loans, consumer goods, and grants for the Afghan populace since the Communist-inspired Saur Revolution of April 1978.

July 19

MILITARY: According to Radio Pakistan, the three-day-old Operation Avalanche, conducted by Soviet and Afghan army troops along a 40-mile stretch of the highway between Kabul and Jalalabad, Afghanistan, has resulted in more than 1,000 casualties at the hands of mujahideen fighters. Parts of this battle were televised on CBS television, and it is believed to be one of the largest deployments of Soviet forces thus far.

July 19–August 10

DIPLOMACY: In Moscow, Soviet Union, President Mohammad Najib arrives for three weeks of discussions with Soviet officials. During a news conference held on July 22, Najib announces his willingness to open 11 cabinet posts to the Afghan opposition, including the vice presidency, should a government of national reconciliation come to pass. Not unexpectedly, such key ministries as defense and foreign affairs remain firmly in the hands of the Communist PDPA. He touts the fact that, since January, 15,000 former guerrillas have laid down their arms.

July 20

DIPLOMACY: In New York City, the UN Security Council passes Resolution 598, which again demands an immediate cease-fire between the belligerents and an exchange of prisoners. A contingent of UN observers would also be deployed to monitor enforcement. Iraq immediately accepts the resolution while Iran balks and insists that the United Nations halt the American naval buildup in the Gulf and stop the flow of French arms to Iraq.

In Bonn, West Germany, the Iranian foreign minister give a radio address with Chancellor Hans Dietrich Genscher, in which the latter openly blames Iraq for starting the present war and accuses it of illegally using banned chemical weapons against Iranian forces.

July 22

NAVAL: In the Persian Gulf, the U.S. Navy begins escorting the first two reflagged Kuwaiti tankers now flying the American flag. It is anticipated this move will deter attacks on them by Iran as they pass through the Strait of Hormuz on their 550-mile voyage to Kuwait.

July 22–December 21
AVIATION: With the Iran-Iraq War now spilling over into the Persian Gulf, Operation Earnest Will unfolds as Air Force E-3A Sentry aircraft begin routine patrols. C-5A Galaxy and C-141 Starlifter transports also convey minesweeping equipment into the region while Air Force tankers support Navy aircraft patrolling the Gulf waters.

July 23
DIPLOMACY: Around this time, the Iranian government dispatches a high-level mission to Kuwait to demand that it abandon its practice of reflagging tankers under the American flag. Iran pledges to stop attacking Kuwaiti shipping, but the government turns down the offer.

POLITICS: In Tehran, Iran, Majlis Speaker Hojatolislam Hashemi Rafsanjani gives a frank interview declaring that the government will continue its present policy of biting off chunks of Iraqi territory with a view toward gradually overthrowing President Saddam Hussein. However, he admits that this relentless attrition is dangerous to the country and war effort.

July 24
AVIATION: After the U.S.-flagged tanker *Bridgeton* strikes a mine in the Persian Gulf, eight RH-53D helicopters begin minesweeping operations to secure the safe passage of neutral shipping.

MILITARY: The 24th Marine Amphibious Unit deploys to the Persian Gulf. It is there to assist the Navy in keeping that valuable waterway open to commercial traffic.

The guided missile frigate USS *Stark* lists to port after being struck by an Iraqi-launched Exocet missile. *(Department of Defense)*

NAVAL: The United States continues Operation Earnest Will by providing protection to reflagged Kuwaiti oil tankers in the Persian Gulf. However, this day the 410,000-ton tanker *Bridgeton* strikes a mine and suffers minor damage, an act placing the U.S. Navy on a collision course with Iranian forces in the Persian Gulf.

In Washington, D.C., the Navy Department announces that it will not be court-martialing Captain Glenn Brindel and the chief weapons officer of the USS *Stark,* but they will receive letters of reprimand before being discharged from the service.

July 27
AVIATION: Helicopter mine-countermeasure squadron HM-14 arrives in the Persian Gulf.

In the Sanglagh Valley, 60 miles west of Kabul, Afghanistan, fighters belonging to the Shiite Harkat-i-Islami claim to have shot down 13 aircraft and four helicopters during three weeks of intense fighting after Soviet forces tried to close off both ends of the valley.

July 30
AVIATION: In the Persian Gulf, an American helicopter from the frigate USS *LaSalle* crashes due to mechanical difficulties, killing one and injuring three.

July 31
DIPLOMACY: In response to the United States's request of several European governments for help in mine-sweeping operations in the Persian Gulf, the British government declines.
POLITICS: In Mecca, Saudi Arabia, 100,000 Iranian pilgrims riot near the Grand Mosque and battle with Saudi police; 275 Iranians, 85 Saudis, and 42 pilgrims from other countries are killed.

August 1
POLITICS: In Tehran, Iran, a mob sacks the Saudi and Kuwaiti embassies over the violence in Mecca. Arab nations begin rallying behind the Saudis and denounce Iran.

August 3
AVIATION: In an ominous development, the Iraqis successfully test-fire a modified Scud-B tactical missile with a range of 380 miles—twice that of ordinary Scuds.
POLITICS: In Tehran, Iran, Ayatollah Khomeini blames the violence in Mecca on the United States. He also denounces the ruling Saudi family as "vile and ungodly" and unworthy of being caretaker of Islam's holiest shrines.

August 4–7
NAVAL: In the Persian Gulf, Iran stages Operation Martyrdom, reportedly training volunteers in high-speed boats to ram into U.S. Navy vessels while carrying explosive charges.

August 5
MILITARY: Intense guerrilla activities around Kabul and Kandahar, Afghanistan, halt all ground traffic and leads to shortages of basic supplies and commodities.

POLITICS: In Saudi Arabia, King Fahd declares his government's intention to "never relent in the defense of our homeland and sacred shrines."

August 8

AVIATION: To counter Iranian mine-laying operations in the strategic Persian Gulf, Special Forces MH-6 Little Bird helicopters begin patrolling the waters at night. They are under orders to stop any Iranian vessel threatening the free transit of merchant ships and tankers through the Gulf.

A Navy F-14 Tomcat fighter perceives an Iranian F-4 fighter acting aggressively and fires two missiles at the intruder, but both malfunction.

August 8–11

NAVAL: In the Persian Gulf, the Navy reflags three more Kuwaiti tankers and escorts them in harm's way.

August 9

MILITARY: A Soviet Afghan offensive north of Kabul, Afghanistan, results in more than 1,000 refugees fleeing into the capital. Survivors of very heavy artillery shelling claim that many people have died and their homes destroyed.

August 10

NAVAL: The tanker *Caribbean,* having just entered the Gulf of Oman, strikes a mine and spills 10,000 barrels of oil. This is the first damage sustained outside the Persian Gulf.

August 11

NAVAL: The governments of Britain and France, reverse themselves and pledge to send minesweeping ships into the Persian Gulf.

POLITICS: In Kabul, Afghanistan, the government allows UN special human-rights investigator Felix Ermacora to visit and interview political prisoners at three detention centers.

August 12

DIPLOMACY: In Tehran, Iran, the government criticizes UN Resolution 598 and blames the United States for imposing its will on the Security Council.

TERRORISM: In Baghdad, Iraq, a bomb explodes downtown, killing 20 people. The act is attributed to al-Daawa militants.

August 14

AVIATION: Near Khost, Afghanistan, a mujahideen Stinger missile downs another Antonov An-26 transport, killing all seven passengers and destroying valuable commodities intended for Kabul.

August 15

NAVAL: The supply vessel *Anita,* flying under the flag of the United Arab Emirates, strikes a mine and sinks in the Gulf of Oman with a loss of one dead and five missing.

August 17

DIPLOMACY: The Afghan government protests to Iran after mortar rounds and surface-to-surface missiles strike the border town of Islam Qillah.

August 19
Naval: The U.S. Navy escorts four more reflagged Kuwaiti tankers into the Persian Gulf.

August 22
Naval: Four reflagged Kuwaiti tankers, including the damaged *Bridgeton,* are escorted out of the Persian Gulf by Navy warships.

August 24
Naval: In a sign of rising tension throughout the Persian Gulf, when the destroyer USS *Kidd* is approached by two Iranian dhows, warning shots are fired to force them back. The frigate *Jarrett* also interposes itself between a convoy it is escorting and an approaching Iranian warship.

August 25
Diplomacy: A gathering of the Arab League foreign ministers results in passage of a resolution condemning Iranian occupation of Iraqi territory, denouncing its mine-laying, and calling upon Iran to accept Security Council Resolution 598 and a cease-fire.

In Riyadh, Saudi Arabia, Interior Minister Prince Nayif ibn Abdul Aziz publicly declares that his kingdom hopes that the Iranian people will overthrow the regime that has sent so many of its people to their needless deaths. The Saudi government also doubles its assistance to Iraq, sending them a grant of $2 billion.

Military: According to Western diplomatic sources, Soviet and Afghan forces have all but destroyed the town of Sheikhabad in the Shomali region of Afghanistan.

August 26
Military: North of Kandahar, Afghanistan, mujahideen mortars bombard an Afghan army base for five straight hours.

August 28
Terrorism: Radio Pakistan airs a report suggesting that more than 150 Afghan government officials were killed in a large bomb blast at Jalalabad, Afghanistan.

August 29
Aviation: Iraq ends a 45-day crease-fire when its jets attack Iranian oil installations in the Persian Gulf; a supertanker is set ablaze.

August 30
Politics: In a sign of political thaw in Moscow, Soviet Union, a demonstration is held by military veterans of the Afghan war to highlight both human and social costs of that conflict.

Majlis Speaker Hojatolislam Hashemi Rafsanjani gives another frank interview in the *Tehran Times,* whereby he bemoans the lack of a clear strategy on how to best prosecute and win the war with Iraq. He argues the nation can either resort to complete mobilization of military and population resources to deliver a single crushing blow, or maintain the present war of attrition.

August 31

NAVAL: In The Persian Gulf, Iranian high-speed vessels attack Arab tankers outside the Strait of Hormuz.

September 4

DIPLOMACY: In New York City, the UN Security Council approves a peace mission to Iran and Iraq by Secretary-General Javier Pérez de Cuéllar.

September 4–7

AVIATION: Iran ups the ante in the Persian Gulf by firing one of its Chinese-supplied Silkworm anti-shipping missiles at Kuwaiti targets; however, the missile malfunctions and falls into coastal waters. More missiles are fired over the next three days and strike several targets, whereupon the Kuwaitis expel six of seven Iranian diplomats.

September 5

DIPLOMACY: In a surprising turn of events, Afghan dignitaries request that peace talks in Geneva, Switzerland, be resumed. This is the first time the Communist regime has made such a request, and the governments of Pakistan and the United States anticipate eventual Soviet concessions respecting the withdrawal of all troops from Afghanistan.

September 7

DIPLOMACY: In Geneva, Switzerland, the fourth phase of the seventh round of UN-sponsored peace talks resumes. Special envoy Diego Cordovez is of the opinion that the regime in Kabul, Afghanistan, is prepared to compromise on the date and conditions of any future Soviet troop withdrawal from Afghanistan.

September 7–10

DIPLOMACY: In Geneva, Switzerland, Pakistani foreign minister Shahabzada Yaqub Khan and Afghan foreign minister Abdul Wakil fail to achieve accord over a proposed timetable for a Soviet troop withdrawal. Wakil insists that 16 months are required to effect a complete withdrawal, twice what the Pakistanis are willing to allow.

September 9

AVIATION: In Baghdad, Iraq, the government claims to have avenged the recent missile strike against Kuwait by bombing no fewer than 13 cities, oil facilities, and other targets throughout Iran.

September 10

DIPLOMACY: In Geneva, Switzerland, UN-sponsored peace talks between Afghanistan and Pakistan break off after only four days of discussions. Special envoy Diego Cordovez is disappointed that no agreement has been reached over a timetable for Soviet troop withdrawals but concedes that Kabul has dropped its demand of an 18-month time frame to 16 months, while Islamabad increased its from six months to eight.

In Islamabad, Pakistan, Belgian prime minister Leo Tendemans reiterates his nation's stance that Soviet occupation forces are the root cause of the current problems in Afghanistan.

September 11
DIPLOMACY: In Islamabad, Pakistan, Foreign Minister Shahabzada Yaqub Khan concedes that the latest round of Geneva peace talks have concluded without producing any meaningful concessions by Kabul relative to a Soviet withdrawal.

September 11–15
DIPLOMACY: UN secretary-general Javier Pérez de Cuéllar confers with leaders in both Baghdad, Iraq, and Tehran, Iran, but no diplomatic breakthrough is forthcoming.

September 12
MILITARY: In Faryab Province, Afghanistan, Soviet and Afghan forces capture photographer Alain Guillo, who is then paraded through the streets of Maimana as a warning to local inhabitants. Guillo and a local mujahideen commander had been captured in an ambush arranged by a turncoat working with the KGB and the Afghan secret police.

September 13
AVIATION: In Kunduz Province, Afghanistan, a mujahideen Stinger missile claims another Antonov An-26 transport not far from the provincial airport.

DIPLOMACY: After the Communist regime in Kabul, Afghanistan, resumes diplomatic efforts to improve its international image, both American and Pakistani officials summarize the endeavor as an attempt to acquire legitimacy once Soviet troops have departed.

MILITARY: In southern Kandahar Province, Afghanistan, large numbers of mujahideen fighters from six major resistance groups launch a coordinated ground assault along a 40-mile stretch of highway between Kandahar and Spin Boldak. The rebels eventually overrun six Afghan army posts while also demonstrating their ability to carry out complex military operations.

In Kabul, Afghanistan, the Bakhtar News Agency announces that mujahideen forces fired a number of ground-to-ground missiles on residential areas of Jalalabad.

September 14
MILITARY: In response to mujahideen activities, Soviet forces bulldoze a swath of destruction along the main road running through Kunduz, Badakhshan, and Takhar Provinces, clearing home and vegetation out for a distance of 500 yards from the road.

September 16
MILITARY: French journalist Bertrand Gallet concludes a six-week visit to northern Afghanistan and concludes that mujahideen of the Northern Council under Ahmad Shah Massoud wield effective control of nine provinces. They do so with a unique "four-tier" system that organizes fighters in individual villages, groups of villages,

and entire valleys, with the final and largest tier being field forces that actively seek out and engage Soviet forces. He also claims that Massoud's strategy is to cut off all road transportation between Kabul, the Soviet Union, and Pakistan.

TERRORISM: In Peshawar, Pakistan, Gulbuddin Hekmatyar narrowly escapes death after a pickup truck explodes as his car passes.

September 21

AVIATION: An Army Special Forces MH-6 Little Bird helicopter launched from the frigate USS *Jarrett* attacks and damages the Iranian transport *Iran Ajr* at night while it is caught deploying mines in the Persian Gulf. The vessel is then stormed by SEALs and taken under tow. The crew of 26 Iranians is released shortly afterward, and 10 mines are retrieved; three of the crew are killed. The United States is slowly becoming an active participant in the Iran-Iraq War.

DIPLOMACY: In New York City, President Ronald W. Reagan and Pakistani Prime Minister Mohammad Khan Junejo arrive to address the UN General Assembly. Here Reagan reaffirms his support for Pakistan and the Afghan resistance, and both leaders insist that the immediate removal of all Soviet forces from Afghanistan is essential for any peace process.

September 22

MILITARY: The seventh anniversary of the Iran-Iraq War finds Iran suffering from the effects of an invigorated Iraqi Air Force, which has been built up to 400 combat aircraft, and facing potentially hostile actions from the U.S. Navy in the Persian Gulf.

September 24

DIPLOMACY: In New York City, Prime Minister Mohammad Khan Junejo of Pakistan addresses the UN General Assembly and insists that the current problems in Afghanistan are caused by the presence of foreign forces, that they should depart immediately, and, once they are gone, an agreement on a future Afghan government would be reached quickly.

September 27

DIPLOMACY: In New York City, Pakistani prime minister Mohammad Khan Junejo suggests that the United Nations deploy peacekeeping forces to Afghanistan if and when the Soviets withdraw all their forces.

September 28

MILITARY: In Afghanistan, Western diplomatic sources report that 100 Afghan army troops surrendered to the mujahideen the moment that their convoy was attacked near Ghazni.

September 29

DIPLOMACY: In New York City, Afghan foreign minister Abdul Wakil addresses the UN General Assembly and formally requests that the government of Pakistan and the mujahideen leadership support a broad-based coalition government in Kabul, Afghanistan.

MILITARY: On the Logar Road north of Pul-i-Alam, Afghanistan, mujahideen forces ambush a large Soviet convoy; they claim to have destroyed 20 to 25 armored vehicles.

Reports surface that Soviet forces have redeployed from certain advanced bases because mujahideen air defenses have made resupplying them difficult, if not impossible by air. At this time a large number of Soviet troops are also gathered at Darul Aman military base outside Kabul, Afghanistan.

September 30

DIPLOMACY: In New York City, Afghan foreign minister Abdul Wakil again addresses the UN General Assembly with some stark statistics concerning the war in Afghanistan. In additional to a devastated national economy, he says 2,000 schools, 350 bridges, 131 hospitals, 224 mosques, 258 factories, 50 cultural centers, thousands of trucks, and hundreds of miles of roads and communication lines have been destroyed in the fighting. These numbers, he says, represents three-fourths of the total development investment made in his country over the past five decades. However, Wakil is quick to note that the 3,200 national reconciliation commissions functioning throughout Afghanistan have resulted in the peaceful return of 83,000 refugees, while nearly 30,000 guerrillas have laid down their arms.

In Washington, D.C., Congress suspends military aid to Pakistan for six weeks while reviewing a six-year old waiver exempting that nation from a ban on aid to countries pursuing nuclear weapons. This waiver originated because Pakistan serves as a major base for anti-Soviet guerrillas and the government has cooperated closely with the United States in supplying the guerrillas with arms to fight the Soviets.

POLITICS: In Kabul, Afghanistan, President Mohammad Najib further consolidates his grip on national power by being elected president of the Revolutionary Council. This is part of an ongoing purge of Babrak Karmal supporters, including Mahmoud Baryalay and Anahita Ratebzad.

October 1

POLITICS: In Kabul, Afghanistan, President Mohammad Najib, in a nod to mounting Muslim fundamentalism, reverts back to the Islamic form of his name; Najibullah.

October 2

POLITICS: In Faryab Province, Afghanistan, a 5,000-man opposition group led by Abdul Rasul Pahlawan accepts national reconciliation and lays down its arms.

October 3

NAVAL: Near Farsi Island in the Persian Gulf, the Iranians stage naval exercises with their armed speedboats. Their potential for mischief attracts several U.S. Navy vessels, which begin patrolling the area.

October 5

AVIATION: In a bid to increase pressure on Iran, Iraqi warplanes strike at Iranian oil facilities on distant Larak Island, damaging three tankers.

October 8

AVIATION: In the Persian Gulf, an Army MH-6 Little Bird helicopter attacks a group of four Iranian speedboats after one of their number shoots at it. Three boats are sunk, two Iranians are captured, and two die of their wounds.

NAVAL: The U.S.-owned tanker *Sungari*, under the Liberian flag, is struck by an Iranian Silkworm missile in the Persian Gulf near Kuwait.

TERRORISM: In the Shahr-i-Nau section of Kabul, Afghanistan, a large car bomb explodes, killing 27 people and wounding more than 30. This is also reputedly the largest such explosive device detonated in a car to date.

October 10
POLITICS: In Kabul, Afghanistan, President Mohammad Najibullah announces that his government is willing to pay mujahideen fighters to turn over their weapons.

October 11
MILITARY: In Paghman, Afghanistan, a Soviet/Afghan army ambush takes the life of Lee Shapiro and James Lindelof, two members of an American television team, along with two Hezb-i-Islami escorts. The team had been active in the region for five months prior to their deaths.

October 12
DIPLOMACY: In Karachi, Pakistan, Soviet ambassador Abdul-Rahman Vezirov addresses the Pakistan Institute of International Affairs and insists that, while his government is serious about withdrawing its "limited contingent" from Afghanistan, it will only do so on a condition of absolute noninterference in that nation's internal affairs.

A tanker convoy in the Persian Gulf composed of the guided-missile frigate USS *Hawes*, the reflagged tanker GAS *King*, and the guided missile cruiser USS *William H. Standley (Department of Defense)*

October 13

AVIATION: In Islamabad, Pakistan, Hezb-i-Islami leader Yunnis Khalis denies to the Kuwait News Agency that two of his mujahideen commanders recently sold 16 advanced Stinger missiles to the Iranian government for $1 million.`

In Baghdad, Iraq, an Iranian surface-to-surface missile explodes near a school, killing 32 children and wounding 218 en route to class.

October 15

DIPLOMACY: In New York City, the Soviet Union elects to back the UN secretary-general's plan to implement Resolution 598, which includes an Iranian demand to found an impartial commission to establish war guilt, and an Iraqi demand that a troop withdrawal occur immediately after a cease-fire is implemented.

October 16

DIPLOMACY: In light of the latest Iranian attack an neutral shipping, the governments of Kuwait and Saudi Arabia urge the United States to take firm, retaliatory action against Iran lest it be emboldened to take more drastic measures. President Ronald W. Reagan, deciding that the bombing of Iranian oil facilities on the mainland or the elimination of Iranian Silkworm sites on the Fao Peninsula and near the Strait of Hormuz too provocative—and potentially costly in terms of American lives—settles upon destroying several offshore facilities.

NAVAL: In the Persian Gulf, an Iranian battery on the Fao Peninsula fires a Chinese-supplied Silkworm missile at the American-reflagged Kuwaiti tanker *Sea Isle City,* then anchored in Kuwaiti waters, damaging it and wounding 18 seamen.

October 17

POLITICS: In Peshawar, Pakistan, Yunnis Khalis is elected chairman of the mujahideen alliance. In new rules recently adopted, he will serve for one year. Resistance leaders also reiterate that peace is not possible as long as Soviet troops occupy the country, and, furthermore, they will not enter into a coalition arrangement with any government containing Communists.

October 18

POLITICS: In Kabul, Afghanistan, 15 politicians with close political ties to former president Babrak Karmal are dismissed from office.

October 19

DIPLOMACY: In Tehran, Iran, the government admits that the loss of two offshore platforms costs $500 million and denounce the act as a violation of its sovereignty. Moreover, it vows that retaliation will be swift.

NAVAL: In the Persian Gulf, the guided-missile destroyers USS *Hoel* and *Kidd,* and the destroyers USS *John Young* and *Leftwich,* attack two older Iranian oil platforms at Resalat and Reshadat in retaliation for missile attacks against neutral shipping. No casualties are reported. The platforms had been rigged for military purposes and were singled-out for destruction. However, the Navy fired more than 1,000 high-explosive rounds into the platform and it refused to collapse, so a demolition team was sent over to complete the task.

POLITICS: In Kabul, Afghanistan, President Mohammad Najibullah goes on national radio for three hours to push for his plan of national reconciliation. He also makes it clear that only the PDPA will decide who will be allowed to join the coalition and in what capacity.

October 21
POLITICS: In Kabul, Afghanistan, the PDPA concludes its national conference, at which point mass arrests of politicians loyal to dismissed president Babrak Karmal occur. Rumors surface that no fewer than 2,000 party members have been expelled.

October 22
AVIATION: An Iranian Silkworm missile crashes into Kuwait's Sea Island oil terminal, 10 miles offshore from the port of Mina Ahmadi.

DIPLOMACY: Because China supplied Silkworm missiles to Iran, President Ronald W. Reagan announces restrictions on high-tech exports to China. The Chinese government still denies all allegations of selling missiles to Iran.

October 23
MILITARY: In light of the ongoing military crisis, the regime in Kabul, Afghanistan, reinstitutes conscription for all males age 16 or older. Moreover, government and KHAD officials will visit schools and conscript students directly from classrooms.

POLITICS: Reports surface that Siditqullah, youngest brother of President Mohammad Najibullah, has defected to the Afghan resistance in the Panjshir Valley. Apparently, he had been threatened by Najibullah for harboring "unorthodox" views on national matters.

October 24
POLITICS: In Tehran, Iran, a new alliance of seven Afghan Shiite mujahideen groups is announced.

October 26
DIPLOMACY: In Washington, D.C., President Ronald W. Reagan announces a near-complete ban on all Iranian exports, including oil.

October 27
DIPLOMACY: Marek Slewinski of the University of Geneva and Ijaz Gilani of Gallup Pakistan release a preliminary survey of Afghan refugees and conclude that no fewer than 1.5 million have been killed, injured, or incapacitated since communists came to power following the Saur Revolution of 1978. This is 9 percent of the entire Afghan population, or one in every 11 family members.

POLITICS: In Kabul, Afghanistan, Western diplomatic sources confirm that their East European counterparts told them that upwards of 2,000 PDPA politicians face expulsion from the party based on their prior associations. Others will be forced from office if they fail to sign a loyalty oath to the government and abandon factionalism.

October 29
MILITARY: In Badakhshan Province, Afghanistan, mujahideen under Ahmad Shah Massoud storm the Afghan military police garrison at Keran.

October 30

POLITICS: In Kabul, Afghanistan, the Revolutionary Council decrees an amnesty for all Afghan refugees and invites them to come home without recrimination. Those returnees subject to conscription will have a six-month grace period, during which they are free to depart the country.

October 31

DIPLOMACY: At Kabul, Afghanistan, President Mohammed Najibullah departs for Moscow for celebrations marking the 70th anniversary of the October Revolution.

November 1

DIPLOMACY: In New York City, the UN General Assembly adopts a resolution demanding the immediate withdrawal of foreign forces from Afghanistan. This is the ninth passage of such legislation and it passes on a vote of 123 to 19 with 11 abstentions, its largest margin to date. Apparently, intense lobbying by the Soviet Union and Afghanistan failed to sway many votes.

November 3

AVIATION: At Kabul, Afghanistan, mujahideen rocket fire destroys two government helicopters and three military aircraft at the national airport.

November 5

POLITICS: In New York City, Afghan resistance leader Yunnis Khalis holds a news conference at the United Nations and rejects attempts at national reconciliation out of hand. He also denounces peace negotiations held under UN auspices between Afghanistan and Pakistan and insists that the resistance will only deal directly with the Soviet Union.

November 8

AVIATION: In Paktia Province, Afghanistan, mujahideen rocket fire destroys two helicopters and one large transport at Khost military base.

November 8–11

DIPLOMACY: In Amman, Jordan, 16 heads of state from the Arab League formally back Iraq in its struggle with Iran. King Hussein warns delegates that Iran's aggressive expansionism threatens the existing Arabic order. In a major turnaround, the government of Syria, heretofore a supporter of Iran, reverses positions and now supports Iraq. This shift is largely due to the fact that the Syrian economy was in the doldrums and the Saudis, who oppose Iran, have been providing financial support. All delegates present demand that Iran accept Security Council Resolution 598 and an immediate cease-fire; Iran refuses.

November 9

DIPLOMACY: In New York City, Pakistani minister of foreign affairs Zain Noorani opens the UN General Assembly's ninth debate over Afghanistan. He reiterates that the presence of "foreign military forces is the root cause of conflict in that nation."

November 10
DIPLOMACY: In New York City, U.S. Ambassador Herbert Okun addresses the UN General Assembly and challenges the Soviet Union "to match its words with deeds" and speedily withdraw all forces from Afghanistan. He states that adoption of a short timetable for removing troops would demonstrate genuine desire to end the Afghan crisis.

POLITICS: In Kabul, Afghanistan, the Revolutionary Council Presidium endorses a decree encouraging the formation and registration of new political parties.

November 12
DIPLOMACY: In Washington, D.C., President Ronald W. Reagan confers with Afghan resistance leaders. Presently, there are signs of mounting pressure for the mujahideen to make concessions and facilitate a Soviet withdrawal. However, Reagan assures resistance leader Yunnis Khalis that as long as Soviet troops remain in Afghanistan, American military assistance will be strengthened, not slackened.

November 13
DIPLOMACY: In Washington, D.C., a State Department spokesman says that morale among the Afghan resistance is at an "all time high" and that it appears the Soviets have suffered major setbacks of late. Moreover, the mujahideen have performed very well throughout 1987 and are expected to carry that performance level well into 1988. He further says that the recent visit to the United Nations by Afghan leaders is significant seeing since they were headed by an elected leader, Yunnis Khalis.

POLITICS: In Tehran, Iran, Majlis speaker Hojatolislam Hashemi Rafsanjani declares that another "Karbala-style" offensive would take events into unknown regions. The Iraqis are sufficiently spooked into placing all units along the Iranian border on high alert.

November 15
DIPLOMACY: In Italy, former Afghan monarch Mohammad Zahir Shah declares that the current crisis in Afghanistan can only be achieved by direct negotiations between the mujahideen leadership and the Soviet Union. Moreover, he insists that the present regime in Kabul is not legitimate and should expect to share power after the Soviets have departed.

MILITARY: In Paktia Province, Afghanistan, 130 Afghan army troops defect to Hezb-i-Islami forces under Nizamuddin Haqqani.

November 16
NAVAL: In the Persian Gulf, Iranian gunboats attack three tankers conveying Saudi oil. However, bowing to pressure from Syria, they refrain from striking Kuwaiti targets.

November 17
AVIATION: In Washington, D.C., an analyst for the Rand Corporation states that the Soviets have lost 300 military aircraft over the previous year, representing a loss of $2.5 billion. When the expenses of training and equipping flight personnel are factored in, this represents a considerable financial burden for the Soviet economy.

DIPLOMACY: In New York City, Afghan foreign minister Abdul Wakil addresses the UN General Assembly and claims that 90,000 Afghan refugees have returned home from Iran and Pakistan under the government amnesty. Moreover, 30,000 fighters representing 174 armed groups have also laid down their arms.

MILITARY: Eager to keep the Iraqis unbalanced, the Iranians commit several localized offensives in the central sector while renewing their prolonged artillery bombardment of Basra. That city, having been struck by 61,979 shells, has had 90 percent of all dwellings damaged or destroyed.

November 18

DIPLOMACY: An upswing in activity by Soviet diplomats seems indicative of a new willingness to compromise on fixed timetables for the removal of all troops from Afghanistan.

In Washington, D.C., an independent group of six jurists releases a report that forcefully accuses the Soviet Union and the Afghan government of gross human-rights violations and says that the implementation of national reconciliation has done little to ameliorate such transgressions. It also estimates that 10,000 refugees arrive in Pakistan every month.

MILITARY: In Badakhshan Province, Afghanistan, mujahideen loyal to Ahmad Shah Massoud attack and capture the Soviet/Afghan army base at Tappeh-i-Khana. They take several hundred prisoners, including some Soviet advisers. Elimination of this stronghold eliminates a two-week, roundabout detour through the mountains in favor of a two-day passage across open country.

November 19–January 1988

MILITARY: In Paktia Province, Afghanistan, Operation Magistral commences as several divisions of the Soviet army and Afghan forces drive down the road from Gardez to Khost in order to lift the mujahideen siege of the latter. By November 28, the Afghan troops have cleared the base of the Shabek Khel Valley while flanking forces have entered the nearby Kanai Valley. Resistance forces continue falling back before them, counterattacking at night where possible.

November 22

POLITICS: Throughout the Soviet Union, veterans of the Afghan war form a national organization to assist other veterans of that conflict who are being neglected by the government. They also have obtained permission to use public funds to construct the first war memorial to those who have fallen. Western analysts estimate that roughly half-a-million Soviet soldiers have served in Afghanistan, and 12,000 have been killed in combat there.

November 24

MILITARY: In the wake of a failed offensive against the Afghan resistance, Lieutenant General Mohammad Nabi Azimi commits suicide.

November 25

MILITARY: In Herat Province, Afghanistan, Ahmad Abbas and 300 of his fighters surrender to government authorities as part of national reconciliation.

November 27

POLITICS: In Afghanistan, mujahideen loyal to Ahmad Shah Massoud confirm the defection of Siditqullah, younger brother of President Mohammad Najibullah.

November 28

DIPLOMACY: In New York City, the UN General Assembly votes to condemn human-rights violations and atrocities committed by Soviet forces and Afghan army troops.

MILITARY: In Jowzjan Province, Afghanistan, mujahideen fighters capture the Afghan army garrison at Sangcharak. They also claim to have shot down one jet and destroyed seven tanks.

POLITICS: Afghan rebel leader Samruddin directs 650 of his fighters to lay down their arms and participate in the government's national reconciliation program.

November 28–29

MILITARY: In Paktia Province, Afghanistan, Soviet general Boris V. Gromov orders an attack upon mujahideen forces holding the strategic Satukandav Pass between Kabul and Khost. Dummy paratroopers are dropped in the area, whereupon the resistance units fire upon them, revealing their positions to concentrated Soviet air strikes and artillery bombardments. However, a ground assault by a motorized rifle regiment is rebuffed, and the Soviets withdraw.

November 29

DIPLOMACY: Rumors abound that the Soviet Union is eager to find a way out of Afghanistan, especially since U.S. supplied Stinger missiles have largely neutralized their helicopter gunships, the best available weapon for combating the mujahideen. Analysts anticipate that General Secretary Mikhail Gorbachev might offer a 12-month timetable for withdrawing troops at the upcoming summit with President Ronald W. Reagan.

POLITICS: In Kabul, Afghanistan, the government officially summons a Loya Jirga (tribal assembly) to approve a new constitution.

November 29–30

DIPLOMACY: Pakistani president Zia al-Haq tells the *London Sunday Telegraph* that an international presence in Afghanistan is essential to making sure that the Soviets are withdrawing their forces as promised and preventing the clandestine return of any such forces. He further suggests that the composition of an interim government should consist of equal parts from the rebels, the refugees, and the present regime.

MILITARY: President Mohammad Najibullah admits that the important city of Khost, Paktia Province, Afghanistan, is besieged by mujahideen fighters. The Soviets are flying in 50 tons of food every night to keep the population of 40,000 adequately fed.

POLITICS: In Kabul, Afghanistan, a *loya jirga* (tribal assembly) convenes on the campus of the Polytechnic Institute. The 1,860 delegates have been summoned from around the country to approve a new constitution, which officially invokes "Allah, the Bountiful, the Merciful" in its preamble. However, as President Mohammad Najibullah rises to address the gathering, he is interrupted by the sound of rockets fired by nearby mujahideen units. Military aircraft circling the capital are heard for the remainder of his presentation. Nonetheless, Najibullah is elected president under the "Islamized" constitution, which still gives him considerable powers.

November 30

MILITARY: In Paktia Province, Afghanistan, 900 Afghan commandos are helicoptered into the Shabek Khel Valley and engage mujahideen forces still lurking there. Both sides suffer heavy losses as the drive to relieve Khost continues.

POLITICS: During the recent session of the *loya jirga* (tribal assembly), President Mohammad Najibullah introduces a new constitution to legitimize his crumbling regime. The assembly ratifies the document, which reaffirms him as president of the Republic of Afghanistan. Najibullah also proposes a 12-month timetable for the withdrawal of all Soviet troops from the country, noting that this suggestion has already been "negotiated" with Moscow.

TERRORISM: In Kabul, Afghanistan, General Esmat Muslim, a former resistance leader, attempts to shoot his way through a police cordon at the Polytechnic Institute. He dies in a hail of bullets and a further 20 people are killed or wounded.

December 1

DIPLOMACY: In Washington, D.C., President Ronald W. Reagan states that he will insist to General Secretary Mikhail Gorbachev that the time has come for the Soviets to set a firm timetable for the withdrawal of all forces from Afghanistan. The two are slated to meet at an upcoming summit.

MILITARY: In Paktia Province, Afghanistan, General Boris V. Gromov orders another assault against Satukandav Pass with an airborne battalion and Afghan army commandos, which seize the high ground above the pass. The local mujahideen units are taken by surprise and hastily retreat, abandoning heavy equipment and supplies.

POLITICS: In Kabul, Afghanistan, President Mohammad Najibullah announces that captured French journalist Alain Guillo faces trial by an Afghan tribunal for having illegally entered the country and performed "illegal activities." Najibullah also confirms the recent defection of his younger brother Siditqullah.

December 2

DIPLOMACY: In Washington, D.C., an administration spokesman dismisses President Mohammad Najibullah's withdrawal proposal as "inadequate."

December 4

DIPLOMACY: The director of the Soviet Institute of World Economic and International Relations, a chief adviser to General Secretary Mikhail Gorbachev, informs the news media that he fully expects the Soviet government to withdraw all its forces from Afghanistan sometime in 1988.

December 5

DIPLOMACY: In Washington, D.C., the State Department declares that the upcoming summit between President Ronald W. Reagan and General Secretary Mikhail Gorbachev is essential for defining the terms and conditions of a Soviet pullout from Afghanistan.

December 6

POLITICS: In Peshawar, Pakistan, Chairman Yunnis Khalis of the mujahideen alliance states that entering a coalition government with Afghan communists, as proposed by President Zia ul-Haq of Pakistan, is tantamount to accepting communism and betraying thousands of Afghan martyrs. Therefore he adamantly refuses to do so.

December 7

DIPLOMACY: General Secretary Mikhail Gorbachev arrives in the United States, the first Soviet head of state to call in 14 years. During his three-day summit with President Ronald W. Reagan, the two men will map out proposals for arms reductions and the removal of Soviet troops from Afghanistan.

MILITARY: In Herat Province, Afghanistan, mujahideen leader Abdul Rahman orders his 600 fighters to lay down their weapons as part of the government's national reconciliation program.

Afghan resistance activity halts all road traffic along the Kabul-Torkham highway while heavy fighting is also reported at Dakka, Kama Daka, Monau, and Nazian.

December 8

DIPLOMACY: In Paris, France, Professor Marek Slewinski of the University of Geneva addresses the Senate about his year-long demographic study of conditions in Afghanistan. He calculates that a decade of war has cost 1.2 million Afghan lives,

Iranian command-and-control platforms on fire after being shelled by four U.S. Navy destroyers in response to a recent Iranian missile attack on a Kuwaiti super tanker *(Department of Defense)*

nearly 10 percent of the population. This amount exceeds the percentage of Soviets killed during World War II.

December 9

MILITARY: The German newspaper *Die Welt* reports that the Soviets have introduced new types of weapons in the northern provinces of Afghanistan, despite the government's cease-fire and talk of national reconciliation. The fighting is apparently so intense that Soviet villagers on the opposite side of the Amu Darya River have been evacuated from the border.

December 10

DIPLOMACY: In Washington, D.C., General Secretary Mikhail Gorbachev proposes a 12-month timetable for the withdrawal of Soviet troops from Afghanistan, which the Americans reject as inadequate. At this juncture, the three-day summit concludes without any major agreement on ending the Afghan problem.

UN special envoy Diego Cordovez initiates talks with former Afghan king Mohammad Zahir Shah on the formation of a transitional coalition government.

December 10–31

AVIATION: To sustain the surrounded garrison in Khost, Afghanistan, the Red Air Force is directing 20 military transports to make daily flights there.

MILITARY: Several thousand Soviet and Afghan forces begin a concerted drive to relieve the siege of Khost, Afghanistan. On December 27, Radio Kabul declares that the siege has been broken and that a truck convoy made it inside the city. A resistance spokesman declares that the main roads in and out of Khost are still under their control and that the Soviets were forced to use a little-known subsidiary route. By year's end, television footage is aired to prove that the battle is still raging there over the winter months and that the garrison still has to be resupplied by air.

December 12

NAVAL: In the Persian Gulf, the destroyer USS *Chandler* deploys its helicopters to evacuate 11 crew from the sinking Cypriot tanker *Pivot* after it is attacked by Iranian speedboats.

December 14

DIPLOMACY: In Washington, D.C., Robert Peck, deputy assistant secretary of state for Near Eastern and South Asian affairs, declares that the United Nations entertains high hopes that 1988 will be the year that Soviet forces are withdrawn from Afghanistan.

December 15

DIPLOMACY: In Washington, D.C., government officials reflect on the recent failure of the Reagan/Gorbachev summit and conclude that a tough stance by the United States will result in greater compromises from Moscow on the time and manner of a Soviet troop withdrawal.

December 19

MILITARY: In Badghis Province, Afghanistan, mujahideen fighters attack a Soviet convoy entering the country from Marsik across the border. Through the use of heavy weapons, the rebels destroy seven tanks and 11 trucks. In retaliation, Soviet jets and helicopters bomb and strafe nearby villages on the following day. Word of this action does not filter out until the following January 14.

December 20

MILITARY: In southeastern Afghanistan, Afghan army troops begin an offensive against an estimated 9,000 mujahideen operating there.

December 21

DIPLOMACY: In Washington, D.C., Under Secretary of State for Political Affairs Michael Armacost mentions that the United States hopes that the upcoming Geneva talks on Afghanistan in February will be the last. He also mentions that General Secretary Mikhail Gorbachev recently proposed to have Soviet forces refrain from combat operations throughout any period that a troop withdrawal is agreed upon.

December 22

AVIATION: In Parvan Province, Afghanistan, a mujahideen Stinger missile downs a large transport aircraft.

December 24

MILITARY: Soviet news sources are quoted as reporting that 1,500 Afghan rebels were killed or wounded in the recent struggle for Khost.

In Baghlan Province, Afghanistan, resistance fighters capture the military garrison at Burka. Among the materiel captured are two tanks, three mortars, eight heavy machine guns, 60 light weapons, and much ammunition. Both sides incur heavy losses.

In Parvan Province, Afghanistan, mujahideen forces unleash rockets against Bagram Air Base.

December 25

MILITARY: In Peshawar, Pakistan, mujahideen alliance spokesmen deny the Soviet claim of heavy losses in the struggle for Khost, Afghanistan.

NAVAL: In the Persian Gulf, the frigates USS *Elrod* and HMS *Scylla* use helicopters to rescue 20 crewmen from the South Korea-flagged tanker *Hyundai* after it was attacked by an Iranian frigate.

December 26

DIPLOMACY: In New York City, the UN General Assembly again votes to condemn the Soviet occupation of Afghanistan.

MILITARY: In Kapisa Province, Afghanistan, mujahideen fighters loyal to Ahmad Shah Massoud capture the army garrison at Shaba, outside Kabul. Their haul includes three tanks, 14 heavy and light machine guns, more than 100 AK-47 assault rifles, radios, and ammunition. In related operations, the resistance also overruns outposts in Manjawoon, Parandeh, and Hesai Doo, along with a Soviet communications center at Anaba.

POLITICS: In Kabul, Afghanistan, government radio announces that 13 armed groups from four tribes in Ghazni Province have laid down their arms in favor of national reconciliation. It says that 6,000 fighters laid down their arms in 728 villages.

December 27

AVIATION: A mujahideen Stinger missile downs a MiG fighter near Kabul, Afghanistan.

MILITARY: Afghan resistance fighters launch continuing hit-and-run raids against military installations at Kabul, Khairkhana, and Mirbachakot, Afghanistan.

In Parvan Province, Afghanistan, mujahideen forces launch another rocket attack against government aircraft parked at Bagram Air Base.

In Logar Province, Afghanistan, a large Soviet convoy of 400 vehicles, escorted by eight helicopter gunships, is struck by mujahideen fighters near Kalingar. Several tanks and oil tankers are reported destroyed.

POLITICS: In Moscow and Leningrad, Soviet Union, antiwar demonstrations protesting the war in Afghanistan are broken up by riot police.

December 28

MILITARY: In Parvan Province, Afghanistan, Afghan resistance fighters stage another rocket attack against Bagram Air Base and a number of security posts surrounding it. Soviet aircraft counter by flattening villages around Bagram.

In Wardak Province, Afghanistan, mujahideen fighters strike a military convoy moving down the Kabul-Kandahar highway.

POLITICS: Throughout Pakistan, thousands of Afghan refugees hold demonstrations and rallies to protest the Soviet occupation of Afghanistan.

December 29

DIPLOMACY: In Washington, D.C., a government spokesman charges the Soviet Union with mounting a winter offensive in Afghanistan rather than working toward a withdrawal.

MILITARY: Mujahideen fighters use surface-to-surface missiles to strike a military base at Grishik along the Kandahar-Kabul highway, Afghanistan.

December 30–31

MILITARY: Near Khost, Afghanistan, Soviet and Afghan army troops wage a major offensive against nearby resistance units. At least 155 government trucks then roll into the city, bringing food and other provisions to the garrison and the populace. Because talks about a troop withdrawal are intensifying at the international level, both sides are intent on seizing as much favorable territory before a settlement is agreed upon. This action also concludes Operation Magistral, which was the biggest Soviet land victory of the war, but it occurred far too late to change the outcome of events.

1988

January 1

AVIATION: A major Soviet offensive to clear the Gardez-Khost highway involves 60 military aircraft in various support roles.

A rebel bombardment of Bagram Air Base in Parvan Province, Afghanistan, destroys or damages three parked Soviet warplanes.

In Kapisa Province, Afghanistan, a mujahideen Stinger missile brings down a Soviet Su-25 ground-support aircraft.

DIPLOMACY: In Washington, D.C., Secretary of State George Shultz states that the Americans seek a firm Soviet schedule for withdrawing troops from Afghanistan. Moreover, such a schedule would have to be "front-end loaded," remove the bulk of combat forces as soon as possible, and not be slowed or stopped once begun.

MILITARY: Throughout Paktia Province, Afghanistan, a force of 30,000 Soviet and Afghan forces conducts a month-long offensive to clear the strategic Gardez-Khost highway of an estimated 5,000 mujahideen fighters. This is undertaken to relieve the Khost garrison from a lengthy siege by the resistance. Casualties on both sides throughout this operation are believed to be extremely heavy as the terrain is rugged and the resistance fanatical.

In Herat Province, Afghanistan, reports surface that Afghan rebels destroyed nine Soviet tanks and armored personnel carriers. The Soviets retaliated with heavy air raids against the Pashtoon and Zarghoon districts.

January 2

DIPLOMACY: The government of Saudi Arabia pledges to end its support of the Afghan resistance and says it would coordinate its oil policy with the Soviet Union should Soviet forces be withdrawn from Afghanistan.

MILITARY: Afghan mujahideen attack an army position within Herat city, claiming its destruction along with six tanks, five personnel carriers, three jeeps, and nine trucks.

Mujahideen fighters claim to have captured an Afghan army outpost in the Panjshir Valley northeast of Kabul, Afghanistan. This represents their first successful action here in two years and may have been undertaken to divert Soviet attention from the ongoing struggle near Khost.

January 3

DIPLOMACY: In Washington, D.C., President Ronald W. Reagan sends a message to the chairman of the Islamic Alliance of the Afghan Mujahideen, pledging unstinting military and political support for as long as Soviet forces occupy their country.

MILITARY: In Badakhshan Province, Afghanistan, which borders the Soviet Union, mujahideen fighters shell the capital of Faizabad and put the local airport out of commission for a week. In retaliation, Soviet jets bomb the surrounding suburbs and destroy numerous houses.

A report surfaces on Radio Tehran that Afghan government forces are abandoning their attempt to recapture the Zerkoh region of Farah Province, Afghanistan, from mujahideen forces. Apparently, their month-long offensive cost them hundreds of casualties along with 25 tanks and other vehicles. It also mentions that resistance fighters have overrun nine military posts in the province and taken 180 military deserters into their ranks.

In Bamiyan Province, Afghanistan, mujahideen fire rockets at a Soviet encampment as forces were celebrating the anniversary of the Afghan occupation.

January 4

AVIATION: In Paktia Province, Afghanistan, mujahideen Stinger missiles shoot down two MiG aircraft over the Sarobi and Shamal areas. Another warplane is apparently downed over the rebel center at Jehad Wal.

In Laghman Province, Afghanistan, mujahideen fighters destroy two military helicopters near Mehtarlam, one of which was attacking their position.

MILITARY: A report surfaces on Agence France-Presse that 1,500 mujahideen are attacking key Soviet and Afghan positions near strategic Herat, Afghanistan. Moreover, the garrison at Ghurian, 30 miles west of Herat, is reportedly surrounded and has lacked an airlift of supplies for the past four months.

In Kabul Province, Afghanistan, mujahideen fighters launch rockets against government and Soviet installations in the capital, along with security posts at Qila Rustan, Goga Manda, and Yousaf Khel nearby.

January 5

DIPLOMACY: In Kabul, Afghanistan, President Mohammad Najibullah confers with Soviet foreign minister Eduard Shevardnadze about the ongoing crisis and the national reconciliation program.

MILITARY: Mujahideen fighters attack a Soviet convoy proceeding down the Gardez-Kabul highway, forcing it to return to the capital.

January 6

DIPLOMACY: In Kabul, Afghanistan, Soviet foreign minister Eduard Shevardnadze concludes three days of talks then flies back to Moscow. Before departing he declares that 1988 will be the last year of Soviet occupation and that an impending withdrawal is not contingent upon a favorable political settlement beforehand. However, he links all troop withdrawals to an end of U.S. aid to the Afghan resistance.

In Islamabad, Pakistan, Under Secretary of State Michael Armacost confers with members of the Afghan alliance; representatives from all seven mujahideen groups are in attendance.

January 7

AVIATION: In Kandahar Province, mujahideen Stinger missiles bring down two Soviet helicopters while a rocket attack on the local airport destroys a military aircraft. Another large transport aircraft is apparently destroyed north of Kabul.

In Parvan Province, Afghanistan, Afghan rebels attack Bagram Air Base with rockets, destroying eight aircraft and helicopters parked on the ground.

DIPLOMACY: In Washington, D.C., Secretary of State George Shultz declares that the United States might be willing to suspend military aid to the mujahideen once a Soviet withdrawal commences. However, he insists that, once begun, the withdrawal cannot be halted.

In Moscow, Soviet Union, Foreign Minister Yuri Alekseyev states that all Soviet troops will probably be removed from Afghanistan by the end of the year, and it is not contingent upon formation of a coalition or transitional government. He also mentions that American willingness to halt aid to the guerrillas is essential to any Soviet withdrawal.

MILITARY: In Logar Province, mujahideen fighters intercept all traffic along the main highway between Kolangar and Gardez for three days before being driven off.

January 7–8

MILITARY: In Khost Province, Afghanistan, a company of the 345th Independent Guards Airborne Regiment assumes dug in, defensive positions on Hill 3234. Here they are attacked by approximately 400 mujahideen commanded by Jalaluddin Haqqani over the next two days. Assisted by artillery fire, the badly outnumbered Soviets beat off continual attacks, with 34 out of 39 men becoming casualties, including six dead. All receive the Order of the Red Banner and the Order of the Red Star. Mujahideen losses are estimated at 200 dead and injured.

January 8

DIPLOMACY: In Washington, D.C., Secretary of State George Shultz states that a final Afghan agreement will probably entail the withdrawal of Soviet troops, an end to U.S. military aid to the resistance, and an end to Soviet military assistance to the Kabul regime. Moreover, he considers a neutral, nonaligned Afghanistan the goal for both nations.

Western analysts believe that Moscow's recent offer to withdraw troops, whether or not a friendly government is installed in Kabul, Afghanistan, is a tacit admission that military victory eludes them.

MILITARY: Western military analysts predict the speedy disintegration of the Afghan national army once the Soviets withdraw their troops and support.

In Paktia Province, Afghanistan, mujahideen fighters destroy 16 Afghan army outposts in the Shamal, Sarobi, and Zadran regions. Rocket attacks are also launched at Soviet and Afghan bases at Khal, Basat, Ali Shero, and Tarigai.

In Ghazni Province, Afghanistan, mujahideen units operating along the Kandahar-Kabul highway destroy an Afghan army headquarters at Moqar, along with five tanks and other vehicles.

January 9

MILITARY: In Afghanistan, mujahideen fighters attack a Soviet convoy on the Herat-Islamqila highway, destroying 20 personnel carriers.

At Takhseerak, Afghanistan, 17 Afghan army troops defect to the resistance, bringing along a truck loaded with guns and ammunition.

POLITICS: In light of an impending Soviet troop withdrawal, members of the Afghan government grow concerned for their safety, so the Soviet government issues them special identity cards to facilitate their speedy evacuation if necessary.

January 10

DIPLOMACY: In Washington, D.C., an administration spokesman voices skepticism over the Soviet Union's pledge to remove its forces from Afghanistan in 1988.

In Hanoi, Vietnam, Afghan president Mohammad Najibullah declares that the Soviet Union might embrace a broad policy for ending many conflicts in the developing world, especially Vietnam and Afghanistan.

MILITARY: In Konar Province, Afghanistan, large numbers of Soviet and Afghan forces begin massing near Asadabad and Asmar, apparently in preparation for an offensive aimed at rescuing the trapped garrison at Barikot. The road leading through the mountains to that destination has been blocked by the Afghan resistance for the past eight years.

In Faryab Province, Afghanistan, Afghan rebels attack the capital of Maimana with mortars, prompting 200 Afghan soldiers to defect with their weapons and ammunition.

January 12

MILITARY: At Asadabad, Konar Province, Afghanistan, heavy fighting is reported between Soviet-Afghan forces and mujahideen fighters, with casualties on both sides. The Soviets employ at least 10 helicopters to evacuate their wounded while 800 rockets rain down upon the provincial capital, destroying an ammunition dump and an oil reservoir.

A reports on Voice of America says that sporadic fighting continues in and around Kabul, Afghanistan, with several rocket attacks being carried out over the past four days. Violence at Shakardara and Guldara north of the capital has also resulted in an influx of new refugees into the city.

Western diplomats confirm recent reports that mujahideen activity has stopped all traffic along the highway between Kabul and Gardez in Logar Province. This fighting is apparently directed at government attempts to send reinforcements to the garrison of Khost, 69 miles distant.

POLITICS: In Peshawar, Pakistan, unity among the mujahideen alliance begins splintering as the Soviets dangle the prospect of a troop withdrawal. Heated debate also ensues over the potential role of former monarch Mohammad Zahir Shah in a future government.

In Moscow, Soviet Union, the party paper *Pravda* states that troops could begin departing Afghanistan as early as May should an agreement be reached in early March.

January 13

DIPLOMACY: In Islamabad, Pakistan, President Zia ul-Haq and Prime Minister Mohammad Khan Junejo state that present members of the pro-Soviet regime in Kabul, Afghanistan, should be allowed to participate in a successor government following the Soviet withdrawal. They profess the belief that the Soviets will not withdraw if it means leaving behind a hostile government in place. This position differs sharply from that held by the United States and the Afghan alliance.

January 14

MILITARY: In Paktia Province, Afghanistan, heavy fighting continues outside the strategic town of Khost. Moreover, the mujahideen have taken up positions along nearby mountaintops, from which they continually shell the airport. Soviet convoys traveling along the Gardez-Khost highway are also subject to repeated ambushes.

Radio Kabul announces that Soviet and Afghan army forces have broken the siege of Khost, Afghanistan, in which retreating mujahideen units abandoned tons of heavy weapons such as rocket launchers and recoilless rifles. No sooner do government forces reoccupy the city than rebel units launch rockets from neighboring mountaintops.

January 15

AVIATION: Soviet and Afghan air force jets attack and destroy a village near Delarm, Farah Province, Afghanistan, following an attack against Soviet commandoes there. Reputedly the entire town is leveled.

DIPLOMACY: A report in the *Kabul New Times* notes that Soviet general secretary Mikhail Gorbachev has met with U.S. industrialist Armand Hammer in Moscow, in which Hammer declared that the American government is awaiting a goodwill gesture from the Soviets, such as the commencement of a troop withdrawal. Gorbachev counters that such a withdrawal is only possible if linked to an end to outside interference, namely, American military aid to the Afghan resistance.

In Washington, D.C., the administration expresses bewilderment over recent Pakistani statements inferring that Communists should be part of any future Afghan government as a precondition for a Soviet troop withdrawal. Not only does the United States reject such a view, but it also refuses to impose it upon the Afghan resistance.

MILITARY: In Jowzjan Province, Afghanistan, mujahideen fighters damage a stretch of natural gas pipelines near Qarquin along the Amu Darya River.

In Faryab Province, Afghanistan, mujahideen attack five military bases in the towns of Daulatabad and Shirin Taghab.

January 17

AVIATION: A report surfaces that Soviet jets attacked an Afghan resistance caravan, killing eight mules. In return, rebel Stinger missiles downed one jet and a helicopter.

DIPLOMACY: In Geneva, Switzerland, the latest round of UN-sponsored peace talks is announced for February. The withdrawal of all Soviet forces is expected to dominate discussion between representatives of Afghanistan and Pakistan. UN officials also note that the Soviets have withdrawn their prior insistence that they will not withdraw troops until a coalition government is in place at Kabul.

MILITARY: In Kunduz Province, Afghanistan, 53 Afghan army soldiers kill their officers and defect to the mujahideen.

POLITICS: Voice of America reports that Yunnis Khalis, head of the seven-party mujahideen alliance, flatly rules out any possibility of a coalition government with the Communist regime in Kabul, Afghanistan. Moreover, he maintains that a transitional government can only be properly formed after the Soviets have withdrawn and would require outside military assistance to ensure the restoration of peace. Meanwhile, the mujahideen will maintain their struggle against the present regime to the bitter end.

TERRORISM: In Khartoum, Sudan, Ayatollah Mahdi Hakim, a proposed member of the Iranian-sponsored Iraqi government in exile, is assassinated, presumably on the orders of Iraqi president Saddam Hussein.

January 18

MILITARY: Mujahideen units rain down rockets on Jalalabad and Khogiani, Afghanistan, destroying several tanks and military vehicles.

January 19

MILITARY: In Kabul, Afghanistan, the government puts on a brave front by staging a large military parade.

January 20

AVIATION: In Herat Province, Afghanistan, Shindand Air Base is struck by 122mm artillery fire fired by rebels; three Soviet jets are claimed to have been damaged or destroyed.

DIPLOMACY: In Kabul, Afghanistan, President Mohammad Najibullah declares that his government is committed to a nonaligned stance following the removal of Soviet forces and will accept foreign aid from anyone willing to offer it.

In Islamabad, Pakistan, Hezb-i-Islami leader Gulbuddin Hekmatyar informs a French news service that the Soviet Union is willing to hold direct talks with the mujahideen alliance. This was confirmed during a recent meeting between the Soviet ambassador in Pakistan and Jamiat-i-Islami leader Qazi Hussain Ahmad. Hekmatyar also maintains that mujahideen's morale is high, and they will continue the struggle against Soviet troops until they are completely withdrawn from Afghanistan.

In Peshawar, Pakistan, mujahideen leaders decline to meet with UN special envoy Diego Cordovez. They insist upon direct negotiations with the Soviets or none at all.

MILITARY: In Kandahar Province, Afghanistan, Soviet and Afghan army units besiege mujahideen positions at Mohallajat, west of the capital. The former are employing large numbers of armored units, backed by air power, to break rebel resistance in what has been a traditional stronghold. An estimated 1,500 rebels are holed up in the region and running short of food and ammunition.

In Herat Province, Afghanistan, resistance fighters ambush a military convoy in the Sabool Rozanak area along the Herat-Islamqila highway. They claim to have destroyed one tank and three trucks in heavy fighting.

POLITICS: In Kabul, Afghanistan, President Mohammad Najibullah pledges to pursue a nonaligned policy once Soviet forces have withdrawn from the country.

January 22

DIPLOMACY: In public, Soviet officials insist that a troop pullout from Afghanistan is predicated upon an end to Western military assistance to the rebels. Privately, they state that the withdrawal will begin this year with or without a political settlement.

MILITARY: In Nangarhar Province, Afghanistan, mujahideen forces observe a truce during the burial of noted leader Khan Abdul Ghaffar. Soviet and Afghan army forces, however, attack elsewhere in the province by hitting rebel pockets in the Nazian and Maro areas. The resistance retaliates by launching rockets at military targets in Jalalabad.

TERRORISM: In Jalalabad, Afghanistan, the funeral of Khan Abdul Ghaffar is rocked by an explosion that kills 17 people.

January 24

DIPLOMACY: In Kabul, Afghanistan, UN special envoy Diego Cordovez arrives for talks after a brief stay in Islamabad, Pakistan.

January 25

MILITARY: In Afghanistan, mujahideen forces attack a military base along the Kabul-Kandahar highway, destroying seven tanks and military vehicles.

January 27

AVIATION: In Paktia Province, Afghanistan, a mujahideen Stinger missile brings down a Soviet jet near the Zuokh area. The airport in Urgoon Province is also closely besieged by rebel forces, and no aircraft have been able to take off or land for several weeks.

POLITICS: Reports begin reaching Pakistan that the capital of Kabul, Afghanistan, is experiencing extreme shortages of food and fuel.

January 29

AVIATION: Near Kabul, Afghanistan, mujahideen forces launch several rocket attacks against Kabul airport, damaging several parked aircraft.

January 30

MILITARY: In Nangarhar Province, Afghanistan, the city of Jalalabad is bombarded by mujahideen rockets that strike various government installations. Soviet jets counter by bombing nearby residential areas.

January 31

MILITARY: In Kandahar Province, Afghanistan, mujahideen forces launch rockets against Soviet and Afghan forces, along with Pakistani Baluchi tribesmen assisting them. Several thousand Baluchis have migrated into Afghanistan since the Soviet invasion, and they have become a prime target of resistance forces in this region.

In Herat, Afghanistan, Afghan rebels attack Soviet and government forces deployed in the Andraskhan area. The Red Air Force retaliates by bombing nearby residential areas, inflicting heavy loss among civilians.

POLITICS: In Peshawar, Pakistan, the seven-member mujahideen alliance announces that it is forming a government in exile even though Soviet troops have yet to depart Afghanistan. They also appeal to foreign governments for assistance in reconstruction efforts and reiterate their determination not to enter a coalition government with communists in Kabul.

Western analysts predict that any negotiations on troop withdrawals from Afghanistan will be determined by the perception that both superpowers want to project. For the Soviets, this means appearing that it is withdrawing on its own volition, while the Reagan administration seeks to assure its conservative base that it is not abandoning the Afghan resistance under any circumstances.

February 2

AVIATION: In Farah Province, Afghanistan, a mujahideen Stinger missile brings down a large Soviet transport airplane.

DIPLOMACY: In Kabul, Afghanistan, President Mohammad Najibullah receives UN special envoy Diego Cordovez. Pakistani Minister of State for Foreign Affairs Zain Noorani also confers with Cordovez later that day. Noorani notes that the issues surrounding a Soviet withdrawal and the nature of an interim government will undoubtedly complicate UN-sponsored peace talks slated for Geneva this month. However, Cordovez states that the UN remains confident of a Soviet pullout this year and has begun to appoint observers for both sides of the Afghan-Pakistani border to ensure compliance.

MILITARY: A report is aired by the Voice of America suggesting that mujahideen forces have again cut the road linking the city of Khost, Paktia Province, with the capital at Gardez. This comes only a month after a major Soviet operation raised the eight-month long siege of Khost by rebel forces.

In Baghlan Province, Afghanistan, reports surface that intense muajhideen activity has closed movement along the Salang highway linking Kabul with the Soviet Union. This is the most important supply route for Soviet forces in Afghanistan, and it traverses mountainous terrain 3,600 meters above sea level.

In Kapisa Province, Afghanistan, mujahideen forces attack Afghan army security posts around the town of Najrab.

February 3
AVIATION: In Paktia Province, Afghanistan, mujahideen forces apparently bring down a Soviet jet fighter operating near the Khost airport.
MILITARY: Heavy fighting continues to close down the Salang highway north of Kabul, Afghanistan. Heavy fighting is also reported in the vicinities of Qarabagh, Shakardara, Mir Badsah Kot, and Daccus in Kabul Province.

In Balkh Province, which borders the Soviet Union, mujahideen fighters capture five Afghan army security posts in the Aqcha district after four days of heavy fighting.

February 5
MILITARY: Soviet forces begin intensifying efforts to root out Afghan resistance centers in Jowzjan and Balkh Provinces, Afghanistan, as these border the Soviet Union's Central Asian republics.

February 6
POLITICS: In Tehran, Iran, Ayatollah Khomeini, determined to end a legislative impasse between the Majlis and the Council of Guardians, creates a new entity, the 13-member Council for the Expediency of Islamic Order. This body, whose members include the president, the prime minister, and the Majlis speaker, is tasked with settling the passage of bills rejected by the guardian council to ensure the supremacy of Islamic governance.

February 7
MILITARY: In Paktia Province, Afghanistan, the mujahideen claim to have shot down a military transport and destroyed seven tanks and other vehicles in the vicinity of Zadran.
POLITICS: Freedom House, a human-rights group, reports that a young Soviet soldier who deserted to the West has composed an open letter to fellow Soviet soldiers and urges them to resist the war in Afghanistan.

February 8
AVIATION: Over Maidan, Paktia Province, Afghanistan, mujahideen fighters down a Soviet aircraft near the Pakistan border.
DIPLOMACY: In Moscow, Soviet Union, General Secretary Mikhail Gorbachev goes on television to declare his willingness to begin withdrawing Soviet troops from Afghanistan beginning May 15 if a peace accord is signed no later than March 15.

Moreover, the presence of a favorable regime in Kabul is no longer a prerequisite for departing. Gorbachev unhesitatingly characterizes the conflict in Afghanistan as a "bleeding wound."

MILITARY: In Helmand Province, Afghanistan, mujahideen forces ambush a large military convoy near Kajaki, destroying 10 trucks and tanks. A Soviet helicopter is also downed by a Stinger missile in the same area.

In Ghazni Province, Afghanistan, mujahideen fighters clash with Soviet commandos in the village of Shalezi, forcing them to withdraw. The following day Soviet artillery pounds the village, destroying most of the dwellings.

February 9

AVIATION: Over the Persian Gulf, the Iranians claim to have shot down three Iraqi F-1 Mirages in a single engagement.

DIPLOMACY: Radio Moscow announces that General Secretary Mikhail Gorbachev has agreed to a May 15 date to begin withdrawing Soviet troops from Afghanistan, with a view toward completing the maneuver in 10 months. He does so to facilitate a rapid conclusion of Afghan-Pakistani peace talks in Geneva and further notes that the Soviet government would be quite happy with a neutral, nonaligned Afghanistan on its southern border. Gorbachev apparently also accepts U.S. secretary of state George Shultz's suggestion for "front loading" the pullout so that the majority of combat units are removed first.

In Moscow, Soviet Union, Deputy Foreign Minister Anatoly Kovaley characterizes the Soviet peace effort as a unique opportunity to conclude one of the world's most divisive and bitter regional conflicts.

In Washington, D.C., a Reagan administration spokesman is skeptical over the Soviet announcement and notes that other pressing issues, such as ending military aid to Kabul, are still pending.

In Islamabad, Pakistan, Foreign Minister Zain Noorani is encouraged by Soviet offers to withdraw troops from Afghanistan. However, the issue of a post-Soviet, broad-based coalition government remains unaddressed by ongoing negotiations in Geneva.

February 10

AVIATION: Iraq breaks a four-week lull in the tanker war by unleashing its warplanes at targets in the Persian Gulf.

DIPLOMACY: In Washington, D.C., the Reagan administration backtracks slightly and welcomes the Soviet offer to withdraw troops as a positive step but raises questions regarding the actual timetable.

MILITARY: In Takhar Province, astride the Soviet border, Soviet and Afghan army units attack a mujahideen center at Dashti-Qila; the rebels claim to have shot down a helicopter and that Soviet warplanes bombed residential areas of the town.

February 11

DIPLOMACY: In Islamabad, Pakistan, Soviet First Deputy Foreign Minister Yuli Vorontsov declares that the Afghanistan documents in Geneva are ready to be signed.

In Washington, D.C., administration officials declare that they will not cut off military assistance to the Afghan resistance until the last Soviet troops are withdrawn from Afghanistan.

In Islamabad, Pakistan, President Zia ul-Haq confers with Soviet First Deputy Foreign Minister Yuli Voronstov over Afghanistan. Vorontsov reiterates his government's position of seeking to commence a complete withdrawal as of May 15, 1988, should the Geneva accords be signed no later than March.

In Washington, D.C., a Reagan administration spokesman states that the United States will offer to serve as a guarantor of the Afghan settlement, provided that it includes a complete Soviet pullout, Afghan neutrality, the right of self-determination, and the repatriation of 5 million Afghan refugees.

TERRORISM: In Peshawar, Pakistan, Sayyid Bahauddin Majruh, head of the Afghan Information Office, is killed by unknown assailants.

February 12

AVIATION: Waves of Soviet and Afghan warplanes bomb suspected mujahideen positions in the Khinjan Valley, Afghanistan, destroying an estimated 200 houses.

DIPLOMACY: East European diplomats in Kabul, Afghanistan, are growing anxious over the pending Soviet withdrawal and have begun sending family members home and selling off their belongings before fleeing the country.

MILITARY: In Kabul, Afghanistan, mujahideen rockets land near the Soviet embassy while Soviet artillery fires upon rebel positions south and west of the city. Afghan army units are also strengthening their positions in advance of the ultimate Soviet withdrawal.

In Baghlan Province, Afghanistan, mujahideen forces fight with Soviet and Afghan army units along the strategic Salang highway. This is the second Communist attack in Baghlan since the rebels caught and executed the governor, Sultan Mohammad Khan, and other authorities.

Soviet troops turn over security of the Kabul-Kandahar highway to units of the Afghan army.

February 13

DIPLOMACY: With a Soviet withdrawal from Afghanistan pending, the United States, Pakistan, and the Afghan resistance begin demanding that negotiations over creation of a coalition government be settled before the withdrawal agreement is signed in Geneva.

MILITARY: In Faryab Province, Afghanistan, mujahideen forces launch a heavy attack upon government installations at Maimana; they claim to destroy four tanks, a personnel carrier, and supplies of ammunition.

February 14

DIPLOMACY: Western political analysts state that they perceive signs of internal disagreements in the Soviet Union over the withdrawal from Afghanistan.

MILITARY: In Nimruz Province, Afghanistan, mujahideen forces attack government outposts near the capital of Zaranj. Soviet and Afghan forces subsequently attack and bomb the village of Morkali as a suspect rebel center.

February 15

MILITARY: In a major development, Soviet forces begin shipping quantities of supplies and military hardware to Faizabad, Badakhshan Province, Afghanistan, where

2,000 troops are already concentrated. Mujahideen leaders believe that this is in preparation for a drive to break the rebel blockade of Kasham on the road connecting Faizabad with Taliqan, Takhar Province.

February 16
MILITARY: In the Dand and Arghandab suburbs of Kandahar, Afghanistan, mujahideen groups infiltrate close enough to attack Soviet installations. They claim to have inflicted 13 casualties and destroyed an armored vehicle.

February 17
DIPLOMACY: The Soviet government accuses Pakistan of obstructing an end to the Afghan conflict through its insistence that a change of government in Kabul take place before troops are withdrawn.
MILITARY: The Afghan government claims that resistance fighters have launched more than 200 ground-to-ground missiles at various locales within Kandahar Province, Afghanistan.

February 18
DIPLOMACY: In Washington, D.C., Secretary of State George Shultz states that he is willing to present Pakistan's demand for a coalition government in upcoming talks with Soviet foreign minister Eduard Shevardnadze.

February 19
AVIATION: Over Kabul Province, Afghanistan, a flight of eight Soviet warplanes strikes a mujahideen position; one jet is apparently struck by a missile and was last seen struggling to return to Bagram Air Base.

In Herat Province, Afghanistan, mujahideen fighters attack the Soviet base at Adratkhan, 48 miles south of the provincial capital; they claim to destroy four tanks.
POLITICS: In Peshawar, Pakistan, rifts begin showing in mujahideen ranks as some faction leaders state they are willing to abide by a coalition arrangement with members of the communist regime in Kabul.

February 20
DIPLOMACY: In Islamabad, Pakistan, Foreign Minister Zain Noorani fears that a terrible civil war will sweep Afghanistan if the Soviet-backed regime in Kabul, Afghanistan, is allowed to remain in power once Soviet troops have departed. In that case, the 5 million Afghans living in refugee camps abroad cannot be expected to return home and will, in all likelihood, be joined by even more refugees.
MILITARY: In Helmand Province, Afghanistan, Soviet and Afghan army units commence offensive operations against nearby mujahideen units near the Pakistani border. The attack is supported by 60 warplanes and assault helicopters. The action was apparently triggered by a rebel attack along the Lashkargah highway, which had destroyed 30 tanks and other vehicles.

In the Moosa-Kala, Zamandawer, Sangli, and Qadirki areas, Afghanistan, an estimated 10,000 resistance fighters were besieged by superior Soviet forces until this day, when a mujahideen counterattack broke the siege and forced Soviets and Afghans to fall back on Qadirki. This is one of the largest conventional actions of the war thus far, and the fighters claim to have shot down two jets and a helicopter, and also destroyed 40 tanks and other vehicles.

February 22

AVIATION: In Paktia Province, Afghanistan, a mujahideen missile downs a Soviet-supplied MI-8 helicopter near the Jaji cantonment. Apparently, a high-ranking Soviet officer was on board and is among the casualties.

DIPLOMACY: In Beijing, the Chinese government declares its support for Pakistan's position on Afghanistan. It also continues to participate in military supply efforts for the mujahideen.

In New York City, the UN Commission on Human Rights passes a resolution, 31 votes to five, calling for the immediate removal of foreign troops from Afghanistan. The Soviet Union, which voted against it, said the document is imbalanced and does not take into account recent and more positive trends.

MILITARY: In Parvan Province, Afghanistan, Afghan troops abandon the 12 security posts they had been manning and defect to the mujahideen.

February 23

DIPLOMACY: In Moscow, Soviet Union, government radio announces that Sayyed Aminuddin Amin, the Afghan foreign minister, is due to visit for discussions on future cooperation between the two nations.

In Moscow, U.S. secretary of state George Shultz concludes the latest round of talks with Foreign Minister Eduard Shevardnadze and states that both countries are in general agreement over terms for ending the conflict in Afghanistan.

MILITARY: Near Baghlan City, Afghanistan, mujahideen fighters capture four Soviet and Afghan army outposts. This settlement is on the strategic Salang highway, running north from Kabul, and traffic along its winding path is subject to frequent attack from resistance fighters.

In Herat Province, Afghanistan, mujahideen fighters drive Soviet and Afghan army troops out from six villages. They also capture nine posts in the suburbs of Herat.

POLITICS: In Peshawar, Pakistan, the mujahideen alliance declares it is forming an interim government in anticipation of a Soviet pullout.

TERRORISM: In Kabul, Afghanistan, a pair of bombs apparently kill several Soviet advisers.

February 24

AVIATION: Over Logar Province, mujahideen missiles bring down two military jets.

DIPLOMACY: In Peshawar, Pakistan, mujahideen leaders equate a recent slowdown in weapons deliveries to an agreement between the United States and the Soviet Union regarding the withdrawal of all foreign forces. They make their discomfiture known to Texas representative Charlie Wilson, who has long been their benefactor in Washington.

In Brussels, Belgium, U.S. secretary of state George Shultz confers with European officials and remains buoyant over the fact that Soviet forces in Afghanistan appear to be withdrawing to their bases.

In Rome, Italy, Afghan chargé d'affaires Mohammad Nasir Fedai reportedly disappears from his post; he has apparently defected and taken asylum in the West.

MILITARY: A report on Radio Dubai says that rebel attacks are increasing in the vicinity of Kabul, Afghanistan. Over the past week eight explosions rocked the capital, including one close to the Soviet embassy and another near government-controlled Radio Afghanistan.

In Herat Province, Afghanistan, a large Soviet convoy is attacked by nearly 400 mujahideen fighters near Atkharma, 90 miles south of the provincial capital. Fighters from four different groups trapped them in a narrow pass, destroying eight tanks and 15 trucks with rockets and heavy weapons.

Generally speaking, Soviet forces are beginning to turn over various security posts to the Afghan army, although the Soviets still dominate defensive positions in and around the capital of Kabul. This might account for the recent increase of attacks on the city.

TERRORISM: In Kabul, Afghanistan, a bomb explodes in the Directorate of Transport just as a Soviet delegation is arriving from Moscow.

February 25

DIPLOMACY: In Peshawar, Pakistan, Under Secretary of State Michael Armacost meets with mujahideen alliance representatives respecting Soviet troop withdrawals. Gulbuddin Hekmatyar resents the fact that the Americans and Russians have concluded some kind of an agreement by going over the heads of the alliance.

In Washington, D.C., a government spokesman vehemently denies that the United States is cutting off military assistance to the Afghan resistance as part of a deal with the Soviets.

In Moscow, Soviet Union, the government rejects a mujahideen demand for an interim government in Kabul, Afghanistan, to monitor the withdrawal of Soviet forces.

February 26

AVIATION: In Kabul, Afghanistan, mujahideen rockets slam into the airport, damaging two parked aircraft.

DIPLOMACY: Some U.S. analysts ponder the fate of the mujahideen alliance once the Soviets have withdrawn from Afghanistan and wonder what the Reagan administration has agreed to in secret talks with Moscow.

In Tehran, Iran, mujahideen leader Burhanuddin Rabbani arrives to discuss the Afghan crisis and also praises Iran for its role in supporting the Afghan resistance.

February 27

AVIATION: In Kabul Province, Afghanistan, mujahideen forces bombard Bagram airport, destroying five aircraft on the ground.

In the northern sector, Iraq resumes its "War of the Cities" by launching missiles at the Iranian town of Saqqez, killing 26 people.

February 28

DIPLOMACY: In New York City, the Iranian delegate informs UN secretary-general Javier Pérez de Cuéllar that since Iran has accepted the 10-point plan necessary to implement Resolution 598 there is no need for the Security Council to impose a weapons embargo against it.

February 29
AVIATION: Iran responds to missile attacks against its cities by launching three Scud-B missiles at Baghdad.

March 1
AVIATION: Over the Asadabad and Para areas of Konar Province, Afghanistan, two Afghan army helicopters are downed by mujahideen forces.

The Iraqis retaliate immediately by striking back at Tehran with 16 Al-Hussein missiles of its own, so-named after the most revered Shiite prophet.
DIPLOMACY: In Moscow, Soviet Union, Afghan foreign minister Abdul Wakil confers with Foreign Minister Eduard Shevardnadze over prospects for a comprehensive political settlement for the Afghan conflict.

In Washington, D.C., the U.S. Senate passes a motion that totally opposes any lessening of military aid to the Afghan resistance during the proposed Soviet withdrawal. It also endorses the deployment of UN peacekeeping forces and the creation of an interim government in Kabul that is acceptable to the resistance. Finally, the motion opposes pressuring Pakistan into accepting Soviet terms for a settlement of the conflict.

In Tehran, Iran, the government protests that the Soviet Union is selling tactical missiles to Iraq for the first time.
POLITICS: Disagreement between resistance groups based in Iran and Pakistan hampers direct negotiations with the Soviet Union over troop withdrawals.

March 2
AVIATION: Iraqi tactical missiles strike the Shiite holy city of Qom, Iran, for the first time.
MILITARY: In Logar Province, Afghanistan, mujahideen forces attack Soviet headquarters at Puli-i-Alam and other military installations at Mohammad Agha township; heavy Soviet casualties are reported.

March 3
MILITARY: In Takhar Province, Afghanistan, a Soviet officer of Tajik descent crosses the Amu Darya River and defects to the Afghan resistance.

March 4
AVIATION: In Kabul Province, Afghanistan, Soviet warplanes strike residential areas of Guldara, destroying many houses and other buildings.
DIPLOMACY: In Washington, D.C., President Ronald W. Reagan declares that the United States will not halt arms shipments to the Afghan resistance until the Soviets stop supplying the regime in Kabul, Afghanistan.
MILITARY: In Kabul Province, Afghanistan, mujahideen fighters bombard Soviet security posts at Mirbachakot near Bagram Air Base. Rebel rockets also land in a Soviet camp at Khair Khana elsewhere in the province. Soviet casualties are reported in both instances.

March 5
DIPLOMACY: The United States, intent on increasing pressure on the Soviets, reverses itself and declares that it will not lessen or suspend military aid to the

Afghan resistance until the Soviets cease supplying the regime in Kabul, Afghanistan. Previously, the Americans hinted that they would suspend assistance as the Soviets withdrew.

In Geneva, Switzerland, UN special envoy Diego Cordovez declares that Afghanistan and Pakistan have eliminated all major obstacles relative to a Soviet withdrawal. Meanwhile, Afghan foreign minister Abdul Wakil announces that his government is willing to see them withdrawn over a nine-month period, instead of 10, with the bulk of 115,000 combat troops departing in the first three months. The United States cautions that obstacles remain, especially regarding the continuing shipment of arms to either side.

POLITICS: In Kunduz and Faryab Provinces, Afghanistan, five armed groups led by Mohammad Ismail, Baz Mohammad, Abdul Samad, and Abdul Hakim have agreed to a peace initiative with the government.

March 6

DIPLOMACY: In Moscow, Soviet Union, the government charges that the resistance is moving large quantities of arms and ammunition from Pakistan and into Afghanistan, even as negotiations to end the conflict are under way. This charge is leveled only after the United States declares it will not stop arming resistance fighters unless Moscow ends military aid to Kabul.

MILITARY: In Nangarhar Province, Afghanistan, a two-week Soviet and Afghan army offensive stalls in the face of fierce resistance from the mujahideen. A counterattack by Afghan rebels captures security posts in the Ghani Khel, Babra Tangi and Nazian regions. Heavy fighting and losses in men and equipment are reported on both sides.

POLITICS: In Tehran, Iran, a mob attacks the Soviet embassy over the continual supplying of tactical missiles to Iraq.

March 8

AVIATION: Mujahideen sources report that rocket attacks on the main airport at Kandahar, Afghanistan, destroyed four Soviet MIGs, two helicopters, and three tanks.

MILITARY: In Helmand Province, Afghanistan, mujahideen strike a Soviet encampment near the provincial capital of Lashkargarh, causing several casualties.

Soviet forces have been observed stockpiling large quantities of fuel, food, and ammunition in the provincial capital of Kandahar, Afghanistan. Large-scale construction of defensive works also points to an eventual Soviet withdrawal from the region and their replacement by Afghan army groups.

A Soviet convoy of more than 100 military vehicles is attacked by mujahideen along the Salang highway in Baghlan Province, Afghanistan. The convoy manages to fight its way through, assisted by artillery fire and air cover.

In Parvan Province, Afghanistan, mujahideen fighters strike at a Soviet base near Kabul, reportedly destroying two tanks and a truck.

March 9

DIPLOMACY: In Geneva, Switzerland, the Afghan delegation insists that it will not forgo continuing Soviet military aid to reach a peace agreement. Concurrently, the

United States insists it will not halt arms shipments to the resistance until Moscow stops arming the Kabul regime. Meanwhile, Pakistan is also insisting that an interim government be in place and functioning while Soviet forces are withdrawn.

In Moscow, Soviet Union, the government finally acknowledges that it has been supplying Iraq with short-range tactical missiles. These weapons have been wreaking havoc on Iranian towns and cities of late.

MILITARY: A mujahideen ambush in Kandahar Province, Afghanistan, results in the defection of 66 Afghan army troops to the resistance.

March 10

DIPLOMACY: In Kabul, Afghanistan, Foreign Minister Abdul Wakil warns that a Geneva peace settlement appears unlikely by March 15 owing to new conditions imposed by the United States and Pakistan.

POLITICS: In Kabul, Afghanistan, Noor Ahmad Noor, a former associate of former president Babrak Karmal, founds a new opposition group, called Anjuman-i-Najat-i-Milli. Several former government ministers have since joined in opposition to the regime of President Mohammad Najibullah.

The two factions of the PDPA are still uneasy with each other. Today troops belonging to the secret police, loyal to the Khalq faction, engage in a firefight with forces belonging to the Interior Ministry and the Pacham faction. This occurs at a time when the government is attempting to display national solidarity to the world.

March 11

DIPLOMACY: The Soviet government declares that it will not stop arming the government of President Mohammad Najibullah as demanded by the Reagan administration. It also accuses Pakistan of complicity with the United States by introducing its own new demands at Geneva.

Iran and Iraq agree to a truce in the latest round of the "War of the Cities" following a visit and an appeal by Turkish prime minister Turgut Ozal and renewed pressure by the Soviet Union.

March 12

MILITARY: In Nimruz Province, Afghanistan, mujahideen fighters storm the provincial capital of Zaranj, destroying a military camp and several armored vehicles with rockets. The nearby security posts of Chaghan, Sore, and Nimruz were also captured.

In Kandahar Province, Afghanistan, severe fighting continues unabated throughout the Panjawi district. It is reported that, over the previous month, more than 100 Soviet and Afghan troops have been killed, along with 17 tanks and six military vehicles destroyed. The resistance also notes that 150 Afghan soldiers defected to their ranks during this period.

March 13

AVIATION: Over Paktia Province, Afghanistan, mujahideen missiles shoot down a jet fighter attacking their position.

In Parvan Province, Afghanistan, resistance fighters claim to shoot down two MiG fighters and two helicopters near the Kohistan area.

MILITARY: Mujahideen fighters claim to have surrounded Afghan army headquarters at Ghowr Band.

In the northern sector, Iranian forces backed by Kurdish guerrillas launch Operation Bait al Muqaddas-3 north of Suleimaniya in Iraqi Kurdistan and seize several villages.

March 14
POLITICS: In Peshawar, Pakistan, Gulbuddin Hekmatyar gains appointment as spokesman for the mujahideen alliance.

March 14–19
AVIATION: Soviet and Afghan warplanes continually bomb mujahideen positions at Mani, Kandau, Zhwara, and Bari in Paktia Province, Afghanistan.

MILITARY: A large force of Afghan troops, supported by Soviet commandos, are engaged by mujahideen fighters as they advance from Ghazni to Urgun, Paktia Province. The ensuing struggle lasts five days, after which the commandos withdraw to Sharana after suffering 300 casualties and losing 20 tanks.

March 15
DIPLOMACY: In Moscow, Soviet Union, the government appeals to Pakistan to sign the Geneva peace accord as presently written. However, Pakistan insists on the creation of a broad-based coalition government before the Soviets actually withdraw.

MILITARY: In Takhar Province, Afghanistan, the mujahideen capture 70 Afghan army soldiers and claim to have downed two Soviet helicopters.

POLITICS: In Peshawar, Pakistan, Gulbuddin Hekmatyar of Hezb-i-Islami states that if the Pakistani government signs the Geneva peace accord, the Afghan alliance will not make trouble, but rather, shift the bulk of its organization back into Afghanistan. He also reiterates that the alliance will not enter into any coalition arrangement with the present regime in Kabul.

In the northern sector, Iranian forces and Kurdish guerrillas launch Operation Wa al Fajr 10, in which Halabja, a city of 70,000 people, is captured.

March 16
AVIATION: Over Herat Province, Afghanistan, a mujahideen Stinger missile brings down a Soviet MiG-27 fighter bomber near Shindand airport.

DIPLOMACY: In Geneva, Switzerland, UN special envoy Diego Cordovez declares that peace talks are experiencing "serious difficulties." The Soviet Union also delays the withdrawal of its forces from Afghanistan, angrily accusing the United States of reneging on its prior "understanding" to stop military aid to the resistance movement.

MILITARY: Responding to the emergency situation in Iraqi Kurdistan, President Saddam Hussein orders chemical weapons and nerve agents dropped on the Kurdish town of Halabja, Iraq, one day following its capture by Iranian forces. An estimated 5,000 civilians are killed.

March 17
DIPLOMACY: In Geneva, Switzerland, Pakistani foreign minister Zain Noorani suggests that the United States and the Soviet Union adopt a "symmetrical" cutoff of aid to their respective sides in the Afghan conflict. However, the United States remains adamant that it will continue arming the mujahideen for as long as Moscow arms the Afghan regime in Kabul.

In Tehran, Iran, the government formally accuses Iraq of employing poison gas against its forces.

MILITARY: In Faryab Province, Afghanistan, mujahideen fighters attack armored units in Shirin Taghab along the Soviet border. Heavy losses are reported on both sides. Resistance fighters also use heavy artillery to shell Maimana, the provincial capital.

In Herat Province, mujahideen rockets fall upon Soviet encampments at Ghoriyan and Zinda Jan, destroying three tanks near the city of Herat. The Soviets respond by shelling suspected rebel positions in the suburbs of Herat.

March 19
AVIATION: Soviet and Afghan warplanes continue pounding mujahideen targets in Panjwai, Kandahar Province, Afghanistan. Heavy fighting over the past month has resulted in losses to both sides.

DIPLOMACY: In Peshawar, Pakistan, mujahideen spokesman Gulbuddin Hekmatyar accuses the United States of negotiating with the Soviet Union behind the alliance's back. He also firmly opposes the Geneva peace accord and vows to continue fighting whether they are signed or not.

POLITICS: In Kabul, Afghanistan, a delegation of the All Workers Union of Bulgaria arrives to pay its respects to President Mohammad Najibullah.

MILITARY: In Herat Province, Afghanistan, mujahideen fighters overrun eight Afghan army security posts in the Darb Malik area.

March 20
DIPLOMACY: In Washington, D.C., Soviet foreign minister Eduard Shevardnadze arrives to negotiate a compromise respecting a Soviet withdrawal; the Americans also insist on a complete end to Soviet aid to the Kabul regime.

A report to the U.S. Senate Committee on Foreign Relations suggests that American insistence that Moscow end military aid to Kabul could be a major impediment to a Soviet troop withdrawal.

POLITICS: In an interview for the Russian magazine *Ogonyok,* General Valentine Varennikov, chief of Soviet Land Forces, mentions that the Soviet General Staff had opposed intervening in Afghanistan in 1979, but it was overruled by political leadership, including Defense Minister Dimitri Ustinov. Varennikov is also critical of Babrak Karmal, who headed the puppet Afghan regime from 1979 to 1986. This is also the first time that a ranking member of the Soviet staff has gone on record opposing the Afghan conflict.

March 21

DIPLOMACY: A report surfaces that Mohammad Ghous Amir, chief of legal affairs of the Afghan Foreign Ministry, has defected in Peshawar, Pakistan, and requested asylum.

MILITARY: Jalalabad, Afghanistan, is the scene of a heavy mujahideen attack, which inflicts heavy losses upon Afghan army forces.

In Baghlan Province, Afghanistan, Afghan resistance fighters capture 12 security posts in the region between Aluadin Qala and Gardab, along with mortars, heavy machine guns, and tons of ammunition. Three tanks are also claimed to have been destroyed and 50 army deserters recruited.

March 21–23

POLITICS: Iranian authorities permit Western journalists to visit Halabja, in Iraqi Kurdistan, to show off thousands of victims of chemical weapons, still prostrate on the streets.

March 22

AVIATION: Soviet warplanes catch a mujahideen unit out in the open at Aab-Khurma, outside the Shindand Air Base, and inflict heavy losses.

DIPLOMACY: In Washington, D.C., Soviet foreign minister Eduart Shevardnadze and Secretary of State George Shultz conclude two days of talks, whereupon the latter declares that whenever the Soviets are ready to begin withdrawing, both sides can agree to a "moratorium on military assistance."

MILITARY: Outside Jalalabad, Afghanistan, a Soviet convoy traveling down the Herat highway is attacked by mujahideen fighters, who destroy 23 tanks and eight trucks.

In Logar Province, Afghan rebels attack Soviet/Afghan army security posts, capturing four with quantities of arms and ammunition.

March 23

AVIATION: In retribution for rebel gains in the Sangeen district, Helmand Province, Afghanistan, Soviet warplanes bomb nearby residential areas, destroying scores of houses and irrigation systems.

Over Paktia Province, Afghanistan, Soviet warplanes bomb suspected mujahideen positions in the Ahawar, Ghulam Khan, and Raghbela areas near the Pakistan border.

DIPLOMACY: Peace talks in Geneva, Switzerland, are threatened after Afghanistan threatens to raise an old border dispute with Pakistan relative to the 1893 Duran Line dividing them.

MILITARY: A Soviet convoy of 600 trucks and tanks braves repeated attacks by mujahidden units and fights its way into Urgun, Ghazni Province, Afghanistan, ending a three-year blockade. The trip took six weeks from Gardez, and 42 tanks and trucks were destroyed en route.

In Helmand Province, Afghanistan, mujahideen forces evict Soviet and Afghan troops from the Sangeen district. They seized 33 Soviet and Afghan army posts in the past two days, along with three tanks, heavy machine guns, five mortars, 300 assault rifles, and tons of ammunition and food supplies.

In the Mohallajat area of Kandahar City, Afghanistan, roughly 100 Afghan army troops defect to local mujahideen forces.

March 24
MILITARY: The Afghan resistance claims to have captured the important region of Sangeen, Helmand Province, Afghanistan.
POLITICS: In Baluchistan, Pakistan, tensions are mounting between the native population and numerous Afghan refugees living there. The locals fear that the refugees will never leave while the refugees, distrusting the Kabul regime, are disinclined to return home under national reconciliation.

March 25
DIPLOMACY: Pakistan, probably responding to American pressure, drops its earlier insistence that Afghanistan adopt a transitional coalition government before Soviet troops withdraw and agrees to sign the Geneva peace accord if Kabul simply consents to forming an interim government.

March 26
AVIATION: A report surfaces that the United States is suspending shipments of advanced Stinger missiles to the Afghan resistance to cultivate a favorable atmosphere for peace talks in Geneva, Switzerland.
MILITARY: In Kandahar Province, Afghanistan, mujahideen fighters storm into three security posts at Spin Boldak along the Pakistani border.

March 27
MILITARY: In the central sector, the Iraqi-sponsored National Liberation Army, composed entirely of Iranian expatriates and armed and trained by the Mujahideen-i-Khalq, attacks in the Fakkeh region with a view toward seizing Dezful. It claims to quickly seize 370 square miles of Iranian territory.
POLITICS: Western analysts predict that the removal of Soviet troops will not end the violence in Afghanistan, but instead, trigger a new wave of civil war between the government in Kabul and the Afghan resistance.

March 28
MILITARY: In Parvan Province, Afghanistan, a major offensive by Soviet and Afghan army troops results in a two-week struggle to regain control of Ghowr Band.

March 29
DIPLOMACY: In Geneva, peace talks are stalemated once the Soviets refuse to consider American demands for an end of military aid to the regime in Kabul, Afghanistan.
MILITARY: In Paktia Province, Afghanistan, Soviet forces are seen strengthening fortifications and cantonments with heavy arms and armored vehicles. This is viewed as preparation for turning the region over to Afghan army units.

In Wardak Province, Afghanistan, mujahideen fighters attack a Soviet convoy heading west from Kabul to Ghazni.
POLITICS: In Kabul, Afghanistan, President Mohammad Najibullah promises Afghan resistance leaders that they will receive 54 out of 229 seats in the lower

house and 18 out of 62 seats in the new senate if they participate in forthcoming national elections.

TERRORISM: In Kabul, Afghanistan, the BBC reports that a car bomb has killed four Soviet advisers in a shopping district. The bomb could have been set by the resistance or rival factions within the ruling party.

March 30

POLITICS: In the Soviet Union, new information surfaces that suggests that the decision to invade Afghanistan was made by a handful of officials and did not include Anatoly Dobrynin, Soviet ambassador to the United States.

In Peshawar, Pakistan, the mujahideen alliance summarily rejects an offer by the Afghan government to serve in a coalition parliament.

March 31

AVIATION: Over Logar Province, Afghanistan, mujahideen fighters bring down a Soviet warplane as it attacks their position near Burki Burk.

DIPLOMACY: In Washington, D.C., administration officials state that the Soviets may be willing to compromise on a cutoff date for military assistance to the mujahideen. The American position is that Washington should continue supplying the guerrillas until the last Soviet soldier departs. However, as weapons have also been flowing in from China and Saudi Arabia, it is not known how a compromise will be crafted.

April 1

DIPLOMACY: In Washington, D.C., Secretary of State George Shultz declares that a new negotiating formula will allow the United States to keep arming the mujahideen while the Soviets continue military aid to the Kabul regime.

The government of Pakistan declares its unwillingness to sign any treaty for a Soviet withdrawal unless the United States serves as the guarantor.

MILITARY: In the Qaisar district of Faryab Province, Soviet units are establishing a chain of new security posts. This area borders the Soviet Union and its own oil-producing region.

POLITICS: Western analysts believe that the creation of Sar-i Pul Province, Afghanistan, is part of a Soviet strategy to carve out and retain a military zone should peace talks in Geneva collapse.

In Tehran, Iran, government radio tests its new radio alert tone in the event that the Iraqis launch missiles with chemical weapons against the capital.

April 2

MILITARY: A Voice of America report suggests that mujahideen fighters fired powerful BM-12 rockets against the Kandahar airport in Afghanistan. The rebels claim to have destroyed a helicopter, two tanks, and stockpiled ammunition.

In Bamiyan, Afghanistan, a large mujahideen assault is heavily repulsed by Soviet and Afghan forces. Sixty guerrillas are reported to have died with a large number captured and flown to Kabul. Observers believe that the Soviets had been tipped off in advance about the upcoming attack, a fact subsequently confirmed by Kabul Radio.

In Logar Province, Afghanistan, mujahideen forces bombard Soviet and Afghan army units near Pul-i-Alam. Soviet artillery retaliates by shelling residential areas of nearby Baraki Barak, killing several civilians.

POLITICS: In Kabul, Afghanistan, national radio states that mujahideen leader Haji Ghausuddin and 70 followers have laid down their arms to embrace national reconciliation. Ghausuddin, whose three-party opposition group is based in New Delhi, India, had previously urged other leaders to do likewise.

April 3

DIPLOMACY: In Geneva, Switzerland, peace negotiations between Afghan and Pakistani delegates enter their fifth week without making noticeable progress.

In Kabul, Afghanistan, Soviet foreign minister Eduard Shevardnadze arrives for discussions concerning the withdrawal of Soviet forces. He also mentions "serious difficulties" in peace talks at Geneva.

MILITARY: In the Ghowr Band region of Parvan Province, Afghanistan, 5,000 Soviet and Afghan forces conduct a major operation against local mujahideen units.

POLITICS: In Afghanistan, Sar-i-Pul becomes the 30th province and is adjacent to Samangan, Balkh, Jowzjan, and Faryab Provinces. Gharib Husain becomes the first governor.

April 4

MILITARY: In Kandahar Province, Afghanistan, mujahideen attacks on Panjwai Woleswali accounts for eight Soviet tanks.

In Farah Province, Afghanistan, Afghan rebels seize the subdivisional towns of Qila Kah and Khawke-Sufaid, which are quickly bombed in turn by Soviet warplanes. Several fighters and civilians are killed.

Kabul, Afghanistan, is bombarded by 122mm rockets aimed at Soviet positions around the city.

POLITICS: In Kabul, Afghanistan, government radio officially announces creation of Sar-i-Pul Province, which has been carved from the southernmost portions of Balkh and Jowzjan Provinces.

TERRORISM: An explosion at a customs checkpoint at Kabul airport kills three Afghan army officers.

April 5

DIPLOMACY: In Washington, D.C., an administration spokesman notes that the Soviets appear to be making preparations to withdraw from Afghanistan despite obstacles in Geneva. At this time both nations are funneling enormous amounts of military supplies to their respective combatants.

MILITARY: In Ghazni Province, 105 Afghan army recruits flee from their training camp to join the mujahideen.

By this time, the Soviets have turned over responsibility for all military bases in Logar Province, Afghanistan, to Afghan army troops while making similar preparations in Paktia Province. In the latter region, Afghan rebels go unchallenged along many points on the Gardez-Khost highway.

April 6

DIPLOMACY: Soviet general secretary Mikhail Gorbachev arrives in Tashkent, Soviet Uzbekistan, for talks with Afghan president Mohammad Najibullah, then in Kabul, Afghanistan, still discussing matters with Foreign Secretary Eduard Shevardnadze.

Gorbachev subsequently assures his guest of continuing military assistance following the Soviet pullout.

POLITICS: The Afghan Islamic Press reports that 10,000 refugees rallied at Peshawar, Pakistan, to oppose the Geneva peace process between Kabul and Islamabad. Rebel leaders are demanding direct talks with the Soviet Union.

April 7

AVIATION: In Kandahar Province, Afghanistan, mujahideen Stinger missiles knock down two military helicopters over the Daman region.

DIPLOMACY: In Tashkent, Soviet Uzbekistan, General Secretary Mikhail Gorbachev concludes his discussion with President Mohammad Najibullah. Apparently, the Soviets are prepared to accept the American position that each country can continue to supply its respective side with military aid during and after the Soviet withdrawal.

Spokesmen in both Washington and Islamabad remain confident and optimistic that an agreement leading to the withdrawal of Soviet forces is at hand.

POLITICS: In Washington, D.C., Senator Gordon Humphrey urges President Ronald W. Reagan to reject the Geneva peace agreement if its terms would hinder Washington from honoring America's commitment to the Afghan resistance.

April 8

DIPLOMACY: The governments in Moscow and Kabul declare that conditions are sufficient for a Soviet withdrawal to commence by May 15. These include a nine-month suspension of arms to either side during the period of the withdrawal, with shipments able to be resumed if either side violates the agreement.

In Washington, D.C., Defense Secretary Frank Carlucci states that an agreement to withdraw all Soviet forces from Afghanistan is at hand.

In Islamabad, Pakistan, President Zia ul-Haq estimates that 3 million Afghan refugees could begin returning in five to six months.

In Peshawar, Pakistan, mujahideen alliance spokesman Gulbuddin Hekmatyar rejects a plea by UN special envoy Diego Cordovez to support the Geneva peace accord and vows to fight on.

MILITARY: In Kandahar Province, Afghanistan, fighting begins to intensify prior to the pullback of Soviet forces, and two military posts north of Kandahar city have been heavily hit with numerous Soviet casualties reported. Rebels also attack all eight voting centers throughout Kandahar to disrupt government-sponsored elections.

In Nangarhar Province, Afghanistan, several Soviets are killed when their vehicle hits a land mine outside a military post at Daulat Zay.

A report on the Voice of America suggests that intense fighting rages throughout Herat Province, Afghanistan, in such regions as Qarabagh and Chah-i-Sheen and on the outskirts of Herat city.

April 9

DIPLOMACY: In Geneva, Switzerland, a full agreement is announced relative to the withdrawal of 115,000 Soviet troops from Afghanistan. Its also covers the return of Afghan refugees and the establishment of Afghanistan as a neutral, nonaligned state. The signatories include Pakistan and Afghanistan with Washington and Moscow acting as guarantors.

In Peshawar, Pakistan, the mujahideen alliance forcefully reiterates that it is not beholden to any agreement reached at Geneva, Switzerland.

MILITARY: In Konar Province, a Soviet convoy is attacked in the Khas Konar region by mujahideen fighters as it rolls toward Jalalabad. A total of 25 vehicles are claimed to have been destroyed.

In Bamiyan Province, Afghanistan, the township of Ghulghuah falls to a major mujahideen assault. The rebels claim to have shot down one jet and destroyed two tanks

In Kabul, Afghanistan, mujahideen forces target the offices of Soviet advisers and the Ministry of Defense for a rocket bombardment.

In Logar Province, Afghanistan, a recent mujahideen attack on Pul-i-Alam results in a retaliatory raid by Soviet and Afghan troops against Kolangar village, destroying several homes and killing numerous civilians.

April 10

DIPLOMACY: The Soviet government seems to approve of the U.S. compromise proposal allowing the former to maintain military assistance to the Kabul regime, while the latter continues aiding the mujahideen. However, the Americans are demanding further clarification from Moscow.

MILITARY: Outside Islamabad, Pakistan, a series of explosions rips through a mujahideen ammunition dump at Owjeri near Rawalpindi, killing several hundred people. The stockpile contained weapons delivered there in anticipation of a diplomatic agreement to stop all such arms shipments. Its destruction is believed to be the work of Afghan secret police.

In Parvan Province, Afghanistan, mujahideen forces manage to maintain control of the region despite attacks by Soviet and Afghan forces; the rebels claim to have downed a Soviet jet.

In the northern sector, massed Iranian forces, backed by Kurdish guerrillas, launch Operation Bait al Muqaddas-5 in the Panjwin area of Iraqi Kurdistan. It is hoped that a threatened advance toward the Kirkuk oil fields would compel the Iraqi high command to shift troops northward from the Basra sector. Their progress prompts a visit by Iraqi defense minister Adnan Khairallah to the region to stiffen the troops.

POLITICS: In Peshawar, Pakistan, mujahideen spokesman Gulbuddin Hekmatyar again rejects the Geneva peace accord and threatens to foment instability in Pakistan should Islamabad sign on to it.

April 11

AVIATION: In Takhar Province, Afghanistan, the BBC reports that mujahideen Stinger missiles have downed another Antonov An-26 transport as it flew from Maimana to Mazar-i-Sharif.

MILITARY: In Kunduz Province, Afghanistan, mujahideen forces ambush a military convoy moving south toward Kabul from the river port of Sher Khan. The rebels claim to have captured five trucks and 40 tons of wheat.

April 12

DIPLOMACY: The governments of the United States and the Soviet Union finalize terms for a Soviet withdrawal from Afghanistan within nine months, along with continuing military assistance to their respective sides.

In light of the Afghanistan breakthrough, General Secretary Mikhail Gorbachev announces that Moscow is willing to take Israeli interests into account during any Soviet role in the Middle East peace process.

POLITICS: In the Soviet Union, news of the impending withdrawal from Afghanistan generates mixed feelings among military personnel, ranging from relief to disgrace over being defeated by ragged bands of rebels.

April 13

DIPLOMACY: In Washington, D.C., President Ronald W. Reagan declares that he expects the Afghan resistance to continue fighting after the Soviets have withdrawn from Afghanistan and that the United States will continue supplying their military needs.

April 14

AVIATION: In the Logar Valley south of Kabul, Afghanistan, mujahideen missiles bring down a military jet.

DIPLOMACY: The Soviet Union, having invaded Afghanistan in December 1979 and then been thwarted by Afghan freedom fighters bolstered by U.S. military aid, signs an agreement with the United States, Pakistan, and Afghanistan to remove 115,000 troops from the region beginning May 15. Half of this total is to be gone no later than August 15. U.S. secretary of state George Shultz and Soviet foreign minister Eduard Shevardnadze also conclude a separate "understanding" that pledges non-interference in Afghan affairs, but also allows each nation to continue military aid to their respective sides. This is a major cold war victory for the United States and its allies although the political instability wreaked by the Soviet invasion portends ill for the future.

In Peshawar, Pakistan, the mujahideen alliance denounces the Geneva peace accord and vows to keep fighting until the Kabul regime is toppled.

MILITARY: North of Kabul, Afghanistan, intense fighting is reported between Afghan army forces and mujahideen units; government helicopters are observed transporting many casualties from Shakardara.

In Kabul, Afghanistan, while word of the Geneva peace accord was announced with great excitement, residents were greeted by an intense clash between Soviet and mujahideen forces that lasted throughout the night and until the following dawn.

NAVAL: In the Persian Gulf, the frigate USS *Samuel B. Roberts,* sister ship of the ill-fated USS *Stark,* strikes a supposed Iranian mine, which injures 10 sailors and causes a 21-foot-long hole in the hull and extensive damage. The incident occurs 70 miles east of Bahrain, and the vessel makes its way to Dubai on auxiliary engines.

POLITICS: In Washington, D.C., members of Congress are effusive in their praise for the Afghan peace accord.

April 15

AVIATION: In the Speena Boora area of Nangarhar Province, Afghanistan, an Afghan militia outpost is accidentally bombed by Soviet warplanes. Several bombs also land in the nearby Hagum subdistrict.

MILITARY: In Washington, D.C., President Ronald W. Reagan meets with Pentagon officials to devise a proper military response to continued Iranian mining of the Persian Gulf. They decide upon Operation Praying Mantis, whereby the U.S. Navy would destroy several Iranian oil platforms, then engage and possibly sink any Iranian warship sailing forth to challenge it.

NAVAL: U.S. Navy vessels uncover and destroy two mines floating near where the frigate USS *Samuel B. Roberts* was damaged.

POLITICS: In Peshawar, mujahideen leader Gulbuddin Hekmatyar asks the Council of Justice within the Islamic Alliance of Afghan Mujahideen to issue a decree to try all individuals suspected of collaborating with the Soviets during their occupation. He also declares that no Soviet prisoners in the rebels' possession will be returned until all Afghans who have fled to the Soviet Union are returned to face trial.

April 16

DIPLOMACY: In Tehran, Iran, the government denounces the Geneva peace accord and vows to continue aiding the Afghan resistance.

MILITARY: In Washington, D.C., Department of Defense officials conclude that the recent explosion in the Owjeri munitions dump in Rawalpindi, Pakistan, was most likely the handiwork of Afghan intelligence operatives.

In Zabol Province, Afghanistan, mujahideen fighters capture Soviet outposts at Darwazgai, only 15 miles from the Pakistani border. The garrison was evacuated by helicopter prior to falling, after which Soviet jets bombed the area, striking an ammunition dump.

April 16–18

MILITARY: In the southern sector, Iraqi president Saddam Hussein, who is determined to wrest back the Fao Peninsula from Iran, launches a nighttime artillery attack, featuring conventional and chemical weapons. This is followed swiftly by a helicopter commando attack on the scattered 5,000 defenders, then an all-out attack by 40,000 troops backed by tanks. The surprised Iranians quickly withdraw across the Shatt al Arab waterway to safety. This is one of the most stunning tactical upsets of the entire war.

April 17

MILITARY: In Herat Province, Afghanistan, resistance fighters destroy an oil pipeline passing through the western parts of the country.

April 18

AVIATION: U.S. Air Force tankers are actively engaged refueling U.S. Navy aircraft in a confrontation with Iranian forces.

During Operation Praying Mantis, a Marine Sea Cobra helicopter is lost; apparently the crew of two suffered from vertigo and crashed in the predawn darkness. The aircraft is recovered with no physical signs of combat damage.

DIPLOMACY: It is reported that American military assistance to the Afghan mujahideen over the past eight years cost more than $2 billion, with Saudi Arabia providing matching funds. It is one of the Central Intelligence Agency's largest and most successful operations of the cold war.

MILITARY: In Peshawar, Pakistan, spokesmen for the mujahideen alliance declare that the Afghan army garrison at Darwazgai, Zabol Province. Afghanistan, has been eliminated after several days of intense fighting. Previously, this outpost was used to interdict resistance supply routes in several directions.

In Baghdad, Iraq, the government radio declares that it has recaptured the strategic Fao Peninsula from Iranian forces. News of the victory triggered spontaneous celebrations in Baghdad and elsewhere throughout Iraq. In Tehran, Iran, Ayatollah Khomeini upbraids his military leaders for having grown "arrogant."

NAVAL: In the Persian Gulf, Operation Praying Mantis unfolds as U.S. Navy warships and jet bombers conduct a retaliatory action for the recent mine strike on the frigate USS *Samuel B. Roberts*. Initially, the destroyer *Merrill* shells and destroys the Sassan oil platform, heretofore employed as a command and control center for attacks on neutral shipping. Once it is evacuated by the crew, a detachment of marines goes on board to plant satchel charges, and the huge platform is destroyed. A second platform of Sirri Island is likewise eliminated by the guided-missile cruiser *Wainwright* and the frigates *Simpson* and *Bagley*.

Meanwhile, A-6 Intruders launched from the carrier *Enterprise* fire Harpoon missiles that sink the fast patrol boat *Joshan* and the frigate *Sahand* 10 miles southwest of Larak Island. Navy A-6 aircraft are also fired upon by the Iranian frigate *Sahand*, which is quickly disabled and sunk by repeated bomb and missile strikes. Finally, the destroyer *Joseph Strauss* joins A-6 and A-7 aircraft in pummeling the Iranian frigate *Sabalan*, which is allowed to return to port in severely damaged condition upon the orders of the U.S. secretary of defense. The action serves to highlight the intractable hostility between Iran and America.

POLITICS: In Peshawar, Pakistan, the Islamic Unity of Afghan Mujahideen convenes the first meeting of what it deems as its interim government cabinet. It discusses the formation of a new government in Afghanistan along with a host of related problems.

April 19

AVIATION: In Helmand Province, Afghanistan, waves of Soviet jets attack the Sangeen district, killing many villagers and destroying scores of buildings. A mujahideen Stinger missile also brings down a Soviet warplane in the vicinity of Mossa Kala.

Reports surface from Jalalabad, Afghanistan, that a military convoy carrying "three-meter-long rockets" has departed recently for Sanakel, 15 miles east of the city. This is apparently the site of a large Soviet storage facility.

MILITARY: Soviet and Afghan forces sweep through Helmand Province, Afghanistan, to clear the region of mujahideen fighters after they captured the Sangeen district on March 23.

In Kabul Province, Afghanistan, a force of 100 Afghan soldiers at Chehar Deh defects to the mujahideen with two truckloads of food and ammunition.

NAVAL: In Tehran, Iran, the Iranian government admits that 15 of its sailors had died in recent clashes with the U.S. Navy.

POLITICS: In Kabul, Afghanistan, the recent Geneva peace accord has triggered great anxiety among the residents, with many fearing that a Soviet withdrawal will precipitate additional fighting inside the city.

April 20

POLITICS: In Tehran, Iran, the resistance group Harkat-i-Islami condemns the Geneva peace accord and insists it will wage a jihad against the Kabul regime until an Islamic government is established.

April 21

AVIATION: In Faryab Province, Afghanistan, a mujahideen Stinger missile brings down a MiG fighter jet that was attacking their position.

MILITARY: In Nangarhar Province, Afghanistan, a large Soviet convoy bound for Jalal-abad departs, jamming traffic along the Torkham-Jalalabad road fro several hours.

Reports surface in Quetta, Pakistan, that the township of Khawk-i-Sufaid, Farah Province, Afghanistan, was recently captured in some of the fiercest fighting of the entire war. Both sides suffered heavy casualties, including scores of civilians, but the rebels ended up seizing large quantities of arms, vehicles, and food.

In Laghman Province, Afghanistan, mujahideen fighters size Dusaraka and Qala-i-Arsallah; these are two important outposts along the strategic Kabul-Jalal-abad highway.

POLITICS: In Kabul, Afghanistan, President Mohammad Najibullah declares that 1.5 million Afghans voted in recent national elections.

April 22

DIPLOMACY: In Washington, D.C., President Ronald W. Reagan cautions his fellow Americans that the Soviet withdrawal from Afghanistan does not spell the end of Soviet involvement in southwest Asia. He says he is very concerned over the security of Pakistan.

MILITARY: In Konar Province, Afghanistan, the Afghan resistance captures the Barikot cantonment after four days of heavy fighting. This post, directly on the border with Pakistan, was guarded by a brigade of Afghan army troops, the majority of whom were evacuated by helicopter, while others simply defected to the muja-hideen. Immediately afterward, Soviet and Afghan air force jets bomb the base and the neighboring villages in retaliation.

A report on Voice of America says that the mujahideen have sustained heavy losses from a large Soviet/Afghan army offensive in northern Helmand Province, Afghanistan. At least 10,000 troops and 1,200 tanks and armored vehicles were involved in the attack, which was aimed at capturing the Kajaki Dam on the Helmand River since it supplies power to several areas in Helmand and Kandahar Provinces. The Afghan resistance has apparently destroyed the installation. This is the fourth large operation undertaken to capture the dam in three months.

April 24

MILITARY: In Logar Province, Afghanistan, the Bakhtar News Agency reports that a major mujahideen base has fallen to government forces. They apparently captured 124 missile launchers, three light guns, 50 ground-to-ground rockets, 1,400 land mines, and 60 hand grenades.

In Parvan Province, Afghanistan, a large Soviet and Afghan army convoy is ambushed near the Salang Tunnel, underscoring its status as a vulnerable transit point between Kabul and the Soviet Union.

NAVAL: Determined not to be cowed by the presence of American warships in the Persian Gulf, Iranian speedboats attack a Saudi-owned tanker off Dubai.

April 25

DIPLOMACY: In Islamabad, Pakistan, a group of UN monitors under Finnish general Rauli Helminen arrives to begin supervising implementation of the Geneva peace accord.

MILITARY: The BBC reports that Maroof and Adgahr, Kandahar Province, Afghanistan, have been evacuated in the face of constant mujahideen pressure. The garrisons were evacuated by helicopter and flown directly to Kandahar city. Word of the government abandonment of three similar garrisons in the past 48 hours suggests that the Kabul regime is shortening and shoring up its lines of defense prior to a Soviet withdrawal.

POLITICS: Throughout Pakistan, the mujahideen mark the ninth anniversary of the Soviet invasion by staging huge rallies in numerous refugee camps.

April 26

DIPLOMACY: In New York City, UN secretary-general Javier Pérez de Cuéllar appoints Diego Cordovez as his personal representative for the remainder of the Afghan crisis. He also designates General Rauli Helminen of Finland to serve as deputy for military affairs, and Benon Vahe Sevan, a director within the UN secretariat, to be senior political deputy. The establishment of UN observer posts in Kabul, Afghanistan, and Islamabad, Pakistan, is expected to cost $7 million.

The government of Saudi Arabia announces that it is breaking off relations with Iran to protest the Iranian-instigated riots in Mecca in 1987 that cost 400 lives. It is also angered by the sacking of its embassy and recent Iranian attacks on neutral shipping in the Persian Gulf.

MILITARY: In Paktia Province, Afghanistan, the security post at Ghulam Khan falls bloodlessly to mujahideen fighters after 80 Afghan army soldiers defect.

POLITICS: In Peshawar, Pakistan, the mujahideen alliance rejects Afghan president Mohammad Najibullah's suggestion for a demilitarized zone along the Pakistani border to facilitate the return of refugees.

April 27

AVIATION: In Parvan Province, Afghanistan, a mujahideen missile downs a Soviet Su-25 ground-attack aircraft near Bagram Air Base.

DIPLOMACY: Saudi Arabia finally severs all diplomatic and political ties to Iran over the latter's refusal to reduce the amount of pilgrims sent on the hajj from 155,000 to 45,000, based on a new formula of 1,000 pilgrims per million Muslims in a country. The Iranians accuse the United States of being behind both moves.

MILITARY: In Kabul, Afghanistan, the government stages a huge military parade to celebrate the 10th anniversary of the Communist revolution, but the Soviets are represented by only two low-level dignitaries. This seems to confirm Moscow's intention to distance itself from the Kabul regime, and the civil strife that will follow a Soviet withdrawal.

In Kunduz Province, Afghanistan, a body of 100 Afghan army troops defects to the mujahideen from its post along the strategic Salang highway. It is also reported that the governor of Kunduz was captured by the Afghan resistance, after resistance members feigned interest in national reconciliation, then seized him and several high-ranking officials when they appeared for talks with rebel leaders.

In Baghlan Province, Afghanistan, a Soviet supply convoy is struck by mujahideen rockets near Qila Gai, damaging four tanks and 18 trucks.

Afghan rebels have closed the strategic Salang highway between Kabul and Charikar.

April 28

MILITARY: In Kabul, Afghanistan, President Mohammad Najibullah declares that Soviet military advisers will remain behind despite the withdrawal of their troops. However, they are not expected to hand over their weapons to the Afghan national army. Najibullah also expresses confidence that government troops can defeat the Afghan resistance.

In Logar Province, Afghanistan, pitched battles between mujahideen fighters and government forces result in the destruction of 10 tanks and other vehicles. Heavy casualties are also reported for both sides.

TERRORISM: Kabul, Afghanistan, is rocked by one of the biggest bomb blasts of the entire war, but there is no word on casualties.

April 29

NAVAL: In Washington, D.C., the Pentagon announces its intention to protect all neutral shipping in the Persian Gulf. Henceforth, any neutral vessel under attack can call upon U.S. warships for protection.

POLITICS: In Kabul, Afghanistan, President Mohammad Najibullah states that government forces currently control all 34 provinces in Afghanistan and that the pullout of Soviet forces will not alter that situation.

April 30

DIPLOMACY: In Washington, administration spokesmen disagree that according to the Geneva peace accord Soviet military advisers can remain behind in Afghanistan.

MILITARY: Soviet troops begin withdrawing from Baharak, Badakhshan Province, and Rustaq, Takhar Province, Afghanistan. Both regions are directly on the Soviet border.

In Nangarhar Province, Afghanistan, mujahideen forces bombard Soviet garrisons at Lalpura, Sarhadari, Farsh, and Landai Kyber along the Pakistani border.

May 1

DIPLOMACY: In Kabul, Afghanistan, a UN team arrives to monitor Soviet compliance with the Geneva peace accord.

MILITARY: Reports surface in Quetta, Pakistan, that the Afghan army has abandoned Showalikot, 20 miles north of Kandahar, Afghanistan, following mass defections to the mujahideen. The garrison were airlifted out by helicopter, abandoning a year's worth of food and ammunition to the resistance.

In Konar Province, Afghanistan, Afghan army forces abandon Asmar and relocate the garrison to the provincial capital of Chagha Sarai.

Throughout western Afghanistan, Soviet and Afghan army forces are strengthening security posts in the vicinity of Herat, and the highways connecting it to the Soviet Union, Iran, Mazar-i-Sharif, Kabul, and Kandahar.

Reports surface that Afghan army general Fazal Ahmad, who had previously served in the Defense Ministry as chief of logistics, has defected to the mujahideen in Herat Province. He is last reported as being in Iran.

Kabul, Afghanistan, is hit by the heaviest rocket barrage of the year, in which residential areas of Soviet technical staff were targeted. Apparently, the mujahideen possess weapons capable of striking targets from well beyond the city's perimeter.

May 2

DIPLOMACY: In Moscow, Soviet Union, Western diplomats, including U.S. Ambassador Jack Matlock, attend the May Day parade for the first time in eight years. This is apparently a goodwill gesture aimed at improving ties prior to the next Reagan-Gorbachev summit.

May 3

DIPLOMACY: In Kabul, Afghanistan, President Mohammad Najibullah invites Mohammad Zahir Shah to return home from Italy and partake of a new coalition government once the Soviets withdraw. However, the former monarch declares that the time is not yet right for him to return.

MILITARY: At Takhta Pul, Kandahar Province, Afghanistan, mujahideen forces attack a Soviet garrison, apparently inflicting 20 casualties.

The districts of Maruf, Shahwalikot, and Taghar in Kandahar Province, Afghanistan, have been seized by resistance forces. Shortly before, the garrison at nearby Arghastan was evacuated by helicopter. This is the third town in the region to fall, in addition to Noroz and Shah Wali.

Fighting has apparently broken out in regions bordering the Soviet Union, including Kunduz, Takhar, and Baghlan Provinces.

A report surfaces from Baghlan Province, Afghanistan, that mujahideen forces have executed the provincial governor and also seized several army posts around the city.

May 4

DIPLOMACY: The group Amnesty International accuses the Soviet and Afghan armies of grossly violating human rights, including deliberate attacks upon civilians, in their war against the mujahideen.

May 5

AVIATION: In Parvan Province, Afghanistan, mujahideen rockets slam into Bagram Air Base, destroying a military aircraft on the ground.

DIPLOMACY: In Washington, State Department officials declare that the United States would support the Afghan resistance if it chose to form a coalition government, once it had consolidated its control over most of the countryside.

In New Delhi, India, Afghan president Mohammad Najibullah arrives to confer with Prime Minister Rajiv Gandhi and President Ramaswamy Venkataraman.

MILITARY: Near Spin Bolak, Afghanistan, 600 Afghan soldiers from the Kakazi tribe defect to the mujahideen, bringing all their rifles, rocket launchers, and heavy machine guns on eight trucks.

In Ghazni Province, Afghanistan, a military aircraft is shot down by Afghan rebels over the Gailan subdivision, and the rebels also claim the destruction of two Afghan army tanks.

In Faryab Province, Afghanistan, the mujahideen fire a dozen rockets against Soviet positions in the provincial capital at Maimana.

May 6

DIPLOMACY: In New Delhi, India, the government declares that Afghan president Mohammad Najibullah is willing to share power with guerrilla groups, provided India serves as mediator.

May 7

MILITARY: Kandahar City, Afghanistan, experiences the heaviest rocket bombardment since the war commenced.

In Paktia Province, Afghanistan, the garrison at Share Nau, Chamkani district, is overrun by Afghan rebels, who kill 100 Afghan soldiers, capture another 100, and destroy 50 vehicles.

In Baghlan Province, Afghanistan, mujahideen fighters attack an Afghan supply center directly on the Soviet border, destroying four tanks and 18 military vehicles.

POLITICS: In Kabul, Afghanistan, President Mohammad Najibullah appeals to moderate factions among the mujahideen to join his government. He also insists that the Afghan army can maintain power even after the Soviets have withdrawn.

May 8

MILITARY: In Kandahar City, Afghanistan, mujahideen infiltrate close enough to attack a PDPA party meeting, killing eight high-ranking officials.

In Takhar Province, Afghanistan, the mujahideen finally capture the Dashti Qala district after a week of intense combat. Previously, they had eliminated 25 security posts during their advance.

POLITICS: Western journalists are allowed in Kabul, Afghanistan, to witness the withdrawal of Soviet forces. The BBC reports that both local residents and the Soviet troops themselves are very happy over the prospect of leaving. However, the only people not sharing such sentiments are the Afghan Communists, who worry for their safety in a post-Soviet nation.

May 9

AVIATION: A report surfaces on Radio Tehran that the mujahideen shot down a Soviet helicopter in eastern Jalalabad, Afghanistan, as it escorted a Soviet convoy heading for Kabul.

MILITARY: Kabul, Afghanistan, is struck by seven large mujahideen rockets, killing 23 people in residential areas.

May 10

AVIATION: According to Radio Tehran, Soviet and Afghan air force jets staged 30 sorties over two targets in the Barikot region of Konar Province, along the Pakistani border.

POLITICS: In Gorki Park, Moscow, Victory Day demonstrations are organized by the government in support of the Afghan war.

May 11

DIPLOMACY: In Kandahar, Afghanistan, the tempo of mujahideen attacks on the city forces the Indian government to close its consulate. It had shuttered its Jalalabad consulate in April.

MILITARY: The first trickle of Soviet troops departs Kabul, Afghanistan, and wends its way north along the Salang highway toward the Soviet Union.

POLITICS: In Peshawar, Pakistan, the mujahideen alliance declares its intention to attack Soviet forces in Afghanistan, even while in the act of withdrawing.

In Kabul, Afghanistan, the government declares that all commercial traffic will be forbidden on the Salang highway north of the capital as of May 14. This is undertaken for the protection of Soviet forces departing the country.

Soviet forces are observed turning over security posts and other facilities to Afghan army units prior to their departure as they begin concentrating in major urban areas. Locally, Soviet officials have been attempting to reach interim truces

Damaged by a mine in the Persian Gulf, the guided-missile frigate USS *Samuel B. Roberts* is transported by the carrier *Mighty Servant II* to Newport, Rhode Island. *(U.S. Navy)*

with local mujahideen leaders, and, in one instance, the Soviet commander at Bagram Air Base promises that his aircraft will not attack civilian localities if the rebels stop shelling that facility.

May 12
DIPLOMACY: In New York City, UN High Commissioner Prince Sadruddin Aga Khan is tasked with coordinating international relief and resettlement efforts for the United Nations in Afghanistan.

May 13
AVIATION: Mujahideen missiles down two military helicopters in Nangarhar Province, Afghanistan, as they cover the withdrawal of Soviet and Afghan forces from the region.

MILITARY: As Soviet troops gather in eastern Afghanistan and prepare to evacuate Jalalabad, Nangarhar Province, Western analysts say that the mujahideen are expected to attack the city soon and that this will be the first test of the Afghan national army to resist them. Meanwhile, a convoy of more than 100 tanks and trucks was seen departing Kabul, headed north, while 4,000 Soviet troops are headed from Shel Khel, eight miles from Jalalabad, as part of the overall evacuation.

In Nangarhar Province, Afghanistan, Afghan and Soviet troops abandon security posts in the Mainkhel and Chelgazi region of Hissarik district on the Pakistan border.

POLITICS: In Kabul, Afghanistan, government-sponsored demonstrations are held in front of the U.S. and Pakistan embassies to protest the latest rash of mujahideen rocket attacks on the city. Meanwhile, a total of 65 journalists from Japan, the Soviet Union, Canada, the United States, Britain, Austria, Spain, Jordan, and Poland arrive in Kabul, Afghanistan, to cover ceremonies marking the Soviet withdrawal.

In Peshawar, Pakistan, the mujahideen alliance rejects proposed talks with UN special envoy Diego Cordovez regarding formation of an interim government in Kabul, Afghanistan.

May 14
TERRORISM: In Kabul, Afghanistan, a bomb explodes near reviewing stands prepared for farewell ceremonies to Soviet troops; eight people are killed and 20 wounded.

May 15
AVIATION: In Kandahar Province, Afghanistan, Soviet aircraft launch a punitive air strike against Loikariaz village a day after 200 Afghan soldiers defected to the local mujahideen; 82 civilians are killed.

DIPLOMACY: In Washington, D.C., an administration spokesman declares that it will promote unity among all mujahideen groups until the communist regime in Kabul, Afghanistan, is overthrown and a broad-based Afghan government succeeds it.

MILITARY: In Kabul, Afghanistan, Soviet troops begin their official withdrawal, and Western journalists are invited to observe and report. The first detachment, which recently evacuated from Jalalabad, arrives in the capital en route to the Soviet Union.

General Boris V. Gromov, commander of Soviet forces in Afghanistan, announces that one-fourth of his men and equipment will be withdrawn from the country by the end of the month whether the mujahideen suspend their attacks or not. He also notes that 170 bases are being turned over to the Afghan national army, and the total amount of equipment left behind is valued at $1 billion.

At this stage of the war, Western military analysts estimate that from 12,000 to 18,000 Soviet troops have been killed or wounded in Afghanistan since 1979.

In light of mujahideen inroads throughout Kapisa, Afghanistan, Soviet and Afghan forces begin construction of new security posts along the Salang highway to protect withdrawing Soviet troops.

In Moscow, Soviet Union, the state-run media announce that the first convoy of Soviet troops departing Jalalabad was attacked by mujahideen rockets. General Vladimir Lobov also goes on the airwaves to discuss the harshness of the Afghan terrain, which greatly facilitates guerrilla attacks, and to say that strict discipline will be maintained throughout the withdrawal.

POLITICS: In Kabul, Afghanistan, President Mohammad Najibullah declares that his regime will survive the impending Soviet withdrawal, and he appeals to the Afghan resistance to cooperate.

May 16

DIPLOMACY: In Kabul, Afghanistan, the government accuses the Pakistani government of violating the Geneva peace accord by supplying the Afghan resistance with arms.

Marines inspect a ZU-23 automatic antiaircraft gun located on an Iranian Sassan oil platform, which they attacked as part of Operation Praying Mantis. *(Department of Defense)*

MILITARY: Now that the Soviet Union has begun withdrawing its 115,000 combat troops from Afghanistan, the process is expected to unfold across nine months. The mujahideen are also expected to quickly topple the regime of President Mohammad Najibullah once they are gone.

Mujahideen leader Ahmad Shah Massoud declares his intention to attack Jalalabad, Afghanistan, as soon as the Soviets have departed the city.

In Farah Province, Afghanistan, 500 Afghan soldiers from the Bowadi tribe defect to the mujahideen with 600 weapons and 30 vehicles.

The former Soviet Afghan army base at Jaji, Afghanistan, falls to a concerted mujahideen offensive after a week of fierce fighting that produced hundreds of casualties on both sides. Tons of food, supplies, and weapons are summarily abandoned to the rebels as a convoy of 1,200 Afghan and Soviet troops evacuates in a 45-truck convoy headed from Gardez. The resistance also claims to have picked up 110 Afghan deserters, including 16 officers.

POLITICS: In Peshawar, Pakistan, the Islamic Union, one of the seven mujahideen groups, declares its intention to relocate operations back to Afghanistan once the Soviets depart.

May 17

MILITARY: Soviet troops complete their pullback from the eastern portions of Nangarhar Province, Afghanistan, where they served as a barrier protecting Kabul from Pakistan-based rebels.

On the Jalalabad-Kabul highway, mujahideen fighters capture the town of Hesarak after trading fire with retreating Soviet forces.

Radio Kabul confirms a mujahideen rocket attack on Kandahar, Afghanistan, in which 12 122mm projectiles hit the headquarters of government forces, killing Major General Abdul Mutabil, an important member of the Mujahideen-Khalq faction.

In a significant defeat for the Kabul regime, mujahideen fighters storm into the Afghan army garrison at Alikhel, Afghanistan, seizing a large stockpile of weapons, supplies, and vehicles. The resistance now enjoys unfettered control of the Jaji district near the Pakistani border, which means that resupply efforts have been cut from six days to one by utilizing open roads instead of mountain passes. To date the Afghan resistance is acquiring greater mobility, better logistical support, and a large number of defections from its adversaries.

May 18

MILITARY: In Balkh Province, Afghanistan, the first convoy of 1,200 Soviet troops crosses the border and back into the Soviet Union at Hayratan. They receive a hero's welcome.

The government garrison at Chambkani, Afghanistan, becomes the fifth such post to be evacuated in the past two weeks. Afghan rebels had been attacking the base for the past several days, causing heavy losses on both sides.

May 19

DIPLOMACY: In Washington, D.C., Assistant Secretary of State Robert Peck testifies before a congressional hearing and clarifies that the United States remains at liberty to continue aiding the Afghan resistance without violating the Geneva peace accord. As guarantors, both the United States and the Soviet Union are free to give military assistance to their respective sides.

MILITARY: In Afghanistan, Major General Fazil Ahmad Samadi defects to the Afghan resistance.

May 20

AVIATION: Because the hills surrounding Jalalabad, Afghanistan, are full of mujahideen fighters, the regional airport has all but ceased functioning. All civilian flights have been suspended indefinitely while military flights are executed under perilous circumstances.

DIPLOMACY: Western analysts express concern over northern Afghanistan, which has been closely linked economically to Soviet Central Asia and might possibly serve as a buffer zone protecting Soviet strategic interests should a hostile regime emerge in Kabul.

MILITARY: In Moscow, Soviet Union, the TASS news agency reports that casualties in the Afghan war amount to 15,000. Western analysts believe this figure has been revised downward for political reasons.

North of Kabul, Afghanistan, mujahideen fighters attack a Soviet military convoy as it moves along the Salang highway and through the Shakardara area. This route, which passes through the strategic Panjshir Valley, affords the quickest exodus from Afghanistan but also the most perilous one.

May 21

MILITARY: The BBC reports that mujahideen fighters have captured an important garrison in the Panjshir Valley, through which passes the Salang highway. Ahmad Shah Massoud is intent on gaining control of the entire region with a view toward the post-Soviet period.

In Ghowr Province, Afghanistan, fierce fighting is reported between Afghan army troops in the Sarchashma area of Shahrak district and mujahideen fighters attempting to evict them. A Soviet aircraft flying in support has reportedly been shot down by the rebels.

NAVAL: In the Persian Gulf, the Iranians maintain their militant stance by staging a 10-day combined arms exercise labeled Zulfikar (Sword of Islam), which involves 50 naval vessels and marine, army, and air force units that might have been better employed elsewhere. Iraqi president Saddam Hussein is aware that all these military assets are tied up in the Gulf region and decides to strike near Basra.

May 22

DIPLOMACY: The regime in Kabul, Afghanistan, accuses the Pakistani government of violating the Geneva peace accord by supplying weapons and supplies to the mujahideen.

MILITARY: The second group of Soviet troops departs Afghanistan for the Soviet Union. Jalalabad also becomes the first Afghan city that the Soviets have completely evacuated.

POLITICS: At this critical juncture, continued infighting is reported by factions within the PDPA, with fissures along ideological, class, and ethnic lines.

May 23

MILITARY: With Afghan army units arrayed along the Pakistani border weakening through combat and desertion, the mujahideen begin moving up additional units to besiege Jalalabad.

A report surfaces on the Voice of Germany that the mujahideen have acquired another strategic post in the Panjshir Valley, Afghanistan, following the defection of 50 Afghan army soldiers.

In Herat, Afghanistan, mujahideen rockets slam into an Afghan army munitions dump, which spreads exploding munitions over a four-mile area over the next three hours.

In Kotai-i-Herat pass, five miles east of Herat, a Soviet convoy is struck by mujahideen rockets. Meanwhile, in the Ghorian district east of Herat, a group of border militia under Haji Sher Jan Alizai defects with their weapons to the resistance.

In Moscow, Soviet Union, state-run television announces that the Soviet evacuation of Nangarhar Province, Afghanistan, is complete. The withdrawing units were attacked en route by mujahideen fighters armed with surface-to-surface missiles.

POLITICS: Western diplomats in Kabul, Afghanistan, report that the prevailing mood in the city is grim as Soviet forces withdraw and leave it vulnerable to attacks by the resistance.

May 24

MILITARY: In Herat, Afghanistan, several security posts garrisoned by Afghan army troops are handed over to the local mujahideen without a struggle. A handful of other positions have to be carried by force, but military defections continue to be a serious problem for the Kabul regime.

In Helmand Province, Afghanistan, Soviet and Afghan forces have begun pulling back while mujahideen forces launch several attacks against Kalat, capital of Zabol Province.

May 25

AVIATION: In the fight for Shalamche, Iraq, the Iraqis unveil a new tactical weapon with a range of 35 miles and whose warhead explodes 500 feet above a target, showering the area with 200 antipersonnel bomblets.

MILITARY: In Moscow, Soviet Union, General Alexi Lizichev, chief of the main political directorate of the Soviet army, declares that 13,310 Soviet soldiers have died in Afghanistan, 35,478 have been wounded, and 311 remain unaccounted for. He further states that, as of today, 9,500 troops have been returned to the Soviet Union, along with 1,000 tanks and other pieces of equipment.

In Kabul, Afghanistan, Radio Kabul intimates that fighting broke out between the resistance groups of Gulbuddin Hekmatyar and Javed Nasir in the Karagagh district of Ghazni Province.

In Kandahar Province, Afghanistan, mujahideen rockets strike Soviet tanks in the vicinity of Hazraji Baba, prompting a retaliatory attack by Soviet jets on nearby civilian targets.

In the southern sector, the Iraqi Third Army Corps, bolstered by the elite Presidential Guard, maintains the strategic initiative by beginning a large and determined offensive to recapture Shalamche, east of Basra. The attack kicks off with a huge artillery bombardment that dumps tons of conventional and chemical ordnance on the defenders. The searing desert heat precludes the use of protective clothing, and Iranian defenses are further upended by helicopter-borne Iraqi commandos followed by closely coordinated tank assaults. The Iraqi front line advances a further 25 miles eastward to Kut Suwadi and Bublyan.

May 26

AVIATION: In Moscow, Soviet Union, Soviet deputy defense minister Sergei F. Akhromeyev says that 70 helicopters have returned from Afghanistan. He also notes that Soviet troop strength there stands at 100,300 men.

DIPLOMACY: The Soviet government reiterates that Pakistan's continuing military aid to the mujahideen violates the Geneva peace accord and is unacceptable.

MILITARY: The BBC airs a report suggesting that the mujahideen have captured six security posts along the Kabul-Kandahar highway, either through combat or outright defection. The two posts, at Ishare Safa and Janda, contained garrisons of 200 men apiece.

In Ghazni Province, Afghanistan, Afghan army troops evacuate the Shahjoi and Kara Bagh posts following a four-day engagement. Resistance fighters have also apparently captured the town of Saidabad. It is feared that the government's shaky control of the highways may ultimately impede the Soviet withdrawal from Ghazni.

Northwest of Kabul, Afghanistan, mujahideen fighters attack a Soviet convoy as it passes through the Mashwanri area; they claim six military vehicles are destroyed.

POLITICS: In Kabul, Afghanistan, Mohammad Hassan Sharq replaces Sultan Ali Keshtmand as prime minister, while the latter becomes secretary of the PDPA Central Committee.

May 27

MILITARY: In Pakistan, a gathering of 45 mujahideen leaders formulates a strategy for the post-Soviet period.

May 28

DIPLOMACY: In Moscow, Soviet Union, President Ronald W. Reagan and General Secretary Mikhail Gorbachev open another summit meeting.

MILITARY: In Zabol Province, Afghanistan, mujahideen fighters attack Kalat, the provincial capital.

POLITICS: It is reported that, throughout the month of May, tribal elders and chieftains convened jirgas (meetings) to voice support for the Geneva peace accord.

In Tehran, Iran, Ayatollah Khomeini, though disheartened by the loss of the Shalamche pocket, calls for renewed sacrifice by insisting that "the outcome of the war will be decided on the battlefields, not through negotiations."

May 30

POLITICS: In Kabul, Afghanistan, President Mohammad Najibullah summons the first parliament in 15 years. He also asks resistance members to stop fighting and to assume seats established for their representation.

May 31

DIPLOMACY: In Washington, D.C., an administration spokesman declares that military aid to the mujahideen will continue since the Soviets are leaving $1 billion in military hardware behind for the regime in Kabul, Afghanistan.

MILITARY: In Kabul, Afghanistan, Western diplomatic sources suggest that the second Soviet troop withdrawal is under way following the departure of forces from Ghazni, 81 miles south of the capital, and Gardez, only 60 miles south. Both cities are considered essential to the government's national defense and are now entrusted to Afghan army troops.

In Kandahar Province, Afghanistan, mujahideen forces strike Soviet forces in the Panjwai region and at Spin Boldak near Pakistan. Fighting around the latter position is described as fierce, with many casualties on both sides, and the main road between Spin Boldak and Kandahar remains blocked.

June 1

AVIATION: In Helmand Province, Afghanistan, mujahideen forces shell an Afghan air base, destroying three helicopters on the ground.

MILITARY: Fighting at Spin Boldak, Afghanistan, is reported so intense that shells and rockets are falling on the nearby Pakistani town of Chaman.

POLITICS: The Afghan resistance declares the appointment of an Islamic governor and judge at Kalat, the capital of Zabol Province, Afghanistan.

June 2

POLITICS: In Pakistan, resistance leader Gulbuddin Hekmatyar declares that the Kabul regime will be toppled by his fighters the moment the last Soviet soldier departs. He also observes that the alliance enjoys greater unity than before, that an interim government is bring formed, and that military commanders in Afghanistan will be seated on the ruling council once an Islamic government is established.

In Balkh Province, Afghanistan, the border town of Shadian is captured by the mujahideen. This places rebel forces only 10 miles south of Mazar-i-Sharif and allows them to blockade the city.

MILITARY: In Tehran, Iran, Ayatollah Khomeini, determined to bolster a sagging war effort, appoints Majlis speaker Hojatolislam Hashemi Rafsanjani to serve as commander in chief in place of President Ali Khamenei. He is tasked with creating a command headquarters to better orchestrate activities of the Iranian military, the Revolutionary Guards, the Basij, and internal security forces.

June 3

DIPLOMACY: In New York City, UN officials confirm that the Soviet Union has removed 10,000 troops since May 15, and the pace has shown no sign of slackening.

In Moscow, Soviet Union, General Secretary Mikhail Gorbachev threatens to slow the pace of the Soviet withdrawal from Afghanistan if the government of Pakistan does not cease weapons shipments to the resistance.

MILITARY: *Izvestia* reports that mujahideen rockets have struck Kabul, Afghanistan, causing several civilian casualties. It goes on to state that neither Washington nor Islamabad is taking the Geneva peace accord seriously, and they are responsible for whatever casualties are incurred.

June 4

DIPLOMACY: In Moscow, Soviet Union, President Mohammad Najibullah arrives for talks with General Secretary Mikhail Gorbachev. Meanwhile, five Soviet soldiers are reported killed in Afghanistan by the resistance.

MILITARY: In Kandahar, Afghanistan, mujahideen rockets slam into Soviet positions over the next three days.

June 5

AVIATION: In Faryab Province, Afghanistan, waves of Soviet warplanes attack villages around Maimana, forcing the residents to flee prior to a Soviet offensive there.

DIPLOMACY: In Moscow, Soviet Union, Afghan president Mohammad Najibullah confers with General Secretary Mikhail Gorbachev over the latter's recent talks with President Ronald W. Reagan.

MILITARY: A RAND Corporation study suggests that the Red Army has performed very poorly over the past eight years, largely due to poor training and low morale. However, it cautions against underestimating Soviet military capabilities.

In Faryab Province, Afghanistan, Soviet and Afghan army troops mount a joint offensive against mujahideen units operating near Maimana.

June 6

MILITARY: Western diplomats inform the BBC that the Soviets have nearly completed their withdrawal from Gardez and Ghanzi, Afghanistan, even though numerous convoys were ambushed during the process. No sooner did the Soviets depart than local mujahideen overran two security posts.

June 7

AVIATION: A report surfaces that Major General Mohammad Aziz Sarwai, chief of staff of the Afghan air force, was killed in severe fighting around Kandahar, Afghanistan.

Over Khost, Afghanistan, a mujahideen Stinger missile damages a Soviet transport plane as it was flying back to Kabul.

MILITARY: In Herat and Kandahar, western Afghanistan, Soviet troops begin pulling out. However, diplomatic sources caution that the withdrawal from Kandahar may be delayed over continuing concern for the city's safety. Afghan army troops have also deployed closer to the southern periphery of Kandahar and constructed new defensive positions.

Izvestia reports that five Soviet soldiers died when their convoy was ambushed by rebels as it rolled along the main Kandahar-Kabul highway.

Radio Tehran announces that the Afghan resistance has stepped up attacks in Konar, Logar, Paktia, and Badakhshan Provinces, Afghanistan

June 8

AVIATION: Outside Kandahar, Afghanistan, rebel commanders report that an average of three Soviet transports arrive and depart the city airport every night, bringing in supplies and evacuating casualties.

At Qalat Ghilzai, Zabol Province, mujahideen rockets destroy two helicopters on the ground.

DIPLOMACY: In New York City, Afghan president Mohammad Najibullah addresses the UN General Assembly and warns that the Soviets might postpone their withdrawal should Pakistan continue arming the Afghan resistance. He also accuses Pakistan of violating the Geneva peace accord by continuing to supply weapons to the Afghan resistance.

MILITARY: In Kandahar, Afghanistan, heavy fighting erupts between mujahideen units and a thick belt of Afghan army troops defending that city. This, in turn, has delayed the scheduled evacuation of Soviet troops, who, in any event, face the likely prospect of being ambushed by rebels entrenched in many mountain passes leading out of the region.

Rebel forces have shut down the road between Kandahar and Makur, Afghanistan, while Kalat, provincial capital of Zabol Province, is under siege.

June 9

DIPLOMACY: In New York City, Afghan president Mohammad Najibullah again addresses the UN General Assembly to declare that 243,900 soldiers and civilians have died in fighting throughout Afghanistan.

June 10

DIPLOMACY: In Moscow, Soviet Union, Foreign Minister Eduard Shevardnadze accuses the United States and Pakistan of grossly violating terms of the Geneva peace accord.

June 11

DIPLOMACY: In New Delhi, India, Prime Minister Rajiv Gandhi is optimistic that Afghan president Mohammad Najibullah will survive the withdrawal of Soviet forces from Afghanistan. He fears that the rise of a fundamentalist Islamic regime there would destabilize the entire region, including India, where 12 percent of the population is Muslim.

To date, Pakistan has formally lodged 800 protests over border violations and other acts of aggression from neighboring Afghanistan. By the end of 1987, these resulted in 700 deaths and more than 1,000 injured.

MILITARY: A report on the Voice of America indicates that a retaliatory Soviet artillery bombardment has killed or injured 50 villagers near Kandahar, Afghanistan. The Soviets were apparently responding to a mujahideen attack against Soviet forces at Jakan on June 6. Other reports from Quetta, Pakistan, indicate that hundreds of casualties go untreated in Kandahar City. A picture emerges whereby the bulk of Afghan forces have withdrawn toward the city's interior because the population in outlying regions openly supports the resistance.

Northwest of Kandahar, Afghanistan, mujahideen forces attack the Afghan army garrison at Baba Shah Wali, and seven out of 16 security outposts are captured. The fighting has closed several routes to Pakistan, leading to shortages of food and cooking oil in nearby Spin Boldak.

In Pakistan, government officials confirm an artillery exchange between Pakistani artillery units and those of the Afghan army between Chaman and Spin Boldak. Soviet aircraft also apparently bombed the outskirts of the former.

June 12
AVIATION: Mujahideen rockets rain down on Khost airport, Afghanistan, destroying a helicopter and a transport aircraft.

Over Spin Boldak, Afghanistan, a mujahideen Stinger missile brings down a Soviet-built fighter plane.

DIPLOMACY: In Moscow, Soviet Union, Afghan president Mohammad Najibullah arrives after attending a conference in Havana, Cuba, and confers with General Secretary Mikhail Gorbachev for a second time.

Gorbachev warns of "resolute retaliatory steps" should Pakistan continue arming the Afghan resistance.

MILITARY: One result of the Soviet departure from Afghanistan is that mujahideen field commanders operating in Pakistan are becoming less dependant on the alliance leadership in Peshawar, Pakistan. There is also increasing resentment between commanders who actively battle Soviet and Afghan forces and those who have not left Pakistan. Western analysts conjecture that field commanders will gradually demand to share political power with alliance members in the post-Soviet period.

In Kapisa Province, Afghanistan, Soviet and Afghan army forces commence a major offense against mujahideen units besieging the garrison town of Gulbahar. Heavy fighting and losses are reported on both sides.

In Paktia Province, Afghanistan, the Afghan resistance cuts off all major roads leading to Khost Uluswali.

In Kabul Province, Afghanistan, Soviet and Afghan army units indiscriminately attack Shadaidara, killing civilians and destroying crops and other property. This apparently comes in retaliation for recent guerrilla attacks thought to have been supported by the populace.

In the southern sector, Iranian forces are ordered back into the Shalamche region by Majlis speaker Hojatolislam Hashemi Rafsanjani to improve military morale. They claim a penetration of seven miles and the infliction of 18,000 casualties on the Iraqis before withdrawing voluntarily.

June 14
MILITARY: In Badghis Province, Afghanistan, Afghan forces, backed by Soviet troops, attack mujahideen units in the Ghoormach district; combat reportedly lasts over the next 10 days.

POLITICS: In Moscow, Soviet Union, a group of former prisoners of war hold a news conference to remind the public of the 311 soldiers still missing in action.

June 15
DIPLOMACY: France and Iran resume diplomatic ties under the new Socialist government of François Mitterrand. After the Soviet Union, France is the second-largest supplier of weapons to Iraq and will remain so.

MILITARY: Soviet media report that Soviet troops have completely pulled out from Logar, Nangarhar, and Paktia Provinces, along the Pakistani border.

POLITICS: In Peshawar, Pakistan, Sayyed Ahmed Gailani of the National Islamic Front of Afghanistan replaces Gulbuddin Hekmatyar as spokesman of the International

Union of Afghan Mujahideen. The notoriously outspoken and unpredictable Hekmatyar has made several enemies during his tenure as spokesman.

June 16

POLITICS: In Kabul, Afghanistan, President Mohammad Najibullah declares that he is forming a new government, which will include opposition elements.

According to Radio Beijing, Gulbuddin Hekmatyar declares that Soviet prisoners held by the mujahideen alliance will only be released after all Soviet forces have departed Afghanistan. He does not rule out a request by the International Committee of the Red Cross to negotiate their release.

June 17

AVIATION: Over Faryab Province, Afghanistan, mujahideen fighters bring down two military aircraft.

Over Paktia Province, Afghanistan, resistance fighters claim to have downed a military transport as it was on its landing approach at Khost.

MILITARY: In the Shamali region north of Kabul, Afghanistan, a report surfaces that Soviet and Afghan army forces have abandoned the Panjshir Valley while the mujahideen claim to have seized the Tayes garrison in Badakhshan Province.

In Konar Province, Afghanistan, mujahideen forces ambush a large military convoy, destroying four tanks and nine trucks between Soorai Teeqa and Speen Jumat.

POLITICS: In Moscow, Soviet Union, the Communist Party leadership makes a rare admission of errors that led to military intervention in Afghanistan. They claim that previous leaders erred in thinking that a primitive, tribal land like Afghanistan would be ready for socialism.

June 19

DIPLOMACY: In Washington, D.C., a State Department official declares that the Communist regime in Kabul, Afghanistan, will not long survive the pullout of Soviet forces. However, mujahideen leaders believe that overoptimism on the part of the Americans will lead to an unnecessary reduction of military aid. Pakistan also indicates concern that the Soviet pullout will cause the United States to lose interest in the region.

MILITARY: In the central sector, Iraqi forces fire artillery shells laced with cyanide gas and nerve agents at Iranian positions in the Mehran region. Once the town and surrounding area are captured, they are handed over to the Mujahideen-i-Khalq's National Liberation Army. However, the army withdraws three days later.

POLITICS: In Peshawar, Pakistan, mujahideen spokesman Sayed Ahmad Gilani requests resistance leaders to remove all obstacles in the path of withdrawing Soviet forces to expedite their departure.

June 20

MILITARY: The BBC airs a report in which the regime in Kabul, Afghanistan, claims to have recaptured Kalat, provincial capital of Zabol Province. In fact, the mujahideen have retreated to nearby hills but continue shelling the city.

In Parvan Province, Afghanistan, a large oil convoy is struck by Afghan guerrillas, destroying 10 tankers and a large quantity of fuel.

POLITICS: The BBC learns that mujahideen groups in Afghanistan and Iran do not recognize the interim government established by the leadership in Peshawar, Pakistan.

June 21

DIPLOMACY: Somewhere in Afghanistan, a UN representative meets for the first time with a mujahideen field commander who informs him the United Nations should withhold assistance to the country until an acceptable government has been established in Kabul.

MILITARY: In Kandahar Province, Afghanistan, mujahideen fighters simultaneously strike at the city and the local airport.

In Paktia Province, Afghanistan, mujahideen fighters employ rockets and mortars against government bases. Soviet aircraft retaliate by hitting rebel positions.

June 22

MILITARY: In Peshawar, Pakistan, Jamiat-i-Islami leader Burhanuddin Rabbani informs a news conference that 30 fortified towns have fallen to the Afghan resistance since the start of the Soviet withdrawal. They have also destroyed or captured 150 security posts. Rabbani also criticizes Indian prime minister Rajiv Gandhi for fearing the creation of a fundamentalist regime in Afghanistan and insists that regional security has already been threatened by the Soviet invasion and Indian troops in Sri Lanka.

June 23

MILITARY: In Washington, D.C., Under Secretary of State Michael Armacost testifies before a Senate panel that the Soviet withdrawal is proceeding on time and notes that 25,000 troops have withdrawn from their garrisons, with half that number crossing back over into the Soviet Union. The cities of Jalalabad, Ghazni, and Gardez in the eastern and southeastern parts of the country have been entirely turned over to Afghan army troops.

In New York City, mujahideen leader Abdul Haq informs the United Nations that its first priority should be the establishment of a broad-based coalition government in Afghanistan and a halt to continuing aid to the country, which only helps to prop up the present Kabul regime.

In the Panjshir Valley, Afghanistan, the mujahideen capture the garrison at Gulbahar. In light of Soviet vulnerability along the Salang highway, which passes through this strategic region, the Soviets are eager to work out a truce in advance with local mujahideen leader Ahmad Shah Massoud.

June 24

AVIATION: Over Khost, Afghanistan, a mujahideen Stinger missile brings down a large military transport.

June 25

MILITARY: In the Salizak region of Badakhshan Province, a retaliatory air raid and artillery shelling by Soviet forces from across the border kills 25 civilians. This action comes in response to the recent mujahideen ambush of a Soviet convoy.

In the southern sector, Iraqi forces follow up on earlier successes by staging a quick, overpowering offensive on Majnoon Island in the Persian Gulf. Massed armor, artillery, and the first use of Iraqi paratroops completely outgun and outmaneuver the defenders. Even units of the elite Presidential Guard arrive on the island by hovercraft. Within a day, the Third and Sixth Army Corps have eliminated all resistance on the island.

POLITICS: Word of success on Majnoon Island, which has estimated oil reserves of seven billion barrels, sets off a frenzy of celebrations in war-weary Baghdad.

June 26

MILITARY: Mujahideen forces claim to have captured Maidan Shehr, provincial capital of Wardak Province, and only 25 miles from Kabul, Afghanistan. This follows the capture of Kalat in Zabol Province a few days earlier. A report surfaces on Radio Moscow that Afghan army units quickly recaptured the city, which straddles the strategic Kabul-Kandahar highway.

The TASS News Agency reports that mujahideen fighters assaulted Kote Ashrow in Wardak Province over the past 24 hours but were unable to capture it from Afghan army troops. The agency insists that the resistance, unable to subdue major cities, is concentrating its efforts on smaller towns for propaganda purposes.

June 28

AVIATION: Over Jaghori, Afghanistan, mujahideen Stinger missiles bring down a Soviet-built MiG fighter.

POLITICS: A BBC report suggests that mujahideen leader Ahmad Shah Massoud has established a supervisory council over an eight-day period to review strategy while Soviet units withdraw from Afghanistan. The council also decided to divide the northern reaches of the country into four administrative units, each with its own commander and fighting units, which will independently attack Afghan army garrisons within their grasp. Furthermore, all four regions will receive their own Ulema (religious courts) to settle local disputes. Finally, the mujahideen leadership connected to Massoud stridently opposes any moves toward coalition government and vows to keep fighting until the Kabul regime is toppled.

June 29

AVIATION: Over Paghman, Afghanistan, a mujahideen missile downs a Soviet helicopter as it attacks its position.

MILITARY: In Kabul, Afghanistan, Soviet general Matvei Zekharov informs the news media that, to date, 20,000 troops have been withdrawn while an additional 12,000 civilian personnel have also departed.

In Arghandi, Afghanistan, resistance fighters attack a Soviet convoy, destroying four tanks.

In Starghich, Afghanistan, a body of 100 government militia under Khawaja Mira Jan defects to the mujahideen.

Reports surface in Islamabad, Pakistan, that the defensive perimeter around Kabul, Afghanistan, has shrunk from three rings to two and that mujahideen forces are presently within nine to 12 miles of the center of town. North of the city, the resistance claims control of an 18-mile strip reaching from Paghman to outside Bagram Air Base.

Diplomats familiar with matters in Kandahar, Afghanistan, claim that Afghan army forces have condensed their defensive line into a single ring around the city. Only 2,000 Soviet troops remain, and they are concentrated around the vital airport. The Soviet withdrawal in this part of the country appears to be well under way, with 8,000 troops departing since May.

June 30

MILITARY: Radio Moscow airs a report from General Boris V. Gromov, commander of Soviet forces in Afghanistan, that 20,000 soldiers and 3,000 pieces of military hardware have been removed from Afghanistan.

In Shibargan, Jowzjan Province, Afghanistan, mujahideen fighters attack the residences of Soviet personnel, killing several. The fighting continues for 24 hours before the rebels withdraw.

In the central sector, a determined Iraqi offensive ejects Iranian forces from the town of Mawet.

In Tehran, Iran, the Supreme Council for War Support concedes recent military defeats and blames the United States, the Soviet Union, and the Arab states for forcing the nation to "step back." Moreover, new calls for volunteers are unheeded owing to the Iranian media's obsession with showing the effects of Iraqi chemical weapons.

POLITICS: In Tehran, Iran, the radical Hossein Musavi wins an election in the Majlis to serve as prime minister, 217 votes to 13.

July 1

MILITARY: In the Daryem district of Badakhshan Province, Afghanistan, the Afghan resistance attacks Soviet forces, killing 20 and capturing four. In retaliation, the village of Daryem is heavily bombed by Soviet warplanes.

In Logar Province, Afghanistan, mujahideen forces consolidate at Mohammed Agha, only 20 miles south of Kabul, which also cuts off the main route between the capital and Gardez. Fleeing Afghan army forces abandon scores of guns and trucks to the rebels, and Soviet aircraft retaliate by bombing nearby villages.

Mujahideen loyal to Ahmad Shah Massoud claim to operate administrative governments in 11 northern provinces of Afghanistan.

July 2

MILITARY: At Faizabad, Badakhshan Province, Afghanistan, 10 Soviet soldiers surrender to local mujahideen units.

In the Qadis district of Badghis Province, Afghanistan, local mujahideen units move in and establish local control. This area is directly on the Soviet border, and units from all seven major alliance members participate.

NAVAL: In the Persian Gulf, an Iranian speedboat fires on a Danish supertanker and is driven off by warning shots from the frigate USS *Elmer B. Montgomery.*

July 3

AVIATION: In the Persian Gulf, Iranian speedboats fire on American helicopters patrolling the region. The guided missile cruisers USS *Vincennes* and *Elmer Montgomery* arrive shortly after and drive off the offenders, sinking or damaging three of

The Ticonderoga Class Aegis guided-missile cruiser *Vincennes* fires an antisubmarine rocket as part of seatrials prior to its commissioning in July 1985. *(Department of Defense)*

them. At 10:49 A.M., the *Vincennes* picks up a radar contact, apparently a large aircraft approaching them at high speed. This turns out to be an Iranian A-300 Airbus headed for Dubai, and it is mistaken at long range for an Iranian F-14 fighter. The craft is immediately shot down by a missile six miles out over the Strait of Hormuz, killing all 290 passengers and crew. In fairness to the commander, the aircraft was warned off repeatedly on various frequencies but did not respond. Rather than risk a potential suicide attack on his vessel, the captain ordered the target destroyed. This policy was a direct outgrowth of the Iraqi attack on the *Stark* in 1987, and the vessel's commander was authorized to shoot any craft that failed to heed warnings or appeared to be threatening.

DIPLOMACY: In Washington, D.C., President Ronald W. Reagan expresses deep regret for the downing of the Iranian airliner while the Iranian government denounces the accident as a "barbaric massacre."

MILITARY: Near Spin Boldak, Afghanistan, a government deserter admits to local mujahideen units that morale is low and that Afghan army units suffered heavy losses from continued attacks against regimental headquarters.

TERRORISM: A report surfaces on the BBC that a large car bomb exploded outside a cinema in Jalalabad, Afghanistan, killing more than 30 people and injuring scores more.

July 4

NAVAL: The U.S. Navy opens a formal investigation of the shoot-down of the Iranian airliner, which President Ronald W. Reagan labels as tragic but an "understandable accident." The board concludes that Captain Will C. Rodgers acted responsibly, given the information he had at his disposal.

POLITICS: In Washington, D.C., administration officials and members of Congress lament new American commitments in the Persian Gulf. Both blame the lack of a systematic strategy of policy for the region.

In Moscow, Soviet Union, the government announces a blanket amnesty for deserters from the Afghan war

July 5

AVIATION: At Char, Afghanistan, waves of Soviet jets bomb village complexes, destroying 100 houses and killing 16 rebels and 56 civilians.

In New York City, the Iranian government calls for an urgent meeting of the UN Security Council for the first time since October 1980

DIPLOMACY: In Washington, D.C., President Ronald W. Reagan sends a note to the Iranian government as an apology for the downing of its airliner.

MILITARY: In Quetta, Pakistan, rumors surface that Afghan army troops had executed 40 mule drivers and four truck drivers in the Arghandab region north of Kandahar, Afghanistan. They apparently were employed in relocating people to Kak-Khais to dodge daily raids and fighting.

A report on Radio Kabul suggests that mujahideen factions loyal to Gulbuddin Hekmatyar and Burhanuddin Rabbani have fought each other in Faizabad, Badakhshan Province, Afghanistan.

Military analysts conclude that the strategic Panjshir Valley of northeastern Afghanistan is now completely controlled by mujahideen loyal to Ahmad Shah Massoud of Jamiat-i-Islami. Moreover, refugees who fled to Kabul to escape earlier fighting are filtering back into the region under Massoud's security. In light of serious differences between Massoud and Gulbuddin Hekmatyar, representatives of the two leaders are meeting in Islamabad, Pakistan.

In Islamabad, Pakistan, Western diplomats state that Soviet and Afghan forces have bombed and shelled Maidan Shehr, Wardak Province, Afghanistan, following its capture by Afghan resistance. Damage inflicted on the settlement was extensive and probably performed as a warning to other settlements.

A report on the Voice of America says that sharp disagreements have arisen over the Soviet tactic of indiscriminate bombing of Afghan civilians. Reportedly, the Kabul regime has protested the tactic, insisting that there is no need to subject Afghan civilians to military action, which only fuels the resistance and causes a new flood of refugees in the capital. Soviet advisers have ignored the protest and continued their air campaign against Maidan Shehr, Wardak Province.

July 6

MILITARY: In Kabul, Afghanistan, Soviet soldiers shoot and kill a 17-year-old youth, apparently mistaking him for a guerrilla.

Mujahideen attacks on Afghan army outposts have again closed the Kabul-Jalalabad highway.

July 7

AVIATION: In Farah Province, Afghanistan, mujahideen missiles bring down a government aircraft.

Twelve 122mm rockets launched from Shakardara, Afghanistan, strike the Kabul airport, 12 miles distant, destroying several parked aircraft.

In Parvan Province, Afghanistan, mujahideen missiles down two government helicopters.

DIPLOMACY: In Kabul, Afghanistan, President Mohammad Najibullah confers with UN special envoy Diego Cordovez and complains about Pakistan's violation of the Geneva peace accord.

MILITARY: In Moscow, Soviet Union, government radio announces that the Afghan resistance has increased its activities throughout the countryside, aided and abetted by Pakistan, and in violation of the Geneva peace accord.

TERRORISM: In Kabul, Afghanistan, a car bomb explodes outside PDPA offices, causing considerable damage.

Mujahideen fighters attack a Soviet-Afghan convoy as it rolls along the Kabul-Jalalabad highway; the rebels claim seven tanks and three military trucks were destroyed.

July 9

MILITARY: In Kabul, Afghanistan, government radio announces that Afghan and Soviet units have commenced a large ground offensive against resistance fighters in the mountains of Khuiastan, Helmand Province. Apparently they were guided to rebel positions by numerous civilians, and the civilians were abandoned with tons of supplies and weapons left behind. A report also surfaces of fighting between mujahideen loyal to Jamiat-i-Islami and Harkat-i-Enqelabi.

The Voice of Germany reports that the mujahideen have launched a major attack to capture Jalalabad, capital of Nangarhar Province, Afghanistan. The Hezb-i-Islami movement also claims to have attacked four other key installations in the same region.

In the central sector, a resurgent Iraqi army recaptures 14 mountain peaks in the Panjwin district.

July 10

MILITARY: In Logar Province, Afghanistan, mujahideen forces ambush an Afghan military convoy, destroying 12 tanks, five trucks, and three personnel carriers.

POLITICS: In Moscow, Soviet Union, state television broadcasts a warning to mujahideen units to cease attacking army units as they are removed from Afghanistan. Failure to do so will result in a possible end to the withdrawal.

July 11

AVIATION: In Takhar Province, Afghanistan, waves of Soviet jets level Chah Aab village, destroying 500 houses.

DIPLOMACY: In Peshawar, Pakistan, the mujahideen alliance rejects a UN proposal for the creation of an impartial, coalition government in Kabul along with a cease-fire as of September 1.

In Washington, D.C., President Ronald W. Reagan issues a formal apology to the Iranian people for the downed airliner and offers compensation to families of the deceased, which come from seven nations. This act was done less on the basis of a legal liability than for humanitarian reasons.

MILITARY: Radio Tehran reports that mujahideen fighters have began a major campaign to capture Jalalabad, Nangarhar Province, Afghanistan, and have to date eliminated 13 security posts on the highway leading to the city.

Radio Moscow announces that guerrillas belonging to Jamiat-i-Islami and Hezb-i-Islami have surged into Parvan Province, Afghanistan, where their Stinger missiles are a threat to civil and military aviation at Bagram Air Base.

POLITICS: Radio Moscow protests that arms and supplies continue reaching the resistance movement in Afghanistan through Pakistan. It also reports that recently two convoys of hundreds of pack animals delivered 500 rockets to Taliqan, Takhar Province, directly on the Soviet border.

July 12

AVIATION: Over the Paghman area of Kabul, Afghanistan, mujahideen Stinger missiles bring down a helicopter and a MiG fighter as they prepared to land at Kabul airport.

MILITARY: In Kabul Province, Afghanistan, 150 Afghan army troops desert and go over to the mujahideen with their weapons and equipment. Desertion continues to be a chronic problem among demoralized Afghan soldiers.

TERRORISM: In Kabul, Afghanistan, at least 20 Afghan and Soviet troops are killed when a bomb explodes in the city. The incident occurs as Foreign Minister Adbul Wakil is meeting with UN special envoy Diego Cordovez.

The Iraqi Fourth Army Corps, backed by units of the elite Presidential Guard, attack and drive back Iranians from the Musian border region in the south-central sector; they eventually push 30 miles into Iranian territory and capture Dehloran.

Iranian forces voluntarily depart Halabla in Iraqi Kurdistan, while Iraqi forces withdraw from the Naft-e-Shah region.

July 13

DIPLOMACY: In Peshawar, Pakistan, the mujahideen alliance demands direct talks with the Soviet Union over the release of prisoners of war.

The Soviet government lodges an official protest to the United States regarding Pakistan's violations of the Geneva peace accord.

MILITARY: The city of Kandahar, Afghanistan, is the focus of BBC report showing the relative ease and mobility that mujahideen fighters enjoy there. At one point resistance leader Ismail Gilani of the Mazhaz-i-Mili is shown meeting with local commanders amid the sound of gunfire and combat in the background. Numerous destroyed Soviet tanks and other vehicles suggest heavy losses in that quarter.

July 14

DIPLOMATIC: In New York City, Vice President George H. W. Bush addresses the UN Security Council, calling the shoot-down of the Iranian airliner a tragic accident, nothing more.

MILITARY: Mujahideen fighters storm into seven security posts in the Khake Jabbar district of Kabul, Afghanistan, following two days of fighting.

Along the Ghazni-Kandahar highway, the Afghan resistance captures two important Afghan army bases, then ambushes a government convoy intending to reinforce them. The rebels also pick up 90 defectors, 113 rifles, six trucks, and stores of ammunition and food.

POLITICS: In Tehran, Iran, a gathering of top government and political figures, having weighed all their strategic options, finally and unconditionally endorses Security Council Resolution 598.

July 15

AVIATION: Near Kabul, Afghanistan, a mujahideen Stinger missile brings down a Soviet Mi-25 helicopter.

DIPLOMACY: In Moscow, Soviet Union, government radio again formally accuses the United States and Pakistan of blatantly violating the Geneva peace accord.

MILITARY: Mujahideen units begin occupying the mountains ringing Kabul, Afghanistan, and commence a lengthy bombardment with rockets. Near the Salang tunnel, Afghanistan, resistance fighters ambush an oil convoy, destroying six tankers and a quantity of fuel.

POLITICS: In Tehran, Iran, Majlis speaker Hojatolislam Hashemi Rafsanjani meets with chairmen of various committees and endorses the decision to accept the UN-sponsored cease-fire. That evening a delegation also visits Ayatollah Khomeini to announce and discuss their consensus with him.

July 16

MILITARY: Victorious Iraqi forces voluntarily abandon the Dehloran-Musian area, handing back 2,260 square miles of terrain to Iran, and withdraw to their own border.

POLITICS: In Tehran, Iran, high-ranking clerics from the Assembly of Experts formally adopt the opinion that Iran should accept the UN-sponsored cease-fire resolution. The decision is then conveyed to Ayatollah Khomeini by Majlis Speaker Hojatolislam Hashemi Rafsanjani.

July 17

AVIATION: The airport at Khost, Afghanistan, is struck by mujahideen rockets; one aircraft is reported destroyed on the ground.

After Soviet security posts around Baghlan, Afghanistan, are struck by guerrillas, Soviet warplanes retaliate by bombing residential areas believed to be sympathetic to the rebels.

MILITARY: Reports circulate that Pakistan is lowering the amount of weapons and supplies provided to the mujahideen in Afghanistan, since they possess sufficient quantities of both to carry on the fight. Their continual attacks on Soviet forces might also delay an ultimate withdrawal from the region.

Mujahideen spokesmen announce that they have captured a government outpost in Farah Province, Afghanistan, destroying 10 tanks. Heavy losses are reported for both sides.

POLITICS: In Baghdad, Iraq, President Saddam Hussein uses celebrations marking the 20th anniversary of the Baath revolution to urge the Iranians to agree to the UN sponsored cease-fire, and he reiterates his own five-point peace program. This comprises a return to the international frontier, an immediate exchange of prisoners, a peace treaty, and a nonaggression pact, coupled with a mutual agreement not to meddle in the countries' respective domestic affairs. Thereafter, both nations are to strive for stability and security throughout the region.

July 18

AVIATION: Mujahideen rockets rain down on Kandahar airport, Afghanistan, destroying a Soviet helicopter and two oil tankers nearby.

DIPLOMACY: In Peshawar, Pakistan, UN special envoy Diego Cordovez proposes peace in Afghanistan through the creation of a neutral government. Sabghatul-lah Mojaddidi of the National Front for the Liberation of Afghanistan and Sayyed Ahmad Gailani of the National Islamic Front of Afghanistan both endorse the plan.

In New York City, a letter is delivered to UN secretary-general Javier Pérez de Cuéllar by the Iranian delegation, announcing Iran's unconditional acceptance of Security Council Resolution 598. This occurs slightly less than a year after it was unanimously adopted on July 20, 1987.

In Tehran, Iran, Ayatollah Khomeini informs his countrymen that he is unconditionally accepting the UN-sponsored cease-fire with Iraq.

MILITARY: Moqar city falls to the Afghan resistance, the third such settlement along the Kabul-Kandahar highway to be seized.

July 19

DIPLOMACY: In Baghdad, Iraq, the parliament dismisses Iranian acceptance of a UN-sponsored cease-fire and vows to keep fighting. This comes despite a token endorsement by Sadaam Hussein.

MILITARY: In the Arghandab region of Kandahar Province, Afghanistan, a major battle erupts between resistance fighters and Afghan army units; heavy losses are reported on both sides while three tanks and 16 vehicles are reported destroyed.

In Baghlan Province, Afghan rebels ambush a military convoy, destroying 13 tanks and five heavy machine guns.

July 20

AVIATION: Mujahideen missiles bring down a Soviet jet over the Satu Kandau area of Paktia Province, Afghanistan, while another is claimed while landing at Khost airfield.

DIPLOMACY: In Peshawar, Pakistan, mujahideen leader Burhanuddin Rabbani claims that the best way of restoring peace in Afghanistan is for direct talks between the resistance and the Soviet Union. He also plays down reports of simmering differences between mujahideen factions and leaders.

POLITICS: In Tehran, Iran, Ayatollah Khomeini reaffirms that he is accepting the terms of a UN cease-fire unconditionally but considers this act "more deadly for me than taking poison." Apparently, his nation is war-weary, tired of heavy losses in men and materiel, and greatly concerned about economic problems that jeopardize the future of the Islamic revolution.

In New York City, the UN Security Council passes a resolution regretting the shoot-down of the Iranian airliner by the frigate USS *Vincennes*, but placing no blame on the United States.

July 21

AVIATION: At Kandahar airport, Afghanistan, mujahideen rockets destroy two parked aircraft on the field.

The resistance claims to have shot down six Soviet-Afghan warplanes over the Bagh Tira area, Paktia Province, the Ainak area of Logar Province, and the Asadabad area of Konar Province.

MILITARY: In Paktia Province, Afghanistan, Afghan rebels ambush a military convoy in Dand and lob rockets at security posts near Spin Boldak.

POLITICS: In Kabul, Afghanistan, President Mohammad Najibullah approves the creation of another new province, Nurestan.

July 22

MILITARY: Communist news sources in Moscow and Kabul trumpet the fact that a mujahideen supply convoy was intercepted in Herat Province, Afghanistan, whereby some Stinger missiles, rocket launchers, and several machine guns were captured.

An invigorated Iraqi army commences offensives across the northern, central, and southern sectors, intent on recapturing as much territory as possible before the cease-fire is enacted. The Iranians repel a determined attack in the Shalamche area, but Iraqi armored units thrust to within 15 miles of Ahvaz, capital of Khuzestan Province.

In Tehran, Iran, Revolutionary Guards commander Muhsin Reazai meets with Ayatollah Khomeini and composes a letter accepting the latter's decision to embrace a cease-fire. This is done to quash any possible discontent in the military.

July 23

MILITARY: In the Konar Valley, Afghanistan, mujahideen rockets fall on Pashad over a period of 24 hours without letup.

Kabul, Afghanistan, is the target of increasing activity by the Afghan resistance. On this day diplomats report that at least 60 rockets have hit western and southwestern parts of the city, before switching over to the northern and northwestern sectors. Beforehand, resistance agents distributed pamphlets in city mosques warning the citizens to take shelter. Mujahideen forces also seize 14 security posts around Kabul's periphery.

POLITICS: In Kabul, Afghanistan, creation of the Self-Sacrificing Afghan People's Solidarity Movement is approved by President Mohammad Najibullah.

July 24

MILITARY: In an interview, Soviet major general Kim Tsagolov predicts that the Communist regime in Kabul, Afghanistan, will not long survive the removal of Soviet ground forces due to the loss of public trust through mismanagement of land distribution and other failed social reforms. Moreover, the major general anticipates that a fundamentalist Islamic regime will be established in its wake. Western analysts believe that the extraordinary decision to publish Tsagolov's diatribe indicates that the government is most likely bracing the Soviet public for imminent disaster south of the border.

In Moscow, Soviet Union, the TASS news agency declares that Tsagolov's opinion was strictly personal, and that an official from the Foreign Ministry has pronounced the Kabul regime stable and thriving.

A report in *Izvestia* notes that Soviet troops have defused 500 American, Italian, and Chinese-made mines along the road from Faizabad to Kunduz, Afghanistan.

July 25

DIPLOMACY: The Soviet government reiterates its intention to withdraw all troops from Afghanistan and criticizes Pakistani president Zia ul-Haq for behaving "irresponsibly" throughout the Afghan crisis.
MILITARY: In Washington, D.C., Defense Secretary Frank Carlucci declares his belief that the Soviets are sticking to their timetable and withdrawing troops from Afghanistan as promised. However, other U.S. officials profess belief in Pakistan's claim that thousands of Soviet troops are returning to the theater of operations.

In Parvan Province, mujahideen fighters again ambush a military convoy near the Salang tunnel, which remains a strategic choke point for withdrawing Soviet forces.

In Khuzestan Province, Iran, Iranian forces counterattack outside of Ahvaz, recapturing 230 square miles of territory.

July 26

AVIATION: Soviet aircraft heavily bomb the Urgoon district of Paktia Province, Afghanistan.
DIPLOMACY: In Tehran, Iran, the government declares its willingness to help free American hostages still held in Lebanon if the United States would unfreeze Iranian assets frozen since 1979.
MILITARY: In Kandahar Province, Afghanistan, resistance fighters attack a military convoy outside of Jaldak, claiming three tanks destroyed and two oil tankers set afire.

In the central sector, the Iraqi-sponsored National Liberation Army, composed of dissident Iranians, advances upon Karand and Islamabad-e-Gharb on the Baghdad-Tehran highway. Both towns are taken under heavy Iraqi air support, and the rebels begin pressing onto Bakhtaran.

July 27

AVIATION: A report on the BBC says that a fire at the Kabul airport, Afghanistan, has destroyed five Soviet Su-25 jet bombers on the ground and damaged three others. It is reported that the fire was started by mujahideen rockets launched from 18 miles away.

Over the Chehar Deh region of Kabul, Afghanistan, mujahideen forces bring down two Soviet jets attacking their position.

MILITARY: At this time, the Afghan resistance claims to control 21 miles of road along the highway between Kabul and Jalalabad.

The Afghan resistance abandons Maidan Shehr, Afghanistan, after holding it for 24 hours. The withdrawal is in the face of continuing Soviet air strikes.

In Kabul, Afghanistan, Western diplomats report that the city has been more heavily hit by rockets over the past few weeks than during the past four years.

A report surfaces that mujahideen fighters have killed 18 Soviets in a single action, the highest toll by the mujahideen since the withdrawal began.

In a rare turn of events, mujahideen units are ambushed by Soviet forces in Baba Hussain Wali, Kabul Province, taking heavy losses.

POLITICS: In Kabul, Afghanistan, the Ittehadia-ye Ansarullah (Union of God's Helpers), a new political party, receives government approval.

July 28

AVIATION: At Kandahar airport, Afghanistan, mujahideen Stinger missiles down two Soviet aircraft attempting to land.

July 29

DIPLOMACY: In Washington, D.C., Pakistani foreign minister Sahabzada Yaqub Khan retracts an earlier statement that the Soviets were actually introducing additional combat forces into Afghanistan.

MILITARY: In Kabul, Afghanistan, President Mohammad Najibullah proudly announces that half the Soviet garrison has departed his country and that 19 of 35 provinces are completely free of Soviet forces.

Around Kandahar City, Afghanistan, Afghan rebels continue launching attacks on Soviet garrisons around the city. It is also rumored that the Soviets are increasingly resorting to evacuation by air because leaving by ground is unsafe.

In Kabul, Afghanistan, Afghan soldiers reportedly discover arms caches intended for Gulbuddin Hekmatyar's fighters in the fifth and sixth wards of the city, including several rockets and explosives.

In Iran's central section, a sharp Iranian counterattack supported by jets and helicopter gunships routs the National Liberation Army outside Bakhtaran. The rebels are pushed back to the Iraqi border with 4,500 casualties.

July 30

DIPLOMACY: In New York City, the Afghan Foreign Ministry formally lodges two complaints regarding Pakistani violations of the Geneva peace accord.

MILITARY: At Pul-i-Alam, Afghanistan, the Soviets begin concentrating several hundred trucks, tanks, and personnel carriers in anticipation of a drive down the highway linking Kabul with Kandahar and Gardez. As the force pulls out, it is supported by scores of jet bombers and helicopter gunships.

July 31

DIPLOMACY: In London, United Kingdom, the British Foreign Office declares that it is evacuating embassy dependents due to increasing mujahideen attacks on Kabul, Afghanistan. The Kabul regime condemns such evacuations, declaring them unnecessary and an inducement to panic.

POLITICS: Amid continuing rocket attacks on Kabul, Afghanistan, President Mohammad Najibullah seeks help from tribal elders living near the city.

A report on the Voice of America suggests that Paghman, Afghanistan, has been besieged by thousands of mujahideen fighters over the past two weeks. This has closed the Kabul-Paghman highway, and the government is presently massing reinforcements in an attempt to lift the siege.

Kabul, Afghanistan, is struck by another round of mujahideen rockets fired at Soviet installations and official buildings.

August 1

DIPLOMACY: In Peshawar, Pakistan, the mujahideen alliance releases two Soviet prisoners as a goodwill gesture.

MILITARY: Western military intelligence confirms that the mujahideen are equipped with a new type of surface-to-surface rocket that has a range of 12 miles. Such weapons have been fired on Kabul, Afghanistan, from the distant Khak-i-Jabar and Kohi Pashaye regions. The Soviets retaliate with air strikes against suspected rebel launch sites.

A report on Radio Beijing says that the Afghan resistance has completely surrounded the major southern city of Kandahar, Afghanistan, the nation's second-largest city.

Soviet forces have by and large evacuated Takhar Province, Afghanistan, along the Soviet border, but they still maintain garrisons at the provincial headquarters of Taliqan and several important airfields.

In Baghlan Province, Afghanistan, the mujahideen attack Soviet garrisons in Kelagai, destroying an ammunition dump and five helicopters on the ground.

In Parvan Province, Afghanistan, Afghan resistance fighters fire rockets at Bagram Air Base, destroying three aircraft and four armored vehicles.

POLITICS: In Kabul, Afghanistan, the Constitution Council is founded to examine the constitutionality of laws as well as the compliance of treaties and laws.

August 2

AVIATION: In Nangarhar Province, Afghanistan, a mujahideen missile brings down a Soviet jet fighter over the Khogiani district.

DIPLOMACY: In New York City, the United Nations declares that the Soviet Union has reiterated its intention to withdraw from Afghanistan by February 1989.

In Kabul, Afghanistan, foreign embassies continue evacuating unnecessary personnel because of increasing rocket attacks by the Afghan resistance. The Soviet embassy is also deliberately struck by mujahideen rockets.

MILITARY: To end rebel rocket bombardments of Kabul, Afghanistan, Soviet and Afghan army units begin sweeping through hills adjoining the city.

August 3

AVIATION: In Ghazni Province, waves of Soviet warplanes strike mujahideen positions near Tochi; one Soviet aircraft is claimed by Stinger missiles.

MILITARY: In Bamiyan Province, Afghanistan, a conglomeration of several resistance groups jointly attacks the provincial capital of Bamiyan City, which finally falls to them on August 21. Throughout this period, Soviet aircraft continually pound the surrounding regions.

August 4

AVIATION: Over Pakistan, a Pakistani Air Force F-16 fighter downs an Afghan warplane over Miram Shah in the North Waziristan tribal agency. At the time it was bombing Afghan refugee camps 30 miles inside the border. The Soviet pilot was captured alive and handed over to government officials in return for 50,000 rupees ($2,700), a promise to construct a road for the village, and two seats in the local administration.

In Paktia Province, Afghanistan, mujahideen missiles down two military helicopters over Khost.

DIPLOMACY: In Kabul, Afghanistan, Soviet foreign minister Eduard Shevardnadze arrives and accuses Pakistani foreign minister Yaqub Khan of aiding and abetting terrorism by helping the Afghan resistance in the face of international attempts to end the war.

August 5

DIPLOMACY: In New York City, UN secretary-general Javier Pérez de Cuéllar says that he will deploy 250 military monitors along the borders of Iraq and Iran to observe the cease-fire there.

MILITARY: A report in the Soviet army newspaper *Red Star* suggests that helicopter, mechanized, and paratroop units have all been removed from Kandahar, Afghanistan, as part of a bigger move to withdraw all Soviet units from southern Afghanistan.

In Bangi, Afghanistan, reports surface that 500 Afghan army soldiers defected to the local mujahideen units over the past five weeks. A further 100 defectors apparently deserted their units in Herat Province.

A mujahideen ambush on the highway from Paktia Province to Kabul, Afghanistan, destroys 30 vehicles of various descriptions.

August 6

MILITARY: In Paktia Province, Afghanistan, Afghan army units attack a mujahideen base near Balti. The fight continues for 24 hours, and two Soviet jets are shot down, with the pilots captured.

TERRORISM: As Soviet foreign minister Eduard Shevardnadze prepares to leave Kabul, Afghanistan, the city is rocked by a large car bomb in his vicinity.

August 7

AVIATION: Heightened mujahideen activity in Kunduz Province, Afghanistan, directly on the Soviet border, leads Red Air Force units to conduct air strikes directly from Soviet bases.

DIPLOMACY: In Kabul, Afghanistan, Soviet foreign minister Eduard Shevardnadze concludes talks with Afghan authorities, and they then issue a joint statement condemning Pakistani subversion of the country's internal affairs. They also hint at some kind of retaliatory action should such behavior continue.

MILITARY: In Kandahar, Afghanistan, Afghan army troops uncover a cache of 52 ground-to-ground rockets in a residential area. This is conclusive proof that the mujahideen have infiltrated deep into the city.

The city of Kunduz, Afghanistan, is easily infiltrated by mujahideen forces, who disperse Afghan army troops nearby, seizing 1,600 light weapons and 67 heavy weapons. Government reinforcements and Soviet air strikes force the resistance to abandon the city on August 17, 10 days later, but the incident highlights the vulnerability of Afghan cities without direct Soviet support. Kunduz is also the first major urban area to fall since the Soviets commenced their withdrawal in May.

Near Farah, Afghanistan, mujahideen forces attack a number of Soviet and Afghan targets, killing one Soviet officer and taking three captive. The Soviets subsequently pay out $180,000 in ransom to recover the body and prisoners.

In Kabul Province, Afghanistan, the mujahideen unleash a large rocket bombardment on the Shakardara district.

August 8

DIPLOMACY: In Moscow, Soviet Union, Foreign Minister Eduard Shevardnadze reiterates that troop withdrawals from Afghanistan are continuing on time and on schedule.

In New York City, UN Secretary-General Javier Pérez de Cuéllar announces that the Iran-Iraq cease-fire is effective as of August 20 and that the two sides will begin discussions regarding a final settlement. He also plans to gather 350 military observers from 25 nations to form the United Nations Iran-Iraq Military Observer Group (UNIIMOG), and have them on the borders by the cease-fire date.

MILITARY: The first trickle of Soviet forces begins pulling out of Kabul, Afghanistan.

August 9

DIPLOMACY: In New York City, the UN Security Council passes Resolution 619 to establish the UN Iran-Iraq Military Observer Group to monitor the upcoming cease-fire in the Persian Gulf region. Secretary-General Javier Pérez de Cuéllar also reports that the UN lacks the funding to deploy military observers because the United States has fallen behind on its dues. However, President Ronald W. Reagan counters that he will not ask Congress to release any UN funding until administrative reforms intending to stamp out waste and inefficiency have been adopted by that body.

MILITARY: Moscow television declares that, in light of its recent failure to capture Jalalabad, the Afghan resistance is redoubling its effort to take Kandahar. It cites convoys of arms and ammunition arriving in the region from Pakistan.

The mujahideen have cut off large sections of the Jalalabad-Asadabad highway from regular traffic.

In Tehran, Iran, Majlis Speaker Hojatolislam Hashemi Rafsanjani orders Iranian forces to refrain from offensive operations against Iraqi troops.

NAVAL: In light of the cease-fire between Iran and Iraq, the United States announces that it is reducing its naval presence in the Persian Gulf from 27 warships to the prewar level of only five.

POLITICS: In Baghdad, Iraq, President Saddam Hussein declares a three-day holiday to celebrate a "great victory." Massive public demonstrations of joy and relief break out after eight years of war.

August 10

MILITARY: The Soviet newspaper *Pravda* interviews a Colonel Nasir of the Afghan Ministry of State Security in Kandahar, Afghanistan, who states that widespread desertion is dogging the Afghan army in its attempt to beat back the resistance. He also notes that the Islamic clergy strongly oppose the notion of national reconciliation, seeing it as a ploy to strengthen the government's weakening hand. A report in *Pravda* also suggests that the withdrawal of Soviet forces has triggered fighting among various mujahideen factions.

The Soviet state-controlled media states that mujahideen forces are massing outside Kandahar, Afghanistan, in preparation for a major attack. They apparently are awaiting new shipments of arms from Pakistan, especially Milan antitank guided missiles. The Soviets claim that the resistance is also aided by a host of American, Chinese, German, Pakistani, Iranian, and Saudi advisers.

No sooner does the Soviet garrison withdraw from Taliqan, Takhar Province, Afghanistan, than mujahideen under Ahmad Shah Massoud attack and capture it, greatly aided by mass defections from the Afghan army.

The BBC reports that thousands of mujahideen fighters are gathering only 15 miles south of Kabul, Afghanistan, despite repeated Afghan army operations against them. All main highways in and out of the area are also apparently under their firm control.

August 11

MILITARY: In Kandahar, Afghanistan, the final detachment of 1,200 Soviet troops departs and begins moving in the direction of Herat. Afghan resistance fighters continue attacking them over a distance of 12 miles, allegedly destroying 14 tanks, two airplanes, and a helicopter. Meanwhile, the Afghan army garrison in the city is beefed up to 7,000 men in anticipation of a major mujahideen assault.

In Baghlan Province, Afghanistan, rebel rockets set off a munitions and fuel depot near the provincial capital, creating a tremendous explosion that kills an estimated 800 people and destroys 200 tanks and other vehicles. This apparently was the principal depot for the Soviet Fortieth Army in Afghanistan, and several hundred Soviets perished in the blast.

In Konar Province, Afghanistan, resistance fighters capture a significant outpost at Shigal Thana after two weeks of fighting. Its fall facilitates the siege of the strategic city of Asmar near the Pakistani border.

August 12

AVIATION: Over the outskirts of Kabul, Afghanistan, mujahideen missiles bring down a Soviet military aircraft bombing their position.

MILITARY: It is believed that the Soviets have evacuated 19 Afghan provinces during the past week. Their remaining 60,000 soldiers in 11 provinces are due to be withdrawn no later than February 1989.

Across Kabul, Nangarhar, Balkh, and Kandahar Provinces, Afghanistan, mujahideen units strike at Soviet and Afghan army installations in Jawara, Shakadara, Panichat, and Kandrab. They claim to have destroyed 14 outposts, along with tanks, trucks, and other military hardware.

In Farah Province, Afghanistan, the Soviet garrison of 10,000 troops begins withdrawing; the rebels do not impede their retreat.

POLITICS: In Tehran, Iran, President Ali Khamenei conducts prayer services and addresses the crowd, insisting that Iran had won a "moral victory" in its eight-year ordeal with Iraq.

August 13

MILITARY: In Herat Province, Afghanistan, the final detachment of Soviet troops is withdrawn amid expectation that the city will fall to resistance fighters relatively soon.

Mujahideen fighters attack two Soviet convoys near the Salang tunnel as they return home from eastern Afghanistan.

August 14

DIPLOMACY: The Soviet Union trumpets that fact that it has withdrawn half of its 100,000 combat troops from Afghanistan a full day before the deadline agreed to in the Geneva peace accord.

MILITARY: Near Puli-i-Khumri, Baghlan Province, Afghanistan, mujahideen fighters attack a Soviet convoy of 200 vehicles over a period of two days.

American authorities state that between 10 million and 16 million land mines have been laid in Afghanistan and pose a danger to returning refugees and their livestock. Virtually all have been buried without their whereabouts being recorded.

August 15

MILITARY: In Washington, D.C., State Department spokesman Charles Redman estimates that there are presently between 10 million to 20 million land mines in Afghanistan, with the majority placed by Soviet and Afghan army forces.

Mujahideen field commanders Amin Wardak and Abdul Haq become known for their cooperation in military matters and demonstrate considerable independence from the alliance leadership in Pakistan.

Lieutenant General Boris V. Gromov, commanding all Soviet forces in Afghanistan, notes that the Afghan resistance has captured the town of Kunduz, but the Soviet withdrawal will nonetheless continue on time.

In Kabul, Afghanistan, government radio announces that at least 40 mujahideen rockets have struck areas of eastern Jalalabad.

In Takhar Province, Afghanistan, mujahideen fighters overrun government positions in the Yangi Qala district, capturing 15 vehicles and more than 800 small arms. The Soviets respond by launching air strikes at residential targets nearby.

In Bamiyan Province, Afghanistan, resistance fighters capture Bamiyan city, which enhances their prospects for controlling the entire region.

August 16

DIPLOMACY: In New York City, UN secretary-general Javier Pérez de Cuéllar declares that he is satisfied with the progress of the Soviet pullout from Afghanistan, in accordance with conditions spelled out in the Geneva peace accord. The UN

Goodwill Mission to Afghanistan and Pakistan also certifies that the withdrawal is consistent with the accords.

In Moscow, the Soviet government again warns Pakistan against its continuing aid to the Afghan resistance.

MILITARY: In Kabul, Afghanistan, President Mohammad Najibullah declares that Afghan army forces have recaptured the town of Kunduz, near the Soviet border, from the resistance.

In Paktia Province, Afghanistan, the local tribal militia defects to the mujahideen, giving them effective control of the Chamkani and Mirzaka regions.

The BBC reports that a Soviet officer said that a mujahideen missile ignited the Afghan government's primary ammunition dump at Kalagi, just off the Salang highway. At the time, this was also a Soviet base with hundreds of families stationed there; at least 500 people were killed or injured in the conflagration, which flung live ordnance over a large area. Several helicopters and tanks were likewise destroyed by the explosion, along with a vast quantity of fuel stored there by the Afghan regime.

August 17

DIPLOMACY: The U.S. government criticizes the Soviet Union for rejecting an offer of American help to remove the millions of land mines from Afghanistan.

MILITARY: In Kabul, Afghanistan, Lieutenant General Shahnawaz Tania becomes the new defense minister and Major General Mohammad Asef Delawar becomes chief of the armed forces General Staff.

President Zia ul-Haq of Pakistan is killed when his C-130 transport plane explodes in midair and crashes shortly after takeoff. Among those killed are Arnold L. Raphel, the U.S. ambassador, the chairman of the U.S. Joint Chiefs of Staff Committee, the U.S. Army chief of general staff, and several other top policy makers. Brigadier General Herbert M. Wassom, the U.S. military attaché, is also among those killed. Sabotage by Afghan or Soviet intelligence agents is immediately suspected.

At Kandahar, Afghanistan, word of the death of Pakistani president Zia ul-Haq induces Afghan army troops to fire guns into the air. The mujahideen retaliate by shelling large parts of the city throughout the night. This is apparently the heaviest bombardment experienced during the last 10 years, and four helicopters and eight tanks are claimed to have been destroyed.

Mujahideen forces are forced to abandon the town of Kunduz, Afghanistan, in the face of Soviet air strikes and Afghan army attacks; they had been in control of the town since August 8.

August 19

DIPLOMACY: The Soviet government expresses its condolences over the death of Pakistani president Zia ul-Haq and expresses hope that relations between their two nations will improve. Previously, they considered Zia a driving force behind Islamic extremism in Afghanistan.

Saddiqui, the younger brother of President Mohammad Najibullah who defected in 1987, arrives in the United States with his family and requests asylum.

August 20

DIPLOMACY: In concert with UN Security Resolution 598, Iran and Iraq officially enact a cease-fire. This concludes a horrific eight-year conflict that cost hundreds of thousands of lives without appreciable gains for either side. Western observers calculate that Iran lost 262,000 people and Iraq 105,000. When the estimated 700,000 injured are factored in, the Iran-Iraq War, one of the most prolonged conventional struggles of the 20th century, inflicted at least 1 million casualties.

MILITARY: In Baghlan Province, Afghanistan, mujahideen forces continue pressuring Pul-i-Khumri until 160 militiamen desert. This city lies on the route of the Soviet withdrawal and contains large stocks of fuel and ammunition.

POLITICS: Saddiqui, younger brother of President Mohammad Najibullah, denounces the Afghan regime by stating it has little popular support and will not likely survive a Soviet pullout. Moreover, he accuses his brother of being a sadistic liar and a puppet of Moscow.

August 21

AVIATION: Over Khost airport, Afghanistan, a mujahideen Stinger missile downs a large military transport.

MILITARY: In Kabul, Afghanistan, the Bakhtar News Agency reports that severe outbreaks of violence have occurred between mujahideen groups in Arghandab and Bakhtar Uluswah; apparently 21 people were killed and a number wounded.

In Kandahar Province, Afghanistan, mujahideen fighters assume control over the Arghandab district after two months of combat. Consequently, Soviet troops are flown back in Kandahar as reinforcements.

The Afghan government radio acknowledges that the city of Bamiyan has fallen to the Afghan resistance. The Soviets respond by heavily bombing the city.

August 23

AVIATION: Over Kunduz, Afghanistan, a mujahideen Stinger missile knocks down a Soviet transport plane, killing 120 Afghan and Soviet soldiers.

DIPLOMACY: In Moscow, Soviet Union, the government denies that it was in any way involved in the recent death of Pakistani president Zia ul-Haq and the U.S. ambassador.

MILITARY: In Baghlan Province, Afghanistan, government militia from the Dooshi and Dahan-i-Ghoori districts attack mujahideen positions, backed by Soviet warplanes.

August 25

DIPLOMACY: In Geneva, Switzerland, representatives from Iran and Iraq meet face-to-face for the first time in eight years and begin final peace negotiations.

MILITARY: Herat, Afghanistan, continues to be an object of mujahideen attention, especially since 3,000 government soldiers have defected since April. Despite the presence of four distinct lines of defense, resistance fighters apparently have little difficulty infiltrating Afghan army lines and firing rockets at close range. Refugees fleeing the area claim that the rebels control the city's residential areas.

A report on Radio Kabul says that conflicts have erupted between mujahideen groups loyal to Gulbuddin Hekmatyar in Narkh Alaqadari, Afghanistan.

August 26

DIPLOMACY: In New York City, the UN Security Council passes Resolution 620, which condemns the use of chemical weapons in war, consistent with the 1925 League of Nations Protocol against such devices.

POLITICS: It is reported that the Afghan government officially welcomed the death of Pakistani president Zia ul-Haq as a setback for the Muslim insurgency and a turning point in the Afghan conflict.

August 27

AVIATION: Mujahideen launch their heaviest rocket attack to date against the Kabul airport, destroying eight Soviet aircraft on the ground.

MILITARY: Having struck the Kabul airport, mujahideen fighters move out against the city's outskirts. The Soviet garrison responds by rushing up tanks, backed by helicopter gunships, and chasing them back into the surrounding hillsides.

In Baghlan Province, Afghanistan, mujahideen fighters lash out at a military convoy moving north of the Salang tunnel; six oil tankers are reported hit.

August 28

MILITARY: Throughout Kandahar Province, Afghanistan, mujahideen forces seize control of the Baba Sahib, Shorawak, Maruf, Tabush, Panjwai, Ghorak, Khakriz, Shavalikot, and Arghastan districts. The rebels subsequently warn the populace to begin moving away from government installations in the city as they are slated to be attacked.

In Baghlan Province, Afghanistan, 125 Afghan army soldiers apparently defect to the mujahideen near the Salang tunnel. This brings the total number of defections to 2,000 since the Geneva peace accord were signed.

Along the Iran-Iraq border, the UN-sponsored cease-fire formally goes into effect, closely monitored by the UN Iran-Iraq Military Observer Group.

POLITICS: Despite recent and intensifying mujahideen attacks against Kabul, Afghanistan, the Communist regime declares that there is no danger that the city will fall.

August 30

DIPLOMACY: In Kabul, Afghanistan, Prime Minister Mohammad Hassan Sharq says he hopes that the United States and Pakistan collaborate on the foundation of a coalition government that would include moderates and mujahideen, along with members of the existing Communist regime.

MILITARY: Bagram military airport, Afghanistan, is struck by 107mm rockets that land among parked helicopters and trucks.

In Islamabad, Pakistan, Western diplomats confirm that Taliqan, capital of Takhar Province, Afghanistan, has fallen to fighters of Jamiat-i-Islami.

August 31

AVIATION: Soviet transports fly 4,000 Afghan army reinforcements into Kunduz, Afghanistan, to prevent its recapture by mujahideen forces.

Over Asmar, Afghanistan, a mujahideen missile downs a Soviet MiG fighter, and its pilot is captured.

In Kandahar Province, Afghanistan, the mujahideen manage to shoot down a military aircraft near Jalalabad.

DIPLOMACY: The recent downing of a Soviet M-32 transport aircraft to a mujahideen Stinger missile prompts Soviet Foreign Ministry spokesman Gennady Gerasimov to accuse the Pakistani government of violating the Geneva peace accord. He calls upon the U.S. government to stem the flow of illegal weapons to the resistance. Gerasimov states that these large aircraft are used to supply Soviet forces in Kunduz, Afghanistan, in their struggle against the Afghan resistance.

MILITARY: The popular resort town of Garam Chasma, Pakistan, now functions as a major staging area for guerrillas of Jamiat-i-Islami, which is planning a major offensive into northern Afghanistan.

A report on Radio Kabul suggests that clashes have occurred between the forces of Gulbuddin Hekmatyar and those of Jamiat-i-Islami under Burhanuddin Rabbani. Both sides apparently suffered losses.

In Kandahar Province, Afghanistan, Afghan rebels capture the Silo and Gongyan security posts, along with five tanks, two trucks, four howitzers, and 100 Afghan deserters.

POLITICS: Western analysts believe that the Soviets are trying to establish economic dependancy by linking parts of northern Afghanistan directly to Soviet Central Asia. Presently, an estimated 8,000 Afghans are studying to be civil servants in Soviet schools.

September 1

AVIATION: The Soviet government acknowledges that it is sending warplanes from Soviet bases in Central Asia to attack mujahideen positions in and around Kunduz, Afghanistan. However, insomuch as such tactics are intended to allow the safe withdrawal of Soviet troops from Afghanistan, they do not violate the Geneva peace accord.

Over Peshawar, Pakistan, six Afghan government jets attack an Afghan refugee camp 12 miles into Pakistani airspace. All the casualties are Pakistani, and this action represents the deepest violation of Pakistani air space since the war began.

MILITARY: In Herat Province, Afghanistan, the mujahideen step up their activities to relieve the pressure by government forces operating in Kandahar Province.

Moscow television carries a report of 50 Afghan rebel rockets striking Kabul airport, touching off fires and destroying three parked aircraft. Several residential areas of the city are also hit, with numerous Soviet casualties reported.

In Mir Bachakot, Afghanistan, fighting erupts between mujahideen forces loyal to Gulbuddin Hekmatyar and the Harkat-i-Inqilabi Islami.

September 2

AVIATION: In Kabul, Afghanistan, Western diplomats report that a recent mujahideen rocket attack has destroyed two transport aircraft and a helicopter at Kabul airport, killing nine people and injuring 24.

Over Nangarhar Province, Afghanistan, Soviet aircraft bomb rural areas near the Pakistani border, killing 10 rebels and injuring 25.

Four Afghan Air Force jets drop bombs on the North West Frontier Province of Pakistan, killing one person and wounding 23.

DIPLOMACY: Radio Moscow reports that Pakistan has increased the flow of weapons to the Afghan resistance in violation of the Geneva peace accord.

MILITARY: In Badakhshan Province, Afghanistan, a government militia commander defects to the mujahideen with 400 men and their weapons. Fighting in the Kisham district, southwest of Faizabad, costs the resistance 29 fighters, but it captured six tanks and a large quantity of ammunition and acquired a member of the Afghan secret police, who joined them with an additional 200 men. A total of 360 government troops have been killed and 21 security posts captured.

POLITICS: In Peshawar, Pakistan, a mujahideen alliance spokesman rejects an American suggestion for direct talks with the regime in Kabul, Afghanistan.

September 3

DIPLOMACY: In Islamabad, the Pakistani government rejects an Afghan proposal for a conference among Pakistani, Afghan, U.S., and Soviet foreign ministers to discuss alleged violations of the Geneva peace accord.

POLITICS: In Baghdad, Iraq, Foreign Minister Tariq Aziz declares that the recent Kurdish rebellion against the government has been completely crushed.

September 4

AVIATION: In Bamiyan Province, Afghanistan, the mujahideen claim to have shot down two Soviet warplanes and helicopters in heavy fighting.

A rocket attack Kabul airport, Afghanistan, destroys three army helicopters and two jet fighters on the ground.

MILITARY: In Helmand Province, Afghanistan, mujahideen forces besiege the city Girishk, located along the Kandahar-Herat highway. The action commenced on August 17, and since then several hundred Afghan soldiers have defected to the resistance. All roads having been closed by the rebels, the Soviets have been airlifting in supplies and reinforcements to the garrison.

In the Spin Boldak region of Kandahar Province, Afghanistan, scores of government militia and 60 trucks defect to the mujahideen. They also turn over their base and several security posts to the rebels. This gives them control of a 73-mile strip of highway linking Afghanistan to Pakistan. Soviet aircraft retaliate by attacking the defectors, killing eight mujahideen and 33 militiamen and their families.

In a related action at Spin Boldak, resistance fighters capture a security post despite three days of bombings by Soviet warplanes. Sources in Quetta, Pakistan, report 400 Afghan soldiers either died or defected during this action.

In Kunduz Province, Afghanistan, the mujahideen capture Imam Sahid and Neiki Kala, enlarging their control over the region. A large body of Afghan soldiers defects to the resistance, apparently after killing their officers.

POLITICS: In Bamiyan Province, Afghanistan, a three-day conference is convened by the Pasdaran-i-Jihad and Nasir Organization, during which the Geneva Peace Accords are denounced as a conspiracy of world imperialism. The group also rejects a suggestion by UN envoy Diego Cordovez for an impartial transitional government and vows to keep fighting until the Communist regime in Kabul is toppled and an Islamic government is in place.

September 5

AVIATION: The village of Duqai in the Dir District of the Pakistani tribal areas is struck by eight Afghan air force jets, which intrude 27 miles past the border.

DIPLOMACY: In Baghdad, Iraq, April C. Glaspie presents her credentials to the government as the new U.S. ambassador.

MILITARY: Radio Moscow reports that heavy fighting took place in the Qarabagh district of Ghazni Province, Afghanistan, among competing mujahideen groups. Among those involved are the Movement for Islamic Revolution of Afghanistan, the National Islamic Front of Afghanistan, and the Nasir Organization. Gul Moham-mad, a commander of the National Islamic Front, is among the slain, along with two Arab advisers. Other internecine fighting is reported among resistance groups in Parvan, Samangan, Laghman, and Logar Provinces, apparently over weapons supplies and territorial disputes.

September 6

MILITARY: In Farah Province, Afghanistan, mujahideen forces capture 11 Afghan army outposts with little difficulty.

September 7

AVIATION: The TASS news agency reports that an American-supplied Stinger missile downed a military transport over Kunduz Province, Afghanistan, killing all 16 passengers, including two brigadier generals and a political commissar. Stingers remain among the most lethal weapons in the mujahideen inventory.

POLITICS: The Swedish Committee for Afghanistan issues a report highlighting the brutal Soviet tactic of "systematic destruction" of Afghan farms, irrigation systems, and livestock.

MILITARY: In Badakhshan Province, Afghanistan, resistance fighters capture the Baharak district along the highway connecting Faizabad with Wakhan. This province is on the Soviet, Chinese, and Pakistan borders.

September 8

AVIATION: Three Afghan air force jets bomb several Pakistani villages near the border, but a Pakistani jet manages to down one of the intruders over Nawaqai in the Bajaur tribal agency.

DIPLOMACY: In Washington, D.C., Secretary of State George Shultz meets for an hour with Iraqi minister of state for foreign affairs Saddoun Hammadi and expresses his earnest desire to pursue improved relations, but not if the Iraqis continue using chemical weapons against the Kurds.

MILITARY: In a major development, mujahideen forces storm into Spin Boldak, Kandahar Province, seizing 600 rifles, tanks, armored personnel carriers, and artillery of varying calibers. At least 150 rebels die in the fighting, along with 200 Afghan soldiers, while a further 1,000 defect to the resistance.

Afghan refugees intent upon returning home are instructed in mine- and bomb-disposal techniques by teams from Pakistan, France, Britain, Turkey, and New Zealand. Experts believe that millions of land mines still litter the Afghan countryside, with a potential for killing and maiming thousands of people for years to come.

TERRORISM: In Kabul, Afghanistan, a bomb explodes downtown, killing 10 people and injuring 22.

September 9
POLITICS: In Washington, D.C., Congress passes a watered-down resolution condemning Iraqi chemical attacks against the Kurds, along with a weakened set of economic sanctions.

September 10
DIPLOMACY: In Washington, D.C., the Senate Foreign Relations Committee contemplates imposing stricter sanctions against Iraq because of its use of chemical weapons against the Kurds.

September 11
POLITICS: In Baghdad, Iraq, thousands of Iraqis protest outside the U.S. embassy over the Senate's condemnation of chemical weapons employed against rebellious Kurds.

September 12
AVIATION: In the Bajaur tribal agency, Pakistan, six Soviet jets bomb Nawaqai and are intercepted by Pakistani F-16s; two Soviet jets are reportedly hit by missiles.
DIPLOMACY: In New York City, the United States asks the UN Security Council to investigate whether Iraq employed poison gas against its Kurdish population.
MILITARY: Soviet and Afghan troops are flown back into Kandahar, Afghanistan, thwarting mujahideen plans to storm the city. Political authorities believe that if Kandahar remains in government hands, it may spur local tribes to turn out and oppose the resistance.

In Takhar Province, Afghanistan, Soviet and Afghan forces retake the city of Taliqan from the mujahideen, which had seized it in August. The ensuing battle costs the rebels 63 dead and 120 injured, principally from nonstop Soviet bombing raids launched from across the border in Soviet Central Asia. In return, the fighters claim to have downed one military jet.

In Herat Province, Afghanistan, mujahideen forces continue to besiege Herat, prompting Soviet warplanes to continually bomb nearby residential areas in retaliation.
TERRORISM: In Kabul, Afghanistan, two bombs explode inside KHAD (secret police) interrogation headquarters, killing 25 people and injuring 42. Forty nearby shops are also destroyed by the ensuing fire.

September 13
DIPLOMACY: In Washington, D.C., Secretary of State George Shultz announces that the United States possesses incontrovertible proof that the Iraqis used illegal chemical weapons against the Kurds.
MILITARY: In Helmand Province, the mujahideen capture Girishk on the Kandahar-Herat highway. Farther north, they also claim to have gained control of Oruzgan Province.

Reports on Radio Moscow say that Afghan army troops continue to battle guerrillas in Kunduz, Parvan, and Paktia Provinces, all recently evacuated by Soviet forces.

September 14

AVIATION: In Logar Province, Afghanistan, a mujahideen missile brings down a Soviet-made jet fighter near the provincial capital of Pul-i-Alam.

MILITARY: In Konar Province, Afghanistan, Afghan government forces launch local offensives in the Shindara and Asmar regions. Similar spoiling attacks are also conducted in Kunduz and the Paghman district of Kabul Province.

September 15

AVIATION: The BBC claims that a mujahideen missile brought down a Soviet MiG-27 fighter bomber over Farah Province, Afghanistan.

September 16

POLITICS: In Kabul, Afghanistan, UN special envoy Diego Cordovez declares that he is willing to assist in the formation of a *loya jirga* (assembly) to form a new coalition government following the Soviet withdrawal.

In Peshawar, Pakistan, Hezb-i-Islami leader Gulbuddin Hekmatyar states that the time has long since passed for a *loya jirga* and that Afghanistan's problems can best be addressed by the formation of an Islamic government. Other Afghan leaders criticize the UN special envoy's proposal, and Ahmed Shah, leader of the interim government, dismisses it as interference in Afghanistan's internal affairs.

September 17

AVIATION: In Nangarhar Province, Afghanistan, mujahideen fighters launch rockets against Jalalabad airport, destroying a parked aircraft on the ground.

DIPLOMACY: In Baghdad, Iraq, Foreign Minister Tariq Aziz declares that the 1975 Algerian Accord between Iran and his nation is null and void. He maintains that Iran's violation of a provision that orders it to refrain from interference in Iraq's internal affairs negates the agreement entirely.

POLITICS: A mujahideen spokesman declares that the Afghan resistance will continue bombarding Jalalabad, Afghanistan, until the remaining Communists have departed.

September 18

AVIATION: A recent rocket bombardment of Kandahar airport, Afghanistan, destroys two jet fighter bombers, one helicopter gunship, and one military transport. Parts of the airstrip are also severely damaged; because Afghan rebels ring the city, the airport is the only way to bring in troops and supplies to assist Afghan troops garrisoned there.

MILITARY: In Farah Province, Afghanistan, Afghan rebels attack a military depot at Karah, which ignites and destroys several buildings, along with 18 troops.

September 19

AVIATION: Over Ghazni City, Afghanistan, a mujahideen missile brings down a military helicopter as it attacks rebel positions in a nearby village.

MILITARY: In Nangarhar Province, Afghanistan, serious infighting breaks out at Chaparhar Alaqadari between mujahideen loyal to Gulbuddin Hekmatyar and those of Yunis Khalis; eight fighters are reported killed.

September 20

MILITARY: The Soviet TASS news agency confirms that the capital of Kabul, Afghanistan, is routinely bombarded by mujahideen rockets.

POLITICS: In Moscow, Soviet Union, Afghan prime minister Mohammad Hassan Sharq meets with General Secretary Mikhail Gorbachev and signs a long-term economic, trade, and technical-assistance agreement.

September 21

AVIATION: Kabul, Afghanistan, is struck by 10 S-20 rockets launched by mujahideen forces; these are specifically aimed at the presidential palace and military sites.

MILITARY: In Paktika Province, Afghanistan, mujahideen forces capture the city of Sharna and a neighboring community, Gadoon.

Paghman, Parvan Province, Afghanistan, falls to Afghan resistance forces after they storm into five security posts.

September 22

AVIATION: A rocket attack against Kandahar airport, Afghanistan, destroys two military helicopters on the ground.

MILITARY: In Logar Province, mujahideen forces bombard a military target in the provincial capital of Pul-i-Alam and are struck in turn by Soviet air raids.

These abandoned Soviet military artillery pieces, most of them unserviceable, were found as NATO forces moved into Afghanistan during Operation Enduring Freedom. *(Department of Defense)*

September 23

AVIATION: The mujahideen claim to have shot down a helicopter over Herat Province, Afghanistan, with two more claimed over Pul-i-Alam, in Logar Province. All were destroyed with American-supplied Stinger missiles.

MILITARY: Infighting among competing mujahideen groups results in 50 dead fighters in Faryab, Herat, and Kapisa Provinces, Afghanistan.

September 24

MILITARY: In Nangarhar province, Afghanistan, an Afghan rebel attacks destroys a major government arms depot at Samarkhel, seven miles southeast of Jalalabad. Among the equipment destroyed are 28 Soviet-supplied tactical missiles and a number of trucks and tankers. The group Hezb-i-Islami under Yunnis Khalis claims responsibility for the act.

September 25

DIPLOMACY: In Washington, D.C., the government announces that Edmund McWilliams is being appointed special envoy to the mujahideen alliance.

POLITICS: Tension arises between mujahideen leaders and their American sponsors over how to best expedite a Soviet withdrawal from Afghanistan. The Americans are leaning heavily on the guerrillas to halt attacks on withdrawing Soviet forces.

September 26

AVIATION: In Ghowr Province, Afghanistan, Soviet-made aircraft bomb several villages, killing 66 rebels and civilians. The raid apparently comes in retaliation for recent gains by the mujahideen, which wield a strong hold on the area.

The village of Parachinar, Pakistan, is attacked by six Afghan air force jets, which penetrate three miles over the border to deliver their bombs.

MILITARY: In Paktia Province, Afghanistan, mujahideen fighters capture five additional Afghan army military posts near the Pakistani border.

POLITICS: In New Delhi, India, the *Hindustan Times* reports that Afghan president Mohammad Najibullah has rejected proposals for a neutral, nonaligned government in Afghanistan.

TERRORISM: In Nangarhar Province, Afghanistan, a bomb explodes at the Afghan army's 11th Infantry Division at Samarkhel, killing 40 soldiers and wounding more than 200. The Hezb-i-Islami group claims responsibility for the attack.

September 27

DIPLOMACY: In Washington, D.C., the House of Representatives approves stricter economic sanctions against Iraq over its illegal use of chemical weapons against the Kurds.

MILITARY: The Soviet news agency Izvestia states that since the first stage of the military withdrawal from Kunduz, Afghanistan, and other northern provinces, hostilities and violence in those regions have been sharply on the upswing.

POLITICS: In Islamabad, Pakistan, diplomatic sources confirm that the inhabitants of Kabul, Afghanistan, face shortages of basic commodities like meat, flour, and sugar. This deprivation is the result of rebel attacks on supply convoys north and east of the city, along with heavy snowfall along the Salang highway.

September 28

DIPLOMACY: In New York City, Soviet foreign minister Eduard Shevardnadze asks the UN Security Council to address gross violations of the Geneva Peace Accords.

Pakistani foreign minister Yaqub Khan addresses the UN General Assembly and urges that body to continue playing a role in the Afghan crisis until Soviet troops are completely withdrawn and a broad-based coalition government is functioning in Kabul.

MILITARY: The Soviet government, responding to increased mujahideen attacks throughout Afghanistan, declares that it is suspending the troop withdrawal.

September 29

AVIATION: In Paktia Province, Afghanistan, a mujahideen missile brings down an Afghan army helicopter, killing 30 soldiers, the provincial governor's wife, and their two sons, as it lifts off from Gardez.

MILITARY: The Soviet TASS news agency claims that a single mujahideen rocket launched at Kabul, Afghanistan, has killed 35 people and injured more than 150.

September 30

DIPLOMACY: The Soviet government criticizes the United Nations for what it calls indifference toward Pakistan's alleged violations of the Geneva Peace Accords by allowing weapons to flow to the Afghan resistance. In turn, Pakistan and the United States charge the Soviets with violating the accords by entering Pakistani airspace.

MILITARY: In Ghazni Province, Afghanistan, mujahideen fighters overrun a military base near Gilan and capture a truck with 40 assault rifles. This places rebel forces along the strategic Kabul-Kandahar highway.

The city of Asmar, Afghanistan, falls to the Afghan resistance, which also strengthens its positions in Badakhshan, Laghman, and Parvan provinces.

In Konar Province, Afghanistan, fighting between the Afghan resistance and government forces escalates as the town of Asadabad is besieged by the resistance, which claims to have recently destroyed 12 tanks and shot down an airplane.

POLITICS: In Moscow, Soviet Union, a special Central Committee meeting results in the forced retirement of iconic figures such as Anatoly Dobrynin, Andrei Gromyko, and Mikhail Solomentsev from the Politburo. This is a major shakeup of national leadership by the reformists under General Secretary Mikhail Gorbachev.

October 1

AVIATION: In Paktia Province, Afghanistan, mujahideen missiles down a military transport near Khost.

In Nangarhar Province, Afghanistan, mujahideen forces unleash 11 BM-12 rockets against the cantonment and airport at Jalalabad.

DIPLOMACY: In New York City, Afghan foreign minister Abdul Wakil addresses the UN General Assembly, accusing Pakistan and the United States of violating the Geneva Peace Accords.

MILITARY: In Helmand Province, Afghanistan, the provincial capital of Lashkar falls to the resistance.

In Parvan Province, Afghanistan, the Afghan resistance ambushes a military convoy south of the Salang tunnel, destroying eight oil tankers.

Mujahideen fighters set up a roadblock that cuts the Jalalabad-Kabul highway at Surkhakan, Laghman Province, Afghanistan.

POLITICS: In Moscow, Soviet Union, General Secretary Mikhail Gorbachev is named Soviet president to replace the deposing Andrei Gromyko; he will hold the two posts simultaneously.

October 2

MILITARY: A report on Radio Moscow states that eight rockets recently fell on Jalalabad, Nangarhar Province, Afghanistan, killing 70 people and wounding 34. Recent artillery bombardments of Kabul have also resulted in 50 killed and 150 injured.

In Konar Province, Afghanistan, mujahideen forces capture the Asmar cantonment, seizing eight tanks, 11 armored vehicles, four trucks, and large amounts of arms and ammunition. They also take 200 Afghan army soldiers captive. Apparently, members of all seven resistance groups were present during this crucial operation.

In Baghlan Province, Afghanistan, an Afghan rebel ambush of a military convoy north of the Salang tunnel results in four oil tankers destroyed, along with 10 tons of fuel.

Afghan army units sweeping through the Karez-Mir region north of Kabul, Afghanistan, capture a large cache of mujahideen weapons, including rockets, mortars, several machines guns, and land mines.

October 3

AVIATION: In Helmand Province, Afghanistan, three Soviet helicopters are brought down by mujahideen Stinger missiles. The craft were apparently conveying food and supplies to Afghan forces nearby.

POLITICS: In Moscow, Soviet Union, American Vietnam veterans meet with Soviet soldiers recently returned from Afghanistan. The Americans bring with them specialists in psychology, computers, and artificial limbs. This exchange enhances popular perceptions that Afghanistan represents to the Soviet people what Vietnam was for the United States.

MILITARY: Mujahideen forces continue their attacks upon Kandahar, especially the airport and outlying military posts; three ammunition depots are reported destroyed.

October 4

AVIATION: In Helmand Province, Afghanistan, Soviet warplanes bomb mujahideen positions following the loss of three supply helicopters; 24 fighters are reported killed.

DIPLOMACY: In Lausanne, Switzerland, a collection of 50 Afghans from moderate mujahideen groups, calling themselves the Afghan Committee, petition former monarch Mohammad Zahir Shah to return home and convene a loya jirga, or tribal assembly.

In Kandahar, Afghanistan, mujahideen fighters begin using captured tanks to attack government outposts around the city. Recent rocket attacks on the city killed 298 people during the month of September.

In Paktia Province, Afghanistan, the Afghan resistance captures the Urgoon military cantonment, along with five tanks, eight armored vehicles, 15 trucks, several heavy machine guns and mortars, and more than 1,000 assault rifles. The fighting kills 15 and injures more than 50. This was previously one of the most fortified government posts in all Afghanistan.

In Kabul, Afghanistan, the government radio disputes rebel claims of having captured Urgoon in Paktia Province. However, the Voice of America announces that all Afghan army troops have abandoned the province, which is completely in the hands of the resistance.

A report on Radio Moscow declares that the mujahideen are receiving large surface-to-surface tactical missiles from Pakistan, in direct violation of the Geneva peace accord.

In Baghlan Province, Afghanistan, mujahideen fighters ambush a military convoy north of the Salang tunnel and claim 21 personnel carriers were destroyed along with five oil tankers.

October 5

MILITARY: The Afghan resistance captures two additional security posts along the Jalalabad-Kabul highway; it also claims to have destroyed several important bridges.

Kabul, Afghanistan, is hit by rebel rockets that come down in four different districts during rush hour.

In Nerjab, Afghanistan, mujahideen loyal to Gulbuddin Hekmatyar attack and kill Maulawi Zahir, a commander fighting under Burhanuddin Rabbani.

October 6

AVIATION: To offset recent rebel gains throughout Paktia Province, Afghanistan, waves of Soviet warplanes bomb the provincial capital at Sharana, destroying 150 homes and killing 21 civilians.

In Paktia Province, Afghanistan, mujahideen missiles strike at the Gardez airfield, damaging two parked aircraft.

MILITARY: In Paktia Province, Afghanistan, the resistance captures General Sahib Jan Wiziri and 600 soldiers, militiamen, and KHAD officials. Fighting during the previous week also killed 300 Afghan government soldiers.

Mujahideen units have keep the Jalalabad-Kabul highway closed, which increases pressure on the capital by disrupting food supplies.

October 7

AVIATION: In Nangarhar Province, Afghanistan, mujahideen missiles bring down a government jet fighter.

October 8

AVIATION: In Herat Province, Afghanistan, mujahideen rockets and mortar shells rain down on the airport at Shindland; the Soviets retaliate by dispatching bombers from neighboring Herat to attack rebel positions.

MILITARY: In Paktia Province, Afghanistan, the mujahideen score another important victory by seizing the provincial capital at Sharana. Tons of supplies and equipment also are seized, and the Soviets counter by launching high-altitude bombing raids.

In Pakistan, American bomb-disposal instructors arrive to help Afghan refugees recognize and disarm the million or so land mines still buried in Afghanistan.

Many of these devices are made of plastic and are impossible to uncover with metal detectors.

October 9

MILITARY: In Baghlan Province, Afghanistan, Afghan rebels launch a two-day strike against a military convoy south of the Salang tunnel, destroying 18 tankers and 100 tons of oil.

In Faryab and Parvan Provinces, Afghanistan, internecine fighting breaks out among mujahideen loyal to Gulbuddin Hekmatyar and Burhanuddin Rabbani; 18 fighters are reported slain.

POLITICS: A report surfaces on the Voice of Germany that mujahideen leader Gulbuddin Hekmatyar is calling upon the Soviet Union to abandon the Kabul regime and commence direct negotiations with the Afghan resistance.

October 10

MILITARY: In Helmand Province, Afghanistan, a force of 114 Afghan army troops defects to the mujahideen. The Afghan resistance also seizes the Qlla Murad encampment, Kandahar Province, which cuts the road between the city and the airport.

Asadabad, Afghanistan, is finally secured after the Soviets airlift the garrison out of the surrounded city.

October 12

POLITICS: In Kabul, Afghanistan, Afghan prime minister Mohammad Hassan Sharq informs foreign journalists that the present government will not attempt to retain power in any coalition arrangement with mujahideen factions. He insists that he will resign if the PDPA attempts to retain power and that most people have no faith in either the party or the resistance.

In Logar Province, Afghanistan, the deputy governor surrenders to the Afghan resistance in Kulangar.

October 13

AVIATION: The Tarinkot airstrip in Oruzgan Province, Afghanistan, is struck by mujahideen rockets and mortar shells; three parked aircraft are reported destroyed.

DIPLOMACY: In Moscow, Soviet Union, the government states that it is sending $600 million in food aid to Afghanistan to mitigate circumstances there. The United Nations is also seeking $1.1 billion to help rebuild the war-torn countryside and resettle millions of refugees. However, Western leaders question the quality of Soviet goods being offered and alliance leaders protest that the aid only reinforces the present regime in Kabul, thereby perpetuating the problem.

In Washington, D.C., the United States pledges $150 million for reconstruction efforts in Afghanistan, albeit only after the Soviets have departed.

In Kabul, Afghanistan, Prime Minister Mohammad Hassan Sharq extends an invitation to exiled former monarch Mohammad Zahir Shah to meet with him to discuss ways of ending the conflict in Afghanistan.

In Moscow, Soviet Union, First Deputy Foreign Minister Yuli Vorontsov, a highly skilled negotiator with prior experience in Geneva, gains appointment as the new Soviet ambassador to Afghanistan. He receives considerable latitude for negotiating between the Kabul regime and opposing mujahideen groups.

October 14

AVIATION: Over Parvan Province, Afghanistan, mujahideen missiles down three government aircraft near Charikar.

MILITARY: In Paktia Province, Afghanistan, mujahideen fighters fire several rockets at military installations in Gardez.

A report on Radio Beijing suggests that seven senior Afghan officers have defected to the resistance, including a brigadier general, a colonel, two majors, and a captain.

October 15

MILITARY: In Logar Province, Afghanistan, Soviet and Afghan forces strengthen the defenses of the Logar Copper Mine Complex, given its importance to the national economy. Apparently, new posts are constructed while tanks and other armored vehicles are deployed nearby.

October 16

AVIATION: In Farah Province, Afghanistan, a mujahideen missile brings down an Afghan jet aircraft near the Shindland air base. Another aircraft is shot down in Paktia Province.

DIPLOMACY: In Kabul, Afghanistan, President Mohammad Najibullah receives new Soviet ambassador Yuli Vorontsov. The Soviet government is increasingly alarmed over the crisis in Afghanistan and what it deems are violations of the Geneva peace accord.

October 17

AVIATION: In Kabul Province, Afghanistan, a Soviet fighter accidentally bombs an army security post at Deh Sabz, inflicting several casualties.

MILITARY: In the new province of Sar-i-Pul, Afghanistan, several Afghan resistance fighters put down their arms and embrace national reconciliation.

POLITICS: In Peshawar, Pakistan, Burhanuddin Rabbani of Jamiat-i-Islami becomes the new spokesman for the seven-member mujahideen alliance. He informs the news media of his willingness to negotiate directly with Moscow but rules out any governmental role for former monarch Mohammad Zahir Shah.

October 18

DIPLOMACY: In Islamabad, Pakistan, mujahideen spokesman Burhanuddin Rabbani suggests that direct talks between the Afghan resistance and the Soviet Union might happen soon.

In Moscow, Soviet Union, a government spokesman declares that the Soviets will withdraw their forces from Afghanistan whether or not there is a peace agreement in Geneva. Previously, the Soviets had publicly insisted that Pakistan and the United States must agree to end the fighting in advance.

MILITARY: In Kabul, Afghanistan, the government radio announces that the mujahideen have fired 38 ground-to-ground missiles at the city, one of which struck the Kabul airport terminal.

In Parvan Province, Afghanistan, resistance fighters ambush a military convoy near the Salang tunnel, destroying or capturing 40 vehicles.

In Kapisa Province, Afghanistan, the mujahideen capture the provincial capital of Mahmood Raqi, only 80 miles north of Kabul. Rebel losses are not announced, but they claim to have killed 100 Afghan soldiers and destroyed more than 20 tanks. Significantly, this is the sixth provincial capital to fall to the resistance in the past two months.

In Kandahar Province, Afghanistan, mujahideen fighters capture a district headquarters near the provincial capital of Kandahar.

The Islamic Press reports that Commander Haji Mohammad claims that rebels have seized Afghan army headquarters in Panjwai, Kandahar Province, Afghanistan, along with eight tanks and 165 light and heavy weapons.

POLITICS: In Peshawar, Pakistan, Gulbuddin Hekmatyar becomes the new chairman of the seven member mujahideen alliance. He again declares that there is no possibility for entering into a coalition government with communists or even negotiating with the regime in Kabul. Hekmatyar insists that only a government composed of resistance members is acceptable and that they will continue fighting Soviet forces until that objective is achieved.

October 19

DIPLOMACY: Despite allegations of Soviet sabotage in the death of Pakistani president Zia ul-Haq, the United States appears reluctant to openly criticize the Soviet government. Apparently, the Americans are putting greater emphasis on smooth working relations with the Soviets for the post-Afghanistan period, a position eliciting harsh commentary from conservative hard-liners.

MILITARY: In Balkh Province, Afghanistan, the mujahideen launch 103 rockets at Mazar-i-Sharif, while an additional 60 are directed against Kabul's airport, forcing its closure.

POLITICS: In Kabul, Afghanistan, factional fighting is reported in the ranks of the PDPA, which further complicates the Soviet withdrawal and weakens President Mohammad Najibullah's overall position.

October 20

MILITARY: In Kabul, Afghanistan, government radio announces that 81 rebels have been killed and 64 wounded in military operations around Kandahar. A further 24 mujahideen strongholds are also reported to have been captured or destroyed.

Mujahideen rockets continue to slam into Kabul, Afghanistan, for a second straight day.

October 21

DIPLOMACY: In Kabul, Afghanistan, a UN special representative requests that former king Mohammad Zahir Shah participate in founding a government of national reconciliation.

October 22

AVIATION: Kandahar, Afghanistan, is struck by a salvo of BM-1 rockets that destroy a helicopter at the nearby airport while Radio Tehran reports that three jet fighters were also wrecked.

DIPLOMACY: In Rome, Italy, UN officials appeal to former Afghan monarch Mohammad Zahir Shah to assist in the formation of a coalition government in Afghanistan before the Soviets withdraw. The king has been living in exile there since 1973, and he states his willingness to assist any process provided that the principles of consensus and self-determination are respected.

MILITARY: The state-controlled media announce that Afghan army troops have killed a total of 530 resistance fighters in Kandahar, Kunduz, and Paktia Provinces. They also claim to have seized 23 ground-to-ground rockets in a sweep of the Paghman district of Kabul Province.

In Kunduz Province, Afghanistan, mujahideen fighters fire an estimated 40 rockets and 30 mortar shells at military installations in Kunduz City.

October 23–31

MILITARY: In Laghman Province, Afghanistan, mujahideen forces under Abdul Rahim Wardak, a former Afghan army officer, commence Operation Ghashev (Arrow) to seize part of the strategic Kabul-Jalalabad Road. They engage Afghan army elements deployed in various small outposts, 16 of which are quickly taken through infiltration. Six major bases are also captured in heavy fighting.

October 24

MILITARY: In Nangarhar Province, mujahideen fighters capture two more security posts along the Jalalabad-Kabul highway, destroying several tanks and cutting down power lines.

POLITICS: In Kabul, Afghanistan, President Mohammad Najibullah accuses members of the PDPA of conspiring behind his back. Recent party purges in March and July have done little to quell in-fighting, and opponents of the regime still manage to create disturbances within the Afghan army. Apparently, factionalism is on the rise again throughout the Afghan government.

October 25

DIPLOMACY: In Peshawar, Pakistan, mujahideen spokesman Burhanuddin Rabbani sends a complaint to UN special envoy Diego Cordovez regarding statements he made to the BBC and the *New York Times.* Apparently the envoy was disappointed by the lack of progress toward a solution to the Afghan crisis, which he attributed to Islamic fundamentalists in the Afghan resistance, and he called upon more moderate elements, such as former king Mohammad Zahir Shah, to become involved and end the gridlock.

MILITARY: In Helmand Province, Afghanistan, the mujahideen claim to have destroyed eight Soviet tanks in the regions of Lashkargh and Kajakai.

The Afghan resistance captures five more security posts along the strategic Jalalabad-Kabul highway, blocking traffic and cutting power lines from Sarobi to the capital.

October 26

DIPLOMACY: In Moscow, Soviet Union, the government agrees to hold direct talks with the mujahideen alliance for the first time. At issue is the release of Soviet and Afghan prisoners of war.

POLITICS: In Kabul, Afghanistan, President Mohammad Najibullah finally admits that his program of national reconciliation has failed. Western diplomats in the city also express doubt that Americans have been killed or captured while assisting the mujahideen in battle.

In Herat Province, Afghanistan, Governor Fazulhaq Khaliqyar is appointed to head up Badghis and Ghowr Provinces.

October 27
POLITICS: In Kabul, Afghanistan, President Mohammad Najibullah informs state-run radio that dissatisfaction exists among high-ranking army officials and that an attempted military coup has been quashed.

October 28
DIPLOMACY: The regime in Kabul, Afghanistan, dispatches an envoy to Rome to confer with former monarch Mohammad Zahir Shah.

MILITARY: Radio Moscow reports that the city of Balkh, Afghanistan, has been bombarded by Afghan rebels operating out of nearby Paktia Province. It also accuses the United States of increasing arms shipments to the resistance in violation of the Geneva peace accord.

A large influx of mujahideen fighters apparently are entering Nangarhar Province, Afghanistan, in preparation for an attack on the city of Jalalabad.

October 29
DIPLOMACY: In Washington, D.C., the State Department accuses the Soviet Union of violating the Geneva peace accord by deploying 30 new MiG-27 attack jets in Afghanistan. The agreement specifically states that only defensive weapons will be allowed into Afghanistan during the Soviet withdrawal.

October 30
AVIATION: In Kandahar, Afghanistan, newly arrived MiG-27 attack jets drop laser-guided bombs on mujahideen positions around the city, in an attempt to break the rebel siege and reopen the airport road.

October 31
MILITARY: In Nangarhar Province, Afghanistan, mujahideen fighters storm into the garrison of Landi Khyber, only three miles from the Pakistani border; 80 Afghan soldiers are captured, along with quantities of light and heavy equipment.

November 1
AVIATION: In Kabul, Afghanistan, Western diplomatic sources report that a shipment of two Soviet-made S-1 (Scud) tactical missiles has arrived.

MILITARY: In Oruzgan Province, Afghanistan, mujahideen loyal to Gulbuddin Hekmatyar skirmish heavily with fighters from the Ismail; 49 rebels are killed along with 60 civilians.

POLITICS: In Peshawar, Pakistan, the mujahideen leadership announces plans to elect a new government as soon as the Soviets have departed.

November 1–5
MILITARY: In Laghman Province, Afghanistan, Afghan army units attack and try to reopen portions of the Kabul-Jalalabad Highway severed by the mujahideen.

Overall, they are repelled by severe resistance opposition, losing several tanks and engineering vehicles in the process.

November 2

DIPLOMACY: In Washington, D.C., the government accuses the Soviets of deploying advanced tactical missiles to Afghanistan, which also pose a threat to Pakistan.
MILITARY: It is generally acknowledged that the Soviets are increasing the flow of heavy and sophisticated weapons to the Kabul regime before they depart.

A report from TASS suggests that the Afghans have developed a new kind of long-range missile and will be test-firing it shortly.

At the Khyber Pass, Afghanistan, the mujahideen capture the Tor Khan border post in addition to several select points along the Torkham-Jalalabad highway.

November 4

AVIATION: Pakistan claims that two of its F-16 jet fighters have brought down a Soviet-built MiG-23 of the Afghan air force near Thal, six miles into their territory. Radio Kabul disputes this and claims that Pakistani jets downed two Afghan jets over Khost in Afghanistan.

Afghan forces fire six to eight SS-1 (Scud) tactical missiles from Kabul, Afghanistan, at mujahideen positions ringing the city.
DIPLOMACY: In New York City, the UN General Assembly votes again to condemn the continuing Soviet presence in Afghanistan while calling for a broad-based coalition government in Kabul.

In Moscow, Soviet Union, First Deputy Foreign Minister Alexander Bessmertnykh informs journalists that Soviet forces in Afghanistan will be withdrawn once "suitable conditions" have been met, but prevailing conditions will not permit it. He mentions in passing that some motorized Soviet units are being replaced by their Afghan equivalents.
MILITARY: The Soviet government, citing Pakistan's alleged violations of the Geneva peace accord, declares that it is suspending its withdrawal.

November 5

DIPLOMACY: In Moscow, Soviet Union, Deputy Foreign Minister Alexander Bessmertnykh reiterates his government's determination to suspend all troop withdrawals from Afghanistan and to supply the Afghan army with more powerful weapons in light of escalating guerrilla activities. Pakistan and the United States are also blamed for violating the Geneva peace accord.

In Washington, D.C., President Ronald W. Reagan professes disappointment over the Soviet suspension of troop withdrawals from Afghanistan.
MILITARY: In Laghman Province, Afghanistan, units of the Afghan army advance toward sections of the Kabul-Jalalabad highway closed by mujahideen forces. Using strict radio silence, the resistance fighters allow them to enter, then attack. Heavy fire rakes the military convoys, and a traffic jam ensues as they try to flee the area. This section of the highway consequently remains under mujahideen control.

November 6

AVIATION: American military analysts postulate that the recent Soviet escalation of the air war in Afghanistan is undertaken to prevent the pending collapse of the Kabul regime.

DIPLOMACY: Soviet ambassador Yuli Vorontsov confirms that his government's suspension of troop withdrawals is a direct outcome of American and Pakistani arms shipments to the Afghan resistance and the resistance's continuing attacks upon Soviet forces as they withdraw north to their own border.

In Islamabad, Pakistan, Foreign Minister Sahabzada Yaqub Khan states that the Soviet suspension of troop withdrawals violates the Geneva peace accord and raises doubts as to Moscow's commitment to end the crisis.

POLITICS: In Kabul, Afghanistan, Prime Minister Mohammad Hassan Sharq declares that both he and President Mohammad Najibullah will retain power until a coalition government can be implemented. He also states that the Soviets will resume troop withdrawals once Pakistan cuts off arms supplies to the resistance and persuades its leaders to negotiate with his government.

November 7

POLITICS: In Peshawar, Pakistan, the mujahideen alliance declares that the deployment of new Soviet missiles will not deter it, although it will ask the United States to supply more advanced weapons.

November 9

DIPLOMACY: In Washington, D.C., mujahideen spokesman Burhanuddin Rabbani confers with President Ronald W. Reagan and Secretary of State George Shultz. Afterward, Reagan issues a statement declaring that the United States will never abandon the Afghan people's struggle for freedom.

POLITICS: The mujahideen leadership announces that it is commencing a new offensive against Soviet forces along the route from Kabul to the Soviet border. They also threaten to close the strategic Salang tunnel, through which all Soviet troops must pass.

November 10

DIPLOMACY: In New York City, Afghan prime minister Mohammad Hassan Sharq addresses the UN General Assembly, calling for demilitarization of his country under international supervision and formation of a coalition government before the Soviets depart the country.

POLITICS: President-elect George H. W. Bush, in his first news conference, makes clear his intent to hold the Soviet Union to its pledge to withdraw from Afghanistan. Still, he is eager to pursue improved relations with the Soviet Union.

November 12

DIPLOMACY: In Peshawar, Pakistan, mujahideen spokesman Burhanuddin Rabbani declares that the alliance is ready to commence direct negotiations with the Soviet Union regarding the release of Soviet prisoners. However, he repeats that the resistance will not enter into a coalition arrangement with the present regime in Kabul.

November 13

MILITARY: In Afghanistan, the mujahideen report that they are blocking the route north from Kabul to the Soviet Union. Since 1979 this has been the principal route for Soviet troops and supplies flowing in and out of the country.

November 16

AVIATION: Afghan troops fire an SS-1 (Scud) tactical missile at the Bajaur district north of Peshawar, Pakistan, which kills 10 people. Pakistan is experiencing greater violations of its airspace and territory than at any other period in the Afghan war.

November 17

DIPLOMACY: Afghan deputy foreign minister Abdul Ghaffer Lakanwal and Foreign Ministry deputy director Sayyed Kamaluddin defect to the United States; these are the most high profile defectors since 1979.

November 18

DIPLOMACY: In Kabul, Afghanistan, Soviet ambassador Yuli Vorontsov hints that his government is pursuing direct contacts with Afghan field commanders to try and draw them into a coalition government. He also expresses contempt for the mujahideen leadership in Pakistan, which Western diplomats consider a divisive ploy to divide the Afghan resistance.

November 19

MILITARY: Soviet general Boris V. Gromov warns the Afghan resistance against further escalation, noting that it threatens to nullify the Geneva accords and, with it, the Soviet pullout.

November 20

AVIATION: A report on Radio Pakistan suggests that ground fire downed an Afghan air force jet near Parachinar in the Kurrum agency, Pakistan.

DIPLOMACY: In Moscow, Soviet Union, President Mikhail Gorbachev suggests that the United States and Pakistan are trying to force his country to abandon the Geneva peace accord through their illegal support for the Afghan resistance.

November 21

DIPLOMACY: President Mikhail Gorbachev arrives in New Delhi, India, and suggests an international conference be held to preserve Afghanistan's nonaligned status. He also criticizes the United States and Pakistan for their continual aid to the Afghan resistance.

November 22

AVIATION: In Kabul, Afghanistan, the government announces that a transport plane has been shot down by Pakistan, killing 30 people.

November 24

MILITARY: Fighting continues unabated throughout Afghanistan, seven months after the Geneva peace accord were signed. Record numbers of refugees also continue flowing into Pakistan, while mine fields pose great danger to those wishing to return home.

November 26
DIPLOMACY: In Kabul, Afghanistan, a leading Politburo figure states that the Soviets will honor their commitment to be out of the country no later than February 15.

In Moscow, Soviet Union, newly returned president Mikhail Gorbachev declares his continued willingness to honor the Geneva peace accord, once all other signatories have.

MILITARY: The Afghan resistance reports capturing the Afghan army outpost at Torkham on the Khyber Pass, along with 184 soldiers. The latter capitulated after the mujahideen captured all four districts between Torkham and Jalalabad, which effectively cut off their food and ammunition supplies.

November 27
DIPLOMACY: In Washington, D.C., administration officials anticipate that, during the upcoming summit between Presidents Ronald W. Reagan and Mikhail Gorbachev, the Soviets may request American help in removing their troops from Afghanistan.

In Pakistan, Soviet officials prepare to meet with mujahideen alliance leaders to discuss the release of Soviet prisoners.

November 28
DIPLOMACY: In Islamabad, Pakistan, Soviet representatives confer with their mujahideen opposites regarding the release of 311 Soviet prisoners held by the Afghan resistance.

POLITICS: A report surfaces that Brigadier General Muhammad Gul of the KHAD (Afghan secret police) has defected to the mujahideen. He is also a cousin of President Mohammad Najibullah.

November 30
DIPLOMACY: In Pakistan, Soviet and mujahideen leaders discuss the possibility of high-level talks in Saudi Arabia.

MILITARY: In a published interview, Major General Lev Serebrov declares that the Afghan army does not face imminent collapse following a Soviet pullout from Afghanistan.

POLITICS: In Afghanistan, Mohammad Gul, a cousin of President Mohammad Najibullah, defects to the Afghan resistance.

December
NAVAL: With the end of the Iran-Iraq War, tensions in the Persian Gulf decline to the point where the role of the U.S. Navy is reduced to monitoring American-flagged vessels.

December 1
DIPLOMACY: In northern Afghanistan, the mujahideen release three Soviet prisoners in exchange for 30 captive rebels. This swap seems to indicate that a deal has been arranged between Peshawar and Moscow.

MILITARY: In Afghanistan, roving mujahideen hijack a UN relief convoy carrying aid to other rebel groups.

In Torkham, Afghanistan, a further 170 Afghan soldiers defect to the mujahideen, underscoring low morale in the national army.

December 3–5

DIPLOMACY: In Taif, Saudi Arabia, mujahideen leaders confer with Soviet ambassador Yuli Vorontsov. These are the first formal contacts between the Soviets and the resistance since the invasion began in 1979. Among the topics discussed are war reparations, safe passage for retreating Soviet forces, prisoner exchanges, and the transitional government.

December 4

DIPLOMACY: In Kabul, Afghanistan, President Mohammad Najibullah states that high-level discussions are unfolding in Saudi Arabia between Soviet ambassador Yuli Vorontsov and the Afghan resistance.

In Islamabad, Pakistan, the new prime minister, Benazir Bhutto, pledges to continue existing policies toward Afghanistan for as long as the crisis exists.

December 5

MILITARY: In Afghanistan, the UN relief convoy is released after being held by resistance fighters over the past four days.

December 6

DIPLOMACY: In Washington, D.C., President Mikhail Gorbachev arrives for a three-day summit with President Ronald Reagan.

In Taif, Saudi Arabia, Soviet and mujahideen representatives end their talks without announcing any agreements.

MILITARY: Near Kunduz, Afghanistan, resistance fighters allegedly attack a passenger bus, killing 42 people.

December 7

DIPLOMACY: In New York City, Soviet president Mikhail Gorbachev addresses the UN General Assembly and proposes a cease-fire in Afghanistan commencing January 1 and monitoring by UN peacekeeping forces. This is an apparent reversal on the part of the Soviets, who previously believed that the Afghan army was strong enough to underwrite Soviet security as Soviet forces withdrew.

In Peshawar, Pakistan, the mujahideen alliance leadership denounces Soviet calls for a cease-fire. Moreover, it pledges to fight until the Soviets have departed Afghanistan and the regime of President Mohammad Najibullah is overthrown.

POLITICS: In Kabul, Afghanistan, the University of Kabul announces dramatic curriculum changes by dropping required courses in Marxism-Leninism and related forms of "scientific materialism."

December 8

AVIATION: In Pakistan, an Afghan air force pilot defects with his MiG-21 fighter and lands on an airfield.

POLITICS: In Kabul, Afghanistan, Vice President Abdul Hamid Mohtat says his foremost goal for the government in talks between Moscow and the mujahideen is a lasting cease-fire. However, because the Kabul regime has been excluded from the talks, he cannot predict their duration or outcome.

December 10
POLITICS: In Kabul, Afghanistan, President Mohammad Najibullah nervously awaits the outcome of talks between the Soviets and the mujahideen. He appears upset that the two sides express satisfaction with the progress of their discussions and agree on certain issues.

December 11
AVIATION: Over Paktia Province, Afghanistan, mujahideen missiles bring down a transport aircraft over Khost.

DIPLOMACY: In Kabul, Afghanistan, foreign embassies are swamped by Afghans seeking exit visas. The word on the street is that chaos will erupt in the streets once the Soviets have withdrawn from the capital.

December 12
POLITICS: In Afghanistan, women's groups fear that the little progress they have made since the Soviet invasion will be erased after the Soviets are gone and an Islamic regime arises in Kabul.

December 17
DIPLOMACY: In Washington, D.C., President Ronald W. Reagan expresses concern over broken Soviet promises concerning Afghanistan yet is confident that they will depart the country by February 15 as anticipated.

December 18
DIPLOMACY: In Islamabad, Pakistan, Soviet negotiators and mujahideen representatives convene for a second round of prisoner-exchange discussions. A dispute arises when Moscow asserts that 311 captives are in question, while the resistance maintains the number is much lower.

December 20
MILITARY: Outside Kabul, Afghanistan, mujahideen units continue their hard fight against Soviet and Afghan army units, with many field commanders expressing doubts that the Soviets actually intend to leave.

December 21
POLITICS: In Peshawar, Pakistan, divisions again surface in mujahideen ranks over the nature of the post-Soviet government. Several resistance leaders oppose any formal contacts with the Soviets for any reason.

December 25
DIPLOMACY: In Rome, Italy, Soviet ambassador Yuli Vorontsov confers with former monarch Mohammad Zahir Shah and requests that he participate in a new coalition government; the king politely holds back, biding his time.

December 28
DIPLOMACY: In Washington, D.C., Under Secretary of State Michael Armacost warns that Soviet failure to withdraw all troops from Afghanistan by February 15,

1989, would cast an enormous pall over relations with the incoming administration of George H. W. Bush, as well as alienate the Chinese and Muslims worldwide. He also says that the current regime in Kabul does not enjoy popular support and is likely to tumble soon.

In Los Angeles, California, President Ronald W. Reagan gives a speech marking the ninth anniversary of the Soviet invasion of Afghanistan and denounces Moscow's continued military operations, the introduction of new and stronger weapons, and all the death, destruction, and refugees they generated. Reagan ends by declaring that the United States is proud to support the Afghan resistance and that such support will continue unabated.

December 30
POLITICS: In Kabul, Afghanistan, President Mohammad Najibullah unveils a new national reconciliation program, coupled with a unilateral cease-fire, to take place on January 15. He also remarks that a general amnesty will be declared at that time, along with a new constitution making Islam the official religion of Afghanistan.

December 31
MILITARY: In Kabul, Afghanistan, President Mohammad Najibullah declares that the Afghan army will implement a cease-fire if the resistance does the same. However, a mujahideen spokesman states that the resistance will go on fighting until the present regime is eliminated from power.

1989

January 1
DIPLOMACY: In Moscow, Soviet Union, government radio announces that Ambassador Yuli Vorontsov is in Tehran, Iran, negotiating with mujahideen groups operating there. His highest priority is getting resistance leaders to accept the cease-fire proclaimed by the Kabul government.

January 2
POLITICS: In Peshawar, Pakistan, Sibghatullah Mojaddedi replaces Burhanuddin Rabbani as spokesman for the mujahideen alliance.

January 4
DIPLOMACY: In Islamabad, Afghanistan, a second round of discussions opens between Soviet representatives and the mujahideen alliance. Ambassador Yuli Vorontsov also confers with Pakistani foreign minister Yaqub Khan regarding a resumption of the Soviet withdrawal.
AVIATION: Several Navy F-14 Tomcats of VF-32 from the carrier *John F. Kennedy* engage two Libyan MiG-23 jets over the Gulf of Sidra after a tense standoff. The Libyan jets apparently had approached the American jets in a hostile manner before the incident and were promptly shot down.

January 5
DIPLOMACY: Soviet ambassador Yuli Vorontsov declares that the Soviet deadline for departing Afghanistan may not be honored if mujahideen attacks continue.

MILITARY: In Tashkent, Soviet Uzbekistan, a large group of Afghan cadets studying at the Soviet police academy riot, leaving one dead and several injured. Speculation surfaces that the tension was caused by anxieties over the Soviet withdrawal from Afghanistan and the expected collapse of the Kabul regime.

In Kandahar, Afghanistan, the Afghan resistance reports capturing five more Afghan army security posts.

January 7
DIPLOMACY: In Islamabad, Pakistan, a mujahideen leader states that Soviet ambassador Yuli Vorontsov assured him that Soviet forces would be gone from Afghanistan by February 15.

January 8
DIPLOMACY: In Islamabad, Pakistan, Soviet ambassador Yuli Vorontsov meets with the new Pakistani prime minister, Benazir Bhutto, and invites her to visit Moscow. However, he states to the news media that the solution to the crisis in Afghanistan must be political in nature, not military. He also characterizes violence committed by the resistance as reminiscent of the "Middle Ages."

In Paktia Province, Afghanistan, land mines kill 43 people, mostly civilians. The rebel forces also capture Abdul Rahim of the University of Kabul's engineering department, who had previously disarmed 3,000 mines.

MILITARY: In Nangarhar Province, Afghanistan, the mujahideen claim to have captured 1,000 Afghan army troops along with their Khiva district headquarters.

POLITICS: In Kabul, Afghanistan, a senior member of the PDPA declares that President Mohammad Najibullah will not resign from office, regardless of the government that arises following the Soviet pullout.

January 9
DIPLOMACY: Mujahideen representative Karim Khalili arrives in Islamabad, Pakistan, for talks with Soviet ambassador Yuli Vorontsov. He reiterates that under no circumstances will the resistance share power with the communist regime in Kabul, Afghanistan.

MILITARY: The Afghan resistance sells a Soviet-made T-64 tank it captured to the United States; it subsequently announces that captured Soviet helicopters are for sale.

January 10
DIPLOMACY: In Islamabad, Pakistan, mujahideen leader Sibghatullah Mojaddedi announces his decision to break off direct negotiations with Soviet diplomats and refuses to halt attacks on withdrawing Soviet forces. He also criticizes Soviet ambassador Yuli Vorontsov for characterizing the resistance as living in the Middle Ages.

January 11
AVIATION: Over Landi Khyber, Afghanistan, a mujahideen missile brings down an Afghan air force jet.

DIPLOMACY: Soviet ambassador Yuri Vorontsov warns that the Soviet Union may not meet its February 15 withdrawal deadline if the resistance continues fighting. His remarks are viewed as a threat to Western governments to pressure the Afghan resistance into a political settlement.

MILITARY: In Kabul, Afghanistan, the Soviets shut down their military hospital and withdraw most military advisers from the city.

In Nangarhar Province, Afghanistan, a strong mujahideen offensive captures the Gushta, Ganda Ghar, Girdab, and Arhkhi districts in heavy fighting. The Soviets retaliate by bombing the Gushta and Ghazi Abad areas.

January 12

DIPLOMACY: In Washington, D.C., the administration encourages the Soviets to stick to their February 15 deadline and withdraw all forces from Afghanistan. Despite recent tough talk about suspending the withdrawal, there has yet to be any official indication from Moscow that this might actually transpire.

In Islamabad, Pakistan, Soviet ambassador Victor Yakunin anticipates that relations between Pakistan and the Soviet Union will improve in the future. He attributes this to the growth of democracy in Pakistan and the new government there.

A report on Radio Netherlands says that the Soviets have resumed withdrawing their military forces from Afghanistan.

In Peshawar, Pakistan, mujahideen leader Sibghatullah Mojaddedi declares that the Soviet Union cannot be trusted to abide by the Geneva peace accord.

POLITICS: In Kabul, Afghanistan, Deputy Trade Minister Fateh Mohammad Tareen declares the food situation in the city to be worse than the 1972 drought. He also notes that roughly 20,000 containers of oil, flour, and rice are stranded near the Soviet border in Herat thanks to mujahideen interference.

January 13

AVIATION: In Nangarhar Province, Afghanistan, a Soviet-built SS-1 (Scud) ballistic missile crashes into the village of Hazarnau, killing several civilians. Soviet forces have fired about 65 missiles at suspected mujahideen positions and supporters and plan to provide the Afghan government with 250 of them.

DIPLOMACY: In Peshawar, Pakistan, mujahideen leader Gulbuddin Hekmatyar insists that the impending Soviet withdrawal is inevitable because the Soviet Union has failed to impose its will on the Afghan people. He considers recent threats to suspend the withdrawal as political posturing.

In Washington, D.C., the State Department announces that the Soviets have resumed their pullback of troops from Afghanistan, despite the recent breakdown in talks between Moscow and the mujahideen.

MILITARY: At a news conference in Moscow, Soviet Union, Deputy Defense Minister General Vitali Shabanov declares that the next stage of the Soviet withdrawal from Afghanistan will commence "soon."

POLITICS: In Malaysia, a group of Afghan students burn the Soviet flag in front of the Soviet embassy there. Six members of the Muslim Youth Movement subsequently enter the embassy and hand a note to Ambassador Anatoly Ivanovich Khmelritsky.

TERRORISM: A report surfaces on TASS that a car bomb in Herat, Afghanistan, has killed or wounded 20 people.

January 14

DIPLOMACY: In Kabul, Afghanistan, Soviet foreign minister Eduard Shevardnadze drops in for an unannounced visit.

January 15
DIPLOMACY: In Kabul, Afghanistan, Soviet foreign minister Eduard Shevardnadze declares that Soviet aid will continue to the Afghan regime even after all Soviet forces have departed.

Soviet efforts to bring the mujahideen alliance and the Kabul regime together for talks have failed, and the attempt ends.

In Peshawar, Pakistan, mujahideen spokesmen inform an American delegation that Soviet troops will in all likelihood depart Afghanistan by February 15, simply because they have lost the war. Furthermore, they now state they will not harass Soviet personnel attempting to leave the country.

In Tehran, Iran, Abdul Karim Khalili, head of the eight-party alliance sheltered there, declares that since the Soviets have accepted defeat in Afghanistan, it is impossible for them to remain any longer.

Confusion reigns in Moscow, Soviet Union, as Ambassador Yuli Vorontsov insists that the withdrawal of troops from Afghanistan could be delayed if the rebels keep fighting, while Deputy Foreign Minister Vladimir Petrovsky says that Moscow will uphold the Geneva peace accord and that the withdrawal will continue.

MILITARY: In Faryab Province, Afghanistan, the mujahideen attack the Shereen Tagab district, capturing a number of outposts and destroying 16 tanks and other military vehicles.

In Parvan Province, Afghanistan, resistance fighters cut the natural gas pipeline in the Pule Mattak region; this line runs directly into the Soviet Union.

POLITICS: Reports surface that the inhabitants of Gardez, Paktia Province, Afghanistan, face a famine owing to Afghan rebels besieging the city and blocking all transportation routes to it.

In Soviet Central Asia, the mujahideen have been publishing and passing out Islamic books to the inhabitants of Uzbekistan, Tajikistan, Azerbaijan, Kazakhstan, Kyrgyzstan, and Turkmenistan.

January 16
AVIATION: Soviet and Afghan air force jets bomb a rebel district in Dara-i-Noor, Nangarhar Province, Afghanistan, causing many civilian casualties.

DIPLOMACY: In Kabul, Afghanistan, Soviet foreign minister Eduard Shevardnadze concludes his latest visit by insisting that all Soviet troops will depart the country no later than February 15. He also makes a plea for the mujahideen leadership to resume negotiations while promising continuing Soviet aid to the Kabul regime.

In an interview for the French paper *Le Point*, former monarch Mohammad Zahir Shah states that the United Nations should become more involved with the Afghan crisis in order to end it.

January 17
DIPLOMACY: In Tehran, Iran, mujahideen spokesman Sibghatullah Mojaddedi declares that direct negotiations with the Soviets are not possible as long as their troops occupy Afghanistan. Spokesmen for the Shiite resistance groups in Iran also refuse to join an interim Afghan government.

MILITARY: In Afghanistan, Soviet general Boris V. Gromov declares that the Soviets will complete their withdrawal from the country by the middle of next month.

January 18

AVIATION: Increased aerial activity by Soviet aviation units is noted in Afghanistan, usually in the form of bringing in ammunition and supplies while flying troops back home. Reporters also observe 18 SS-1 (Scud) missiles being transported from Kabul airport to the Darulaman region.

In Kunduz, Afghanistan, mujahideen rockets hit the regional airport, destroying two government helicopters.

DIPLOMACY: In Islamabad, Pakistan, government officials warns a U.S. congressional delegation that the mere withdrawal of Soviet forces from Afghanistan does not signal an end to the threat they pose to the region.

January 19

DIPLOMACY: In Moscow, Soviet Union, Foreign Ministry spokesman Gennady Gerasimov accuses the Afghan resistance of imposing an economic blockade and food shortages on Kabul. In effect, he says he is applying pressure on the existing regime even before the Soviets have completed their withdrawal.

MILITARY: On the road between Kabul and Mazar-i-Sharif, Afghanistan, the mujahideen ambush a government military convoy, reportedly capturing 50 vehicles.

In Kunduz Province, Afghanistan, the resistance claims to have captured the Kunduz airport after three days of intense combat.

January 20

AVIATION: Airline flights shuttling between New Delhi, India, and Kabul, Afghanistan, must carry sufficient fuel for return flights because of shortages of aviation gas in Kabul.

The Red Air Force begins a massive airlift in and out of Kabul, Afghanistan, in an attempt to prop up the Communist regime there as Soviet troops are withdrawn.

DIPLOMACY: The British government is advising all British nationals in Afghanistan to evacuate as soon as possible. London has not yet decided whether to shutter the embassy there.

MILITARY: The media in Moscow indicate that the Afghan resistance is stepping up military activity along the strategic Salang highway running through the Hindu Kush mountains to the Soviet border. Consequently, Kabul, Afghanistan, is experiencing severe shortages in food and fuel at the height of winter.

The latest intelligence places Afghan rebels only three miles from Jalalabad, Afghanistan, despite intense aerial bombardment from Soviet and government warplanes.

The Soviet newspaper *Pravda* states that all troops have departed from 26 of 31 Afghan provinces and the defenses of Kabul are being turned over to the national army.

POLITICS: In Washington, D.C., President George H. W. Bush is sworn in as the new president to succeed Ronald W. Reagan.

January 21

DIPLOMACY: In Washington, D.C., the State Department announces that the Soviets are dropping new and heavier types of ordnance on the mujahideen to protect their withdrawing ground forces.

In Kabul, Afghanistan, the government of West Germany, citing the increase in violence around the capital, announces that it is removing its three remaining diplomats.

January 22

AVIATION: TASS reports that the Soviets have begun an extensive airlift of supplies to Kabul, Afghanistan, to alleviate chronic food shortages.

DIPLOMACY: In Kabul, Afghanistan, West Germany closes its mission and orders its staff home out of fear of rising violence once Soviet forces depart.

In Washington, a State Department official suggests that the United States may close down its mission once Soviet forces depart Kabul, Afghanistan.

January 23

AVIATION: In Washington, D.C., the State Department says that the Soviets have introduced a new, heavy bomb to Afghanistan, possibly weighing as much as 12,000 pounds. This weapon is so large it can only be delivered by large Tu-22 Backfire bombers flying from bases in Soviet Central Asia. These new weapons are used to cover the withdrawal of Soviet ground forces.

DIPLOMACY: Western military experts acknowledge that the Soviets have withdrawn half of their 30,000-man garrison from Kabul, Afghanistan. The State Department consequently states that it will request a relaxation of East-West trade controls once the Soviets are completely gone from the country.

MILITARY: In Moscow, Soviet Union, Major General Lev Serebrov admits that Soviet forces departing Afghanistan share a deep sense of failure.

January 24

AVIATION: Soviet military transports are observed dropping large bundles of flares to thwart mujahideen missile fire as they approach and land at Kabul, Afghanistan.

DIPLOMACY: In Peshawar, Pakistan, mujahideen spokesman Sibghatullah Mojaddedi declares his willingness to resume talks with the Soviet government, provided they meet his conditions, primarily the removal of all forces and an end to military aid to the Kabul regime.

MILITARY: Mujahideen pressure along the Salang highway continues to exert pressure on Kabul, Afghanistan, by restricting food and fuel supplies. Soviet troops are obliged to dig in north of the Salang pass to secure the region for withdrawing forces to pass through.

POLITICS: In Peshawar, Pakistan, the seven-member mujahideen alliance is growing frayed as differences appear over the future of governance once the Soviets are gone. The biggest source of friction originates with field commanders in Afghanistan itself, who are beginning to demand a political say in any future regime.

January 25

AVIATION: Over Kandahar, Afghanistan, a mujahideen Stinger missile brings down a large military transport as it attempts to land. Soviet and Afghan jets retaliate by bombing residential areas around the airport.

DIPLOMACY: In Washington, D.C., Secretary of State George Shultz states that the Soviets should be rewarded for departing Afghanistan by easing trade controls imposed after their 1979 invasion.

MILITARY: Afghan army troops claim to have killed 377 resistance fighters after they refused to allow food to be shipped through the mountain passes to Kabul, Afghanistan.

In Islamabad, Afghanistan, U.S. ambassador Robert Oakley states that the Soviets are continually laying land mines in Afghanistan, even while they withdraw. Oakley notes that mines will greatly impede postwar reconstruction efforts in that country and result in hundreds of civilian casualties.

January 26

AVIATION: As fighting flares near the Soviet border, the Afghan resistance claims to have downed three military aircraft over Kunduz Province, Afghanistan.

DIPLOMACY: In Washington, D.C., the government appeals to the Soviets to halt all aerial bombing of Afghanistan and complete withdrawing its troops.

In Tehran, Iran, another mujahideen deputation under Gulbuddin Hekmatyar arrives to confer with the Iranian foreign minister.

MILITARY: Soviet and Afghan forces level several villages along the strategic Salang highway to keep it passable to withdrawing Soviet troops; several hundred civilians are reported killed in the attack.

January 27

AVIATION: As conditions continue deteriorating in Kandahar, Afghanistan, Soviet transport planes are seen rushing a new influx of supplies and Afghan soldiers to bolster the garrison.

DIPLOMACY: In Washington, D.C., Secretary of State James A. Baker announces the closure of the American embassy in Kabul, Afghanistan, due to increasing instability following the Soviet pullout. The decision comes in the wake of reports of a major Soviet and Afghan army offensive north of the capital to clear the Salang highway of Afghan resistance fighters; several hundred civilians are purportedly killed.

The State Department accuses the Soviet Union of bombing areas of Afghanistan where there are no Soviet ground troops, which is a violation of the Geneva peace accord. These air raids are launched from Soviet territory and include targets in the cities of Kandahar, Jalalabad, and Kunduz.

In Moscow, Soviet Union, Foreign Ministry spokesman Gennady Gerasimov admits that the Afghan rebels have continued their blockade of Kabul, Afghanistan.

In Kabul, Afghanistan, the governments of Japan, Britain, the United States, Italy, and France are evacuating their key diplomatic personnel for fear of an upcoming mujahideen offensive against the capital. Japan and France also announce the closure of their embassies.

MILITARY: Western military observers comment on the difficulties the Soviets are experiencing while withdrawing from Afghanistan. The harsh terrain, weather, and resistance fighters are all compounding their problems.

In Kabul, Afghanistan, Soviet defense minister Dimitri Yazov flies in to observe the final stages of Soviet troop withdrawals scheduled for the following month. He also reiterates continuing military support for the Communist regime.

POLITICS: Western analysts observe that Soviet officials have all but admitted that the collapse of the Communist regime in Kabul, Afghanistan, is inevitable following the removal of Soviet forces. They also discuss the Soviet Union's pressing economic problems at home and the unjustified expenses of the Afghan adventure.

In light of the mounting humanitarian crisis in Afghanistan, Prince Sadruddin Aga Khan, coordinator of the UN relief effort, convenes a meeting to find the best ways of dispatching food to the starving populace.

January 29
AVIATION: Roughly 15 to 20 Soviet Ilyushin IL-76 jet transports arrive in Kabul, Afghanistan, every day, bringing in supplies for the Afghan army and returning home with Soviet troops on board. In light of the mujahideen threat, each IL-76 jettisons antimissile flares as it lands and takes off.

In northern Afghanistan, the mujahideen loyal to Ahmad Shah Massoud experience the heaviest aerial bombardment of the war. Apparently this display of firepower is to force him into truce talks with Soviet defense minister Dimitri Yazov, currently in Kabul.

DIPLOMACY: In Peshawar, Pakistan, mujahideen leader Burhanuddin Rabbani declares that the Soviet Union and the resistance had previously agreed at Taif, Saudi Arabia, that there would be no direct talks between Moscow and individual Afghan leaders. Hence, trying to pressure Ahmad Shah Massoud into truce talks is a futile gesture.

In Vienna, Austria, the government announces that it is shutting down its embassy in Kabul, Afghanistan; this leaves Italy as the only West European country with a functioning embassy there.

MILITARY: In Kabul, Afghanistan, Soviet defense minister Dimitri Yazov concludes two days of talks with President Mohammad Najibullah; both men agree that the Soviet troop withdrawal will be completed by February 15.

In Farah Province, Afghanistan, roughly 400 Afghan army soldiers defect to the mujahideen near the provincial capital. They bring with them their weapons and a large quantity of supplies.

In Jalalabad, Afghanistan, a government convoy of 70 trucks and tanks fights its way past the mujahideen blockade and rescues the garrison.

January 30
AVIATION: Reports surface of intense Soviet aerial bombing along the Salang highway between Kabul, Afghanistan, and the Soviet border. Many villages have been completely destroyed in an attempt to keep that route open to retreating Soviet forces.

DIPLOMACY: In Washington, D.C., spokesman Richard W. Murphy of the Department of State declares that the United States is not positioned to stop the Afghan resistance from besieging Kabul, Afghanistan, once the Soviets have departed the country. He also criticizes the Soviet "scorched earth" policy of destroying anything of value in the retreat from Afghanistan.

In Kabul, Afghanistan, the Soviet Union begins reducing the number of personnel at its embassy.

MILITARY: The TASS news agency reports that mujahideen rockets are continually slamming into Kabul, Afghanistan, causing several civilian casualties.

January 31

DIPLOMACY: In Kabul, Afghanistan, the United States closes its embassy but cannot remove its personnel because of a blizzard that halts all air travel. Meanwhile, the Afghan Foreign Ministry charges that nations who have recently shut their embassies are only doing so to discredit the Kabul regime and boost Afghan resistance morale.

In New Delhi, India, the government orders its embassy in Kabul, Afghanistan, to send home all nonessential personnel, including wives and children.

Soviet foreign minister Eduard Shevardnadze arrives in Beijing, China, becoming the first Soviet diplomat to hold talks there in 30 years. The removal of Soviet forces from Afghanistan was a Chinese precondition for the discussions.

February 1

AVIATION: The Red Air Force intensifies bombing efforts throughout the Panjshir Valley to ensure the safe passage of Soviet troops en route home. The air force apparently is dropping new and more effective types of ordnance upon civilians and resistance fighters.

DIPLOMACY: In Kabul, Afghanistan, Soviet deputy prime minister Yuri Maslyukov confers with President Mohammad Najibullah about cooperation in a number of economic, cultural, and trade matters. The Soviets are attempting to buoy sagging Communist morale throughout the country as their military withdrawal nears completion.

In Washington, D.C., the State Department accuses the Soviet Union of conducting a deliberate scorched-earth policy through extensive aerial bombardment launched from inside the Soviet Union.

Italy becomes the last West European country to shutter its embassy in Kabul, Afghanistan.

POLITICS: A report in the *New York Times* suggests that as the pace of the Soviet withdrawal from Afghanistan accelerates, so too do the friction and hostility among competing mujahideen groups over the nature of a post-Communist government.

As fighting between the Afghan resistance and the Afghan national army intensifies, new waves of refugees begin descending upon camps in Pakistan.

February 2

AVIATION: Large military transports evacuate the few remaining Soviet troops from Kabul, Afghanistan, which are flown direct to Tashkent, Soviet Uzbekistan, and other cities in Central Asia. Returning aircraft invariably bring tons of food, supplies, and weapons for the Kabul regime.

DIPLOMACY: In Kabul, Afghanistan, President Mohammad Najibullah denounces the closure of Western embassies in Afghanistan, claiming it is a form of psychological warfare.

MILITARY: Playing down recent U.S. criticism, General Bronislav Omelichev, first military chief of the Soviet armed forces, declares that all recent Soviet military

activities throughout Afghanistan are meant solely to guarantee the safe return of
departing Soviet forces.

POLITICS: U.S. official Jon Glassman, who has recently departed Afghanistan, warns
of a possible military coup against the regime of President Mohammad Najibullah
by either Communist extremists or resistance sympathizers.

In Peshawar, Pakistan, large numbers of Afghan refugees stage demonstrations
calling for the return of former monarch Mohammad Zahir Shah.

February 3

AVIATION: In Kabul, Afghanistan, a Soviet convoy delivers 360 rockets to Afghan
government forces only days before the last Soviet troops are to depart. The 15
trucks are mounted with BUM-27 multiple launcher systems, which are being
introduced in the war for the first time.

MILITARY: In Peshawar, Pakistan, mujahideen leader Gulbuddin Hekmatyar predicts that Kabul, Afghanistan, will fall in a matter of weeks following the Soviet
withdrawal, and not months as predicted. He also declares that the majority
of Afghan cities will also be taken shortly thereafter. Furthermore, Hekmatyar
insists that his fighters will attack Soviet territory directly should the Soviet Union
launch attacks on Afghanistan from across the Oxus River, which divides the two
countries.

POLITICS: Western analysts say that the Soviet Union has abandoned any hope for
a political solution to the Afghan crisis and is concentrating on removing its forces
without suffering additional casualties. It is likewise assumed that the Soviets will
continue efforts at forming a coalition government in Kabul, behind the scenes,
after they have departed.

In Kabul, Afghanistan, President Mohammad Najibullah declares that his
regime will survive the Soviet withdrawal and that he also anticipates a political
settlement with the Afghan resistance to avoid a protracted civil war. Najibullah
expresses confidence that the Soviet Union has not deserted him and repeats the
recent closure of Western embassies in Kabul represents "psychological warfare"
against the government.

The United Nations seeks to deliver humanitarian relief to the city of Kabul,
Afghanistan, by chartered airlift, even as it is besieged by the Afghan resistance. The
mujahideen, for their part, are willing to tolerate such flights provided the United
Nations increases allotments of aid to them as well.

The Soviet government complains that the mujahideen are holding up thousands of trucks laden with food for the inhabitants of Kabul, Afghanistan. The Foreign Ministry maintains that mujahideen have caused a crisis in the capital region
and several metropolitan areas.

February 4

AVIATION: The Soviet army paper *Krasnaya Zvezda* (Red Star) reports that 24,443
soldiers have been evacuated by airlift from Afghanistan over the past six months.
Meanwhile, the ongoing airlift has delivered 3,500 tons of flour to Kabul and 3,475
tons of ammunition to Kandahar.

DIPLOMACY: In London, United Kingdom, the government begins pressing to lift Western economic sanctions against the Soviet Union that were imposed after it invaded Afghanistan.

In Islamabad, Pakistan, Soviet foreign minister Eduard Shevardnadze arrives, becoming the first high-ranking Soviet official to visit in more than two decades.

MILITARY: In Kabul, Afghanistan, a Soviet troop convoy pulls out from the city during a snowstorm; no more than 1,500 troops are garrisoned in the capital.

February 5

DIPLOMACY: In Islamabad, Pakistan, Soviet foreign minister Eduard Shevardnadze confers with Prime Minister Benazir Bhutto and all but admits that the Communist regime in Kabul, Afghanistan, is imperiled once Soviet forces depart.

In Tehran, Iran, Soviet envoy Yuli Vorontsov promises that all Soviet forces will be out of Afghanistan within the next four days.

MILITARY: Kabul, Afghanistan, is placed under martial law following the departure of the last remaining Soviet troops.

POLITICS: In Washington, D.C., President George H. W. Bush has yet to articulate a new Afghan policy following the Soviet withdrawal, including whether to continue military aid to the resistance.

A report on the Voice of Germany says that large, progovernment demonstrations are being held in Kabul, Afghanistan.

February 6

DIPLOMACY: In Islamabad, Pakistan, Soviet foreign minister Eduard Shevardnadze remains a few extra days, attempting to salvage some kind of future role for the regime of President Mohammad Najibullah. The Soviet embassy also releases a statement saying that Moscow seeks a cease-fire in Afghanistan, proof that the Russians are desperately attempting to find a role for themselves in these final proceedings.

In Kabul, Afghanistan, the only remaining embassies still open are from the Soviet Union and East European, Islamic, and Third World nations.

In New Delhi, India, the family of Afghan prime minister Mohammad Hassan Sharq arrives, with the wives and children of other leading Afghan families. Reports indicate that Kabul, Afghanistan, is facing acute shortages of food and fuel.

MILITARY: Radio Moscow declares that the final contingent of Soviet troops has departed from Kabul, Afghanistan, and is wending its way north and home. It also declares that the city is in a state of chaos and that civil war between competing Afghan factions is most likely inevitable.

The Soviet media broadcast footage of large military convoys motoring through the Salang pass, en route to home. Large convoys of troops and military equipment are also reported on the move from eastern and western reaches of the country.

POLITICS: A report from Western relief organizations states that two or three years are required for all 5 million Afghan refugees in Pakistan and Iran to be resettled back home.

In Moscow, Soviet Press spokesman Boris Pradishev appears on the popular television program *Look* and states that the decision to invade Afghanistan was undertaken by Soviet leader Leonid Brezhnev without consulting members of the Politburo. He also salutes Mikhail Gorbachev for the courage to order a complete military withdrawal. Pradishev concludes by insisting that, despite a decade of war, the reasons and logic behind the Afghan war are still unknown to the populace.

February 7

DIPLOMACY: In Islamabad, Pakistan, Soviet foreign minister Eduard Shevardnadze departs with little to show for his efforts after mujahideen leaders fail to materialize for talks. Before departing he reiterates that no broad-based coalition government is possible in Kabul without the participation of the Communists already in power. He also suggests that relations between his country and Pakistan could be improved through several proposed joint ventures and an overall expansion of trade and economic cooperation between the two.

MILITARY: In Termiz, Soviet Union, ceremonies unfold for a Soviet regiment that has arrived back from Afghanistan. It is suggested that as many as 20,000 troops are still marooned there, awaiting ground or air transportation back home. Meanwhile, a steady stream of Afghan army trucks continues driving toward Kabul, delivering food and military supplies to the hard-pressed garrison there. There remains a distinct air of bitterness among Soviet officers about the retreat and the lack of official support for the 10-year campaign.

In Afghanistan, a mujahideen commander goes on record stating that the Pakistanis are pressuring them to attack Jalalabad, despite its strong garrison.

NAVAL: In Washington, D.C., the U.S. Maritime Commission agrees to return the registry of 11 Kuwaiti tankers back to their owners.

February 8

AVIATION: In Moscow, Soviet Union, the government refuses to back down from its intense aerial bombardment campaign against the Afghan resistance because of the cover it provides withdrawing Soviet forces. It also bolsters the Afghan national army for the time being.

In Afghanistan, the Red Air Force finally abandons its air bases at Sheen Dhand and Bagram.

The first aircraft chartered to carry 32 tons of emergency relief supplies to Afghanistan is grounded at Islamabad, Pakistan, for safety reasons.

DIPLOMACY: In Washington, D.C., President George H. W. Bush begins weighing the lifting of export controls on high-technology items that have been banned from the Soviet Union since 1979.

MILITARY: In Kabul, Afghanistan, the government begins arming 30,000 PDPA members to help defend the city during an anticipated mujahideen siege.

POLITICS: In Detroit, Michigan, former secretary of state Henry Kissinger freely predicts that the Communist regime in Kabul, Afghanistan, will not survive for many months following the Soviet withdrawal.

UN relief coordinator Prince Sadruddin Aga Khan declares there is a severe shortage of food and essential commodities in Kabul, Afghanistan, which can only be partially rectified by an emergency airlift.

February 9

AVIATION: In Islamabad, Pakistan, a chartered Egypt Air cargo plane carrying UN relief supplies to Kabul, Afghanistan, cancels its flight for safety reasons.

MILITARY: Although the mujahideen leadership openly predicts the fall of Jalalabad, Afghanistan, shortly, they are resisting Pakistani pressure for an all-out, frontal assault. Meanwhile, many Afghan army soldiers are continuing to defect to the resistance in large numbers.

February 10
DIPLOMACY: The Soviet Union appeals to Western nations to expedite emergency shipments of food supplies to Kabul, Afghanistan, and to break the blockade there by the Afghan resistance.

February 11
DIPLOMACY: In Washington, D.C., President George H. W. Bush elects to continue military assistance and supplies to the Afghan resistance for as long as Moscow keeps assisting the Communist regime in Kabul, Afghanistan. The National Security Council, the State Department, the Pentagon, and the Central Intelligence Agency all concur that it is essential to continue military aid.

MILITARY: In Moscow, Soviet Union, the government media announce that 89,000 soldiers have recently departed Afghanistan, leaving only 11,000 in place. Footage is aired of a paratroop unit and motorized contingents crossing the Amu Darya bridge linking Hayratan, Afghanistan, with Termiz in Soviet Central Asia.

February 12
DIPLOMACY: In Kabul, Afghanistan, President Mohammad Najibullah accuses Pakistan of planning to invade and annex his country.

In Beijing, China, Pakistani prime minister Benazir Bhutto arrives for high-level talks. Pakistan is under heavy Soviet pressure to moderate its support for the Afghan resistance, so Bhutto seeks reassurance and support from China to continue with her policies.

MILITARY: The final Soviet motorized unit begins wending its way through the strategic Salang pass, only 120 miles south of the Soviet border. There remains only a small group of security personnel at Kabul airport to ensure the safety of cargo planes arriving from the Soviet Union.

POLITICS: The *New York Times* reports there is sometimes "fierce" competition among the rapidly unraveling mujahideen alliance in Pakistan.

February 13
AVIATION: The United States suspends its delivery of relief goods to Kabul, Afghanistan, once airliners begin refusing to land in the capital.

DIPLOMACY: In Washington, D.C., President George H. W. Bush reiterates his pledge to support the Afghan resistance for as long as the Soviet Union props up the Communist regime in Kabul, Afghanistan. He signs a National Security Directive to that effect.

Western analysts detect signs that the Soviet government has begun distancing itself from the regime of President Mohammad Najibullah in Afghanistan. The Soviets remain vague about continuing support to the regime and silent as to continuing American aid to the resistance.

Despite Soviet reassurances, a steady stream of Afghan officials and their families are seen departing the capital of Kabul, Afghanistan.

February 14

DIPLOMACY: In Tehran, Iran, Ayatollah Khomeini accuses British author Salman Rushdie, author of the novel *The Satanic Verses,* of blasphemy toward Islam and sentences him to death.

MILITARY: Kabul airport, Afghanistan, is the site of a final ceremony marking the removal of the last detachment of Soviet troops from Afghanistan.

Twenty-four hours before the official deadline, Lieutenant General Boris V. Gromov becomes the last Soviet soldier to leave Afghanistan by personally walking across the international bridge separating Afghanistan from the Soviet Union. This decade-long military intervention cost the Soviets 15,000 lives and untold billions of rubles, along with condemnation by the United States, China, the Western community, and the Islamic world. However, Western analysts conclude that at least 250 Soviet diplomats, secret agents, and military advisers have remained behind to assist the Kabul regime.

POLITICS: In Peshawar, Pakistan, the mujahideen formally announces the creation of an Afghan interim government with Sibghatullah Mojaddedi as president.

February 15

AVIATION: At Kabul airport, Afghanistan, a final barrage of mujahideen rockets hits as the last detachment of Soviet troops is flown out of the country for home.

DIPLOMACY: In Washington, D.C., a Bush administration spokesman flatly refuses to halt arms shipments to the Afghan resistance as long as the Soviets continue supplying the regime in Kabul, Afghanistan.

In Tehran, Iran, an aide of Ayatollah Khomeini offers $1 million for the murder of British author Salman Rushdie.

MILITARY: Reports in Soviet newspapers say that Afghan army units are looting their bases and defecting to the resistance. The Soviet government is also apparently bracing itself for a rapid collapse of its puppet regime.

Massed mujahidden forces begin probing the outer perimeter of Kabul, Afghanistan, in anticipation of a final attack. The Soviet Foreign Ministry declares that 30,000 rebels are massed around the capital while an additional 15,000 have surrounded Jalalabad.

February 16

DIPLOMACY: In Washington, D.C., President George H. W. Bush determines to continue supplying the Afghan resistance with guns, ammunition, and supplies despite the recent Soviet pullout. Secretary of State James A. Baker also states that the Soviets are obliged to aid in the reconstruction of Afghanistan.

MILITARY: In the Soviet Union, a newspaper carries the first published account of atrocities by Soviet forces against Afghans, a remarkably candid admission.

In Takhar and Badakhshan Provinces, Afghanistan, 10,000 Afghan soldiers stage the biggest mass defection of the nine-year-old war by joining the mujahideen under Ahmad Shah Massoud. The rebels thus acquire 15 tanks, 40 trucks, 50 tractors, 10,000 assault rifles, 850 heavy machine guns, and several grenade launchers.

POLITICS: With their Afghan ordeal concluded, the Soviet Union prepares to confront and bind the social and political wounds inflicted over the past 10 years. The government also announces that the war cost 45 billion rubles, or $75 billion.

February 18
DIPLOMACY: In the United Kingdom, author Salman Rushdie apologizes for inadvertently insulting Muslims with his book *The Satanic Verses.*
POLITICS: In Kabul, President Mohammad Najibullah declares a state of emergency and imposes martial law throughout the capital.

In Peshawar, Pakistan, Mohammad Nabi Mohammadi is appointed the new spokesman for the mujahideen alliance.

February 19
DIPLOMACY: In Tehran, Iran, Ayatollah Khomeini rejects British author Salman Rushdie's apology for insulting Islam and renews his death threat.

February 20
DIPLOMACY: In Tehran, Iran, 12 nations of the European Economic Community (ECC) recall their ambassadors home in light of death threats against author Salman Rushdie.
POLITICS: In Kabul, Afghanistan, Prime Minister Mohammad Hassan Sharq resigns as the government reverts over to a military council.

February 21
POLITICS: In Kabul, Afghanistan, Sultan Ali Keshtmand is appointed chair of the executive committee within the Council of Ministers.

February 22
DIPLOMACY: In Washington, D.C., President George H. W. Bush regards Ayatollah Khomeini's death threats against author Salman Rushdie as "deeply offensive to the norms of civilized behavior."

February 23
POLITICS: In Peshawar, Pakistan, the Afghan Interim Government appoints Abdul Rasul Sayyef as acting prime minister and Sibghatullah Mojaddedi as acting president. The remaining portfolios are spread around other mujahideen leaders from the seven resistance groups present. However, Sayyed Ahmed Gailani challenges their legitimacy.

February 26
DIPLOMACY: In Tehran, Iran, Ayatollah Khomeini informs Soviet foreign minister Eduard Shevardnadze that the withdrawal from Afghanistan will facilitate closer relations between their two nations.

March 5–20
MILITARY: Outside Jalalabad, Afghanistan, mujahideen forces commence a major operation to take the city; it is ultimately repelled with considerable loss. It is reported that Afghan army defenses are directed by Chief of Staff Lieutenant General Asef Delawar.

March 7
DIPLOMACY: The Iranian government breaks off diplomatic relations with Britain after it fails to meet Iran's demands to condemn British author Salman Rushdie and his novel *The Satanic Verses.*

March 24
MILITARY: A combined Soviet and Afghan army relief convoy of 84 trucks breaks through mujahideen lines and relieves the garrison at Jalalabad, Afghanistan.

March 27
POLITICS: In Kabul, Afghanistan, President Mohammad Najibullah offers all mujahideen commanders autonomy if they lay down their arms; a council of 35 commanders rejects the offer.

April 6
DIPLOMACY: In Washington, D.C., Secretary of State James H. Baker recommends Peter Tomsen to serve as special envoy to the mujahideen with a rank of ambassador.

April 12–15
POLITICS: It is reported that the Afghan Interim Government has held its first three-day meeting in Afghanistan.

April 17
AVIATION: Over Saudi Arabia, the Boeing E-3A Sentry aircraft christened Elf One returns to Tinker Air Force Base, Oklahoma, after serving eight years on station.

April 23
MILITARY: The *New York Times* reports that the recent mujahideen attack against Jalalabad, Afghanistan, was instigated by the Pakistani government and against the advice of its own Inter-Services Intelligence Service.

April 24
DIPLOMACY: In Kabul, Afghanistan, Foreign Minister Abdul Wakil accuses Pakistan of continuing aggression against it.

May 6
MILITARY: In Kabul, Afghanistan, Soviet deputy minister of defense Valentin L. Varennikov concludes four days of discussions with Afghan authorities.

May 9
POLITICS: In Peshawar, Pakistan, Sayyed Ahmed Gailani continues challenging the legitimacy of the new Afghan Interim Government.

May 16
POLITICS: Reports surface that Abdul Rahman, head of the KHAD (Afghan secret police), has defected to mujahideen loyal to Yunis Khalis.

May 17
MILITARY: A determined thrust by Soviet/Afghan forces reopens a stretch of the Kabul-Jalalabad highway.

May 21
POLITICS: In Kabul, Afghanistan, President Mohammad Najibullah reiterates his call for mujahideen participation in a *loya jirga*.

May 24
POLITICS: In Kabul, Afghanistan, the government again offers autonomy to mujahideen leaders if they would stop fighting.

June 3
POLITICS: In Tehran, Iran, the 87-year-old Ayatollah Khomeini, founder of the Islamic Republic of Iran, dies. His successor is Ayatollah Ali Khamenei.

June 4
DIPLOMACY: In Washington, D.C., President George H. W. Bush says that, with the passing of Ayatollah Khomeini, Iran may cease being a terrorist state and act responsibly within the community of nations.

June 6
POLITICS: In Tehran, an estimated 3 million people turn out for the funeral procession of the late Ayatollah Khomeini. At one point, hysterical onlookers seize the body and carry it off.

June 20
DIPLOMACY: In Moscow, Soviet Union, President Mikhail Gorbachev welcomes the Iranian speaker of parliament and speaks of his desire for closer relations. The recent Soviet withdrawal from Afghanistan has led to a thaw in relations.

June 21
DIPLOMACY: In Moscow, Soviet Union, President Mikhail Gorbachev declares that railway service with Iran is being restored.

June 24
POLITICS: In Kabul, Afghanistan, President Mohammad Najibullah appoints Mahmud Baryalai to serve as first deputy prime minister.

July 5
MILITARY: The city of Tor Kham, Afghanistan, is wrestled back by Afghan army forces.

July 19
MILITARY: In Helmand Province, Afghanistan, a territorial dispute leads to fighting between mujahideen loyal to Burhanuddin Rabbani and Mohammad Nabi Mohammadi.

July 24
MILITARY: In Kabul, Afghanistan, Defense Minister Shanawaz Tanai is arrested and detained.

July 26
POLITICS: In Kabul, Afghanistan, Najmuddin Kawiani, the head of the foreign relations committee of the National Assembly, announces secret talks with the "opposition."

July 28
POLITICS: In Tehran, Iran, Hojatolislam Hashemi Rafsanjani, the current Majlis speaker, is elected president in a landslide election.

July 29
DIPLOMACY: In Kabul, Afghanistan, Nur Ahmad Nur is appointed ambassador and permanent Afghan representative to the United Nations.

August 1
POLITICS: In Kabul, Afghanistan, former defense minister Shanawaz Tanai is accused of attempting a coup against the government.

August 3
POLITICS: In Tehran, Iran, Hojatolislam Hashemi Rafsanjani is sworn into office as Iran's new president. He is considered to be a moderate reformer.

August 7
MILITARY: Haji Abdul Latif, a commander of the National Islamic Front, is poisoned by his two bodyguards; they later are both executed.

August 11
POLITICS: Abdul Rasul Sayyaf, acting prime minister of the Afghan Interim Government, rejects a suggestion by Gulbuddin Hekmatyar that he seize power by backing an Afghan army coup against the government.

August 14
MILITARY: In Kabul Afghanistan, government spokesman Muhammad Nabi Amani declares that 183 civilians have been killed from mujahideen rocket attacks against the capital.

August 17
MILITARY: Near al-Hillah, Iraq, a massive explosion occurs at an Iraqi military facility, and Western sources say that several hundred people died. This plant was the brainchild of Gerald Bull, a weapons designer who was known to be manufacturing a supergun, or huge artillery piece, capable of striking targets in Israel.

August 20
MILITARY: In Afghanistan, Major General Muhammad Faruq Zarif defects to the mujahideen.

August 25
POLITICS: Mujahideen leader Ahmad Shah Massoud of Jamiat-i-Islami accuses the Islamic Unity Party of collusion with the regime in Kabul, Afghanistan.

August 29
MILITARY: In Helmand Province, Afghanistan, mujahideen loyal to Abdul Rasul Sayyaf and Mohammad Nabi Mohammadi battle for control over collecting taxes and tolls.

POLITICS: In Tehran, Iran, the Majlis approves all 22 of President Hashemi Rafsanjani's cabinet nominees, which may be interpreted as an endorsement of his moderate approach to policies.

August 30
POLITICS: In Peshawar, Pakistan, Gulbuddin Hekmatyar withdraws his group from the mujahideen alliance.

September 15
POLITICS: Iraqi authorities arrest Farzad Bazoft, an Iranian journalist working for the *London Observer,* and charge him with espionage after he visits the destroyed munition works at Al-Hillah. Daphne Parish, a British nursing administrator who accompanied him, is likewise apprehended

October 11
POLITICS: In Afghanistan, Muhammad Ashgar, president of the National Salvation Society, asks for a peaceful resolution to the fighting.

October 17
DIPLOMACY: In Kabul, Afghanistan, Soviet ambassador Boris Nikolayevich Pashtukov presents his credentials to the government.

November 7
MILITARY: In Kandahar, Afghanistan, intense combat between mujahideen fighters and Afghan army troops results in the death of Lieutenant General Ali Akbar.

November 14
MILITARY: Outside Jalalabad, Afghanistan, the mujahideen launch a three-pronged attack to capture the city and are repelled again.

November 21
POLITICS: In Kabul, Afghanistan, President Mohammad Najibullah declares that he is extending the state of emergency by an additional six months.

November 30
POLITICS: Gulbuddin Hekmatyar and Burhanuddin Rabbani agree to an immediate cease-fire and an exchange of prisoners and territory.

December 2
MILITARY: In Jalalabad, Afghanistan, Brigadier General Ghulam Haidar is killed fighting the mujahideen.
POLITICS: In Kabul, Afghanistan, the government rounds up 127 people and accuses them of plotting a coup.

December 5
AVIATION: The Iraqi government claims to have successfully tested a new, three-stage missile capable of launching satellites into space. It also has a 1,200-mile range and is able to hit targets in Israel; possession of this weapon, however, is viewed as a warning more to neighboring countries such as Iran and Syria than to the Jewish state.

December 7
NAVAL: In the Persian Gulf, the battleship USS *New Jersey* arrives on a five-day goodwill cruise to Bahrain and the United Arab Emirates. It is the first battleship to visit these waters since the end of World War II, and its passage sends a message to potentially hostile powers that the United States will protect its interests in the region.

December 21
MILITARY: Sayyed Jamal and three other commanders of the Islamist Movement are executed by the Islamic Party for having ambushed several of its commanders. Continuing infighting among various mujahideen groups threatens the unity necessary to confront the Marxist regime in Kabul, Afghanistan, which is still propped up by lavish Soviet military support.

December 31
POLITICS: In Kabul, Afghanistan, President Mohammad Najibullah seeks to soften his regime's image by calling on the PDPA to change its name.

1990

January 24
POLITICS: In Kabul, Afghanistan, President Mohammad Najibullah pledges to resign should he lose UN-sponsored elections.

February 2
POLITICS: In Quetta, Pakistan, 10,000 refugees demonstrate while demanding the return of former monarch Mohammad Zahir Shah.

February 12
POLITICS: In Kabul, Afghanistan, Farid Ahmad Mazdak is appointed acting chair of the National Front Central Council.

March 5
POLITICS: In Kabul, Afghanistan, trials begin for 124 Afghans arrested last December and accused of plotting to overthrow the government.

March 6
MILITARY: In Kabul, Afghanistan, Defense Minister Shanawaz Tanai attempts a military coup against President Mohammad Najibullah.

March 7
POLITICS: In Peshawar, Pakistan, mujahideen leader Gulbuddin Hekmatyar declares his support for General Shanawaz Tanai's attempted coup against the Afghan government.

March 9
MILITARY: In Afghanistan, Bagram Air Base is recaptured by forces loyal to the Kabul regime while, in Pakistan, other mujahideen leaders refuse to support General Shanawaz Tanai's coup.

March 15
TERRORISM: In Baghdad, Iraq, the government hangs the Iranian-born British journalist Farzad Bazoft for alleged espionage.

March 18
POLITICS: In Kabul, Afghanistan, the PDPA expels 24 members for treachery against party and country.

April 2
DIPLOMACY: In Baghdad, Iraq, President Saddam Hussein threatens to "burn half of Israel" should it attempt a preemptive strike against his budding chemical weapons industry.

April 6
MILITARY: In Afghanistan, supposed peace talks with mujahideen forces break down when the latter suddenly fires on the government deputation, killing two generals and 11 troops. Fazl Haq Khaliqyar, governor of Herat, is among those wounded.

April 9
DIPLOMACY: Word surfaces that an unnamed American diplomat has been expelled from Baghdad, Iraq, in retribution for an Iraqi diplomat's expulsion from the United Nations in New York City.

April 14
DIPLOMACY: In Kabul, Afghanistan, the government accuses the United Nations of failing to adequately police the Geneva peace accord.

May 21
POLITICS: In Kabul, Afghanistan, a new government is chosen with the appointment of Fazulhaq Khaliqyar as prime minister.

May 28
POLITICS: In Kabul, Afghanistan, the government summons a *loya jirga* (national assembly) to contemplate proposed amendments to the new constitution.

May 29
POLITICS: In Kabul, Afghanistan, a new multiparty system is formally announced by President Mohammad Najibullah.

June 4
POLITICS: An essay in *U.S. News and World Report* brands Saddam Hussein of Iraq as "The World's Most Dangerous Man," noting that his army, 1 million strong, is the fourth largest in the world.

June 16
POLITICS: The nine Shiite mujahideen groups stationed in Iran unite into the new Islamic Unity Party, or Hezb-i-Wahdat.

June 21–22
POLITICS: Northwestern Iran is struck by a major earthquake registering 7.3 on the Richter scale; an estimated 40,000 people are killed with thousands of buildings also damaged or destroyed. A global relief effort is mounted to aid the survivors.

President Ali Akbar Hashemi Rafsanjani accepts aid from the United States despite the lack of official diplomatic relations.

June 22
POLITICS: In Paktia Province, Afghanistan, various mujahideen commanders convene a strategy conference.

June 27
POLITICS: In Kabul, Afghanistan, the PDPA holds a second party congress, reelects Mohammad Najibullah as president, and votes to change its name to Herb-i-Watan (Homeland Party).

June 30
POLITICS: A meeting takes piece among former government authorities, President Sibghatullah Mojaddedi of the Interim Government, and members of the new Islamic Unity Party.

July
DIPLOMACY: Sometime during this month Iraqi foreign minister Tariq Aziz visits Cairo and presents his case against Kuwait and the United Arab Emirates to the Arab League. Iraq is pressing for compensation over allegedly lost oil revenues.

July 15–30
MILITARY: U.S. satellite intelligence shows unmistakable signs of an Iraqi military buildup along the Kuwaiti border, although most authorities believe President Saddam Hussein is simply bluffing his neighbor into making oil concessions.

July 17
DIPLOMACY: In an ominous televised speech commemorating Revolution Day, President Saddam Hussein of Iraq demands that Kuwait reduce its oil production from Rumalia Field, which extends under Iraqi territory, and settle ongoing border disputes. Failing this, he intends to invade; this is a threat that few take seriously at the time.

July 18
DIPLOMACY: In Baghdad, Iraq, President Saddam Hussein releases a letter charging that Kuwait and the United Arab Emirates have cooperated in a scheme to deliberately depress oil prices through overproduction. It also claims that Kuwait stole $2.4 billion worth of oil through oblique drilling into an Iraqi oil field.

Foreign Minister Tariq Aziz dispatches a memorandum to the Arab League secretary, in which he accuses Kuwait of encroaching upon clearly defined Iraqi territory.

July 24
NAVAL: In Washington, D.C., President George H. W. Bush dispatches six U.S. Navy warships to the Persian Gulf region as a precaution after information of Iraqi troops massing on the Kuwaiti border is more closely scrutinized.

July 25
DIPLOMACY: In Cairo, Egypt, President Hosni Mubarak tells journalists that, in a recent meeting, Iraqi president Saddam Hussein assured him that he had no intention of invading Kuwait.

In Baghdad, Iraq, U.S. ambassador April C. Glaspie confers with President Saddam Hussein for the first time, informing him that the United States has no interest in getting involved in intra-Arab conflicts. Saddam Hussein mentions the same to her, citing the U.S. withdrawal from Lebanon after the bombing of the marine barracks there in October 1983, as an example of American's lack of resolve.

POLITICS: In Pakistan, the UN-sponsored repatriation of Afghan refugees to their homeland commences.

July 27

DIPLOMACY: In Geneva, Switzerland, OPEC ministers agree to increase the price of oil from $18 to $21 a barrel, which is still less than what Iraqi president Saddam Hussein had demanded.

July 29–August 25

POLITICS: In Kabul, Afghanistan, as President Mohammad Najibullah departs for extended talks in Moscow, Abul Rahim Hatef is appointed the acting president in his absence.

July 30

DIPLOMACY: In Jeddah, Saudi Arabia, representatives from that nation, Kuwait, and Iraq meet to discuss reconciliation, but no progress is made.

August 1

DIPLOMACY: Talks between Iraq and Kuwait regarding oil production and border disputes are suddenly broken off.

MILITARY: The Central Intelligence Agency deduces that at least 100,000 Iraqi troops are now poised on the borders of Kuwait and an invasion seems imminent. Kuwait's military establishment, only 20,000 strong, is not expected to put up serious resistance.

August 2

DIPLOMACY: In New York City, Resolution 660 passes the UN Security Council on a vote of 14–0 and calls for the immediate withdrawal of Iraqi forces from Kuwait. Iraqi president Saddam Hussein defiantly refuses to relinquish the country, which he is reclaiming as an oil-rich part of Basra Province.

In Colorado, President George H. W. Bush gives a joint news conference with British prime minister Margaret Thatcher, both of whom condemn Iraq's invasion of Kuwait in the harshest terms. They also speak of enlisting collective action to expel him.

MILITARY: In one of the gravest military miscalculations of the 20th century, Iraqi president Saddam Hussein orders his forces to occupy Kuwait, an American ally and major oil exporter. A force of 110,000 troops manages to overrun the country and capture all its objectives in only 10 hours. Kuwait's emir escapes in his helicopter to Saudi Arabia just ahead of the invaders.

President George H. W. Bush issues several executive orders declaring a national emergency while the Joint Chiefs of Staff review Centcom Operations Plan 1002–90, a highly classified contingency plan for transferring major American forces into the Middle East region over a period of three to four months.

The Soviet Union, which is Iraq's largest supplier of military hardware, declares it is suspending all future sales until Kuwait is evacuated.

POLITICS: To justify his invasion of Kuwait, President Saddam Hussein claims that he was answering the call of Kuwaiti revolutionaries to overthrow the monarchy there.

In Washington, D.C., the government bans most trade with Iraq and freezes Iraqi and Kuwaiti assets in the country. The U.S. Senate also adopts a resolution commending the president for his handling of the crisis and calls for the departure of Iraq from Kuwait.

Industry analysts compute that if Iraq is allowed to abscond with Kuwait's oil supplies, it will become the world's second-largest oil supplier after Saudi Arabia.

August 3

DIPLOMACY: In Moscow, Soviet Union, Secretary of State James A. Baker and Soviet foreign minister Eduard Shevardnadze issue a joint statement condemning the Iraqi invasion of Kuwait.

In Washington, D.C., a visibly angry President George H. W. Bush informs reporters that the Iraqi invasion of Kuwait "will not stand."

The Arab League votes to oppose Iraq's actions, but only on a vote of 14 to 7. Many of the poorer Arab states, and the Palestinians, are openly sympathetic toward Iraqi president Saddam Hussein.

MILITARY: Having invaded and subdued Kuwait, massed Iraqi forces position themselves menacingly along the border with Saudi Arabia, further alarming the world community.

TERRORISM: Within Kuwait City, Kuwait, Iraqi troops conduct a campaign of killing, raping, and pillaging. Their excesses cause a mass exodus of refugees from the country.

August 4

DIPLOMACY: In Rome, Italy, the 12-member European Community votes to boycott the import of Kuwaiti and Iraqi oil, ban all arms sales, and suspend all trade. Its alacrity in adopting such measures is unusual.

MILITARY: In New York City, General H. Norman Schwarzkopf briefs the National Security Council about the military options available for Kuwait. He maintains that it will take a minimum of 17 weeks to build up sufficient military forces in the theater to drive the Iraqis out. The possibility that President Saddam Hussein will use chemical weapons is also discussed.

At Fort Benning, Georgia, the Army Central Command under Lieutenant General John Yeosock begins preliminary planning for action in the Persian Gulf region. He is assisted by Major General William G. Pagonis, director of logistics, and other high-ranking staff officers.

This abandoned and ruined Russian T-55B Soviet tank, a remnant of the failed Soviet occupation in the 1980s, rusts near Bagram Air Base in Afghanistan. *(Department of Defense)*

In Kuwait, Iraqi forces begin entrenching themselves and building fortifications.

POLITICS: In Kuwait, a "provisional government" is formed around a nine-man military cabinet.

August 6

DIPLOMACY: In New York City, the UN Security Council votes 13 to 0 in favor of Resolution 661, which imposes strict trade and financial boycotts on Iraq and Kuwait. Turkey announces that it is cutting the flow of Iraqi oil across its territory in pipes running to the Red Sea.

In Saudi Arabia, Defense Secretary Richard Cheney arrives and consults with King Fahd; in an unprecedented move for a Saudi leader, he grants the United States and its allies permission to station troops on its soil for the first time.

MILITARY: The U.S. Army kicks into high gear as several divisions receive their deployment orders to Saudi Arabia. They include the 82nd Airborne Division and the 24th Infantry Division. Within 24 hours the 1st Cavalry Division, the 1st Brigade, the 2nd Armored Division, the 101st Airborne Division, and the 3rd Armored Cavalry Regiment are also ordered to ship out as part of Operation Desert Shield.

August 7

AVIATION: At Langley Air Force Base, Virginia, the 71st Tactical Fighter Squadron, 1st Tactical Fighter Wing, begins deploying 24 F-15C Eagles on an 8,000-mile flight to Dhahran, Saudi Arabia. The flight is made in 15 hours with the help of 12 inflight refuelings.

DIPLOMACY: In Washington, D.C., President George H. W. Bush reiterates that Iraqi aggression against Kuwait "will not stand" and formally orders a buildup of American military forces in the region to drive Iraqi president Saddam Hussein out of that strategic oil-producing country.

MILITARY: The U.S. Army begins gearing up for Operation Desert Shield to protect Saudi Arabia and its oilfields from a possible Iraqi attack.

NAVAL: The carrier *Dwight D. Eisenhower* passes through the Suez Canal and enters the Red Sea, where it joins the carrier *Independence* in the Gulf of Oman. Their combined air wings are presently the only coalition aircraft available for immediate use in the Persian Gulf region.

August 8

AVIATION: In Dhahran, Saudi Arabia, the first Air Force Reserve C-141 Starlifter lands, becoming the first American aircraft to deploy in the theater. They are joined shortly afterward by F-15Cs from the 1st Tactical Fighter Wing and additional AWACS aircraft arrive to assist Saudi AWACS already flying over the kingdom.

In response to a request from General H. Norman Schwarzkopf, Air Force vice chief of staff Lieutenant General Mike Loh orders the Air Staff Planning Group (Checkmate) under Colonel John Warden to initiate plans for conducting a strategic air war against Iraqi forces.

DIPLOMACY: In London, United Kingdom, Prime Minister Margaret Thatcher orders British land, naval, and air assets deployed to Saudi Arabia at the request of King Fahd.

In Lajes, Azores, Secretary of State James A. Baker informs the news media that the Americans are approaching the governments of Syria and Turkey in an attempt to politically isolate Iraq.

In Baghdad, Iraq, the government declares that it has formally annexed Kuwait as it 19th province, an act confirmed by a vote in the National Assembly.

MILITARY: In Savannah, Georgia, the 2nd Brigade, 24th Infantry Division, boards transports for a rapid transit to Saudi Arabia. The entire division is assembled there by September 12.

POLITICS: In Washington, D.C., President George H. W. Bush makes a televised address to the American people, declaring that he seeks the withdrawal of all Iraqi troops from Kuwait, the restoration of legal governance, stability in the Persian Gulf, and protection for Americans living throughout that region. He unequivocally insists that the United States is not at war and says he hopes that the present crisis can be resolved peacefully.

The new puppet regime in Kuwait promptly endorses the recent forced merger with Iraq.

August 8–9

MILITARY: In Dhahran, Saudi Arabia, the 2nd Brigade, 82nd Airborne Division, under Colonel Richard Rokosz becomes the first large American unit airlifted into the theater. Shortly afterward, it is joined by staff officers of the soon-to-arrive XVIII Airborne Corps.

August 9

DIPLOMACY: In New York City, the UN Security Council votes 15 to 0 to pass Resolution 662, which declares "null and void" the Iraqi claim of annexing Kuwait. Furthermore, it calls on all nations not to recognize the annexation.

MILITARY: General H. Norman Schwarzkopf, who goes by the moniker "Stormin' Norman" and has a particular expertise in this region, is chosen as commander of coalition forces. The Americans are acting under a tight deadline to secure the Saudi oil fields from a potential Iraqi attack.

POLITICS: In Iraq, the government announces that it is sealing off its borders and only foreign diplomats will be allowed to depart. This raises security questions about thousands of foreigners still trapped in that country and Kuwait.

In Washington, D.C., President George H. W. Bush gives a televised news conference in which he reiterates that American forces in the Persian Gulf are not necessarily committed to an active military mission, and that he hopes that economic sanctions alone will evict Iraq from Kuwait.

August 10

AVIATION: At Central Command, MacDill Air Force Base, Florida, Colonel John Warren of the Air Staff Planning Group presents a preliminary draft for air operations in the Persian Gulf to General H. Norman Schwarzkopf. General Charles Horner also begins drawing up contingency plans for air power in the event that Iraqi forces attack Saudi Arabia before the Americans can deploy there in force.

Detachments of F-16s from Shaw Air Force Base, South Carolina, and C-130s from Pope Air Force Base, North Carolina, begin filtering into Saudi Arabia.

DIPLOMACY: An emergency meeting of the Arab League summoned by Egyptian president Hosni Mubarak votes 12 to 3 to dispatch forces to defend Saudi Arabia. The resolution is opposed only by Libya, Iraq, and the Palestine Liberation Organization.

MILITARY: In accordance with Operation Desert Shield, the 7th Marine Expeditionary Brigade begins airlifting from the United States to Al Jubayl, Saudi Arabia. Once there it will join up with its assigned Marine Prepositioning Force squadron.

POLITICS: In Baghdad, Iraq, President Saddam Hussein calls upon the "Muslim masses" to embark on a jihad (holy war) against corrupt Arab leaders and infidel foreign forces.

August 11

MILITARY: In Saudi Arabia, Colonel David Whately and the 7th Transportation Group arrive from Fort Eustis, Virginia. They are tasked with managing the huge influx of men and materiel en route to the theater.

The first detachments of Egyptian and Moroccan forces begin deploying to Saudi Arabia.

August 12

AVIATION: At Dhahran, Saudi Arabia, the first 32 KC-135 tanker aircraft arrive, the first of more than 300 KC-135s and KC-10s scheduled to deploy. These are shortly joined by MH-53J Pave Low helicopters from the 1st Special Operations Wing.

DIPLOMACY: In Washington, D.C., President George H. W. Bush invokes a ban on Iraqi oil and most exports.

In Baghdad, Iraq, President Saddam Hussein links Iraqi withdrawal from Kuwait to Israeli withdrawal from the occupied West Bank.

NAVAL: To enforce a UN embargo of Iraq, U.S. Navy vessels begin a naval quarantine of the Persian Gulf region. President George H. W. Bush authorizes them to use force if necessary.

August 12–14

MILITARY: In Saudi Arabia, Operations Dragon I and II unfold as the 82nd Airborne Division forms a defensive perimeter around the ports of Al-Jubayl, Dhahran, and Ad-Damman. They have on hand 4,575 soldiers, a company of M551 Sheridan light tanks, and a battalion of 105mm howitzers.

August 13

DIPLOMACY: In Washington, D.C., an administration spokesman declares that King Hussein of Jordan has been approached to join the anti-Saddam alliance, despite his public posturing for Iraq. He also states that the Americans are actively discouraging Israel from joining the coalition, so it can attract broad-based Muslim support.

MILITARY: Because the Iraqi army employs hundreds of Soviet-made Scud ballistic missiles, the U.S. Army deploys its first PAC-2 Patriot surface-to-air missile unit, Battery B, 2nd Battalion, 7th Air Defense Artillery.

August 14

AVIATION: In Washington, D.C., the Department of Defense announces the presence of E-3 AWACS, KC-10s, KC-135s, and RC-135s in the Persian Gulf theater.
DIPLOMACY: Ships from the Soviet Union join the naval quarantine against Iraq.
MILITARY: In Saudi Arabia, deployment of the XVIII Airborne Corps is assisted by photo intelligence provided by an army satellite.

The first detachment of Syrian troops arrives in Saudi Arabia.

August 15

AVIATION: Top secret F-117 stealth aircraft belonging to the 37th Tactical Fighter Wing deploy from Tonopah, Nevada, and they are soon joined by F-4G Wild Weasels flying in from George Air Force Base, California.
DIPLOMACY: In an attempt to mend his fences with Iran, Iraqi president Saddam Hussein offers to accept a 1975 decision equally dividing the Shatt al Arab waterway and to remove all Iraqi soldiers from disputed Iranian territory.
MILITARY: In Saudi Arabia, the 1st and 3rd Brigades, 82nd Airborne Division, deploy for battle.
POLITICS: In a televised address to the nation, President George H. W. Bush stresses "access to energy resources" to preserve the current way of life as a main factor behind intervening in the Persian Gulf region.

August 16

AVIATION: At Myrtle Beach Air Force Base, South Carolina, the first wave of Fairchild A-10 Thunderbolt IIs departs for service in Saudi Arabia.
DIPLOMACY: In Kuwait, Iraqi authorities order all foreign embassies closed and the 6,500 Britons and Americans present to assemble at two designated hotels.

August 17

AVIATION: In Washington, D.C., President George H. W. Bush mobilizes the Civil Reserve Air Fleet for the first time since 1952. These aircraft are pressed as troop carriers to accelerate the buildup of forces in the Persian Gulf.

Once General H. Norman Schwarzkopf approves the initial air campaign strategy, Colonel John Warden is dispatched to Saudi Arabia to personally brief General Charles Horner about it.

The Defense Satellite Communications Systems is established by the Air Force Space Command to facilitate command links to Operation Desert Storm.
DIPLOMACY: In Tehran, Iran, the Majlis speaker announces that Iraq is "playing host" to foreign citizens within its boundaries and that they would be lodged at military installations while acting as human shields. This information prompts the UN Security Council to pass a resolution demanding the release of all foreigners in Iraq and warning the Baghdad regime not to harm them.
MILITARY: Iraqi forces occupying Kuwait are heavily reinforced and begin constructing defensive structures, or sand berms, along the Saudi border.

The military buildup in Saudi Arabia continues as a brigade of the 101st Airborne Division deploys from Fort Campbell, Kentucky. The remaining two brigades are embarking on ships at Jacksonville, Florida, and all three will assemble with their equipment by September 22.

In accordance with Operation Desert Shield, the 4th Marine Expeditionary Brigade begins sailing on vessels from Morehead City, North Carolina, for the Persian Gulf.

August 18

DIPLOMACY: In Washington, D.C., President George H. W. Bush denounces Iraq's use of foreign citizens as human shields and labels the practice as contrary to "all accepted norms of international conduct."

In Paris, France, the government warns Iraq of "grave consequences" if any of its 560 citizens in Kuwait are harmed.

NAVAL: In the Persian Gulf, the guided-missile frigate *Reid* and frigate *Bradley* fire warning shots across the bows of two Iraqi tankers attempting to leave. The guided-missile cruiser *England* and the guided-missile destroyer *Scott* also divert freighters from docking in the Persian Gulf and the northern Red Sea.

August 19

AVIATION: A force of 18 F-117 Nighthawks from the 415th Tactical Fighter Squadron arrives at Mushait Air Base, Saudi Arabia, for service during Operation Desert Shield.

MILITARY: On Okinawa, the 1st Battalion, 6th Marines, begins embarking for service in Operation Desert Shield.

August 20

AVIATION: In Saudi Arabia, General Charles Horner declares that there is sufficient American air power in Saudi Arabia to defend it against any Iraqi attack. At this time he is also briefed by Colonel John Warden as to the overarching campaign for waging a strategic air war.

MILITARY: In Saudi Arabia, Lieutenant General Walter E. Boomer arrives to take charge of I Marine Expeditionary Force. He is ordered to command all marine units in Operation Desert Shield except those still afloat.

Off Liberia, units belonging to the 26th Marine Expeditionary Unit arrive to replace the 22nd Marine Expeditionary Unit as part of Operation Sharp Edge.

In Baghdad, Iraq, the government announces that it is positioning Western hostages at strategic sites throughout the country to serve as "human shields."

August 21

AVIATION: By this date, the U.S. Air Force has deployed A-10s, C-130s, E-3 AWACS, F-4Gs, F-15s, F-15Es, F-16s, F-117s, KC-135, KC-10s, and RC-135s in the theater. This is the largest concentration of military aircraft outside the United States since the Vietnam War.

When the air force requests the services of 6,000 reservists, 15,000 people volunteer to serve with Operation Desert Shield.

DIPLOMACY: In Aden, Yemen, dock workers refuse to unload oil from recently arrived Iraqi tankers.

August 22

AVIATION: By this date, Air Force Reserve personnel have flown 8,000 soldiers and 7 million tons of military cargo into Saudi Arabia for service in Operation Desert Storm. Moreover, 20,000 reservists and 12,000 Air National Guardsmen will be called up for service in the Persian Gulf.

DIPLOMACY: The United States and other nations choose to defy Iraqi's ultimatum and keep their embassies open in Kuwait.

MILITARY: In Washington, D.C., Executive Order 12727 is signed by President George H. W. Bush to mobilize 200,000 army reservists for six months of active service. This is the largest activation of reservists since the Korean War, although most are expected to assume noncombat support functions.

In Saudi Arabia, a brigade of the 82nd Airborne Division is redeployed to an advance position in the desert (Forward Operating Base Essex) to help blunt any possible Iraqi attack. Operating temperatures at the time exceed 100 degrees Fahrenheit.

President George H. W. Bush orders 31,000 marine Reservists mobilized for active duty in Operation Desert Shield.

August 23

AVIATION: In Washington, D.C., Secretary of Defense Richard Cheney authorizes the air force to mobilize its Reserve components for service in the Persian Gulf; 20,000 are called to the colors to serve in the Persian Gulf crisis.

DIPLOMACY: In Baghdad, Iraq, President Saddam Hussein makes a televised appearance with a group of British detainees, insisting that they are "guests, not hostages." The British government immediately denounces the display as a "repulsive charade."

POLITICS: By this date, the price of oil has risen from $14 to $32 a barrel due to the Gulf crisis.

August 24

AVIATION: At Birmingham, Alabama, the 117th Tactical Reconnaissance Wing dispatches six of its RF-4C Phantom II aircraft to the Persian Gulf region, to be joined by similar aircraft sent by the 67th Tactical Reconnaissance Wing, Bergstrom Air Force Base, Texas.

DIPLOMACY: In Kuwait, Iraqi military forces surround several foreign embassies after they refused orders to shut down. The government also announces that while the wives and children of American and British citizens are free to go, the men are required to remain behind.

August 25

DIPLOMACY: In New York City, the UN Security Council votes 13 to 0, with two abstentions, to pass Resolution 665, which grants the United States the right to enforce the UN embargo by any means. This is the first time that the United Nations has approved a military force not under its flag. The support of the Soviet Union is also unprecedented and crucial to its passage.

MILITARY: In Hawaii, men of the 1st Marine Expeditionary Brigade begin flying out to al-Jubayl, Saudi Arabia, where its ships await.

August 26
MILITARY: In Saudi Arabia, General H. Norman Schwarzkopf arrives to take charge of Operation Desert Shield. In a nod to Saudi sensibilities, however, Prince Khalid bin Sultan is named joint commander.

August 27
DIPLOMACY: In Kennebunkport, Maine, President George H. W. Bush, speaking to reporters from his private residence, states that Iraq's recent conciliatory moves, like allowing its vessels to be searched by ships at sea, does not alter the American demand that it unconditionally depart Kuwait.

August 28
AVIATION: In Torrejon, Spain, F-16 fighters are sent in a new deployment to airfields in Qatar, another Persian Gulf ally.
DIPLOMACY: The Iraqi government again declares that Kuwait is its 19th province. President Saddam Hussein also decides to release all foreign women and children being detained in Iraq.
POLITICS: In Washington, D.C., President George H. W. Bush meets with 170 congressional members and delineates U.S. objectives in Kuwait: the unconditional withdrawal of all Iraqi forces and restoration of the legitimate Kuwaiti government. Security for the Persian Gulf region and the protection of Americans abroad are also highlighted. Congress overwhelmingly supports the president's actions.

August 29
AVIATION: At Ramstein Air Base, West Germany, a C-5 Galaxy, laden with military supplies for the Persian Gulf, crashes on takeoff, killing 13 people. Staff Sergeant Lorenzo Galvin Jr. wins the Airman's Medal for heroic efforts to assist crash victims.
DIPLOMACY: The Organization of the Petroleum Exporting Countries authorizes an increase in production levels to maintain a steady, worldwide supply during the present crisis.

August 31
MILITARY: Colonel Jesse Johnson leads the 5th Special Forces Group to Saudi Arabia to train various Arab coalition armies. In time, it is joined by the 3rd and 10th Special Forces Group and some Delta Force contingents.
NAVAL: In the Persian Gulf, the guided-missile cruiser *Biddle* stops and searches the Iraqi freighter *Al Karamah;* it is found empty and allowed to proceed to Jordan.

September 1
DIPLOMACY: In Cairo, Egypt, 12 members of the Arab League vote to call on Iraq to abandon Kuwait, pay reparations, and free all foreign nationals in its grasp. Libya votes against the resolution while eight other member nations boycott the proceedings.

In Iraq, the first of several hundred foreigners are released, but the United States calculates that 2,500 Americans, including women and children, are still detained in Iraq and Kuwait. By this date 100,000 refugees, mostly Palestinians, are stranded in relief camps throughout Jordan.

MILITARY: At Forward Operating Base Essex, Saudi Arabia, men of the 82nd Airborne Division are relieved by the 101st Airborne Division, who promptly rename the position Forward Operating Base Bastogne.

September 2
MILITARY: Once near Kuwait, the 7th Marine Expeditionary Brigade is disbanded and incorporated into the I Marine Expeditionary Force, which now consists of the 1st Marine Division and 1st Marine Air Wing.

September 3
MILITARY: In the Saudi Arabian desert, Operation Desert Dragon II unfolds as the 101st Airborne Division erects two addition Forward Operating Bases called FOB Normandy and FOB Carentan to the west of FOB Bastogne.

September 4
DIPLOMACY: In Washington, D.C., President George H. W. Bush asks that Egypt's $7 billion debt with the United States be waived as a reward for supporting the U.S. position in Kuwait.

MILITARY: In Afghanistan, an armed clash between mujahidden loyal to the Islamist Movement and the Islamic Party results in 16 deaths.

September 5
AVIATION: Five C-130 units from the Air National Guard begin arriving in Saudi Arabia.

DIPLOMACY: In Washington, D.C., the U.S. Congress passes the Iraqi Sanctions Act, which imposes a strict trade embargo in concert with UN resolutions.

MILITARY: In Kabul, Afghanistan, government forces expel armed militias from the capital.

September 6–7
DIPLOMACY: Secretary of State James A. Baker makes and concludes two visit to the Middle East and returns with pledges of financial support from King Fahd of Saudi Arabia and Kuwait's exiled emir.

September 7
MILITARY: In the Saudi Arabian desert, the 1st and 2nd Brigades of the 24th Infantry Division deploy, and they are soon joined by the 12th Aviation Brigade.

The special operations-capable 13th Marine Expeditionary Unit deploys in the Persian Gulf, where it will remain under navy control.

September 8
AVIATION: The first wave of AC-130H gunships from the 16th Special Operations Squadron arrives in Saudi Arabia.

September 9
DIPLOMACY: In Helsinki, Finland, President George H. W. Bush and Soviet president Mikhail Gorbachev pledge to take joint action to undo Iraq's conquest of Kuwait; Bush consequently drops his prior opposition to high-level Soviet participation in Middle Eastern peace talks. Gorbachev also declares that Soviet participation in the Persian Gulf will be restricted to two modest naval vessels.

September 10
DIPLOMACY: The Arab League, torn by dissension over how to handle the Kuwait crisis, relocates its headquarters from Tunis to Cairo, Egypt.

In Brussels, Belgium, Secretary of State James A. Baker addresses a NATO foreign ministers meeting and calls the Soviets reliable partners in the present crisis. He also declares that Saudi Arabia, Kuwait, and the United Arab Emirates have pledged $12 billion in financial assistance to cover U.S. military expenditures.

September 11
POLITICS: In Kabul, Afghanistan, President Mohammad Najibullah declares the legalization of all political parties.

In Washington, D.C., President George H. W. Bush addresses a joint session of Congress, declaring that the United States would never allow a ruthless character like Iraqi president Saddam Hussein to control the world's oil supply. He also states that he will not be deterred by Iraq's blatant use of Western hostages as human shields.

September 12
DIPLOMACY: In Tehran, Iran, Iraq reestablishes diplomatic relations with its former enemy. Iran's supreme religious leader, Ayatollah Ali Khamenei, also states that a jihad is justified to combat the U.S. military buildup in the Gulf.

In Iraq, state television carries a speech by President George H. W. Bush in which he speaks to the Iraqi people.

September 13
AVIATION: In Riyadh, Saudi Arabia, U.S. Air Force brigadier general Buster Glosson, deputy commander of the Joint Task Force Middle East, briefs General H. Norman Schwarzkopf and General Colin Powell on the operational air war plan that will follow Operation Desert Shield.

DIPLOMACY: In Washington, D.C., administration officials note with disappointment that Jordan is not changing its favorable stance toward Iraq. King Hussein probably had no choice because the bulk of his population consists of poor Palestinians who, tired of wealthy Kuwaitis' condescension toward them, overwhelmingly favor the Iraqi action. The officials also reiterate that Israel's help in the present crisis is unwanted as it would alienate Muslim support for a broad-based coalition.

September 14
DIPLOMACY: In Kuwait City, Iraqi forces seize the French embassy and take several French citizens prisoner. They are then released, but President François Mitterrand is so angered by the breach of diplomatic etiquette that he orders 4,000 troops and a contingent of tanks and aircraft to Saudi Arabia.

MILITARY: The 197th Infantry Brigade makes its appearance in the Saudi Arabian desert, having shipped in from Fort Benning, Georgia. It is attached to the 24th Infantry Division until that formation's 48th Infantry Brigade deploys on November 30.

Camps Red, Gold, and White are founded by the 82nd Airborne Division at Ab Qaiq, Saudi Arabia.

The British government announces that it is sending an armored brigade of 8,000 men and 120 tanks to Saudi Arabia.

NAVAL: In the Gulf of Oman, an Iraqi tanker refuses to halt when ordered to by U.S. and Australian naval vessels, so shots are fired across its bow. Only then does it consent to being searched and, when found not to be carrying contraband, is allowed to proceed.

September 15

DIPLOMACY: In Bonn, the West German government announces that it is donating $2 billion in aid to support military efforts in the Persian Gulf region.

MILITARY: In Paris, France, the government responds angrily to Iraq's decision to forcibly enter its embassy in Kuwait by dispatching thousands of troops and warplanes to Saudi Arabia.

POLITICS: In Kuwait, Iraqi troops open the border with Saudi Arabia, allowing thousands of Kuwaiti refugees to flee. However, the Iraqis stop and detain all men of military age. Those arriving report widespread abuses, torture, and execution by the occupiers.

September 16

DIPLOMACY: In Baghdad, Iraq, the government allows an eight-minute taped broadcast by President George H. W. Bush, in which he declares that President Saddam Hussein has brought their nations to the brink of war and that Iraq must abandon Kuwait to prevent it.

MILITARY: At Fort Hood, Texas, the 1st Cavalry Division begins shipping out men and equipment under the aegis of Brigadier General John Tilleli. Once deployed, it is joined by the 1st Brigade, 2nd Armor Division, until the 155th Armored Brigade is ready for service overseas.

NAVAL: In the Persian Gulf, the Bahama-rigged tanker *Daimon* is intercepted by the destroyer *O'Brien*, becoming the 1,000th vessel to be stopped and searched.

POLITICS: In Washington, D.C., President George H. W. Bush addresses the nation, warning that the United States stands on the "brink of war."

September 17

AVIATION: In Washington, D.C., Secretary of Defense Dick Cheney relieves U.S. Air Force chief of staff Michael J. Dugan for unauthorized comments made to the media relative to Operation Desert Shield. He also mentioned a contingency plan to kill Iraqi president Saddam Hussein, if necessary.

MILITARY: Final elements of the 4th Marine Expeditionary Brigade deploy in the Persian Gulf and are retained under navy command.

September 18–28

AVIATION: Transports of the 436th and 438th Military Airlift Wings deliver tons of blankets, tents, cots, and other equipment for the 100,000 foreign workers fleeing Kuwait for Jordan.

September 20

DIPLOMACY: In Baghdad, Iraq, the Revolutionary Command Council announces that a withdrawal from Kuwait is impossible and that the "mother of all battles" is shaping up.

In Beijing, China, Asian countries remove their athletic teams from the Regional mini-Olympics unless Iraq withdraws from Kuwait.

September 23
DIPLOMACY: In Baghdad, Iraq, President Saddam Hussein warns that his troops might attack oil fields in Saudi Arabia and elsewhere if economic sanctions "strangled" Iraq.

September 25
DIPLOMACY: In New York City, the UN Security Council votes 14 to 1 to enforce an embargo on all Iraqi air traffic. Soviet foreign secretary Eduard Shevardnadze also warns the General Assembly that war in the Gulf region is inevitable unless Iraq evacuates Kuwait.

In Baghdad, Iraq, President Saddam Hussein makes a broadcast in which he addresses the American people.

September 27
DIPLOMACY: In London, United Kingdom, the government is convinced that Iranian leaders will no longer attempt to kill author Salman Rushdie, so diplomatic relations are resumed.
NAVAL: In the Gulf of Aqaba, Jordan, the Iraqi tanker *Tadmur* is intercepted by the frigate *Elmer B. Montgomery,* which places a boarding crew on board after firing shots across the bow.

September 29
DIPLOMACY: In New York City, the UN Security Council approves Resolution 642, which extends the Iran-Iraq Military Observer Group for another six months.

October 1
DIPLOMACY: In New York City, President George H. W. Bush addresses the UN General Assembly, expressing his desire for a diplomatic solution to the Kuwaiti crisis.
POLITICS: In Washington, D.C., the Democratic-controlled House of Representatives votes 380 to 29 to endorse President George H. W. Bush's handling of the Iraqi crisis.

October 1–4
NAVAL: The carrier *Independence* passes through the Strait of Hormuz and enters the Persian Gulf, marking the first time a vessel of this kind has operated in such cramped waters since 1974. The visit is deemed successful, and the vessel departs three days later.

October 2
POLITICS: In Washington, D.C., the Democratic-controlled U.S. Senate votes 96 to 3 in support of President George H. W. Bush's handling of the Kuwaiti crisis.

October 3
POLITICS: In Kuwait City, Kuwait, President Saddam Hussein arrives and vows not to give up a "single inch" of what he deems the 19th Iraqi province.

October 5

MILITARY: In Oruzgan Province, Afghanistan, mujahideen fighters storm into the capital at Tirin Kot.

October 10

AVIATION: In the Persian Gulf, U.S. Air Force fighter and fighter bomber units begin training exercises to familiarize themselves with desert warfare. To underscore that point, F-15Cs are already performing combat air patrols.

DIPLOMACY: In a humanitarian gesture, the Iraqi government allows 360 American men of Arabic descent to depart Kuwait.

October 15

POLITICS: In Islamabad, Pakistan, mujahideen leader Ahmad Shah Massoud arrives for talks with the Pakistani president and Gulbuddin Hekmatyar.

October 16

DIPLOMACY: Secretary of State James A. Baker announces that he rejected a recent Iraqi proposal to withdraw from Iraq if it could retain possession of a strategic island in the Persian Gulf.

October 19

POLITICS: In Baghdad, Iraq, the government introduces gasoline rationing due to a lack of chemicals necessary for refining oil into fuel.

October 25

MILITARY: In Washington, D.C., Defense Secretary Richard Cheney announces that American manpower levels in the Persian Gulf region would be boosted by 100,000, bringing the total number to 340,000 troops. U.S. forces are beginning to acquire an offensive capacity.

POLITICS: In Washington, D.C., Congress votes to pare down military assistance to the Afghan resistance.

October 28

POLITICS: In Baghdad, Iraq, President Saddam Hussein repeals gasoline rationing, declaring it a mistake. He also fires his oil minister.

October 29

DIPLOMACY: In New York City, the UN Security Council votes 13 to 0 in passing Resolution 674, which warns Iraq that "further measures"—a veiled hint at military action—might be invoked under the UN charter. It also holds Iraq accountable for all damages incurred by Kuwait in the invasion.

POLITICS: In Washington, D.C., President George H. W. Bush warns that, in light of Iraq's actions of late, military force remains a distinct possibility.

October 30

AVIATION: To expedite the shipment of certain crucial items to the Persian Gulf, air force transports commence Operation Desert Express.

NAVAL: In the Persian Gulf, the amphibious assault ship *Iwo Jima* experiences a steam leak in its fire room, which kills 10 sailors.

November 5

DIPLOMACY: In Saudi Arabia, Secretary of State James A. Baker confers with King Fahd, who declares, in the event of war, the Saudis would have primary responsibility for defending their own kingdom, but that coalition forces have permission to launch an attack upon Kuwait from Saudi territory.

In Washington, D.C., Congress passes additional public laws restricting trade with Iraq with and imposing economic sanctions on all countries with commercial ties with Iraq.

November 7

DIPLOMACY: In London, United Kingdom, Prime Minister Margaret Thatcher addresses the House of Commons by delivering an ultimatum to Iraqi president Saddam Hussein, namely, if he does not evacuate Kuwait voluntarily, he will be removed by force.

November 8

DIPLOMACY: In Moscow, Soviet Union, Secretary of State James A. Baker confers with General Secretary Mikhail Gorbachev and Foreign Minister Eduard Shevardnadze; he subsequently announces that the use of force against Iraq "cannot be ruled out."

MILITARY: Gearing up for an inevitable showdown with Iraqi president Saddam Hussein, President George H. W. Bush orders an increase in American and allied forces in the Persian Gulf to 430,000 men. Part of this entails shipping the VII Corps under Lieutenant General Frederick M. Franks from Germany to Saudi Arabia. A total of 200,000 men, 6,000 tracked vehicles, and 59,000 wheeled vehicles are relocated by mid-February 1991.

At Fort Riley, Kansas, the 1st Infantry Division (Mechanized) under Major General Thomas G. Rhame is ordered to prepare for deployment overseas. Because only two brigades can be organized in time, the third brigade will be supplied by the 2nd Armored Division.

As part of a general buildup in the Persian Gulf, the 2nd Marine Division, 5th Marine Expeditionary Brigade, and 2nd Marine Air Wing are ordered deployed with I Marine Expeditionary Force.

POLITICS: In Washington, D.C., President George W. Bush assures the American people that the country possesses both the will to go to war and the means to do so. However, Defense Secretary Richard Cheney declares that a decision on whether to commence military operations is still weeks away.

November 13

DIPLOMACY: Secretary of State James A. Baker justifies the current U.S. mobilization in one word: "jobs." He maintains that control of the world's oil supply by Iraqi president Saddam Hussein could trigger a worldwide recession.

November 13–14

MILITARY: In Washington, D.C., President George H. W. Bush extends the service term for reservists in Operation Desert Shield by an additional 180 days. Within hours, Secretary of Defense Dick Cheney mobilizes an additional 80,000 reservists and National Guard troops.

November 14

POLITICS: In Washington, D.C., President George H. W. Bush promises congressional leaders that he will consult with Congress before resorting to force against Iraq.

November 16

DIPLOMACY: In Amman, Jordan, the Iranian foreign minister announces that his talks with his Iraqi counterpart, Tariq Aziz, had led to measures that will end a series of lingering disputes dating back to the 1980–88 war between them.

November 17

AVIATION: To enhance Desert Shield communications, a DSCS II satellite is placed above the Indian Ocean by the Air Force Space Command.

November 19

DIPLOMACY: In Geneva, Switzerland, Afghan president Mohammad Najibullah arrives for talks with exiled Afghan notables in order to form a coalition government back in Kabul. Syrian president Hafez al-Assad also meets with President George H. W. Bush, whereupon he announces that he is joining the anti-Saddam coalition.

November 20

POLITICS: In Washington, D.C., 45 members of the U.S. House of Representatives file suit to require the chief executive to seek congressional approval for any military action in the Persian Gulf.

November 21

AVIATION: A-10 Thunderbolt IIs from Davis Monthan Air Force Base, Arizona, deploy to Saudi Arabia.

November 21–24

DIPLOMACY: President George H. W. Bush begins a tour of Middle Eastern nations for talks with prominent Arab heads of state.

November 22

MILITARY: President George H. W. Bush and First Lady Barbara Bush visit four military camps in the Persian Gulf to celebrate Thanksgiving with the troops. He also mentions Iraqi president Saddam Hussein's quest to obtain nuclear weapons as another justification for possible war with Iraq.

November 23

DIPLOMACY: In Geneva, Switzerland, President George H. W. Bush confers with presidents Hosni Mubarak and Hafez al-Assad of Egypt and Syria, respectively, on the ongoing military buildup in the Gulf.

November 27

MILITARY: At Fort Bragg, North Carolina, the 1st Special Operations Command is reorganized and redesignated the U.S. Army Special Operations Command (Airborne). The U.S. Army Reserve Special Operations Command is also retitled the U.S. Civil Affairs and Psychological Operations Command.

November 29

DIPLOMACY: In New York City, the UN Security Council passes Resolution 678, authorizing the use of force against Iraqi forces in Kuwait, by a vote of 12 to 2 (Cuba and Yemen), with one abstention (China); a deadline is set for January 15, 1991. This is also the first time since 1950, at the onset of the Korean War, that such authority has been granted. Meanwhile, Iraq's UN ambassador, Abdul Amir al-Anbari, insists that the council pursue an "integrated" Middle East peace plan that includes the Palestinians.

POLITICS: In Iraq, President Saddam Hussein, unfazed by the military buildup against him, declares to an Arab youth group that "Iraq is neither shaken nor panicked by the air and sea fleets of America and its aides."

November 30

DIPLOMACY: In Washington, D.C., President George H. W. Bush declares his willingness to dispatch Secretary of State James A. Baker to Baghdad, Iraq, in an attempt to circumvent war. However, he reiterates that a total Iraqi withdrawal from Kuwait is mandatory.

December 1

MILITARY: In Washington, D.C., Secretary of Defense Dick Cheney enlarges the reservist call-up to 115,000 men and women.

In California, the 5th Marine Expeditionary Brigade and the special operations-capable 11th Marine Expeditionary Unit set sail for the Persian Gulf.

December 4

POLITICS: In Washington, D.C., Democrats in the U.S. House of Representatives, aware of their inability to curb the president as commander in chief, vote 177 to 37 on a policy statement urging him not to commence hostilities in the Persian Gulf without congressional consent.

December 5

AVIATION: The 152nd Tactical Reconnaissance Group dispatches its RF-4Cs to airfields in Saudi Arabia.

December 6–7

DIPLOMACY: In Baghdad, Iraq, President Saddam Hussein announces that he is releasing all foreign hostages in Iraq and Kuwait, including 900 Americans, 1,200 Britons, and 200 Japanese. The Iraqi National Assembly subsequently rubber-stamps this decision with its approval.

December 11

DIPLOMACY: In Washington, D.C., the administration announces that about 500 Americans have elected to remain behind in Iraq and Kuwait because of dual citizenship or longtime residency.

December 19

MILITARY: In Saudi Arabia, Lieutenant General Calvin Waller, commanding general in the Persian Gulf region, states that coalition forces would not be ready to move against Iraq before January 15. This is the same date as the UN deadline for Saddam Hussein to withdraw from Kuwait.

General H. Norman Schwarzkopf, writing an internal memo, estimates that forcefully evicting the Iraqis from Kuwait may entail 20,000 coalition casualties, including 7,000 dead.

December 20
DIPLOMACY: In an interview with German television, Iraqi president Saddam Hussein says that the United States is unwilling to fight a war if it might suffer 5,000 casualties.

December 21
DIPLOMACY: In Baghdad, Iraq, President Saddam Hussein unequivocally declares that his forces will not withdraw from Kuwait by January 15, 1991, the deadline set by the United Nations.

December 22
MILITARY: In Saudi Arabia, the first unit of the VII Corps, the 2nd Armored Cavalry Regiment under Colonel Don Holder, arrives from Germany.

December 24
DIPLOMACY: In an interview with Spanish television, Iraqi president Saddam Hussein declares that Israel will be his first target, whether it attacks him or not.

December 25
MILITARY: In Washington, D.C., the Pentagon orders all U.S. forces in the Gulf region to observe Christmas celebrations discreetly so as to not offend their Saudi hosts.

December 26
NAVAL: In the Arabian Sea, an international flotilla, including the destroyers *Fife* and *Oldendorf,* the guided-missile frigate *Trenton,* and the amphibious transport dock *Shreveport* intercept and board the so-called peace ship *Ibn Khaldoon.* Tense moments result after the crew on the latter attempt to grab weapons from the boarding crew, and warning shots are fired in the air. The vessel is found to be carrying contraband cargo and redirected into a port.

December 27
MILITARY: In Riyadh, Saudi Arabia, General Colin Powell and Secretary of Defense Dick Cheney are briefed by General H. Norman Schwarzkopf on his forthcoming strategy. He intends to launch a vast flanking movement by the VII Corps and XVIII Airborne Corps from the western desert that will decisively turn the Iraqi right flank before the soldiers can react to it.

December 29
AVIATION: The 169th Tactical Fighter Group becomes the first Air National Guard unit deployed in the Persian Gulf for active duty.

December 31
MILITARY: In Washington, D.C., the Pentagon states that 52 U.S. servicemen have died in the Persian Gulf region during the military buildup there, largely through accidents.

1991

January
MILITARY: At this critical juncture, the U.S. Army has 200,000 troops deployed in the Arabian desert with many more en route.

January 1
MILITARY: At Tactical Assembly Area (TAA) Thompson, northwest of King Khalid Military City, Saudi Arabia, elements of the 1st Armored Division, VII Corps, arrive and deploy under Major General Ronald H. Griffin. As the men settle into TAA Thompson, they begin an extensive set of drills and maneuvers with live gunnery.

The 24th Marines are deployed to al-Jubayl, Saudi Arabia, where they will provide rear-area security throughout the I Marine Expeditionary Force area.

January 2
AVIATION: In Saudi Arabia, the 4th Tactical Fighter Wing (Provisional) is cobbled together from Air National Guard F-16s of the 174th Tactical Fighter Wing and the 169th Tactical Fighter Group.
MILITARY: On this day, the Central Command reveals U.S. military strength in the Persian Gulf to be 350,000, with more on the way. They are bolstered by 250,000 soldiers from allied nations.

January 3
DIPLOMACY: In Washington, D.C., President George H. W. Bush, seeking to avert the outbreak of hostilities, proposes that Secretary of State James A. Baker and Iraqi foreign minister Tariq Aziz meet in Geneva for a last chance at negotiated settlement. However, he maintains there will be no compromises in negotiations.

January 4
DIPLOMACY: In Baghdad, Iraq, the government agrees to a final, face-to-face meeting between foreign minister Tariq Aziz and Secretary of State James A. Baker.
NAVAL: A Spanish naval vessel halts the Soviet freighter *Dmitri Firmanov* in the Red Sea. The vessel is then boarded by Spanish and U.S. naval personnel, who uncover military equipment not listed on the cargo manifest. The vessel is detained.

January 7
MILITARY: According to the U.S. Central Command's intelligence section, Iraqi president Saddam Hussein has deployed 452,000 Iraqi troops (35 divisions), bolstered by 4,300 tanks and 3,100 artillery pieces.

January 8
MILITARY: At Riyadh, Saudi Arabia, Operation Quick Silver unfolds as the 3rd Brigade, 82nd Airborne Division, deploys in response to a terrorist threat to the capital.
POLITICS: In Washington, D.C., President George H. W. Bush formally asks Congress for authorization to commit American forces to military action in the Persian Gulf if Iraq refuses to relinquish Kuwait.

In a nationwide editorial, former president Richard M. Nixon endorses President George H. W. Bush's military and diplomacy policies.

January 9

DIPLOMACY: In Geneva, Switzerland, Secretary of State James A. Baker and Iraqi foreign minister Tariq Aziz discuss the Persian Gulf crisis for six and a half hours without resolution; the latter flatly refuses to believe that the United States will enforce UN Resolution 678. As neither side will budge from previously staked-out positions, armed conflict appears inevitable.

MILITARY: In Afghanistan, General Hashim is captured by mujahideen forces, then executed.

POLITICS: In Washington, D.C., the Pentagon institutes war coverage by pools of reporters, along with security review of all dispatches sent; the media complains but complies.

January 10

DIPLOMACY: In Washington, D.C., President George H. W. Bush calls Israeli prime minister Yitzhak Shamir and urges him to remain out of any conflict with Iraq, even if his country is attacked by missiles.

MILITARY: The 1st Brigade, 2nd Armored Division ("Tiger Brigade") under Colonel John B. Sylvester, is removed from the 1st Cavalry Division and reassigned to the 2nd Marine Division, I Marine Expeditionary Force, to provide them with enhanced firepower. At the time the marines are still saddled with M60A3 Patton tanks instead of more modern M1A1 Abrams tanks. Meanwhile, the British 7th Armoured Brigade rejoins the British 1st Armoured Division, then part of VII Corps.

POLITICS: A declassified letter from William Webster, director of the Central Intelligence Agency, reveals that economic sanctions alone could not force Iraq to relinquish Kuwait over the next 12 months.

   In Washington, D.C., the U.S. Congress begins debating the use of force in the Persian Gulf.

January 11

AVIATION: At Riyadh, Saudi Arabia, two pre-production E-8A JSTARS aircraft are deployed for eventual use against Iraq. This highly advanced reconnaissance platform is capable of real-time surveillance over a battlefield situation.

January 11–12

MILITARY: The I Marine Expeditionary Force is reinforced by the II Marine Expeditionary Force and the 5th Marine Expeditionary Brigade. This assemblage constitutes one of the largest amphibious task forces since the Inchon operation of 1950.

POLITICS: In Washington, D.C., Congress hotly debates authority for U.S. military action against Iraq, although, as commander in chief, President George H. W. Bush does not need its permission to engage. Nonetheless, the House of Representatives votes 250 to 183 and the Senate votes 52 to 47 to implement UN Resolution 678 against Iraq.

January 12

DIPLOMACY: In Baghdad, Iraq, the United States shutters its embassy and removes all diplomatic personnel.

POLITICS: In Washington, D.C., Congress begins debating to authorize President George H. W. Bush to use military force against Iraq. National polls indicate that 63 percent of the American people support action against Iraq.

January 13
DIPLOMACY: In Baghdad, Iraq, UN Secretary-general Javier Pérez de Cuéllar holds emergency talks with President Saddam Hussein for two hours but cannot persuade him to withdraw his forces from Kuwait.

January 14
MILITARY: The 1st Armored Division under Major General Ronald H. Griffin makes a reconnaissance of terrain west of the Saudi-Iraqi border, concluding it is passable for tanks and other tracked vehicles. This information, plus that subsequently obtained by U-2 overflights of enemy positions, allows the 1st and 3rd Armored Divisions to deploy farther west to avoid troop congestion on the ground.

January 15
DIPLOMACY: The deadline for Iraqi forces to evacuate Kuwait, per UN Resolution 678, expires. There is no reaction from Iraq.

MILITARY: In light of the threat of chemical warfare against coalition forces by Iraqi president Saddam Hussein, men of the XVIII Airborne Corps begin taking anti-nerve-agent pills as a precaution.

POLITICS: In London, United Kingdom, Parliament authorizes the use of force against Iraq.

January 16
AVIATION: The first aerial mission of Operation Desert Storm commences as seven B-52Gs of the 2nd Bomb Wing launch from Barksdale Air Force Base, Louisiana, carrying new AGM-86C conventional air-launched cruise missiles. With 35 hours of flight time ahead of them, round-trip, this is also history's longest bombing mission.

DIPLOMACY: In Baghdad, Iraq, the national media report that President Saddam Hussein has drafted a letter to President George H. W. Bush, denouncing him as an "enemy of God and colleague of the Devil."

MILITARY: On the eve of hostilities, Central Command declares that 425,000 U.S. troops are in the Persian Gulf region, along with forces of 19 nations and naval forces of 14 nations.

In Saudi Arabia, convoys begin transporting men and equipment of the VII Corps and XVIII Airborne Corps down the Tapline Road, gradually stretching in length to 120 miles. Operation Desert Shield is about to give way to Operation Desert Storm.

POLITICS: In Washington, D.C., President George H. W. Bush informs the American people that coalition aircraft have begun raiding Iraqi military targets. He hopes that victory in the Persian Gulf will be a major step in establishing a "new world order" based on law.

In Paris, France, the National Assembly authorizes the use of military force against Iraq.

In Baghdad, Iraq, President Saddam Hussein takes to the airwaves and again refers to the upcoming strife as the "mother of all battles."

January 17

AVIATION: With the UN deadline for evacuating Kuwait having passed, Operation Desert Shield yields to Operation Desert Storm as American and coalition aircraft begin a concerted bombardment of Iraqi military targets, missile sites, communications facilities, and other targets deemed useful to Saddam Hussein's occupying forces. On the first day alone, coalition forces launch 750 sorties while carrier aircraft contribute a further 228. This aerial onslaught continues relentlessly for the next 38 days with devastating results and relatively light losses.

Among the first wave of aircraft to go in are AH-64A Apache helicopter gunships from the 1st Battalion, 101st Aviation Regiment, 101st Airborne Division, under Lieutenant Colonel Richard A. Cody. Early shots fired by the laser-guided Hellfire missiles destroy two Iraqi early-warning radar sites, paving the way for additional coalition aircraft to launch strikes. Army air crews are guided to their targets by Air Force MH-53 Special Operations helicopters.

Aircraft from six carriers launch strikes against targets in Kuwait and Iraq as part of Operation Desert Storm. One F/A-18 Hornet flown by Lieutenant Commander Michael S. Speicher of VFA-81 (Saratoga) is shot down, and the pilot is declared killed in action. This status is revised in time to missing/captured, but his remains are not recovered until 2009.

Seven B-52Gs from Barksdale Air Force Base, Louisiana, unleash a salvo of 35 super-accurate cruise missiles against communications and radar targets in Iraq.

F-117 light bombers steal past Iraqi radar defenses and begin bombing strategic targets throughout Baghdad while intense antiaircraft fire lights up the darkness. They account for 31 percent of all targets struck on the first day.

As General H. Norman Schwarzkopf begins his "Hail Mary maneuver," a massive outflanking movement, air force C-130 transports deliver 14,000 troops and 9,000 tons of cargo belonging to the army's XVIII Airborne Corps. This forward deployment suddenly places them on the Iraqi right flank.

An F-16C flown by Captain Jon K. Kelk, 3rd Tactical Fighter Wing, gains the distinction of bagging the first Iraqi MiG-29 jet fighter.

The Iraqis launch eight Scud missiles at Israel, which fall in the Tel Aviv-Haifa region; the Israelis, under American pressure, do not respond militarily. The Americans also shoot down an Iraqi Scud with Patriot missiles over Dhahran, Saudi Arabia.

In Washington, D.C., Defense Secretary Richard Cheney and Joint Chiefs of staff chairman General Colin L. Powell describe Iraqi antiaircraft fire as heavy, but the Iraqi air force itself has made few appearances.

DIPLOMACY: After some hesitation, the Turkish government votes to allow air force warplanes stationed at Incirlik Air Base to be used against targets in northern Iraq.

MILITARY: The 2nd Battalion, 34th Armor (1st Division), begins rehearsing attacks on Iraqi earthen positions using plows and armored combat earthmovers.

NAVAL: Within hours of the decision to go to war, navy vessels in and around the Persian Gulf fire off 122 precision-guided Tomahawk cruise missiles. The honor of firing the first missile goes to the cruiser *San Jacinto* serving in the Red Sea.

POLITICS: In Baghdad, Iraq, an interesting turn of events is the government's decision to allow CNN correspondents Peter Arnett and Bernard Shaw to televise live coverage of Operation Desert Storm for the first 16 hours. The images of Iraqi antiaircraft fire racing into the nighttime sky over the city are simultaneously captivating and terrifying.

January 17–February 28

AVIATION: The Air Force Reserve is extremely active during Operation Desert Storm. Various C-130 transports complete 3,200 combat sorties while A-10 Thunderbolt IIs from the 706th Tactical Fighter Squadron fly 1,000 sorties against enemy targets. Despite this level of involvement, no Reserve aircraft are lost and no personnel are killed.

January 18

AVIATION: In a series of air battles over Iraq, coalition aircraft shoot down eight Iraqi MiG-29 and Mirage F-1 fighters, with the first two falling to a pair of F/A-18s piloted by Commander Mark I. Fox and Lieutenant Nick Mongillo of VFA-81 (*Saratoga*).

Air force jets flying from Incirlik Air Base, Turkey, strike at military targets in northern Iraq to prevent forces there from concentrating against forces moving up from Saudi Arabia.

Over Dhahran, Saudi Arabia, Patriot missiles fired by Battery A, 2nd Battalion, 7th Air Defense Artillery, shoot down a Scud ballistic missile fired by Iraqi forces. Several other Scuds strike Tel Aviv, Israel, as the Patriot battalions there are not yet operational. When the government requests additional defenses against missiles, the army dispatches Task Force Patriot Defender, consisting of two battalions from the 10th Air Defense Brigade, from Germany.

Battery A, 1st Battalion, 27th Field Artillery, fires the first army tactical missile system rockets at Iraqi targets in occupied Kuwait, destroying an SA-1 missile battery. This event marks the debut of the multiple-launch rocket system in combat.

DIPLOMACY: In Tel Aviv, Israel, despite cries for revenge for Iraqi Scud missile attacks, the government heeds American advice not to strike back and possibly shatter the delicate anti-Iraq coalition of Western and Muslim nations.

MILITARY: In Washington, D.C., President George H. W. Bush signs an executive order extending the tour of army reservists beyond 180 days. He also authorizes the call up of 1 million reservists as needed.

NAVAL: In the Persian Gulf, the destroyer *Moosbrugger* dispatches a SEAL team that boards the Sudanese vessel *El Obeid;* this is the first vessel apprehended since the commencement of hostilities.

In the Persian Gulf, the guided-missile frigate *Nicholas,* assisted by Helicopter Antisubmarine Squadron 44 (Light) and a Kuwaiti patrol boat, neutralize several Iraqi oil platforms with enemy troops firing shoulder-launched missiles at coalition aircraft. Five Iraqis are killed, eight are wounded, and 23 are taken captive.

January 19

AVIATION: Over Iraq, A-6 Intruder and A-7 Corsair II aircraft from the carriers *John F. Kennedy* and *Saratoga* fire new standoff land attack missiles against military targets for the first time.

Iraqi surface-to-air missiles shoot down two F-16Cs belonging to the 614th Tactical Fighter Squadron and the pilots are captured. They are paraded before Iraqi television along with six other coalition airmen.

The Iraqis launch 10 Scud missiles into Israeli territory, injuring 10 civilians.

NAVAL: In the Red Sea, the submarine *Louisville* fires the first submerged Tomahawk cruise missile in history against targets in Iraq.

January 20

AVIATION: Over Dhahran, Saudi Arabia, several Iraqi Scud missiles are downed by Patriots fired by Batteries A and B, 2nd Battalion, 7th Air Defense Artillery.

In Baghdad, Iraq, the government broadcasts a videotape showing three American and two British pilots, along with one each from Italy and Kuwait, all of whom had been shot down and captured.

In Kuwait, General H. Norman Schwarzkopf declares that air superiority has not yet been achieved over Iraq since antiaircraft missiles are still being fired at coalition warplanes.

MILITARY: Artillery units attached to the I Marine Expeditionary Force commence bombarding Iraqi units on Kuwaiti soil.

January 21

AVIATION: An A-10 Thunderbolt II flown by Captain Paul T. Johnson braves intense antiaircraft fire to destroy an Iraqi vehicle threatening a downed navy F-14 pilot; he wins the Air Force Cross. Meanwhile, an MH-53J Pave Low helicopter piloted by Captain Thomas J. Trask, 20th Special Operations Squadron, flies in under fire to extract the pilot. Trask and his crew win the Mackay Trophy for their efforts.

DIPLOMACY: In Jerusalem, Israel, Deputy Secretary of State Lawrence Eagleburger announces that Israeli leaders have agreed not to enter the Gulf War despite random and provocative Iraqi missile attacks.

MILITARY: In Baghdad, Iraq, the government announces that is dispersing allied prisoners of war to various strategic site to discourage air strikes against them.

January 22

AVIATION: Over Iraq, an F-15E flown by Colonel David W. Eberly and Lieutenant Colonel Tom Griffith is shot down in combat; Eberly and Griffith evade capture for the next three days but are finally taken near the Syrian border.

Over the Persian Gulf, A-6 Intruder aircraft attack and disable an Iraqi T-43 class vessel, which has a mine-laying capability.

Another Iraqi Scud missile is launched at Israel; the Israelis do not respond to this provocation.

MILITARY: Six Iraqi prisoners are taken in a sweep by the 3rd Armored Cavalry Regiment.

In Afghanistan, Esmat Muslim, chief officer of progovernment militia forces, dies.

January 22–27

AVIATION: MiG-29 aircraft sequestered in hardened aircraft shelters at Al Asad Air Base, Iraq, are hammered by F-111F "Aardvarks" using laser-guided "smart" bombs. Many grounded aircraft are destroyed in this fashion.

January 23

AVIATION: General Colin Powell, chairman of the Joint Chiefs of Staff, declares that air superiority has been achieved over Iraq. Enemy positions are now being bombed with virtual impunity. Moreover, Iraq's two nuclear facilities have been wiped out and its chemical and biological warfare capabilities have been badly damaged.

In the Persian Gulf, A-6 Intruders attack an Iraqi *Al Qaddisiyah*-class tanker that was apparently collecting military intelligence and disable it. An enemy hovercraft and a patrol ship moored alongside are also sunk.

A week of intense coalition aerial attacks leaves Iraq with only five air bases still functioning. Their surviving aircraft are reduced to 40 sorties per day.

By this date, Saudi-based Patriot missile batteries have downed 18 Iraqi Scud missiles.

In the period of coalition-building before attacking Iraq's forces in Kuwait, President George H. W. Bush meets with Jabir al-Ahmad al-Sabah, emir of Kuwait, at the White House, where the leaders wave at photographers in a show of unity. *(George Bush Presidential Library)*

DIPLOMACY: In Khartoum, Sudan, an Afghan resistance embassy is opened by Burhanuddin Rabbani.

MILITARY: Near Objective Falcon, Saudi Arabia, scouts of the 1st Battalion, 325th Infantry, 82nd Airborne Division, begin nightly reconnaissance sorties to observe enemy positions.

TERRORISM: In Kuwait, Iraqi forces begin dumping millions of gallons of Kuwaiti oil into the Persian Gulf and torching hundreds of captured oil wells.

January 24

AVIATION: In the Persian Gulf, A-6 Intruder aircraft sink an Iraqi minelayer and minesweeper, and 22 survivors are airlifted to safety by an SH-60 Seahawk helicopter from the guided missile frigate *Curts*.

Over the Persian Gulf a Saudi F-15C shoots down two Iraqi Mirage F-1 fighters armed with Exocet antishipping missiles.

Today air forces mount 2,570 sorties; over the past eight days, the number was a staggering 14,750.

NAVAL: A SEAL team lands on a small island in the Persian Gulf and captures 51 Iraqis who had been shooting at coalition aircraft. All are evacuated by helicopter from the destroyer *Leftwich* and the guided-missile frigate *Nicholas*. This is also the first portion of Kuwaiti territory to be liberated.

January 25

AVIATION: Air force fighter bombers begin employing new I-2000 bombs against hardened Iraqi aircraft shelters, destroying several MiG 29s inside.

Iraqi Scuds launched at Israel and Saudi Arabia kill one person in each nation.

DIPLOMACY: In Washington, D.C., the administration accuses the Iraqis of committing "environmental terrorism" by deliberately pumping millions of gallons of oil into the Persian Gulf.

January 26

AVIATION: With the Iraqi air force effectively neutralized, coalition forces begin concentrating their attacks on enemy ground forces in Kuwait.

In Washington, D.C., the Pentagon announces that two dozen Iraqi warplanes have flown to Iran to escape the fighting. The Iranian government says these aircraft will be impounded and returned after the war, but they are subsequently added to the Iranian air force.

January 27

AVIATION: Coalition forces acknowledge their air supremacy over Iraqi after 10 days of combat, freeing their aircraft to attack enemy targets at will. F-111s also hit oil-pumping manifolds in Kuwait's main terminal at al-Ahmadi with guided GBU-15 bombs to halt the flow of crude oil into the Persian Gulf; this is also the worst deliberately set oil spill ever created.

January 27–February 1

AVIATION: Seriously outgunned, roughly 75 pilots of the Iraqi air force fly their aircraft to neutral Iran, where they are interned for the conflict. The pilots are released at the end of the war, but their aircraft remain behind in Iran.

January 29

AVIATION: Over Al Khafji, Saudi Arabia, an AC-130H gunship is shot down with a loss of all 14 crew members, but other air force planes continue pounding Iraqi forces and pin them in place for a counterattack.

In the Persian Gulf, helicopters from the amphibious assault ship *Okinawa* attack Iraqi small craft around Umm al Maradum Island, sinking four.

DIPLOMACY: In Washington, D.C., Secretary of State James A. Baker and new Soviet foreign minister Aleksandr Bessmertnykh issue a joint statement that holds out the possibility of a cease-fire should Iraqi forces quit Kuwait.

MILITARY: Detachments from the amphibious assault ship *Okinawa* seize Umm al Maradum Island in the Persian Gulf; this is the second small portion of Kuwaiti territory liberated by coalition forces.

Inexplicably, Iraqi president Saddam Hussein orders three brigade-size night attacks across the Kuwaiti border, one of which captures the Saudi town of Al Khafji. A total of 11 marines are killed in the fighting, mostly by friendly fire.

POLITICS: In Washington, D.C., President George H. W. Bush delivers his State of the Union address, insisting that the recent war in the Gulf region is to liberate Kuwait, and not to cause "the destruction of Iraq, its culture, or its people."

January 31

MILITARY: In Iraq, two American soldiers from the 233rd Transportation Company, including Specialist Melissa A. Rathbun-Nealy, stray into Iraqi territory and are taken prisoner. Rathbun-Nealy is also the first female prisoner of the conflict.

In order to prevent further Scud attacks upon Saudi Arabia and Israel, Major General Wayne A. Dowding of the Joint Special Operations Task Force is ordered to hunt down Scud launchers and either destroy them or point them out to coalition air forces. On hand are two squadrons from Delta Force, a company from the 1st Battalion, 75th Rangers, some Navy SEALS, and elements of the army's 160th Special Operations Aviation Regiment or "Night Stalkers." The endeavor is moderately successful as Scud launchers are mobile and difficult to track down.

The town of Al Khafji, Saudi Arabia, is retaken by coalition forces after they kill 200 Iraqis and capture an additional 500.

February 1

AVIATION: By this date in the aerial offensive, coalition forces announce that they have achieved complete control of the airspace over Iraq. To date they have also unloaded more tons of ordnance against targets than was dropped in all of World War II.

MILITARY: Along Phase Blue Line, Saudi Arabia, a 15-minute firefight erupts between Iraqi forces and men from the 4th Battalion, 325th Infantry, 82nd Airborne Division. No losses are incurred by either side.

In Saudi Arabia, Saudi and Qatari troops take the village of Al Khafji from Iraqi forces, backed by Marine Corps air, artillery, and observer support.

February 2

AVIATION: Over the Indian Ocean, a B-52 bomber based on Diego Garcia experiences electrical problems while returning from a bombing mission over Iraq and crashes. Three crew members are rescued, but three are lost.

February 3
MILITARY: By this date, the ground phase of Operation Desert Shield is concluding, as most allied ground units have completed their deployments to assigned assembly areas. Foremost among these are the VII Corps and the XVIII Airborne Corps in northwestern Saudi Arabia, which will figure prominently in Operation Desert Storm.

February 4
AVIATION: A remote-controlled Pioneer observation vehicle is used to spot artillery targets for the battleship *Missouri* for the first time.

NAVAL: In the Persian Gulf, the battleship *Missouri* fires its 16-inch guns in anger for the first time since World War II. Accurate shelling destroys several Iraqi command-and-control bunkers.

POLITICS: Severe flooding in southwestern Afghanistan inflicts extreme hardship on the inhabitants there.

February 5
POLITICS: In Baghdad, Iraq, the government suspends the sale of fuel due to coalition air attacks. This is on top of persistent shortages of food, water, and electricity.

February 6
AVIATION: An A-10 Thunderbolt II flown by Captain Robert R. Swain Jr. shoots down an Iraqi Gazelle helicopter with a 30mm cannon. This is the first aerial victory attributed to a "Warthog."

Over Iraq, a navy F-14 Tomcat from Fighter Squadron/carrier *(Ranger)* shoots down an Iraqi Mi-8 helicopter.

DIPLOMACY: In Amman, Jordan, King Hussein abandons his former neutrality and complains that the nations allied against Iraq are attempting to place the Arabs "under direct foreign hegemony."

MILITARY: Final elements of the 3rd Armored Division under Major General Paul F. Funk arrive in Saudi Arabia and begin deploying. This is the final unit belonging to VII Corps.

Marines of the Direct Support Command begin constructing a new forward logistics base dubbed Al Khanjar, which is fully operational within six days.

February 7
DIPLOMACY: In New York City, UN secretary-general Javier Pérez de Cuéllar states that Iraqi civilian casualties in the Persian Gulf War will run into the thousands.

MILITARY: Along the Kuwaiti-Iraqi border, the first artillery raids of Desert Storm are conducted by the VII Corps and 1st Cavalry Division. These actions also mark the debut of the laser-guided Copperhead missile, which knocks out an enemy observation tower. These harassment attacks convince the Iraqi high command that coalition forces are planning a major push through the Wadi al-Batin, and they reinforce the area ahead of time.

February 8
MILITARY: In Pakistan, a group of 300 mujahideen fighters are sent to Saudi Arabia to help oust Iraqi forces from Kuwait. Both Abdul Rassul Sayyaf and Gulbuddin Hekmatyar oppose the move.

In Saudi Arabia, Defense Secretary Richard Cheney and Joint Chiefs of Staff chairman General Colin L. Powell arrives for talks with Saudi officials and coalition commanders.

February 9

AVIATION: Iraqi Scud missiles continue raining down on Israel, wounding 26 civilians.

A-10 Thunderbolt IIs begin the process of "tank plinking" or destroying individual targets with precision-guided munitions, or "smart weapons." At this juncture, roughly 600 enemy tanks and armored vehicles have been destroyed, representing 15 percent of Iraq's overall military strength.

DIPLOMACY: The Iraqis finally break off diplomatic relations with the United States and close their embassy in Washington, D.C.

MILITARY: Coalition commander General H. Norman Schwarzkopf suggests that the opening phase of Operation Desert Storm commence between February 21 and 25, and President George H. W. Bush agrees.

February 11

AVIATION: Coalition forces mount 2,900 strike sorties. A grand total of 61,862 have been flown over a 26-day period. They also announce that, to date, 39 Iraqi aircraft have been shot down while an additional 142 planes have sought asylum in Iran.

February 12

AVIATION: Over Baghdad, Iraq, air force fighter bombers use "smart bombs" to bring down the Martyr's Bridge, the Republic Bridge, and the July 14 Bridge.

February 13

AVIATION: Acting upon a tip from military intelligence, F-117s bomb the Al Firdos bunker in downtown Baghdad, Iraq, suspected of housing President Saddam Hussein. The building, a civilian communications center, is flattened, with the loss of more than 400 civilians, but the elusive dictator is not there. Thereafter, coalition air authorities more closely supervise combat strikes in the capital city.

MILITARY: Another large artillery raid commences as three rocket batteries from the 42nd Field Artillery Brigade and the 1st Cavalry Division fire 216 rounds at Iraqi artillery positions. These, in turn, drop 140,000 "bomblets" on exposed enemy positions.

February 14

AVIATION: An air force EF-111A electronic countermeasures aircraft crashes in Saudi Arabia after a bombing mission over Iraq; the two-man crew ejects but is apparently killed upon landing.

MILITARY: The 1st Armored Division, 9,000 vehicles strong, rumbles toward Tactical Assembly Area Garcia, just below the 2nd Armored Cavalry's position. Concurrently, the 3rd Armored Division positions itself to the west of this armored concentration.

The U.S. Command announces that, to date, coalition forces have destroyed 1,300 of 4,280 Iraqi tanks, 800 of 1,870 armored personnel carriers, and 1,100 of 3,110 artillery pieces.

February 15

DIPLOMACY: In Baghdad, Iraq, the five-man Revolutionary Council declares that it is willing to consider the UN resolution requiring Iraq to withdraw from Kuwait. However, it insists that all sanctions be lifted and all reparation issues be dropped. President George H. W. Bush dismisses the offer as a "cruel hoax" and encourages the Iraqi people to overthrow their government.

MILITARY: Coalition commander General H. Norman Schwarzkopf is briefed on the condition and morale of Iraqi prisoners. He learns that the Iraqis are tired of incessant warfare and would surrender readily except for minefields in their path, possible execution by the Republican Guard, and threats against family members. Many are of the opinion that the bulk of Iraqis will surrender the moment serious fighting starts.

February 16

AVIATION: An AH-64A Apache helicopter gunship from the 1st Infantry Division accidentally fires Hellfire missiles at American personnel carriers as they work their way through a sand berm along the Iraqi border. Two soldiers are killed and six others wounded in the first of several "friendly fire" episodes that follow.

February 17

AVIATION: A wave of AH-64A Apaches from the 2nd Battalion, 229th Aviation Regiment (101st Airborne Division) begins attacking and reducing Iraqi bunker complexes near the soon-to-be designated Main Supply Route New Market. They are joined by additional Apaches from Company C, 3rd Battalion, 502nd Infantry; around 40 Iraqis from the 45th Infantry Division surrender.

MILITARY: The VII Corps unleashes its largest bombardment to date with five battalions of artillery that smash various Iraqi air defenses. This allows AH-64A Apaches of the 2nd Squadron, 6th Cavalry (11th Aviation Brigade), to slip into enemy lines unopposed and destroy several communication facilities.

February 18

AVIATION: The XVIII Airborne Corps swings into action as helicopters from the 1st Battalion, 82nd Aviation Regiment (82nd Airborne Division), conduct a reconnaissance in force over Objective Rochambeau while other Apaches belonging to the 12th Aviation Brigade maul Iraqi troops at Objective White.

An MH-60 Black Hawk from the 3rd Battalion, 160th Special Operations Battalion, swoops in and rescues a downed F-16 pilot 40 miles north of the Iraqi border.

NAVAL: In the Persian Gulf, the amphibious assault ship *Tripoli* and the guided-missile cruiser *Princeton* strike mines and suffer damage. A total of seven crewmen are injured.

February 19

AVIATION: Baghdad, Iraq, is struck by a combination of F-4Gs and F-16s launched from Turkish air space. Today coalition forces mount a record 3,000 sorties for a total of 83,000 since the war began.

DIPLOMACY: In Washington, D.C., President George H. W. Bush looks askance at a Soviet proposal that allows a gradual Iraqi withdrawal from Kuwait.

MILITARY: The 24th Infantry Division (Mechanized) rumbles forward to engage Iraqi troops while its attached aviation brigade provides support. An Iraqi border post is also eliminated by a direct hit from a Copperhead missile courtesy of Battery B, 4th Battalion, 41st Field Artillery.

In Saudi Arabia, General H. Norman Schwarzkopf announces that the Iraqi army is on the "verge of collapse." Meanwhile, Lieutenant General Thomas Kelly, chief of operations for the Joint Chiefs of Staff, mentions that the coalition is now ready to attack Iraqi forces on the ground.

February 20

AVIATION: Attack helicopters from the 82nd and 101st Airborne Divisions ravage Iraqi positions near the Saudi border, inducing more than 400 soldiers to surrender. Meanwhile, the Iraqi 45th Infantry Division is bombarded by the 1st Battalion, 201st Field Artillery.

MILITARY: At Wadi al-Batin, Kuwait, the 1st Battalion, 5th Cavalry, 1st Cavalry Division, forces its way through the Iraqi sand berm and begins fanning out into the desert, looking for enemy positions. They are subsequently attacked by Iraqi artillery and antitank guns before pulling back with three killed and nine injured.

February 22

DIPLOMACY: In Baghdad, Iraq, President Saddam Hussein voices his support for a Soviet proposal allowing a gradual withdrawal from Kuwait.

In Washington, D.C., President George H. W. Bush espouses strong doubts about the plan and insists that if Iraq has not completely withdrawn its forces by 8 P.M. on February 23, a ground offensive will commence. He also denounces the Iraqis for setting fire to Kuwaiti oil installations, which has caused inky black smoke to cloak half of Kuwait.

February 23

AVIATION: Air force B-52Gs continue pounding Iraqi Republican Guard positions as other Iraqi troops continue setting Kuwaiti oil wells on fire.

MILITARY: In Washington, D.C., President George H. W. Bush declares to the world that the liberation of Kuwait is at hand and that fighting will continue until the last Iraqi unit is forcibly ejected from that captured nation.

Teams of Special Forces fan out in the Euphrates River valley, Iraq, seeking intelligence as to Iraqi troop movements. The three-man team headed by Master Sergeant Jeffrey Sims is uncovered and battles superior enemy forces for several hours until MH-60 Black Hawks of the 160th Special Operations Aviation Regiment swoop in to rescue them.

In Kuwait, General H. Norman Schwarzkopf decides that Iraqi positions have been sufficiently "softened up" and the moment of decision to launch an all-out ground offensive is at hand.

February 24

AVIATION: Over the next three days, coalition aircraft are responsible for flying 3,000 combat sorties, including reconnaissance, close air support, and interdiction.

MILITARY: At 4:00 A.M., American and coalition ground forces under General H. Norman Schwarzkopf unleash their long-anticipated ground offensive against Iraqi forces holding Kuwait. The XVIII Airborne Corps under Lieutenant General Gary E. Luck, supported by the 82nd Airborne Division and the French 6th Light Armored Division, moves forward almost unopposed and easily takes its objectives. Simultaneously, the 101st Airborne Division employs 66 UH-60 Black Hawk and 39 CH-47 Chinook helicopters to air assault its way deep inside Iraqi territory and establish Forward Operating Base Cobra; 340 prisoners are seized in the process.

As the flanking movement continues, Schwarzkopf orders his main strike force, VII Corps under Lieutenant General Tommy Franks, directly into the fray. Spearheaded by the 2nd Armored Cavalry Regiment—and preceded by a massive bombardment of 11,000 artillery rounds and 414 MLRS rockets—tanks and infantry of the 1st Infantry Regiment surge forward and breach Iraqi defenses. The only resistance comes from a handful of Iraqi T-55 tanks that are quickly dispatched by the 2nd Armored Cavalry. VII Corps seizes all its objectives in only two hours instead of the 18 anticipated.

The I Marine Expeditionary Force, numbering 84,515 men, steps over the front line during Operation Desert Storm. Here the 1st and 2nd Marine Divisions, assisted by armor of the Tiger Brigade, penetrate numerous belts of Iraqi defenses while advancing upon Kuwait City. Simultaneously, the 5th Marine Expeditionary Brigade disembarks to function as the I Marine Expeditionary Force reserve. Other marine units remain afloat in the Persian Gulf to act as a deception. The overall operation is directed by Major General Walter E. Boomer.

February 25
AVIATION: As Iraqi forces surround and prepare to attack an Army Special Forces team, they are struck by Air Force F-16Cs while a UH-60 Black Hawk helicopter swoops in to rescue the Americans.

In Dhahran, Saudi Arabia, an Iraqi Scud missile slams into a warehouse occupied by the 14th Quartermaster Detachment, killing 28 soldiers (including the first enlisted female soldier to die in combat) and wounds 97. Nearby Patriot antimissile batteries were experiencing software problems and unable to deal with incoming projectiles.

MILITARY: As the VII Corps marches forward, General H. Norman Schwarzkopf expresses concern that the elite Iraqi Republican Guard is trying to escape in the direction of Basra. He consequently orders Lieutenant General Tommy Franks to turn his armored units eastward and cut them off.

President Saddam Hussein, speaking on Baghdad radio, orders his remaining forces out of Kuwait.

February 25–26
MILITARY: Colonel Robert Clark leads the 3rd Brigade, 101st Airborne Division, on a 150-mile penetration of Iraqi territory. This not only is the longest air assault in history, but it also severs Highway 8 and cuts off all enemy supplies and reinforcements below it.

February 26

AVIATION: The Iraqi Adnan Division is attacked by Lieutenant Colonel William Hatch and AH-64A Apaches of the 3rd Battalion, 1st Aviation Regiment. In a one-sided engagement, the Americans account for 38 T-72 tanks, 14 BMP fighting vehicles, and 70 trucks.

As most surviving Iraqi forces abandon Kuwait, they are savaged by coalition-force warplanes, which kill thousands along what becomes known as the "Highway of Death." The four-lane passage is literally gutted by the wreckage of tanks, personnel carriers, trucks, and looted civilian automobiles. The aerial attacks stop on the orders of President George H. W. Bush.

DIPLOMACY: In Baghdad, Iraq, several radio spokesmen mention that the country is ready and willing to withdraw from Kuwait per the terms of UN Resolution 660.

MILITARY: At a region denoted as 73 Easting, M1A1 Abrams tanks of the 2nd Armored Cavalry Regiment engage the Republican Guard Tawakalna Division in a standup fight; the Americans destroy 28 Russian-built T-72 tanks and 16 other armored vehicles at a cost of three dead. This encounter demonstrates in stark relief just how superior American armor is over its Soviet counterparts.

At Salman Airfield, Iraq, the 1st Platoon, Company A, 27th Engineering Battalion suffers seven dead while clearing unexploded cluster-bomb submunitions off a runway.

February 26–27

MILITARY: The Battle of Objective Norfolk unfolds as the 1st and 3rd Brigades, 1st Infantry Division, race through the 2nd Armored Cavalry Regiment and engage the Republican Guard Tawakalna Division, and the 37th Brigade of the 12th Armored Division, head on. The swirling engagement results in the destruction of both Iraqi forces and scores of tanks, with hundreds killed or injured. The Americans lose six dead along with a handful of Abrams and Bradleys, all through friendly fire.

February 27

AVIATION: The air force successfully delivers two 4,700-pound GPU-28 bombs that demolish the so-called impregnable Iraqi command bunker at Al Taji. Total air sorties mounted this day top 3,500, a new record.

A UH-60 Black Hawk helicopter from the 2nd Battalion, 229th Aviation Regiment, en route to rescue a pilot downed behind enemy lines, is itself hit by Iraqi forces. Five Americans die in the crash, and three are captured; among the latter is Major Rhonda Cornum, flight surgeon, the second female prisoner of the war.

DIPLOMACY: In New York City, the United Nations receives a letter from Iraqi foreign secretary Tariq Aziz, declaring that his government will accept all 12 UN resolutions and conditions for a cease-fire. The Iraqis will also annul their annexation of Kuwait and agree to pay reparations. However, UN officials demand that Iraq agree to all 12 previous Security Council resolutions passed since August 2, 1990.

In Washington, D.C., President George H. W. Bush announces that Kuwait is finally free of Iraqi troops, and he calls an end to military operations at 8 P.M., only 100 hours after Operation Desert Storm commenced.

MILITARY: Along Medina Ridge, the biggest tank fight of the war erupts as the 1st Armored Division rolls forward to engage the Republican Guard's Medina Division and the remnants of the 12th Armored Division. Supported by artillery and helicopter fire, the Americans devastate their opponents, destroying more than 300 Iraqi vehicles; one American is killed, and a handful of vehicles are damaged.

Major General Barry R. McCaffrey leads the 24th Infantry Division (Mechanized) on a jaunt into Iraqi territory near Basrah, capturing Jalibah Air Base and destroying several MiG-29 fighters on the ground. They then dash down Highway 8, capturing several supply depots and sweeping aside resistance from remnants of the al-Faw, Nebuchadnezzar, and Hammurabi Divisions.

In Saudi Arabia, General H. Norman Schwarzkopf informs journalists that the Iraqi collapse was due to abysmally poor military leadership, and he openly mocks President Saddam Hussein as a strategist. He also concedes that while the low allied casualty count appears to be "miraculous," that is meaningless to families who lost loved ones in the war.

The first American column enters Kuwait City and finds it completely abandoned by Iraqi forces.

February 28
AVIATION: With the terminus of Operation Desert Storm set for 8 A.M., the air force has flown 59 percent of all coalition force sorties, while its 2,000 aircraft represent 75 percent of all machines involved. For all their media celebrity, precision-guided "smart bombs" comprise only 10 percent of ordnance dropped or fired. However, the elusive F-117s account for 40 percent of all Iraqi strategic targets knocked out by flying 1,270 combat sorties and dropping 2,041 tons of bombs. This is also the first "space war," judging from the extensive use of satellite technology.

Jets, aircraft, and helicopters of the 3rd Marine Air Wing fly several hundred missions, mostly ground support. Their losses total four AV-8B Harriers and two OV10 Broncos shot down; five marine aviators are also captured and released within days.

During the 100 hours of Desert Storm, the Air Force Space Command satellite systems were extremely active in relaying meteorological information to combat headquarters along with alerts of short-range ballistic missile launches.

DIPLOMACY: In Baghdad, Iraq, the government announces that a cease-fire is in place.

MILITARY: With Kuwait completely free of Iraqi units, President George H. W. Bush declares a unilateral cease-fire after only 100 hours of fighting. Considering the devastation wrought on Iraqi forces since January 17, the toll is astonishingly light: 98 dead (21 through friendly fire) and 352 wounded. A further 126 died in non-combat-related accidents. In sum, the army deployed 227,800 men in theater, of which 35,158 were from the Army Reserve and 37,692 came from National Guard formations.

Operation Desert Storm concludes just as the I Marine Expeditionary Force recaptures Kuwait City along with 22,000 prisoners. Marine casualties in the 100-hour campaign are 24 dead and 92 wounded.

Iraqi casualties in Operation Desert Storm are estimated at more than 100,000 dead and wounded, with a further 175,000 captured. Experts surmise that 29 Iraqi divisions have been destroyed along with all but 500 of Iraq's 4,200 tanks and other armored vehicles.

March 1

DIPLOMACY: Iraqi and coalition authorities meet at Safwan, Iraq, and propose cease-fire terms for the first time.

March 2

DIPLOMACY: In New York City, the UN Security Council approves Resolution 686, which spells out terms for a cease-fire with Iraq, which includes rescinding its annexation of Kuwait, the release of all prisoners, the return of all property, and an end to all military action.

MILITARY: As elements of the Hammurabi Division flee inland from Basra, they fire upon the 24th Infantry Division, whose return fire through tanks, artillery, and helicopters bags an additional 185 Iraqi armored vehicles, 400 trucks, and 34 pieces of artillery.

March 3

MILITARY: At Safwan, Iraq, General H. Norman Schwarzkopf and coalition leaders under Lieutenant General Khalid ibn Sultan meet with their Iraqi counterparts to hammer out cease-fire terms, including immediate repatriation of all captives. The Iraqis, led by Lieutenant General Hashim Ahmad al-Jabburi, agrees to all U.S. demands unconditionally. Schwarzkopf then announces that coalition forces, which occupy 20 percent of Iraq, will pull back once the cease-fire is in effect. A one-kilometer separation zone between contending forces is also put in place.

Once military operations have concluded, U.S. Army civil-affairs units swing into action, providing food, medicine, and shelter to thousands of Iraqi and Kuwaiti refugees while engineer and explosive ordnance disposal units begin the arduous task of disarming thousands of mines and unexploded ordnance still littered about the desert.

Central Command estimates that coalition forces have destroyed 3,300 tanks, 2,100 armored vehicles, and 2,200 artillery pieces. A total of 80,000 Iraqi prisoners have also been taken, although the death toll is less precise and looms upward of 100,000.

March 4–5

MILITARY: The Iraqis release 45 coalition prisoners, including two female captives, and insist that it holds no more. Coalition forces are preparing to process 175,000 Iraqi captives. However, the Red Cross says that 7,000 Kuwaitis are still unaccounted for.

March 4–12

MILITARY: At Khamisiyah, Iraq, engineers from the 82nd Airborne Division discover and destroy a huge Iraqi bunker complex/weapon cache. They are unaware that chemical weapons and nerve agents are present, exposing many soldiers to low-level doses. This is the origin of what becomes known as Gulf War Syndrome, which ultimately affects 100,000 service personnel.

March 5
DIPLOMACY: In Baghdad, Iraq, the government officially voids its annexation of Kuwait per the cease-fire agreement.
MILITARY: In Basra, Iraq, Shiite Iraqis, long oppressed by the Sunni-dominated government, rise in rebellion.

March 6
POLITICS: In Washington, D.C., President George H. W. Bush triumphantly addresses a joint session of Congress. Bush orders the return of U.S. military forces from the Persian Gulf but pledges to maintain a strong diplomatic presence throughout the Middle East. He also lauds the Gulf War, insisting that the allies have passed the first major test of the new world order.

March 7
MILITARY: In Washington, D.C., Defense Secretary Richard Cheney announces that the bulk of the 450,000 Americans in the Persian Gulf will be brought home no later than midsummer.

March 8
MILITARY: At Andrews Air Force Base, Maryland, 21 former American prisoners of war arrive.

March 8–December
AVIATION: The Military Airlift Command again demonstrates its strategic flexibility by flying a host of supplies, personnel, and even environmental cleanup equipment into the Persian Gulf region. Accordingly, 42 C-5 Galaxies and three C-141 Starlifters of the 60th and 436th Military Airlift Wings fly in more than 1,000 tons of firefighting equipment and crews necessary to extinguish 517 oil wells set alight by retreating Iraqi forces. They also deliver 7,000 tons of relief supplies to Kurdish refugees in southeastern Turkey.

March 9
MILITARY: The first units of the I Marine Expeditionary Force begin withdrawing to the United States; all will have departed by August 27.

March 10
AVIATION: Iraq releases another 21 prisoners, including eight air-force members.
DIPLOMACY: The governments of six Arab countries strongly endorse President George H. W. Bush's plans for the Middle East.

March 12
MILITARY: In Washington, D.C., President George H. W. Bush authorizes the Southwest Asia Service Medal for any military personnel participating in Operations Desert Shield or Desert Storm.

March 13

AVIATION: In Baghdad, Iraq, President Saddam Hussein orders helicopter gunships to advance on Basra against the Shiite insurgents, an act that President George H. W. Bush cautions might be a violation of the recent cease-fire.

March 15

AVIATION: In Kuwait, General H. Norman Schwarzkopf tells Iraq that the use of fixed-wing aircraft against Shiite rebels in Basra is a violation of the cease-fire.

March 16

MILITARY: In Baghdad, Iraq, President Saddam Hussein announces that the Shiite rebellion in Basra has been completely crushed. UN officials subsequently conclude that as many as 20,000 Iraqis fled to Iran to escape the fighting and persecution.

March 17

MILITARY: At Fort Stewart, Georgia, elements of the 24th Infantry Division are the first American military units to return from the Persian Gulf.

March 20

AVIATION: Over northern Iraq, a Su-22 caught violating the cease-fire agreement is promptly shot down by an air force F-16C.

March 21

DIPLOMACY: In Iraq, a UN survey team pronounces the damage inflicted by the Gulf War upon that society as "near apocalyptic."

MILITARY: The human-rights group Middle East Watch states that Kuwaiti soldiers and other vigilantes tortured and beat 400 people, mostly Palestinians, suspected of collaborating with the Iraqis.

March 21–22

DIPLOMACY: In Washington, D.C., former ambassador to Iraq April Glaspie testifies before the House Foreign Affairs Committee about her prewar interview with President Saddam Hussein.

March 22

DIPLOMACY: In New York City, the United Nations ends its food embargo against Iraq.

MILITARY: In Washington, D.C., General Colin Powell, chairman of the Joint Chiefs of Staff, declares that U.S. forces will remain in southern Iraq for several months until the United Nations can impose a better security arrangement there.

March 26

MILITARY: In a news conference, General H. Norman Schwarzkopf admits that he recommended continuing Desert Storm further, but President George H. W. Bush disputes this.

March 27

DIPLOMACY: In Washington, D.C., President George H. W. Bush adopts a "wait and see" attitude toward the Shiite and Kurdish uprising in Iraq and says that the regime of President Saddam Hussein will fall of its own accord.

In Tehran, Iran, the government denies that it is arming Iraqi Shiites and Kurds and encouraging them to rebel against the central government.

March 28
MILITARY: In Basra, Iraq, a spokesman for Iraqi Shiites declares that local guerrillas are still waging war against the government of Saddam Hussein.

March 30
MILITARY: The city of Kirkuk, Iraqi Kurdistan, falls to Iraqi government forces, triggering an exodus of thousands of refugees into neighboring mountains. This latest Kurdish uprising has been brutally suppressed.

March 31
MILITARY: The city of Khost, Afghanistan, long an object of the Afghan resistance, finally falls to mujahideen under Commander Haqani. They take 2,500 government soldiers captive, along with seven generals, including Colonel General Muhammad Zahir Solamal, deputy minister of defense; Major General Ghulam Mustafa, chief of political affairs; Major General Muhammad Azam of the Afghan Air Force; and Lieutenant General Shirin, commander of militia units around Khost. This is a major blow against the Kabul regime.

April 1
DIPLOMACY: In northern Iraq, a coalition of Kurdish insurgent forces appeals to the West for humanitarian assistance in the wake of the latest failed rebellion against the central government.

April 2
DIPLOMACY: In Washington, D.C., the administration reiterates its hands-off approach to the insurgencies in Iraq by Shiites and Kurds. However, the governments of France and Turkey appeal to the United Nations for humanitarian assistance.
POLITICS: In Kabul, Afghanistan, the government declares a day of mourning after the fall of Khost to the resistance movement.

April 3
DIPLOMACY: In New York City, the UN Security Council approves Resolution 687, which imposes harsh financial and military conditions on Iraq as part of the cease-fire agreement. Henceforth President Saddam Hussein is to renounce terrorism, pay billions in restitution to Kuwait, and accept the 1963 border resolution with that nation. Moreover, he is required to destroy all stocks of chemical and biological weapons of mass destruction and cooperate completely with the International Atomic Energy Agency. Finally, a special UN commission is established to closely monitor Iraqi compliance with all of the above; Saddam Hussein complies but considers the conditions unjust.
POLITICS: As the monthlong Kurdish rebellion against President Saddam Hussein continues, thousands of civilians begin a mass exodus into Turkey and Iran.

In Washington, D.C., President George H. W. Bush repeats his neutralist stance toward the insurgencies in Iraq and notes that the coalition cannot solve all the internal problems there.

April 5

AVIATION: In Washington, D.C., President George H. W. Bush orders the Air Force to begin an airlift of food, medicine, and relief supplies to the Kurdish refugees of northern Iraq.

DIPLOMACY: In New York City, the UN Security Council condemns Iraq's brutal suppression of Kurds and Shiites by passing Resolution 668, which also mandates the deployment of humanitarian assistance units. Presently there are 1 million Kurdish refugees in Turkey and Iran.

April 6

DIPLOMACY: In Baghdad, Iraq, the government accepts the harsh UN terms for a permanent cease-fire but also denounces them as unfair and vindictive.

POLITICS: In Kabul, Afghanistan, Muhammad Nurzad is elected major of the capital following the defection of Abdul Karim Misaq to West Germany.

April 6–July 24

MILITARY: In northern Iraq, Operation Provide Comfort is executed to bring humanitarian assistance to thousands of Kurdish refugees. Joint Task Force Provide Comfort consequently is created at Incirlik Air Base, Turkey, where elements of the 3rd Infantry Division (Mechanized) distribute food, water, and shelter. By the time the operation concludes, more than 17,000 tons of relief supplies have been distributed.

April 7

AVIATION: Six U.S. Air Force transports commence Operation Provide Comfort to assist the Kurds in northern Iraq; part of this effort entails enforcing a "no-fly zone" above the 36th parallel, which is in the making.

A Patriot missile is fired from its mobile launcher. Although the Patriot had only mixed success against the Scud, it was the best antimissile artillery that the United States could deploy at the time. *(Defense Imagery)*

April 8

DIPLOMACY: In northern Iraq, Secretary of State James A. Baker inspects a Kurdish refugee camp firsthand and promises to help organize an international relief effort.

In Luxembourg, the European Community endorses the concept of a safe haven for Kurdish refugees north of latitude 16 degrees south.

April 9

DIPLOMACY: In New York City, the UN Security Council approves plans to deploy a 1,440-member peacekeeping force along the Kuwait-Iraq border.

April 10

DIPLOMACY: In Washington, D.C., the administration warns Iraqi president Saddam Hussein not to commence military activities in the northeastern section of Iraq, where the majority of Kurdish refugees are located. Presently, sickness and malnourishment are killing 1,000 Kurds along the border of Iraq and Turkey.

In Baghdad, Iraq, the government formally accepts cease-fire terms first proposed on March 1.

POLITICS: In Kabul, Afghanistan, Vice President Sultan Ali Keshtmand is dismissed from office.

April 16

AVIATION: Acting under the aegis of UN Resolution 668, the United States, Britain, and France begin patrolling the northern reaches of Iraq to keep Iraqi warplanes from entering and attacking the Kurds. This is the first so-called no-fly zone.

DIPLOMACY: In Washington, D.C., President George H. W. Bush announces that U.S., French, and British forces will be establishing camps in northern Iraq to assist thousands of Kurdish refugees. An estimated 10,000 U.S. troops will be deployed there to administer the effort, which will accommodate 100,000 refugees.

POLITICS: In Kabul, Afghanistan, President Mohammad Najibullah extends amnesty to all Afghan refugees who agree to come home.

April 17

MILITARY: In northern Iraq, the first teams of U.S. Army Special Forces arrive to scout out locations for refugee facilities.

April 18

DIPLOMACY: The Iraqi government and the United Nations agree to allow refugee centers to be established in northern and southern Iraq to assist thousands of refugees gathered there.

April 19

DIPLOMACY: In compliance with UN Resolution 687, the Iraqi government informs the United Nations of its chemical and biological warfare programs. However, it denies possessing any nuclear stocks.

April 20

MILITARY: In northern Iraq, the first detachment of U.S. Marines arrives to establish refugee camps for thousands of displaced Kurds.

TERRORISM: In Konar Province, Afghanistan, an explosion wrecks the headquarters of the Wahhabi movement in Asadabad, killing 500 and wounding 700, including many Arabs and Pakistanis. The attack was apparently carried out by a powerful car bomb, but the Wahhabis insist it was a Scud missile attack.

April 23
MILITARY: Because of the decisive nature of Operation Desert Storm, which does much to revive America's military spirits, Congress votes to award Generals Colin Powell and H. Norman Schwarzkopf a special gold medal.

April 24
DIPLOMACY: As U.S. forces continue constructing refugee camps in northern Iraq, the first UN observers begin arriving to monitor them.

POLITICS: In Baghdad, Iraq, Kurdish leaders meet with their Iraqi counterparts and receive assurances of safe passage back to their homes.

April 26
DIPLOMACY: In Geneva, Switzerland, representatives from Pakistan's intelligence services and members of the Kabul regime meet.

MILITARY: In northern Iraq, Iraqi troops are withdrawn from the town of Zakho, where their presence discouraged the return of numerous Kurdish refugees.

POLITICS: In Iraq, UN observers calculate that Kurdish refugees are dying at the rate of 4,000 per day.

April 29–30
POLITICS: In northern Iraq, thousands of Kurdish refugees, buoyed by the presence of U.S. troops, begin returning to the region of Zakho. UN observers estimate that 25,000 Kurds are returning to Iraq every day.

May 5
MILITARY: U.S. forces begin moving into northern Iraq from southern Turkey to create a safe haven in the vicinity of Dahok for the return of Kurdish refugees.

May 7–9
MILITARY: Troops and equipment of the U.S. 3rd Armored Division pull back across the Iraqi-Kuwaiti border, thereby ending their occupation of southern Iraq.

May 14
DIPLOMACY: In Washington, D.C., the State Department declares that 250,000 Kurdish refugees had departed the border and mountain regions of southern Turkey and returned to their homes in Iraqi Kurdistan.

Iraqi foreign minister Tariq Aziz and UN secretary-general Javier Pérez de Cuéllar agree to terms for allowing UN Special Commission weapons inspectors into Iraq. The measures include unrestricted freedom of entry and exit for all personnel and whatever equipment they require.

May 16
DIPLOMACY: In Baghdad, Iraq, the government submits a revised declaration of its chemical weapons and missile systems, per Resolution 687.

MILITARY: In Germany, the 11th Armored Cavalry Regiment receives orders to ship out to Kuwait as part of Operation Positive Force, the high-profile continuing presence of U.S. forces there.

May 18
DIPLOMACY: In Baghdad, Iraq, the government agrees to allow the United Nations to deploy 500 lightly armed guards to oversee refugee centers in northern and southern Iraq.

May 20
POLITICS: Queen Elizabeth II grants General H. Norman Schwarzkopf an honorary knighthood for his command of coalition forces in the Gulf War.

May 21
DIPLOMACY: In New York City, UN secretary-general Javier Pérez de Cuéllar promulgates a five-point proposal for a political settlement in Afghanistan. However, the Afghan Interim Government categorically rejects any compromise with the regime of President Mohammad Najibullah.

May 22–24
MILITARY: In northern Iraq, an agreement between coalition and Iraqi military leaders results in the allied occupation of Dahok, while all Iraqi military and secret police are withdrawn. Within two days an estimated 50,000 refugees return to the region.

May 27–28
DIPLOMACY: In Moscow, Soviet Union, representatives from Pakistan arrive for talks about the future of Afghanistan.

May 31
TERRORISM: In Nowshera, Pakistan, a mujahideen ammunition dump explodes, probably the work of Afghan secret police operatives.

June 4
MILITARY: In Washington, D.C., the Pentagon releases estimate of Iraqi casualties from the Gulf War: 100,000 dead and 300,000 wounded.

June 9
DIPLOMACY: In Iraqi, UN weapons inspectors begin their first search for illegal chemical weapons.

June 13
MILITARY: In Kuwait, the 11th Armored Cavalry Regiment relieves the 1st Brigade, 3rd Armored Division, and assumes responsibility for the defense of that nation.

June 14
DIPLOMACY: In Iraq, UN weapons inspectors charge that the government is understating both its nuclear weapons program and the amount of weapons-grade nuclear material it has on hand. The Iraqis deny both counts.

June 17
DIPLOMACY: In New York City, the UN Security Council reaffirms the mission of the Special Commission to monitor Iraqi weapons and disarmament.

June 21
MILITARY: Coalition forces reach an agreement to maintain a sizable military presence in southern Turkey to monitor the Kurdish safe zones in northern Iraq.

June 25
MILITARY: The coalition powers announce that 5,000 U.S., British, Dutch, and French troops will be stationed in southern Turkey to safeguard Kurdish safe zones. They are to be backed up by U.S. warplanes operating out of Incirlik Air Base, Turkey.

June 28
DIPLOMACY: In light of the latest round of obstructionism, the UN Security Council orders Iraq to turn over all suspicious equipment to UN inspectors.
MILITARY: East of Baghdad, Iraq, Iraqi soldiers fire weapons over the heads of UN inspection teams and forbid them from examining machinery suspected of manufacturing nuclear weapons.

The trail of destroyed vehicles, including trucks and buses, on the so-called highway of death shocked even hardened veterans. *(DOD Defense Information Center, March ARB, California)*

June 30

DIPLOMACY: In Iraq, UN weapons inspectors begin their first search for Iraqi missiles.

July 3

MILITARY: In Washington, D.C., President George H. W. Bush awards the Presidential Medal of Freedom to Generals Colin Powell and H. Norman Schwarzkopf for outstanding military leadership during the recent events in Kuwait.

July 8

DIPLOMACY: In Baghdad, Iraq, the government admits to three clandestine programs to produce enriched uranium. However, it strenuously denies it has any programs capable of producing nuclear weapons.

July 15

MILITARY: In northern Iraq, coalition forces have completely withdrawn from the safe zone established for Kurdish refugees.

July 17–18

DIPLOMACY: In Iraq, UN weapons inspectors declare that bombings in the recent Gulf War have destroyed Iraq's facilities for enriching uranium.

July 18–20

AVIATION: In Iraq, UN weapons inspectors gather up and destroy undeclared Iraqi missiles and all ground equipment.

July 19

MILITARY: In northern Iraq, fighting resumes between Kurdish fighters and Iraqi military forces; an estimated 500 people are killed in the exchange.

July 22

MILITARY: In Afghanistan, mujahideen loyal to Ahmad Shah Massoud capture Jahkashem and the Wakhan Corridor from government forces.

July 29

POLITICS: In a surprising move, President Saddam Hussein takes to the airwaves in Iraq and flatly declares that he refuses to admit a defeat. He also makes the extraordinary claim that, in light of Iraq's continuing independence and his unaffected tenure in office, he actually won the Gulf War.

July 30

DIPLOMACY: In Iraq, chief of UN weapons inspectors Rolf Ekeus informs the Security Council that Iraq possesses four times as many chemical weapons as it had admitted having. He also notes that the government had buried machinery and equipment in order to hide its nuclear ambitions.

August 2–8

DIPLOMACY: In Iraq, UN weapons inspectors commence their first search for biological weapons.

August 5
DIPLOMACY: In Iraq, the government informs UN inspectors that its scientists have extracted small amounts of weapons-grade material from spent nuclear fuel.

August 9
TERRORISM: Outside Paris, former Iranian prime minister Shahpur Bakhtiar, 75 years old, is stabbed to death.

August 13
MILITARY: In Washington, D.C., a Pentagon report states that 35 of the 148 American fatalities in the Gulf War were caused by friendly fire, as were 72 of the 467 wounded.

August 15
DIPLOMACY: In New York City, the UN Security Council allows existing Iraqi sanctions to remain in place but will let the government sell $1.6 billion in oil to buy food and medical supplies for the general population. However, 30 percent of the revenues must go to a special fund established for Kuwaitis whose relatives died as a result of the recent invasion.

The UN Security Council also expresses its disapproval of Iraqi noncompliance with cease-fire terms by passing Resolution 707. This comes only four months after a severe drubbing in the Gulf War and a cease-fire.

August 26
DIPLOMACY: In New York City, the United Nations establishes the second "no-fly zone" south of latitude 32 degrees, this time with a view toward protecting Iraqi Shiites.

August 30
TERRORISM: In Konar Province, Afghanistan, Jamilur Rahman, self-proclaimed chief of the Wahhabi Republic, is assassinated by unknown gunmen.

September 6–13
DIPLOMACY: In Iraq, the government blocks a UN inspection that was supposed to have been conducted by helicopter. It also refuses to release documentation relative to efforts to obtain nuclear materials. The standoff ends only following a Security Council threat to resort to military action.

September 13
DIPLOMACY: The United States and the Soviet Union agree in principle to end all arms shipments to Afghanistan on January 1, 1992.

In Iraq, UN inspection teams conclude that Iraqi president Saddam Hussein possessed sufficient nuclear material to construct two or three small nuclear devices per year in the 1990s before the facilities were destroyed.

September 18
AVIATION: In Washington, D.C., President George H. W. Bush authorizes U.S. warplanes to fly in Iraqi airspace to protect UN weapons investigators. The order comes following President Saddam Hussein's refusal to allow helicopter inspections of his military facilities.

DIPLOMACY: In New York City, Thomas Pickering, U.S. ambassador in the United Nations, declares that Iraq's repeated obstruction of Security Council resolutions releases all other parties from the cease-fire obligations.

September 23
DIPLOMACY: In Baghdad, Iraq, the government detains 40 UN weapons inspectors for attempting to remove evidence of its nuclear weapons program.

September 24
DIPLOMACY: In New York City, the UN Security Council declares that the Iraqi government has agreed to allow helicopter inspections of various facilities without challenging them. Iraq also releases the 40 weapons inspectors under detention, but only after a direct threat of military enforcement.

September 25
MILITARY: In Washington, D.C., Chairman of the Joint Chiefs of Staff General Colin Powell informs a House of Representatives subcommittee that, based on a recent inspection of two Iraqi facilities, Iraq was, in fact, attempting to acquire nuclear capabilities.

September 27
DIPLOMACY: In Iraq, the government accedes to UN Security Council demands and releases secret documents relative to its nuclear weapons program.

September 28
DIPLOMACY: In Iraq, UN investigators are allowed to leave the country with documentation highlighting that country's nuclear ambitions.

October 7
MILITARY: In Iraq, UN inspectors uncover a top-secret document revealing that the center of President Saddam Hussein's nuclear weapons program was located 40 miles southwest of the capital and was only slightly damaged during the Gulf War.

October 8
DIPLOMACY: In Washington, D.C., Assistant Secretary of State Richard Clarke gives a televised interview in which he accuses Iraqi president Saddam Hussein of deliberately hiding weapons of mass destruction from UN inspectors.
MILITARY: In Iraqi Kurdistan, a spokesman for the Kurds states that recent fighting with Iraqi forces has produced 400 casualties, including 60 captured soldiers.

October 11
DIPLOMACY: In New York City, the UN Security Council unanimously approves Resolution 715, which insists that Iraq accept all inspection personnel without reservation.

October 14
POLITICS: In Kabul, Afghanistan, the supreme court tries to curry favor with the Afghan resistance by declaring that all legal decisions must conform to Islamic law.

October 17

DIPLOMACY: In Washington, D.C., a member of the International Atomic Energy Agency testifies before Congress that Iraq is withholding information relative to its nuclear ambitions.

November

AVIATION: This month the Military Air Lift Command performs its 100th humanitarian flight by assisting Afghan refugees fleeing to camps in Pakistan. Since March 1986, air force transports have delivered more than 1,000 tons of relief aid to the region.

November 4

TERRORISM: In Italy, former Afghan monarch Mohammad Zahir Shah survives an assassination attempt and is only slightly wounded.

December 5

POLITICS: In New York City, the United Nations agrees on a solution for transferring the government of Afghanistan from the Communists to the mujahideen.

In Washington, D.C., Congress passes Public Law 102–190 to authorize "all necessary means" to force Iraq to comply with UN Resolution 687.

December 6

DIPLOMACY: In Washington, D.C., an administration official bemoans the conditions of Kurdish refugees in northern Iraq. Over 200,000 had fled Iraqi attacks in that region over the past few weeks.

December 14

POLITICS: In Baghdad, Iraq, President Saddam Hussein is televised freely chatting informally with his senior military advisers. This is a clear signal to the Iraqi people—and the rest of the world—that he remains in firm control of his nation.

December 15

MILITARY: In Moscow, Soviet Union, the government announces that it has stopped all arms shipments to the Kabul regime.

December 31

DIPLOMACY: The Soviet flag is lowered from the Kremlin for a final time, marking the end of the Soviet Union. It is replaced with the new Commonwealth of Independent States, marking a complete victory for the United States and the West in the cold war.

1992

January 1

DIPLOMACY: In Moscow, Russia, the government reiterates it has terminated all military assistance to the Kabul regime.

January 3

DIPLOMACY: In Washington, D.C., the State Department accuses Iraq of interfering with international aid slated for its own people. The suggestion is made that

President Saddam Hussein be allowed to sell crude oil under UN inspection in order to purchase humanitarian aid for the populace.

January 13
DIPLOMACY: In Iraq, government officials inform UN weapons inspectors that they had acquired technologies for constructing uranium enrichment plants, but they insist that these devices have all been destroyed since the cease-fire.

January 14
POLITICS: In Kabul, Afghanistan, President Mohammad Najibullah annuls the decree confiscating all property belonging to the royal family.

February 4
DIPLOMACY: In Baghdad, Iraq, the government redoubles its recalcitrance by balking at a UN plan for monitoring its armament industry. It also suspended negotiations about selling oil for food and medicine for the Iraqi people.

February 6
MILITARY: In Afghanistan, General Abdul Rashid Dostum defects to the mujahideen, joined by leaders Shah Nasir Naderi and general Abdul Momen.

February 26–27
DIPLOMACY: In Iraq, UN weapons inspectors are denied access to various facilities or to observe Scud missiles being dismantled, in violation of the 1991 cease-fire agreement.

February 28
DIPLOMACY: In New York City, the UN Security Council criticizes Iraqi president Saddam Hussein's unwillingness to destroy his ballistic missile arsenal and related weapons of mass destruction. It gives Iraq until March 8 to comply or face "serious consequences."

March 11
DIPLOMACY: In New York, City, Security Council president Diego Arria urges that existing sanctions against Iraq remain in place until that government complies fully with the cease-fire terms that ended the 1991 Gulf War. President Saddam Hussein is still not allowing UN weapons inspectors access to suspected military sites.

March 12
DIPLOMACY: In New York City, the UN Security Council rejects Iraqi foreign minister Tariq Aziz's assertions that his nation has fully compiled with all UN cease-fire resolutions.

March 13
NAVAL: In the Persian Gulf, the *America* carrier battle group deploys in a none-too-subtle hint to Iraq that punitive measures will be the result of continuing obstructionism and noncompliance with UN resolutions.

March 15
MILITARY: In Afghanistan, the mujahideen capture all of Samangan Province.

March 18

POLITICS: In Kabul, Afghanistan, President Mohammad Najibullah agrees to step down once the Interim Government is installed.

March 19

AVIATION: In Baghdad, Iraq, the government announces that it has unilaterally destroyed most of its 89 missiles capable of carrying chemical or biological agents.

In Washington, D.C., Pentagon officials inform President George H. W. Bush that a bombing campaign is available to enforce Iraqi compliance on destroying weapons of mass destruction and on UN resolutions.

March 20

DIPLOMACY: In New York City, the UN Security Council declares that Iraq has agreed to destroy all its ballistic missiles per terms of the cease-fire resolution that ended the Persian Gulf War. It also agrees to provide a full accounting of its nuclear, biological, and chemical warfare programs.

March 29

MILITARY: Sari-i-Pul, Afghanistan, falls to mujahideen of the National Unity Party (Wahdat).

April 2

DIPLOMACY: In Warsaw, Poland, 27 nations, including the United States, are prompted by Iraqi machinations to sign an accord to halt the spread of nuclear weapons.

April 8

AVIATION: In Washington, D.C., the administration expresses concerns that Iraq relocated missiles and missile launchers into the northern reaches of the country.
MILITARY: In Afghanistan, Uzbek militia under General Abdul Rashid Dostum capture Mazar-i-Sharif.

April 9–10

POLITICS: In Afghanistan, the government and several mujahideen leaders begin negotiations for an orderly transitional government. However, the followers of Gulbuddin Hekmatyar refuse to participate.

April 10

AVIATION: In Washington, D.C., the Pentagon releases its final assessment of the Gulf War and concludes victory was in large measure the product of effective air power. Because of this, casualties, previously estimated at 10,000, were only 220.

After the United Nations reveals that American U-2 spy planes are flying over Iraq, that nation calls for their immediate halt and threatens to down them. However, the Security Council reiterates the right to undertake such activity.

April 12

MILITARY: In Afghanistan, mujahideen loyal to Ahmad Shah Massoud take control of the strategic Salang tunnel north of Kabul.

POLITICS: In Iran, moderate cleric Hashemi Rafsanjani wins a resounding landslide election over more strident, anti-Western opponents.

April 15
MILITARY: Continuing his offensive, General Abdul Rashid Dostum's Uzbek militia capture Kabul airport.

April 16
MILITARY: In Afghanistan, various mujahideen groups storm into the cities of Gardez, Ghazni, and Herat as government resistance collapses.

POLITICS: In Kabul, Afghanistan, President Mohammad Najibullah resigns from power, then tries to flee, but he is forced to seek refuge in a UN compound. He is replaced by Abdul Rahim Hatif, who serves as interim president. Meanwhile, a military junta of mujahideen and rebellious army units takes control of the city.

April 18
MILITARY: Mujahideen forces capture Kunduz and Jalalabad, Afghanistan.

POLITICS: In Kabul, Afghanistan, Abdul Rahim Hatef is nominated to serve as interim president in the absence of Mohammad Najibullah.

April 21
MILITARY: In Logar Province, Afghanistan, Pul-i-Alam falls to the mujahideen of the Islamic Party (Hezb-i-Islami).

April 22
MILITARY: Gardez, Afghanistan, is captured by mujahideen loyal to Jalaluddin Haqani.

April 23
MILITARY: In Washington, D.C., a report issued by the House Armed Services Committee states that U.S. military intelligence overestimated the number of Iraqi troops in Kuwait by one-third.

April 24
MILITARY: In Kabul, Afghanistan, thousands of victorious mujahideen from the six major opposition groups stream into the capital and outlying neighborhoods.

POLITICS: To facilitate the upcoming transition to power, the mujahideen leadership in Pakistan establishes an interim Islamic Council of 51 members under Sibghatullah Mojaddedi. Free elections are planned, but mujahideen leader Gulbuddin Hekmatyar calls for the creation of a fundamentalist Islamic state.

April 25
MILITARY: Mujahideen units continue filtering into Kabul, Afghanistan, and occupying government buildings; fighting immediately breaks out between fighters loyal to Gulbuddin Hekmatyar and to Ahmad Shah Massoud.

April 26
MILITARY: In Kabul, Afghanistan, the mujahideen of Ahmad Shah Massoud seize control of the presidential palace and ousts those of Gulbuddin Hekmatyar from

nearby military barracks. Shiite militia of Narakat-i-Islami also seize control of a missile base at Darulaman.

April 28

POLITICS: In Kabul, Afghanistan, Sibghatullah Mojaddedi arrives and proclaims the foundation of an Islamic state, along with a general amnesty for all, expect Moham-mad Najibullah.

April 29

MILITARY: In Kabul, Afghanistan, additional fighting results in the expulsion of Hezb-i-Islami fighters from the Ministry of the Interior. Mujahideen leader Ahmad Shah Massoud also arrives in the capital.

May 3

DIPLOMACY: The government of Egypt lends diplomatic recognition to the new Islamic republic of Afghanistan.

POLITICS: Mujahideen leader Gulbuddin Hekmatyar threatens to attack the capital unless the Uzbek militia of General Abdul Rashid Dostum depart immediately.

Kurdish women and children in the northern section of Iraq had long been endangered by Saddam Hussein's regime, but following Operation Desert Storm they were protected by a UN-sponsored resolution that forbade Iraqi planes from flying over the region. *(Defense Imagery)*

May 5
POLITICS: In Kabul, Afghanistan, the various rival factions conclude a peace settlement whereby Sibghatullah Mojadeddi becomes interim president and appoints a 36-member temporary cabinet. Gulbuddin Hekmatyar also stops shelling the city and begins negotiations with the new ruling coalition.
MILITARY: In Kabul, Afghanistan, Ahmad Shah Massoud gains appointment as the Afghan defense minister.

May 6
POLITICS: The first meeting of the Islamic Council is convened by Burhanuddin Rabbani.

May 10
POLITICS: In Kabul, Afghanistan, mujahideen leader Sayyid Ahmed Gailani arrives with his fighters.

May 19
DIPLOMACY: In Vienna, Austria, reports emerge that a gathering of nuclear specialists from the United States, France, Britain, and Russia, meeting under the aegis of the International Atomic Energy Agency, concluded that Iraq was far from acquiring nuclear weapons prior to the Gulf War. In 1990, the Bush administration raised the specter of an Iraqi nuclear bomb within six months.

May 21
MILITARY: In Afghanistan, mujahideen leaders Gulbuddin Hekmatyar and Ahmad Shah Massoud agree to a cease-fire between them.
POLITICS: In Kabul, Afghanistan, mujahideen leader Yunnis Khalis arrives with his fighters.

May 25
POLITICS: In Kabul, Afghanistan, a settlement is reached between the ruling coalition and Gulbuddin Hekmatyar, calling for an immediate end to the fighting and national elections within six months.

May 30
MILITARY: In the Karte Nau district of Kabul, Afghanistan, an armed clash erupts between the mujahideen of Gulbuddin Hekmatyar and General Abdul Rashid Dostum.

June
POLITICS: In Vienna, Austria, the exiled Iraqi National Congress is founded by members of two Kurdish groups; within four months they are joined by various Shiite dissenters.

June 15
POLITICS: In Washington, D.C., a National Intelligence Estimate portrays President Saddam Hussein as actually more in control of Iraq than he was a year previously. In addition, the UN sanctions in place are adversely affecting the populace but have no discernible effect on the president himself.

June 19

MILITARY: Armed clashes are reported between the mujahideen fighters of Ahmad Shah Massoud and General Abdul Rashid Dostum.

June 28

POLITICS: In Kabul, Afghanistan, Sibghatullah Mojaddedi resigns from the presidency in favor of Burhanuddin Rabbani.

July 2

MILITARY: In London, United Kingdom, Iraqi dissenter Ahmed Chalabi says that a recent attempted military coup against President Saddam Hussein was promptly and ruthlessly crushed by loyalist security forces. Intelligence is subsequently received that suggests as many as 145 army officers were rounded up and executed in consequence.

July 3

POLITICS: In Baghdad, Iraq, the government news agency denies that there has been a coup attempt against President Saddam Hussein, but rumors persist that he has violently purged his officer corps of hundreds of men.

July 4

MILITARY: In Washington, D.C., declassified documents from the Pentagon, dated 1985, reveal that American nuclear technology exported abroad could easily be adapted to producing nuclear weapons.

Near Kabul, Afghanistan, tension between mujahideen loyal to Gulbuddin Hekmatyar and forces under General Abdul Rashid Dostum erupts into an artillery duel.

July 6

TERRORISM: In Iraqi Kurdistan, a bomb explodes near the motorcade of Danielle Mitterrand, wife of the French president, and six people are killed.

July 6–29

DIPLOMACY: In Baghdad, Iraq, the government refuses to grant the UN weapons inspection team permission to visit the Ministry of Agriculture. After a three-week impasse, a UN threat of force finally gains them the access they required.

July 7

POLITICS: In Denver, Colorado, a federal grand jury indicts former U.S. ambassador to Kuwait Sam Z. Sakhem of absconding with millions of dollars paid to him for an anti-Iraq propaganda campaign.

July 17

DIPLOMACY: In Washington, D.C., an administration spokesman warns Iraqi president Saddam Hussein of a possible military response if Iraq fails to honor terms of the UN-sponsored cease-fire. The Pentagon also notes that it has 250 warplanes in the region ready to back up UN demands with force, if necessary.

July 26

DIPLOMACY: In Baghdad, Iraq, the government finally allows UN weapons monitors access to specific government buildings, thereby ending a longstanding diplomatic impasse. However, team members must be from nations that did not fight Iraq in the recent war.

July 27

DIPLOMACY: In Washington, D.C., the administration issues a statement noting that President George H. W. Bush and his national security advisers have been discussing the wide range of options open to them to enforce Iraqi's compliance with UN resolutions.

July 28

DIPLOMACY: The United States adopts a three-point program to pressure Iraq to allow UN weapons inspections without interference, refrain from attacking Kurds and other minorities, and legalize opposition political groups.

July 28–29

DIPLOMACY: In Baghdad, Iraq, the UN weapons inspection team combs through the Ministry of Agriculture building without finding incriminating evidence.

July 29

MILITARY: In Sulaimaniya, Iraq, military units apparently fire on Kurdish demonstrators, killing several and also wounding some UN workers and guards.

August 2

POLITICS: In Kabul, Afghanistan, Yunnis Khalis resigns his seat on the Islamic Council.

August 2–20

AVIATION: In Kuwait, Operation Intrinsic Action unfolds as transports of the Air Mobility Command arrive with army reinforcements. The move is made in response to recent threats made to Kuwait by Iraq.

August 3–4

MILITARY: In Kuwait, a force of 2,000 Marines and other troops participate in joint operations over the next two weeks that are intended as a show of force against Iraq.

August 10

POLITICS: In Washington, D.C., the Justice Department denies House Democrats the appointment of a special investigator to look into whether administration officials violated the law prior to the Persian Gulf War.

August 15

DIPLOMACY: In Kabul, Afghanistan, the escalation of violence induces the United Nations to begin reducing its staff.

August 16

DIPLOMACY: In Paris, France, a gathering of Iraqi dissidents says that U.S. air strikes against Iraq will have a counterproductive effect on affairs since they are viewed as being directed against the people instead of President Saddam Hussein.

In Amman, Jordan, Gulf nation officials conclude that Saddam Hussein's grip on power leaves but two options for Western powers: his death or the partitioning of Iraq into Kurdish, Shiite, and Sunni enclaves.

August 17
DIPLOMACY: In Iraq, UN weapons inspectors halt plans to inspect a building that the government had declared off-limits. Meanwhile, coalition powers threaten to resume bombing if access is denied.

August 20
DIPLOMACY: In Baghdad, Iraq, the government declares that it will resist any attempt to impose a "no fly zone" over the southern third of the country.

August 24
POLITICS: In Baghdad, Iraq, President Saddam Hussein goes on record as maintaining he will prevail in any confrontation over the establishment of "no-fly zones."

August 26
AVIATION: Over Iraq, coalition aircraft commence Operation Southern Watch to enforce a "no-fly zone" to keep Iraqi aircraft from flying below the 32nd parallel. Naval aircraft involved are operating from the carrier *Independence.* They are eventually joined by warplanes from France and Britain. This joint deployment is undertaken to prevent President Saddam Hussein from attacking the large Shiite community residing in the southern marshes of Iraq.

POLITICS: In Washington,. D.C., President George H. W. Bush informs a news conference that the "no fly zone" was conceived after receiving credible intelligence of harsh repression against Iraqi Shiites by the central government. Apparently, Iraqi warplanes are the chief means for enforcing the central government's will.

August 27
POLITICS: In Kabul, Afghanistan, President Burhanuddin Rabbani arranges a cease-fire with the mujahideen of Gulbuddin Hekmatyar.

In Baghdad, Iraq, the government puts on a brave face and insists that it will confront "colonialists" at a time and place of its own choosing.

September 5
MILITARY: In Kabul, Afghanistan, the Uzbek militia of General Abdul Rashid Dostum depart the capital, probably because of a cease-fire with Gulbuddin Hekmatyar.

September 6
DIPLOMACY: In Baghdad, Iraq, the UN weapons inspection team leader notes that the government refuses to identify foreign suppliers of nuclear materials, another violation of UN resolutions.

The annual Arab Economic Report reveals that the cost of the recent Gulf War to Arab nations was $620 billion, including a $51 billion subsidy to support U.S. and coalition forces in the Persian Gulf.

September 8
DIPLOMACY: In Baghdad, Iraq, the government appoints Nizar Hamdoun, previously ambassador to the United States, to serve as Iraqi envoy to the United Nations.

September 17

POLITICS: In Paghman, Afghanistan, President Burhanuddin Rabbani and Gulbuddin Hekmatyar agree to allow the national assembly to select the former's successor.

October 27

POLITICS: In Kabul, Afghanistan, the Leadership Council, headed by President Burhanuddin Rabbani, approves a two-month extension of his term in office.

December 12

POLITICS: In Kabul, Afghanistan, President Burhanuddin Rabbani declares he will remain in office beyond his present term until a successor is agreed upon.

December 27

AVIATION: Over southern Iraq, an F-16C shoots down an Iraqi MiG-25 Foxbat that had violated the UN no-fly zone. This is also the first aircraft destroyed by the new AIM 120 AMRAAM air-to-air missile, or "Slammer," a weapon that greatly extends the reach of F-16s and enhances their lethality.

December 30

POLITICS: In Kabul, Afghanistan, the Resolution and Settlement Council votes to keep President Burhanuddin Rabbani in power, although five of nine mujahideen factions boycott the proceedings.

1993

January 2

POLITICS: In Kabul, Afghanistan, President Burhanuddin Rabbani resigns as head of the Jamiat Party.

January 6

DIPLOMACY: The United States and the United Nations deliver Iraq an ultimatum: Remove all antiaircraft missiles in the southern "no-fly zone" or face a major bombing campaign.

January 9

DIPLOMACY: In Iraq, the government says that it is removing all threatening antiaircraft missiles from the southern "no-fly zone." The White House says that it is convinced that stern coalition ultimatums produced Iraqi compliance in this matter, although several missile batteries remain in place.

January 13

AVIATION: Air Mobility Command transports fly in forces to support Southern Watch II, the "no-fly zone" in southern Iraq near Kuwait and Saudi Arabia.

A force of 100 American, British, and French warplanes attacks 32 Iraqi antiaircraft missile sites discovered south of the 32-degree north latitude line. Thirty-five of these are launched from the carrier *Kitty Hawk*.

MILITARY: In Washington, D.C., President George H. W. Bush orders the deployment of 1,250 U.S. Army troops to guard Kuwait from border incursions.

January 17
AVIATION: Over Iraq, an F-16 tasked with covering a F-4G Wild Weasel mission against Iraqi antiaircraft sites in the northern "no-fly zone" detects a MiG-23 and destroys it with an AIM-210 "Slammer" missile.
NAVAL: In the Persian Gulf, the destroyers *Caron, Hewitt,* and *Stump* launch 45 Tomahawk cruise missiles against the Iraqi Zafaraniyah nuclear fabrication plant in Baghdad. This attack comes in response to Iraqi noncompliance with UN resolutions.

January 18
AVIATION: In separate actions, F-4G Wild Weasels return fire on an Iraqi missile site that fired on them while F-16s bomb an airfield whose antiaircraft sites had fired upon them. They are joined by British and French aircraft.

January 19
DIPLOMACY: In Baghdad, Iraq, the government orders a cease-fire against coalition aircraft and also declares that it will allow UN inspectors into the capital without interference. The Iraqi ruling council maintains its actions are intended as a goodwill gesture toward the incoming presidential administration of Bill Clinton.
MILITARY: On the outskirts of Kabul, Afghanistan, mujahideen loyal to Burhanuddin Rabbani attack those of Gulbuddin Hekmatyar, who responds by launching rockets against the capital.

January 23
AVIATION: Over the Iraqi southern "no-fly zone," a U.S. Navy jet pilot bombs an Iraqi antiaircraft position after its radar "locks on" to his aircraft.

February 3
DIPLOMACY: In light of the deteriorating security situation, the United Nations suspends all aid shipments through southern and eastern Afghanistan.

February 5
DIPLOMACY: In Kabul, Afghanistan, the escalating violence persuades the Indian government to withdraw its diplomats.

February 6
MILITARY: In Kabul, Afghanistan, various groups of mujahideen occupying the Soviet embassy commence fighting among themselves.
POLITICS: In Kabul, Afghanistan, General Abdul Rashid Dostum is appointed as deputy defense minister.

February 8
DIPLOMACY: In Kabul, Afghanistan, the Turkish government closes its embassy.

February 11
POLITICS: In Kabul, Afghanistan, the imam of al-Azar University pleads with various mujahideen groups to stop fighting among themselves.

February 13
DIPLOMACY: In Baghdad, Iraq, President Saddam Hussein makes an overture to President Bill Clinton to resume bilateral relations and reopen diplomatic talks.

February 16
POLITICS: The city of Kabul, Afghanistan, enjoys the first day of peace since the mujahideen arrived in January.

February 23
MILITARY: In Iraq, local troops point weapons at helicopters carrying UN inspectors scouting out Scud missile sites.

March 7
POLITICS: In Afghanistan, the Islamabad Accord goes into effect with Burhanuddin Rabbani nominated to serve as president for 18 months while Gulbuddin Hekmatyar serves as prime minister. Furthermore, a council of all mujahideen parties will jointly be in charge of the Ministry of Defense. Pakistan and various Afghan groups will also help supervise the cease-fire among them. Finally, a council is to be elected in eight months, and national elections for the presidency and legislature will be held by mid-1995. However, Yunnis Khalis and Abdul Rashid Dostum are not among the signatories.

March 8
MILITARY: Kabul, Afghanistan, is attacked by rocket's launched by the Hezb-i-Islami and the Islamic Unity Party of Yunnis Khalis.

March 11
DIPLOMACY: In Mecca, Saudi Arabia, various Afghan leaders confer with King Fahd over details of the Islamabad Accord. Among the topics discussed is the relative power of the Uzbek militia under General Abdul Rashid Dostum.

March 19
MILITARY: In Washington, D.C., the U.S. Army releases a report first compiled in January 1992 that concludes that Iraq had, in fact, committed war crimes against Kuwaitis and prisoners of war during the Gulf War.

March 19–20
POLITICS: A conference held in Jalalabad, Afghanistan, fails to iron out differences among various mujahideen groups.

March 22
MILITARY: In Kabul, Afghanistan, fighting resumes between members of the Ittihad (Islamic Union for the Liberation of Afghanistan) and Wahdat (the Islamic Party).

March 23
MILITARY: Fighters from Hezb-i-Islami seize the Naghu Dam from Harakat-e-Inqulabi-i-Islami.
POLITICS: Pakistani authorities seize Stinger missiles from Mullah Abdul Salam, a local mujahideen leader. The mullah quickly takes 27 hostages to get them back.

March 28
POLITICS: In Afghanistan, a spokesman for General Abdul Rashid Dostum insists that genuine peace is impossible unless there is adequate Uzbek representation in the Kabul government.

April 1–2
POLITICS: A committee is formed between members of the Hezb-i-Islami (Islamic Unity Party) and the Jamiat (Islamist Movement); they ultimately agree to a cease-fire and an exchange of prisoners.

April 7
POLITICS: In Kabul, Afghanistan, the government accuses both the Islamic Party of Gulbuddin Hekmatyar and the Islamic Unity Party of funneling arms to insurgents in Tajikistan.

April 9
AVIATION: U.S. and coalition warplanes bomb Iraqi antiaircraft sites that fired on patrols in the northern "no-fly zone." The Iraqis deny initiating this, the first such action in 10 days.
POLITICS: In Afghanistan, the short-lived cease-fire between the Islamic Unity Party and the Islamist Movement is called off.

April 13
TERRORISM: In Kuwait, authorities arrest 17 conspirators who planned to assassinate former president George H. W. Bush with a car bomb during a previous ceremonial visit. U.S. intelligence subsequently concludes that the Iraqi government was behind the plot.

April 15
DIPLOMACY: The governors of Herat, Afghanistan, and nearby Khorsan, Iran, agree in principle to cooperate in antidrug smuggling operations.

April 25
MILITARY: Mujahideen loyal to Gulbuddin Hekmatyar begin a blockade of Kabul, Afghanistan.

May 3
MILITARY: In Tajikistan, roughly 50 fighters of the Shia-oriented Islamic Unity Party are killed fighting rival groups.

May 9–10
MILITARY: In Kabul, Afghanistan, a major clash develops between mujahideen loyal to Burhanuddin Rabbani and those Allied to Gulbuddin Hekmatyar.

May 11
MILITARY: As fighting rages in Kabul, Afghanistan, between competing groups, the Kabul Museum suffers heavy damage.

May 12

AVIATION: Kabul, Afghanistan, suffers another round of rocket attacks from Gulbuddin Hekmatyar's forces.

May 13

MILITARY: The mujahideen of General Abdul Rashid Dostum and Ahmad Shah Massoud forge an alliance to oppose Gulbuddin Hekmatyar's Hezb-i-Islami.

May 19

POLITICS: Once again, Gulbuddin Hekmatyar and Burhanuddin Rabbani agree to a cease-fire between their forces.

TERRORISM: In Kuwait, an Iraqi terrorist suspect admits that he was part of a 10-man team attempting to assassinate former president George H. W. Bush during a recent visit there.

May 20

MILITARY: In Kabul, Afghanistan, Ahmad Shah Massoud resigns as defense minister.

June 5

POLITICS: In Kuwait City, 14 suspects charged with plotting to assassinate former president George H. W. Bush with a car bomb go on trial. One of them testifies that they acted upon the orders of Iraqi intelligence.

June 6

POLITICS: In Charasyab, Afghanistan, Gulbuddin Hekmatyar presides over the first ad hoc meeting of his new government.

June 17

POLITICS: In Paghman, Afghanistan, the new government assembles, and Gulbuddin Hekmatyar is sworn in as prime minister.

June 21

POLITICS: In Darulaman, Afghanistan, the Council of Ministers convenes its first meeting.

June 23–28

MILITARY: Mujahideen of Ahmad Shah Massoud and the Wahdat Islamists engage in heavy fighting.

June 26

DIPLOMACY: In Washington, D.C., President Bill Clinton makes a televised address to the nation, stating that the Iraqi plot against former president George H. W. Bush was an attack against the entire nation. He is consequently ordering retaliatory action against Iraqi intelligence facilities.

June 27

AVIATION: Two U.S. warships in the Persian Gulf and Red Sea fire 23 Tomahawk missiles at Iraqi intelligence facilities in Baghdad, Iraq. The Iraqis subsequently claim that eight civilians were killed. Senior Arab officials in Egypt, Sudan, and

Jordan comment that the attacks were not well-received by the Arab public, and such attacks are contributing to ill will toward America.

June 29

AVIATION: In southern Iraq, a U.S. warplane fires a missile at an Iraqi antiaircraft site after it allegedly locks its radars on it.

July 1

DIPLOMACY: In Baghdad, Iraq, Foreign Minister Tariq Aziz hopes that better relations can be cultivated with Washington and that the Iraqis will not retaliate for the June 27 missile attack against the capital.

July 3

POLITICS: President Burhanuddin Rabbani and General Abdul Rashid Dostum meet and attempt to settle their differences peacefully.

TERRORISM: In Kuwait City, five Iraqi defendants and one Kuwaiti declare their innocence in planning to assassinate former president George H. W. Bush.

July 5

DIPLOMACY: In Baghdad, Iraq, UN weapons inspectors withdraw from the country after the government prevents them from installing monitoring cameras at missile sites. Meanwhile, the Security Council maintains that Iraq is in material breach of the 1991 cease-fire agreement.

July 9

POLITICS: Acting upon news that Iraq and the United Nations have reopened talks on resuming limited oil exports, the price per barrel drops to $17.79 on the spot market.

July 11

DIPLOMACY: In Iraq, the government blocks a UN weapons inspection team from sealing a missile site, whereupon the inspectors depart the country.

July 12

POLITICS: After lengthy negotiations in Kabul, General Abdul Rashid Dostum and Gulbuddin Hekmatyar agree to a cease-fire.

July 15

MILITARY: Around Kabul airport, Afghanistan, fighting continues between the forces of Ahmad Shah Massoud and Gulbuddin Hekmatyar.

July 17

POLITICS: In Baghdad, Iraq, President Saddam Hussein accuses the Clinton administration of "radical fanaticism," but he makes no mention of the latest impasse over UN weapons inspections.

July 19

DIPLOMACY: In Baghdad, Iraq, the government again bows to the threat of UN punitive action and readmits UN weapons inspection teams looking for weapons of mass destruction.

July 26
MILITARY: The mujahideen of Ahmad Shah Massoud eject forces of Gulbuddin Hekmatyar from Bagram Air Base north of Kabul, Afghanistan.

July 29
AVIATION: Over southern Iraq, Navy EA-6B Prowlers unleash HARM missiles at Iraqi antiaircraft sites after their radar locks onto them.

August 24
DIPLOMACY: In London, United Kingdom, the Iraqi ambassador to Canada and the former envoy to Tunisia defect; they quickly join the ranks of the exiled Iraqi National Congress there. Since 1991 a total of five Iraqi ambassadors have changed sides.

August 31
POLITICS: In Afghanistan, a cease-fire is arranged between mujahideen of Burhanuddin Rabbani and those of the Islamic Unity Party.

September 14
MILITARY: Kabul, Afghanistan, is again shelled by mujahideen of Gulbuddin Hekmatyar's Islamic Party.

September 15
POLITICS: Rumors surface that the defunct Afghan Communist Party has secretly met at Microrayon to elect Mahmaud Baryalai as its head.

October 2
MILITARY: In Tajikistan, reports surface that as many as 300 Islamic fighters are operating there.

October 19
POLITICS: After considerable delays, the Kabul-Jalalabad highway reopens to commercial traffic.

October 24
DIPLOMACY: An agreement is signed between Afghanistan and Tajikistan for exporting natural gas from the former to the latter.

November 9
DIPLOMACY: In Kabul, Afghanistan, Robin Raphel, the U.S. under secretary of state, pays a visit for talks about humanitarian and economic aid with Burhanuddin Rabbani, Gulbuddin Hekmatyar, Abdul Rashid Dostum, and Ahmad Shah Massoud.

November 21
POLITICS: In Kabul, Afghanistan, the noted Islamist ideologue Hasan al-Turabi arrives for talks with various leaders.

November 26
DIPLOMACY: In Baghdad, Iraq, the government finally agrees to honor the terms of UN Resolution 715, first adopted on October 11, 1991.

November 27

DIPLOMACY: In New York City, an American UN official declines to discuss lifting the oil embargo with the visiting Iraqi deputy prime minister, despite the fact that the four other members of the permanent Security Council had done so. The Americans insist that sanctions and diplomatic isolation are forcing Iraq into compliance with UN disarmament resolutions and should not be modified.

December 23

MILITARY: The town of Sher Khan Bandar, Afghanistan, is occupied by the Uzbek militia of General Abdul Rashid Dostum without a fight.

1994

January 1

MILITARY: Mujahideen loyal to General Abdul Rashid Dostum and Gulbuddin Hekmatyar ally to oust Burhanuddin Rabbani's forces from Kabul, Afghanistan.

January 5

MILITARY: During intense combat around Kabul, Afghanistan, the mujahideen of Burhanuddin Rabbani capture Kabul airport.

January 6

MILITARY: In the Microrayon and Bala Hissar areas of Afghanistan, additional fighting breaks out once the fighters of Sibghatullah Mojaddidi join the alliance against Burhanuddin Rabbani.

January 10

MILITARY: The mosque at Pul-Khisti, Afghanistan, is destroyed during combat between feuding mujahideen.

February 28

DIPLOMACY: In New York City, a UN commission declares that Iraqi forces had not employed chemical weapons against Shiites in the southern marshlands the previous September. However, it did find that President Saddam Hussein ordered 40 percent of the delicate marshlands drained in order to facilitate military operations against the inhabitants.

April 2

DIPLOMACY: In Kabul, Afghanistan, a UN emissary arrives for cease-fire discussions with Gulbuddin Hekmatyar, Burhanuddin Rabbani, and Ahmad Shah Massoud.

April 4

MILITARY: The town of Pul-i-Khumri, Afghanistan, is attacked by mujahideen under Ahmad Shah Massoud to drive out the fighters of General Abdul Rashid Dostum and Gulbuddin Hekmatyar.

April 6

MILITARY: In Afghanistan, the UN emissary departs without achieving a cease-fire between feuding factions.

April 14
AVIATION: Tragedy strikes over northern Iraq as a pair of patrolling U.S. Air Force F-15s mistakenly shoot down two U.S. Army UH-60 Black Hawk helicopters carrying 26 officials from four allied nations. The pilots apparently mistook them for Iraqi Russian-built Mil-17 helicopters.

April 15
AVIATION: In Washington, D.C., the Pentagon states that air force pilots involved in the Black Hawk shoot down violated the rules of engagement by failing to issue a warning before shooting.

April 19
POLITICS: In Kabul, Afghanistan, President Burhanuddin Rabbani declares his intention to extend the mandate of his office until December 1994 since opposing groups will not honor the Islamabad agreement of March 1993.

Forces loyal to Mullah Salam take two Chinese engineers and 10, Pakistanis hostage, then demand that the Pakistani government return the mullah's brother along with three Stinger missiles that had been appropriated from him.

April 27
DIPLOMACY: The International Committee of the Red Cross issues a report that places the number of casualties resulting from this latest round of civil strife at 2,500 dead, 17,000 injured, and 632,000 made refugees since the start of the year. They also estimate that 20,000 households and dwellings have been destroyed.

April 30
DIPLOMACY: In Washington, D.C., Congress supports legislation that says the United States should continue supporting Iraq's territorial integrity and its gradual transition to a peaceful democracy.

May 1
MILITARY: In Afghanistan, an offensive against Kabul launched by the mujahideen of Gulbuddin Hekmatyar is blunted.

May 9
AVIATION: The handful of jet aircraft still available to the Afghan government bombs the rebel outposts at Mazar-i-Sharif and Pul-i-Khumri.

May 13–14
MILITARY: The government garrison at Qargha, outside Kabul, Afghanistan, is bombarded by units loyal to General Abdul Rashid Dostum.

May 17–18
MILITARY: At Maidan Shahr, Afghanistan, mujahideen loyal to Abdul Rasul Sayyaf drive out those belonging to Gulbuddin Hekmatyar.

May 21–22
AVIATION: Two government aircraft are claimed to have been shot down by Stinger missiles operated by mujahideen of General Abdul Rashid Dostum.

May 22

AVIATION: In Afghanistan, General Ali Ahmad Jalali, purportedly the head of aviation forces under General Abdul Rashid Dostum, claims to have 32 operational aircraft, 100 pilots, and a considerable amount of bombs.

May 28

MILITARY: Within the Islamic Unity Party, fighting breaks out between factions headed by Mohammad Akbari and Abdul Ali Mazari.

May 29

POLITICS: In Baghdad, Iraq, President Saddam Hussein also assumes the title and functions of prime minister, another sign of his consolidation of political power there.

June 3

AVIATION: Military aircraft operated by the forces of General Abdul Rashid Dostum bomb factional positions in Herat, Afghanistan.

MILITARY: At Shindand, Afghanistan, heavy fighting is reported by groups loyal to General Abdul Rashid Dostum and mujahideen leader Ismail Khan.

June 5

TERRORISM: In Kuwait, six Iraqis and a Kuwaiti receive death sentences for their roles in the failed plot to assassinate former president George H. W. Bush with a car bomb. Seven other defendants receive jail sentences while one is acquitted.

June 8

POLITICS: In Kabul, Afghanistan, President Burhanuddin Rabbani proposes that a *loya jirga* (assembly) select his successor.

June 10

MILITARY: After a few weeks of peace, skirmishing among rival factions begins anew in Kabul, Afghanistan.

June 15

POLITICS: In Kabul, Afghanistan, President Burhanuddin Rabbani formally extends his term of office by six more months.

June 19

TERRORISM: In Afghanistan, mujahideen leader Ismail Khan survives a failed assassination attempt.

June 20

TERRORISM: In (Mashhad), Iran, a bomb explodes in a prayer hall, killing 25 people and wounding 75. At the time, Shiites were marking the death of one of their holiest figures.

June 25

MILITARY: In Afghanistan, the Darulaman Palace, previously garrisoned by the Islamic Party, is captured by fighters of the Shiite Harakat (Islamic Revolutionary Movement).

June 26
MILITARY: In severe fighting, mujahideen under Burhanuddin Rabbani expel those of General Abdul Rashid Dostum from Bala Hissar and Maranjan Hill.

June 27
POLITICS: In Afghanistan, Yunnis Khalis appoints himself to serve as interim president.

July 8
POLITICS: In Afghanistan, a commission forms among the forces of Abdul Rashid Dostum, Gulbuddin Hekmatyar, and others to negotiate a cease-fire with the alliance of Burnuddin Rabbani and Abdul Rasul Sayyaf.

July 13
AVIATION: In Washington, D.C., the Pentagon releases a report on the tragic April 14 downing of two army helicopters over northern Iraq by air force jets. The accident is attributed to the fact that the helicopters' IFF (Identification Friend or Foe) transponders were set to frequencies assigned to Turkey, not Iraq, hence the jets mistakenly identified them as Iraqi.

July 14
DIPLOMACY: In Islamabad, Pakistan, the minister of foreign affairs promises to close the office of Mullah Salam (Roketi) if he does not release his hostages immediately.

July 20
POLITICS: In Herat, Afghanistan, a *loya jirga* attracts 700 participants and proceeds to debate a political solution to the internecine violence of late.

July 24
POLITICS: In Herat, Afghanistan, President Burhanuddin Rabbani arrives but fails to participate in the assembly convening there.

July 29
MILITARY: In a region controlled by mujahideen of Gulbuddin Hekmatyar, BBC correspondent Mir Wais Jalil is inexplicably killed.

August
POLITICS: In Kandahar, Afghanistan, Mullah Mohammad Omar, a one-eyed veteran of the Soviet invasion, founds the new Taliban movement.

August 2
AVIATION: Two B-52s from the 2nd Bomb Wing fly a record world circumnavigation mission in 47 continuous hours with five aerial refuelings. They land in Kuwait on the fourth anniversary of the Iraqi invasion.

August 7
POLITICS: In Kabul, Afghanistan, extended talks unfold between President Burhanuddin Rabbani and Ahmad Gailani, Mohammad Nabi Mohammadi, and Harkat Muhseni.

August 16
AVIATION: In Islamabad, Pakistan, the government bans Afghanistan's Ariana Airlines for various breaches of international regulations.

September 8
MILITARY: The town of Khenjan, north of the strategic Salang Pass, Afghanistan, is captured by mujahideen of the Hezb-i-Islami.

September 12
MILITARY: In Darulaman, Afghanistan, combat breaks out between fighters belonging to the Islamic Unity Party and the Islamic Revolutionary Party.

September 25
POLITICS: A cease-fire among feuding Shiite mujahideen factions is brokered by the Iranian government.

October
MILITARY: In an ominous but little-appreciated development, a militia force consisting of religious students headed by Mullah Omar seizes Kandahar, Afghanistan. They call themselves the Taliban, or "Students of Religion."

October 2
POLITICS: In Islamabad, Pakistan, the government announces that it is seizing and holding Afghan transit goods for security reasons.

October 6
MILITARY: Without warning, Iraqi president Saddam Hussein orders his army along the Kuwaiti border. It is not clear if he intends to invade or simply apply pressure to his southern neighbor.

October 7
DIPLOMACY: In New York City, the Security Council passes Resolution 949 to condemn Iraq's deployment along the Kuwaiti border and orders their removal.
MILITARY: In response to President Saddam Hussein's order that Iraqi military forces move to the Kuwaiti border, President Bill Clinton deploys navy and marine forces into the theater. The president warns that the United States will defend all its Gulf allies.

October 8–December 22
DIPLOMACY: In Kuwait City, Western diplomats are incredulous that Iraqi president Saddam Hussein appears bent on provoking a new military confrontation with the same powers that so completely humbled him three years previously. It appears the crisis has been manufactured to protest existing economic sanctions that are still in place.
MILITARY: The 15th Marine Expeditionary Unit (SOC) positions itself off Kuwait City in the Persian Gulf in the event of hostilities with Iraq.
NAVAL: In light of recent Iraqi maneuvers near the Kuwaiti border, the guided-missile cruiser *Leyte Gulf,* the *George Washington* carrier battle group, and the *Tripoli* amphibious ready group begin deploying in the Red Sea region.

October 9
DIPLOMACY: In Washington, D.C., President Bill Clinton explicitly warns Iraqi president Saddam Hussein that if his forces invade Kuwait again, they would likewise be expelled by another massive armed response.

October 10
AVIATION: Air force warplanes begin arriving in Kuwait during Operation Vigilant Warrior to deter possible Iraqi aggression in the Persian Gulf region. Within days, the number of aircraft in the theater has increased from 77 to 270, including F-15s, F-16s, and A-10s.

MILITARY: In response to recent Iraqi movements toward the Kuwaiti border, President Bill Clinton orders the deployment of 36,000 American troops to the Persian Gulf, backed by warships and hundreds of aircraft. Meanwhile, elements of the 24th Infantry Division (Mechanized) deploy with Kuwaiti units as a precaution.

POLITICS: In Washington, D.C., President William J. Clinton makes a televised address, saying that President Saddam Hussein of Iraq cannot be trusted so existing UN sanctions against Iraq will not be lifted until that country fully complies with UN resolutions.

October 11
DIPLOMACY: The International Committee of the Red Cross estimates that, to date, the latest round of civil strife in Afghanistan has killed 1,100 people and wounded 23,000 during the month of September alone.

October 12
MILITARY: In Washington, D.C., the Pentagon reports that Iraqi forces have pulled back from the Kuwaiti border. Also, the six nations of the Gulf Cooperation Council—Bahrain, Kuwait, Oman, Qatar, Saudi Arabia, and the United Arab Emirates—have all agreed to pay the costs associated with the U.S. deployment.

October 14–16
AVIATION: At Langley Air Force Base, Virginia, a pair of C-17 Globemaster IIIs fly their first logistical mission by conveying military supplies to Saudi Arabia.

October 16
DIPLOMACY: In Baghdad, Iraq, the government-controlled media announce that Iraq will comply with UN demands to withdraw all military forces from the Kuwaiti border.

In New York City, the UN Security Council votes to condemn Iraqi president Saddam Hussein's threatening moves in the Persian Gulf region. However, U.S. officials declare that Iraq appears to be backing down by withdrawing its forces.

October 28
MILITARY: In Kuwait, President William J. Clinton pays a visit to troops deployed at Camp Doha; critics charge he is trying to improve his ratings at home by going abroad.

October 31–November 1
AVIATION: At Ellsworth Air Force Base, North Dakota, a pair of B-1B Lancers fly nonstop for 25 hours to reach a bombing range in Kuwait. This mission also marks their operational debut in the Persian Gulf region.

November 2

MILITARY: Between Spin Boldak and Kandahar, Afghanistan, a Pakistani convoy headed for Turkmenistan is accosted by various Afghan mujahideen groups; fighting breaks out between the guerrillas over what to do with their captives.

November 5

MILITARY: In Kandahar, Afghanistan, the newly formed Taliban, who preach an extreme form of Sunni Islam, execute a number of defenders who had previously opposed them. Their ruthlessness is pronounced, even by rough-and-tumble Afghan standards.

November 7

DIPLOMACY: In Kabul, Afghanistan, the government accuses Uzbekistan of interfering in its internal affairs by supplying General Abdul Rashid Dostum with 30 tanks.

November 8

DIPLOMACY: For the first time in seven months, a UN deputation arrives at Kabul, Afghanistan, for talks.

November 10

DIPLOMACY: In Baghdad, Iraq, the National Assembly formally recognizes Kuwaiti independence and its existing borders; President Saddam Hussein also signs a decree to the same effect.

November 11

DIPLOMACY: In New York City, the United Nations appeals for $106.4 million in humanitarian aid to assist the people of Afghanistan.

November 13

MILITARY: In Kandahar, Afghanistan, Taliban forces repel an attack launched by various factions. The city subsequently serves as the movement's spiritual center.

November 14

DIPLOMACY: In New York City, the UN Security Council elects to keep all economic sanctions in place against Iraq, especially those pertaining to oil exports. Evidence has been obtained that President Saddam Hussein is living lavishly while most of Iraq's population lacks adequate food and medicine.

November 17

DIPLOMACY: In Islamabad, Pakistan, the minister of the interior declares that his government will begin repairing the road from Kandahar to Kabul, Afghanistan. The government in Kabul denounces this move as an "invasion."

November 25

MILITARY: Helmand Province, Afghanistan, is taken over by a Taliban offensive.

December 5
POLITICS: In Kabul, Afghanistan, a convoy of 64 UN trucks delivers aid for the first time in six months. However, its cargo is divided between the followers of President Burhanuddin Rabbani and his opponents.

December 12
DIPLOMACY: In Kabul, Afghanistan, President Burhanuddin Rabbani departs for Morocco to attend the Organization of the Islamic Conference.

December 13
POLITICS: In Kunduz, Afghanistan, the first UN aid convoy in two years arrives.

December 15
MILITARY: In Washington, D.C., Defense Secretary William Perry declares that Kuwait is no longer in military danger of being invaded.

December 19
DIPLOMACY: In New Delhi, India, the government announces that it is reopening its embassy in Kabul, Afghanistan.

December 20
DIPLOMACY: In Islamabad, Pakistan, General Abdul Rashid Dostum arrives for peace talks with various leaders.

December 28
DIPLOMACY: In Islamabad, Pakistan, a UN emissary arrives to reopen and facilitate peace talks among feuding mujahideen factions.

December 30
DIPLOMACY: In Afghanistan, a delegation from Sudan arrives for talks with Prime Minister Gulbuddin Hekmatyar.

1995

January 1
MILITARY: In Pakistan, around 3,000 armed Taliban fighters, mostly ethnic Pashtuns, begin filtering back into southern Afghanistan.
POLITICS: In Kabul, Afghanistan, President Burhanuddin Rabbani announces that he is not stepping down from office at the end of his term. UN peace envoys are called in to help find a peaceful solution. Meanwhile, mujahideen leader Yunnis Khalis returns to Jalalabad following a 19-year hiatus.

January 4
DIPLOMACY: In Jalalabad, Afghanistan, the UN envoy opens a new office and begins negotiating with Gulbuddin Hekmatyar. Meanwhile, in Kabul, President Burhanuddin Rabbani meets with the U.S. ambassador to Pakistan.

January 6
DIPLOMACY: In Paris, France, French officials meet with a high-ranking Iraqi diplomat and agree to open a diplomatic office in Baghdad. The decision is openly criticized by officials in Washington and London.

January 10
POLITICS: In Kabul, Afghanistan, President Burhanuddin Rabbani offers to hand over his office to a UN-brokered interim administration provided that the forces of Gulbuddin Hekmatyar stop shelling the city.

January 12
POLITICS: In Afghanistan, a cease-fire is announced contingent upon Burhanuddin Rabbani stepping down from the presidency.

January 17
POLITICS: In Sarobi, Afghanistan, a UN aid convoy is plundered by mujahideen loyal to Gulbuddin Hekmatyar.

January 19
AVIATION: Kabul, Afghanistan, is shelled by mujahideen loyal to Gulbuddin Hekmatyar; 22 people are reported killed and many more wounded.

January 22
MILITARY: Kabul, Afghanistan, is once again surrounded and blockaded by the forces of Gulbuddin Hekmatyar.

January 24
MILITARY: The city of Ghazni, Afghanistan, is captured by a Taliban offensive.

January 26
MILITARY: In Kunduz Province, Afghanistan, heavy fighting erupts between the forces of General Abdul Rashid Dostum and the Afghan army; at least 100 soldiers are reported killed and 120 injured.

In Miami, Florida, the Teledyne Corporation agrees to pay $13 million in fines after being charged with selling tons of materials to Iraq capable of being used in cluster bombs.

January 27–31
MILITARY: In Ghazni Province, Afghanistan, the forces of Gulbuddin Hekmatyar are forced from their positions by an alliance between the mujahideen of Burhanuddin Rabbani and the Taliban. Apparently, Hekmatyar sustains heavy losses in terms of men and equipment.

January 28
POLITICS: In Afghanistan, the United Nations declares that plans are being formalized to allow Burhanuddin Rabbani to resign from the presidency while power is transferred to an interim council of opposition leaders.

February 5
MILITARY: Kunduz, Afghanistan, falls to the forces of General Abdul Rashid Dostum, after which widespread looting is reported.

February 10
MILITARY: In Warduk Province, Afghanistan, Maidan Shahr falls to a surging Taliban offensive; previously, it was a stronghold of Gulbuddin Hekmatyar.
POLITICS: In Kabul, Afghanistan, the UN envoy declares that President Burhanuddin Rabbani will hand over his office to a committee of 20 people as of February 20.

February 11
MILITARY: In Logar Province, Afghanistan, the Taliban claim to have seized controlled of Pul-i-Alam, the provincial capital.

February 13
MILITARY: In Afghanistan, a prompt counterattack by mujahideen loyal to Burhanuddin Rabbani retakes Kunduz from the Uzbek militia.

February 14
MILITARY: In Logar Province, Afghanistan, the Taliban storm into the Charasyab headquarters of Gulbuddin Hekmatyar; having abandoned his heavy weapons, Hekmatyar withdraws to Sarobi and thereafter ceases to be a major factor in the Afghan civil war.

February 15
DIPLOMACY: In Paris, France, industry sources indicate that Iraq has arranged to sell $700 million of crude oil in violation of UN sanctions.
MILITARY: In Logar Province, Afghanistan, Taliban forces occupy the major settlements of Puli-i-Charkhi and Khost, driving Hezb-i-Islami fighters before them.

February 17
AVIATION: In Kabul, Afghanistan, the Kabul airport reopens for service following a year of closure.

February 19
MILITARY: In southern Afghanistan, a surging Taliban offensive seizes control of Sharan in Paktika Province and Gardez in Paktia Province.

February 20
POLITICS: In Kabul, Afghanistan, once President Burhanuddin Rabbani fails to step down from power, the UN envoy concedes his transfer of power plan has failed.

February 22
POLITICS: In Kabul, Afghanistan, President Burhanuddin Rabbani again refuses to step down unless the Taliban participate in interim administration discussions.

February 23
DIPLOMACY: In Washington, D.C., Russian deputy foreign minister Georgi Mamedov informs the United States that his country will continue assisting Iran to obtain a nuclear-powered reactor on the Persian Gulf for commercial usage.

February 25

POLITICS: The growing Taliban movement threatens to attack Kabul, Afghanistan, if President Burhanuddin Rabbani does not lay down his arms.

February 25–27

MILITARY: In southwestern Afghanistan, mujahideen loyal to Burhanuddin Rabbani and the Hezb-i-Wahdat struggle to control the areas of Karte Seh, Kote Sangi, and Karte Chahar.

February 27

TERRORISM: In Zakho, Iraq, a car bomb explodes, killing 54 Kurds and injuring 80. This town is under UN protection, and it is immediately suspected that Iraqi government operatives were behind the blast.

March 5

POLITICS: Shiite leader Abdul Ali Mazari announces that he will recognize the regime in Kabul, Afghanistan, if the minority Hazara receive an automatic 25 percent representation.

March 6–10

MILITARY: Fighting against the Hezb-i-Wahdat continues, so they strike a deal with the Taliban, which had been blocking their escape routes. Henceforth, Taliban fighters advance into Darulaman and occupy the Wahdat front lines, disarm forces loyal to Abdul Ali Mazari, and launch attacks against the forces of Burhanuddin Rabbani. Casualties are reported as 100 to 150 fighters killed and more than 1,000 civilians wounded.

March 9

POLITICS: Harakat leader Mohammad Nabi Mohammadi enters into discussions with the Taliban, withdrawing his support from President Burhanuddin Rabbani; several members of the administration also resign.

March 11

MILITARY: A prompt counterattack by Jamiat forces captures territory previously claimed by Wahdat, including a Scud missile base at Darulaman.

March 12

DIPLOMACY: In Tehran, Iran, the government declares that it will repatriate 500,000 Afghan refugees this year. To that end, it withdraws temporary living permits, declines to renew work permits, and scales back welfare facilities.

In New York City, the United States, bolstered by satellite intelligence that Iraqi president Saddam Hussein is quietly rebuilding his military at the expense of the civilian population, turns back attempts by France, Russia, and China to remove UN economic sanctions against Iraq.

MILITARY: Mujahideen loyal to President Burhanuddin Rabbani attack Taliban forces in the Karte Seh region, driving them out. Reports surface that the city's Hazara (Shiite) population was roughly handled by Rabbani's forces. In return, Taliban artillery shells Kabul, Afghanistan, as their fighters withdraw.

March 13
POLITICS: The Shiite Hezb-i-Wahdat leader Abdul Ali Mazari dies under mysterious circumstances while in Taliban custody. His successor, Karim Khalili, cannot prevent splits from occurring in the party.

In Iraq, two American employees of the McDonnell Douglas Corporation are arrested after they accidentally stray across the border from Kuwait.

March 14
POLITICS: In Afghanistan, the Taliban claim to have complete control of Ghowr and Nimruz Provinces.

March 16
POLITICS: In Kabul, Afghanistan, President Burhanuddin Rabbani declares that he is delaying his resignation, slated for March 21, by 15 days.

March 19
MILITARY: In Logar Province, Afghanistan, fighters loyal to Ahmad Shah Massoud force Taliban fighters to abandon their headquarters at Charasyab.

March 20
MILITARY: All Taliban forces are expelled from the region of Kabul, Afghanistan, following the apparent murder of Abdul Ali Mazari, the Shiite mujahideen leader.

March 25
POLITICS: In Baghdad, Iraq, a court sentences two Americans accused of illegally entering the country to eight years in jail. President William J. Clinton condemns the decision.

March 30
TERRORISM: In Charasyab, Afghanistan, a mass grave of 22 Hazara (Shiite) males, bound and executed, is uncovered. It is impossible to ascribe the killings to either the Taliban or forces of Burhanuddin Rabbani, as both of them had recently occupied the town.

April 1
POLITICS: In Afghanistan, Gulbuddin Hekmatyar is replaced as head of the anti-Rabbani alliance. His successor is Sibghatullah Mojaddedi of the Jabhayi Najati Milli Afghanistan.

April 4
DIPLOMACY: In Washington, D.C., President William J. Clinton formally accuses Iraq of attempting to rebuild its capacity to possess weapons of mass destruction (WMD). His cabinet also advises him on the desirability of a near-total trade ban with Iran.

MILITARY: Fighting in Farah Province, Afghanistan, takes the lives of 400 Taliban fighters and 800 mujahideen loyal to Burhanuddin Rabbani. The Taliban also launch several attacks against Shindand Air Base.

April 6–7
DIPLOMACY: In New York City, several UN biological weapons experts announce that Iraq has an undeclared biological weapons program.

April 7
POLITICS: In light of escalating violence, the government of Iran forbids commercial travel there.

April 11
POLITICS: In Washington, D.C., the Central Intelligence Agency asks Congress to appropriate $19 million to fund covert operations against Iraq and Iran.

April 12
POLITICS: In Tashkent, Uzbekistan, Abdul Rahman of Jamiat confers with General Abdul Rashid Dostum over a possible alliance against the Taliban.

April 13
DIPLOMACY: In Afghanistan, the Taliban's leaders insist that foreign countries not reopen their embassies in Kabul.

April 14
DIPLOMACY: In New York City, the UN Security Council passes Resolution 986 to allow Iraq to sell oil to meet emergency food and medical needs. The Iraqi government rejects the resolution and does not accept its terms until December 1996.

April 19
MILITARY: Kabul, Afghanistan, suffers from a fuel blockade imposed by the Taliban.

April 26
MILITARY: In northern Iraq, Turkish forces pull out after destroying base camps and supply depots used by Kurdish guerrillas.

April 27
MILITARY: In Afghanistan, the Taliban release 300 prisoners loyal to General Abdul Rashid Dostum.

April 30
DIPLOMACY: In Washington, D.C., President William J. Clinton declares that the United States is suspending all trade with Iran unless it halts its support of terrorism and intention to acquire nuclear weapons. The president also criticizes ongoing Russian assistance to help Iran obtain a nuclear reactor.

May
MILITARY: At Maidan Shahr, Afghanistan, mujahideen loyal to President Burhanuddin Rabbani continue pressuring Taliban forces to retreat from the capital region.

May 1
DIPLOMACY: In Baghdad, Iraq, spouses are allowed to visit two Americans serving eight years in prison for illegally entering the country.

May 3–4
DIPLOMACY: The governments of India and Pakistan agree to reopen their embassies in Kabul, Afghanistan.

May 5
POLITICS: In Kabul, Afghanistan, militants raid offices of the newspaper *Subh Omid* over its anti-government views.

May 8
DIPLOMACY: In Washington, D.C., President William J. Clinton signs an executive order authorizing a complete trade ban with Iran.

May 9
DIPLOMACY: In Kabul, Afghanistan, the Pakistani ambassador returns to his embassy.
MILITARY: In Farah Province, Afghanistan, mujahideen loyal to President Burhanuddin Rabbani and Jamiat governor Ismail Khan attack and eject Taliban forces from the region.

May 13
DIPLOMACY: In Baghdad, Iraq, the government contests U.S. charges that it plans to obtain nuclear weapons and reveals plans to construct 10 nuclear power plants over the next two decades.

May 15
MILITARY: In Helmand Province, Afghanistan, combined action by forces loyal to Burhanuddin Rabbani and Ismail Khan results in a Taliban withdrawal.

May 16
MILITARY: Nimruz Province, Afghanistan, falls to fighters of the anti-Taliban alliance.

May 24
POLITICS: Prolonged negotiations between Afghan president Burhanuddin Rabbani and General Abdul Rashid Dostum result in the Salang Highway being reopened. A fatwa proclaiming a jihad against the latter is also rescinded.

June 5
MILITARY: In Samangan and Baghlan Provinces, Afghanistan, forces loyal to General Abdul Rashid Dostum attack mujahideen of President Burhanuddin Rabbani.

June 9
POLITICS: In Afghanistan, a 10-day truce is arranged by the Taliban and its opponents to allow a prisoner exchange, free movement by civilians, and an extension of peace talks.

June 15
AVIATION: Warplanes operated by General Abdul Rashid Dostum carry out bombing raids against Kabul and Kunduz, Afghanistan.

MILITARY: In Washington, D.C., administration spokesmen mention a failed military uprising against Iraqi president Saddam Hussein by an elite Republican Guard unit at the Abu Ghraib prison. The revolt is ruthlessly crushed but does indicate mounting dissatisfaction with the current regime.

June 20

AVIATION: A court-martial clears Captain James Wang, an air force officer, of charges associated with the shooting down of two army helicopters over northern Iraq in April 1994 and the resulting 26 deaths. He was senior officer of a nearby AWACS aircraft and failed to alert intercepting fighters that the helicopters were friendly.

DIPLOMACY: In New York City, a ranking UN monitoring official informs the Security Council that Iraq's biological warfare program is larger than previously estimated.

MILITARY: The town of Bamiyan, Afghanistan, falls to a combined assault by forces loyal to President Burhanuddin Rabbani and the Akbari faction of the Shiite Wahdat. They evict fighters of the hostile Khalili faction within Wahdat.

June 22

POLITICS: Iran begins the forced repatriation of 400,000 Afghan refugees through Herat, Afghanistan.

June 29

MILITARY: In Maidan Shahr, Afghanistan, fighting resumes between Taliban forces and fighters loyal to Burhanuddin Rabbani.

POLITICS: In Islamabad, Pakistan, an envoy from former monarch Mohammad Zahir Shah meets with Afghan officials. He indicates the king's willingness to be a participant in the ongoing peace process.

July 1

MILITARY: In Baghdad, Iraq, the government admits for the first time that it had developed offensive biological agents such as anthrax and botulism on the cusp of the Gulf War. However, it denies incorporating the substances into weapons systems.

July 11

DIPLOMACY: In New York City, the Security Council unanimously votes against lifting economic sanctions against Iraq, based on new information that it has been less than forthcoming with its biological weapons program.

July 16

DIPLOMACY: In Baghdad, Iraq, President Saddam Hussein orders the release of two Americans, William Barloon and David Daliberti, who were held captive since they accidentally strayed into Iraqi territory in March. However, U.S. officials view the move as a ploy to get the United Nations to ease or drop existing economic sanctions.

July 23

MILITARY: Bamiyan Province, Afghanistan, falls to the forces of General Abdul Rashid Dostum and the Khalili faction of Wahdat.

July 30

POLITICS: In Kabul, Afghanistan, President Burhanuddin Rabbani urges the United Nations to establish a commission of intellectuals to form a grand assembly (*loya jirga*) for a year, elect a new leader, draft a new constitution, and institute a parliament from commission members.

August 3

AVIATION: In Kandahar, Afghanistan, the Taliban hijack a Russian cargo plane carrying arms for President Burhanuddin Rabbani. The hijackers demand the release of all Afghans being held in Russian jails; the crewmen remain hostage for a year.

August 8

POLITICS: In Iraq, Lieutenant General Hussein Kamel Hassan al-Majid and Lieutenant Colonel Saddam Kamel Hassan al-Majid, both sons-in-law of President Saddam Hussein and highly placed officials in national weapons programs, defect to Jordan with wives and families in tow. They are also accompanied by several senior officers. The act is considered a blow to Iraq's international standing, and the elder brother is expected to shed new light on Iraq's chemical, biological, and nuclear programs, all of which he helped direct.

August 10

DIPLOMACY: In Washington, D.C., President William J. Clinton pledges his support for King Hussein of Jordan after he grants political asylum to Saddam Hussein's defecting sons-in-law.

August 12

DIPLOMACY: In Amman, Jordan, newly defected Lieutenant General Hussein Kamel Hassan al-Majid calls upon the Iraqi army to overthrow the regime of President Saddam Hussein.

August 13

DIPLOMACY: In Baghdad, Iraq, Deputy Prime Minister Tariq Aziz declares that Iraq will release information it had been withholding from the United Nations. This change of heart is brought about by the defections of President Saddam Hussein's sons-in law.

August 14

DIPLOMACY: In Amman, Jordan, King Hussein states that it is time for a change of leadership in Iraq.

August 17

NAVAL: Threatening Iraqi troop movements along the Kuwaiti border result in the deployment of the *Abraham Lincoln* and *Independence* carrier battle groups, assisted by the *New Orleans* amphibious ready group. The carrier *Theodore Roosevelt* is also put on alert in the eastern Mediterranean.

POLITICS: In Sistan Province, Iran, the government purges itself of additional Afghan refugees by forcibly sending them home.

August 17–20

DIPLOMACY: In Baghdad, Iraq, UN special chairman Rolf Ekeus meets with Iraqi officials and acquires new information concerning Iraq's biological and nuclear weapons programs.

August 20

DIPLOMACY: In Baghdad, Iraq, UN inspectors obtain huge amounts of documentation purportedly pertaining to several prohibited weapons programs. Agents in the field also learn that specific biological agents had been destroyed after the 1991 Gulf War, and before, as maintained by the government. Anxiety grows that such weapons remain hidden within Iraq's military arsenal.

August 21

POLITICS: In a sign of rising Islamization, all cinemas in Kabul, Afghanistan, are shut down by the government to halt the spread of immorality. Moreover, foreign videos are destroyed, and female singers are banned from the media.

August 22

DIPLOMACY: In Baghdad, Iraq, the government admits it has manufactured lethal botulinum and anthrax bacteria as part of a comprehensive biological weapons program.

Internally displaced persons and returning refugees from Afghanistan wait outside a mobile clinic run by Relief International, during the fighting that unsettled Afghanistan before the Taliban seized power in 1998. *(Photo by R. Colville/United Nations)*

August 25
DIPLOMACY: In Baghdad, Iraq, UN special chairman Rolf Ekeus says that Iraq began a crash program to acquire nuclear weapons in 1990, but it was bombed out of existence during the 1991 Gulf War.

August 25–29
AVIATION: In their first major exercise as an operational unit, 11 new C-17 Globemaster IIIs of the 315th and 437th Airlift Wings haul 300 tons of troops and equipment to Kuwait.

August 28
MILITARY: Girishk village, Helmand Province is captured from the Taliban by the Afghan army, although the settlement is recaptured two days later.

August 31
MILITARY: In Erbil, northern Iraq, Iraqi military units launch an all-out attack against the Kurds by capturing this, their largest city, even though it is under the protection of the northern "no-fly zone."

POLITICS: In Kabul, Afghanistan, the nation's female delegation is banned from attending the World Conference on Women in Beijing, China. The government cites the un-Islamic nature of the agenda, namely, family planning and abortion.

September
MILITARY: The forces of General Abdul Rashid Dostum are gradually driven out of Badghis Province, Afghanistan, by the Taliban.

September 2
MILITARY: A resurgent Taliban offensive captures Farah Province, Afghanistan, along with the city of Shindand. The nation's largest air force base is located here.

September 3
AVIATION: In New York City, the UN Security Council decrees that the Iraqi southern "no-fly zone" is to be extended to latitude 33 degrees north.

September 5
MILITARY: Herat, Afghanistan, is captured by the Taliban, forcing Governor Ismail Khan to flee to Iran. Observers comment that its capture could not have been possible without the assistance of Gulbuddin Hekmatyar and General Abdul Rashid Dostum. Presently the Taliban control 13 provinces out of 30.

September 6
DIPLOMACY: After the Afghan government complains about Pakistani interference in its affairs, a mob estimated at 5,000 attack the Pakistan embassy in Kabul, killing one staff member and injuring 26. Pakistan closes the embassy but does not sever diplomatic relations.

POLITICS: Iran closes its borders and blocks the repatriating refugees following the fall of Herat, Afghanistan, to the Taliban.

September 7
MILITARY: Ghowr Province, Afghanistan, falls to a Taliban offensive.

September 8
DIPLOMACY: In New York City, the UN Security Council again extends existing economic sanctions against Iraq after the government reveals that it had secretly produced biological warfare agents. Unconfirmed information has also surfaced intimating that President Saddam Hussein is secretly pursuing nuclear weapons.

September 15
TERRORISM: In Herat, Afghanistan, a number of bombs aimed at the Taliban explode; casualties are not reported.

September 16
POLITICS: In Herat, Afghanistan, the Taliban expel BBC reporter Kasra Naji on account of what they perceive as "biased reporting."

September 21
AVIATION: The Taliban force down an Ariana airliner carrying spare parts over Kandahar, Afghanistan.
DIPLOMACY: In Islamabad, Pakistan, the government suddenly expels 13 Afghan diplomats without explaining why.

September 24
TERRORISM: In Herat, Afghanistan, more explosive devices are aimed at the Taliban, and reports of sabotage are reported.

October 9
DIPLOMACY: In Islamabad, Pakistan, the government expels Afghan ambassador Masud Halili; another six diplomats follow him on October 18.

October 11
MILITARY: The city of Charasyab, Afghanistan, falls to the latest Taliban offensive; large numbers of civilians are reported killed and injured in the shelling.
POLITICS: In Kabul, Afghanistan, the National Reconciliation Commission shows its peace proposal to President Burhanuddin Rabbani prior to presenting it to leaders in other provinces.

October 15
MILITARY: The town of Bamiyan, Afghanistan falls to a Taliban offensive, but mujahideen loyal to Burhanuddin Rabbani capture the Sanglakh Valley, very close to Maidan Shahr.
POLITICS: In Iraq, a national referendum authorizing Saddam Hussein to remain as president for another seven years is passed by almost 100 percent of the voters.

November
AVIATION: In Amman, Jordan, the government reportedly confiscates a shipment of missile parts headed for Iraq.

November 6
POLITICS: In Kabul, Afghanistan, President Burhanuddin Rabbani informs the United Nations that he is willing to resign immediately if a cease-fire can be arranged with the Taliban and all foreign intervention halts. However, the offer is suspended once fighting erupts in the capital.

November 10
DIPLOMACY: Responding to the closure of girls' schools in Herat and Jalalabad, Afghanistan, by Taliban forces, UNICEF terminates all education and training programs in the region.

November 11
MILITARY: Kabul, Afghanistan, is struck by Taliban rockets that inflict widespread damage and kill a reported 35 civilians.

A determined offensive by government forces loyal to President Burhanuddin Rabbani drives the Uzbek militia of General Abdul Rashid Dostum from several towns and regions in Balkh Province, Afghanistan.

November 13
MILITARY: Kabul, Afghanistan, is again shelled by Taliban forces, which kill another 21 civilians.

TERRORISM: In Riyadh, Saudi Arabia, a bomb explodes outside a Saudi National Guard facility, killing a soldier and four civilians attached to the U.S. Army Materiel Command. Another 60 people, mostly Saudis, are injured, and intelligence points to a little-known Saudi dissident named Osama bin Laden.

November 26
AVIATION: Warplanes operated by the Taliban attack various targets in Kabul, Afghanistan, killing 40 civilians and wounding 140.

November 27
POLITICS: In Kabul, Afghanistan, Sibghatullah Mojaddidi resigns as president of the Supreme Coordination Council while leadership of the Jabha faction withdraws completely.

November 30
MILITARY: Kabul, Afghanistan, is subject to another intense Taliban bombardment, resulting in the deaths of 17 civilians and an additional 26 wounded.

December 1
AVIATION: Warplanes flown by government pilots drop bombs on Taliban positions outside of Kabul, Afghanistan. The Taliban retaliate by shelling residential areas and the local airport.

December 5
POLITICS: In Kabul, Afghanistan, demonstrations erupt to protest the ongoing civil war and bombing of residential areas. A petition is also handed to UN representatives demanding action to prevent further attacks on civilians.

December 9
AVIATION: Afghan air force jets bomb Taliban targets in Charasyab, Afghanistan; 37 Taliban fighters are reported killed along with several civilians.

December 12
MILITARY: Kabul, Afghanistan, receives another heavy shelling at the hands of the Taliban; heavy property damage and loss of life are reported.

December 19
MILITARY: Taliban units inflict another heavy bombardment on Kabul, Afghanistan; casualties are not known but are presumed significant.

December 25–30
MILITARY: Taliban units unleash intermittent rocket attacks on Kabul, Afghanistan, further underscoring the government's impotence.

December 30
POLITICS: At Mazar-i-Sharif, Afghanistan, a deputation from President Burhanuddin Rabbani meets with aides of General Abdul Rashid Dostum about a possible negotiated settlement. Surging Taliban strength has many factions worried about the future.

1996

January 2–3
MILITARY: Kabul, Afghanistan, is staggered by another round of Taliban rocket fire that kills 24 civilians; the government claims the attack was aimed at derailing peace proposals.

January 10
POLITICS: In Kabul, Afghanistan, the government tenders a peace offer to the Taliban and all opposition groups, calling for a cease-fire, a prisoner exchange, and peace talks. President Burhanuddin Rabbani, however, makes no mention of resigning his office.

January 10–12
MILITARY: The Taliban launch another round of rocket attacks on residential areas of Kabul, Afghanistan.

January 14
MILITARY: The Taliban tightens its grip around Kabul, Afghanistan, and the inhabitants suffer from a lack of food and fuel.
POLITICS: President Burhanuddin Rabbani concludes a peace agreement with the Khalili faction of the Shiite Hezb-i-Wahdat, which covers a cease-fire, a prisoner exchange, and reopening of the Kabul-Bamiyan road.

January 17
DIPLOMACY: In New York City, Iraq and the United Nations agree to consider talks on the sale of $1 billion in oil-for-food, in which the proceeds would fund the purchase of food and medicine for the population under strict UN supervision.

January 20
MILITARY: In Afghanistan, reports surface of intense fighting between Taliban factions in Kandahar, Ghazni, Wardak, and Logar Provinces. The struggle erupts over Mullah Omar's desire to hold peace talks with President Burhanuddin Rabbani; the hard-core faction of Mullah Borjan seeks to keep on fighting.

January 29
MILITARY: Kabul, Afghanistan, is struck by another round of Taliban rocket attacks.
POLITICS: Demonstrations erupt in Kabul, Afghanistan, over President Burhanuddin Rabbani's continuation in office, with many calling for him to turn power over to an interim government.

February 1
MILITARY: Continued shelling of Kabul, Afghanistan, by Taliban forces results in heavy damage in the area of the Grand Mosque, with scores of civilian casualties.

February 3
AVIATION: In Kabul, Afghanistan, the International Committee of the Red Cross manages to land aircraft from Peshawar, Pakistan, carrying sufficient food to feed 100,000 people.

February 6
POLITICS: A relief convoy of 400 trucks finally pulls into Kabul, Afghanistan; they had been delayed when militias on roads from Pakistan and Jalalabad demanded a bounty for each vehicle.

February 11
MILITARY: Afghan forces engage Taliban units on the fringes of southern Kabul, Afghanistan.

February 13
POLITICS: In Kabul, Afghanistan, Sibghatullah Mojaddidi decides to rejoin the Supreme Coordinating Council.

February 14
POLITICS: In Islamabad, Pakistan, UN-sponsored peace talks are arranged between the Taliban and all major opposition parties, but they conclude without an agreement being reached.

February 22
POLITICS: In Kabul and Sarobi, Afghanistan, President Burhanuddin Rabbani attempts a new series of peace talks with mujahideen leader Gulbuddin Hekmatyar.

February 23
POLITICS: In Baghdad, Iraq, the two sons-in-law of President Saddam Hussein, who defected to Jordan then returned home under a government pardon, are killed by family members for being "traitors" to the nation. A third brother, the defectors' father, and two of the attackers are also slain.

February 26

MILITARY: In Baghlan Province, Afghanistan, severe fighting ensues among numerous factions, and hundreds of deaths and injuries are reported.

February 27

DIPLOMACY: The UN High Commissioner for Refugees reports that 391,000 Afghans were repatriated in 1995, but there are still 400,000 internal refugees residing in the vicinity of Jalalabad.

March

POLITICS: It is reported that in all Taliban-controlled regions, each household must contribute one family member to perform hard labor, a 10 percent tax is imposed on all earnings, and all vehicles are confiscated.

March 4

POLITICS: In Afghanistan, the organization Save the Children suspends operations in Taliban-controlled areas due to restrictions placed upon them.

March 7

POLITICS: A treaty between President Burhanuddin Rabbani and mujahideen leader Gulbuddin Hekmatyar commits them to an alliance to fight the Taliban. They also agree to restore all electricity to Kabul.

March 12–13

AVIATION: Afghan air force warplanes attack Taliban forces in the settlements of Charasyab and Muhammad Aga.

March 13

DIPLOMACY: In Tehran, Iran, the government declares that another 250,000 Afghan refugees are to be repatriated to northern Afghanistan through Turkmenistan.
MILITARY: As Taliban forces shell Kabul, Afghanistan, they are attacked by government warplanes.

March 17

DIPLOMACY: In Baghdad, Iraq, authorities deny UN weapons inspectors access to five inspection sites for over 17 hours.

March 19

DIPLOMACY: In New York City, the UN Security Council issues a formal complaint that Iraq's obstruction of weapon inspection teams violates agreed-to resolutions. However, no punitive actions are mentioned at this time.

March 30

POLITICS: In Kandahar, Afghanistan, the Taliban leadership calls for a council of 1,000 ulema (clerics) to establish future policy.

April 3

POLITICS: In Kandahar, Afghanistan, a gathering of 1,000 Muslim clergy elect Mullah Omar as "commander of the faithful," although the Supreme Coordination Council (SCC) rejects this appointment.

April 8
AVIATION: In Amman, Jordan, the government of King Hussein makes a distinct reversal in policy by allowing U.S. warplanes to fly patrols over southern Iraq from Jordanian air bases.

April 11
MILITARY: In Washington, D.C., the Pentagon issues a 63-page report outlining the apparent spread of weapons of mass destruction. They believe this trend represents as much of a military threat to U.S. survival as did the Soviet Union during the cold war.

    In Ghowr Province, Afghanistan, government forces capture the Saghar district from the Taliban, but the Taliban strike back by seizing the Sharak district.

April 18
POLITICS: In Herat, Afghanistan, the Taliban order all civil servants to grow their beards or lose their jobs.

May–June
MILITARY: At al-Hakam, Iraq, UN weapons inspectors direct the dismantling of Iraq's main facility for manufacturing biological warfare agents. The site is only 50 miles southwest of Baghdad, and concerns will arise that the Iraqis are now employing mobile tractor-trailer labs to avoid detection.

May 4
MILITARY: In Kabul, Afghanistan, Taliban gunners shell the Iranian embassy, wounding two staff members.

May 12
MILITARY: In Kabul, Afghanistan, mujahideen loyal to Gulbuddin Hekmatyar are allowed into the city to help President Burhanuddin Rabbani's forces defend it against the Taliban.

May 20
DIPLOMACY: In New York City, the United Nations and Iraq come to an agreement to sell $2 billion worth of oil supplies every 90 days over the next six months and under strict UN supervision. This is done to mitigate the suffering of the Iraqi populace, who have endured six years of economic sanctions. A portion of the sales is also to be set aside for Kuwaitis who lost relatives in the 1991 Gulf War.

POLITICS: In Tehran, Iran, the government announces that the Taliban have executed Mullah Abdul Rahman, their own commander in Wardak Province, Afghanistan, for attempting to contact the opposition.

May 24
POLITICS: In Kabul, Afghanistan, Gulbuddin Hekmatyar and Burhanuddin Rabbani give mutual consent to national elections to form a "real Islamic government." In response, the Taliban forms a counter-meeting with Yunnis Khalis, Mohammad Nabi Mohammadi, Ahmad Gailani, and General Abdul Rashid Dostum.

May 30
POLITICS: In Kabul, Afghanistan, popular demonstrations outside of UN offices demand international aid for mine-clearing operations.

June 1
MILITARY: In Ghowr Province, Afghanistan, a surging Taliban offensive storms into Chaghcharan, the provincial capital.

June 5
DIPLOMACY: In Vienna, Austria, the Organization of the Petroleum Exporting Countries meets to discuss how to cope with falling oil prices once newly released Iraqi oil hits the spot market.

In Washington, D.C., the State Department declares that U.S. oil companies will be allowed to purchase Iraqi oil as it appears on the world market.

June 7
POLITICS: The Supreme Coordination Council rejects Gulbuddin Hekmatyar's membership due to his recent alliance with President Burhanuddin Rabbani.

A UN inspector uses a chemical air monitor to detect leakage from a CS-filled 120mm mortar shell at Fallujah Chemical Proving Ground. *(UN Photo)*

June 11
AVIATION: General Abdul Rashid Dostum founds Balkh Airlines to ferry passengers and freight between Mazar-i-Sharif, Pakistan, Iran, and Central Asia. The Pakistani government subsequently grants him landing rights in Peshawar.

June 12
DIPLOMACY: In New York City, the UN Security Council passes Resolution 1060, which condemns Iraq's refusal to cooperate fully with UN weapons inspectors. Moreover, the head of the UN Special Commission informs the news media that, in light of his inspectors' inability to do their task, suspicions are strong that President Saddam Hussein still possesses weapons of mass destruction and a clandestine armament program.

June 13
DIPLOMACY: In Baghdad, Iraq, the government again obstructs a weapons inspection team from completing its mission. This prompts the UN Security Council to ask the UN Special Commission's executive chairman to visit Iraq in person and demand access to all sites of interest.

June 17
DIPLOMACY: In New York City, the Banque Nationale de Paris is selected by the United Nations to maintain sales accounts of Iraqi oil exports, from which proceeds food and medical supplies are to be purchased.

June 18
MILITARY: The ongoing Taliban offensive captures various government outposts in Nimruz Province.

June 19
POLITICS: In Kabul, Afghanistan, a new political deal is cut between President Burhanuddin Rabbani and Gulbuddin Hekmatyar, which allows the latter to serve again as prime minister.

June 22
DIPLOMACY: In Baghdad, Iraq, the chief executive of the UN Special Commission declares that Iraqi officials have agreed to grant weapons inspectors access to areas suspected of containing illegal weapons materials. In exchange, the commission is to take into consideration the country's "sensitive areas," a euphemism for legitimate security concerns.

June 24
MILITARY: In the Shor Desert near Mazar-i-Sharif, the northern warlord Rasul Pahalwan is ambushed and killed by unknown assailants.

June 25
TERRORISM: The Khobar Towers, an American apartment complex in Dhahran, Saudi Arabia, is struck by a terrorist truck bomb that kills 19 air force personnel and wounds 300. Most of the casualties were present in support of Operation Southern

Watch, and, again, the name of Osama bin Laden is mentioned as a facilitator of the blast.

June 26
POLITICS: In Kabul, Afghanistan, Gulbuddin Hekmatyar is formally sworn in as prime minister. The Taliban counter by shelling the city, killing 60 people and wounding 150.

July 1
DIPLOMACY: In Washington, D.C., the administration objects to Iraqi plans to distribute humanitarian supplies obtained from oil exports, mostly on the grounds that it allows the government unsupervised control over their distribution. Certain loopholes also allow Baghdad to evade certain economic sanctions.

July 3
POLITICS: In Kabul, Afghanistan, President Burhanuddin Rabbani appoints 10 broadly based cabinet members. However, a further 12 portfolios are left open for factions not yet present in the capital.

July 10
DIPLOMACY: German diplomat Norbert Holl is nominated to serve as the new UN special representative to Afghanistan.

July 18
POLITICS: In Afghanistan, the Islamic National Front coalesces around the parties headed by Ahmad Gailani, General Abdul Rashid Dostum, Sibghatullah Mojaddidi, Abdul Karim Khalili, and Saiq Moddabir to strive for a broad-based national government. Haji Qadir is chosen as head of the alliance.

July 22
POLITICS: In Kabul, Afghanistan, Prime Minister Gulbuddin Hekmatyar orders all cinemas in the city closed and bans music and television broadcasts as un-Islamic. Women are ordered to dress modestly, but he does not impose Taliban-like restrictions on work or education.

July 27
DIPLOMACY: In Kabul, Afghanistan, UN special representative Norbert Holl arrives and takes up residence.

July 31
DIPLOMACY: In New York City, the U.S. delegation to the Security Council vetoes adopting procedures that would allow Iraq to sell oil on the international market.

August 5
MILITARY: Heavy fighting breaks out in Paktia, Paktika, Nimruz, and Ghowr Provinces, Afghanistan, as the Taliban intensify their offensive.
POLITICS: In Afghanistan, opposition parties accuse the Taliban of forced conscription and levying taxes to support their war effort.

August 8

DIPLOMACY: In New York City, once the United Nations has approved a scheme for an Iraqi distribution plan for dispersing humanitarian aid, the United States formally drops its opposition to the plan.

MILITARY: Chaghcharan, capital of Ghowr Province, Afghanistan, changes hands several times before the Taliban finally seize it. The victors then round up and execute several people who cooperated with opposition forces; they also fire on women protesting their policies, killing five.

August 13

POLITICS: Prime Minister Gulbuddin Hekmatyar and General Abdul Rashid Dostum agree to a cease-fire that allows the reopening of the Salang Highway, which runs north from Kabul, Afghanistan.

August 14

DIPLOMACY: In Kabul, Afghanistan, the Pakistani embassy is reopened.

August 16

POLITICS: The crew of a Russian air transport hijacked by the Taliban in 1995 escapes captivity and returns home from the United Arab Emirates.

August 17

MILITARY: In Iraqi Kurdistan, fighting erupts between two factions of Kurds, and several attempts by the United States to broker a cease-fire fail.

August 28

DIPLOMACY: In Washington, D.C., the State Department declares that it has evidence that Iraq is smuggling refined oil products to the black market. Kamal Kharazi, the Iraqi delegate to the United Nations, denies the charge, and the United Nations requests that the Americans spell it out in writing.

POLITICS: In eastern Afghanistan, Laghman, Nangarhar, and Nurestan Provinces declare their neutrality in the war between the government of President Burhanuddin Rabbani and the Taliban.

August 29

POLITICS: North of Kabul, Afghanistan, the strategic Salang Highway running north from the capital reopens for the first time in several months.

August 31

MILITARY: In northern Iraq, President Saddam Hussein orders his armored forces to seize Ebril, a Kurdish enclave that also functioned as their de facto capital. Despite the fact that this region is under the protection of the northern "no-fly zone," he ignores a warning from President William J. Clinton to desist and begins rushing additional troops and aircraft into the region.

September 1

DIPLOMACY: In New York City, UN secretary-general Boutros Boutros Ghali suspends the recent oil-selling agreement with Iraq over their seizure of the Kurdish city of Ebril. President William J. Clinton also vows to punish the Iraqis for their aggression and orders naval forces into the region.

In Baghdad, Iraq, Defense Minister Lieutenant General Sultan Hashim Ahmed declares that President Saddam Hussein has ordered the removal of military forces from Ebril.

September 2

MILITARY: In Ebril, Iraqi Kurdistan, Iraqi troops begin pulling back after seizing the city to assist the Kurdish Democratic Party. Before departing, they allegedly conduct house-to-house searches, killing several hundred Kurds.

September 3–4

AVIATION: Following the Iraqi seizure of the city of Ebril, two B-52Hs depart Guam on Operation Desert Strike, fly to the Middle East, and launch 13 cruise missiles against antiaircraft and command-and-control centers in Iraq. This action requires the assistance of 29 tanker aircraft and wins the crew of Duke 01 the Mackay Trophy. This is also the first combat mission of the B-52H.

Reacting to an Iraqi occupation of Kurdish territory in northern Iraq, Operation Desert Strike commences as the guided-missile cruiser *Shiloh*, the guided-missile destroyers *Laboon* and *Russell*, the destroyer *Hewitt*, and the nuclear-powered submarine *Jefferson City* fire 31 Tomahawk missiles against air defense targets.

In Washington, D.C., Defense Secretary William Perry declares that the targets struck by American missiles were chosen less to assist the Kurds than to damage President Saddam Hussein's ability to harm oil-producing nations to the south.

DIPLOMACY: In Baghdad, Iraq, Deputy Premier Tariq Aziz states that his country was well within its rights to come to the "assistance" of the Kurds.

September 4

AVIATION: In Washington, D.C., President William J. Clinton expands the northern "no-fly zone" in Iraq from the 32nd to the 33rd parallel. Britain agrees to the change, but France protests the move and declares that its aircraft will not patrol the new region.

U.S. warplanes and vessels launch another 17 cruise missiles against command-and-control centers throughout Iraq.

DIPLOMACY: A letter is submitted to UN secretary-general Boutros Boutros Ghali concerning the restrictive nature of Taliban rule in Afghanistan.

POLITICS: In Kabul, Afghanistan, female demonstrators protest the restrictions placed on them by the Taliban. Among the groups represented are the Afghan Women's Islamic Movement and the Afghan Women's Islamic Renaissance.

September 5

MILITARY: The Taliban offensive gathers strength and expands throughout eastern regions of the country.

In northern Iraq, President Saddam Hussein formally orders his troops out of Ebril and the Kurdish enclaves.

POLITICS: In Washington, D.C., the U.S. Senate approves a resolution commending recent American air strikes against radar and air defense installation in northern Iraq.

September 9

AVIATION: Iraqi antiaircraft defenses fire several missiles at U.S. warplanes patrolling the northern "no-fly zone."

MILITARY: In Iraqi Kurdistan, fighters of the Kurdish Democratic Party wrest control of Sulaymaniyah, the Kurdish cultural capital, from the rival Patriotic Union of Kurdistan.

September 11

MILITARY: In Nangarhar Province, Afghanistan, Taliban forces storm into the provincial capital of Jalalabad. The road from Kabul to Peshawar, Pakistan, is also cut, leading to a mass influx of war refugees from the city toward the latter. The United Nations temporarily closes down its office to protect staff workers.

September 12

AVIATION: Afghan government warplanes bomb Taliban positions around Jalalabad, Afghanistan, as they advance upon Sarobi, the only access route to Bagram airport.

MILITARY: In Nangarhar Province, Afghanistan, Afghan government forces are rushed to the town of Sarobi in anticipation of a Taliban attack there.

Mehtarlam, capital of Laghman Province, Afghanistan, falls to a surging Taliban offensive.

September 13

MILITARY: After Iraq stops firing on coalition aircraft in the northern and southern "no-fly zones," President William J. Clinton reconsiders launching further attacks.

September 15

DIPLOMACY: In Tehran, Iran, the government reiterates its intention to repatriate 250,000 refugees back to northern Afghanistan through Turkmenistan. The United Nations is cooperating with the effort.

September 15–19

AVIATION: In northern Iraq, air force transports begin Operation Pacific Haven by air-lifting 2,000 Kurdish refugees for processing at Anderson Air Force Base, Guam, prior to settlement in the United States.

September 16

POLITICS: In Tashkent, Uzbekistan, emissaries from President Burhanuddin Rabbani arrive to secure greater military support from General Abdul Rashid Dostum.

September 22

MILITARY: Konar Province, Afghanistan, falls to a surging Taliban offensive.

September 25

MILITARY: In Nangarhar Province, Afghanistan, the Taliban capture the strategic town of Sarobi, along with considerable military supplies and equipment.

September 26

MILITARY: Kabul, Afghanistan, is attacked by Taliban forces approaching from the southeast and southwest, triggering a huge exodus of refugees toward Mazar-i-Sharif. Their advance sparks a withdrawal of mujahideen loyal to Burhanuddin

Rabbani, Gulbuddin Hekmatyar, and Ahmad Shah Massoud from the capital, and they regroup at Jabal Seraj.

POLITICS: The Taliban leadership brands Burhanuddin Rabbani, Gulbuddin Hekmatyar, and Ahmad Shah Massoud as national criminals.

September 27

MILITARY: Kabul, Afghanistan, falls to Taliban forces, who then declare that sharia law will dominate throughout the country. Thousands of civilians begin fleeing the city.

POLITICS: With the capital region firmly under control, the Taliban appoint Mullah Mohammad Rabbani as head of a six-man ruling council. Their first act is to declare an Islamic state and offer amnesty to all government prisoners in Kabul and Kandahar. However, former president Mohammad Najibullah and his brother Shapur Ahmadzai, a former national security chief, are grabbed from the UN compound, then tortured and executed. Their bodies are subsequently hung on public display.

September 28

POLITICS: In Kabul, Afghanistan, the Taliban regime decrees that women are required to wear body-length burqas and be accompanied by a male relative outside the home. They are also forbidden from working or attending school. Moreover, all film, music, television, cassettes and video recorders are summarily banned, as are kites. In a nod to prevailing realities, Sibghatullah Mojaddidi declares his support for the Taliban.

September 29

POLITICS: In Kabul, Afghanistan, civil servants are given six weeks to allow their beards to grow or face dismissal and punishment.

September 30

MILITARY: Once Kapisa Province, Afghanistan, falls to the Taliban, along with the towns of Charikar and Jabal Seraj, the mujahideen of Ahmad Shah Massoud withdraw toward their base in the Panjshir Valley. Pursuing Taliban forces are halted by troops loyal to General Abdul Rashid Dostum.

POLITICS: In Afghanistan, the Taliban leadership announces salary payments for women who are no longer allowed to work, although no mention is made of the time limit.

October 3

POLITICS: In Kabul, Afghanistan, a teacher shortage brought on by the ban against female workers closes most schools and colleges. Hospitals also suffer from a shortage of nurses, though women are still allowed to work at all-female hospitals. The Taliban also order all males to wear turbans and grow beards.

October 7

DIPLOMACY: In Kabul, Afghanistan, Taliban cleric Mullah Mutai scoffs at foreign criticism of the Taliban's treatment of women, insisting that "Islamic principles have not changed in the last 1,400 years."

MILITARY: The Council for the Defense of Afghanistan arises as Burhanuddin Rabbani, General Abdul Rashid Dostum, Abdul Karim Khalili, and Ahmad Shah Massoud form an anti-Taliban alliance.

POLITICS: In Kabul, Afghanistan, the UN High Commissioner for Refugees closes down its offices due to a shortage of female workers, while Save the Children ceases its mine awareness program. Meanwhile, the Taliban impose a 9:00 P.M. to 4:00 A.M. curfew in the city.

October 12–19
MILITARY: North of Kabul, Afghanistan, forces loyal to Ahmad Shah Massoud storm back into the towns of Jabal Seraj and Charikar, ejecting Taliban defenders.

October 14
MILITARY: In Afghanistan, the Taliban are accused of forcibly conscripting young men into their ranks from bazaars and mosques. They also press men charged with being former government sympathizers into changing sides.

October 15
DIPLOMACY: In Islamabad, Pakistan, the government offers to broker peace by sending Minister of the Interior Baban Naseerullah to deal with the Taliban in Kabul.
MILITARY: Taliban forces retake Qara Bagh, Afghanistan, but it is retaken on the 19th by mujahideen loyal to General Abdul Rashid Dostum and Ahmad Shah Massoud. Meanwhile, Bamiyan is again captured by the Taliban, but forces loyal to President Burhanuddin Rabbani occupy the Sanglakh Valley.

October 16
DIPLOMACY: In Geneva, Switzerland, UN officials deny an Iraqi request to use revenue accrued from the oil-for-food program to defray the legal costs of defending itself against claims from the 1991 Gulf War.

October 18
AVIATION: In Afghanistan, Bagram Air Base is recaptured by forces loyal to General Abdul Rashid Dostum and Ahmad Shah Massoud.

October 20
MILITARY: North of Kabul, Afghanistan, the mujahideen of Ahmad Shah Massoud capture Hussein Kot, 12 miles from the capital, after which they fire rockets against Kabul airport. Simultaneously, the forces of General Abdul Rashid Dostum advance on the city from the northeast.

October 21
POLITICS: In Afghanistan, General Abdul Rashid Dostum proposes a cease-fire with Pakistani interior minister Naseerullah serving as intermediary. Ahmad Shah Massoud accepts the terms outright, but, after the Taliban insist on a prisoner exchange and a commission to monitor the cease-fire, the proposal collapses.

October 22
MILITARY: Taliban forces destroy the village of Sar Cheshma, five miles north of Kabul, Afghanistan, as collective punishment for allowing the forces of Ahmad Shah Massoud to shell the capital.

October 22–30

MILITARY: The anti-Taliban alliance, meeting increasing resistance as it draws nearer to Kabul, Afghanistan, finally stalls.

October 23

POLITICS: In Mazar-i-Sharif, women clad in Western-style clothing protest Taliban excesses against them.

October 25

MILITARY: Taliban claim of capturing Qala-i-Nau in Badghis Province, Afghanistan, is disputed by General Abdul Rashid Dostum.

October 27–28

MILITARY: Another attack aimed at Kabul, Afghanistan, by the anti-Taliban alliance is repulsed.

October 29

DIPLOMACY: In Tehran, Iran, the government sponsors a regional conference to achieve peace in Afghanistan, but the attempt fails when Pakistan, Saudi Arabia, and Uzbekistan refuse to attend.

October 30

MILITARY: In Afghanistan, the town of Dar-ye-Nur is captured by anti-Taliban alliance forces but is soon retaken by the Taliban.

October 30–November 3

MILITARY: In Badghis Province, Afghanistan, heavy fighting between Taliban and anti-Taliban forces results in a stalemate. Former Herat governor Ismail Khan had his troops flown in from Iran to take part in this battle.

November 1

POLITICS: In Kabul, Afghanistan, the Taliban decree that girls can resume attending school as fighting has apparently stopped around the city. There are also indications that women might be allowed to work outside the home again.

November 4

AVIATION: Warplanes of the Afghan air force bomb Herat airport and nearby Taliban positions.
MILITARY: In Konar Province, Afghanistan, troops of the anti-Taliban alliance capture the Mangoi district but lose it to a Taliban counterattack shortly afterward.
POLITICS: General Abdul Rashid Dostum again calls for a cease-fire, but the Taliban, who insist on a prisoner exchange in advance, reject the offer.

November 5

POLITICS: General Shanawaz Taina, former defense minister under President Mohammad Najibullah, endorses the Taliban.

November 9

AVIATION: In Afghanistan, warplanes operated by General Abdul Rashid Dostum's forces bomb Taliban positions at Kabul airport.

November 10

POLITICS: The outbreak of fighting near the capital results in a new flood of refuges fleeing north. However, there is little shifting in the front lines.

November 11–16

POLITICS: In Badghis Province, Afghanistan, renewed fighting results in 50,000 refugees fleeing toward Herat and Qala-i-Nau Afghanistan. Because most of them are Pashtuns, the UN High Commissioner for Refugees considers this move the result of ethnic cleansing.

November 17

DIPLOMACY: In Kabul, Afghanistan, the Taliban regime demands that the United Nations recognize it as legitimate and provide a seat to its representative.

November 18

DIPLOMACY: In New York City, the United Nations sponsors a one-day conference on Afghanistan, which calls for an immediate cease-fire and demilitarization of Kabul. Delegates from 19 countries attend, but no representatives from belligerent factions.

November 20

POLITICS: In Kabul, Afghanistan, the UN High Commissioner for Refugees suspends activities following the arrest of four staff members by the Taliban. However, operations resume after December 11, following their release.

November 23–24

MILITARY: North of Kabul, Afghanistan, Taliban forces claim to have captured Mir Bachakot and Guldra. This marks the first major shift in the front lines in two months.

November 26

POLITICS: In Jalalabad, Afghanistan, the Taliban arrest 60 people, charging them with failure to attend regular prayers.

November 27

MILITARY: In Badghis Province, Afghanistan, forces loyal to General Abdul Rashid Dostum capture the Bala Morghab region, triggering the flight of 10,000 Pashtun refugees to Turkmenistan.

North of Kabul, Taliban forces seize the villages of Kalakan and Istalif, pushing the front lines forward another 10 miles.

December 4

POLITICS: In Kabul, the Taliban regime decrees that the traditional *chandari* is not in conformity with Islamic requirements and that women are required to wear full-length burqas outside of the home.

December 7

POLITICS: In Kabul, Afghanistan, the Taliban regime forbids women from working for relief agencies.

December 9

DIPLOMACY: In New York City, the UN secretary-general Boutros Boutros Ghali again allows Iraq to sell off $2 billion worth of oil every six months to purchase food, medicine, and other supplies for its people. Iraq reports that oil production is at 600,000 barrels per day, only 20 percent of its pre-Gulf War level.

POLITICS: Throughout Afghanistan, reports surface that the Taliban are harassing non-Pashtun minorities such as Hazara, Tajiks, and Uzbeks.

UN envoy Norbert Holl meets separately with representatives from the Taliban, Ahmad Shah Massoud, and General Abdul Rashid Dostum to arrange a cease-fire. The Taliban deny that progress has been made toward establishing a commission.

December 10
POLITICS: In Iraq, the order goes to begin pumping oil for sale for the first time in a decade.

December 18
POLITICS: In Kabul and Herat, Afghanistan, the Taliban execute several people in public for various offenses.

December 21–22
POLITICS: In Herat, Afghanistan, large numbers of women demonstrate against the Taliban and demand aid from international organizations. The Taliban militia violently disposes of the protesters, arresting 20 women, imposing a curfew, and patrolling the street with tanks.

December 23
MILITARY: The U.S. Army agrees to investigate the precise nature of sickness among Gulf War veterans, especially if there are bacteriological causes. It is determined that thousands of service members were exposed to low levels of Iraqi nerve agents as stockpiles were being destroyed.

December 24
MILITARY: In Wardak Province, Afghanistan, armed clashes are reported between different factions within the Islamic Unity Party; 17 people are reported killed.

December 27–28
AVIATION: In Afghanistan, warplanes operated by the anti-Taliban alliance strike Taliban targets in Kabul and near the airport.

MILITARY: A major Taliban offensive recaptures Bagram Air Base along with the towns of Qara Bagh, Kalakan, and Istalif.

December 30
DIPLOMACY: In New York City, the United Nations declares that 21 contracts have been signed regarding limited Iraqi oil sales under the food-for-oil program.

1997

January 1
AVIATION: In northern Iraq, Operation Provide Comfort is superceded by Operation Northern Watch to enforce "no-fly zone" conditions north of the 36th north latitude line.

January 2
POLITICS: In Kabul, Afghanistan, the Taliban warn that failure to pray five times a day will result in severe punishment.

January 4
POLITICS: In light of drought conditions in the south, Mullah Omar orders people to pray for rain and snow.

January 5
AVIATION: Warplanes operated by General Abdul Rashid Dostum bomb the Wazir Akbar suburb of Kabul, Afghanistan, killing four people and wounding 10.
MILITARY: In Kabul, Afghanistan, the Taliban threaten to hang their alliance prisoners if aerial attacks continue.

January 6
POLITICS: In Jalalabad, Afghanistan, the medical school of the local university opens without any female students.

January 7
DIPLOMACY: In Pakistan, an American deputation confers with Mullah Hasan, vice president of the Taliban Council. They engage him in talks regarding the drug trade and the elimination of global terrorism.
MILITARY: In Washington, D.C., the Presidential Advisory Committee on Gulf War Veterans' Illnesses releases an inconclusive report on the many ailments affecting large numbers of troops who served in the Persian Gulf in 1990 and 1991. It declares it found little to indicate pollution or chemical weapons as the root cause, but it does not rule out stress.

January 9
POLITICS: In Kabul, Afghanistan, the Taliban regime decrees that nonobservance of Ramadan is punishable by two months' imprisonment. Two men are charged for not meeting their religious obligations.

January 9–14
MILITARY: In Badghis Province, Afghanistan, intense combat continues between the Taliban and mujahideen loyal to General Abdul Rashid Dostum.

January 13–15
POLITICS: Taliban and anti-Taliban delegates meet in UN-sponsored peace talks; the former appear agreeable toward negotiation but refuse to demilitarize Kabul, Afghanistan, as demanded by the opposition.

January 16
MILITARY: In Afghanistan, the most recent Taliban offensive recaptures Bagram Air Base along with Charikar, capital of Parvan Province. The Taliban begin a forced evacuation of Tajik villagers to preclude any possibility of their supporting Ahmad Shah Massoud.
POLITICS: A good indication of Afghanistan's feeble economy is that the national currency, the afghani, has sunk to 28,200 for $1.

January 17–18
MILITARY: In Kapisa Province, Taliban forces surge northward and continue capturing several towns and other key sites, such as Mahmud Raqi.

January 21
POLITICS: Heavy fighting near Charikar, Parvan Province, leads to a new flood of refugees headed south to Kabul, Afghanistan.

January 21–22
DIPLOMACY: In Ashgabat, Turkmenistan, a UN-sponsored forum on international aid for Afghanistan convenes; donor countries and relief agencies agree to continue their work despite spiraling violence in Afghanistan.

January 22
DIPLOMACY: In Washington, D.C., the State Department refuses to extend diplomatic recognition to the Taliban regime in Afghanistan.

January 23
MILITARY: In northern Afghanistan, a surging Taliban offensive captures Jabal Saraj close to the strategic Salang Pass and the town of Gulbahar, at the mouth of the Panjshir Valley. This places Taliban forces at the doorstep of Ahmad Shah Massoud's power base. To curtail further advances, alliance forces begin blasting hillsides in the pass to halt the enemy advance.
POLITICS: In Kabul, Afghanistan, the UN High Commissioner for Refugees reports that 30,000 Afghans have recently streamed into the city from the north.

January 25–26
POLITICS: In Tehran, Iran, a peace conference opens among representatives of Burhanuddin Rabbani, Gulbuddin Hekmatyar, and General Abdul Rashid Dostum. They agree upon an immediate cease-fire, a prisoner exchange, and a safe environment for Kabul, Afghanistan, but because the Taliban fail to attend, nothing is achieved.

January 26
MILITARY: Taliban forces claim to have seized Shinwari and Siagird in the Ghorband Valley from fighters of the Islamic Unity Party.
POLITICS: The Taliban are accused of ethnic cleansing in Gulbahar by removing Tajiks who might otherwise side with Ahmad Shah Massoud's forces.

January 27
MILITARY: In northern Afghanistan, alliance forces continue blowing up parts of the Salang highway to stem the Taliban advance.
POLITICS: In Kabul, Afghanistan, the torrent of refugees in the city is so great that local aid agencies are being overwhelmed. Consequently, large numbers are moving off toward Jalalabad and even Peshawar, Pakistan.

January 28
AVIATION: Government warplanes attack Taliban positions near the town of Jabal Seraj, killing at least three civilians.

DIPLOMACY: In Baghdad, Iraq, the government news agency announces that crude oil exports from the Mina al Bakr terminal reached 11.5 million barrels.

POLITICS: In Kabul, Afghanistan, the UN High Commissioner for Refugees states that scores of refugees are dying from exposure and malnutrition as new fighting increases their number daily.

January 29

DIPLOMACY: In Washington, D.C., administration officials deny that Iraq was threatening Kuwait but reiterate American willingness to respond militarily if necessary.

POLITICS: Taliban forces continue advancing along the Salang highway and are accused of ethnic cleansing by forcibly relocating Tajik communities to forestall any rebellions. The Taliban show no interest in the surge of refugees their activities are generating.

January 30–31

MILITARY: Taliban forces push north through the Ghorband Valley, 80 miles north of Kabul, Afghanistan, and seize the towns of Chardehi and Bakhan.

February 2

DIPLOMACY: A Taliban deputation arrives in the United States for low-level talks.

MILITARY: In Parvan Province, Afghanistan, surging Taliban forces storm into the Hazara (Shiite) districts of Shekali and Sorkhi Parsa.

In Bamiyan Province, fighters of the Islamic Unity Party under Karim Khalili gird themselves for the inevitable Taliban offensive there.

POLITICS: In Kabul, Afghanistan, the Taliban regime declares that Shiite residents of Tagab and Behsoud, Wardak Province, have rebelled against Karim Khalili's Islamic Unity Party.

February 15

POLITICS: In Kabul, Afghanistan, the Taliban regime forbids government workers or military men from smoking.

February 27

POLITICS: In Kabul, Afghanistan, the Taliban regime proscribes the owning of foreign magazines and books.

March 3

DIPLOMACY: In New York City, the UN Security Council votes to maintain existing economic sanctions against Iraq. This is the 36th time that the country has come up for review for this purpose since 1990.

March 18

DIPLOMACY: In Baghdad, Iraq, the government grants Russia "most favored nation" status for receiving oil under the oil-for-food program. The Russians eventually pick up seven of 37 contracts tendered by the United Nations.

March 19

MILITARY: In Jalalabad, Afghanistan, an ammunition dump explodes, killing 50 people and destroying scores of local residences. However, this is viewed as an accident, not sabotage.

March 20

MILITARY: In Afghanistan, General Abdul Malik Pahlawan seizes Badghis, Faryab, and Sar-i-Pul Provinces; he also captures and turns over Ismail Khan and 700 captives to the Taliban.

POLITICS: In Kabul, Afghanistan, the Taliban regime outlaws all new year's celebrations.

May 1

DIPLOMACY: In New York City, the UN Security Council again votes to maintain existing economic sanctions against Iraq.

May 13

POLITICS: In Mazar-i-Sharif, Afghanistan, a new government is formed by President Burhanuddin Rabbani to oppose the Taliban.

May 19

MILITARY: In Faryab Province, Governor Abdul Malik Pahlawan mutinies and formally joins the Taliban. This prompts General Abdul Rashid Dostum to seek refuge in Turkey and then Uzbekistan.

May 24

MILITARY: At Mazar-i-Sharif, Afghanistan, Taliban forces enter without a struggle with the help of their new ally, the Shiite Abdul Malik Pahlawan. They are perilously close to uniting the entire country under one rule for the first time in two decades.

POLITICS: In Iran, moderate cleric Mohammad Khatami wins a landslide election for the presidency; he campaigned on a platform of religious tolerance and social reform.

May 25–26

DIPLOMACY: The governments of Saudi Arabia, Pakistan, and the United Arab Emirates extend recognition to the Taliban regime in Afghanistan.

May 27

DIPLOMACY: In Tehran, President-elect Mohammad Khatami states that relations with the United States could improve provided that the latter changes its attitude toward Iran.

May 28

MILITARY: In Mazar-i-Sharif, Afghanistan, Governor Abdul Malik Pahlawan, alarmed that his Shiite forces are being systematically disarmed by the Taliban, suddenly turns on his allies and attacks. Several hundred Taliban are reported killed, and 2,000 become captives.

May 30

MILITARY: The anti-Taliban alliance scores some minor gains when mujahideen from the Islamic Unity Party seize the Ghorband Valley, and forces loyal to Ahmad Shah Massoud storm into Jebal Saraj.

June 21
DIPLOMACY: In New York City, the UN Security Council reacts to the latest round of Iraqi obstructionism by passing Resolution 1115, which demands unconditional, unrestricted access to sites of interest to the UN Special Commission.

July 4
POLITICS: In Mazar-i-Sharif, Afghanistan, General Abdul Malik Pahlawan forces the closure of the Pakistani consulate.

July 20–24
MILITARY: The mujahideen of Ahmad Shah Massoud retake several areas north of Kabul, Afghanistan, pushing their advanced columns to within 12 miles of the city.

July 29
MILITARY: The drive on Kabul, Afghanistan, by the anti-Taliban alliance stalls in the face of stiffening resistance north of the city.

August
MILITARY: Throughout the month, the Taliban maintain a land blockade of Shiite-dominated Hazarajat, whose inhabitants are considered heretical.

August 4
DIPLOMACY: In New York City, UN Secretary-General Kofi Annan approves a new aid distribution plan enabling Iraq to sell off $2 billion of oil every six months.

August 5
DIPLOMACY: In Baghdad, Iraq, Iraqi leaders express defiance and decide to end all cooperation with the UN Special Commission and the International Atomic Energy Agency until the United Nations lifts its oil embargo. They also insist that the commission relocate its office to either Geneva, Switzerland, or Vienna, Austria.

August 11
POLITICS: At Salang Pass, northern Afghanistan, opposition leaders Ahmad Shah Massoud, Burhanuddin Rabbani, Abdul Malik Pahlawan, and Abdul Karim Khalili meet to ponder their strategic options against the Taliban.

August 12
DIPLOMACY: In New York City, Richard Butler, the UN Special Commision director, informs UN Security Council members that Iraq has greatly diminished the effectiveness of his operations by blocking or interfering with monitoring functions.

August 14
DIPLOMACY: In Kabul, Afghanistan, the United States shuts down its embassy to avoid the appearance of recognizing the Taliban regime.

August 21
MILITARY: Just as the Taliban begin to lose ground north of Kabul, Afghanistan, fighting erupts in Mazar-i-Sharif between the forces of Abdul Malik Pahlawan and General Abdul Rashid Dostum.

POLITICS: Over Bamiyan, Afghanistan, prime minister Abdul Rahim Ghafurzai of the Northern Alliance, a patch-work alliance of anti-Taliban warlords, is killed when his plane crashes.

September 5
DIPLOMACY: In New York City, Afghan deputy foreign minister Abdullah Abdullah, who represents the government of President Burhanuddin Rabbani, takes his seat in the UN General Assembly.

September 8–11
MILITARY: Vengeful Taliban forces clamp down on Mazar-i-Sharif by besieging it.

September 12
MILITARY: The Taliban recapture Mazar-i-Sharif, Afghanistan, and restore order, but the population remains restive; General Abdul Malik Pahlawan flees the area.
POLITICS: General Abdul Rashid Dostum returns from Kabul, Afghanistan, to his northern power base.

October 3
NAVAL: President William J. Clinton orders the *Nimitz* carrier battle group into the Persian Gulf, ostensibly as a warning to Iran, but also to Iraq.

October 4
MILITARY: Outside Mazar-i-Sharif, Afghanistan, alliance forces counterattack and drive the Taliban from the local air base. This is a signal for the city's inhabitants to rise against the Taliban militia in their midst; an estimated 2,000 fighters are rounded up and massacred.

October 14
MILITARY: In Mazar-i-Sharif, Afghanistan, General Abdul Rashid Dostum returns from exile abroad and resumes control of Uzbek militia forces.

October 19
POLITICS: In Kabul, Afghanistan, the Taliban order female patients removed from Wazir Akbar Khan and Karte Seh hospitals and interned at medical facilities reserved for women.

October 23
DIPLOMACY: In New York City, the UN Security Council, reacting to the latest incident of Iraqi noncooperation, begins weighing restrictions on Iraq's top military officials.

October 26
POLITICS: In Kabul, Afghanistan, the Taliban regime orders that the country be renamed the Islamic Amirat (Emirate) of Afghanistan.

October 27
DIPLOMACY: In Baghdad, Iraq, the parliament votes to recommend that all weapons inspectors be turned back until the United Nations produces a timetable for ending all economic sanctions in place since 1990.

October 29

DIPLOMACY: In New York City, the United Nations receives a letter from Iraqi deputy prime minister Tariq Aziz, which claims that the UN Special Commission was under American influence and, hence, intractably hostile to Iraq. He also insists that the United States end all surveillance flights. This same day, the Iraqi government also orders all American inspectors out of the country within one week; only six of the 100 inspectors in place are American. The ensuing impasse lasts nearly a month.

October 30

DIPLOMACY: The Iraqi government forbids three American weapons inspectors working for the United Nations from entering the country.

November 3

AVIATION: In Baghdad, Iraq, President Saddam Hussein threatens to attack American U-2 spy planes operating in his airspace. These aircraft are used to assist UN monitoring efforts, and the Security Council insists that the flights be allowed to continue.

November 3–12

DIPLOMACY: In Iraq, the government prevents American weapons inspectors from attending UN-sanctioned investigations over a period of nine days.

November 10

AVIATION: The United States, ignoring Iraqi threats to shoot them down, resumes high-level U-2 reconnaissance flights.

November 12

DIPLOMACY: In New York City, the UN Security Council votes to ban foreign travel for Iraqi officials who supported President Saddam Hussein's hard-line obstructionism.

November 13

DIPLOMACY: In Iraq, the government formally expels six American weapons inspectors by driving them 400 miles overnight to the Jordanian border.

November 16

POLITICS: Near Mazar-i-Sharif, Afghanistan, General Abdul Rashid Dostum publicly reveals mass graves holding 2,000 Taliban bodies.

November 18

DIPLOMACY: In Washington, D.C., the State Department condemns the Taliban's treatment of women.

November 20

DIPLOMACY: In Baghdad, Iraq, the government agrees to allow UN weapons inspectors to resume their work following negotiations with the Russian government.

November 21

DIPLOMACY: In New York City, with Iraq apparently willing to cooperate with UN inspectors again, the United States claims a victory for the United Nations. However, the claim rings hollow since President Saddam Hussein gained a valuable delay and his diplomatic opposition may have weakened.

December 4
DIPLOMACY: In New York City, the UN Security Council votes unanimously to allow Iraq to continue selling $2 billion worth of oil to obtain food, medicine, and other humanitarian supplies.

December 9
POLITICS: In Tehran, Iran, the Organization of the Islamic Conference opens its annual summit with Ayatollah Ali Khamenei denouncing Western civilization and claiming that the United States is attempting to dominate Middle East peace negotiations. However, President Mohammad Khatami announces his willingness to broaden communications with the West.

December 11
POLITICS: In Tehran, Iran, the Organization of the Islamic Conference adopts a resolution condemning terrorism as incompatible with Islam.

December 14
DIPLOMACY: In Tehran, Iran, President Mohammad Khatami expresses his hope for a "thoughtful dialogue" with the United States.

December 16
POLITICS: In Kabul, Afghanistan, a UN spokesman admits that hundreds of Taliban prisoners were massacred near Mazar-i-Sharif the previous September; the majority of bodies were flung into well pits.

December 23
DIPLOMACY: In New York City, UN resolve to confront Iraq appears to buckle when, upon being informed by Richard Butler, head of the UN Special Commission, that the government again blocked weapons inspectors, the Security Council votes to criticize—not condemn—the action. This softening came at the behest of Russia and other member nations.

December 27
DIPLOMACY: In Baghdad, Iraq, the government declares it is ready to resume exports under the UN oil-for-food program.

1998

January 6
DIPLOMACY: President Burhanuddin Rabbani, eager to convene a regional conference on Afghanistan, visits Iran, Pakistan, and Tajikistan.
MILITARY: In Faryab Province, Afghanistan, accusations arise that the Taliban recently massacred 400 civilians.

January 12

MILITARY: In response to Iraqi president Saddam Hussein's refusal to admit a UN weapons inspection team, more than 27,000 American and British troops are rushed to the Persian Gulf for possible action against Iraq.

NAVAL: The *Guam* amphibious ready group, 24th Marines Expeditionary Unit (SOC), deploys in the Persian Gulf in response to Iraqi intransigence regarding weapons inspections.

January 13

DIPLOMACY: In Iraq, UN weapons inspector Scott Ritter Jr. is accused of being an American spy. The Iraqi government also stops weapons inspectors from searching for outlawed chemical and biological weapons. Furthermore, it announces that it is ceasing all cooperation with the commission because too many American and British members are present.

January 17

DIPLOMACY: In Baghdad, Iraq, President Saddam Hussein threatens to expel all UN arms inspectors in six months if Iraq is not cleared of suspected arms violations and all sanctions are not lifted.

January 27

DIPLOMACY: In Washington, D.C., the House of Representatives approves a resolution expressing the need for a war crimes tribunal to try senior members of the Iraqi government.

January 28

DIPLOMACY: In Cairo, Egypt, senior members of the Arab League and the Egyptian government declare their opposition to military action against Iraq to force Iraqi president Saddam Hussein to comply with UN sanctions and inspections.

February 1

DIPLOMACY: In Kuwait, U.S. secretary of state Madeleine Albright receives permission from the emir to launch an attack upon Iraq to enforce compliance with UN resolutions. However, she acknowledges that France, Russia, and China prefer pursuing diplomacy.

February 4

POLITICS: Takhar, Afghanistan, is hit by a large earthquake that kills an estimated 5,000 people and destroys 1,500 dwellings; at least 15,000 people are made homeless in midwinter.

February 17

DIPLOMACY: In Washington, D.C., President William J. Clinton warns Iraq that he is prepared to order another round of air attacks to enforce its compliance with UN resolutions.

February 20
DIPLOMACY: In New York City, the UN Security Council more than doubles the amount of oil that Iraq is authorized to sell from $2.14 billion worth to $5.2 billion worth under the oil-for-food program. It is feared that the Iraqi people are suffering from a severe nutritional crisis brought on by sanctions.

February 22
DIPLOMACY: In New York City, UN secretary-general Kofi Annan and Iraqi deputy prime minister Tariq Aziz sign an agreement allowing weapons inspectors to investigate various presidential properties in Iraq. This agreement defuses the crisis for the time being.

February 23
DIPLOMACY: In Moscow, Russia, President Boris Yeltsin applauds the new UN agreement to allow UN inspectors into Iraq; the United States and Britain are withholding judgment at present.

In Baghdad, Iraq, UN secretary-general Kofi Annan signs a memorandum of understanding with Iraqi officials on the thorny issue of UN inspections of alleged weapon sites.

In Washington, D.C., President William J. Clinton informs a news conference that the new memorandum of understanding reached with Iraq hopefully will allow the UN Special Commission to fulfill its mission without further delays.

TERRORISM: In Peshawar, Pakistan, Saudi militant Osama bin Laden calls on all Muslims to attack and kill Americans and their allies. To that end he helps to found the World Front for Jihad Against Jews and Crusaders.

February 25
DIPLOMACY: In New York City, President William J. Clinton solicits support from Britain, France, and Russia for the new Security Council resolution and warns Iraq not to violate it.

March 2
DIPLOMACY: In New York City, the UN Security Council unanimously approves the new deal struck with Iraq to allow weapons inspectors on presidential properties. However, it rejects an American provision calling for a guaranteed military response for failure to comply.

March 5
POLITICS: In Kabul, Afghanistan, the Taliban regime readopts the lunar calendar.

March 13
DIPLOMACY: In Washington, D.C., the Senate passes SR 78, which calls for indicting Iraqi president Saddam Hussein for war crimes.

March 23
POLITICS: In Baghdad, Iraq, the government announces the arrest of Nassir al-Hindwai, a noted germ warfare specialist, who was preparing to flee the country. UN arms inspectors had hoped to talk with him.

March 25
DIPLOMACY: In Kandahar, Afghanistan, the United Nations withdraws its staff members.

April 7
POLITICS: In Kandahar, Afghanistan, Saudi terrorist Osama bin Laden is seen offering public prayers during the Muslim Feast of the Sacrifice.

April 9
POLITICS: Various independent inspection teams dispute that Iraqi president Saddam Hussein has taken measures to eliminate all biological weapons and the means of manufacturing them.

April 13
DIPLOMACY: In New York City, a report issued by the UN Human Rights Commission declares that Iraq has executed at least 1,500 people over the past year, largely for political reasons.

April 16
DIPLOMACY: In New York City, UN inspector Richard Butler reports that Iraq is no closer to meeting the requirements necessary to end all UN sanctions than it was six months ago. He states that Baghdad has failed to provide any new information on weapons holdings and is renewing its opposition to his commission's agenda.

April 17
DIPLOMACY: In New York City, the U.S. ambassador to the United Nations discusses peace with Taliban representatives.

April 22
DIPLOMACY: In New Canaan, Connecticut, the charity organization Americares announces plans to supply 75,000 pounds of medical and hospital supplies to Iraq to help its citizens. The goods are to be shipped to Jordan, then flown to Baghdad by the Royal Jordanian Air Force.

April 23
DIPLOMACY: In Kabul, Afghanistan, U.S. dignitaries arrive for discussions on the apparent increase in poppy cultivation.

April 26
POLITICS: In Islamabad, Pakistan, peace talks open among various Afghan factions and opposition leaders.

May
POLITICS: In Afghanistan, 490 men are punished for cutting off their beards, as are 110 women for appearing "insufficiently veiled" in public.

May 3
MILITARY: In Afghanistan, the Taliban collect their forces and launch a major offensive against what has become the Northern Alliance. This act squelches any chance for peace talks with the United States.

May 25
POLITICS: In Kabul, Afghanistan, the Department for "Enjoining Good and Forbidding Evil" is given the rank of a ministry within the Taliban regime. It is tasked with maintaining public morality.

May 27
TERRORISM: In Khost, Afghanistan, Saudi terrorist Osama bin Laden holds a news conference in which he calls for a jihad against U.S. forces stationed on Saudi Arabian soil.

May 29
POLITICS: In Kabul, Afghanistan, Taliban leader Mullah Omar cancels an amnesty previously offered to former members of the Communist Party.

June 16
POLITICS: In Kabul, Afghanistan, the Taliban regime dictates that all girls' schools in private homes be closed.

June 23
DIPLOMACY: Various UN-sponsored laboratories find concrete evidence of nerve gas in an Iraqi missile warhead, and the case for a complete UN embargo against Iraq is strengthened.

July 5
DIPLOMACY: The governments of Jordan and Iraq announce that they are constructing an oil pipeline between their two nations.

July 8
POLITICS: In Kabul, Afghanistan, the Taliban regime decrees that all television sets are to be destroyed and that henceforth individuals will be tested on their knowledge of Islam.

July 9
POLITICS: In Kabul, Afghanistan, the Taliban regime makes it a crime to convert from Islam to another religion.

July 13
POLITICS: In Jalalabad, Afghanistan, two UN staff members are murdered by unknown assailants.

July 21
DIPLOMACY: In light of escalating violence, many foreign agencies and businesses begin pulling out of Kabul, Afghanistan.

August 3
DIPLOMACY: In Baghdad, Iraq, the government announces it is halting all cooperation with UN weapons inspections unless the United Nations lifts all existing economic sanctions.

August 5
DIPLOMACY: In Baghdad, Iraq, the government also demands that chief UN arms inspector Richard Butler be removed; until then, all cooperation with the weapons inspectors is over.

August 6
DIPLOMACY: In New York City, the UN Security Council rebukes Iraqi president Saddam Hussein and insists that he cooperate with weapons inspectors. However, it takes no other action. Meanwhile, chief inspector Richard Butler reports that Iraq's recent "disclosure" of facts surrounding its biological warfare program is not based on reliable information.

August 7
TERRORISM: U.S. embassies in Nairobi, Kenya, and Dar es Salaam, Tanzania, are struck by truck bombs; 250 people are killed, including 11 Americans and one marine security guard. A further 1,100 are injured. Saudi expatriate Osama bin Laden is believed to have played a role in the attacks.

An F-16CJ "Wild Weasel" pulls up to the refueling boom of a KC-135 Stratotanker over eastern Turkey as part of Operation Northern Watch, which enforced the "no-fly zone" over northern Iraq called for by the agreement that ended Operation Desert Storm. *(Defense Imagery)*

August 9

MILITARY: In Afghanistan, Mazar-i-Sharif again falls to Taliban forces, who proceed to murder 4,000 to 5,000 people, including nine Iranian diplomats.

August 14

POLITICS: In Washington, D.C., Congress passes Public Law 105-235, which declares Iraq in material breach of the 1991 Gulf War cease-fire agreement. It also calls on President William J. Clinton to force Iraq back into compliance.

August 18

DIPLOMACY: In Washington, D.C., Secretary of State Madeleine Albright demands that the Taliban extradite Osama bin Laden, form a broad-based government, and improve human-rights conditions if Afghanistan wants recognition from the United States.

August 20

DIPLOMACY: In New York, the UN Security Council renews all existing sanctions against Iraq after President Saddam Hussein orders all cooperation ended until economic restrictions are lifted. Iraqi foreign minister Tariq Aziz nonetheless maintains that Iraq will not cooperate until the United Nations at least seriously considers lifting the sanctions.

MILITARY: The U.S. Navy, reacting to the bombings of American embassies in Kenya and Tanzania, launches 75 cruise missiles at suspected chemical weapons facilities in Khartoum, Sudan, and terrorist training camps near Khost, Afghanistan.

August 21

DIPLOMACY: Following the murder of another UN official in Kabul, Afghanistan, the United Nations and the International Committee of the Red Cross withdraw all their staff members.

August 26

DIPLOMACY: In Iraq, American weapons inspector William S. Ritter resigns after the United Nations fails to contest Iraqi obstructionism, a fact he considers "a surrender to Iraqi leadership."

August 27

POLITICS: In Jalalabad, Afghanistan, pro-Taliban demonstrators attack UN representatives in retaliation for the U.S. missile attack against Khost.

September

DIPLOMACY: Upon further reflection, Saudi Arabia begins withdrawing diplomats from Kabul, Afghanistan.

September 3

DIPLOMACY: In Iraq, William S. Ritter, the former UN weapons inspector, claims that the government has begun interfering with monitoring operations at specific installations. This causes another souring of relations between Iraq and the United Nations.

September 13
DIPLOMACY: At this juncture, the Taliban regime in Afghanistan is recognized only by Pakistan, Saudi Arabia, and the United Arab Emirates.
MILITARY: Taliban forces storm into Shiite-dominated Hazarajat; they now control 80 percent of the country, though the Northern Alliance continues to offer determined resistance.

September 17
POLITICS: In Washington, D.C., a Department of State spokesman declares that two warring Iraqi Kurdish factions had reached a peaceful settlement and are now fully united against the regime of President Saddam Hussein.

September 22
DIPLOMACY: In Kabul, Afghanistan, the Saudi chargé d'affaires is recalled for consultations.

September 24
DIPLOMACY: In Tehran, Iran, the government retracts its death threat against British author Salman Rushdie over his book *The Satanic Verses;* Britain consequently resumes diplomatic relations.

September 27
POLITICS: In Kabul, Afghanistan, Taliban leader Mullah Omar decrees that any believer who cannot correctly recite the five main Islamic prayers will face punishment.

October 8
MILITARY: In Tehran, Iran, the government announces that its forces have inflicted heavy casualties on Taliban fighters in a heavy border skirmish. Iran had massed 270,000 troops on the border after eight Iranian diplomats were murdered in Afghanistan by Taliban operatives.

October 21
DIPLOMACY: In New York City, the United Nations postpones its decision on granting recognition to the Taliban regime in Afghanistan.

October 22
POLITICS: In Kabul, Afghanistan, the Taliban regime decrees that all Hindus must wear yellow identification marks on their clothing to signify their religion.

October 26
AVIATION: In a setback for UN weapons inspection efforts, three different reports concerning nerve gas in Iraqi missiles reach three entirely different conclusions. The Americans report positive evidence of traces of the gas, a French study mentions the possibility of gas having been present, while a Swiss report states that there is no evidence of a nerve agent.

October 31
DIPLOMACY: In Baghdad, Iraq, the government again announces that it is no longer cooperating with weapons inspectors on the UN Special Commission on Iraq.

POLITICS: In Washington, D.C., the U.S. Congress passes Public Law 105-338, which makes replacing President Saddam Hussein's regime with a democratic government in Iraq a stated objective of the United States. The law is signed by President William J. Clinton, and "regime change" becomes an official government policy. Clinton also signs legislation prohibiting the import of Iraqi oil.

November 1
DIPLOMACY: The UN oil-for-food program coordinator, Denis Halliday, resigns after blaming existing economic sanctions for the deaths of Iraqi children.

In Baghdad, Iraq, the government takes its defiance of the United Nations a step further by expelling all UN and International Atomic Energy Agency inspectors from the country. This also poses a direct challenge to the United States, which had championed both inspections and economic sanctions.

November 5
DIPLOMACY: In New York City, the UN Security Council unanimously approves Resolution 1205, which condemns Iraq's recent decision to end cooperation with weapons inspectors. However, no other action is mentioned or taken.

November 7
DIPLOMACY: In Washington, D.C., a government official says that the United States considers the prevailing system of UN inspections in Iraq insufficient to bringing President Saddam Hussein to heel. Therefore, the Clinton administration is prepared to employ force unilaterally, if need be, to enforce Iraqi compliance.

November 8
DIPLOMACY: In Washington, D.C., the government offers a $5 million reward for the capture of Osama bin Laden.
POLITICS: In Afghanistan, the Taliban offer to "try" Saudi terrorist Osama bin Laden, and by month's end they clear him of all charges.

November 11
DIPLOMACY: In Washington, D.C., President William J. Clinton again warns Iraqi president Saddam Hussein that an aerial attack is imminent unless he complies with all UN resolutions.
MILITARY: In Kuwait, Operation Desert Thunder unfolds as the 1st Brigade, 3rd Infantry Division deploys along the Iraqi border to counter any threatening moves by Iraq.

November 13
MILITARY: Mohammad Akbari, a main leader of the Shiite Hezb-i-Wahdat, finally surrenders to the Taliban.

November 14
AVIATION: In response to Iraq's refusal to allow further UN arms inspection teams into the country, the United States and Britain prepare to launch a wave of air strikes. Only 20 minutes before the attacks begin, President Saddam Hussein changes his mind and allows the teams back in.

DIPLOMACY: In New York City, UN secretary-general Kofi Annan receives a letter from Iraqi deputy prime minister Tariq Aziz declaring that his government will allow UN weapons inspections to resume. This act circumvents, for the time being, what would have been a very large air strike by U.S. bombers and cruise missiles.

November 15

AVIATION: U.S. warplanes were already en route to their targets in Iraq when President William J. Clinton recalls them before cruise missiles could be launched.

DIPLOMACY: In New York City, Iraqi UN ambassador Nizar Hamdoon reaffirms his government's "unconditional" decision to allow weapons inspections to resume.

POLITICS: In explaining the turn of events in Iraq, President William J. Clinton appears to call for the Iraqi people to overthrow President Saddam Hussein.

November 16–17

DIPLOMACY: In Iraq, UN aid workers and weapons inspectors are allowed back into the country for the time being.

December 9

DIPLOMACY: In Stanford, California, a White House aide, while honoring former secretary of state Warren Christopher, asks Middle Eastern nations to back a "regime change" in Iraq by supporting the overthrow of President Saddam Hussein.

December 16–20

AVIATION: Over Iraq, Operation Desert Fox commences in retaliation for Iraqi obstruction and deceit in connection with UN arms inspections. Aircraft from the carrier *Enterprise*, assisted by 325 Tomahawk cruise missiles, strike at Iraqi nuclear, biological, and chemical weapons facilities. This is also the first time that female aviators fly combat missions. The Air Combat Command contributes several B-1B Lancers to the operation, in combat debut in the Persian Gulf. A total of 415 cruise missiles, 100 more than employed during the Gulf War of 1991, are launched at 97 various targets, along with 600 laser guided bombs.

DIPLOMACY: In Washington, D.C., the Russians recall their ambassador to protest the latest round of punitive measures against Iraq.

MILITARY: The 31st Marine Expeditionary Force (SOC) and jets of Marine Corps Fighter Squadron 312 participate in Operation Desert Fox to coax Iraqi cooperation with UN nuclear inspectors. Considerable damage is inflicted, but President Saddam Hussein still refuses to allow inspectors back into the country.

December 17

DIPLOMACY: In Washington, D.C., the House of Representatives approves a resolution supporting the removal of Saddam Hussein from power in Iraq and his replacement by a democratic government.

December 19

POLITICS: In Damascus, Syria, marine guards use tear gas to disperse crowds at the U.S. embassy who are protesting Operation Desert Fox against Iraq.

December 28

AVIATION: U.S. warplanes patrolling the northern "no-fly zone" are fired on by Iraqi antiaircraft missiles, and they shoot back. The Americans regard this attack as a deliberately provocative action.

1999

January 4

DIPLOMACY: In Baghdad, Iraq, the Foreign Ministry asks the United Nations to formally replace all American and British staff members.

January 5

DIPLOMACY: Iraqi president Saddam Hussein finds himself more diplomatically isolated in the Arab world after calling for the overthrow of leaders who have not supported him during the latest round of U.S. aerial attacks.

January 6

DIPLOMACY: In Washington, D.C., the administration admits that it had "spied" on Iraq through the UN Special Commission on Iraq as it conducted weapons inspections. Apparently, agents posing as inspectors had installed communication devices to monitor Iraqi security forces.

January 11

MILITARY: The United States declares that it has received intelligence pointing to the execution of more than 500 Iraqi military officers and dissidents from Shiite-dominated regions of the country.

January 24

AVIATION: Over Iraq, a navy EA-6B Prowler fires an AGM-154A joint standoff weapon at a hostile radar site near Mosul for the first time. After eight years of compliance, the regime of Saddam Hussein is beginning to challenge UN enforcement of Operation Northern Watch.

January 25

AVIATION: Operation Southern Watch commences over Iraq as U.S. and British warplanes continue pounding Iraqi antiaircraft missile sites near Basra. Navy F/A-18 Hornets of VFA-22 and VFA-94 launch the first AGM-154A joint standoff weapons used in combat.

February 2

AVIATION: U.S. pilots receive broadened rule of engagement for attacking Iraqi targets in the northern and southern "no-fly zones."
DIPLOMACY: In Islamabad, Pakistan, U.S. deputy secretary of state Strobe Talbott confers with Taliban officials over the extradition of Osama bin Laden; the Taliban refuse his request.

February 12

DIPLOMACY: The United Nations begins carefully reinserting staff members and aid workers back into Afghanistan.

Politics: In Kabul, Afghanistan, the Taliban regime announces the sudden disappearance of Saudi terrorist Osama bin Laden.

February 19
Politics: In Kabul, Afghanistan, the Taliban regime decrees that all heroin laboratories must be destroyed.
Terrorism: In Najaf, Iraq, the Grand Ayatollah Sayyid Muhammad Sadiq al-Sadr, a leading Shiite religious figure, is gunned down by unknown assailants.

March 14
Politics: In Turkmenistan, delegates from the Taliban and the Northern Alliance convene and agree in principle to a shared government, a prisoner exchange, and other open negotiations.

April 8
Diplomacy: In Baghdad, Iraq, the government rejects a UN proposal to allow the resumption of arms inspections inside the country. This time, the United Nations offered an enlarged food-for-oil arrangement along with a slight easing of sanctions.

April 21
Military: In Bamiyan Province, Afghanistan, Shiite fighters associated with Hezb-i-Wahdat storm back into the town of Bamiyan.

April 26
Politics: In Afghanistan, Shiites are allowed to celebrate their traditional Ashura ceremonies, but not in public.

April 30
Politics: In Rome, Italy, former Afghan monarch Mohammad Zahir Shah proposes that a *loya jirga* be summoned in Afghanistan to help restore peace and stability.

May 17–November 17
Aviation: Continuous Iraqi violations result in four U.S. air strikes against anti-aircraft positions and radar sites in the "no-fly zone." The aircraft involved are navy F/A-18 Hornets and air force A-10 Thunderbolt IIs.

June 9
Terrorism: In Baghdad, Iraq, a bomb explodes next to a bus loaded with members of the exiled Iranian dissident group Mujahideen-i-Khalq, killing and wounding more than 30 people. The blast is attributed to Iranian intelligence operatives.

June 16
Aviation: In the southern "no-fly zone" of Iraq, Iraqi antiaircraft fire prompts a sharp riposte by Navy F/A-18 Hornets and British GR-1 Tornadoes against two radar sites and a missile battery.

June 25
Politics: In Rome, Italy, former Afghan monarch Mohammad Zahir Shah meets with various Afghan dignitaries to help solve the ongoing political crisis in Afghanistan.

July 4

POLITICS: Saudi terrorist Osama bin Laden briefly resurfaces in Jalalabad, Afghanistan.

July 6

DIPLOMACY: In Washington, D.C., the administration of President William Clinton announces the imposition of trade and financial restrictions against the Taliban regime of Afghanistan, due to its apparent support for Saudi terrorist Osama bin Laden.

July 7–8

POLITICS: In Iran, a religious court bans publication of a moderate newspaper, which prompts university students to protest. Police and paramilitary forces attack and savagely beat the protesters, killing at least one. However, student-related disturbances spread to at least 18 cities nationwide.

July 13

POLITICS: In Tehran, Iran, many businesses close down during continuing clashes between students and police.

July 14

POLITICS: In Tehran, Iran, President Mohammad Khatami, wary of a crackdown by hard-line Islamic authorities, condemns the student demonstrations, and they halt three days later.

TERRORISM: In Quetta, Pakistan, chief Abdul Ahmad Karzai of the Popalzai tribe is assassinated with two of his followers.

July 28

MILITARY: In Afghanistan, Taliban forces commence a three-pronged offensive against mujahideen loyal to Ahmad Shah Massoud, recapturing Bagram Air Base.

August 4

POLITICS: Across the Shomali Plain, Afghanistan, the Taliban are accused of ethnic cleansing by forcibly removing Tajik communities.

August 5

DIPLOMACY: In Rome, Italy, former Afghan monarch Mohammad Zahir Shah condemns foreign influences in Afghanistan, a veiled reference to Pakistan.

August 8

DIPLOMACY: Former Afghan president Sibghatullah Mojaddidi angrily departs Pakistan to protest that government's continuing interference in Afghanistan's internal affairs.

August 10

AVIATION: In Iraq, antiaircraft fire directed at coalition aircraft enforcing the southern "no-fly zone" provokes a retaliatory counterattack by F-14D Tomcats, F/A-18 Hornets, and F-16C Falcons, which knock out offending missile and radar sites.

August 15
POLITICS: In Kabul, Afghanistan, Mullah Omar summons 5,000 Afghan and Pakistani madrasah (religious school) students into the country.

August 18
DIPLOMACY: An agreement is reached between the governments of Afghanistan and Pakistan to improve mail services and communications.

August 24
TERRORISM: In Kandahar, Afghanistan, Taliban spiritual leader Mullah Omar survives an assassination attempt.

September 9
POLITICS: In Kabul, Afghanistan, Taliban spokesman Mullah Mutawakkil insists that war is the only solution to Afghanistan's political problems.

September 19
DIPLOMACY: A disturbing UN study suggests that Afghan poppy cultivation has risen to 91,000 hectares in 1999 while opium production has reached 4,600 tons yearly.

September 23
POLITICS: In Charleston, South Carolina, presidential hopeful George W. Bush addresses cadets at the Citadel military academy, stressing homeland defense and the specter of chemical and nuclear terrorism.

October 7
DIPLOMACY: In Islamabad, Pakistan, the Inter-Service Intelligence Agency denounces all terrorist training camps in Afghanistan.

October 13
POLITICS: In Islamabad, Pakistan, Prime Minister Nawaz Harif is overthrown by a military coup and replaced by General Pervez Musharraf.

October 15
DIPLOMACY: In New York City, the UN Security Council endorses economic sanctions against the Taliban regime of Afghanistan if it does not surrender Saudi terrorist Osama bin Laden. They are to take effect on November 14 and include a freeze on Taliban financial resources abroad and an international ban on all Afghan aircraft.

October 19
DIPLOMACY: A ranking American official meets with Taliban officials and warns them of the consequences if they fail to abide by UN demands.

October 27
POLITICS: In Kabul, Afghanistan, Mullah Mutawakkil replaces Mullah Hasan Akhund as minister of foreign affairs.

November 14

DIPLOMACY: All UN sanctions against the Taliban regime in Afghanistan, including an air embargo, come into effect.

November 17

AVIATION: A navy F/A-18 Hornet patrolling the southern "no-fly zone" is locked on by an Iraqi missile radar and retaliates by firing a HARM missile at it.

DIPLOMACY: In Kabul, Afghanistan, the Taliban regime declares that the separatist revolt in Chechnya, Russia, is an Islamic cause.

November 21

DIPLOMACY: In Herat, Afghanistan, the Iranian consulate is allowed to reopen.

November 22

DIPLOMACY: In Rome, Italy, former Afghan monarch Mohammad Zahir Shah assembles 55 Afghan expatriates in preparation for holding a *loya jirga*.

November 28

POLITICS: In Kabul, Afghanistan, the Taliban regime declares its intention to establish scores of Islamic councils throughout the provinces to oversee judicial and administrative matters.

December 11

POLITICS: General Abdul Malik Pahlawan ends his political exile in the United States by reentering Afghanistan and rejoining the forces of Ahmad Shah Massoud. General Abdul Rashid Dostum likewise rejoins his army from Turkey.

December 14

DIPLOMACY: In Washington, D.C., the government warns the Taliban regime that it would be held accountable for any future terror attacks abetted by Osama bin Laden.

December 17

DIPLOMACY: In New York City, the UN Security Council passes Resolution 1284 to establish the new Monitoring, Verification, and Inspection Commission to replace the earlier UN Special Commission. However, Iraq refuses to accept the resolution, which criticizes its failure to cooperate with weapons inspectors.

December 19

DIPLOMACY: In New York City, the UN Security Council warns the Taliban regime in Afghanistan that it will expand existing sanctions if it fails to extradite Osama bin Laden, close all terrorist training camps, and halt illegal drug smuggling.

December 21

DIPLOMACY: The government of Turkmenistan and the Taliban regime in Afghanistan sign a contract whereby the latter provides electricity to Faryab, Sheberghan, and Mazar-i-Sharif.

2000

January 7
DIPLOMACY: In Kabul, Afghanistan, Taliban head Mullah Omar accuses the United States of hostility toward Islam and Muslims.

January 16
DIPLOMACY: In Moscow, Russia, the government accuses the Taliban regime in Afghanistan of aiding and abetting the insurgency in Chechnya. The government of Chechnya opens an embassy in Kabul.

January 27
POLITICS: In Kabul, Afghanistan, the news agencies CNN and al-Jazeera receive permission to open information offices.

February 1
DIPLOMACY: In Kabul, Afghanistan, the Taliban insist that they oppose terrorism, but they will not extradite Osama bin Laden to the United States.
POLITICS: In Afghanistan, the Northern Alliance accuses the Taliban regime of atrocities against Hazara, Uzbek, and Tajik ethnic minorities in Gosfandi; 80 civilians reportedly have been executed.
TERRORISM: In Washington, D.C., the Central Intelligence Agency warns that Osama bin Laden is attempting to obtain biological, chemical, and nuclear weapons. The agency also accuses him of masterminding the hijacking of an Indian airliner by Kashmiri separatists in December 1999.

February 3
DIPLOMACY: In Pakistan, Fransec Vendrell, the new UN representative to Afghanistan, arrives for a tour of the area.

February 6–7
TERRORISM: Over Afghanistan, an Ariana airliner is hijacked over Mazar-i-Sharif by Afghan passengers and made to fly to London. Having landed, they demand that the Taliban release Ismail Khan from imprisonment.

February 7
DIPLOMACY: In Paris, France, a Taliban delegation arrives for talks, whereupon the French take a hard line against international terrorism, the opium trade, human-rights violations, and the treatment of women.

February 9
AVIATION: In New York City, the UN Sanctions Committee, tasked with imposing punitive measures, waives its air embargo against Afghanistan to allow religious pilgrims to perform the hajj.
POLITICS: In Kabul, Afghanistan, the Taliban arrest a number of airport workers, including women, charging them with complicity in the February 6 hijacking of an Ariana airliner.

TERRORISM: In Kabul, Afghanistan, a bomb explodes outside the Ministry of the Interior. The Taliban accuse the Northern Alliance of planting it; the latter rejects any responsibility.

February 10

TERRORISM: In London, United Kingdom, the Afghans who hijacked an Ariana airliner surrender peacefully; Mullah Omar demands that they face English law or international law for their misdeed.

February 11

DIPLOMACY: In Afghanistan, the UN World Food Program predicts a food crisis, specifically, a million-ton shortfall in wheat.

February 12

POLITICS: In Kabul, Afghanistan, the Taliban regime assures the hostages of the Ariana airliner a safe conduct pass should they return home from the United Kingdom. Nonetheless, half of the passengers request political asylum from the British.

February 14

AVIATION: Warplanes operated by the Taliban regime bomb targets in the Panjshir Valley; eight civilians are reported killed.

POLITICS: In London, United Kingdom, 70 hijacked Afghan passengers opt to return home to Afghanistan.

February 17

DIPLOMACY: In New York City, the United Nations condemns the Taliban for bombing and killing eight civilians in the Panjshir Valley.

February 18

POLITICS: In Iran, reform-minded moderates sweep parliamentary elections, winning 141 seats, with 44 for the conservatives and 10 for independents. The results are a political victory for President Mohammad Khatami.

February 23

DIPLOMACY: With opium production in Afghanistan soaring to 75 percent of the world's supply, the government of Pakistan requests global assistance in suppressing it.

February 25

DIPLOMACY: In Kazakhstan, President Islom Nazarbayev complains about the trafficking of opium and terrorism flowing from refugee camps in Afghanistan and Pakistan.

The UN High Commissioner for Refugees announces a deal with Iran and Pakistan to repatriate 200,000 Afghan refugees once the Taliban regime agrees to the settlement; the United Nations will provide all logistical support.

February 26

POLITICS: In Iran, the final tally of national elections places the reformist party firmly in control of the Majlis. This is the first time since 1979 that hard-line conservatives have been ousted from power.

February 27
DIPLOMACY: The International Drug Enforcement Agency declares that 75 percent of the world's opium production originates inside Afghanistan.

February 28
POLITICS: In Afghanistan, various nongovernmental organizations declare their concern for the effects UN sanctions will have on the civilian population.

February 29
TERRORISM: In Kabul, Afghanistan, a bomb explodes outside the Ministry of Information and Culture; the Northern Alliance denies any responsibility for the act.

March 1
DIPLOMACY: In New York City, Hans Blix, a respected scientist, assumes the post of executive chairman of the UN Monitoring, Verification, and Inspection Commission.

MILITARY: North of Kabul, Afghanistan, Taliban forces and mujahideen loyal to Ahmad Shah Massoud skirmish openly for the first time in several months. The

These beggars in the capital city of Kabul reflect the fact that Afghanistan is still a nation with countless unemployed, poor, and disabled people. In particular, many Afghan widows are forced to use their children to attract contributions. *(Photo by Lizelle Potgieter/Shutterstock)*

Taliban also claim to have captured the port of Sher Khan Bandar along the border with Tajikistan.

March 2
DIPLOMACY: In Tehran, Iran, the national police force demands better border security to combat rising drug traffic from Afghanistan.
MILITARY: Fighting between Taliban forces and those of Ahmad Shah Massoud extend into a second day and includes artillery duels in the Shomali Plain near Kabul, Afghanistan.

March 3
DIPLOMACY: In New York City, the UN Security Council insists on an end to Taliban military aggression or further, unspecified sanctions will be imposed.
MILITARY: As Taliban forces consolidate their gains at Sher Khan Bandar and Imam Sahib, Russia sends troops into Tajikistan to help secure its border with Afghanistan.

March 6
POLITICS: In Kandahar, Afghanistan, the Taliban regime publicly destroys large quantities of heroin and hashish.

March 7
POLITICS: The Organization of the Islamic Conference sponsors peace talks among the warring factions in Afghanistan.

March 8
POLITICS: In Kabul, Afghanistan, the UN representative announces that he sees some softening of the Taliban hard line toward women, especially concerning education and access to health facilities.

March 13
DIPLOMACY: In Washington, D.C., President William J. Clinton acknowledges that moderates are now in control of Iran, but oil contracts are nonetheless still banned.
TERRORISM: Near Tehran, Iran, Mujahideeni-i-Khalq operatives use mortars to fire on an army base outside the capital.

March 17
DIPLOMACY: In Washington, D.C., Secretary of State Madeleine Albright announces that some economic sanctions against Iran will be relaxed, and she is seeking to work toward normalized relations. However, she says this can only transpire once Tehran stops supporting terrorism and abandons nuclear weapons.

March 20
POLITICS: In Kabul, Afghanistan, the Taliban regime forbids any New Year's observances.

March 27
POLITICS: In Kandahar, Afghanistan, Ismail Khan, the "Lion of Herat," escapes from Taliban imprisonment after three years; he is accompanied by opposition leader Abdul Zaher.

The UN High Commissioner for Refugees begins repatriating Afghans from Pakistan; each family receives $100, food, and plastic sheeting to provide shelter.

March 28
TERRORISM: In Torkum, Afghanistan, on the famous Khyber Pass to Pakistan, a bomb explodes, killing four people and injuring more.

March 29
DIPLOMACY: In Tehran, Iran, the government announces that Ismail Khan has safely arrived in the country.
POLITICS: The United Nations suspends its operations in southern Afghanistan after the Taliban search several offices for the fugitive Ismail Khan.

March 31
POLITICS: A new anti-Taliban alliance is forged among the mujahideen of Abdul Malik Pahlawan, Abdul Rashid Dostum, and Ahmad Shah Massoud, with the backing of Iran and Russia.

April 4
TERRORISM: In Peshawar, Pakistan, Mohammad Arif Khan, the Taliban governor of Nangarhar Province, is assassinated.

April 5
POLITICS: In Kabul, Afghanistan, Mullah Omar decrees that poppy cultivation is to be reduced by one-third in Nangarhar Province, while poppy fields along the Jalalabad-Pakistan road are to be plowed under.

April 7
MILITARY: There are reports of a military clash between Taliban and anti-Taliban forces in the Nejan district, north of Kabul, Afghanistan, as both sides collect forces for a new spring offensive.

April 8
DIPLOMACY: In New York City, UN officials warn the Taliban regime of additional sanctions unless fighting and human-rights abuses end and Osama bin Laden is extradited.
MILITARY: In the Nejrab district, Afghanistan, Taliban forces storm into the Darra-i-Kalan Valley but are driven back by a prompt alliance counterattack.

April 9
DIPLOMACY: In Islamabad, Pakistan, the government demands that Afghanistan dismantle all terrorist training facilities and extradite all Pakistanis suspected of committing religious attacks in Karachi.

April 12
DIPLOMACY: In Kabul, Afghanistan, the Taliban regime warns Russia not to interfere in the nation's internal affairs.

April 13

MILITARY: In Ghowr Province, Afghanistan, alliance forces claim to have recaptured the Saghar and Sharak districts while heavy fighting is also reported near Albak, capital of Samangan Province.

POLITICS: In Kandahar, Afghanistan, UN teams return to their office following assurances by Taliban authorities.

April 15

POLITICS: In Afghanistan, the Sunni-oriented Taliban regime permits Shiite Muharram celebrations.

April 18

DIPLOMACY: In Washington, D.C., Secretary of State Madeleine Albright and Uzbek president Islom Karimov agree that the Taliban regime in Afghanistan threatens regional stability.

April 19

DIPLOMACY: In Tajikistan, a UN representative meets with mujahideen leader Ahmad Shah Massoud; the latter agrees to peace talks with the Taliban, but no concrete measures are taken.

For the first time in eight years, Iran and Afghanistan allow normal postal services through Herat.

POLITICS: Throughout Afghanistan, food prices rise by 25 percent due to the imposition of taxes by the Taliban, the collapsing Afghan currency, drought conditions in the south, UN sanctions, and the printing of money by the opposition.

April 21

POLITICS: In Afghanistan, all warring parties allow a three-day truce for UNICEF workers to distribute polio vaccines to children.

April 23

POLITICS: In Iran, the conservatively controlled court system takes a slap at moderate reformers by shutting down 12 newspapers that it claims disparaged Islam. Three journalists are also imprisoned.

April 24

TERRORISM: In Peshawar, Pakistan, Maulavi Mohammad Siddiquillah, a mujahideen commander associated with Gulbuddin Hekmatyar, is assassinated.

April 25

DIPLOMACY: The European Union pledges $26 million in aid for displaced Afghan refugees.

April 27

POLITICS: Throughout Iran, hard-line Islamic clerics endorse a political crackdown coupled with the closing of several reformist newspapers.

May

POLITICS: Throughout this month, Taliban forces torture and kill civilians in the Robatak Pass between Baghlan and Samangan Provinces, Afghanistan.

May 1

POLITICS: In Tehran, Iran, 13 Iranian Jews are placed on trial after being charged with spying for Israel.

May 5

POLITICS: In Iran, runoff elections result in a gain of 47 seats for moderate reform ers, 10 for conservatives, and nine for independents.

May 8

POLITICS: In Jidda, Saudi Arabia, the Organization of the Islamic Conference sponsors indirect peace talks between the Taliban and opposition delegates.

May 9

DIPLOMACY: In Washington, D.C., the government announces $4 million for UN refugee efforts in Afghanistan.

POLITICS: In Jidda, Saudi Arabia, peace talks result in an agreement to exchange prisoners.

May 10

POLITICS: In Tehran, Iran, six of 13 Jewish Iranians plead guilty to spying for Israel.

May 17

DIPLOMACY: In Washington, D.C., a delegation representing former Afghan monarch Mohammad Zahir Shah arrives to promote the idea of a *loya jirga* to facilitate creation of a broad-based national government in Afghanistan. Among those in attendance is a minor Pashtun dignitary, Hamid Karzai.

May 18

DIPLOMACY: In Washington, D.C. the government endorses a plan for former Afghan monarch Mohammad Zahir Shah to hold a *loya jirga* in Afghanistan and possibly bring peace.

May 19

DIPLOMACY: In Moscow, Russia, President Vladimir Putin and President Islom Karimov of Uzbekistan pledge to cooperate in the fight against terrorism sponsored by the Taliban regime of Afghanistan.

The Pakistani government and the Taliban regime agree to recognize the Durand Line establishing the boundary between their countries, and Pakistan agrees to close down all mujahideen training camps.

In Washington, D.C., the United States pledges $500,000 to assist emergency drought conditions in southern Afghanistan.

May 20

AVIATION: In Takhar Province, Afghanistan, warplanes operated by the Taliban bomb the alliance-held town of Taliqan, killing a UN aid worker and six children.

May 22

DIPLOMACY: In Moscow, Russia, the government accuses the Taliban regime of funneling arms and supplies to Chechen insurgents. It also warns of preemptive strikes against Afghanistan if that country becomes a threat to Russian security.

May 23

MILITARY: In Afghanistan, Taliban forces claim to have captured the strategic Salang Tunnel after two days of intense fighting with mujahideen loyal to Ahmad Shah Massoud.

May 26

DIPLOMACY: The United States and Russia agree that the UN Security Council must take positive steps against Afghanistan if the Taliban regime continues to ignore world opinion.

TERRORISM: In Kabul, Afghanistan, a bomb explodes at a Taliban ammunition dump; opposition leaders deny any culpability.

May 27

DIPLOMACY: U.S. under secretary of state Thomas Pickering meets with Taliban deputy foreign minister Abdul Jallil and demands the extradition of Saudi terrorist Osama bin Laden.

May 28

DIPLOMACY: In Kabul, Afghanistan, Mullah Omar denies that there are any terrorist training camps in Afghanistan. However, Western and Pakistani intelligence services identify such camps at Rishkor and in Laghman and Khost Provinces.

June 4

POLITICS: In Afghanistan, the Taliban accuses alliance forces of breaking a cease-fire arrangement in Ghorwand, Parvan Province, during the UNICEF vaccination program.

June 7

DIPLOMACY: In New York City, the UN Security Council is feeling increased pressure for tougher sanctions against Afghanistan for its failure to extradite Saudi terrorist Osama bin Laden.

June 10

MILITARY: Taliban forces begin massing in northern Afghanistan in preparation for an offensive against the Northern Alliance. This move induces Uzbekistan to begin reinforcing its border with Afghanistan.

June 14

DIPLOMACY: In New York City, the UN Security Council begins weighing "intelligent" sanctions against the Taliban regime that would protect the general population. However, doubts are expressed concerning Pakistan's commitment to enforcement.

Members of the Central Asian Economic Association insist that the international community is not doing enough to end the strife in Afghanistan.

MILITARY: In Afghanistan, the Northern Alliance claims to have wrested Chaghcharan, capital of Ghowr Province, away from the Taliban.

June 23

DIPLOMACY: The UN High Commissioner for Refugees warns that drought conditions in southern Afghanistan could lead to a massive exodus into Pakistan and Iran unless aid is dispatched. The United States agrees to provide $6 million to assist the region.

June 24

DIPLOMACY: In Kabul, Afghanistan, leaders from the Pakistani Jamiat-i-Islami arrive and argue that the Taliban should not turn Osama bin Laden over to the West.

June 26

DIPLOMACY: In Kabul, Afghanistan, the Taliban regime agrees to stop poppy production as soon as international aid arrives to repair the nation's damaged infrastructure.

MILITARY: In Afghanistan, the Northern Alliance claims that the Taliban is preparing to launch a summer offensive to capture Dara-i-Suf, Samangan Province.

June 30

AVIATION: In Baghdad, Iraq, the government announces that it has resumed development of liquid-fueled ballistic missiles capable of carrying explosives or biological and chemical weapons.

DIPLOMACY: The Organization of the Islamic Conference declares that a military solution to Afghan strife is untenable and also calls for an end to hostilities and a ban of all arms shipments from abroad.

July 1

MILITARY: North of Kabul, Afghanistan, fighting erupts between Taliban and anti-Taliban forces near Bagram; it has the net effect of cancelling the exchange of 4,000 prisoners worked out by the Organization of the Islamic Conference.

POLITICS: In Tehran, Iran, a court finds 10 Jews guilty of spying for Israel, and they receive sentences ranging from four to 13 years in prison; the verdict is criticized by Western governments. Three Jews are also acquitted.

July 4

DIPLOMACY: In Karachi, Pakistan, the U.S. consul general declares that sanctions against Afghanistan will remain in effect until Saudi terrorist Osama bin Laden is handed over by the Taliban.

July 6

DIPLOMACY: The government of Turkmenistan contracts with the Taliban regime to provide electricity to the city of Herat.

July 9

MILITARY: In Afghanistan, the Northern Alliance admits to losing ground north of Kabul to the latest Taliban offensive.

July 10

POLITICS: In Afghanistan, the Taliban bans nongovernmental agencies from employing female workers; it is unclear if the government is referring only to Afghan employees.

TERRORISM: In Kabul, Afghanistan, a bomb explodes outside the Pakistani embassy; the Northern Alliance is blamed for the blast.

July 12

DIPLOMACY: In Tehran, Iran, the government orders its border with Afghanistan sealed to halt the flow of drugs.

POLITICS: In Afghanistan, the United Nations begins negotiating with the Taliban for them to lift their ban on female aid workers.

The Taliban expel American aid worker Mary MacMakin from Afghanistan on the grounds that she was spying for the United States.

July 15

DIPLOMACY: In Kabul, Afghanistan, Mullah Omar refuses to hand over Saudi terrorist Osama bin Laden to American authorities.

July 17

TERRORISM: In Kabul, Afghanistan, the house of a Pakistani diplomat is bombed; the Taliban regime blames opposition forces.

July 18

DIPLOMACY: In New York City, the UN World Food Program announces a major relief operation to assist 1.6 million Afghans imperiled by famine arising from drought conditions.

POLITICS: In Afghanistan, the Taliban arrest members of the Pakistani soccer team for wearing shorts, and their heads are shaved as punishment. The government subsequently apologizes to Islamabad for the incident.

July 20

DIPLOMACY: In Kabul, Afghanistan, the United Nations admits no progress has been made in talks concerning female workers in nongovernmental organizations.

July 21–22

TERRORISM: In Kabul, Afghanistan, responsibility for a spate of bomb explosions is laid on the doorstep of the Northern Alliance.

July 25

DIPLOMACY: In Islamabad, Pakistan, the government demands the extradition of all Pakistanis suspected of terrorist activities; the Taliban regime says it will comply if evidence can be produced.

POLITICS: In Baghlan Province, Afghanistan, the Taliban arrest Commander Bashir Baghlani on suspicion that he was in collusion with alliance forces; the opposition says he was arrested for refusing to provide the Taliban with recruits.

July 28

MILITARY: Intense fighting is reported in Baghlan Province, Afghanistan, as the Taliban offensive continues.

POLITICS: In Kabul, Afghanistan, Mullah Omar decrees a complete ban on poppy and opium production.

July 29
MILITARY: In northern Afghanistan, Taliban forces manage to cut communications between the Panjshir Valley and Takhar Province along the Tajikistan border. This action imperils alliance forces loyal to Ahmad Shah Massoud.

July 30
MILITARY: The Taliban offensive storms into the strategic region of Burqa, Afghanistan.

July 31
POLITICS: Iran, assisted by the United Nations, begins expelling 65,000 illegal Afghan refugees from its territory.

August
AVIATION: This month Baghdad International Airport is allowed to open temporarily to accommodate a number of humanitarian flights.

August 3
MILITARY: In Takhar Province, Afghanistan, Taliban forces capture the strategic town of Ishkamish from mujahideen under Ahmad Shah Massoud.
POLITICS: In Kabul, Afghanistan, the United Nations continues pressing the Taliban to allow it to recruit female workers for all nongovernmental organizations.

August 5
MILITARY: In northern Afghanistan, anti-Taliban forces claim to recapture a strip of territory along the Salang highway.

In Herat Province, Afghanistan, seven members of the Organization for Mine Clearance are killed; the Taliban blame the Northern Alliance for the attack.

August 6
MILITARY: In Takhar Province, Afghanistan, Taliban forces capture the town of Banji from Northern Alliance forces.

August 7
MILITARY: As the Taliban advance on Taliqan, Afghanistan, Northern Alliance opposition stiffens, resulting in heavy casualties to both sides.

August 8
POLITICS: The United Nations demands the arrest and punishment of those responsible for the murder of seven Organization for Mine Clearance workers on August 5.

In Iran, the extremist Islamist judiciary closes down the popular daily *Bahar,* which is also the last reformist newspaper.

August 9
MILITARY: In northern Afghanistan, fighting intensifies near Taliqan.

POLITICS: Due to the current ban on poppy production, the price of opium rises steeply in Afghanistan.

August 10
MILITARY: Fighting around Taliqan, Afghanistan, abates slightly, and the Northern Alliance reiterates its willingness to accept UN mediation.

August 11
DIPLOMACY: In Moscow, Russia, the government says most guerrillas captured or killed in Chechnya are actually Afghan mercenaries.
MILITARY: On the Tajikistan border, Tajik and Russian border guards repel a Taliban attempt to cross over.

August 13
MILITARY: Taliban forces renew their attempt to capture Taliqan, Afghanistan, and make some progress on the ground.

August 16–17
POLITICS: In Kabul, Afghanistan, the Taliban close down all UN World Food Program bakeries due to the ban on female workers. They reverse themselves a day later following strong UN protests.

August 19
DIPLOMACY: In Kabul, Afghanistan, the Taliban regime reaffirms its decision not to extradite Saudi terrorist Osama bin Laden.
MILITARY: In Afghanistan, Northern Alliance forces claim to capture the Daray-i-Noor district near Jalalabad, along with parts of the Khiva district.

August 21
POLITICS: In Samangan Province, Afghanistan, the UN World Food Program delivers emergency relief supplies to the inhabitants of alliance-held Dara-i-Suf, then besieged by Taliban forces.

August 22
DIPLOMACY: In New York City, the UN Security Council is alerted that the Afghan population could not withstand imposition of further sanctions, save for arms embargos.

August 25
MILITARY: Northeast of Kabul, Afghanistan, mujahideen allied with Ahmad Shah Massoud make continued progress against the Taliban.

August 26
POLITICS: In Kabul, Afghanistan, the Taliban regime, pointing to the suffering of the people, calls for an end to economic sanctions.

August 30
DIPLOMACY: Turkmenistan advances peace proposals that the Taliban appear willing to embrace, including the release of some political prisoners.

August 31

DIPLOMACY: In Islamabad, Pakistan, the government endorses an Afghan peace plan promulgated by Turkmenistan.

MILITARY: In Afghanistan, the Northern Alliance claims to have captured Baghlan Province back from the Taliban.

September 1

DIPLOMACY: In Afghanistan, the UN-sponsored land-mine-clearance program is threatened by a lack of funding

TERRORISM: In Jalalabad, Afghanistan, the Pakistani embassy is damaged by a bomb.

September 2

POLITICS: In Turkmenistan, mujahideen leader Ahmad Shah Massoud meets with officials regarding a possible end to the civil war in Afghanistan.

September 4

MILITARY: In western Iran, mujahideen leader Ismail Khan begins recruiting fighters from refugee camps in order to fight the Taliban.

September 4–6

MILITARY: Taliban forces, including Arab and Pakistani fighters, start an all-out drive to capture Taliqan that culminates in its capture. The fighting leads to a wave of refugees headed for Tajikistan and Pakistan.

September 9

MILITARY: Taliban forces continue fighting to clear away alliance forces from the outskirts of Taliqan, Afghanistan.

September 10

MILITARY: North of Kabul, Afghanistan, fighting begins anew around Bagram Air Base.

September 13

MILITARY: Ballistic rockets slam into Kabul airport from surrounding villages, a good indication of how far south alliance forces have infiltrated.

September 14

POLITICS: In Tobat-e-Heydarieh, Iran, Iranian police corner and kill 11 Afghan bandits.

Opium production drops 28 percent in Afghanistan, but that country continues to be the world's biggest supplier.

September 15

DIPLOMACY: In Kabul, Afghanistan, Sadako Ogata, the UN High Commissioner for Refugees, discusses the issue of women's rights with the Taliban regime.

September 17

MILITARY: Northern Alliance forces have settled into the hills surrounding Taliqan while the Taliban offer to hold peace talks with Ahmad Shah Massoud.

September 18

DIPLOMACY: In Kabul, Afghanistan, the Taliban regime presses the UN High Commissioner for Refugees to lift economic sanctions and provide political recognition.

September 19

MILITARY: In Kunduz Province, Afghanistan, Taliban forces capture the Imam Sahib district and further imperil the supply lines of Ahmad Shah Massoud; the town is recaptured the following day.

POLITICS: In Taliqan, Afghanistan, the UN World Food Program arrives to assist civilians displaced by the recent fighting.

September 21

MILITARY: A surging Taliban offensive seizes Hazarbagh, north of Taliqan, Afghanistan, along with the Khawajaghar airport.

POLITICS: In Tehran, Iran, an appeals court reduces the sentences of 10 Jews convicted of spying for Israel.

September 22

DIPLOMACY: In Kabul, Afghanistan, the Taliban seek international aid to compensate farmers for cutbacks in the production of poppy, the sole cash crop in many regions. They also protest the UN decision to cut back on substitute crops.

The government of Tajikistan warns that its stability is threatened by Islamic extremists trained and supplied by the Taliban.

President Burhanuddin Rabbani appeals for international aid in getting the Taliban regime out of Afghanistan; he warns that the entire region will pay a steep price should an extremist Islamic state take root there.

MILITARY: In northern Afghanistan, Taliban forces continue making impressive gains by capturing the port of Sher Khan Bandar on the Amu Darya River, the Imam Sahib and Dashti Archi districts of Kunduz Province, and the Ali Khanoum border area of Takhar Province.

September 23

POLITICS: In Kabul, Afghanistan, two men are publicly executed by the Taliban for having carried out bombing operations in the capital.

September 28

DIPLOMACY: In Rome, Italy, the government suggests establishing a humanitarian corridor in Afghanistan to allow all factions to have access to humanitarian aid.

September 29

POLITICS: An estimated 8,000 Afghan refugees flee to Pakistan to escape the latest round of combat.

TERRORISM: In Kabul, Afghanistan, bombs explode at the offices of the Al-Rasheed Trust aid agency and a newspaper that supports the Taliban movement.

September 30

MILITARY: Taliban forces storm into the Karkhar Gorge east of Taliqan, Takhar Province. This passage leads directly into Badakhshan Province, the seat of the Northern Alliance.

October

AVIATION: This month Iraq is allowed to reestablish air links by scheduling domestic passenger flights for the first time since 1991. Destinations include Russia, Ireland, and several Middle Eastern countries.

October 1

DIPLOMACY: The government of Uzbekistan opens discussions with the Taliban regime to address security concerns in Central Asia.

October 2

POLITICS: In Kandahar, Afghanistan, two men accused of murder and robbery are publicly hung by the Taliban.

October 5

DIPLOMACY: In Kabul, Afghanistan, a UN special envoy arrives for talks with the Taliban and discovers that the regime is interested in peace talks and a possible political settlement.

October 6

POLITICS: In Iran, anti-Taliban leaders meet to form the new United Front in exile.

October 7

POLITICS: In Meshhed, Afghanistan, Ahmad Shah Massoud, Abdul Rashid Dostum, and Ismail Khan gather to open a united front against the Taliban.

October 8

DIPLOMACY: Mujahideen leader Ahmad Shah Massoud urges the international community to continue pressuring Pakistan into ending the Afghan civil war.

October 9

MILITARY: Firing along the Tajikistan border results in the death of a Russian border guard, and five Tajiks are wounded.

October 12

TERRORISM: At Aden, Yemen, a terrorist attack on the guided-missile destroyer *Cole* kills 17 sailors and wounds 39. The ship itself is also seriously damaged by an inflatable speedboat laden with a half ton of high explosives, which rips out a 40-foot hole in its port side. The *Cole* returns to the United States atop the Norwegian commercial heavy-lift ship *Blue Marlin,* and it is repaired in Pascagoula, Mississippi. The vessel resumes active duty with the fleet on April 19, 2002. Surprisingly, no terrorist network claims responsibility for the attack, but American intelligence points to fugitive Saudi Osama bin Laden.

DIPLOMACY: In Washington, D.C., the government warns the Taliban that Afghanistan faces a military response if Saudi terrorist Osama bin Laden is behind the attack on the USS *Cole.*

October 15
MILITARY: In northern Afghanistan, the Northern Alliance counterattacks and makes gains in the Khoja Ghar district of Takhar Province and the Imam Sahib and Dashti Archi districts of Kunduz Province.
TERRORISM: In Kabul, Afghanistan, a bomb explodes outside the Ministry of Communications.

October 16
DIPLOMACY: In Kabul, Afghanistan, the Taliban regime denies that Osama bin Laden had any role in the attack on the USS *Cole* in Yemen.

October 19
POLITICS: The UN High Commissioner for Refugees criticizes the effects of religious extremism in Afghanistan.

October 20
DIPLOMACY: In New York City, the United Nations releases figures showing that a combination of drought and anti-drug measures on Afghan borders have brought opium revenues down from $230 million to $90 million.
TERRORISM: In New York City, Ali A. Mohamed, a former U.S. Army sergeant, pleads guilty to assisting in the bombings of the U.S. embassies in Kenya and Tanzania. He

The crew of the USS *Cole* escort their damaged ship aboard a U.S. Navy tug vessel in the harbor of Aden, Yemen. On October 12, 2000, al-Qaeda terrorists exploded a small boat against the side of the *Cole,* killing 19 U.S. sailors. *(Department of Defense)*

says the purpose of the bombings was to persuade Western nations to remove themselves from the Middle East.

October 23
DIPLOMACY: Afghan president Burhanuddin Rabbani entreats Pakistan to stop providing arms to the Taliban. He also predicts that the Northern Alliance will mount a major offensive against them before the onset of winter but believes that outright revolts in Taliban areas are necessary to bring them to the negotiating table.
MILITARY: In Afghanistan, opposition forces storm across a river near Taliqan, cutting off the Taliban-held city of Kunduz.

October 24
DIPLOMACY: The United Nations estimates that the latest round of fighting in Afghanistan has displaced another 60,000 people with winter fast approaching.

October 26
DIPLOMACY: The Russian defense minister meets with Ahmad Shah Massoud, a redoubtable adversary during the Soviet invasion years, while the Taliban warns them against providing arms to the Northern Alliance.
MILITARY: In Afghanistan, mujahideen loyal to Ahmad Shah Massoud begin shelling Taliban positions in and around Taliqan.

October 27
POLITICS: The UN World Food Program predicts that thousands of Afghans will not survive the upcoming winter unless they receive immediate funding to support emergency food distribution.

October 29
POLITICS: In Kabul, Afghanistan, the Taliban regime decrees a ban on all poppy-seed planting in the following season.

November
DIPLOMACY: Throughout the month, the Baghdad regime balks at new weapons inspections proposed by the United Nations.

November 2
DIPLOMACY: In Islamabad, Pakistan, U.S. and Taliban ambassadors meet to discuss issues pertaining to the drug trade and Saudi terrorist Osama bin Laden.

November 3
POLITICS: The Taliban and opposition leaders finally agree to UN-sponsored peace talks.

November 6
DIPLOMACY: The government of Kazakhstan advises the Taliban regime it is willing to engage in talks for pragmatic reasons.

POLITICS: In Kabul, Afghanistan, Mullah Muhammad decrees that men without beards are banned from seeking employment or any governmental services.

November 7
DIPLOMACY: In New York City, the United Nations votes against recognizing the Taliban regime in Afghanistan and its seat remains held by opposition members.
POLITICS: In a battle along their mutual border, Iranian police kill 13 Afghan drug smugglers.

November 9
DIPLOMACY: In Moscow, Russia, the government refuses to negotiate with the Taliban and urges that existing sanctions be intensified.
POLITICS: In Islamabad, Pakistan, the government bans any further influx of Afghan refugees into the North-West Frontier Province for security reasons. This decision is applauded by the Taliban regime and criticized by the opposition.

November 10
DIPLOMACY: In Islamabad, Pakistan, British and Taliban ambassadors meet to discuss a wide range of issues.
MILITARY: In Tajikistan, Taliban mortar rounds land and result in a retaliatory threat from Russia.

November 12
DIPLOMACY: In Kabul, Afghanistan, the Taliban regime threatens Russia and all Central Asian allies if they continue supplying arms to Ahmad Shah Massoud. It also requests Pakistan to withdraw its ban on refugees.

November 13
MILITARY: In Samangan Province, Afghanistan, opposition leader Paydel Pahlwan joins the Taliban with 150 fighters due to Russian support for Ahmad Shah Massoud.

November 14
DIPLOMACY: In Rome, Italy, former Afghan monarch Mohammad Zahir Shah meets with opposition leaders over the possibility of holding a *loya jirga* to decide the future of Afghanistan; the Taliban oppose the process.

November 17
DIPLOMACY: The United Nations requests Pakistan to reopen its borders to Afghan refugees.

November 18
DIPLOMACY: In Kabul, Afghanistan, the Taliban regime refuses to extradite 18 Pakistani militants accused of political assassinations in their home country.

November 19
POLITICS: In Islamabad, Pakistan, the government says it will open its borders to Afghan refugees who carry relevant documentation.

November 20

MILITARY: Intense fighting resumes around Taliqan in northern Afghanistan, with conflicting claims regarding casualties and territorial gains.

POLITICS: In Kabul, Afghanistan, the Taliban regime rejects former king Mohammad Zahir Shah's offer of a peace proposal.

November 21

DIPLOMACY: The governments of India and Russia begin pushing for greater economic sanctions against the Taliban if they fail to stop their violence.

November 22

TERRORISM: In Kabul, Afghanistan, an explosion rocks the Ministry of Information.

November 23

DIPLOMACY: In Kandahar, Afghanistan, the UN special envoy and the Taliban foreign minister engage in discussions about possible peace talks.

November 24

DIPLOMACY: In Kabul, Afghanistan, the Taliban regime accuses Russia of supplying the Northern Alliance with weapons and ammunition throughout its attack on Taliqan.

November 26

POLITICS: In Afghanistan, several foreign aid workers are detained by the Taliban because of alleged irregularities in their paperwork.

November 27

POLITICS: The Russian government reports that Afghan refugees on the border of Tajikistan have been fired upon by Taliban border guards.

November 28

DIPLOMACY: In New York City, the United Nations says it requires $229 million for emergency relief efforts in Afghanistan. Pakistan claims the funding is necessary to help it support an estimated 2.6 million refugees within its borders.

November 30

DIPLOMACY: In Kabul, Afghanistan, the Taliban regime condemns additional sanctions enacted against it, pointing to the suffering of average citizens. It also again refuses to extradite Saudi terrorist Osama bin Laden, insisting that a ban on his supposed activities will suffice.

In Tehran, Iran, the government announces that Afghan drug smugglers will be shot on sight in an attempt to halt the flow of illegal drugs and violence across the border.

December

DIPLOMACY: This month the Baghdad regime halts all oil exports after the United Nations refuses to allow a 50-cents-a barrel surcharge on all foreign oil transactions not under direct UN supervision.

December 1

DIPLOMACY: The European Parliament passes a resolution demanding that all members of the European Union break diplomatic ties with the Taliban regime.

December 10–19

POLITICS: In Afghanistan, the United Nations and nongovernmental agencies begin withdrawing their staff out of fear of Taliban reprisals.

December 20

DIPLOMACY: In New York City, the UN Security Council renews existing sanctions against the Taliban regime and this time includes a complete arms embargo, the closure of all Taliban offices abroad, and a refusal to let Taliban officials leave the country. It also demands that the Taliban extradite fugitive Saudi terrorist Osama bin Laden.

December 28

MILITARY: In Bamiyan Province, Afghanistan, intense combat breaks out near Imam Sahib, Taliqan, and the Panjshir Valley; the Northern Alliance claims to have made some territorial gains.

2001

January 2

POLITICS: In Kabul, Afghanistan, Taliban leader Mullah Omar decrees that any conversion from Islam to Christianity is punishable by death.

January 4

DIPLOMACY: In Islamabad, Pakistan, Foreign Minister Abdul Sattar announces that Pakistan will comply with the latest round of UN sanctions against Afghanistan.

January 6

POLITICS: In Afghanistan, President Burhanuddin Rabbani promises to end mandatory veil use by women once the Taliban are ejected from power.

January 7

MILITARY: In Bamiyan Province, Afghanistan, Taliban forces recapture Yakaolang, whereupon they are accused of atrocities against Shiite Hazaras.

January 8

DIPLOMACY: The latest round of UN-imposed sanctions are enacted against the Taliban regime of Afghanistan.

January 9

POLITICS: In Yemen, government authorities say that Saudi terrorist Osama bin Laden was probably involved in the attack on the USS *Cole*.

January 10

POLITICS: Throughout Pakistan, religious groups rally to the side of the Taliban due to the UN sanctions.

January 31

POLITICS: In Herat, Afghanistan, the United Nations reports that 110 people have died of cold and hunger.

February 2

DIPLOMACY: In New York City, the United Nations publishes the names of 54 Taliban diplomats whose accounts are to be frozen.

February 7

DIPLOMACY: In Kabul, Afghanistan, Interior Minister Muinuddin Haidar of Pakistan arrives to demand the extradition of 60 Pakistanis suspected of religious terrorism in the homeland.

February 9

DIPLOMACY: In New York City, the United States shuts down the Taliban office despite UN protests.

POLITICS: In Islamabad, Pakistan, the government declares a ban on the admission of new Afghan refugees.

February 10

POLITICS: In Afghanistan, Northern Alliance leaders offer to engage in peace talks with the Taliban.

February 14

DIPLOMACY: In Kabul, Afghanistan, the Taliban shut down the UN office in retaliation for the closure of their own office in New York City.

MILITARY: In Afghanistan, the Northern Alliance claims to have recaptured Bamiyan City, Bamiyan Province, but is retaken by the Taliban within three days.

February 16

AVIATION: Over Baghdad, Iraq, 24 aircraft from the carrier *Harry S. Truman* strike radar sites and air-defense command centers in retaliation for a series of violations in the northern and southern "no-fly zones." These sites were judged potentially menacing for aircraft patrolling the zones.

February 19

DIPLOMACY: The organization Human Rights Watch releases its report on Taliban atrocities for May 2000 and January 2001. It characterizes the regime as brutal toward all political opposition.

February 20

DIPLOMACY: In New York City, the United Nations reiterates its warning of starvation conditions throughout Afghanistan.

February 22

AVIATION: In Washington, D.C., President George W. Bush gives his first news conference and mentions his concerns that the Chinese are assisting Iraq with radar defense systems.

February 24
DIPLOMACY: In Cairo, Egypt, Secretary of State Colin Powell mentions that Iraqi president Saddam Hussein has yet to develop meaningful weapons of mass destruction and is still unable to project conventional military power against neighboring countries.

February 26
POLITICS: In Kabul, Afghanistan, Mullah Omar orders the destruction of all statues, an act that brings condemnation from the international community.

March 1
POLITICS: In Bamiyan Province, Afghanistan, the Taliban begin destroying giant Buddha statues in defiance of world opinion.

March 2
DIPLOMACY: UNESCO requests that the Taliban stop destroying all pre-Islamic statues. It also begins a series of international visits but is ignored by local authorities.

March 5
POLITICS: In a radio broadcast from Kabul, Afghanistan, Mullah Omar decries the giant Buddha statues as "idols" whose destruction was warranted.

March 12
AVIATION: In Kuwait, during Operation Desert Spring, a live-fire exercise at night, an F/A-18 Hornet from the carrier *Harry S. Truman* accidentally drops a 500-pound bomb on allied personnel, killing five Americans and a New Zealand army officer; an additional five Americans and two Kuwaitis are injured.
DIPLOMACY: In Moscow, Russia, President Vladimir Putin declares his intention to resume the sale of conventional weapons to Iran following a five-year hiatus.

March 13
POLITICS: In Bamiyan Province, Afghanistan, an Afghan freelance photographer records the destruction of the giant Buddhist statues.

March 20
POLITICS: In Afghanistan, the Taliban again prohibit the celebration of the New Year.

March 28
POLITICS: In Kabul, Afghanistan, the religious police order primary students to wear white turbans and secondary students to wear black ones.

April 3–7
DIPLOMACY: Northern Alliance leader Ahmad Shah Massoud begins a tour of European capitals to raise cash and arms for anti-Taliban forces. He also wants them to pressure Pakistan to stop interfering in Afghanistan's internal affairs.

April 10
POLITICS: Several conservative religious organizations in Pakistan convene a conference, after which they read friendly messages to Osama bin Laden and Mullah Omar of Afghanistan.

May 1
DIPLOMACY: In Washington, D.C., the State Department accuses Pakistan of providing military support to the Taliban regime in Afghanistan.

May 5
POLITICS: In Kabul, Afghanistan, the Taliban regime summarily forbids foreigners from alcohol, pork, loud music, or consorting with the opposite sex.

May 17
POLITICS: Ismail Khan returns to Afghanistan from Iran to lead a united front against the Taliban regime from western portions of the country.

May 18
POLITICS: In Kabul, Afghanistan, the Ministry of Enjoining Good and Forbidding Evil closes an Italian-financed hospital because male and female nurses ate together.

May 22
POLITICS: In Kabul, Afghanistan, Mullah Omar again orders that Hindus are forbidden from wearing turbans and must wear yellow identification marks on all clothing.

May 24
POLITICS: In Kabul, Afghanistan, the Taliban regime orders all Afghan Hindu women to wear yellow identification marks as well as full-length Afghan burqas.

May 31
POLITICS: In Kabul, Afghanistan, the Taliban regime orders all female foreign workers to stop driving.

June 3
POLITICS: In Afghanistan, the Taliban approve a yearly budget that includes $14 million for religious primary education and $1.14 million for secondary education.

June 4
POLITICS: In Kabul, Afghanistan, the Taliban regime formalizes a code for foreign nationals that forces them to obey Islamic rules and outlaws adultery, missionary activities, music, television, pork, and "immoral clothing."

June 8
POLITICS: In Iran, President Mohammad Khatami is overwhelmingly reelected with 76 percent of votes cast and vows to pursue greater freedom and social reforms. However, the country is still effectively run by the Ayatollah Ali Khamenei, the conservative courts, and the military.

June 20
DIPLOMACY: In Washington, D.C., the Senate passes a resolution condemning Taliban policies toward women and minorities.

June 26
POLITICS: In Kabul, Afghanistan, the Taliban regime appoints Mullah Muhammad Taher as minister of planning, Mullah Saduddin Said as minister of public works, and Ahmatullah Matih as minister of agriculture.

June 27
DIPLOMACY: Responding to a firestorm of international criticism, the Taliban regime withdraws its requirement that Afghan Hindus wear yellow identification marks.

June 29
DIPLOMACY: In Washington, D.C., the government reiterates its warning to the Taliban that they would be held accountable for any future attacks by Osama bin Laden.

July
POLITICS: In Afghanistan, the Taliban arrest eight international aid workers, charging them with spreading Christianity.

July 2
DIPLOMACY: In Islamabad, Pakistan, U.S. ambassador Wendy Chamberlain and Under Secretary of State Richard Armitage again warn the Taliban ambassador of military retaliation should Osama bin Laden launch any terror attacks.

July 4
DIPLOMACY: Taliban representatives in Saudi Arabia and the United Arab Emirates are called home.

July 12
POLITICS: In Kabul, Afghanistan, the Taliban regime prohibits the use of the Internet and orders all state employees to wear black clothing.

August 7
MILITARY: Forces loyal to General Abdul Rashid Dostum begin massing for a renewed offensive against Taliban forces.
POLITICS: In Kabul, Afghanistan, Taliban authorities refuse outside access to the eight incarcerated aid workers accused of preaching Christianity.

August 8
POLITICS: In Tehran, Iran, Mohammad Khatami is inaugurated for his second term as president and vows to continue along the path of social reform.

August 10
AVIATION: Over Iraq, 50 F-14 and F/A-18 aircraft launched from the carrier *Enterprise* join British jets in the latest round of punitive strikes against Iraqi antiaircraft emplacements southeast of Baghdad. This is the 25th retaliatory strike for Iraqi violations of Operations Northern and Southern Watch.

August 13
POLITICS: In Afghanistan, mujahideen commander Abdul Haq demands the formation of a broad-based, national union government in Kabul.

August 27
POLITICS: In Kabul, Afghanistan, a diplomatic delegation is allowed access to eight aid workers charged with preaching Christianity.

September 4

POLITICS: In Kabul, Afghanistan, trials begin for eight foreign aid workers charged with preaching Christianity. They consist of four Germans, two Americans, and two Australians working for Shelter Now International.

September 7

POLITICS: In Kabul, Afghanistan, the Taliban minister of justice informs fellow Afghans that Islam prohibits friendship with infidels and that they should avoid all contact with them.

September 9

TERRORISM: Mujahideen leader Ahmad Shah Massoud is assassinated by two Arabs posing as journalists; a bomb hidden in their videocamera explodes, killing all three. The attack is viewed as an al-Qaeda operation, performed on behalf of the Taliban by Osama bin Laden. Massoud is succeeded by General Mohammad Qasim Fahim.

September 11

MILITARY: In Washington, D.C., a hijacked airliner flown by terrorists slams into the Pentagon, killing 125 military and civilian personnel. Among them is Lieutenant General Timothy J. Maude, deputy chief of staff for personnel and the highest-ranking fatality since World War II.

NAVAL: In the wake of devastating terrorist attacks in New York City and Washington, D.C., several navy vessels patrol coastal waters. The attack on the Pentagon took the lives of 33 sailors and six civilian workers, while wounding four sailors and two navy civilians.

TERRORISM: A defining tragedy in American history unfolds as two hijacked airliners, commanded by Muslim fanatics, crash into New York's World Trade Center, collapsing both towers and killing 3,000 people. Another airliner crashes into the Pentagon in Washington, D.C., while a fourth crashes in a field in rural Pennsylvania as the passengers attempt to wrest control from their abductors. President George W. Bush immediately declares these terrorist acts, the largest in human history, to be the work of Saudi fugitive Osama bin Laden and his al-Qaeda ("The Base") terrorist network.

September 12

DIPLOMACY: In New York, a UN resolution calls for all nations to collaborate in punishing those responsible for the 9/11 terrorist attacks.

A New York City firefighter looks up at what remains of the World Trade Center after the terrorist attack of September 11, 2001. It was this incident that led to the invasion of Afghanistan that October. *(U.S. Navy)*

Smoke and flames rise over the Pentagon during the night of September 11, 2001, after terrorists crashed an airliner into the building. *(U.S. Navy)*

In Washington, D.C., President George W. Bush addresses the nation on television to declare war on terrorism and all parties responsible for it.

POLITICS: In Afghanistan, thousands of Afghans and international aid workers begin flooding over the border into Pakistan out of fear of what will happen if the Taliban do not extradite Saudi terrorist Osama bin Laden. Defense Secretary Donald Rumsfeld also allegedly suggests that the overall response against terrorism gave the United States an opportunity to confront the menace posed by Iraqi president Saddam Hussein.

September 13

DIPLOMACY: As the United States begins mobilizing for war against the Taliban, Pakistani president Pervez Musharraf declares his support for American military actions launched from Pakistani soil.

In Brussels, Belgium, NATO secretary-general George Robertson states that the organization will invoke a clause stating that an attack on one of its 19 constituent members is an attack on the entire alliance.

In Kabul, the Taliban regime declares that it will turn Osama bin Laden over to the United States if Washington presents convincing evidence he was behind the attack.

September 14

DIPLOMACY: In Washington, D.C., and London, United Kingdom, the respective governments accuse Saudi terrorist Osama bin Laden of being the architect of the 9/11 attacks.

In Washington, D.C., a State Department official warns representatives from 15 Arab nations to either join the coalition against global terrorism or face diplomatic isolation. Deputy Defense Secretary Paul Wolfowitz comments that combating terrorism includes ending any nation-state that supports it.

POLITICS: In Kabul, Afghanistan, Mullah Omar calls on Muslims worldwide to prepare for a jihad, or holy war.

September 15

POLITICS: In Afghanistan, the death of Ahmad Shah Massoud is publicly confirmed by the Northern Alliance. The Taliban also order all foreigners out of the country.

September 16

DIPLOMACY: In Washington, D.C., President George W. Bush addresses a joint session of Congress and issues an ultimatum to the Taliban in Afghanistan: Either surrender fugitive terrorist Osama bin Laden or face war with the United States.

September 17

DIPLOMACY: In Kabul, Afghanistan, a delegation of Pakistani government representatives arrives to demand the extradition of Osama bin Laden within three days, but Mullah Omar refuses.

MILITARY: In Washington, D.C., President George W. Bush orders a highly classified, worldwide military response against global terrorism, and Afghanistan, home of the radical Taliban movement, becomes the first priority.

September 18

TERRORISM: In Washington, D.C., President George W. Bush announces that he wants Osama bin Laden "dead or alive."

September 20

AVIATION: Over southern Iraq, U.S. and British warplanes bomb a number of missile sites that had apparently locked onto them. The administration denies any link between this action and the September 11 attack.

September 20–21

DIPLOMACY: In his address to a special session of Congress, President George W. Bush reiterates demands that the Taliban regime of Afghanistan surrender Osama bin Laden or face immediate military action. The Taliban refuse to comply, setting the stage for a major military response.

POLITICS: In Afghanistan, a gathering of mullahs requests that Saudi terrorist Osama bin Laden be "invited" to leave the country to circumvent U.S. military action. The Taliban agree to consider their edict but request additional time.

September 22

DIPLOMACY: The United Arab Emirates breaks off diplomatic relations with Afghanistan.

September 24

DIPLOMACY: In Kabul, Afghanistan, Pakistan begins withdrawing its diplomatic personnel from the country. The United States also begins freezing the accounts of individuals and organizations suspected of supporting terrorism.

In Moscow, Russia, the government promises to allow the United States access to its air space for military actions in Afghanistan.

In Washington, D.C., President George W. Bush declares all terrorist-related assets in the United States frozen and also grants the treasury secretary power to impose sanctions on any bank providing terrorists access to the international financial system.

MILITARY: In Afghanistan, the Taliban admit to losing Zaare, near Mazar-i-Sharif, to the Northern Alliance.

September 25

DIPLOMACY: The government of Saudi Arabia breaks off diplomatic relations with Afghanistan.

September 26
DIPLOMACY: In Islamabad, Pakistan, the government again pledges to cut all ties to the Taliban and cooperate with the United States in the war on terror.

September 28
DIPLOMACY: In Rome, Italy, a delegation under Yunnis Qanuni, representing the United Front, meets with former Afghan monarch Mohammad Zahir Shah. Meanwhile, President Burhanuddin Rabbani declares that he sees no role for the king in a future goverment.

In New York City, the UN Security Council unanimously passes a resolution requiring all 189 member states to take action against global terrorism, especially pertaining to financing, training, and movements.

September 29
DIPLOMACY: In Washington, D.C., King Abdullah of Jordan arrives to sign a free-trade agreement with the United States and also pledges his support for an antiterrorist effort.

MILITARY: In Washington, D.C., the government announces that American and British Special Forces have been deployed inside Afghanistan since mid-September; they are gathering military intelligence and establishing links with the Northern Alliance.

POLITICS: In Kandahar, Afghanistan, Pakistani clerics meet with Mullah Omar in an attempt to get him to surrender Saudi terrorist Osama bin Laden, but he refuses.

September 30
DIPLOMACY: In Washington, D.C., President George W. Bush approves legislation to provide direct military assistance to the Northern Alliance in Afghanistan.

October
AVIATION: The air force and the Central Intelligence Agency jointly begin operations against the Taliban with unmanned, remotely guided RQ-1 Predator aircraft, each armed with deadly and accurate Hellfire missiles.

October 1
POLITICS: In Afghanistan, the United Front decides to constitute an Interim Government following talks with former monarch Mohammad Zahir Shah in Rome, Italy. It also seeks to call a *loya jirga* for establishing a new government in Afghanistan.

October 2
DIPLOMACY: George Robertson, secretary-general of NATO, says that evidence submitted by the United States to prove that al-Qaeda is responsible for the 9/11 terrorist attacks, is "clear and compelling." As a member nation that has been attacked, the United States requests military assistance against terrorist cells in Afghanistan and receives it.

POLITICS: In Kabul, Afghanistan, the Taliban regime once again refuses to extradite Saudi terrorist Osama bin Laden to the United States.

October 4

DIPLOMACY: In London, United Kingdom, the government releases classified files of evidence linking Saudi terrorist Osama bin Laden to the 9/11 attacks. Prime Minister Tony Blair also declares that no one can now doubt Osama bin Laden's role in the attack.

In Washington, D.C., President George W. Bush pledges $320 million in humanitarian aid for Afghanistan, to be delivered before the onset of winter.

October 5

MILITARY: An advance force of 1,000 troops from the U.S. 10th Mountain Division arrives in Uzbekistan to secure airport facilities. These are the first troops to deploy in territory belonging to the former Soviet Union.

October 6

DIPLOMACY: In Kabul, Afghanistan, the Taliban offer to release all eight imprisoned aid workers if the United States will guarantee that it will not attack and the propaganda war against the regime is ended. The offer is completely rejected by the Bush administration.

In Rome, Italy, former Afghan monarch Mohammad Zahir Shah calls for the United Nations to participate in creation of a new Afghan government.

MILITARY: A group of 1,000 Special Forces arrives in Uzbekistan prior to their clandestine deployment in Afghanistan.

October 7

AVIATION: U.S. and British warplanes begin Operation Enduring Freedom, a concerted aerial campaign to drive the Taliban and al-Qaeda from power in Afghanistan. The attacks are run in concert with the Northern Alliance, an anti-Taliban group, and they include aircraft from the carriers *Enterprise* and *Carl Vinson*; 50 Tomahawk cruise missiles are also launched from a variety of vessels. Lieutenant General Charles W. Wald serves as the joint force air component commander throughout this operation.

B-2 Spirit bombers of the 509th Bomb Wing at Whiteman Air Force Base, Missouri, fly to Afghanistan and back on the longest bombing mission in aviation history.

Marine squadrons VMFA-251 and 314, launching from the carriers *Theodore Roosevelt* and *John C. Stennis,* are joined by Harrier jump jets of the 15th Marine Expeditionary Unit (SOC) as part of Operation Enduring Freedom.

MILITARY: Special Forces teams arrive in northern Afghanistan to coordinate anti-Taliban efforts with the Tajiki-based Northern Alliance while also directing close support bombing missions.

Additional elements of the 10th Mountain Division (Light) arrive in Uzbekistan to guard an airfield utilized by U.S. Special Forces for search-and-rescue operations; this is the first American military unit deployed on territory of the former Soviet Union.

POLITICS: A videotape of Osama bin Laden is broadcast, praising the 9/11 attacks on the United States.

October 8

AVIATION: Over Afghanistan, C-17 Globemaster IIIs perform their first combat mission by dropping pallets containing 37,000 "Humanitarian Daily Rations" to territory controlled by the Northern Alliance.

Coalition aircraft begin around-the-clock air strikes against Taliban positions throughout Afghanistan, especially Kabul and Kandahar. This action enables the Northern Alliance to begin counterattacking across a broad front.

October 9

AVIATION: Over Afghanistan, U.S. and coalition warplanes begin their first daylight raids against Taliban targets. The Pentagon also acknowledges the destruction of seven terrorist training camps, although these were probably already vacant when struck.

October 10

AVIATION: In Washington, D.C., the government announces that it has secured complete control of airspace over Afghanistan.

DIPLOMACY: In Qatar, an emergency meeting of the Organization of the Islamic Conference gathers to condemn the recent attacks on the United States. The group avoids directly condemning the ongoing military campaign in Afghanistan.

October 11

AVIATION: An al-Qaeda compound in Kandahar, Afghanistan, and Taliban positions in Kabul are struck by U.S. warplanes in daylight for the first time.

October 12

NAVAL: In the Arabian Sea, the carrier *Kitty Hawk* deploys to serve as a floating base for forthcoming Special Forces operations in Afghanistan. To accomplish this, most of its air assets have been transferred ashore.

October 13

AVIATION: Kabul airport is subject to U.S. bombing raids for the first time; four civilians are reported killed.

DIPLOMACY: In Kabul, Afghanistan, the Taliban regime continues to reject U.S. demands to extradite Saudi terrorist Osama bin Laden.

It is revealed that the government of Uzbekistan will allow U.S. military forces to operate from bases on its soil and against the Taliban in Afghanistan.

October 15

AVIATION: U.S. warplanes continue to pound Taliban and al-Qaeda training camps in Kabul and Jalalabad, Afghanistan.

POLITICS: In Afghanistan, Foreign Minister Abdullah Abdullah of President Burhanuddin Rabbani's government, announces that the Northern Alliance will not occupy the capital of Kabul until an interim government arises.

October 16

AVIATION: In Kabul, Afghanistan, a U.S. air strike inadvertently damages Red Cross warehouses. Taliban positions around Jalalabad are struck by American helicopter gunships for the first time.

POLITICS: The UN World Food Program declares it will restore a supply route to northern Afghanistan; the first Russian aid also arrives in that region.

October 18
AVIATION: U.S. warplanes heavily strike Taliban positions in and around Kabul, Afghanistan; the Northern Alliance declares its intention to march on the city and liberate it.

TERRORISM: Four al-Qaeda members implicated in the bombings of the U.S. embassies in Kenya and Tanzania receive life sentences.

October 19
AVIATION: In Pakistan, an army helicopter involved in Operation Enduring Freedom crashes, killing two soldiers.

DIPLOMACY: In Islamabad, Pakistan, Secretary of State Colin Powell and President Pervez Musharraf pledge to seek a coalition government in Afghanistan. Moderate members of the Taliban might be invited to join.

MILITARY: The first wave of U.S. Special Forces arrives in Afghanistan to cooperate closely with indigenous forces and help guide precision air strikes.

October 20
MILITARY: Southwest of Kandahar, Afghanistan, 100 men of the 75th Ranger Regiment deploy onto a Taliban-held airfield, find it deserted, then search all adjoining buildings for possible military intelligence. Once reinforced by a Delta Force unit, the Rangers subsequently capture a house used by Taliban leader Mullah Omar.

October 21–22
AVIATION: Coalition warplanes strike at Taliban positions north of Kabul, Afghanistan, softening them up for an eventual Northern Alliance offensive. Mazar-i Sharif is struck especially hard as the opposition closes in.

October 22
AVIATION: In Washington, D.C., Defense Secretary Donald Rumsfeld declares that coalition air strikes are presently in support of Northern Alliance forces.

October 24
MILITARY: Northern Alliance forces advance, covered by an umbrella of U.S. air power, yet Taliban forces fiercely resist north of Mazar-i-Sharif.

POLITICS: In Peshawar, Pakistan, Sayyid Ahmad Gailani meets with various tribal chiefs to expand the anti-Taliban alliance.

October 25
AVIATION: Coalition warplanes continue striking Taliban positions at Kabul, Afghanistan, and north of the city to assist the Northern Alliance.

October 26
AVIATION: In Kabul, Afghanistan, U.S. warplanes again accidentally strike Red Cross warehouses.

DIPLOMACY: In Prague, Czech Republic, a government official declares that 9/11 ringleader Mohammad Atta met in the city with an Iraqi intelligence official five months prior to the attack.

TERRORISM: In Afghanistan, former mujahideen leader Adbul Haq and two associates are executed by the Taliban for fomenting a rebellion among fellow Pashtuns.

October 27

AVIATION: Throughout the day, coalition warplanes pound Taliban positions in northern Afghanistan as opposition forces begin driving southward.

MILITARY: In Pakistan, armed militants begin filtering into Afghanistan to support the Taliban regime.

October 28

AVIATION: Along the Kakala River on the border of Tajikistan, U.S. warplanes attack Taliban positions. Beginning this week, coalition aircraft also switch from bombing fixed assets of the Taliban and al-Qaeda to hitting front-line units opposing the Northern Alliance.

October 30

MILITARY: In Afghanistan, Northern Alliance forces begin positioning themselves north of Kabul in preparation for an advance.

October 31

AVIATION: In light of their tenacious resistance, Taliban units in northern Afghanistan are subject to another round of intense aerial bombardment by U.S. warplanes.

November 2

AVIATION: In Afghanistan, the crew of an MH-53J Pave Low helicopter of the 20th Special Operations Squadron braves hazardous weather to fly behind enemy lines and rescue the crew of another MH-53 that crashed. They are awarded a Mackay Trophy.

MILITARY: North of Kandahar, Afghanistan, Hamid Karzai, a noted Pashtun leader, rallies anti-Taliban forces and sentiment among his fellow Pashtuns.

November 3

TERRORISM: The al-Jazeera network airs a videotape by Saudi terrorist Osama bin Laden in which he characterizes American military activity in Afghanistan as an assault against Islam.

November 4

AVIATION: It is reported that American warplanes are dropping large "Daisy Cutter" bombs on Taliban positions in Afghanistan. These fearsome fuel-air explosives can kill people within 100 yards of the drop point.

November 5

AVIATION: Taliban units in Samangan and Balkh Provinces, Afghanistan, withstand a heavy U.S. aerial bombardment, as do some units still garrisoned in Taliqan. The

Pentagon also announces that precision air strikes are being employed against the caves and tunnel systems known to be used by the Taliban and al-Qaeda.

November 5–18
MILITARY: In Afghanistan, the Northern Alliance, buttressed by coalition air power, begins an offensive that quickly overruns half the country. This action has problems of its own as the alliance, based mostly on Tajik, Uzbek, and Hazara tribesmen, has great antipathy for the Pashtun people, who occupy the eastern third of Afghanistan. Fortunately, alliance leaders agree to form an inclusive government once the fighting successfully concludes.

November 6
DIPLOMACY: President George W. Bush addresses a 17-nation antiterrorist summit in Warsaw, Poland, via satellite. He states for the first time that Saudi terrorist Osama bin Laden is trying to obtain chemical, biological, and nuclear weapons technology. He also meets with French president Jacques Chirac and British prime minister Tony Blair.
MILITARY: Heavy fighting, backed by air attacks, erupts outside of Mazar-i-Sharif, Afghanistan, while Northern Alliance forces claim to capture the settlement of Ogopruk.
POLITICS: In Afghanistan, the United Front releases a list of 60 candidates for the upcoming *loya jirga*, most from its own organization.

November 8
AVIATION: Outside Mazar-i-Sharif, Afghanistan, U.S. warplanes catch a group of Pakistani militants out in the open, killing 85.
MILITARY: Massed Northern Alliance forces begin moving in on Mazar-i-Sharif from the south.

November 9
MILITARY: The city of Mazar-i-Sharif, Afghanistan, falls to the Northern Alliance force under generals Abdul Rashid Dostum and Mohammad Mohaqiq; hundreds of Taliban prisoners are apparently massacred by the victors after the surrender.

November 11
MILITARY: Unable to withstand the deluge of aerial assaults, Taliban leader Mullah Omar allegedly orders his forces to abandon the capital of Kabul, Afghanistan, and redeploy closer to Kandahar, their spiritual capital.

November 12
MILITARY: The city of Herat, Afghanistan, falls to Northern Alliance forces under Ismail Khan as their offensive gathers steam; they are assisted by British ground forces.

November 13
MILITARY: Backed by coalition air power, troops and tanks of the Jamiat-i-Islami forces in the Northern Alliance roll into the capital of Kabul, Afghanistan, while Saudi terrorist Osama bin Laden disappears from view. Taliban forces under Mullah

Omar are also in full retreat across the country. The newcomers are enthusiastically greeted as liberators by people who have chafed for several years under severe Taliban restrictions.

November 13–27

MILITARY: The last stand by Taliban, al-Qaeda, and 3,000 foreign fighters (Arabs, Pakistanis, and Chechens) at Kunduz withers under a steady hail of coalition bombs. By the time the city falls, the Northern Alliance has seized 6,000 Taliban prisoners.

November 14

MILITARY: Opposition forces under Haji Qadir and the Shiite-dominated Hazara roll into Jalalabad, Afghanistan, without major resistance. United Front forces also storm into Ghazni and western parts of the country.

In Kunduz, Afghanistan, a raid by U.S. Army rangers rescues eight foreign aid workers, including two American women, who had been arrested by the Taliban for allegedly preaching Christianity.

November 14–December 2

MILITARY: In southern Afghanistan, Pashtun tribes under Gul Agha Sherzai and Hamid Karzai drive the Taliban from their spiritual capital at Kandahar. Both columns receive coalition air support.

November 15

MILITARY: In Washington, D.C., government officials announce that U.S. Army rangers and special forces are on the ground in Afghanistan and looking for Osama bin Laden and other al-Qaeda leaders. By this time, no less than 80 percent of the country is in the hands of Northern Alliance forces, the complete opposite of the situation a month earlier.

It is reported that 150 British and American Special Forces have been deployed north of Kabul, Afghanistan, probably to coordinate air operations with the Northern Alliance.

POLITICS: In Kabul, Afghanistan, Foreign Minister Abdullah Abdullah declares that, with the Taliban clearly defeated, international forces are no longer necessary.

November 16

AVIATION: A U.S. air strike in Afghanistan apparently results in the death of Mohammad Atef, a senior al-Qaeda leader and a close associate of Osama bin Laden.

MILITARY: A force of 100 British Special Forces arrive at Bagram Air Base, Afghanistan.

November 17

DIPLOMACY: The Iranians reopen their embassy in Kabul, Afghanistan.

MILITARY: Forces loyal to Ismail Khan attack and capture Farah Province from Taliban forces.

POLITICS: In Kabul, Afghanistan, former president Burhanuddin Rabbani arrives and promises to establish a broad-based government.

November 18

NAVAL: Petty Officer Vincent Parker and Petty Officer Third Class Benjamin Johnson die aboard an Iraqi tanker they were inspecting when the dangerously overloaded vessel suddenly sinks in heavy seas. Previously, it had been halted by the destroyer *Peterson* on the suspicion that it was smuggling oil out of Iraq.

POLITICS: In Afghanistan, television broadcasting resumes and features two female announcers.

November 19

AVIATION: U.S. warplanes continue bombing Taliban forces in Taliqan, their final stronghold in northern Afghanistan.

DIPLOMACY: In Kabul, Afghanistan, the United States applies direct pressure on the Northern Alliance to establish a broad-based coalition government in the capital.

MILITARY: Northen Alliance forces storm onto Chagatai Ridge overlooking the besieged city of Taliqan, Afghanistan, in preparation for an attack on the city.

TERRORISM: On the road between Kabul and Jalalabad, Afghanistan, armed gunmen seize and execute four Western journalists.

November 21

DIPLOMACY: In Islamabad, Pakistan, the government orders two Taliban consulates to be closed.

November 22

MILITARY: In Kunduz, Afghanistan, fierce fighting erupts in the Taliban garrison between factions that wish to surrender to Northern Alliance forces and those determined to continue fighting.

November 23

AVIATION: In Kandahar, Afghanistan, U.S. warplanes drop 15,000-pound "Daisy Cutter" bombs on Taliban positions.

MILITARY: Taliban forces continue resisting tenaciously in Kunduz, Afghanistan, which leads to another round of heavy aerial bombardment by U.S. warplanes. However, the majority of defenders are preparing to surrender.

November 24

MILITARY: The surviving Taliban forces in Kunduz, Afghanistan, finally capitulate to the Northern Alliance. In true Afghan fashion, roughly 300 fighters change sides and join the victors while 400 die-hard foreign fighters are detained in a local fort.

November 25

MARINES: In Afghanistan, the 15th Marine Expeditionary Unit (SOC) from the *Peleliu* amphibious-ready group helicopters 400 miles inland and deploys at an abandoned airstrip christened Forward Operating Base Rhino. From there the marines begin patrolling the region for Taliban and al-Qaeda fighters as reinforcements are airlifted in from the 26th Marine Expeditionary Unit (SOC) from the *Bataan* amphibious-ready group.

November 25–27

AVIATION: During a prison uprising in Mazar-i-Sharif, Afghanistan, air force jets drop bombs that accidentally wound five Special Forces soldiers; they are immediately evacuated to medical facilities at Landstuhl, Germany.

MILITARY: Hundreds of captured Taliban prisoners held at the fortress of Mazar-i-Sharif rise in revolt. CIA operative Johnny "Mike" Spann also becomes the first American to die during the fighting. Nearly all 600 Taliban captives involved are killed during the rebellion.

November 26

AVIATION: F-14Ds from the carrier *Carl Vinson* wipe out a 15-vehicle Taliban convoy after being directed to it by Marine AH-1W Super Cobra helicopters operating from Forward Operating Base Rhino.

MILITARY: The Taliban stronghold of Kunduz, Afghanistan, is declared secured by the Northern Alliance after a two-week siege.

A force of 500 Marines arrives at Kandahar, Afghanistan, and takes control of a local airfield. Large numbers of Taliban remain in the nearby city but do not attack the marines.

November 27

AVIATION: U.S. warplanes begin a series of air strikes in Kandahar, Afghanistan, against a compound that Defense Secretary Donald Rumsfeld characterizes as "clearly a leadership area."

November 27–December 5

POLITICS: In Bonn, Germany, a gathering of the four leading factions of Afghans from Rome, Peshawar, and Cyprus begin negotiations to establish an interim government in Afghanistan. Their efforts are facilitated by the United Nations.

November 28

AVIATION: Operation Swift Freedom unfolds as Air Mobility Command C-17 Globemaster III transports carry army Special Forces troops to an airstrip near Kandahar, Afghanistan.

MILITARY: At Mazar-i-Sharif, Afghanistan, the first elements of the 10th Mountain Division become the first regular army units to deploy in the theater.

November 30

MILITARY: Northern Alliance forces begin massing for an advance upon Kandahar, Afghanistan, the spiritual center of the Taliban.

TERRORISM: Special Forces fighting in Mazar-i-Sharif, Afghanistan, capture 84 surviving Taliban fighters, among them 20-year-old John Walker Lindh, an American citizen from San Anselmo, California, apparently fighting alongside them. Once returned to the United States, he faces possible treason charges.

December

POLITICS: Throughout the month, the UN World Food Program moves 90,000 tons of wheat into famine-threatened regions of Afghanistan.

December 1–2

AVIATION: Air Force B-52s launch punishing attacks against Taliban positions around Kandahar, Afghanistan, in some of the heaviest raids of the war.

December 4

AVIATION: Coalition aircraft begin pounding the mountain refuge of Tora Bora, a heavily fortified cave complex 55 miles south of Jalalabad, which holds an estimated 2,000 al-Qaeda fighters. Fugitive Saudi terrorist Osama bin Laden is thought to be among them.

MILITARY: Southwest of Kandahar, Afghanistan, U.S. marines occupy another air-field to deny its use to the Taliban as American, British, and Australian forces close in on the city itself.

POLITICS: In Mazar-i-Sharif, the United Nations pulls outs its international staff once fighting breaks out among Northern Alliance factions.

TERRORISM: The *Washington Post* runs a story that Saudi terrorist Osama bin Laden was working on his own "dirty" (radioactive) bomb. Rumors also circulate that CIA director George J. Tenet is investigating the possibility that Iraqi president Saddam Hussein possesses nuclear weapons of any kind.

December 5

AVIATION: In Afghanistan, a 2,000-pound bomb dropped by a B-52 accidentally strikes an American command post, killing three Special Forces soldiers and five Afghan allies; 20 Americans and 18 Afghans are wounded. The Afghans in question were led by Hamid Karzai, newly appointed head of the Afghan government; he is slightly injured.

MILITARY: From Forward Operating Base Rhino, Afghanistan, the 15th Marine Expeditionary Unit (SOC) conducts a motorized convoy of light armored vehicles below Kandahar to interdict any Taliban reinforcements entering the area.

December 5–6

POLITICS: In Bonn, Germany, representatives from the four Afghan factions agree to an interim government headed by Pashtun leader Hamid Karzai for the next six months. After that a *loya jirga* (grand council) will convene to form a new administration to sponsor free elections within two years.

December 6

POLITICS: In Kandahar, Afghanistan, Taliban leader Mullah Omar abrogates power to a local chieftain, then flees for the mountains.

December 7

AVIATION: Coalition aircraft resume bombing the Tora Bora cave complex in southern Afghanistan, to root out any remaining Taliban or al-Qaeda fighters lurking there.

MILITARY: Taliban forces, mercilessly harassed by coalition air power and Northern Alliance ground forces, abandon their traditional stronghold of Kandahar and melt into the mountains along the Pakistan border. Their regime fell after only 62 days of fighting, mostly aerial bombardment.

In southern Afghanistan, marines ambush a Taliban convoy, killing seven fighters and destroying three trucks. Marine aircraft also take out several more vehicles nearby.

December 9
MILITARY: Kandahar, Afghanistan, the spiritual home of the Taliban movement, is completely occupied by Northern Alliance forces.

December 11
MILITARY: In Kabul, Afghanistan, the long-abandoned U.S. embassy is reclaimed by the 26th Marine Expeditionary Unit (SOC). Shortly after, it is relieved by the 4th Marine Expeditionary Brigade.
POLITICS: In Afghanistan, General Abdul Rashid Dostum voices his opposition to the new Bonn agreement.

December 12
AVIATION: Off Diego Garcia in the Indian Ocean, the guided-missile destroyer *Russell* rescues the crew of an air force B-1B bomber, which ditched en route to targets in Afghanistan. This is the first B-1B lost in combat and the first lost during Operation Enduring Freedom.

December 13
POLITICS: In Kabul, Afghanistan, interim president Hamid Karzai arrives for the first time and begins forming a government.
TERRORISM: The U.S. government releases a newly captured videotape of Saudi terrorist Osama bin Laden, in which he extols the casualties inflicted on 9/11. The Americans offer it as proof of his complicity in the attack.

December 14
MILITARY: In Afghanistan, troops from the 26th Marine Expeditionary Unit (SOC) travel overland from Forward Operating Base Rhino to seize the Kandahar airfield. Soon afterward, this location becomes an important detention facility for Taliban captives of interest to U.S. military intelligence.

December 15
AVIATION: The carrier *Enterprise* is relieved by the *John C. Stennis* after its air groups have flown 4,200 sorties and dropped 2 million pounds of bombs on Taliban targets in Afghanistan.
MILITARY: Near the Pakistani border, British troops and Northern Alliance forces attack the last-known remnants of al-Qaeda in Afghanistan while Pakistani army patrols cut off any retreat into their territory.

December 16
MILITARY: Men of the new Pashtun-based Eastern Alliance clear out remaining al-Qaeda pockets at Tora Bora after killing 200 and capturing 11. American and British Special Forces begin combing through the caves over in subsequent weeks, but no trace of Osama bin Laden is found.

POLITICS: In Washington, D.C., Secretary of State Colin Powell declares that "we've destroyed al-Qaeda in Afghanistan." However, the government admits it has no knowledge of Osama bin Laden's whereabouts.

December 17

AVIATION: At Istres Air Base, France, Air Mobility Command (MAC) C-17 Globemaster IIIs begin airlifting French military forces to Afghanistan as part of Operation Enduring Freedom.

DIPLOMACY: In Kabul, Afghanistan, the U.S. embassy, which had been closed since the Soviet withdrawal from Afghanistan on January 31, 1989, is reopened for business.

December 19

MILITARY: An agreement is concluded between the United Nations and the Afghan Interim Government for a British-led, international peacekeeping force to garrison the country; this becomes known as the International Security Assistance Force.

December 20

MILITARY: In Afghanistan, 53 Royal Marines arrive as the spearhead of the International Security Assistance Force. Meanwhile, the final al-Qaeda fighters depart the Tora Bora area and head for Pakistan.

December 21

MILITARY: North of Kabul, Afghanistan, Northern Alliance fighters storm into Pul-i Khumri north of the capital, along with Qala-i-Nau in Badghis Province.

December 22

MILITARY: In Kabul, Afghanistan, General Tommy Franks arrives to attend ceremonies marking the inauguration of an interim government under Hamid Karzai, the acting prime minister. Karzai is installed only 78 days after the commencement of Operation Enduring Freedom, along with 30 cabinet members.

December 24

POLITICS: To help squelch dissent among Northern Alliance members, General Abdul Rashid Dostum is appointed deputy minister of defense.

December 27

NAVAL: In Washington, D.C., the Department of Defense announces that Taliban and al-Qaeda captives seized in Afghanistan will be interned in special facilities at Guantánamo Bay, Cuba.

TERRORISM: The al-Jazeera network broadcasts a videotape of Osama bin Laden, looking gaunt and tired, in which he states his intention to destroy the U.S. economy.

December 28

TERRORISM: The United States begins drawing up rules for military tribunals to try terrorist suspects, although suspects can only face the firing squad through a unanimous tribunal vote.

December 29

AVIATION: Based on bad information given by local warlord Pacha Khan Zadran, U.S. warplanes bomb a suspected Taliban gathering, only to kill 110 Paktia villagers. This raid was apparently manipulated to settle old scores.

December 31

AVIATION: By this date, navy aircraft have accounted for 72 percent of all tactical air strikes and more than half of all precision-guided weapons launched against Taliban and al-Qaeda forces in Afghanistan.

2002

January 1–2

AVIATION: At Kandahar, Afghanistan, U.S. Marines are airlifted to Helmand Province to search for Mullah Omar, now a wanted refugee.

January 3

MILITARY: In Afghanistan, Forward Operating Base Rhino closes once the 15th Marine Expeditionary Unit ships back to its vessels.

January 4

DIPLOMACY: In Kabul, Afghanistan, Interior Minister Yunnis Qanuni signs a security-force deployment agreement with British general John McColl. The 4,500-man force will consist of troops from 17 nations.

TERRORISM: Near Khost, Afghanistan, terrorists shoot and kill army Sergeant Nathan Chapman, who is the first American soldier to die from enemy fire.

January 5

POLITICS: In Kabul, Afghanistan, a government official declares that anti-Taliban operations in the southern mountains have been completed but fugitive Mullah Omar has apparently escaped the noose.

January 7

AVIATION: U.S. warplanes bomb positions near Khost, Afghanistan, apparently trying to kill or flush out Taliban leader Halauddin Haqqani, a wanted refugee.

January 8

MILITARY: At military bases throughout Afghanistan and Central Asia, U.S. forces begin settling in for a long haul in the war against global terrorism.

January 9

AVIATION: In Pakistan, a KC-130R from VMGR-352 crashes near Shamsi military airfield, killing seven marines.

POLITICS: In Kabul, Afghanistan, President Hamid Karzai calls for a new, national army to unite the country.

January 11

AVIATION: At Guantánamo Bay, Cuba, a C-17 Globemaster III arrives with the first 20 of 371 Taliban and al-Qaeda detainees. Defense Secretary Donald Rumsfeld characterizes them as "unlawful combatants," and thus not covered by the Geneva Convention rules respecting prisoners.

POLITICS: In Kandahar, Afghanistan, the governor announces that Mullah Obaidullah, the Taliban minister of defense, Mullah Nooruddin Rurabi, the minister of justice, and Mullah Saadudin, minister of mines and industry, have all surrendered to local authorities. They are soon joined by Mullah Haqani, the former ambassador to Pakistan.

TERRORISM: In Guantánamo Bay, Cuba, terrorist detainees begin arriving for interrogation. The facilities are guarded by the 2nd Marine Expeditionary Force.

January 15–16

TERRORISM: In Alexandria, Virginia, former Taliban John Walker Lindh, 20, is formally charged with conspiring to kill U.S. citizens and abetting terrorism. He appears in court the next day to confront his parents, whom he has not seen in two years.

January 17

DIPLOMACY: In Kabul, Afghanistan, Secretary of State Colin Powell arrives to assure the new government of continuing American assistance, both financial and military.

January 19–February 8

MILITARY: At Kandahar airfield, Afghanistan, the 26th Marine Expeditionary Unit is replaced by the 101st Airborne Division and begins shipping back to the *Bataan*. During these proceedings, a CH-53E Super Stallion crashes on January 20, killing two marines and injuring five.

January 21

AVIATION: After Iraqi antiaircraft weapons fire at coalition aircraft enforcing Operation Southern Watch, American and British jets retaliate by striking weapons emplacements at Tallil, 170 miles southeast of Baghdad.

DIPLOMACY: In Tokyo, Japan, an international conference pledges $2.6 billion in reconstruction aid for newly liberated Afghanistan.

January 24

MILITARY: In Oruzgan Province, Afghanistan, an attack by U.S. Army troops results in the deaths of 16 armed Afghans and the capture of 27, none of whom are Taliban or al-Qaeda fighters.

January 25

POLITICS: In Kabul, Afghanistan, Mohammad Ismail Qasimyar, a noted political figure, heads up a 21-member commission tasked with choosing delegates for a *loya jirga* slated to assemble in June.

January 27

POLITICS: In Afghanistan, the national banner of the 1964 constitution is adopted by the new interim government.

January 28

MILITARY: In Kandahar, Afghanistan, Afghan security forces corner six pro-Taliban Arab fighters in a hospital and kill them all.

January 29

POLITICS: In Washington, D.C., President George W. Bush declares in his State of the Union address that rogue nations such as Iran, Iraq, and North Korea constitute an "axis of evil" in the world. Moreover, he pledges that none of them will be allowed to develop or possess nuclear weapons or other devices of mass destruction. He also says that the war against global terrorism has only begun.

MILITARY: At Kandahar airfield, Afghanistan, the 3rd Brigade, 101st Airborne Division, deploys and replaces marine forces. Under the code name Task Force Rakkaan, it consists of three battalions of the 187th Infantry Regiment.

January 31

DIPLOMACY: Members of the Iraqi opposition call upon President George W. Bush to help them overthrow the regime of President Saddam Hussein.

MILITARY: In Paktia Province, Afghanistan, warlord Padsha Khan is defeated by Saif Ullah, a Pashtun chieftain who seized control following the defeat of the Taliban.

February 4

AVIATION: Over Afghanistan, an MQ-1B Predator unmanned aerial vehicle (UAV) fires a Hellfire missile at a group of senior al-Qaeda figures on the ground, killing them. This is the first combat missile launch by a UAV.

Over Mosul, Iraq, Iraqi antiaircraft weapons fire at coalition aircraft enforcing Operation Northern Watch and are, in turn, attacked by American and British jets.

February 5

AVIATION: South of Khost, Afghanistan, U.S. warplanes strike the Mafazatoo area, Gorboz district, in an attempt to flush out Taliban and al-Qaeda operatives.

TERRORISM: In Alexandria, Virginia, a grand jury indicts 20-year old John Walker Lindh on charges of abetting terrorism and conspiracy to commit murder.

February 8

TERRORISM: In Kandahar, Afghanistan, Mullah Muttawakkil, the former Taliban foreign minister, surrenders to coalition forces.

February 10

DIPLOMACY: In Meshed, Iran, the government closes down the offices of Gulbuddin Hekmatyar.

MILITARY: Control of the International Security and Assistance Force passes to Germany and the Netherlands for the next six months.

February 11–15

DIPLOMACY: In Baghdad, Iraq, a UN human-rights expert makes an official visit for the first time since 1992. He is to check out documented abuses ranging from torture, executions, and discrimination to food and health care.

February 13

TERRORISM: John Walker Lindh, a former Taliban soldier, pleads not guilty that he supported terrorist groups that plotted to kill Americans.

February 14
POLITICS: At Kabul Airport, Afghanistan, a crowd, angered by delays in flights to Mecca for the Hajj, riots and kills Aviation Minister Abdul Rahman.

February 15–16
POLITICS: In Kabul, Afghanistan, acting president Hamid Karzai claims that feuding officials pursuing a vendetta were responsible for the death of Aviation Minister Abdul Rahman; four people are arrested in the city while three more are apprehended after they flee to Saudi Arabia.

February 17
AVIATION: In an attempt to neutralize hostile militia bands not associated with the Taliban or al-Qaeda, U.S. warplanes begin dropping precision-guided "smart weapons" on selected targets.

February 21
POLITICS: Camps in Pakistan are once again swollen by thousands of Pashtun refugees fleeing ethnic cleansing activities performed by Northern Alliance forces.

February 28
AVIATION: For the second time this year, Iraqi antiaircraft weapons in Mosul fire upon coalition aircraft enforcing Operation Northern Watch. U.S. and British jets counter by attacking air defense installations in the region.

March 1
AVIATION: In eastern Afghanistan, the aerial element of Operation Anaconda commences as air force B-52s, B-1Bs, AC-130s, A-10s, and F-15s support ground units attacking Muslim extremists near Gardez. Precision-guided weapons help keep civilian casualties to a minimum while thermobaric bombs are dropped in caves; these kill terrorists by depriving them of oxygen.
MILITARY: In Shah-i-Kot, Afghanistan, 1,000 U.S. troops and Special Forces begin Operation Anaconda to flush out Taliban and al-Qaeda forces lurking in the mountainous terrain there.

March 2–10
AVIATION: An air force AC-130 Spectre gunship is on hand to relieve a detachment of the 10th Mountain Division that was surrounded by enemy fighters. Afterward, two HH-60 Blackhawk helicopters rescue them from rough terrain; the Spectre aircrew wins a Mackay Trophy for its timely support.
MILITARY: Approximately 1,200 army troops and Special Forces soldiers engage Taliban remnants in the Shah-i-Kot Valley, Afghanistan, and Operation Anaconda forces them from their stronghold at Tora Bora. Present are the 1st Battalion, 87th Infantry (10th Mountain Division), the 3rd Brigade, 101st Airborne Division, and the 1st Battalion, 75th Ranger Regiment. The ensuing operation accounts for more than 500 enemy dead at a cost of eight Americans killed and 40 wounded.

March 3
AVIATION: Above Shah-i-Kot, Afghanistan, an army CH-47 Chinook transport helicopter is brought down by Taliban fire, killing seven soldiers.

March 4
AVIATION: Near Gardez, eastern Afghanistan, a helicopter assault on enemy troops results in the deaths of two airmen. They are the first air-force combat losses during Operation Enduring Freedom.

NAVAL: During Operation Anaconda in eastern Afghanistan, Aviation Boatswain's Mate First Class Neil C. Roberts, a navy SEAL, is killed in action.

March 6
AVIATION: Helicopters airlift a large body of U.S. troops and Special Forces to the Tora Bora cave complex in southern Afghanistan to look for any lingering Taliban or al-Qaeda forces still there.

March 10
MILITARY: In the Shah-i-Kot Valley, near Gardez, Afghanistan, Operation Anaconda continues to unfold as U.S. troops battle Taliban and al-Qaeda operatives.

March 11
DIPLOMACY: In London, United Kingdom, Vice President Richard Cheney confers with Prime Minister Tony Blair on the possibility of military action against Iraqi president Saddam Hussein owing to his manufacture of weapons of mass destruction.

March 12
DIPLOMACY: In Amman, Jordan, King Abdullah warns Vice President Richard Cheney that the overthrow of Saddam Hussein in Iraq might greatly destabilize the region. He therefore urges the Americans and British to seek a peaceful settlement to the problem.

MILITARY: Afghan forces surround the Taliban mountain stronghold in the Shah-i-Kot Valley on three sides and capture the local fortress; resistance is light.

POLITICS: In London, United Kingdom, Foreign Minister Jack Straw reports to the House of Commons shared intelligence with the United States relative to Iraq and its clandestine missile program.

March 13
DIPLOMACY: In Cairo, Egypt, President Hosni Mubarak informs Vice President Richard Cheney that he will attempt to defuse the crisis with Iraq by persuading President Saddam Hussein to allow UN weapons inspectors back into the country.

March 14
DIPLOMACY: In Yemen, President Ali Abdullah Saleh informs Vice President Richard Cheney that he opposes any U.S.-led attack on Iraq.

March 16
DIPLOMACY: In Riyadh, Saudi Arabia, Crown Prince Abdullah warns Vice President Richard Cheney that a U.S.-led attack on Iraq is not in the region's best interests.

March 17
DIPLOMACY: In Bahrain, Vice President Richard Cheney mentions during a news interview that the United States is naturally concerned over the prospect of Iraqi president Saddam Hussein acquiring nuclear weapons. He also mentions that Washington has reason to believe that Baghdad is actively trying to acquire such devices.

March 20
TERRORISM: In Khost, Afghanistan, al-Qaeda operatives attack U.S. and coalition forces; no casualties result.

March 25
POLITICS: In the Burqa region of Afghanistan, a 6.1-magnitude earthquake kills 1,200 people while leaving tens of thousands homeless and in dire need of humanitarian aid. The Afghan government begins scrambling to provide assistance with help from the global community.

March 27
NAVAL: Near Kandahar, Afghanistan, Chief Hospital Corpsman Matthew J. Bourgeois, a Navy SEAL, is killed during a small-unit training exercise.

April
MILITARY: In southeastern Afghanistan, Operation Snipe is spearheaded by British Royal Commandos, backed by Afghan forces.

April 3–4
POLITICS: In Kabul, Afghanistan, authorities announce that several hundred people connected to an alleged plot to overthrow the government have been arrested; the following day 150 of 300 taken into custody are released.

April 4
POLITICS: In Kabul, Afghanistan, the government announces a new initiative to curb the production of opium poppies, the raw ingredient for heroin. The decision is badly received in many traditional poppy-growing regions.

April 8
DIPLOMACY: In Baghdad, Iraq, President Saddam Hussein halts all oil exports abroad, allegedly to hurt the U.S. economy in retaliation for its support of Israel. He calls upon other oil-exporting Arabs to do likewise, but none do.

TERRORISM: In Jalalabad, Afghanistan, defense minister Mohammad Qassim Fahim survives a failed assassination attempt when a bomb kills eight people near his motorcade.

April 15
MILITARY: In Kandahar, Afghanistan, four explosive ordnance disposal soldiers die when a cache of 107mm rockets, apparently booby-trapped, explodes in their midst.

In eastern Pakistan, coalition Special Forces commence Operation Mountain Lion against Taliban and al-Qaeda operatives lurking there.

April 16
MILITARY: A corollary to Operation Mountain Lion, Operation Ptarmigan, is begun by British ground forces and commandos.

April 18
AVIATION: In Afghanistan, an American warplane accidentally kills four Canadian soldiers and wounds eight others in an errant bomb drop south of Kandahar. Canadians were then engaged in a live-fire exercise without informing the Americans, but the pilots involved are to face a court of inquiry.

POLITICS: In Kabul, Afghanistan, former king Mohammad Zahir Shah returns home after a 29-year exile and is greeted by thousands of cheering countrymen.

April 26
POLITICS: Former president Burhanuddin Rabbani tenders his allegiance to the forthcoming *loya jirga*.

April 27
POLITICS: In Iraq, the nation officially celebrates President Saddam Hussein's 65th birthday.

April 28
POLITICS: Throughout Afghanistan, slain mujahideen leader Ahmad Shah Massoud is declared a national hero.

April 29
DIPLOMACY: In Ankara, Turkey, the government announces that it will be taking the reins of the International Security Assistance Force from Britain.

MILITARY: Northern Alliance leader General Mohammad Qassim Fahim is promoted to marshal.

April 30
MILITARY: In Washington, D.C., the Defense Department announces that 1,000 troops are being deployed along Afghanistan's eastern border with Pakistan in order to preclude Taliban and al-Qaeda infiltration.

May 2
MILITARY: In southeastern Afghanistan, Royal Marine contingents add their weight to ongoing Operation Snipe.

POLITICS: In Kabul, Afghanistan, a *loya jirga* Independent Commission gathers under UN auspices.

May 14
DIPLOMACY: In New York, the UN Security Council unanimously imposes tighter restrictions on Iraq to cut down on items potentially useful to the military, but it also allows other goods to be imported for civilian use.

May 15
POLITICS: The UN High Commissioner for Refugees seeks to draw world attention to the plight of 500,000 Afghan refugees who have returned home to poverty and deprivation.

May 20
MILITARY: In Kabul, Afghanistan, the government begins forming a national army to transcend sectionalism and local warlords.

May 23
DIPLOMACY: In New York City, the UN Security Council extends Afghanistan's international peace force's mandate by six months.
POLITICS: In northern Afghanistan, the International Committee of the Red Cross helps arrange the release of 512 Taliban prisoners from Sheberghan prison.

May 24
TERRORISM: In Kandahar, Afghanistan, a bomb attack is aimed at a local music shop.

May 26
MILITARY: In Gardez, Afghanistan, U.S. forces raid a compound and seize two Taliban suspects.

May 27
POLITICS: In Kabul, Afghanistan, former monarch Mohammad Zahir Shah declares his willingness to serve as head of state if asked by the *loya jirga*.

May 29
MILITARY: In southeast Afghanistan, British and Afghan forces commence Operation Buzzard in the vicinity of Khost.

May 31
MILITARY: In Bagram, Afghanistan, Lieutenant General Dan K. McNeill assumes command of the newly created Combined Joint Task Force 180; he is tasked with coordinating military moves by coalition forces in the country.

Taking a break here are troops under the command of Afghan general Abdul Rashim Dostum, one of the prominent leaders of the Northern Alliance who joined U.S. and NATO forces in overthrowing the Taliban in fall 2001. *(Department of Defense)*

June 6

TERRORISM: Secretary of Defense Donald Rumsfeld asks NATO members to change their prevailing defensive strategy to reflect present-day realities. He calls for a new, more aggressive approach involving preemptive war against terrorists and rogue nations possessing weapons of mass destruction.

June 11

POLITICS: In Kabul, Afghanistan, the *loya jirga* convenes with 1,598 delegates, including 190 female members, to elect a new head of state and parliament.

June 13

POLITICS: In Kabul, Afghanistan, Hamid Karzai, an ethnic Pashtun, is overwhelmingly nominated to serve as head of the provisional government by the *loya jirga*; his tally is 1,295 ballots out of 1,575, and he will serve until a general election is arranged in 2004.

June 19

POLITICS: In Kabul, Afghanistan, Hamid Karzai is inaugurated by the *loya jirga* as interim president of the new transitional government.

June 20

MILITARY: In Afghanistan, leadership of the International Security Assistance Force for Afghanistan passes from Britain to Turkey.

POLITICS: In Kabul, Afghanistan, General Mohammad Qassim Fahim remains in place as minister of defense and Abdullah Abdullah holds the post of foreign minister. However, Yunnis Qanuni transfers from minister of interior to minister of education, and remains a special adviser on national security.

June 22

POLITICS: In Kabul, Afghanistan, the transitional government begins ruling the nation with a new 29-member cabinet.

June 25

POLITICS: In Kabul, Afghanistan, Sima Samar is transferred from minister of women's affairs to president of the human rights commission.

June 28

TERRORISM: Near Spin Boldak, Afghanistan, an ammunitions dump explodes near the Pakistani border, killing 10 people and injuring 35.

July 1

AVIATION: An Air Force AC-130 gunship, alerted by a military unit that it is under fire, inadvertently attacks a wedding ceremony where participants were firing guns in the air; 40 to 80 villagers are killed. President Hamid Karzai calls for an investigation into the mishap.

POLITICS: At West Point, New York, President George W. Bush tells U.S. Military Academy cadets that the United States will not wait to be struck by terrorists, for circumstances now require America to take the battle to the enemy before bigger threats arise.

July 3
MILITARY: In North-West Frontier Province, Pakistan, four al-Qaeda operatives and three police are killed in a gunfight at the Kohat checkpoint along the Afghan border.

July 5
DIPLOMACY: In New York City, UN secretary-general Kofi Annan meets with Iraqi foreign minister Naji Sabri, and the latter rejects weapons inspection proposals. Sabri subsequently insists that any future inspections are contingent on the United Nations lifting its sanctions, ending all threats of regime change, and disbanding "no-fly zones."

July 6
TERRORISM: Afghan vice president Haji Abdul Qadir, a noted Pashtun leader, and the minister of public works are shot and killed by gunmen; their deaths may be related to government efforts to suppress the drug trade.

July 12
POLITICS: In Afghanistan, six provincial governors demand that United States forces obtain their permission before mounting military operations.

July 13
MILITARY: Outside Bagram Air Base, Afghanistan, a U.S. military convoy comes under fire as it drives toward Kabul.

July 15
TERRORISM: In Alexandria, Virginia, 21-year old former Taliban fighter John Walker Lindh pleads guilty to charges of terrorism and conspiracy; he is to be sentenced on October 4, although several charges, including murder, have been dropped.

July 19
POLITICS: At Fort Drum, New York, President George W. Bush addresses men of the 10th Mountain Division and declares that the United States is compelled to neutralize terrorist threats before they are fully formed.

July 29
MILITARY: At Ab Khail, 10 miles east of Khost, Afghanistan, U.S. forces exchange fire with al-Qaeda operatives.

August 1
DIPLOMACY: In Baghdad, Iraq, foreign minister Naji Sabri invites UN inspector Hans Blix to discuss weapons inspections.

August 2
DIPLOMACY: In Baghdad, Iraq, the government dispatches a letter to UN secretary-general Kofi Annan in which Hans Blix is invited to attend technical discussions on disarmament issues.

August 5

DIPLOMACY: In Baghdad, Iraq, the government announces that it will grant members of the U.S. Congress access to areas suspected of being related to weapons development. The offer is declined.

August 6

DIPLOMACY: In New York City, UN secretary-general Kofi Annan declares that inspectors are willing to return to Iraq, but only if the government sticks to UN inspection rules.

August 8

MILITARY: In Kabul, Afghanistan, Afghan security forces kill 13 al-Qaeda fighters; this group consisted of 12 Pakistanis and one Kyrgyz.

August 9

TERRORISM: In Jalalabad, Afghanistan, a car bomb explodes outside a construction firm building; 10 people are killed, and 25 are injured.

August 13

DIPLOMACY: In Kabul, Afghanistan, President Mohammad Khatami becomes the first Iranian head of state to visit the capital in 40 years.

August 14

MILITARY: In Kabul, Afghanistan, the formation of a French-trained battalion of the Afghan army is attended by ceremonies; a representative of the UN secretary-general is present.

August 18–26

MILITARY: Southeastern Afghanistan is the scene of Operation Mountain Sweep, conducted by men of the 82nd Airborne Division, the 75th Rangers, and accompanying aviation units. Several Taliban weapons caches are captured, but the fighters escape.

August 19

DIPLOMACY: In New York City, UN secretary-general Kofi Annan declines Iraq's most recent disarmament proposals but offers to resume weapons inspections under the terms of Resolution 1284, which was adopted in 1999. This mandates UN inspectors to return and begin free investigations into Iraq's alleged chemical, biological, and nuclear weapons programs.

August 20

POLITICS: In Berlin, Germany, a dissident group opposed to Saddam Hussein briefly takes control of the Iraqi embassy. German police storm the building five hours later, releasing five hostages.

August 26

POLITICS: In Nashville, Tennessee, Vice President Richard Cheney addresses the Veterans of Foreign Wars Convention and states that Iraq undoubtedly possesses weapons of mass destruction. Furthermore, President Saddam Hussein has acquired them for use against the United States and its allies in the Middle East. For this reason, Cheney says, the old policy of containment, which was successfully applied against communism during the cold war, is no longer a valid strategy.

September 3

DIPLOMACY: In Kabul, Afghanistan, French Minister of Foreign Affairs Dominique de Villepin arrives to assure his hosts of France's continuing support.

September 4

MILITARY: While in political exile, Gulbuddin Hekmatyar declares a jihad against American forces in Afghanistan.

POLITICS: In Washington, D.C., President George W. Bush states that he will seek congressional authorization prior to taking any military action against Iraq. He also pledges to consult with U.S. allies before going to war, although German chancellor Gerhard Schroeder says he would not support a war against Iraq, even with UN authorization.

September 5

TERRORISM: In Kandahar, Afghanistan, President Hamid Karzai survives an assassination attempt, presumably by Taliban operatives. His bodyguards kill the assassin. A car bomb also explodes in Kabul, killing 30 people.

September 7–11

MILITARY: In the Bermel Valley, Afghanistan, 175 miles south of Kabul, the 1st Battalion, 504th Parachute Infantry (82nd Airborne Division), makes several ground sweeps, seizing suspected Taliban agents, weapons, and many documents.

September 8

DIPLOMACY: In Washington, D.C., National Security Advisor Condoleezza Rice says during a televised interview that Iraqi president Saddam Hussein is illicitly attempting to procure aluminum tubes necessary for the uranium enrichment process.

September 9

MILITARY: In London, United Kingdom, the International Institute for Security Studies releases a report on Iraq that finds that nation's military strength is less than in 1991, but Iraq has been stockpiling arms since UN inspections ended in 1998. The document is noncommittal on whether action should be taken against President Saddam Hussein.

September 10–11

TERRORISM: Al-Qaeda agent Ramzi bin al-Shibh, the suspected coordinator of the 9/11 terrorist attacks, is arrested in Karachi, Pakistan, and secretly transported to an American military base for questioning.

September 11

NAVAL: In honor of the first anniversary of the 9/11 terrorist attack, the secretary of the navy instructs all vessels to fly the first navy jack (flag) of 1775, consisting of

13 red and white stripes with the motto "Don't Tread on Me," until the war against terrorism has concluded.

September 12
DIPLOMACY: In New York, President George W. Bush addresses the UN General Assembly and calls Iraqi president Saddam Hussein a "grave and gathering danger" to world peace. He insists that the world body pass a resolution requiring Iraq to readmit weapons inspectors and mandating that Iraq continue disarming. Failing that, Bush warns that the United States will intervene unilaterally, if necessary, to secure Iraqi compliance. The president also announces a $180 million donation from the United States, Saudi Arabia, and Japan, for constructing roads in Afghanistan.

September 13
AVIATION: The air force charges Majors Harry Schmidt and William Umbach with involuntary manslaughter and assault for an incident that led to the deaths of four Canadian soldiers the previous April.

In Islamabad, Pakistan, the government announces that it has arrested and detained Ramzi bin al-Shibh, a leading al-Qaeda operative.

September 14
DIPLOMACY: The government of Saudi Arabia offers the United States bases from which it could launch attacks against Iraq if a UN resolution sanctioned the move.

September 16
DIPLOMACY: In Baghdad, Iraq, the foreign minister states that UN weapons inspectors will be allowed in without preconditions or restrictions. The offer is dismissed by President George W. Bush as a time-gaining ploy.

September 17
DIPLOMACY: In Iraq, UN chief weapons inspector Hans Blix arrives in Baghdad to confer with Iraqi officials.

September 18
DIPLOMACY: In Washington, D.C., Defense Secretary Donald Rumsfeld testifies before a Senate committee to state that Iraq possesses a stockpile of chemical and biological weapons and that his operatives know that many are stored in Tikrit (Saddam Hussein's hometown) or Baghdad.

September 19
DIPLOMACY: In Washington, D.C., Defense Secretary Donald Rumsfeld says that several nations have agreed to support the United States in military action against Iraq. President George W. Bush also asks Congress for the authority to use force.

September 21
DIPLOMACY: In Tel Aviv, Israel, Prime Minister Ariel Sharon informs President George W. Bush that his country would retaliate against Iraq if it attacks.

September 22
DIPLOMACY: In London, United Kingdom, Prime Minister Tony Blair releases classified files implying that Iraq possesses significant capabilities in terms of producing and fielding weapons of mass destruction.

POLITICS: In Herat, Afghanistan, the American military arranges a meeting between warlords Ismail Khan and Gul Agha Sherzai to circumvent fighting between their followers.

Nangyar Tarzai is nominated to serve as Afghan ambassador to Pakistan.

September 25
AVIATION: The Afghan national airline, Ariana, resumes weekly flights from Kabul to Frankfurt, Germany.

September 27
TERRORISM: In Washington, D.C., Defense Secretary Donald Rumsfeld states that the United States possesses "solid evidence" of a connection between the al-Qaeda terror network and the Iraqi government.

September 28
DIPLOMACY: In Baghdad, Iraq, the government rejects a proposed UN Security Council resolution granting it 30 days to disclose all weapon inventories and allow UN inspectors unfettered access to weapon sites.

POLITICS: In Washington, D.C., Vice President Richard Cheney gives a televised interview and all but insists that Iraq can field weapons of mass destruction.

September 29
MILITARY: In southeastern Afghanistan, Operation Alamo Sweep begins as parts of the 82nd Airborne Division, the Rangers, and other units are airlifted to the Afghan-Pakistani border to root out any Taliban or al-Qaeda fighters there.

This propaganda poster promoting Osama bin Laden and his cause was found by members of a U.S. Navy SEAL team in a site in eastern Afghanistan where they were seeking intelligence information that might help to track him down. *(Department of Defense)*

October 1
DIPLOMACY: In Baghdad, Iraq, the government says it will allow UN weapons inspectors back into the country within two weeks, but it refuses them access to presidential properties and other sensitive areas.

October 2
MILITARY: In central Afghanistan, Special Forces, acting on a tip, uncover a hidden Taliban cache containing nearly 500,000 rounds of ammunition.

POLITICS: In Washington, D.C., President George W. Bush reiterates to the news media that Iraq currently possesses weapons of mass destruction.

October 4
DIPLOMACY: In Baghdad, Iraq, UN weapons inspector Hans Blix demands that the Iraqi government disclose information on all its weapons programs before additional inspectors arrive.

TERRORISM: In Alexandria, Virginia, John Walker Lindh, who apparently fought alongside Taliban forces in Afghanistan, receives a 20-year jail sentence.

October 7

DIPLOMACY: In Cincinnati, Ohio, President George W. Bush gives a speech declaring that only President Saddam Hussein's removal from power would end the current confrontation with Iraq. He insists that if Iraq has ties to al-Qaeda, it could attack the United States with chemical or biological weapons without warning—the proof would come in the form of a "mushroom cloud."

POLITICS: In Kabul, Afghanistan, the government introduces a new currency, whereby a new afghani can be exchanged for 1,000 older ones.

October 15

POLITICS: In Iraq, Saddam Hussein wins another unopposed election for the presidency.

October 16

DIPLOMACY: In Islamabad, Pakistan, Secretary of State Colin Powell and President Pervez Musharraf declare their intention to seek a coalition government in Afghanistan. Moderate members of the Taliban might be allowed to join.

POLITICS: In Washington, D.C., Congress votes to grant President George W. Bush authorization to deal with the military threat posed by Iraq and enforce any relevant UN sanctions against that nation. The vote is 296–133 in the House and 77–23 in the Senate. The president quickly signs it into law.

October 20

POLITICS: In Baghdad, Iraq, President Saddam Hussein announces that virtually all prisoners held in jail will be released.

October 23

DIPLOMACY: In London, United Kingdom, Afghan defense minister Mohammad Qassim Fahim arrives for talks on military matters.

In New York City, the United States presents the UN Security Council with a resolution mandating military action against Iraq if the latter's weapons of mass destruction are not destroyed immediately.

A recent UN report paints Afghanistan as the world's largest producer of opium once again.

November 3

AVIATION: In Yemen, the CIA fires a missile that kills al-Qaeda leader Qaed Salim Sinan al-Harethi, along with five operatives. This is the first strike against terrorist leaders outside Afghanistan.

POLITICS: In Kabul, Afghanistan, the curfew that has been enforced since 1978 is finally ended.

Former Afghan monarch Mohammad Zahir Shah officiates at opening ceremonies for the new constitutional drafting commission under Nematullah Shahrani.

The organization Human Rights Watch accuses Ismail Khan of establishing his own personal fiefdom in Herat, Afghanistan, whereby civil rights are threatened.

November 7

POLITICS: In Washington, D.C., President George W. Bush addresses the nation on television, in which he calls Iraqi president Saddam Hussein a dire threat because of his possible links to the terrorist group al-Qaeda.

November 8

DIPLOMACY: In New York City, the UN Security Council votes 15 to 0 to pass Resolution 1441, which grants Iraq a "final opportunity" to comply with all previous disarmament resolutions, including those allowing weapons inspectors. Failing this, President Saddam Hussein faces "serious consequences."

November 10

AVIATION: American warplanes begin a concerted series of attacks against Iraqi antiaircraft sites for violating UN-ordered "no fly zones."

DIPLOMACY: In Beirut, Lebanon, a meeting of Arab League foreign ministers votes to support UN inspection of Iraqi weapons but opposes a U.S.-led invasion.

November 11–12

POLITICS: In Kabul, Afghanistan, Afghan police beat and disperse university students protesting inadequate conditions; several end up in the hospital, and one is shot dead.

November 12

TERRORISM: The al-Jazeera network plays an audiotape purportedly made by Saudi terrorist Osama bin Laden in which he threatens any nation that supports a U.S.-led invasion of Iraq.

November 12–13

DIPLOMACY: In Baghdad, Iraq, the state-controlled national parliament votes unanimously to reject the latest UN resolution. However, a day later it switches gears and agrees to host weapons inspectors while denying that Iraq possesses weapons of mass destruction.

November 14

POLITICS: In Washington, D.C., Defense Secretary Donald Rumsfeld gives a radio interview and raises the possibility of an al-Qaeda attack on the continental United States or its military forces abroad with weapons of mass destruction. In that event, he warns, the anticipated death toll could range as high as 100,000.

November 17–18

AVIATION: Iraqi antiaircraft batteries fire on coalition aircraft patrolling the northern "no-fly zone," which prompts a sharp response. Aircraft drop precision-guided munitions on all the offending positions. This comes in the wake of a UN resolution authorizing strong action for Iraqi transgressions.

November 18

TERRORISM: A videotape of Saudi fugitive Osama bin Laden surfaces on the Arabic language al-Jazeera network in Qatar, affording the first proof that the wanted terrorist is still alive.

November 21

DIPLOMACY: In Prague, Czech Republic, a NATO summit meeting votes to condemn Iraq for its recalcitrance on weapons inspections, but Germany remains steadfastly opposed to an invasion.

TERRORISM: In Washington, D.C., government officials announce that wanted terrorist Abd al-Rahim al-Nashiri has been captured. He is suspected of having planned the 1998 attack on the U.S. embassies in Africa.

November 23

DIPLOMACY: In Bucharest, Romania, President George W. Bush appeals to a large audience for support in a war against Iraq.

November 25

DIPLOMACY: In Baghdad, Iraq, the first teams of UN inspectors are allowed to return.

November 27

MILITARY: In New York City, the UN Security Council unanimously extends the International Security Assistance Force's mandate for another year in Afghanistan.

December 2

POLITICS: In Bonn, Germany, Afghan delegates meet to discuss security and reconstruction matters.

In Herat Province, the Afghan government arranges a cease-fire between mujahideen loyal to Amanullah Khan, a Pashtun, and Ismail Khan, a Tajik; a recent outbreak of fighting left 60 people dead.

December 3

DIPLOMACY: In Iraq, UN inspectors make a surprise inspection visit of President Saddam Hussein's presidential palace, which results in the government filing a complaint.

December 6

NAVAL: In the Arabian Gulf, the guided-missile destroyer *Paul Hamilton* is damaged when it accidentally collides with a merchant vessel.

December 7

DIPLOMACY: In Baghdad, Iraq, the government issues a 12,000-page bundle of documents, purportedly a full accounting of all programs related to weapons of mass destruction. Various UN agencies receive copies for their perusal.

December 11

MILITARY: In Paktia Province, Afghanistan, local warlords begin open combat for control of the city of Gardez.

December 12

DIPLOMACY: By this date 98 UN weapons inspectors are active in Iraq.

POLITICS: In Kabul, Afghanistan, the supreme court under Fazl Hadi Shinwari outlaws cable television in Jalalabad.

December 14–17

POLITICS: In London, United Kingdom, a gathering of 330 Iraqi dissidents begins planning for a new government in the event President Saddam Hussein is removed from power. The delegates approve a transitional national assembly and a three-person executive council to facilitate a new constitution and national elections.

December 18

MILITARY: The United States begins deploying 50,000 additional troops in the Persian Gulf region in anticipation of a possible attack upon Iraq.

December 19

DIPLOMACY: In Washington, D.C., Secretary of State Colin Powell denounces the December 7 documents issued by Iraq as disingenuous and warns that it risks war if the pattern of deception and noncooperation continues. President George W. Bush also declares that Iraq is in material violation of Resolution 1441.

In New York, chief UN weapons inspector Hans Blix informs the UN Security Council that Iraq's claim to have abandoned programs for weapons of mass destruction are unsubstantiated. Furthermore, he says, the documents released by the Baghdad regime are simply a rehash of materials handed over in 1997.

December 21

MILITARY: An International Security Assistance Force patrol is ambushed in Kabul, Afghanistan; seven German soldiers are killed.

December 23

AVIATION: The Indian government donates another Airbus 300-B4 to Ariana Airlines.

Over Iraq, an unmanned Predator reconnaissance craft is shot down by an Iraqi fighter jet.

December 25

DIPLOMACY: The governments of Russia and Iran sign an agreement saying the former will construct a nuclear power plant in the latter. Russia also agrees to provide fuel for the reactor. The United States goes on record as opposing the accord because Iran's vast oil and gas reserves negate any need for nuclear power.

December 26

AVIATION: U.S. and British warplanes bomb a military command center southeast of Baghdad, Iraq, in retaliation for an Iraqi jet deliberately straying into a "no-fly zone."

December 27

POLITICS: An accord is concluded among Afghanistan, Turkmenistan, and Pakistan to construct a gas duct from Central Asia to the Indian Ocean; financing has yet to be secured for the 1,200-mile project.

December 31

MILITARY: In an attempt to shore up Afghan civilian support for the war against terror, the army implements its first Provincial Reconstruction Team (PRT) as part of an ongoing civil-military effort to repair the nation's infrastructure. By broadening the reach of the central Afghan government, the team also plays a major role in enhancing national security.

2003

January 3
MILITARY: At Fort Stewart, Georgia, the remainder of the 3rd Infantry Division is ordered to deploy to Kuwait and join the headquarters unit and 2nd Brigade already there. Live-fire exercises have already been completed there.

POLITICS: In Kabul, Afghanistan, 400 Pashtun chiefs arrive to protest the arrest of an Achakzai chief by the Americans.

January 7
MILITARY: In Afghanistan, the American military announces the training of 400 new recruits for the Afghan national army.

January 10
MILITARY: In Washington, D.C., Defense Secretary Donald Rumsfeld authorizes the deployment of an additional 62,000 troops in the Persian gulf over the next 24 hours. This brings available manpower in the region to 80,000.

January 11
NAVAL: In London, United Kingdom, the government announces that it is deploying an aircraft carrier into the Persian Gulf region.

January 13
POLITICS: In key cities throughout Afghanistan, joint regional teams are created by the United States to heighten security and oversee the reconstruction program.

January 14
DIPLOMACY: In New York City, members of the European Union advise against a precipitous intervention in Iraq, insisting that UN weapons inspectors be given more time for their task. UN secretary-general Kofi Annan agrees that the inspectors should be allowed to complete their mission.

January 16
DIPLOMACY: In southern Iraq, UN weapons inspectors announce that they have uncovered 11 empty chemical warheads that were not listed on the Iraqi weapons declaration.

January 17
DIPLOMACY: In Paris, France, Mohamed ElBaradei, the UN nuclear weapons inspector, holds a news conference and demands additional time for his team members to complete their work. He is accompanied by French president Jacques Chirac and UN weapons inspector Hans Blix.

In Vienna, Austria, members of the International Atomic Energy Agency conclude that Iraq's notorious aluminum tubes are not associated with developing nuclear fuels.

In Washington, D.C., President George W. Bush scoffs at the notion of additional time for Iraq, stating that all the accumulating evidence, coupled with Iraqi disingenuousness, cries out for military action.

January 19
DIPLOMACY: In southern Iraq, UN weapons inspectors uncover additional proof of illegal chemical weapon warheads.

In Washington, D.C., President George W. Bush says he might allow Iraqi president Saddam Hussein to relocate to another country as a means of avoiding war.

January 20
DIPLOMACY: In Baghdad, Iraq, the government agrees to allow its nuclear scientists to be interviewed by UN authorities, but only within the confines of the country.

In London, United Kingdom the government announces that it is deploying an additional 26,000 troops to the Persian Gulf region.

In Paris, France, the government declares that it will not support a UN resolution for military action against Iraq.

MILITARY: At Fort Hood, Texas, the 4th Infantry Division (Mechanized) is ordered to deploy to Turkey in anticipation of hostilities with Iraq. The division currently has three brigades at Fort Hood and another at Fort Carson, Colorado.

January 21
DIPLOMACY: The World Bank announces it is providing grant aid totaling $100 million for various projects in Afghanistan.

POLITICS: In Kabul, Afghanistan, the supreme court outlaws all cable television.

TERRORISM: In Kuwait, terrorists shoot and kill Michael R. Pouliot, a civilian contractor, and wound David Caraway, a software engineer. Al-Qaeda is suspected in the attack.

January 23
DIPLOMACY: The *New York Times* prints an op-ed piece by National Security Advisor Condoleezza Rice in which she maintains that Iraq has consistently lied about possessing weapons of mass destruction. She points to that nation's apparent attempts to obtain uranium by purchasing it from abroad.

January 26
TERRORISM: Outside Jalalabad, Afghanistan, a convoy operated by the UN High Commissioner for Refugees is attacked; four terrorists and two police are killed. UN staff workers return to Jalalabad in safety.

January 27
DIPLOMACY: In Baghdad, Iraq, chief UN weapons inspector Hans Blix declares that the government is not fully cooperating with the inspectors, and it has also failed to prove that it has destroyed any banned weapons. Blix also raises the specter that stocks of the deadly contagion anthrax may still be unaccounted for. Conversely, nuclear weapons inspector Mohamed ElBaradei says he has no conclusive proof that Iraq has resumed production of such devices.

January 28

MILITARY: In Spin Boldak, Afghanistan, Special Forces and 82nd Airborne Division soldiers, backed by Afghan militia, begin clearing out caves in the Adi Gahr Mountains; 18 al-Qaeda terrorists are slain.

POLITICS: In his State of the Union address, President George W. Bush accuses Iraqi president Saddam Hussein of hiding biological and chemical weapons of mass destruction from UN inspectors. Bush says that the British government is the source for such allegations. He also advises the United States to prepare for a possible conflict to evict him, but he gives no indication of a timetable for offensive action.

In Kabul, Afghanistan, the government declares that new political parties will not serve in the new legislature until 2004.

In Peshawar, Pakistan, a conference of Afghan tribal elders criticizes the Kabul administration.

January 29

POLITICS: In Kabul, Afghanistan, Ali Ahmad Jalali becomes the new interior minister; he replaces Taj Mohammad Wardak due to discontent over the latter's handling of student protests in November 2002.

In Washington, D.C., President George W. Bush holds a news conference and reiterates his charge, based on British intelligence, that Iraqi president Saddam Hussein tried to purchase uranium in Africa.

January 30

AVIATION: Near Bagram Air Base, Afghanistan, an army UH-60 Black Hawk helicopter crashes due to mechanical failure, and six occupants are killed.

DIPLOMACY: In New York City, the leaders of Britain and seven other European countries take out a full page ad in the *Wall Street Journal* calling upon the global community to stand united against Iraq. France and Germany are not among them.

January 31

TERRORISM: In Kandahar, Afghanistan, a bomb explodes in a bus crossing the Rambasi Bridge; 18 people are killed. The attack was believed mounted by the Taliban and al-Qaeda, and aimed at local Afghan troops.

February 5

DIPLOMACY: In New York City, Secretary of State Colin Powell addresses the UN Security Council and casts Iraqi president Saddam Hussein as a threat to global security for his refusal to cooperate with weapons inspectors, his suspected links to al-Qaeda, and his mobile biological weapons factories. The address was televised and observed by tens of millions of people worldwide. Afterward, representatives from 10 East European countries speak in favor of war, but those from China, France, and Russia oppose military action for the time being.

February 6

DIPLOMACY: NATO member nations Belgium, France, and Germany block the deployment to Turkey of military equipment that might be used by Turkey to defend against an Iraqi attack.

MILITARY: At Fort Campbell, Kentucky, the 101st Airborne Division is ordered to prepare to deploy abroad in the war against terrorism.

NAVAL: In Washington, D.C., Defense Secretary Donald Rumsfeld announces his decision to deploy the carrier *Kitty Hawk* in the Persian Gulf.

February 8

AVIATION: In anticipation of another war with Iraq, the Defense Department begins contracting with commercial airlines to deliver troops and supplies to the Persian Gulf region. This involves activation of the Civil Reserve Air Fleet.

TERRORISM: In northern Iraq, Shawkat Hajji Mushir, a Kurdish member of the Iraqi parliament, is assassinated by the militant group Ansar al-Islam, along with two government officials.

February 9

DIPLOMACY: In Baghdad, Iraq, chief UN weapons inspector Hans Blix states that cooperation with Iraqi officials has improved, and he cites the release of documents pertaining to the destruction of anthrax and nerve agent stockpiles.

February 10

AVIATION: In Baghdad, Iraq, the government agrees to allow unfettered aerial reconnaissance of its territory by U.S., French, and Soviet aircraft.

DIPLOMACY: In Brussels, Belgium, NATO is blocked by France and Germany from developing war plans on an invasion of Iraq. Those nations, joined by Russia, insist on additional weapons inspectors first. A minor crisis arises when France, Germany, and Belgium refuse to assist fellow NATO country Turkey should it be attacked by Iraq.

MILITARY: In Afghanistan, Turkey hands control of the International Security Assistance Force to Germany and the Netherlands.

February 11

TERRORISM: The al-Jazeera TV network releases a voice recording purporting to be of Osama bin Laden, in which he warns the United States of future attacks. He also encourages Iraq to defend itself against any U.S. attack.

February 13

AVIATION: A UN weapons panel concludes that Iraqi al-Samoud 2 ballistic missiles have a range exceeding the 90-mile limit established by the Security Council and issues a deadline to begin destroying them.

MILITARY: In Helmand Province, Afghanistan, a sweep by U.S. forces nets seven terror suspects, but the troops are accused of killing civilians. The Afghan government promises an investigation.

February 14

DIPLOMACY: In Iraq, UN weapons inspectors Hans Blix and Mohamed ElBaradei declare that the Iraqi government has been slightly more cooperative and will allow surveillance flights. However, they report that President Saddam Hussein is still less than forthcoming about disallowed weapons systems and that Iraq recently tested a long-range missile in violation of UN resolutions. This new information spurs greater French and German opposition to military action.

MILITARY: At Fort Carson, Colorado, the 3rd Armored Division is ordered to deploy to Kuwait.

TERRORISM: A tape recording allegedly made by Osama bin Laden is aired by the al-Jazeera network. In it he announces his support for the Iraqi people and calls for attacks on the United States and Israel.

February 16

DIPLOMACY: NATO authorities reach an agreement to help Turkey protect itself against an Iraqi attack, although the arms are to be shipped under the aegis of NATO's Defense Planning Council, and not NATO itself.

MILITARY: The new Afghan army begins to receive shipments of arms and ammunition from the Pakistani military.

POLITICS: In Washington, D.C., President George W. Bush discounts antiwar demonstrations and states that no new UN resolution is necessary to commence military action. However, in deference to British prime minister Tony Blair, Bush begins pursuing a second UN resolution.

February 17

POLITICS: A recording attributed to Mullah Omar entreats fellow Afghans to join a jihad against the United States.

February 19

AVIATION: Over southeastern Iran, a Russian-built Ilyushin IL-62 jet transport of the Iranian air force crashes into a mountainside, killing all 289 Revolutionary Guards on board.

DIPLOMACY: In Ankara, Turkey, the government rejects a U.S. $26 billion aid package as inadequate in exchange for its participation in a war against Iraq.

TERRORISM: Renegade warlord Gulbuddin Hekmatyar is designated a global terrorist by the United States.

February 19–March 3

MILITARY: In the Baghlan Valley, Afghanistan, soldiers from the 2nd Battalion, 504th Parachute Infantry, 82nd Airborne Division, air assault positions ("parachute down") in the search for Taliban and al-Qaeda weapon caches. No resistance is encountered.

February 20

MILITARY: In Kabul, Afghanistan, the Defense Ministry reassigns five Tajik generals and replaces them with Hazara, Pashtun, and Uzbek officers. General Gul Zarak Zadran, an ethnic Pashtun, also becomes the fourth deputy defense minister.

February 22

DIPLOMACY: In Iraq, UN weapons inspector Hans Blix orders the government to destroy its entire stock of al-Samoud 2 missiles.

The United States and Spain draft a letter to the UN Security Council, declaring that Iraq has failed to disarm itself in the time allowed by Resolution 1441. Consequently, it is now necessary to authorize the use of force.

POLITICS: In Tokyo, Japan, a conference on demobilizing and disarming Afghan militias opens.

In Faryab Province, Afghanistan, fighting erupts between the forces of Abdul Rashid Dostum and Ustad Atta Mohammad; six people are killed.

Exiled mujahideen leader Gulbuddin Hekmatyar urges the Afghan people to resist the United States' "invasion" of Afghanistan.

February 24

DIPLOMACY: In New York City, delegates from France, Germany, and Russia present the UN Security Council with a counter-resolution allowing inspection teams in Iraq additional time and scope.

MILITARY: In Afghanistan, U.S. forces trade fire with unidentified assailants at Tarin Kot, Oruzgan Province, and Wazir, Nangarhar Province.

The road between Gardez and Khost, Afghanistan, is blocked by forces loyal to Bacha Zadran, a local warlord, in retaliation for government seizure of several of his vehicles.

At Spin Boldak, Afghanistan, local police arrest five terrorism suspects.

February 25

AVIATION: In the Arabian Sea, Juma Mohammad Mohammedi, the Afghan minister for mines and industry, is killed when his plane crashes on a flight to Pakistan.

MILITARY: In Zabol Province, Afghanistan, Afghan security forces trade fire with Taliban fighters, killing one.

TERRORISM: In Kandahar, Afghanistan, a bomb explodes near the home of the new Afghan education minister Dawood Barak.

February 26

DIPLOMACY: In New York City, the UN Agency for Narcotics Control declares Afghanistan to be the primary producer of opium for 2002, producing in excess of 3,400 tons.

CBS news anchor Dan Rather interviews President Saddam Hussein of Iraq, and the latter denies that his missiles exceed UN-imposed range limits.

MILITARY: In Nangarhar Province, Afghanistan, Afghan security forces uncover a huge cache of weapons at Bander; the haul includes mortars, mines, guns, and ammunition.

February 27

DIPLOMACY: In Iraq, President Saddam Hussein composes a letter to UN weapons inspector Hans Blix and agrees in principle to destroying his stock of ballistic missiles should they exceed the 100-mile range limit imposed by the United Nations in 1991.

MILITARY: In Kandahar, Afghanistan, Afghan security forces arrest seven Taliban suspects and recover a large supply of explosives and land mines.

February 28

POLITICS: In Mazar-i-Sharif, Afghanistan, at the behest of the United Nations, military leaders Abdul Rashid Dostum, Ustad Atta Mohammed, and Saradar Seedi meet and agree to end ethnic-based conflict.

TERRORISM: In Kandahar, Afghanistan, two rockets explode, but no casualties are reported.

March 1

DIPLOMACY: In Baghdad, Iraq, the government orders the dismantling of all al-Samoud 2 ballistic missiles per the orders of UN weapons inspector Hans Blix, who says that the Iraqis have done little to assist the inspectors.

In Sharm al-Sheikh, Egypt, an Arab summit votes to demand that Iraq fully comply with all UN resolutions, but it declines to endorse regime change.

In Ankara, Turkey, the parliament rejects an American plea to station 62,000 troops on Turkish territory as a springboard for invading northern Iraq. This is a considerable diplomatic setback for the United States.

MILITARY: After the Turkish parliament denies the 4th Infantry Division access to its soil for the purpose of invading Iraq, the unit is rerouted to Kuwait.

TERRORISM: In Rawalpindi, Pakistan, the Central Intelligence Agency and Pakistani security forces arrest Khalid Sheikh Mohammad, accused of being al-Qaeda's mastermind behind the 9/11 attacks.

March 3

MILITARY: In Helmand Province, Afghanistan, the United States launches a new anti-Taliban drive in another valley.

POLITICS: A Taliban spokesman claims responsibility for a spate of recent attacks throughout Afghanistan.

March 4

POLITICS: In Boulder, Colorado, a group from the University of Colorado declares that it will help rebuild the village of Farza, north of Kabul, Afghanistan.

March 5

DIPLOMACY: In Baghdad, Iraq, UN weapons inspector Hans Blix says he requires more time to complete inspections.

In New York City, Britain, Spain, and the United States submit a resolution to the UN Security Council declaring that Iraq had missed its final chance to disarm peacefully. The motion is opposed by France, Germany, and Russia.

March 6

DIPLOMACY: In New York City, the Chinese delegation to the United Nations asks for more time before an attack on Iraq is launched.

In Baghdad, Iraq, a UN inspection commission spokesman announces that the government has destroyed 112 missiles with ranges exceeding 100 miles, although an estimated 120 still remain.

In Washington, D.C., Secretary of State Colin Powell declares that the United States is ready to lead a coalition of willing nations that would disarm Iraq by force, if necessary, with or without UN authority.

POLITICS: In Washington, D.C., President George W. Bush addresses the nation on television, characterizes Iraqi president Saddam Hussein as a direct threat to U.S.

national security, and declares that he will attack Iraq unilaterally if necessary to rid the world of him.

March 7

DIPLOMACY: After UN weapons inspector Hans Blix informs the Security Council that Iraqi disarmament will take several months, the United States and Britain present a draft resolution requiring President Saddam Hussein to disarm by March 17 or face war. France indicates that it will veto the resolution in the council.

In New York City, nuclear inspector Mohamed ElBaradei addresses the UN Security Council and claims that letters purportedly showing that Iraq tried to obtain uranium from Niger are forgeries. These letters are a centerpiece in the American case against Saddam Hussein.

March 14

POLITICS: In Washington, D.C., President George W. Bush announces his "road map for peace" in the Middle East, particularly respecting the Arab-Israeli conflict. No specific mention of war with Iraq is made.

March 15

MILITARY: On the cusp of war with Iraq, the army deploys 57,500 men from the 3rd Infantry and 101st Airborne Divisions, while the 4th Infantry Division (Mechanized) is currently en route by water. The entire Third U.S. Army present in theater is commanded overall by Lieutenant General David D. McKiernan.

In ceremonies presided over by President Hamid Karzai, the first two battalions of the new Afghan National Army are sworn in.
POLITICS: In Kabul, Afghanistan, the finance minister presents a $500 million budget for the rest of the year.

March 16

AVIATION: In Iraq, a government spokesman announces that 74 missiles and 42 warheads have been destroyed per UN resolutions.
DIPLOMACY: In Lajes, Azores, President George W. Bush, British prime minister Tony Blair, and Prime Minister Jose Maria Aznar of Spain declare that their diplomatic efforts to disarm Iraq without war have ended. In their quest to secure a peaceful, nonthreatening Iraq, there is little question at this juncture that war is looming.
POLITICS: In Washington, D.C., Vice President Richard Cheney, in a televised interview, predicts that American troops would be hailed as liberators in Iraq. He also says that it is common knowledge that President Saddam Hussein has been actively trying to construct nuclear weapons of his own.

March 17

AVIATION: In Washington, D.C., President George W. Bush delivers a 15-minute televised ultimatum requiring President Saddam Hussein and his sons to depart from Iraq within 48 hours—or face war.
DIPLOMACY: In New York City, delegates from the United States, Britain, and Spain withdraw their resolution authorizing force against Iraq after France makes clear its

intention to veto it. The three nations intend to go to war without Security Council backing.

UN secretary-general Kofi Annan orders the immediate evacuation of all UN personnel from Iraq, including weapons inspectors.

March 18

AVIATION: During the buildup to war in Iraq, air force planes begin dropping informational leaflets on 20 civilian locations. An EC-130 Commando Solo aircraft also broadcasts messages and alerts Iraqi citizens to take cover. Other aircraft begin bombing antiaircraft emplacements placed in violation of the southern "no-fly zone."

DIPLOMACY: In Washington, D.C., the administration draws up a list of 30 countries, members of the "coalition of the willing," that support forcibly disarming Iraq. Another 15 nations also support the effort but declined to be named.

POLITICS: In London, United Kingdom, the House of Commons votes 412 to 149 for Prime Minister Tony Blair to use "all means necessary" to disarm Iraqi president Saddam Hussein.

March 19

AVIATION: Operation Iraqi Freedom commences as U.S. Navy vessels fire a total of 42 Tomahawk cruise missiles at various targets in Iraq. Several buildings thought to house President Saddam Hussein, his two sons, and several ranking government officials are deliberately targeted. Air force F-117 Nighthawks also drop precision-guided munitions at communication and command centers. Coalition forces' aircraft hit artillery, air defenses, and missile sites throughout the country.

The Iraqis launch three missiles at American bases in Kuwait. One misses its intended target while two others are downed by Patriot missile batteries.

MILITARY: Operation Iraqi Freedom begins as 145,000 coalition soldiers, spearheaded by the United States and Britain, invade Iraq to topple the regime of Saddam Hussein. Special Forces are already in theater gathering military intelligence, and President George W. Bush declares that the goal of the war is the removal of Saddam Hussein from power, the destruction of all Iraqi weapons of mass destruction (WMDs), and the elimination of all terrorist elements within Iran.

NAVAL: In the Persian Gulf, the guided-missile destroyers *Donald Cook* and *Milius,* the guided-missile cruisers *Cowpens* and *Bunker Hill,* and the attack submarines *Cheyenne* and *Montpelier* launch cruise missiles against Iraqi targets.

March 20

AVIATION: Approximately 500 coalition aircraft, mostly from Britain and the United States, begin swarming over Iraqi antiaircraft and missile radar defenses, along with command and control centers. All told, coalition air and sea forces unleash 1,000 Tomahawks and more than 3,000 precision-guided munitions against Iraqi forces. The extent of this firepower, dubbed "shock and awe," is intended to stun the defenders into surrendering.

In Kuwait, Patriot PAC-3 missiles fired by Battery D, 5th Battalion, 52nd Air Defense Artillery, shoot down two Iraqi Scud missiles headed toward 101st Airborne Division headquarters at Camp Thunder.

DIPLOMACY: In Ankara, Turkey, the parliament votes to allow coalition aircraft to utilize Turkish air space for the duration of Operation Iraqi Freedom. It also votes to allow Turkish troops to occupy part of northern Iraq, a stance that the United States and Britain oppose.

MILITARY: In Iraq, the 3rd Infantry Division under Major General Buford C. Blount III initiates the ground offensive by crossing into Iraq from Kuwait. Resistance is light and easily dispatched by AH-62 Apache gunships. That afternoon, the first enemy units are engaged by the 3rd Squadron, 7th Cavalry, while the 3rd Battalion, 15th Infantry (3rd Division), neutralizes some enemy armored vehicles.

The Marine 1st Expeditionary Corps, assisted by British Royal Marines, cross into Iraq from Kuwait and turn northeast to take Basra, the country's second-largest city.

East of Kandahar, Afghanistan, U.S. forces commence Operation Valiant Strike against Taliban fighters in the Sami Ghar Mountains.

NAVAL: In the Persian Gulf, the guided-missile destroyer *John S. McCain* and the attack submarines *Columbia* and *Providence*, assisted by two British submarines, unleash an additional 50 Tomahawk missiles at select targets in Baghdad, Iraq. Teams of SEALS and Royal Marines are also helicoptered for raids against the Kaabot and Mabot oil terminals.

March 20–27

MILITARY: Near Kandahar, Afghanistan, men from the 2nd Battalion, 504th Parachute Infantry, 82nd Airborne Division, under Lieutenant Colonel Charles A. Flynn, conduct Operation Valiant Strike in the Sami Ghar Mountains. Resistance is slight, and several weapons caches are seized.

March 21

AVIATION: Launching at night, aircraft from the carriers *Abraham Lincoln, Constellation, Harry S. Truman, Kitty Hawk,* and *Theodore Roosevelt* participate in the "shock and awe" campaign against the Iraqi capital of Baghdad. A further 320 Tomahawk cruise missiles are fired against various military targets.

In the Arabian Gulf, an Iraqi fast-attack patrol boat is detected and tracked by a Navy P-3 Orion of VP-46, then destroyed by an air force AC-130 Spectre gunship.

MILITARY: In southern Iraq, the 101st Airborne Division under Major General David H. Petraeus crosses the border in a mass of helicopters and ground vehicles.

The 3rd Brigade, 3rd Infantry Division, having dashed more than 100 miles into enemy territory, comes under attack at Nasiriyah, Iraq. Its counterfire destroys the Iraqi 11th Infantry Division in short order, and, once the 1st Brigade seizes Jalibah Air Base, it is handed over to the marines.

TERRORISM: At Guantánamo, Cuba, the United States releases 18 prisoners, allowing them to return to Afghanistan.

March 22

AVIATION: Coalition force aircraft fly more than 1,000 sorties and launch a like number of cruise missiles at Iraqi military targets.

Over the Arabian Gulf, two Royal Navy Sea King helicopters collide and crash; an exchange officer, U.S. Navy lieutenant Thomas M. Adams, is among the six servicemen killed.

MILITARY: In a news briefing, General Tommy R. Franks, commander, Central Command, declares that Operation Iraqi Freedom will be waged as a campaign of "overwhelming force." At this juncture, the leading coalition forces are 150 miles from Baghdad and closing in fast.

March 23

AVIATION: In the eastern Mediterranean, the long reach of the Tomahawk cruise missile is amply displayed when the guided-missile cruisers *Cape St. George* and *Anzio,* and the guided-missile destroyer *Winston S. Churchill,* begin launching missiles against targets in Iraq.

Over Karbala, Iraq, an AH-64 Apache Longbow from the 1st Battalion, 227th Aviation Regiment, is badly damaged by heavy fire from Republican Guard units and crash lands; the crew of two is captured. Chief Warrant Officer David S. Williams and Chief Warrant Officer Ronald Young are subsequently paraded on Iraqi television.

Over Kuwait, a Patriot antimissile battery fires and accidentally downs a Royal Air Force GR4 Tornado jet bomber. An American F-16 also knocks out a Patriot battery after its radar locks on to it; no casualties occur.

MILITARY: At Camp Pennsylvania, Kuwait, a disgruntled soldier lobs a grenade into tents, killing an Air National Guard officer and an intelligence officer. The attack wounds 14 others; the soldier is charged with two counts of premeditated murder and faces the death penalty.

Near Nasiriyah, Iraq, an 18-vehicle convoy from the 507th Maintenance Battalion goes down the wrong road and is ambushed. Of 33 soldiers present, 11 are killed and six are captured.

March 24

AVIATION: Coalition force aircraft bombard Iraqi military targets near the oil-producing center of Kirkuk for a 24-hour period.

MILITARY: Near Najaf, Iraq, the 1st Brigade, 3rd Infantry Division, severs Highway 9 as Iraqi irregulars launch waves of suicide attacks against them. These are repelled with heavy losses to the latter, although the soldiers expend so much ammunition that they have to employ captured enemy weapons. The American are now within 50 miles of the Iraqi capital.

NAVAL: In the Khor Abd Allah waterway, Iraq, coalition naval forces board four Iraqi vessels carrying nearly 100 mines. The units involved come from the U.S. Navy and Army, and Coast Guard units from Australia and Kuwait.

POLITICS: In Baghdad, Iraq, President Saddam Hussein goes on television and urges his countrymen to hold firm and resist coalition forces.

March 25

AVIATION: Over Iraq, a Lockheed S-3 Viking from Sea Control Squadron 38 (VS-38) directs a raid by F/A-18 Hornets from VFA-151. This is the first time the 30-year-old Viking design has seen combat and also the first time it released a laser-guided missile. Carrier aircraft also attack the Iraqi presidential yacht *Al Mansur,* sinking it.

MILITARY: As forces begin crossing the Euphrates River at Samawah, Iraq, they are beset by intense sandstorms that make rapid movement impossible. The advance on Baghdad slows necessarily, and intelligence is received that the Iraqis might employ chemical weapons against coalition forces as they approach the city.

In southern Iraq, British forces announce that they have captured the city of Umm Qasr, but Basra itself has yet to fall.

March 26

AVIATION: In northern Iraq, Operation Northern Delay commences as 15 C-17 Globemaster IIIs insert 990 paratroopers and 20 heavy platforms onto Bashur Airfield. This act effectively opens up a second front and is also the first time that parachutists have dropped from C-17s. The crew of the lead aircraft also wins a Mackay Trophy for orchestrating such an intricate maneuver.

MILITARY: The city of Najaf, Iraq, is surrounded by two brigades of the 3rd Infantry Division; American losses are one crewman killed and two M1A1 Abrams tanks and one M2 Bradley disabled. In time, the advances are joined by truckloads of men from the 101st Airborne Division, although the still-intense sandstorms have grounded all of that unit's helicopters.

The 173rd Airborne Brigade drops nearly 1,000 parachute infantry over Bashur Airfield, Iraq, in that unit's first combat jump since Vietnam. They are assisted by roughly 150 men of the 10th Special Forces Group (Airborne) who are helping direct air strikes against nearby targets.

In Washington, D.C., the Pentagon announces that it has captured 4,000 Iraqi troops.

March 27

AVIATION: Over Kuwait, a Patriot missile successfully intercepts and destroys an Iraqi Scud missile.

MILITARY: Once the sandstorms subside, the 3rd Infantry Division resumes its advance on Karbala, Iraq, while Iraqi irregulars tie down other units in severe fighting near Najaf.

In Afghanistan, the 2nd Battalion, 505th Parachute Infantry, 82nd Airborne Division, commences Operation Desert Lion by sweeping through the Kohe Safi Mountains near Bagram Air Base. Resistance is minimal, and the soldiers uncover a large cache of 107mm rockets and machine-gun munitions.

March 28

AVIATION: In the Persian Gulf, minesweeping operations are maintained by helicopters of Mine Countermeasures Squadron 14 (HN-14) and the Commander Task Unit. Consequently, the Royal Navy landing ship *Sir Galahad* is enabled to dock at Umm Qasr with tons of humanitarian aid for the locals.

MILITARY: Around Karbala, Iraq, AH-64 Apache Longbow helicopters from the 101st Airborne Division attack tanks belonging to the Republican Guard Medina Division.

In northern Iraq, U.S. Special Forces, assisted by local Kurds, capture several villages controlled by the terrorist group Ansar al-Islam, which is reportedly linked to the al-Qaeda network.

March 29

MILITARY: As units of the 3rd Infantry Division wage battle against the Republican Guard Medina Division outside Najaf, they are increasingly harassed by irregular fedayeen fighters, who fire at them from schools, hospitals, and mosques. The irregulars are also quick to employ women and children as human shields.

In Helmand Province, Afghanistan, two U.S. Special Forces soldiers are killed in a Taliban ambush.

NAVAL: In the Persian Gulf, the *Nassau* amphibious-ready group unloads the 24th Marines Expeditionary Unit. This is the first sizable troop reinforcement to land in theater.

POLITICS: A *Newsweek* poll finds that 74 percent of the American public feel that the Bush administration is enacting a well-conceived military strategy. President George W. Bush's favorable rating also soars by 15 points to reach 68 percent.

TERRORISM: At Najaf, Iraq, five soldiers from the 1st Brigade, 3rd Division, die at the hands of a suicide bomber.

March 30

MILITARY: In Baghdad, Iraq, a government spokesman declares that 4,000 volunteers from 23 countries are ready to carry out suicide bombings for Iraq.

POLITICS: In Washington, D.C., Defense Secretary Donald Rumsfeld plays down criticism that the United States has failed to deploy adequate forces for the invasion of Iraq.

March 30–31

MILITARY: The American advance on Baghdad, Iraq, continues as the 2nd Brigade, 3rd Infantry Division, seizes a bridge over the Euphrates at Al Hindiyah, only 50 miles from the capital. Meanwhile, the 101st Airborne Division captures the airfield at An Najaf, along with several tanks and prisoners. To the rear, the 82nd Airborne Division, which is tasked with keeping American lines of supply and communication open, destroys several Iraqi artillery batteries with effective counterfire.

March 31

AVIATION: Over northern Iraq, aircraft from the carrier *Theodore Roosevelt* bombard artillery emplacements, barracks, and surface-to-air missile installations.

POLITICS: Another taped message from Taliban leader Mullah Omar reiterates his call for a holy war against American forces occupying Afghanistan.

April 1

AVIATION: Over Iraq, a Patriot missile successfully shoots down a Scud missile fired at American forces. This is the first Patriot success outside of Kuwait.

MILITARY: A quick raid on the hospital at Nasiriyah, Iraq, by Special Forces frees Private First Class Jessica Lynch, who had been wounded and captured when the 507th Maintenance Company was ambushed. A sweep of the hospital ground also uncovers the bodies of seven soldiers killed earlier.

At this juncture of the conflict, U.S. casualties stand at 46 dead, seven captured, and 16 missing; Britain says 27 of its soldiers have been killed.

NAVAL: The raid on the hospital at Nasiriyah, Iraq, is assisted by navy SEALS and marine reconnaissance units.

April 1–2
MILITARY: The U.S. Army 3rd Division is attacking the Republican Guard Medina Division north of Karbala, Iraq, only 50 miles south of Baghdad, while the 1st Marine Division is pressing north, 70 miles south of the capital.

April 2
AVIATION: Over Kuwait, a Patriot missile battery inadvertently locks onto a navy F/A-18 Hornet jet fighter of VFA-195 *(Kitty Hawk),* shooting it down. Apparently, a software error caused the radar to misidentify the aircraft as an incoming missile; Lieutenant Nathan White dies.

Over Iraq, B-52s drop CBU-105 cluster bombs on Iraqi tank units. These armor-piercing, sensor-fused weapons are deadly to massed tank formations.

Iraqi antiaircraft fire downs a U.S. Army UH-60 Black Hawk helicopter, killing all seven passengers.

DIPLOMACY: In Ankara, Turkey, the parliament votes to allow the U.S. military to transport food and nonmilitary supplies across its territory and into northern Iraq.

MILITARY: In the latest friendly fire incident, three soldiers of the 1st Battalion, 39th Field Artillery, are killed when an F-15C fighter bomber mistakes their MLRS missile launcher for a Soviet-designed Iraqi vehicle and directs a laser-guided GBU-12 bomb to it.

April 3
MILITARY: The 1st Brigade, 3rd Infantry Division, rumbles through the Karaba Gap, seizes the Yasin al Khudayr bridge over the Euphrates River, and captures Saddam International Airport. Simultaneously, the 101st Airborne Division and the 2nd Brigade, 82nd Airborne Division, engage Iraqi irregular forces that have emerged in the 3rd Infantry Division's wake.

The 1st Marine Division brushes aside light resistance and begins crossing the Tigris River, only 25 miles south of Baghdad, Iraq.

April 4
MILITARY: Men from the 1st Brigade, 3rd Infantry Division, attack and destroy members of the Special Republican Guards as they occupy Saddam International Airport. A 12-hour battle ensues during which one American dies and eight are wounded while enemy losses are estimated at 250.

In the course of heavy fighting around Saddam International Airport, Sergeant First Class Paul R. Smith, Company B, 11th Engineer Battalion, is killed while manning a .50-caliber machine gun. However, he stopped several Republican Guard attacks while American wounded were being evacuated, and he is the only soldier from Operation Iraqi Freedom to be recommended for the Congressional Medal of Honor.

Baghdad, Iraq, is now completely encircled by U.S. forces and has lost nearly all electrical power.

POLITICS: In Iraq, President Saddam Hussein makes two videotaped broadcasts, but exactly when the tapes were made is not clear.

TERRORISM: Four U.S. soldiers are killed at a highway checkpoint in Iraq when two Iraqi women conduct a suicide car bomb attack.

April 5

MILITARY: The 3rd Infantry Division dispatches two battalions on a quick raid into downtown Baghdad, before withdrawing them to the west to join the 1st Brigade. Meanwhile, Central Command announces that it holds 6,500 Iraqi prisoners. A further 3,000 Iraqis are estimated to have been killed.

April 6

MILITARY: Near Ebril, northern Iraq, artillery attached to the 173rd Airborne Brigade silences Iraqi artillery positions in a short but deadly duel.

On a plateau between Ebril and Makhmur, northern Iraq, a force of 31 Green Berets, reinforced by Kurdish guerrillas, repels attacks by Iraqi infantry and armor with Javelin missiles. Unfortunately, an errant bomb dropped by naval aircraft kills 19 Kurdish fighters and wounds 40.

Basra, Iraq, finally falls to British forces as organized resistance throughout the country begins collapsing.

POLITICS: An air force transport flies Ahmad Chalabi, a leading anti-Hussein figure and leader of the exiled Iraqi National Congress, along with 700 of his fighters, into southern Iraq.

April 7

AVIATION: Acting on a tip that Iraqi president Saddam Hussein and his two sons are lodged in a building in the Mansur district of Baghdad, Iraq, a B-1B Lancer from the 34th Bomb Squadron drops four GBU-31 satellite-guided joint direct-attack munitions on the premises, destroying it. The president is not there, but the attack kills several senior Iraqi leaders.

A C-130 Hercules brings the first army troops to Saddam International Airport, Baghdad, under the cover of darkness.

MILITARY: In a ferocious fire fight, the 2nd Brigade, 3rd Infantry Division, advances into the heart of central Baghdad and crushes remaining resistance from the Republican Guards along Highway 8. Four Americans die and 30 are wounded, while an estimated 600 Iraqis are killed. The Republican Palace, the actual seat of Saddam Hussein's regime, is also captured and occupied.

British forces report the capture and occupation of Basra, Iraq's second-largest city.

TERRORISM: The Associated Press receives a taped audio message purportedly with the voice of Osama bin Laden urging Muslims to seek martyrdom through attacks on U.S. and British forces.

April 7–8

DIPLOMACY: In Belfast, Northern Ireland, President George W. Bush and Prime Minister Tony Blair confer over the future of peace in the Middle East, especially what assistance Iraq will require in the post–Saddam Hussein era.

April 8

AVIATION: Iraqi ground fire brings down an A-10 Thunderbolt II over Baghdad, although the pilot escapes capture and is secured by coalition forces near the airport. However, a surface-to-air missile destroys an F-15E Strike Eagle, killing both crewmen.
MILITARY: The balance of the 3rd Division consolidates its grip on Baghdad, Iraq, by occupying the west bank of the Tigris River. The Iraqis subsequently attack these positions in a variety of trucks, tanks, and buses, but they are repelled by the Americans, backed by U.S. Air Force close air support, losing several hundred men. Two journalists also die when an M1A1 Abrams tank, alerted that there are Iraqis firing from the Palestine Hotel, opens fire.

April 9

MILITARY: As marines advance into Baghdad, Iraq, and link up with elements of the 3rd Division, the city is considered fully occupied. Meanwhile, U.S. troops, search-ing for weapons of mass destruction at a military training site, encounter several barrels containing chemicals related to pesticides.
POLITICS: In Firdos Square, Baghdad, Iraq, viewers around the world are transfixed by the sight of U.S. troops and jubilant Iraqis tearing down a 20-foot statue of Sad-dam Hussein. The image is broadcast around the world and appears to vindicate President George W. Bush's estimation of the former dictator. However, many riot-ers plunder the National Museum of Iraq of highly prized collections dating back to the dawn of civilization.

April 10

MILITARY: As organized Iraqi resistance collapses, American Special Forces and Kurdish fighters occupy the northern city of Kirkuk. They are soon joined by the 173rd Airborne Brigade, which secures several gas-oil separation plants and oil wells. The 82nd and 101st Airborne Divisions continue with mop up operations around Samawah and Karbala, respectively.
POLITICS: Afghanistan applies to become a member of the World Trade Organization.
TERRORISM: In Najaf, Iraq, a riotous mob storms into a mosque and loots it, killing two Shiite clerics in the process.

April 11

AVIATION: Over Iraq, a B-52 employs a Litening II advanced airborne targeting and navigation pod to strike Iraqi facilities at an airfield.
MILITARY: Army and marine forces begin active patrols to discourage widespread looting in Baghdad and Kirkuk, Iraq. However, they react too slowly to prevent the National Museum of Iraq from being repeatedly sacked. Meanwhile, Special Forces teams arrange a truce between themselves and the Iraqi V Corps near Mosul, while an Iraqi colonel surrenders at the border crossing at Highways 10 and 11 near Syria. An active hunt for weapons caches in the area turns up several tons of ballistic mis-siles and heavy weapons.

   Marines capture the city of Tikrit, Iraq, hometown of President Saddam Hussein.

   South of Kabul, Afghanistan, Afghan security forces trade shots with Taliban forces; casualties are not reported.

In Afghanistan, fighting breaks out again between fighters of Abdul Rashid Dostum and Atta Mohammad in Maimana, Faryab Province; four of Atta's soldiers are killed and four are wounded. The United Nations consequently begins evacuating personnel from the region.

In Helmand Province, Afghanistan, U.S. troops begin a sweep near the area where Special Forces were ambushed on March 29; some arrests are made and weapons and explosive seized.

NAVAL: At Naval Amphibious Base Little Creek, Virginia, the amphibious dock landing ship *Portland* is the first vessel to return from active duty during Operation Iraqi Freedom.

POLITICS: In Baghdad, Iraq, U.S. forces release their list of 55 former officials who are fugitives. These are arrayed on a deck of cards with President Saddam Hussein listed as the ace of spades.

In Kabul, Afghanistan, the government announces the new National Solidarity Program to administer $95 million in grants to 4,000 villages over the next three to four years.

In Washington, D.C., Defense Secretary Donald Rumsfeld, when queried about the mass looting and lawlessness in Baghdad, Iraq, simply comments that "stuff happens."

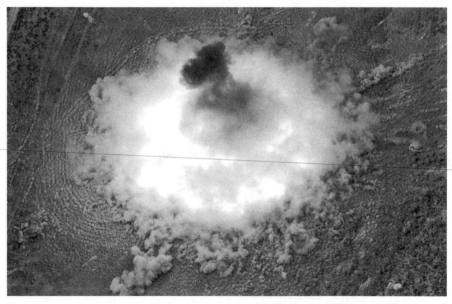

At a test site in Utah, U.S. Air Force personnel dropped a 15,000-pound bomb to test its effectiveness and impact. Known as the Daisy Cutter, this was the most powerful nonnuclear explosive in the U.S. arsenal and was used primarily in Afghanistan against caves and tunnels where al-Qaeda or Taliban members were believed to be hiding. *(U.S. Air Force)*

April 12

MILITARY: American efforts to restore law and order are thwarted by an epidemic of looting in Baghdad, Kirkuk, and Mosul, Iraq. General Amir Saadi is also seized, becoming the highest-ranking Iraqi captured, while the 3rd Infantry Division skirmishes with various militia groups.

In Kabul, Afghanistan, the senior U.S. commander calls for joint U.S.-Afghan patrols along the Pakistani border to circumvent Taliban infiltration.

TERRORISM: In Khost, Afghanistan, hand grenades are thrown at an Italian military patrol; two Afghan soldiers are shot in consequence; one Taliban suspect is arrested. A car loaded with explosives also detonates near the city, killing two Pakistanis, a Yemeni, and a former Taliban intelligence officer.

April 13

DIPLOMACY: In Washington, D.C., President George W. Bush accuses Syria of accepting fleeing Iraqi officials along with shipments of chemical weapons.

MILITARY: Near Samarra, Iraq, several American captives have been released by the Iraqis and are found walking along a road until discovered by marines combing the area. They include the two Apache helicopter crewmen shot down on March 23rd.

POLITICS: In Kandahar, Afghanistan, Governor Gul Agha Sherzai condemns the Taliban for killing several relatives in the border town of Chaman, Pakistan. Pakistani authorities near that settlement also seize drugs that were about to be smuggled through the Murda Karez Mountains and across the border into Afghanistan; a further 1,100 pounds of morphine are also confiscated at an Afghan refugee camp in the Chaghi district.

April 14

DIPLOMACY: In Washington, D.C., Secretary of State Colin Powell warns Syria that the United States is considering diplomatic or economic measures after Damascus granted sanctuary to fleeing Iraqi authorities. Defense Secretary Donald Rumseld also goes on record warning Syria not to accept fleeing Iraqi leaders. The Syrian government denies both charges.

MILITARY: Central Command leader General Tommy Franks declares that all organized resistance in Iraq has ended and that all major towns and cities are under coalition control. Army troops are occupied with searching for weapons of mass destruction while engineers are beginning the task of rebuilding the country's shattered infrastructure.

A rather tardy 4th Infantry Division under Major General Raymond T. Odierno crosses into Iraq from assembly areas in Kuwait. It subsequently forms the core of Task Force Iron Horse in concert with other armored units.

In Baghdad, Iraq, Marine and Iraqi policemen begin joint security patrols to discourage widespread looting.

TERRORISM: In Baghdad, Iraq, Special Forces and 3rd Infantry Division soldiers capture Mohammed Abu Abas (Abu Abbas) who had masterminded the hijacking of the Italian liner *Achille Lauro* and murdered American citizen Leon Klinghofer in 1985.

April 15

DIPLOMACY: In Baghdad, Iraq, retired lieutenant general Jay Garner, head of the U.S.-sponsored Office of Reconstruction and Humanitarian Assistance, arrives to begin repairing the damage caused by war. He meets quietly with Iraqi authorities and pledges to restore essential services as quickly as possible. U.S. authorities also announce that they are shutting down a Syria-Iraq oil pipeline that violates UN sanctions.

In Washington, D.C., President George W. Bush warns Iran not to interfere with Iraqi internal affairs, amid reports that some Iranians are crossing the porous border to agitate for an Islamic state.

POLITICS: Five hundred Afghan refugees are repatriated home from Pakistan by UN authorities.

In several refugee camps near Pakistan's North-West Frontier Province, pamphlets that call for an uprising against President Hamid Karzai and U.S. occupation forces appear; they are attributed to the Taliban.

Throughout Afghanistan, UNICEF commences a three-day program to immunize 6 million Afghan children against polio.

TERRORISM: Near Mazar-i-Sharif, Afghanistan, Commander Shahi and two Uzbek bodyguards working for General Abdul Rashid Dostum are ambushed and killed by unknown assailants.

In Mosul, Iraq, Iraqi gunmen hiding behind crowds of anti-American protestors fire on nearby U.S. forces. The Americans return fire, killing between 10 and 17 people.

April 16

AVIATION: At Baghdad International Airport, Iraq, a P-3 Orion patrol plane of VP-46 is the first navy aircraft to land there. It is carrying the commander of U.S. Naval Forces Central Command, Vice Admiral Timothy Keating.

DIPLOMACY: In Washington, D.C., President George W. Bush calls upon the UN Security Council to end all sanctions imposed against Iraq. He also signs a bill providing $79 billion in supplementary funds for Iraqi occupation and reconstruction.

MILITARY: General Tommy Franks, the senior American ground commander, enters Baghdad for the first time.

In Brussels, Belgium, NATO headquarters announces that it is assuming control of the International Security Assistance Force as of late summer, 2003.

In Ghazni Province, Afghanistan, coalition troops uncover three large weapons caches, including antitank rockets, antiaircraft ammunition, and rocket-propelled grenades, at Karbala.

In Zabol Province, Afghanistan, Romanian troops discover a large supply of weapons at Qalat.

April 17

MILITARY: At Ghulam Khan, Afghanistan, Afghan and Pakistani border forces trade fire, although details on who fired first or why the Pakistanis crossed the border are confused.

In Afghanistan, a large cache of Taliban weapons, including 3,000 107mm rockets, is uncovered by Romanian coalition forces.

POLITICS: South of Kabul, Afghanistan, Afghan security forces apprehend Maulawi Qalamuddin, a former deputy head of the Taliban.

In Maimana, Afghanistan, UN officials arrange the peaceful withdrawal of a rival militia group, whereupon UN offices are reopened.

In Iraq, U.S. forces arrest Barzan Ibrahim al-Tiktriti, Saddam Hussein's brother-in-law and a former intelligence officer.

TERRORISM: In Jalalabad, Afghanistan, a hand grenade is lobbed at UNICEF headquarters; no casualties or damage result.

April 18

POLITICS: In Iraq, Emad Husayn Abdullah al-Ani, who had previously developed nerve agents for use in the 1980s war with Iran, turns himself in to U.S. occupation officials.

April 19

DIPLOMACY: In Kabul, Afghanistan, the U.S. special representative warns Pakistani officials that border clashes threaten to upend Afghan security and stability; a meeting between delegates from both nations smooths over the dispute.

MILITARY: The 4th Division, advancing northward, encounters pockets of resistance from Iraqi paramilitaries between Taji and Samarra; it destroys eight armed trucks and seizes 30 prisoners. An unmanned surveillance drone also captures television images of fedayeen guerrillas loading ammunition stores onto trucks.

In Baghdad, Iraq, soldiers from the 3rd Infantry Division uncover a stash of $656 million in U.S. $100 bills. The neighborhood in question is home to many high-ranking Iraqi officials.

April 20

MILITARY: In Kabul, Afghanistan, a gathering of senior military leaders concurs that a national army is needed to transcend ethnic rivalries.

April 21

POLITICS: In Kabul, Afghanistan, cable television broadcasts, which had been outlawed by the supreme court in January 2003, are allowed to resume.

Afghan authorities announce the arrest of five former Taliban supporters accused of killing four foreign journalists at Tangi Abishu in November 2001.

April 22

DIPLOMACY: In Islamabad, Pakistan, Afghan president Hamid Karzai meets with President Pervez Musharraf and stresses the need to help secure their porous border against future Taliban infiltration.

MILITARY: In southwestern Afghanistan, U.S. forces kill one Taliban fighter and arrest seven more. They also kill a Taliban member thought responsible for the murder of a Red Cross worker in Kandahar in March 2003.

POLITICS: The UN Development Fund for Women announces a research program to determine exactly how disadvantaged Afghan women really are.

April 22–23

POLITICS: In Iraq, thousands of Shiites begin traveling to the holy city of Karbala to observe religious festivals long banned by Saddam Hussein.

April 23

DIPLOMACY: In Islamabad, Pakistan, the government reveals an agreement to train and equip Afghan security personnel. It also pledges to establish a free industrial zone near Torkum and Chaman on the border to assist Afghan economic development.

MILITARY: In Oruzgan Province, Afghanistan, two Afghan soldiers and three Taliban are killed in an armed clash at Tarin Kot.

POLITICS: By this date, U.S. occupation authorities have arrested 11 of the 55 most wanted Iraqi officials.

April 24

POLITICS: In Afghanistan, the government readily embraces the UN-sponsored National Emergency Employment Program to help rural Afghans find work on labor-intensive public-works programs.

In Iraq, former deputy prime minister Tariq Aziz surrenders to coalition authorities.

April 25

POLITICS: In Kabul, Afghanistan, consultations begin on a new draft constitution paving the way for national, free elections in 2004. A Hindu businessman also becomes the first non-Muslim appointed to a commission to examine the draft constitution.

April 27

POLITICS: In Baghdad, Iraq, U.S. forces arrest Mohammad Mohsen Zobeidi, who had proclaimed himself mayor of Baghdad and attempted to seize power.

TERRORISM: In Badghis Province, Afghanistan, the Afghan Human Rights group uncovers the bodies of 26 prisoners who had been bound before being executed.

April 28

MILITARY: In eastern Afghanistan, two U.S. soldiers die during a firefight with Taliban operatives.

Pakistan authorities uncover another huge weapons cache in North-West Frontier Province and reiterate that they are working against the Taliban while denying that Mullah Omar is on Pakistani soil.

POLITICS: In Baghdad, Iraq, 300 Iraqi political figures confer to work out the details of a national conference that will put a transitional government in motion.

TERRORISM: In Fallujah, Iraq, Iraqi gunmen hiding behind a crowd of anti-American protestors open fire on U.S. forces. The Americans return fire, killing 15 people and wounding 65.

April 29

DIPLOMACY: In Washington, D.C., the government announces that all combat troops will be removed from Saudi Arabia by the end of the summer. However, 400 to 500 will remain behind to serve as instructors.

POLITICS: A UN survey indicates that, once again, Afghanistan is the world's largest grower of poppies, with implications for the global opium trade.

April 30
MILITARY: By this date, total American combat-related deaths in Iraq total 138 while British losses are at 32. A further 548 Americans have been wounded in action.
POLITICS: In Kabul, Afghanistan, a Human Rights Department is founded to help train police to respect and safeguard the lives of prisoners.
TERRORISM: In Karachi, Pakistan, authorities apprehend six al-Qaeda suspects, along with weapons and explosives; several of them are believed to have participated in the attack upon the USS *Cole* in Yemen.

May 1
AVIATION: Operation Northern Watch, begun as a "no-fly zone" over northern Iraq on January 1, 1997, ends.
MILITARY: In Kabul, Afghanistan, Defense Secretary Donald Rumsfeld and President Hamid Karzai declare major military operations against the Taliban have ceased. Presently, 8,000 U.S. troops and the 5,500-strong International Security Assistance Force are still deployed there.
NAVAL: President George W. Bush lands on the deck of the carrier *Abraham Lincoln* off the California coast and announces an end to all offensive military operations in Iraq. "Mission accomplished!" he declares to loud applause.

May 2
MILITARY: In Helmand Province, Afghanistan, authorities arrest 60 Taliban suspects following a failed attack on the Kajakai Dam.

May 3
DIPLOMACY: In Damascus, Syria, Secretary of State Colin Powell requests President Bashar al-Assad to detain all Iraqi leaders who may have fled into his country and block any weapons from being transported from there.

May 5
MILITARY: In Wardak Province, Afghanistan, eight fighters loyal to Gulbuddin Hekmatyar are arrested in the wake of an attack on the Afghan Development Agency.

May 6
DIPLOMACY: In Washington, D.C., President George W. Bush, dissatisfied with the pace of Iraqi reconstruction, appoints retired diplomat L. Paul Bremer III as his envoy in Baghdad; he enjoys completely authority over retired general Jay Garner, head of reconstruction efforts.
MILITARY: The American search for Iraqi weapons uncovers a tractor-trailer that might have been used as a mobile laboratory for producing either biological or chemical weapons.
POLITICS: In Kabul, Afghanistan, a small demonstration erupts to protest that the United States needs to do more to rebuild the country and provide jobs and security.

May 8

TERRORISM: In Gardez, Afghanistan, the United Nations complains about increasing attacks against aid workers and local civilians.

May 9

AVIATION: In Helmand Province, Afghanistan, U.S. forces call in an air strike to separate rival factions.

POLITICS: In Washington, D.C., Deputy Defense Secretary Paul Wolfowitz says that weapons of mass destruction were the administration's rationale for war with Iraq and persons in authority endorsed it.

TERRORISM: In Karachi, Pakistan, authorities arrest two former Taliban officials, confiscating their weapons and satellite telephones.

May 10

TERRORISM: North of Kandahar, Afghanistan, Mullah Habibullah, a Muslim cleric and close associate of President Hamid Karzai, is killed outside of a mosque.

In Helmand Province, Afghanistan, two Afghan soldiers die in an explosion outside the governor's residence.

May 11

MILITARY: Near Khost, Afghanistan, an Afghan soldier dies and a U.S. soldier is wounded in a clash with suspected Taliban; two rebels are killed by bullets, and the rest die in a subsequent air strike.

POLITICS: In Baghdad, Iraq, U.S. military commander General Tommy Franks declares that the Iraqi Baath Party has disbanded and is defunct.

In Kabul, Afghanistan, protestors demonstrate against President Hamid Karzai's amnesty offer to all Taliban members who have not killed fellow Afghans.

In Zard, Pakistan, authorities announce the confiscation of 200 pounds of heroin that had been smuggled across the border from Afghanistan.

May 12

MILITARY: In Afghanistan, the British army reveals that a provincial reconstruction team is to be installed at Mazar-i-Sharif to rebuild the area and enhance security measures.

U.S. occupation authorities announce that they have arrested and detained Rihab Rashjid Taha, also known as "Dr. Germ," who played a major role in Iraq's biological weapons program.

May 14

DIPLOMACY: In Moscow, Russia, Secretary of State Colin Powell and President Vladimir Putin continue to disagree on Iraq, but they seek improvements in bilateral issues. The Russian parliament also approves a treaty further reducing U.S. and Russian respective stockpiles of nuclear weapons.

MILITARY: Redeployment of the 3rd Infantry Division is halted in the face of continuing unrest and violence throughout Baghdad, Iraq. Security of the city is the responsibility of the 1st Armored Division under Major General Ricardo S. Sanchez, but the 3rd Infantry will now assist in that task.

May 15
MILITARY: In northern Iraq, Operation Planet X is executed by the 1st Brigade, 4th Infantry Division, against a village 11 miles south of Tikrit. Troops seize 260 suspected Baath Party members along with General Mahdi Adil Abdallah, one of the coalition's most wanted figures.
POLITICS: In Kirkuk, northern Iraq, clashes between Kurds and Arabs take the lives of nine people.

May 16
POLITICS: In Baghdad, Iraq, U.S. envoy L. Paul Bremer III issues Order No. 1, which summarily bans 15,000 to 30,000 senior Baath Party leaders from holding jobs within the new Iraqi government.

May 19
POLITICS: In Baghdad, Iraq, 10,000 Shiites demonstrate against the continuing U.S. presence in the country.

May 21
MILITARY: In Kabul, Afghanistan, U.S. soldiers guarding the American embassy accidentally shoot four Afghan soldiers whom they mistook for guerrillas.

May 22
DIPLOMACY: In New York City, the UN Security Council votes 14 to 0 to pass Resolution 1483 and lift all sanctions imposed on Iraq after the 1991 Gulf War. It also agrees to place the United States and Britain in administrative control of the country until a legitimate democratic government can be formed.
MILITARY: Near Gardez, Afghanistan, Taliban forces attack a party of U.S. troops, and five hostile Afghans are killed in the process.

May 23
POLITICS: In Baghdad, Iraq, Provisional Authority head L. Paul Bremer III institutes Order No. 2, which disbands the Iraqi army, the Interior Ministry (both police and security elements), and the presidential security force.

May 24
POLITICS: In Kabul, Afghanistan, 200 people protest the accidental killing of four Afghans by American soldiers.

May 26
AVIATION: Over Turkey, a military transport crashes, killing 74 Spanish peacekeeping soldiers returning from Afghanistan.

May 27
DIPLOMACY: In Washington, D.C., the Treasury Department complies with UN Resolution 1483 by eliminating most economic sanctions against Iraq, making it legal once again for companies or individuals to conduct business with that nation.

May 28

MILITARY: In Washington, D.C., Bush administration officials declare that several Iraqi tractor-trailer units they have examined were outfitted to produce biological weapons, but there is no evidence they were actually used for that purpose.

TERRORISM: Because of the deaths of four U.S. servicemen in Iraq over the past few days, U.S. officials say they will maintain a larger military force than previously planned.

May 30

DIPLOMACY: In Basra, Iraq, British prime minister Tony Blair is the first Western leader to visit Iraq since the invasion. He is slated to confer with Robin Sawyers, the chief British representative, and Provincial Authority head L. Paul Bremer III.

POLITICS: On Air Force One, Secretary of State Colin Powell, en route to Poland, defends the military intelligence gathered on Iraqi weapons of mass destruction that precipitated the recent invasion. Further, he insists that his presentation before the UN Security Council was based on usually reliable sources.

June 1

MILITARY: Iranians seize four soldiers of the 1092nd Engineer Battalion as they cruise along the Shatt al Arab waterway separating Iran from Iraq. The men are blindfolded and interrogated, then released the following day.

POLITICS: In Baghdad, Iraq, coalition authorities abandon plans to create a large national assembly to serve as a transitional government, due to the acute factionalism inherent in Iraqi society. They therefore settle upon a temporary advisery council of 25 to 30 politicians.

In the Chitral Valley, Pakistan, more than 2,000 Afghan refugees voluntarily return to their homes in Nangarhar and Konar Provinces, Afghanistan.

June 2

DIPLOMACY: In Evian, France, President George W. Bush and French president Jacques Chirac release a joint communiqué declaring terrorism and weapons of mass destruction the "pre-eminent threat to national security." Chirac had previously opposed the war in Iraq.

In a note laced with frustration, UN weapons inspector Hans Blix says that, prior to the war, he had been unable to either prove or disprove the existence of Iraqi weapons of mass destruction.

MILITARY: In Konar Province, Afghanistan, the governor complains that the Taliban are paying poor people $10 to launch rockets against U.S. forces and Afghan army bases.

POLITICS: In London, United Kingdom, Prime Minister Tony Blair is experiencing increasing criticism over the lack of weapons of mass destruction uncovered in Iraq so far, but he says he is "100 percent behind the evidence" produced thus far.

In Herat, Afghanistan, Governor Ismail Khan is ordered to turn over $20 million in customs duty to the Afghan central government.

June 3

MILITARY: In Baghdad, Iraq, army engineers begin searching a large bomb crater for any trace of Saddam Hussein's remains.

Near Spin Boldak, Afghanistan, fighting between rival mujahideen groups leads to four deaths.

In Paktia Province, Afghanistan, a convoy of four Afghan trucks bringing fuel to the U.S. base at Urgan is attacked by Taliban forces; no casualties are reported.

POLITICS: In London, England, the House of Commons convenes a committee to investigate how British intelligence information was employed to justify the invasion of Iraq.

In Herat, Afghanistan, Governor Ismail Khan agrees to hand over $2 million in customs revenues to the central government; these funds will be used to pay the national defense forces.

TERRORISM: In Kandahar, Afghanistan, a bomb explodes near the home of Ahmad Wali Karzai, a relative of President Hamid Karzai, but no damage or casualties are reported.

June 3–6

DIPLOMACY: In London, United Kingdom, President Hamid Karzai pays his respects to Prime Minister Tony Blair and Queen Elizabeth II.

June 4

MILITARY: At Populzai, near Spin Boldak, Afghanistan, troops loyal to the governor of Kandahar trade fire with Taliban insurgents; 47 insurgents are reported killed.

June 5

TERRORISM: On the Gardez highway, Afghanistan, a roadside bomb explodes near a U.S. Special Forces convoy; no casualties are incurred.

June 6

DIPLOMACY: The World Bank reveals a $59.6 million grant for providing health care to women and children throughout Afghanistan.

POLITICS: A September 2002 classified report by the Defense Intelligence Agency is released that states that the agency had no conclusive proof of Iraq "producing or stockpiling chemical weapons."

June 7

TERRORISM: In Kabul, Afghanistan, a suicide bomb explodes near a bus crammed with members of the International Security Assistance Force; four German soldiers die, and 31 Afghans are injured. Tragically, the soldiers were headed for the airport after their tour of duty had ended.

June 8

POLITICS: In Washington, D.C., National Security Advisor Condoleezza Rice admits that the administration's claim that Iraq was attempting to purchase uranium from Niger was based on documents subsequently found to be forgeries.

June 9

MILITARY: In Thuluya, Iraq, north of Baghdad, U.S. Army troops sweep through an entire neighborhood looking for terrorists; some 400 residents are detained for questioning.

POLITICS: In Kabul, Afghanistan, President Hamid Karzai blames the recent attack on a security force bus on "foreign elements."

In Zabol Province, Afghanistan, leaflets appear urging the Afghan police and military to join the Taliban in their struggle against U.S. forces.

June 9–13
MILITARY: In Balad, Iraq, Operation Peninsula Strike unfolds as Task Force Iron Horse, including the 3rd Brigade, 4th Infantry Division, the 173rd Airborne Brigade, and the 3rd Squadron, 7th Cavalry (3rd Infantry Division), execute raids to seize any remaining Baath Party members. On the final day of operations, the 3rd Squadron engages a force of armed Iraqis, killing 20 in a one-sided firefight.

June 10
POLITICS: In Afghanistan, a national debate unfolds over the proposed new constitution, what form of Islam it should embody, and the extent of power that the central government should wield.

June 11
POLITICS: A report issued by the Associated Press estimates that 3,249 Iraqi civilians were killed in the course of Operation Iraqi Freedom.

June 12
MILITARY: U.S. forces attack a secret terrorist training camp northwest of Baghdad, Iraq, killing 68 insurgents and confiscating 70 surface-to-air missiles.
TERRORISM: Iraqi insurgents blow up a section of the oil pipeline running through the north-central section of the country.

June 14
MILITARY: In Baghdad, Iraq, Major General Ricardo S. Sanchez, commanding the 1st Armored Division, gains promotion to lieutenant general in charge of V Corps. He also succeeds General Tommy Franks as head of the Multi-National Force-Iraq.

June 15
MILITARY: In central and northern Iraq, U.S. military forces conduct Operation Desert Scorpion to finally quash remnants of hostile forces still operating there. They will also increase the tempo of humanitarian aid throughout the region.

June 16
MILITARY: In Baghdad, Iraq, Brigadier General Martin E. Dempsey is appointed the new commander of the 1st Armored Division.
POLITICS: In Spin Boldak, Afghanistan, the Taliban circulate leaflets threatening suicide attacks against coalition forces and members of the Afghan government.

June 17
POLITICS: In Kabul, Afghanistan, the government unveils plans to begin a disarmament program for all Afghan militia commencing in July. To that end, President Hamid Karzai also promises to reform the Defense Ministry.

TERRORISM: In Peshawar, Pakistan, authorities apprehend an al-Qaeda suspect who happens to be an Arab national and a leading terror facilitator.

June 18

DIPLOMACY: The Council on Foreign Relations issues a warning that the United States could lose the struggle in Afghanistan due to its lack of control over warlords and the snail-like pace of national reconstruction.

POLITICS: In Washington, D.C., Defense Secretary Donald Rumsfeld characterizes the small number of insurgents attacking U.S. forces as "dead-enders" and insists that the coalition is making good progress in rehabilitating Iraq.

Deputy Defense Secretary Paul Wolfowitz testifies before Congress and states that the violence still being encountered in Iraq is performed by handfuls of insurgents who lack sympathy and support from the local population.

MILITARY: North of Baghdad, Iraq, soldiers of the 4th Infantry Division raid two farmhouses and uncover $8.5 million in U.S. dollars and $400 million in Iraqi dinars. They also take into custody 20 men, including several of Saddam Hussein's personal bodyguards, and seize weapons and another $1 million in jewelry. Among those seized is Abid Hamid Mahmoud, Saddam Hussein's former secretary and a key adviser.

Along the Syrian-Iraqi border, U.S. Special Forces engage in a firefight with Syrian border guards, wounding five.

Soldiers of the U.S. 3rd Infantry Division set up a perimeter defense on March 24, 2003, during their advance through southern Iraq. *(Defense Imagery)*

June 19

DIPLOMACY: In Peshawar, Pakistan, the government requests an increase in the size of coalition forces in Afghanistan to fill the power vacuum outside the capital of Kabul.

June 20

TERRORISM: In Washington, D.C., Defense Department officials announce that, according to Abid Hamid Mahmoud, Saddam Hussein's personal secretary, the former president's two sons had fled the country into Syria.

June 21

MILITARY: U.S. and coalition forces are airlifted into eastern Afghanistan to seal the border with Pakistan from Taliban and al-Qaeda infiltration.

POLITICS: In Kabul, Afghanistan, two journalists are charged with blasphemy and placed on trial; the weekly newspaper *Afaab* is also shut down by the government.

TERRORISM: Insurgents blow up another Iraqi oil pipeline in an attempt to sabotage the national economy, which is dependent upon oil revenues.

June 22

TERRORISM: In Kunduz, Afghanistan, a bomb explodes near a U.S. military base, but no casualties result.

June 24

POLITICS: The Taliban declares it is forming a new leadership council, composed of military commanders from southwest Afghanistan, to combat U.S. and coalition forces in Afghanistan.

The Reuters news agency reports that Taliban leader Mullah Omar has formed an eight-man resistance council to fight the American occupation.

TERRORISM: In Basra, Iraq, six British soldiers are killed by unidentified assailants.

June 25

MILITARY: Outside Spin Boldak, Afghanistan, two Afghan soldiers are killed in a Taliban ambush three miles from a U.S. military base.

In western Afghanistan, an Afghan soldier is wounded during an attack upon a militia commander in the Maruf district northeast of Kandahar.

In Paktia Province, Afghanistan, a U.S. Special Forces soldier is killed in a firefight near Gardez; two more are wounded.

POLITICS: In Kabul, Afghanistan, President Hamid Karzai orders the two journalists charged with blasphemy released on bail.

June 26

DIPLOMACY: In Warsaw, Poland, Afghan president Hamid Karzai, on his first state visit there, muses that Saudi terrorist Osama bin Laden is most likely hiding along the Afghan-Pakistani border. He subsequently addresses a forum in Switzerland, giving an optimistic assessment of Afghanistan's reconstruction and rebirth thanks to international cooperation.

June 27

MILITARY: In Nangarhar Province, Afghanistan, U.S. forces commence Operation United Resolve to root out Taliban elements and prevent them from crossing into the country from Pakistan. While there, they will also assess humanitarian conditions in the region.

TERRORISM: The Taliban announce that Mullah Malang is tasked with recruiting and training a new generation of fighters.

June 28

MILITARY: In Samangan Province, Afghanistan, reports surface of new infighting between Tajik and Uzbek militias; no casualties are reported.

June 29–July 7

MILITARY: In light of continuing insurgent attacks against American convoys on Highways 1 and 2 north of Baghdad, Operation Sidewinder is undertaken by the 4th Division to apprehend the transgressors. When the operation concludes, a total of 282 prisoners have been seized along with many weapons and tons of ammunition.

June 30

TERRORISM: In Jalalabad, Afghanistan, rockets are fired at a military compound near UNICEF offices.

In Kandahar, Afghanistan, a bomb explodes at a mosque, injuring nine worshippers. The attack originated after Mullah Abdullah Fayaz refused Taliban demands to sanction a jihad against the Afghan government.

July 2

POLITICS: Former mujahideen leader Gulbuddin Hekmatyar again calls upon fellow Afghans to expel foreign forces from Afghanistan.

MILITARY: In Washington, D.C., President George W. Bush responds to journalists asking about Iraqi insurgents who have killed 26 U.S. soldiers since major operations concluded three months earlier. If they think they can attack American forces with impunity, Bush declares, "Bring 'em on!"

July 4

MILITARY: In Paktia and Khost Provinces, Afghanistan, U.S. forces commence Operation Haven Denial to root out Taliban elements operating there.

In Iraq, U.S. forces kill 11 insurgents who were attempting to stage a highway ambush.

POLITICS: The al-Jazeera network airs an audiotape purportedly made by Saddam Hussein, who urges all Iraqis to resist the invaders.

July 5

TERRORISM: In Kabul, Afghanistan, an explosion kills three Dutch soldiers working with the International Security Assistance Force.

In Baghdad, Iraq, a bomb explodes during a ceremony for graduating Iraqi policemen, killing seven and wounding 74.

July 6

MILITARY: In Samangan Province, Afghanistan, fighting flares anew between fighters loyal to General Abdul Rashid Dostum and Ustad Atta Mohammad. However, the United Nations manages to arrange a cease-fire between the two in the Shalgara district of Balkh Province.

POLITICS: Retired diplomat Joseph Wilson IV, who was sent to Niger to investigate claims that the Iraqis were attempting to buy uranium from that nation, writes an op-ed piece for the *New York Times* in which he declares he felt that the documents he uncovered were fraudulent, but his report did not reach top administration officials.

July 7

MILITARY: In Baghdad, Iraq, General Tommy Franks is replaced as Central Command commander by General John P. Abizaid, former deputy head of Combined Forces Command.

In Nangarhar Province, Afghanistan, a cross-border shootout between Afghan and Pakistani border forces is confirmed.

POLITICS: In Baghdad, Iraq, various Iraqi political groups endorse the idea of a 37-member governing council, and U.S. governing envoy L. Paul Bremer III introduces a new national currency to replace the dinar.

July 8

DIPLOMACY: In Kabul, Afghanistan, protestors march against what they deem as Pakistan's "invasion" of their nation, then attack the Pakistani embassy, smashing computers and office equipment. Pakistan closes the office in protest while President Hamid Karzai condemns the attack.

The U.S. Agency for International Development grants $553,000 to the Afghan ministry of education to explore the possibility of constructing an American university in Kabul, Afghanistan, similar to those in Egypt and Lebanon.

July 9

MILITARY: In Washington, D.C., Defense Secretary Donald Rumsfeld admits to a Senate committee that the occupation of Iraq is running at $3.9 billion per month, roughly twice what was originally estimated. Former commander General Tommy Franks also informs a Senate committee that U.S. forces in Iraq are not likely to be reduced for "the foreseeable future."

POLITICS: In Washington, D.C., White House spokesman Ari Fleischer states that previous statements about Iraq and Nigerian uranium should have been excluded from last January's State of the Union address.

TERRORISM: The U.S. Court of Appeals upholds the president's right to designate American citizens captured in combat as "enemy combatants" and subject them to indefinite confinement without legal representation.

July 10

DIPLOMACY: In Paris, France, creditor nations learn that Iraq owes them $21 billion as of August 1990, with a like amount due in interest payments for being in arrears. Japan apparently is owed the most money, but this is not revealed at the time.

TERRORISM: In Kandahar, Afghanistan, security forces arrest a senior Taliban official, along with detonators and machine guns; although his name is never publicly revealed, he is believed to be the brother of Taliban defense minister Mullah Obaidullah.

July 11

POLITICS: In Washington, D.C., Central Intelligence Agency director George Tenet accepts responsibility for verifying the apparently bogus letter purporting that Iraq was attempting to purchase uranium from Niger. Defense Secretary Donald Rumsfeld and National Security Advisor Condoleezza Rice insist that the statement about Iraq seeking to build nuclear weapons is technically accurate, since it was based on the British conclusion about evidence.

TERRORISM: In Ghazni Province, Afghanistan, Governor Hajj Asadullah warns of possible Taliban attacks in Ghazni, Khost, Paktia, Paktika, and Wardak Provinces. He further asserts these coordinated efforts could be the result of a recent meeting in Pakistan between Taliban leaders and Gulbuddin Hekmatyar.

July 12

TERRORISM: In Jalalabad, Afghanistan, a UN refugee transit center is struck by a bomb; no casualties are reported.

Bagram Air Base, Afghanistan, is struck by a rocket; no damage is inflicted.

July 12–17

MILITARY: In northern Iraq, Operation Soda Mountain is launched by the 4th Division, the 101st Infantry Division, and the 3rd Armored Cavalry to capture insurgents and their cadres. In 141 raids throughout the region, 600 prisoners are seized, including 62 former regime leaders, along with weapons and ammunition.

July 13

MILITARY: Near Spin Boldak, Afghanistan, Afghan forces raid a Taliban training camp, seizing 300 rocket-propelled grenades, antitank rifles, automatic weapons, and tons of ammunition.

POLITICS: In Baghdad, Iraq, a gathering of 37 national leaders, representing a cross-section of religious and ethnic groups, convenes a governing council of 25 members. This body will act as an interim government until national elections are held; as such, it possesses the authority to operate government ministries, appoint diplomats, approve a budget, and summon a commission to draft a new national constitution. However, final authority for all matters rests in the hands of Provisional Authority head L. Paul Bremer III.

July 14

POLITICS: In London, United Kingdom, Prime Minister Tony Blair stands by the British intelligence assessment that Iraq was actively trying to obtain materials to construct nuclear weapons.

TERRORISM: In Kandahar Province, Afghanistan, five Afghan police are killed in an attack on the Ghorak district police station; police chief Sahak Mam is among the dead.

In Kabul, Afghanistan, a car bomb intended for coalition personnel explodes, but no casualties result.

July 15

DIPLOMACY: In Washington, D.C., Afghan foreign minister Abdullah Abdullah confers with Secretary of State Colin Powell, and reaffirms his belief in America's commitment to Afghan reconstruction and democracy.

In Kabul, Afghanistan, representatives from the United States, Pakistan, and Afghanistan gather to help defuse repeated border incidents between the two neighbors.

POLITICS: Throughout Afghanistan, census teams are deployed to count potential voters for upcoming national elections.

July 16

MILITARY: In Baghdad, Iraq, General John P. Abizaid declares that the Americans are engaged in a "classical guerrilla-type war" with supporters of the previous regime, whose tactics and attacks are increasingly sophisticated. Fanatical Muslims fighting under the banner of al-Qaeda are also entering Iraq from abroad to commit acts of terrorism. In light of declining morale in the 3rd Infantry Division, the general also states that it will be rotating back to the United States by September.

In Kandahar Province, Afghanistan, Afghan security forces conduct house-to-house searches in the Ghorak district looking for gunmen who killed five policemen two days earlier.

POLITICS: In Kabul, Afghanistan, President Hamid Karzai decrees that a *loya jirga* will be assembled; this is to consist of 500 delegates, of whom 450 will be elected and 50 appointed by Karzai.

July 17

DIPLOMACY: In Washington, D.C., British prime minister Tony Blair informs a joint session of Congress that the invasion of Iraq was justified, even if biological, chemical, and nuclear weapons are never found. "History will forgive" the coalition for overthrowing a particularly brutal dictator.

TERRORISM: In Kabul, Afghanistan, the Interior Ministry reveals that four Afghans have been arrested for planning the recent attack on the Pakistani embassy there.

July 18

MILITARY: In Bagram, Afghanistan, an improvised bomb strikes a coalition military convoy, wounding three soldiers. A remote-control mine also kills eight Afghan troops in Khost Province.

July 19

AVIATION: Coalition warplanes are called in to bomb a Taliban position near Spin Boldak on the Pakistani border. Elsewhere a force of 200 Taliban thought to be under Mullah Abdul Razaq attack a government checkpoint.

July 20

MILITARY: In Baghdad, Iraq, ground forces commander General Ricardo S. Sanchez declares that eight battalions of U.S.-trained Iraqis will become the first part of the reconstituted Iraqi defense force.

July 21

POLITICS: In Afghanistan, nongovernmental aid agencies stress the urgency of medical assistance for half of the population, especially women and children. Families who have lost husbands and fathers are also viewed as extremely vulnerable.

July 22

MILITARY: Detachments from the 101st Airborne Division track down and kill Saddam Hussein's two sons, Uday and Qusay, in Mosul, northern Iraq. They received an anonymous tip as to their whereabouts from the local populace. Furthermore, to convince fearful Iraqis that both are dead, U.S. authorities release videotapes showing their bodies.

July 23
AVIATION: In Konar Province, Afghanistan, a B-52 strike is called in against suspected rebel positions near Asadabad.

DIPLOMACY: In Islamabad, Pakistan, government and Afghan delegates convene a meeting and promise to enhance cooperation in the war against terror. General John P. Abizaid also meets with President Pervez Musharraf and praises him for his help against international terrorism.

MILITARY: In Paktia Province, Afghanistan, units of the new Afghan national army embark on Operation Warrior Sweep through the Sumad District.

POLITICS: In Tehran, Iran, the government announces that it has arrested a number of al-Qaeda operatives but releases no names.

July 24
POLITICS: In Kabul, Afghanistan, the Ministry of Communications reveals that Internet service is going to be offered under the auspices of France and the UN Development Program.

July 25
DIPLOMACY: In Kabul, Afghanistan, local aid groups plead with coalition forces for enhanced security to prevent Taliban attacks against national reconstruction projects.

MILITARY: In Paktia Province, Afghanistan, coalition forces sweep through the Zormat region, uncovering a large cache of weapons but no guerrillas.

July 26
MILITARY: In Kabul, Afghanistan, U.S. military spokesman Colonel Rodney Davis warns that continuing Taliban and al-Qaeda terror attacks remain a distinct possibility.

July 27
MILITARY: In Helmand Province, Afghanistan, Taliban and al-Qaeda guerrillas attack a police patrol, killing six officers.

A Taliban spokesman admits that Mullah Abdur Rahim, a leading commander, was severely wounded three months earlier near Spin Boldak, Afghanistan.

POLITICS: In Zabol Province, Afghanistan, politicians plead with coalition forces to eliminate 500 Taliban fighters operating freely out of the Deh Chopin district.

July 28
DIPLOMACY: In Washington, D.C., the government announces plans for a $1 billion aid package to build schools and roads throughout Afghanistan.

POLITICS: The group Human Rights Watch warns that numerous Afghan warlords are creating a climate of intimidation that could jeopardize the drafting of a new constitution and national elections in 2004.

In Afghanistan, Taliban posters and pamphlets are distributed, warning 28 named collaborators that they face death unless they withdraw their support for the government. The intended victims are mostly from the Nurzai tribe near Spin Boldak.

July 29

MILITARY: Taliban forces ambush an Afghan army patrol in Naish, 40 miles north of Kandahar, killing three soldiers.

POLITICS: An audiotape is aired with a voice purported to be that of Saddam Hussein, who extols his sons as martyrs for the cause. As of this date, coalition authorities have captured or killed 36 of the 55 most wanted Iraqi fugitives.

TERRORISM: In Kandahar, Afghanistan, pro-government Mullah Jenab is gunned down outside his mosque by Taliban assassins.

July 30

MILITARY: The United States reports that 50 soldiers have been killed in insurgent attacks since combat operations ended on May 1.

POLITICS: In Afghanistan, a report from the UN Food and Agriculture Organization projects a bumper harvest in Afghanistan, but southern parts of the country are still plagued by drought conditions.

July 31

MILITARY: Near Spin Boldak, Afghanistan, a U.S. Special Forces base is attacked by unknown assailants who withdraw back across the Pakistan border.

In Konar Province, Afghanistan, U.S. forces kill three Taliban fighters near their base in Asadabad.

In Kabul, Afghanistan, the Interior Ministry promises better training for police and border guards to make them a disciplined, nonpartisan agency. President Hamid Karzai also announces reforms in the Defense Ministry that will facilitate a demobilization program.

POLITICS: On the Tajikistan border, Russian security forces seize 1.5 tons of Afghan heroin that had been smuggled in.

August 1

AVIATION: North of Kandahar, Afghanistan, U.S. helicopter gunships attack and kill four Taliban fighters, driving the rest of their party back into Pakistan.

DIPLOMACY: In New York City, UN secretary-general Kofi Annan says that Afghanistan may require international security forces for the foreseeable future.

POLITICS: Northern Alliance leaders Mohammad Qasim Fahim, Abdul Karim Khalili, Abdullah Abdullah, Yunnis Qanuni, and Abdul Rasul Sayyaf, all of whom hold cabinet positions in the government, announce that they are forming a political party.

August 2

MILITARY: North of Kandahar, Afghanistan, U.S. and Afghan forces kill four Taliban fighters in the Tora Ghar Mountains; 12 others are captured.

POLITICS: In Kabul, Afghanistan, the Afghan women's rights group Negar presents a petition to the commission drafting the new national constitution and calls for equals rights for women.

August 3

POLITICS: The United Nations and several nongovernmental aid agencies bemoan deteriorating security conditions throughout Afghanistan, though President Hamid Karzai appears unperturbed. Kandahar Province, spiritual home of the Taliban, is especially experiencing violent incidents.

UNICEF notes that a campaign to help vaccinate millions of Afghan children against measles has cut the death rate from 400 a month to 50 over the past 18 months.

TERRORISM: An audiotape, purportedly with the voice of al-Qaeda's second-in-command, Ayman al-Zawahiri, is aired, in which he warns Americans not to abuse captives held at Guantánamo, Cuba.

August 4

MILITARY: In Jowzjan Province, Afghanistan, warlord Farouq Khan, formerly of the Northern Alliance, refuses to participate in the national demobilization program.

POLITICS: In Baghdad, Iraq, the Provisional Authority reopens a former Baathist prison for suspected terrorists; it is staffed by U.S. troops under high security.

TERRORISM: In Mazar i Sharif, a pile of weapons voluntarily handed over to the government explodes, killing 13 people and injuring 21; however, the incident is viewed by many as accidental.

August 5

MILITARY: In Faryab Province, Afghanistan, fighting recommences between forces loyal to General Abdul Rashid Dostum and Ustad Atta Mohammad.

August 6

AVIATION: The German airline Lufthansa commences weekly flights from Dusseldorf to Kabul, Afghanistan.

MILITARY: In Baghdad, Iraq, men of the 4th Infantry Division discover a large cache of rockets, mortar rounds, small arms, and ammunition.

August 7

MILITARY: In Helmand Province, Afghanistan, Taliban operatives attack government offices, killing six Afghan soldiers and a translator for U.S. forces.

POLITICS: In Kabul, Afghanistan, a pioneering group of 30 women graduate from a business training course and aspire to open small businesses of their own.

TERRORISM: In Baghdad, Iraq, a bomb explodes outside the Jordanian embassy, killing 11 people and wounding 70.

August 8

MILITARY: In Helmand Province, Afghanistan, Afghan army troops begin a sweep through the Deshu district to root out Taliban elements there.

August 9

MILITARY: In Paktia Province, Afghanistan, Taliban rockets are launched at a U.S. base near Shkin; no casualties occur.

POLITICS: In Kabul, Afghanistan, former monarch Mohammad Zahir Shah returns from France, having recovered there from a broken leg.

The Movement for National Unity Party is founded in Afghanistan by Sultan Mahmud Ghazi.

August 9–10
MILITARY: In Basra, Iraq, British soldiers use rubber bullets to quell rioting Iraqis who had been protesting the shortages of power and fuel.

August 10
POLITICS: In Peshawar, Pakistan, Taliban spokesman Mohammad Amin announces that the movement intends to extend its attacks into northern Afghanistan under the command of Mullah Mohammad Asim Muttaqi.

In Kabul, Afghanistan, the United Nations suspends various missions in southern Afghanistan due to incessant attacks against aid workers and a lack of security.

August 11
MILITARY: In Kabul, Afghanistan, NATO General Goetz Gliemeroth takes charge of the International Security Assistance Force, but without a stated mandate.
TERRORISM: In Islamabad, Pakistan, the government announces the arrest of Hajji Jamil, a former mujahideen commander and close associate of the outlawed Gulbuddin Hekmatyar.

August 13
MILITARY: In Herat, Afghanistan, Governor Ismail Khan is stripped of all military responsibilities and rendered a regional administrator. General Baz Muhammad Ahmadi succeeds him as provincial military commander.
TERRORISM: Throughout Afghanistan, a spate of attacks nationwide takes the lives of 60 people in a 24-hour period, the most serious spike in violence since the war ended.

August 14
DIPLOMACY: In New York City, the UN Security Council extends a welcome to the new Iraqi governing council but stops short of granting recognition.

August 15
DIPLOMACY: In Washington, D.C., President George W. Bush nominates Zalmai Khahilzad to serve as the American ambassador to Kabul, Afghanistan.
TERRORISM: In northern Iraq, insurgents blow up part of the oil pipeline running into Turkey.

August 16
TERRORISM: Outside Baghdad, Iraq, insurgents drop mortar rounds on a prison compound, killing six people and injuring 59.

August 17
TERRORISM: In Baghdad, Iraq, a large bomb cuts a water main, cutting off water supplies to an estimated 300,000 homes.

August 18
MILITARY: In Baghdad, Iraq, men of the 2nd Brigade, 1st Armored Division, uncover a large weapons cache, including 20 pounds of C-4 plastic explosives, outside their lines.

August 19
POLITICS: In Iraq, U.S. authorities report the capture of former vice president Taha Yassin Ramadan, a close associate of Saddam Hussein's.

TERRORISM: In Baghdad, Iraq, a suicide truck bomb explodes next to UN headquarters, killing 24 people. Among them is Sergio Vieria de Mello, the UN special representative. More than 100 people are also injured in the blast.

In Afghanistan, nine police officers are killed in a Taliban-style ambush in the eastern part of the country.

August 20
DIPLOMACY: In light of increasing terror attacks in Iraq, the United Nations says it is reducing its staff nationwide. The World Bank and the International Monetary Fund also begin withdrawing staff members for safety reasons.

August 22
MILITARY: Final elements of the 3rd Infantry Division return to Fort Stewart, Georgia, following a two-year deployment in the Middle East in the war against terrorism.

August 23
TERRORISM: An insurgent attack near Basra, Iraq, takes the lives of three British servicemen.

August 26
MILITARY: In Khalis, Iraq, the 2nd Brigade, 4th Infantry Division, under Colonel David Hogg commences Operation Ivy Needle to corral a gang of criminals who have been attacking coalition forces and Iraqi police; 24 members are rounded up.

August 29
MILITARY: U.S. authorities report that the death toll of service personnel in Iraq has risen to 282, including 67 killed in hostile action since hostilities officially ended on May 1.

TERRORISM: In Najaf, Iraq, a car bomb explodes outside the Imam Ali Mosque during Friday prayers, killing more than 80 worshippers. Among the dead is noted cleric Ayatollah Mohammad Bakr al-Hakim, a moderate who urged followers to support the U.S. occupation. Shiites blame supporters of Saddam Hussein for the attack.

September 1
POLITICS: In Baghdad, Iraq, the Governing Council selects a 25-member cabinet and assumes control of most day-to-day functions.

TERRORISM: An audiotape attributed to Saddam Hussein is released, in which he denies any responsibility for the attack on the Imam Ali Shrine.

September 2
TERRORISM: In Baghdad, Iraq, a car bomb explodes outside police headquarters, killing one person and wounding 25.

September 3
DIPLOMACY: In New York City, the U.S. delegation introduces a draft resolution to the UN Security Council, calling upon member nations to support a multinational occupation force in Iraq.

POLITICS: In Washington, D.C., reports surface of a heretofore top-secret memo from the Joint Chiefs of Staff that characterizes planning for the war with Iraq as rushed and poorly conceived. This information partly explains why there have been ongoing problems in Iran since the occupation by coalition forces.

September 4
DIPLOMACY: French president Jacques Chirac and German chancellor Gerhard Schroeder oppose the U.S. initiative to have Iraq occupied by international peace-keepers. They seek to have the United Nations direct the entire reconstruction effort.

September 7
DIPLOMACY: In Kabul, Afghanistan, Defense Secretary Donald Rumsfeld arrives for talks with President Hamid Karzai and pledges increased U.S. military aid.

MILITARY: In Kabul, Afghanistan, Lieutenant General John Vines says that 200 Taliban fighters have been killed by U.S. forces over the past two weeks.

POLITICS: In Washington, D.C., President George W. Bush takes to the airwaves and asks Congress to approve $87 billion in military and reconstruction assistance for Iraq. He compares the effort to those that rebuilt Japan and Germany following World War II, and links such matters directly to the war against terrorism.

September 8
MILITARY: In London, United Kingdom, the government announces that it is dispatching an additional 1,200 peacekeeping troops to Iraq.

POLITICS: In Kabul, Afghanistan, the Afghan Council of Ministers approves a law authorizing the legal formation of political parties.

September 9
DIPLOMACY: In New York City, France, the United Kingdom, and Germany submit a resolution to the UN Security Council that demands that Iran provide accurate information about its nuclear program and allow UN inspectors unfettered access to suspected nuclear sites.

September 10
MILITARY: At Guantánamo, Cuba, James Yee, a Muslim chaplin, is arrested and charged with espionage in connection with aiding Islamic terrorists in captivity and carrying classified information. Yee is a former West Point graduate, and all charges against him are gradually dropped.

TERRORISM: A videotape of Saudi terrorist Osama bin Laden and his associate Ayman al-Zawahiri is aired on the al-Jazeera network.

September 12
MILITARY: At Fort Stewart, Georgia, President George W. Bush awards a Presidential Unit Citation to the 3rd Infantry Division for its lengthy service in Iraq.

In Fallujah, Iraq, U.S. troops engage in a shootout with local police officers after they allegedly fire on them; 10 police are killed. The U.S. government subsequently apologizes for the deaths, but local residents swear to take vengeance.

September 13–14
DIPLOMACY: In Paris, France, French foreign minister Dominique de Villepin urges that an Iraqi interim government that would report directly to the United Nations be installed within a month. A day later, Secretary of State Colin Powell criticizes the suggestion as unrealistic.

September 16
POLITICS: In Washington, D.C., Democratic congressman John P. Murtha, who had previously supported the war, criticizes the administration's handling of postwar affairs and demands that those responsible for it be dismissed.

September 17
POLITICS: In Washington, D.C., President George W. Bush modifies his previous stance and states, "We've had no evidence that Saddam Hussein was involved with September the 11th." Democratic senator Edward Kennedy says that the Iraqi war was fought to give Republicans a political boost.

September 18
TERRORISM: An insurgent attack near Tikrit, Iraq, takes the lives of three U.S. Army soldiers.

September 19
POLITICS: In Mosul, Iraq, former Iraqi defense minister General Sultan Hashim Ahmed al-Tai surrenders to coalition authorities.

September 20
MILITARY: In Kabul, Afghanistan, Tajiki defense minister Bismillah Khan is replaced by Abdul Rahim Wardak, a Pashtun.
TERRORISM: In Baghdad, Iraq, unknown gunmen fatally injure Akila al-Hashemi, one of three women working on the Iraqi Governing Council.

September 22
TERRORISM: In Baghdad, Iraq, a suicide bomber detonates himself outside UN headquarters, killing a guard and wounding 19 people.

September 23
DIPLOMACY: In New York City, President George W. Bush addresses the United Nations, calling on the world to put aside its differences on Iraq and help rebuild that nation. However, UN secretary-general Kofi Annan declares that unilateral military action threatens to undermine the United Nations. French president Jacques Chirac also urges the transfer of national sovereignty back to the Iraqis on a "realistic timetable"—without offering one.

September 24
DIPLOMACY: In Iraq, UN weapons inspectors issue a preliminary report stating that no weapons of mass destruction have been uncovered in the past four months.

September 25
DIPLOMACY: UN officials announce that they are removing additional personnel from Iraq, given the security risks.

In Washington, D.C., Secretary of State Colin Powell grants the Iraqi Governing Council six months to draw up and approve a new constitution.

September 27
DIPLOMACY: Russian president Vladimir Putin tells President George W. Bush that he will cancel the contract to aid Iran's nuclear energy program.

September 30
DIPLOMACY: Afghanistan becomes the 169th nation to agree to the Nuclear Non-Proliferation Treaty.

October 2
TERRORISM: David Kay, the chief U.S. weapons inspector, informs Congress that the 1,400-man Iraq Survey Group has yet to uncover demonstrable proof of weapons of mass destruction, be they biological, chemical, or nuclear. He also notes that an additional nine months may be required to complete the search.

October 6
TERRORISM: Two separate insurgent attacks claim the lives of three U.S. Army soldiers and an Iraqi translator.

October 9
TERRORISM: In Baghdad, Iraq, a suicide truck bomber crashes into a local police station, killing eight officers. Meanwhile, a U.S. soldier dies in a rocket-propelled-grenade attack northeast of the city while a Spanish diplomat is gunned down outside his Baghdad residence.

October 14
TERRORISM: In Baghdad, Iraq, a bomb explodes outside the Turkish embassy, killing one person.

October 16
DIPLOMACY: In New York City, the UN Security Council unanimously approves a U.S.- and British-backed resolution allowing for a U.S.-led multinational force for Iraq. The measure also appeals to member nations to support the occupation with troops and money and urges the Iraqi Governing Council to present a timetable for a new constitution no later than December 15. It also condemns insurgent attacks on UN personnel, a Shiite mosque in Najaf, and the international community. The unanimous vote is seen as a victory for the United States, now that tensions with some of its traditional allies are easing.

TERRORISM: In Karbala, Iraq, three U.S. soldiers die in a firefight with the private army of a Shiite cleric.

October 17
POLITICS: In Washington, D.C., Congress passes an $87 million Iraq aid package requested by President George W. Bush. The margin in the Senate is 87 to 12 and in

the House, 303 to 125. Of this total, $20 billion is reserved for security and reconstruction efforts while the rest will be spent on military operations.

October 19
POLITICS: A news report says that the administration deliberately shunned a State Department assessment predicting much of the postwar instability and tensions inherent in an Iraqi occupation.

October 23–24
DIPLOMACY: In Madrid, Spain, donor countries pledge $13 billion in aid for Iraqi reconstruction, which, when added to the $20 billion provided by the United States, falls sort of the $55 billion estimated by the World Bank to be necessary over the next four years.

October 26
TERRORISM: A rocket attack on the Rashid Hotel in Baghdad, Iraq, kills a U.S. Army colonel and wounds 16 others. The mayor of Baghdad is also assassinated.

October 27
TERRORISM: A string of rocket attacks timed to coincide with the Islamic holiday of Ramadan kills 43 people across Baghdad, Iraq, while another 200 are wounded. Fifteen people alone are killed in a barrage aimed at the headquarters of the International Committee of the Red Cross; this is the bloodiest single day since Saddam Hussein was removed from power.

October 28
POLITICS: In Washington, D.C., President George W. Bush, while acknowledging that Iraq is still a "dangerous place," places the blame on foreign terrorists infiltrating the country. However, he vows that no new troops are necessary and that the United States will "stay the course."

TERRORISM: In Washington, D.C., the Central Intelligence Agency announces that two of its operatives have been killed in Afghanistan three days earlier. The agents were involved in tracking terrorists in the southeastern part of the country.

October 30
DIPLOMACY: The United Nations declares that it is pulling its remaining staff out of Baghdad, Iraq, due to concern for their safety, but it will still maintain staff members in the northern reaches of the country.

October 31
MILITARY: The protracted insurgency in occupied Iraq has resulted in the deaths of 120 American personnel and 1,100 wounded by this date. The most insidious weapon used is the improvised explosive device placed alongside roadways and detonated when military columns pass by.

November 2
AVIATION: Over Fallujah, Iraq, a shoulder-fired surface-to-air missile brings down an army CH-47 Chinook helicopter, killing 16 soldiers and injuring 20. Another missile narrowly misses an accompanying CH-47.

November 3
POLITICS: In Washington, D.C., President George W. Bush gives a speech reiterating his determination that "America will never run" from Iraq.

In Kabul, Afghanistan, the 35-member commission completes drafting a new constitution, and it is presented to former monarch Mohammad Zahir Shah.

MILITARY: In Washington, D.C., Defense Secretary Donald Rumsfeld says that more than 100,000 Iraqi security troops have been trained.

November 5
MILITARY: The army releases a new rotation plan to move troops stationed stateside and in Germany to Iraq and Afghanistan. These plans involve 37,000 National Guard forces.

November 6
POLITICS: President George W. Bush gives a speech calling upon Middle Eastern nations to embrace democracy and recognize that the fall of Saddam Hussein is a "watershed moment in the global democratic revolution." He also signs into law an $87 billion supplemental spending bill to cover additional military and reconstruction expenses in Iraq.

November 7
AVIATION: Over Tikrit, Iraq, a UH-60 Black Hawk helicopter explodes and crashes, killing six soldiers on board.

MILITARY: In Ankara, Turkey, the parliament reverses itself and offers the United States army troops to help garrison Iraq. However, the move is strongly resisted by the Iraqi Governing Council.

November 8
DIPLOMACY: In Washington, D.C., President George W. Bush asks that Congress provide $87 billion for the wars in Iraq and Afghanistan; of this, $11 billion is for the military efforts against the Taliban, $800 million is for reconstruction, and the rest is for Iraq.

MILITARY: In retaliation for the loss of a helicopter near Tikrit, Iraq, U.S. troops, tanks, and artillery begin a series of punishing raids in neighborhoods known to be staging areas for insurgent attacks.

POLITICS: In Afghanistan, national elections are held in all 32 provinces as 500 members of a new *loya jirga* are chosen.

November 11
MILITARY: In Washington, D.C., Defense Secretary Donald Rumsfeld gives a televised interview and states that the United States is embroiled in a "low intensity war" in Iraq. This is the first time such terminology has been used to describe affairs there.

November 12
MILITARY: In Kuwait, the 3rd Brigade, 2nd Infantry Division arrives under the command of Colonel Michael E. Rounds. It is the first organized Stryker brigade deployed abroad; in light of the Iraqi insurgency, many of the wheeled Strykers are equipped with slatted armor to protect them against rocket-propelled grenades.

TERRORISM: In Nasiriyah, Iraq, a truck and a car bomb explode in a building housing Italian military police; 19 Italians and 13 Iraqis are killed in the blast.

November 13
MILITARY: In Iraq, senior U.S. commander General John P. Abizaid states that coalition forces are confronting 5,000 guerrillas in Iraq, who are getting better financed and more sophisticated tactically.

November 14
POLITICS: U.S. officials clarify their position by declaring that Iraqi self-governance is acceptable before a new constitution is drafted. Moreover, total national sovereignty is to be restored in 2004, although occupation forces will remain.

November 15
AVIATION: Over Mosul, Iraq, a pair of UH-60 Black Hawk helicopters collide and crash, killing 17 soldiers and injuring five. The reasons behind the accident are unexplained.
TERRORISM: In Baghdad, Iraq, bombs explode at two police stations, killing 14 people.

November 26
POLITICS: In Iraq, Grand Ayatollah Ali al-Sistani denounces the U.S. plan for a new constitution and demands direct elections now, which, in all likelihood, would result in a Shiite-dominated government.

A U.S. Navy F/A-18F Super Hornet takes off from the flight deck of the aircraft carrier USS *Kitty Hawk*. These planes played an important role in supporting the coalition forces in the early phase of the war in Iraq. *(Defense Imagery)*

November 27
DIPLOMACY: In Kabul, Afghanistan, Senator Hillary Clinton arrives to assure the country's leaders that American aid is forthcoming.
MILITARY: In Baghdad, Iraq, President George W. Bush makes a surprise Thanksgiving appearance at Baghdad International Airport and dines with members of the 101st Airborne Division. This is the first time an American chief executive has visited Iraq in any capacity.

November 29
TERRORISM: South of Baghdad, Iraq, an insurgent attack kills seven Spanish intelligence officers as they drive to work in their SUV.

November 30
MILITARY: The total military losses for the month of November amount to 104 coalition troops dead, of which 79 were American.

Near Samarra, Iraq, insurgents ambush a U.S. military convoy, which promptly turns the tables on the attackers, killing 54 guerrillas.
TERRORISM: Two Japanese diplomats and two South Korean contractors are killed in scattered attacks across Iraq.

December 1
POLITICS: In Herat, Afghanistan, a Provincial Reconstruction Team, consisting of both civilian and military members, is established. It joins similar teams already functioning in Mazar-i-Sharif, Kunduz, Gardez, Kandahar, and Parvan.

December 2
MILITARY: In Tikrit, Iraq, a force of 1,000 U.S. soldiers makes a sudden raid in the hopes of snaring an aide to former president Saddam Hussein.

December 4
DIPLOMACY: In Kabul, Afghanistan, Defense Secretary Donald Rumsfeld meets with President Hamid Karzai over the seeming rise in attacks on U.S. forces. He subsequently ventures to Mazar-i-Sharif for talks with two local warlords in charge of regional security forces.
MILITARY: At Abu Ghraib, Iraq, Operation Bulldog Mammoth unfolds as the 2nd Battalion, 70th Armor, 4th Division; 1st Battalion, 325th Airborne Infantry, 82nd Airborne Division; and the 70th Military Police Battalion raid apartment complexes northwest of Baghdad looking for terrorism suspects; 40 individuals are taken into custody along with numerous weapons.

December 5–6
AVIATION: In Afghanistan, two rounds of U.S. air strikes against Taliban positions are said to have killed 15 Afghan children by mistake.

December 6
MILITARY: In Iraq, Defense Secretary Donald Rumsfeld meets with Lieutenant General Ricardo S. Sanchez, who says that attacks on U.S. forces average 20 per day—roughly half the rate of a few weeks earlier.

December 8

MILITARY: In Ad Duluyiyah, Iraq, two soldiers from the 3rd Brigade, 2nd Infantry Division, are killed when their Stryker vehicle accidentally rolls down an embankment and into a canal. While not combat related, these are the 2nd Infantry Division's first fatalities.

December 9

DIPLOMACY: In Washington, D.C., the Defense Department announces that bids for $18.6 billion worth of reconstruction projects in Iraq would only go to nations that supported the recent war there. This is in accordance with a directive signed by Deputy Defense Secretary Paul Wolfowitz. Nations such as France, Germany, and Russia would only be allowed to bid on subcontracts.

MILITARY: In Tokyo, Japan, the government announces that it is deploying 600 troops to Iraq as peacekeepers, insisting that they would only use force in self-defense.

December 13

MILITARY: A force of 600 soldiers belonging to the 1st Brigade, 4th Division (Mechanized), commences Operation Red Dawn by searching the village of Ad Dawr, nine miles southeast of Tikrit. They capture the bedraggled fugitive Iraqi president Saddam Hussein as he hides in a "spider hole." He is immediately taken into custody and examined by Army medics.

POLITICS: In Baghdad, Iraq, Provisional Authority head L. Paul Bremer III declares to journalists, "Gentlemen, we got him." This concludes an eight-month manhunt for the "Ace of Spades" in the card deck of wanted Iraqi leaders.

December 14

DIPLOMACY: In Washington, D.C., an exultant President George W. Bush holds a televised news conference on Saddam Hussein's capture. He says he believes that a very dark episode in Iraq's history has closed and Iraqis can now reject violence and oppression in building a new country.

POLITICS: In Kabul, Afghanistan, the 500-member *loya jirga* convenes to debate the new constitution, then ratify it.

TERRORISM: West of Baghdad, Iraq, a bomb explosion outside a police station kills 17 people and wounds 33.

December 15

POLITICS: In Washington, D.C., President George W. Bush, while favoring the "ultimate penalty" for captured former Iraqi president Saddam Hussein, pledges to work with Iraqi leaders to convene a war-crime tribunal.

Saddam Hussein was captured December 13, 2003, and pictures showing his disheveled appearance were released around the world. *(Defense Imagery)*

TERRORISM: In Baghdad, Iraq, two additional bombings of police stations kill eight people and wound more than 20.

December 17

MILITARY: In Iraq, U.S. soldiers clash with Iraqi insurgents gathering for an apparent meeting; 17 are killed and 73 arrested.

December 25–26

TERRORISM: Insurgents launch a series of rocket attacks across Iraq; four American soldiers and six Iraqi civilians are killed.

December 26

POLITICS: A violent earthquake strikes the city of Bam, Iran, destroying it and killing more than 26,000 people. Also destroyed was a mud-brick citadel dating back more than 2,000 years.

December 29

MILITARY: *Time* magazine votes "The American Soldier" as "Person of the Year."

December 31

MILITARY: At this time in the Iraqi occupation, American deaths total 486 with a further 2,408 wounded in hostile action.

TERRORISM: In Baghdad, Iraq, a bomb tears through the popular Nabil Restaurant, killing eight Iraqis and wounding 35.

2004

January

MILITARY: Army personnel totals are steady at 494,000 officers and soldiers, though more than 100,000 of these are deployed overseas. Iraq and Afghanistan remain the military's largest focus of operations.

January 2

AVIATION: Near Fallujah, Iraq, ground fire downs an OH-58D Kiowa Warrior helicopter belonging to the 1st Battalion, 82nd Aviation Regiment. Captain and pilot Kimberly N. Hampton is the first female helicopter pilot to die in Operation Iraqi Freedom.

January 4

POLITICS: In Kabul, Afghanistan, three weeks of heated debate conclude as the *loya jirga* grants official approval to establishing an Islamic state, a presidential system of governance, a bicameral legislature, recognition of local languages, and a lifelong title of "Father of the Nation" for former monarch Mohammad Zahir Shah. Significantly, for a Muslim country, women are also accorded equal rights.

January 6

MILITARY: In Afghanistan, the NATO-led International Security Assistance Force expands its authority beyond Kabul and takes charge of seven reconstruction teams operating in the provinces.

TERRORISM: In Kandahar, Afghanistan, two bombs explode, killing 15 people and injuring dozens. Taliban operatives are blamed.

January 7
POLITICS: In Kunduz, Afghanistan, a provincial reconstruction team is established under German auspices.

January 8
AVIATION: Over Fallujah, Iraq a medivac UH-60 Black Hawk helicopter of C Troop, 1st Squadron, 17th Cavalry, goes down, apparently after being hit by a ground-launched missile; all nine occupants are killed.

DIPLOMACY: In Washington, D.C., Secretary of State Colin Powell admits that any proof of an Iraq–al-Qaeda link is still missing.

POLITICS: In Washington, D.C., President George W. Bush gives a televised interview, reiterating his belief that Iraq under Saddam Hussein possessed stockpiles of outlawed weapons.

MILITARY: In Washington, D.C., the government announces that 123,000 troops would begin rotating home from Iraq and Kuwait starting in May and will be replaced by 110,000 fresh troops.

POLITICS: A report issued by the Carnegie Endowment for International Peace claims that the Bush administration strong-armed analysts to exaggerate the threat posed by Iraq's weapons programs.

January 9
MILITARY: In Washington, D.C., the Defense Department declares that former Iraqi president Saddam Hussein is to be designated a prisoner of war, with all the rights accorded one.

TERRORISM: In Baqubah, Iraq, an explosion near a Shiite mosque kills five worshippers.

January 11
MILITARY: An estimated 3,000 soldiers have deserted from the Afghan National Army since its founding in May 2002. Soldiers receive $70 per month while officers are paid $200 for the same period.

POLITICS: In Tehran, Iran, the Religious Council disqualifies 3,600 reformist candidates from running for seats in parliament.

In Basra, Iraq, thousands of Shiites take to the streets to demand direct elections for a new national government. Because they constitute the majority of the population, the long-oppressed Shiites are expected to take control.

In Najaf, Iraq, Grand Ayatollah Ali al-Sistani, the nation's highest Shiite cleric, again calls for direct elections to choose an interim government. This is in direct conflict with the present plan advanced by Provisional Authority head L. Paul Bremer III, which calls for provincial caucuses.

January 12
DIPLOMACY: In New York City, U.S. officials approach the United Nations for possible assistance in mediating the dispute over forming a new Iraqi government.

January 13

DIPLOMACY: In Washington, D.C., President George W. Bush holds out the prospect that Canada might be allowed to bid on reconstruction projects in Iraq, even though it had opposed the invasion.

January 17

AVIATION: In Afghanistan, local authorities blame a U.S. helicopter attack for the deaths of 11 civilians; U.S. authorities claim that only five Taliban fighters were killed.

TERRORISM: North of Baghdad, an insurgent roadside bomb kills three U.S. soldiers.

January 18

POLITICS: In Afghanistan General Abdul Rashid Dostum announces that he will join the government if appointed minister of defense, chief of staff, or commander of 20,000 soldiers.

TERRORISM: In Baghdad, Iraq, a suicide bomber explodes himself inside an American occupation headquarters, killing 20 Iraqis working there and wounding 60.

January 19

MILITARY: At Fort Bragg, North Carolina, the 2nd Brigade, 82nd Airborne Division, arrives home after a long tour of duty in Iraq.

POLITICS: In Baghdad, Iraq, 100,000 Iraqis take to the streets in support of Ayatollah Ali al-Sistani, who is demanding national elections and refuses to meet with American officials on the subject.

January 20

DIPLOMACY: In New York City, the American UN delegation asks Secretary-General Kofi Annan to dispatch officials to Iraq and consult with Ayatollah Ali al-Sistani on the viability of holding national elections.

January 22

POLITICS: In Afghanistan, Mohammad Mohaqiq declares his candidacy for the Afghan presidency.

January 23

DIPLOMACY: David Kay, chief weapons inspector for the Iraqi Survey Group, resigns after his 1,400-man team fails to find any evidence of chemical, biological, and nuclear weapons. He says he doubts any were present at the time of the invasion.

January 25

TERRORISM: In Ramadi, Iraq, seven Iraqi police officers are killed in two separate attacks.

January 26

POLITICS: In Kabul, Afghanistan, President Hamid Karzai and former king Mohammad Zahir Shah preside over public ceremonies marking the adoption of the new constitution.

In Washington, D.C., Vice President Richard Cheney says on National Public Radio that he believes there is overwhelming evidence that Saddam Hussein had extensive links with the al-Qaeda terror network. He is also confident that Iraq, prior to the invasion, possessed mobile biological warfare laboratories.

January 27
DIPLOMACY: In New York City, UN secretary-general Kofi Annan agrees to dispatch a team of specialists to Iraq to evaluate the feasibility of early elections and discuss the matter with leading Shiite officials. However, he insists that the United States and its allies guarantee the team's security ahead of time.

POLITICS: In Washington, D.C., Iraqi Survey Group leader David Kay informs the Senate Armed Forces Committee that his organization was completely incorrect about Iraqi weapons of mass destruction. He now does not expect to find any, and he regards the lapse as a failure of military intelligence. Moreover, Kay calls for an independent investigation into how such intelligence was gathered and utilized prior to the war.

TERRORISM: Southwest of Kirkuk, Iraq, a roadside bomb takes the lives of three U.S. Army soldiers. In Mosul, a suicide car bomber attacks a police station, killing nine people and wounding 45.

January 28
POLITICS: In Kabul, Afghanistan, Interior Minister Ali Ahmad Jalali announces the creation of a 33rd province, Daikondi, which has been carved out of the northern part of Oruzgan Province.

Masuda Jalal becomes the first woman in Afghan history to announce her candidacy for the presidency.

January 29
DIPLOMACY: In Washington, D.C., National Security Advisor Condoleezza Rice notes that although no weapons of mass destruction have been discovered in Iraq, the possibility of them having been transferred to Syria cannot be completely ruled out.

POLITICS: In London, United Kingdom, a committee headed by James Brian Edward Hutton, Baron Hutton, former Lord Chief Justice of Northern Ireland, concludes that Prime Minister Tony Blair did not deliberately exaggerate intelligence estimates respecting Saddam Hussein's programs to acquire weapons of mass destruction. His report also castigates the BBC for raising the issue.

TERRORISM: Outside Ghazni, Afghanistan, an explosion near a Taliban weapons cache kills seven U.S. Army soldiers and wounds three others.

January 30
POLITICS: In Tehran, Iran, the ultraconservative Religious Council reinstates 1,160 reformist candidates for upcoming parliamentary elections.

January 31
MILITARY: In Baghdad, Iraq, reports of prisoner abuses at Abu Ghraib prison result in a far-ranging investigation.

TERRORISM: In Mosul, Iraq, a suicide bomber runs his car into an Iraqi police station, killing nine people and injuring 43.

February 1

MILITARY: In Wurzburg, Germany, the first elements of the 1st Infantry Division begin departing for a tour in Iraq under Major General John R. S. Batiste. Most of the division's heavy equipment will remain behind as it will be utilizing armored humvees and small arms to combat the insurgency. These troops, in concert with the 2nd Brigade, 25th Infantry Division, and the 30th Separate Heavy Brigade, will also form the core element of Task Force Iron Danger to replace Task Force Iron Horse.

POLITICS: In Washington, D.C., Bush administration officials state that a bipartisan commission is being tasked with investigating how prewar military intelligence reports concerning weapons of mass destruction could have erred.

In Tehran, Iran, one-third of Majlis members resign their seats to protest tight restrictions placed on upcoming parliamentary elections. Apparently, 2,000 reformist candidates have been forbidden from running by the ultraconservative Guardian Council.

TERRORISM: In Erbil, northern Iraq, suicide attackers strike the offices of the two leading Kurdish political parties, killing 105 people and wounding 200 more.

February 2

POLITICS: In Washington, D.C., Secretary of State Colin Powell says that he might not have recommended war against Saddam Hussein if he had known with certainty that weapons of mass destruction did not exist, but he concludes that the invasion was nonetheless "the right thing to do." President George W. Bush calls for an independent commission to investigate this failure in military intelligence gathering.

February 3

POLITICS: In London, United Kingdom, Prime Minister Tony Blair seeks an independent investigation of intelligence gathering relative to prewar Iraq.

February 5

POLITICS: In Washington, D.C., Central Intelligence Agency director George Tenet confesses that his agency made errors respecting Iraqi weapons of mass destruction but denies it experienced political pressure to alter its assessments.

February 6

DIPLOMACY: In Brussels, Belgium, Defense Secretary Donald Rumsfeld tries to get NATO further engaged in Afghanistan and to take over military operations there.

POLITICS: In Washington, D.C., President George W. Bush names nine members of his intelligence investigation committee, headed by U.S. Appeals Court Judge Laurence Silberman and former U.S. senator Chuck Robb.

February 8

POLITICS: President George W. Bush, in a live interview on NBC's *Meet the Press*, says that, even though inspectors have yet to turn up evidence of weapons of mass destruction, the invasion of Iraq was justified because Saddam Hussein was fully capable of producing such devices.

February 10

TERRORISM: Outside a police station in Iskandariyah, Iraq, a suicide bomber detonates himself in a line of people looking for work, killing 55 people and injuring 65 more.

February 11–12
TERRORISM: In Baghdad, Iraq, two suicide bombers targeting Iraqi police and recruits seeking to join the army kill 47 people and injure scores more.

February 12
MILITARY: At Fort Lewis, Washington, National Guard Specialist Ryan G. Anderson, Company A, 1st Battalion, 303rd Armor Regiment, is arrested for attempting to pass classified information to al-Qaeda.

In Fallujah, Iraq, General John P. Abizaid comes under hostile rocket and small-arms fire while visiting a civil defense post. Soldiers of the 82nd Airborne Division fire back, but there are no casualties.

At Fort Campbell, Kentucky, the 101st Airborne Division under Major General David H. Petraeus finally rotates home after a lengthy tour of duty in Iraq; the division suffered 58 fatalities during Operation Iraqi Freedom.

February 14
TERRORISM: In Fallujah, Iraq, an estimated 70 insurgents attack an Iraqi police station, killing 25 people and freeing 87 inmates. Four Lebanese and Iranian insurgents are also killed.

February 17
DIPLOMACY: In Kabul, Afghanistan, the European Union dispatches a delegation for official talks.

February 18
TERRORISM: In northern Iran, a train wreck, apparently caused by an explosion, kills 300 people.

February 19
DIPLOMACY: In New York City, UN secretary-general Kofi Annan concludes that Iraqi national elections are not possible before the formal transfer of sovereignty back to Iraq on June 30.
POLITICS: In Konar Province, Afghanistan, a new provincial reconstruction team is created in the capital of Asadabad.

February 20
POLITICS: In Iran, national elections are handily won by religious conservatives, who secure a clear majority in the Majlis. Many moderates decided to boycott the election because the ultraconservative Guardian Council had barred 2,000 moderate candidates from running.

February 23
DIPLOMACY: In New York City, a UN delegation returning from Iraq informs the Security Council that direct elections there are not realistic before late 2004 or early 2005.
TERRORISM: In Kirkuk, northern Iraq, a car bomb explodes near a police station, killing 10 people and injuring 43.

February 26
MILITARY: In Washington, D.C., the Defense Department approves the Global War on Terrorism Expeditionary Medal for personnel deployed to Afghanistan or Iraq,

and the Global War on Terrorism Service Medal for those who participated in any homeland-security activities.

March 1

POLITICS: In Baghdad, Iraq, the Iraqi Governing Council gives its blessing a new draft constitution that will remain in place through 2004 or 2005. The new document maintains civilian control of the military and equal protection for both sexes and all religions. Moreover, Islam is regarded as a "source" for the law, but not the primary source.

March 2

TERRORISM: In Baghdad and Karbala, Iraq, three bombs aimed at Shiite pilgrims celebrating *ashoura* explode, killing 170 people and wounding 200 more. Police arrest a fourth suicide bomber whose vest failed to explode.

March 3

TERRORISM: In Baghdad, Iraqi police announce the arrest of 15 people connected to the recent bombing of Shiite pilgrims.

March 4

MILITARY: At Fort Stewart, Georgia, the 3rd Infantry Division returns after a lengthy tour of duty in Iraq. However, personnel are notified that it will be redeployed there in November 2004.

POLITICS: In Afghanistan, NATO announces the 11th provincial reconstruction team in Ghazni.

March 6

MILITARY: Near the Afghan-Pakistani border, nine Taliban fighters are killed after a group of 40 tries to overrun a Special Forces sniper outpost.

March 8

POLITICS: In Baghdad, Iraq, the Iraqi Governing Council signs an interim constitution that will take effect as soon as U.S. and coalition forces end their occupation. The present document includes a bill of rights along with a system of checks and balances. However, this transpired only after five Shiite hard-liners dropped their opposition to Kurds possessing veto power over legislation.

March 9

TERRORISM: Iraqi police shoot and kill two officials of the coalition Provisional Authority along with their Iraqi translator, 70 miles south of Baghdad. These are the first American civilians to die in the insurgency.

March 10

MILITARY: In Kabul, Afghanistan, the British deploy a 100-man Special Forces team for clandestine operations against al-Qaeda.

March 12

POLITICS: In Herat, Afghanistan, a new provincial reconstruction team under American auspices assembles.

March 14

MILITARY: In northeastern Iraq, a patrol from the 4th Infantry Division exchanges fire with Iranian border guards; no casualties result.

March 17

TERRORISM: In Baghdad, Iraq, a car bomb tears through the popular Mount Lebanon Hotel, killing seven people and wounding 35.

March 19

AVIATION: A Russian An-124 Condor transport aircraft touches down at Kabul airport with a shipment of heavy weapons and supplies for the Afghan National Army. The army still relies on Soviet-era weapon stocks provided to the Kabul regime between 1978 to 1990.

MILITARY: By this date, the first anniversary of Operation Iraqi Freedom, 571 U.S. servicemen have been killed in hostile action.

POLITICS: In Washington,. D.C., President George W. Bush speaks on the first anniversary of the invasion of Iraq, linking it to the ongoing war against terrorism, which he deems inescapable for the present generation.

March 21

MILITARY: A serious outbreak of fighting occurs when militias loyal to Governor Ismail Khan trade shots with the forces of General Abdul Zahir Nayebzadeh; Mirwais Sedeq, the minister of civil aviation and tourism, is killed.

March 22

MILITARY: The Afghan government dispatches a force of 600 soldiers to Herat, Afghanistan, to shore up regional security and protect noncombatants. A cease-fire is concluded through negotiations, and calm returns to the area.

March 23

TERRORISM: In Hillah and Kirkuk, Iraq, two separate attacks take the lives of 11 Iraqi police officers.

March 26–April 10

MILITARY: At the National Training Center, Fort Irwin, California, the 2nd Brigade, 3rd Infantry Division, becomes the first unit selected to be reorganized and tested under the new tactical structure. It is also slated for deployment in Iraq in the fall.

March 28

MILITARY: In Ghazni, Afghanistan, men of the 10th Mountain Division uncover a cache of Taliban grenades, mines, and mortar rounds. Simultaneously, a detachment from the 3rd Battalion, 6th Field Artillery, discovers 2,000 rifles and stores of ammunition while searching a house in Kandahar.

March 31

DIPLOMACY: In Bonn, Germany, an international conference on Afghanistan results in an $8.2 pledge of aid with $4.4 billion earmarked for 2004.

MILITARY: In Baghdad, Iraq, the advance elements of the 1st Cavalry Division under Major General Peter W. Chiarelli arrive in Iraq to replace the 1st Armored Division. Meanwhile, the 1st Brigade, 1st Infantry Division, and the National Guard 81st Armored Brigade join the 1st Marine Expeditionary Force in a sweep against militant strongholds at Fallujah and Ramadi.

TERRORISM: Near Fallujah, Iraq, a roadside bomb takes the lives of five U.S. Army soldiers. A mob also kills four American contract workers then triumphantly drags their bodies through the streets before hanging them on public display. This atrocity prompts President George W. Bush to take retaliatory action against the local militants.

April 1

MILITARY: In Afghanistan, a force of 2,000 marines arrives from the Persian Gulf region to reinforce local security.

April 2

DIPLOMACY: In Brussels, Belgium, NATO headquarters approves a plan to expand the security assistance force's mandate in Afghanistan.

MILITARY: The army announces that its recruitment goals have been met for the previous year, despite the ongoing conflicts in Iraq and Afghanistan. Moreover, it is well on its way to meeting the current year's goals as well.

April 3

POLITICS: In Iraq, an aide to radical cleric Moqtada al-Sadr is arrested for his suspected complicity in the murder of fellow Shiite leader Ayatollah Abdel Majid al-Khoei. This act sets the stage for a showdown between al-Sadr's private militia—the Mahdi Army—and U.S. forces.

April 4

MILITARY: In the Sadr City district of Baghdad, Iraq, men of the 1st Brigade, 1st Cavalry Division, engage a large insurgent force in the downtown area; seven Americans die, and 51 are injured. Enemy losses are unknown. Apparently, these are Shiites loyal to radical cleric Moqtada al-Sadr, and this skirmish forms part of a mass uprising around the country, with similar attacks in Kufah, Karbala, Najaf, and Kut.

April 5

MILITARY: Marines begin surrounding the city of Fallujah, Iraq, long a hotbed of Sunni insurgency. However, several nearby Iraqi security battalions refuse to participate in any attacks there.

POLITICS: In Mazar-i-Sharif, Afghanistan, General Abdul Rashid Dostum's Jumbesh-i-Milli militia holds a conference of 2,000 members to register them for the upcoming election.

April 6–7

MILITARY: In Fallujah, Iraq, U.S. marines surround and attack militants in retaliation for the mutilation of four American contractors. Several hundred Sunni radicals are killed in exchange for 12 marines killed in action.

In Nasiriyah, Iraq, Shiite fighters loyal to radical cleric Moqtada al-Sadr clash with Italian soldiers.

April 7
AVIATION: U.S. warplanes bomb a mosque in Fallujah, Iraq, that was manned and being used for sniping purposes by Sunni insurgents.
DIPLOMACY: The government of Kazakhstan announces that it is withdrawing all of its forces in Iraq as of April 30.

April 8
MILITARY: Uzbek militia under General Abdul Rashid Dostum ejects government forces from Maimana, Faryab Province, only to retreat from there three days later.
POLITICS: In Iraq, U.S. authorities note that Sunni and Shiite radicals have struck a temporary alliance against occupation forces.
TERRORISM: Insurgents kidnap three Japanese civilians and threaten to kill them unless their government withdraws all 550 soldiers from Iraq. However, they are released unharmed on April 15.

April 9
MILITARY: Two soldiers from the 724th Transportation Company are captured by Iraqi insurgents after an ambush; both are subsequently murdered in captivity.

In Baghdad, Iraq, Specialist Michelle Witmer, 32nd Military Police Company (Wisconsin), is killed by an improvised explosive device; she is the first female National Guard soldier killed in army history and the first Wisconsin National Guard member to die since World War II.
TERRORISM: In Baghdad, Iraq, terrorists kidnap American contract worker Thomas Hamil.

April 11
MILITARY: In Fallujah, Iraq, U.S. forces call a cease-fire and halt further military action against Sunni radicals for the time being.

April 12
TERRORISM: In Iraq, insurgents kidnap 11 members of a Russian company, while three Czechs are reported missing.

April 13
POLITICS: In Washington, D.C., President George W. Bush holds his third prime-time news conference to declare that the United States intends to turn sovereignty back over to Iraq on June 30, as promised. He also denies that any mistakes have been committed in the invasion of Iraq or in handling the ongoing insurgency.

In Kabul, Afghanistan, President Hamid Karzai orders the Panjshir area organized into a province.

April 14
POLITICS: In Baghdad, Iraq, UN envoy Lakhdar Brahimi says that the new Iraqi caretaker government is taking shape, with provisions for a prime minister, a president, and two vice presidents.

April 15

DIPLOMACY: In Washington, D.C., the government accepts a UN proposal to replace the Iraqi Governing Council with a caretaker government once the United States returns sovereignty to the Iraqis in June.

MILITARY: An upsurge in violence throughout Iraq results in extended tours for 20,000 soldiers previously scheduled to be rotated home. All have their tours of duty extended by 90 days.

April 16

AVIATION: Near Kharbut, Iraq, two CH-47 Chinook helicopters crash in a sand-storm, but the crews are rescued by MH-53Js. During the operation, the helicopters had to dodge surface-to-air missiles fired from below, along with blinding sand that reduced visibility to zero. The rescue crews win the Mackay Trophy.

MILITARY: U.S. forces surround the holy city of Najaf, Iraq, in an attempt to isolate radical cleric Moqtada al-Sadr, who refuses to disband his Mahdi Army.

April 18

DIPLOMACY: Newly elected Spanish prime minister Jose Luis Rodriguez Zapatero declares that he is withdrawing all Spanish forces from Iraq as soon as possible.

April 19

DIPLOMACY: In Washington, D.C., President George W. Bush appoints John Negro-ponte to serve as the U.S. ambassador to Iraq.

MILITARY: In Fallujah, Iraq, U.S. authorities say they will end all further military operations in the region if Sunni radicals turn over their heavy weapons. The insurgents comply for the time being.

April 20

MILITARY: In Santo Domingo, Dominican Republic, and Tegucigalpa, Honduras, the governments announce that they are withdrawing all their peacekeeping forces from Iraq as soon as possible.

April 21

DIPLOMACY: In Kabul, Afghanistan, U.S. ambassador Zalmai Khalilzad declares the end of American support for militias that had previously assisted in ousting the Taliban.

In New York City, the UN Security Council votes unanimously to endorse investigations into the oil-for-food program first established in 1995 to root out possible corruption.

TERRORISM: In Basra, Iraq, a series of coordinated suicide bombings kills 68 people, including 20 children. Since this is a Shiite-dominated region, the attackers were most likely radical Sunni Muslims.

April 22

MILITARY: At Fort Hood, Texas, the 4th Infantry Division (Mechanized) comes home after a tour of duty in Iraq; it lost 79 soldiers in combat operations.

In Afghanistan, Pat Tillman, a former NFL football player turned U.S. Army ranger, dies in a firefight near the Pakistani border. The circumstances surrounding his death are not immediately clear, and an investigation is launched.

POLITICS: In Baghdad, Iraq, the United States reverses itself and states that Baathist administrators formerly associated with Saddam Hussein's regime will be allowed to work for the government. To date, more than 400,000 party members had been dismissed from the public sector, and they have been a major force in recent unrest.

April 23–24
MILITARY: Outside of Fallujah, Iraq, marines engage and kill a force of 30 insurgents in a firefight. However, the cease-fire still holds.

April 25
POLITICS: In Kandahar, Afghanistan, the United Nations suspends activities after several of its aid workers were attacked.

April 27
POLITICS: In Kabul, Afghanistan, the government marks the 20th anniversary of the mujahideen victory over the Soviet Union with a large military parade. Among the participants are women of the local police corps, who march for the first time.

April 29
MILITARY: Marines begin pulling back from portions of Fallujah, Iraq, and control of the city passes to an Iraqi general.

POLITICS: The *New York Times* reports that a recent report by the Defense Intelligence Agency concludes that the rash of insurgent attacks in Iraq is being coordinated by former members of Saddam Hussein's secret service.

TERRORISM: In Baghdad, Iraq, a roadside bomb kills eight U.S. soldiers.

April 30
DIPLOMACY: In a major flap, pictures surface of U.S. forces abusing Iraqi prisoners at the Abu Ghraib prison. The images spark outrage throughout the Muslim world, and President George W. Bush promises a thorough investigation.

MILITARY: Once the marines have withdrawn from Fallujah, Iraq, a new Fallujah Brigade is cobbled together from militia and former Iraqi army units. Their job is to rid the city of all foreign fighters.

POLITICS: In Kabul, Afghanistan, the interior minister says a special police force has been created for the protection of all historical sites nationwide.

An extended broadcast of ABC's *Nightline* show displays photos of more than 700 U.S. servicemen killed in action in Iraq since the 2003 invasion. Host Ted Koppel says the program was done to honor their sacrifice and highlight the costs of the conflict.

May 3
MILITARY: In Baghdad, Iraq, Lieutenant General Ricardo S. Sanchez reprimands six commissioned and noncommissioned officers for their alleged role in the Abu Ghraib prison scandal.

May 4

MILITARY: In Qatar, Lieutenant General John P. Abizaid, commander of U.S. forces in the Middle East, declares his intention to maintain at least 135,000 soldiers in Iraq for the time being.

POLITICS: In Baghdad, Iraq, 150 Shiite leaders gather to urge cleric Moqtada al-Sadr to surrender his weapons and withdraw all forces from the holy cities of Najaf and Karbala.

May 5

MILITARY: In Iraq, a March 9 classified report by Major General Antonio Taguba identifies several members of the Army's 372nd Military Police Company and 315th Military Intelligence Battalion as culpable in abuses perpetrated at the Abu Ghraib prison in Baghdad. The abuses outlined include kicking and punching prisoners, threatening them with unmuzzled guard dogs, and photographing them in sexually explicit positions.

POLITICS: In Washington, D.C., President George W. Bush gives an interview for Arabic television in which he denounces the abuses of Iraqi prisoners as "abhorrent." He also criticizes Defense Secretary Donald Rumsfeld for not informing him about the notorious photos earlier.

May 6

MILITARY: In an attempt to embarrass cleric Moqtada al-Sadr, U.S. forces seize the governor's office in the holy city of Najaf and install a new governor more friendly to coalition authorities.

POLITICS: The International Committee of the Red Cross says it has found widespread evidence of prisoner-of-war abuse by coalition forces throughout Iraq.

May 7

DIPLOMACY: In Madrid, Spain, the government declares that it will not be sending troops to Iraq, even as part of an international force.

MILITARY: In Iraq, the army charges Private First Class Lynndie England with abusing several Iraqi captives at Abu Ghraib prison.

POLITICS: In Washington, D.C., Defense Secretary Donald Rumsfeld testifies before congressional committees regaining prisoner abuse at Abu Ghraib.

TERRORISM: In Mosul, Iraq, insurgents attack an Iraqi police squad car, killing four officers.

May 10

MILITARY: In Baghdad, Iraq, U.S. authorities report that they have destroyed cleric Moqtada al-Sadr's headquarters and killed 16 of his Mahdi Army followers.

In Fallujah, Iraq, U.S. and Iraqi forces jointly occupy volatile parts of the city, though the cease-fire there is still in effect.

May 11

POLITICS: In Washington, D.C., Major General Antonio Taguba testifies before a Senate committee that the misdeeds at Abu Ghraib could be ascribed to a lack of leadership from the brigade commander on down, and also to a lack of discipline, training, and proper supervision. His "Taguba Report" exposes and catalogs many lapses of discipline and military protocol.

TERRORISM: An Islamist Web site shows videotape of the murder of 26-year-old businessman Nicholas Berg, who was decapitated by suspected Jordanian militant Abu Musab al-Zarqawi.

May 13

MILITARY: In Iraq, military commander Lieutenant General Ricardo S. Sanchez outlaws certain practices, such as sleep deprivation and "stress positions," when handling prisoners of war.

May 17

MILITARY: In Kabul, Afghanistan, the government approves plans to support a 2,000-man Afghan National Guard.

POLITICS: In Baghdad, Iraq, the Iraqi National Congress declares that it is cutting off future subsidies to Ahmad Chalabi, a leading national figure, after his four decades in exile has ended.

TERRORISM: In Baghdad, Iraq, a suicide bomber kills Ezzedine Salim, president of the Iraqi Governing Council, along with six bystanders.

May 19

AVIATION: In western Iraq, U.S. warplanes bomb a suspicious nighttime gathering in the desert, killing 40 people. Survivors claim this was a wedding ceremony, but the military insists that they were insurgents.

MILITARY: In Iraq, army Specialist Jeremy Sivits pleads guilty to several charges associated with the abuse of Iraqi prisoners at Abu Ghraib prison. He receives a dishonorable discharge and a year in prison.

POLITICS: In Washington, D.C., General John P. Abizaid and Lieutenant General Ricardo Sanchez testify before a Senate committee, and the former accepts responsibility for all misbehavior by U.S. troops in the Middle East.

May 20

MILITARY: In Baghdad, Iraq, U.S. and Iraqi forces raid the office of Governing Council member Ahmad Chalabi, a former ally who had been receiving a stipend from the U.S. government. Widespread corruption is suspected along with passing top secret intelligence to Iran.

In Karbala, Iraq, U.S. forces pull out of the center of the city following a week of clashes with Shiite militants.

May 22–23

MILITARY: Around Kufah, Iraq, U.S. forces attack a mosque garrisoned by radical fighters, killing 36.

May 24

DIPLOMACY: In Washington, D.C., President George W. Bush promulgates a five-step plan to help build a secure and democratic Iraq, which includes the restoration of full sovereignty by June 30, rebuilding the infrastructure, and encouraging free elections. "Iraqis will write their own history," he insists, "and find their own way."

MILITARY: The Defense Department announces that Lieutenant General Ricardo S. Sanchez, commander of all coalition forces in Iraq, will be replaced by a more senior officer. However, they deny the action is connected to the revelations of abuse at Abu Ghraib prison.

May 25

MILITARY: In Washington, D.C., President George W. Bush asks for an additional $25 billion for the military budget to sustain present efforts in Iraq and Afghanistan.

POLITICS: An army report dated May 5 reveals that widespread prisoner abuse in Iraq and Afghanistan commenced in late 2002 and continued well into April 2004.

May 26

POLITICS: In Kabul, Afghanistan, President Hamid Karzai approves measures allowing presidential and parliamentary elections.

May 27

POLITICS: In Iraq, the United States agrees to suspend its arrest warrant for militant cleric Moqtada al-Sadr and withdraw all military forces from Najaf after the Shiite militia has disbanded.

May 28

POLITICS: In Baghdad, Iraq, Iraqi Governing Council member Ayad Allawi is chosen as the first interim prime minister until full sovereignty is restored. He is highly regarded as a secular Shiite and a staunch anti-Saddam Hussein former exile.

June 1

POLITICS: In Baghdad, Iraq, an interim government is formed after the Iraqi Governing Council votes to dissolve itself and appoint Shiite Ayad Allawi as prime minister and Sheik Ghazi al-Yawar, a Sunni, the new president. This action takes place under the aegis of UN special envoy Lakhdar Brahimi, who also appointed all 33 members of the new government, including six women. The group represents a cross-section of Iraq's multi-ethnic and multi-religious groupings.

June 2

MILITARY: In Washington, D.C., the Pentagon extends the tours of service for active-duty and reserve U.S. troops in Iraq and Afghanistan.

June 4

MILITARY: In the Sadr City area of Baghdad, Iraq, four U.S. Army troops are killed while fighting various Shiite militias.

POLITICS: In Baghdad, Iraq, Prime Minister Ayad Allawi states that an early pullout by U.S. and coalition forces from the country would be disastrous.

June 5

TERRORISM: In Baghdad, Iraq, a rocket attack kills four Polish and American civilian contractors.

June 6

POLITICS: In Baghdad, Iraq, Secretary of State Colin Powell and Prime Minister Ayad Allawi agree to work closely for passage of a UN resolution outlining the conditions for transferring all authority to Iraq while maintaining coalition forces to assist in security matters.

TERRORISM: In Baghdad, Iraq, insurgent attacks on a police station and a military base kill 19 Iraqis.

June 7

MILITARY: In Iraq, nine large militia groups agree to peacefully disband, but the largest two, the Sunni Fallujah Brigade and the Shiite Mahdi Army, decline to follow suit.

To make up for a shortfall in troop numbers, the U.S. government announces that it is transferring 3,300 soldiers from South Korea to Iraq.

June 8

DIPLOMACY: In New York City, the UN Security Council votes 15 to 0 in favor of a joint American-British resolution transferring power to an interim Iraqi government. This constitutes a major diplomatic victory for the United States.

TERRORISM: An insurgent mortar attack in Iraq kills six Polish, Slovak, and Latvian soldiers, while a bomb in the largely Kurdish city of Mosul kills 10 people and wounds 25.

June 10

POLITICS: In Washington, D.C., President George W. Bush admits that he cannot recall if he had seen two memoranda on how captured enemy combatants were to be handled. He insists that any orders he issued relative to the subject were consistent with international law.

TERRORISM: In Najaf, Iraq, members of cleric Moqtada al-Sadr's Mahdi Army occupy a police station, violating a cease-fire agreement between al-Sadr and U.S. forces.

June 11

POLITICS: In Iraq, cleric Moqtada al-Sadr has second thoughts and orders his followers to observe a cease-fire with the new interim government.

June 12

POLITICS: Shiite cleric Moqtada al-Sadr announces plans to form his own party and participate in the upcoming 2005 national elections.

TERRORISM: In northwest Baghdad, Iraq, Deputy Foreign Minister Bassam Salih Kubba is fatally shot by unknown assassins.

June 13

TERRORISM: In western Baghdad, Iraq, unknown assailants gun down an unnamed ministry official.

June 14–16

TERRORISM: A series of three bombings temporarily closes Iraq's main oil export terminal. In Baghdad, several bombings aimed at police forces kill and injure dozens of innocent bystanders.

June 16

POLITICS: The 9/11 Commission releases its findings, noting the lack of credible evidence of a link among al-Qaeda, Iraq, and the September 11, 2001 attacks.

TERRORISM: In Kirkuk, Iraq, an oil ministry official is killed by unnamed assailants.

Shiite cleric Moqtada al-Sadr orders his Mahdi Army followers to stop participating in street fights with coalition forces and rival militias.

June 17

POLITICS: In Washington, D.C., Defense Secretary Donald Rumsfeld admits that, acting upon the advice of CIA director George Tenet, he failed to announce the name of a suspect captured in Iraq owing to his suspected status as a senior terrorist leader.

In Iraq, more than 90 percent of Iraqis respond to a poll by the Provisional Authority by viewing the United States as an occupying power.

TERRORISM: In Baghdad, Iraq, two suicide car bombers outside a military recruiting center and a city council building kill 41 Iraqis and injure 142 more.

June 18

DIPLOMACY: In New York City, the UN International Atomic Energy Agency criticizes Iran for failing to be more open about its nuclear energy ambitions. Meanwhile, the Iranian government announces its intention to obtain centrifuges for enriching uranium as fuel.

June 22

POLITICS: In Washington, D.C., the Bush administration releases classified documents on the proposed treatment of enemy combatants. In one, he expresses the opinion that the Geneva Convention for prisoners does not apply to al-Qaeda members.

TERRORISM: In Iraq, insurgents kidnap South Korean translator Kim Sun Il and demand that his country withdraw its troops from the country.

June 24

TERRORISM: Around Fallujah, Ramadi, Baqubah, Mosul, and Baghdad, Iraq, a coordinated series of terrorist bombings kills more than 100 people, including three Americans, and injures scores more. Gunmen also seize the main police station in Baquba.

June 28

DIPLOMACY: In Baghdad, Iraq, L. Paul Bremer III, the Provisional Authority's senior U.S. administrator, formally hands sovereignty over to Iraqi prime minister Ayad Allawi and President Ghazi al-Yawar; the low-key ceremony was held two days earlier than announced to preclude any chance of a terrorist attack. Bremer then departs the country and returns home.

MILITARY: In Istanbul, Turkey, NATO leaders decide to lend their military expertise to instructing Iraqi security personnel, but France and Germany insist their soldiers will not teach in Iraq itself.

June 29

DIPLOMACY: In Istanbul, Turkey, President George W. Bush addresses the Muslim world and urges it to put aside its hatred of the West and to support democracy.

In Baghdad, Iraq, John Negroponte presents his credentials as the new U.S. ambassador, the first since 1991.

MILITARY: In light of persistent military manpower shortages, the Pentagon announces that it is calling up 5,600 former soldiers for tours in Iraq and Afghanistan.

June 30

POLITICS: In Iraq, the United States hands legal custody of former dictator Saddam Hussein over to Iraq, along with 11 of his aides. For security purposes, the Americans retain physical custody of the captives. Hussein also appears before an Iraqi judge and is to be arraigned on July 2. Hussein questions the legitimacy of the court, denies any role in the 1988 gas attack against Halabja that killed thousands of Kurds, and says he could not possibly be guilty of invading Kuwait as it is part of Iraq.

July

MILITARY: This month the Iraqi Civil Defense Corps is disbanded and replaced by the new Iraqi National Guard. This is augmented by the 6,000-man Iraqi Intervention Force, a 1,600-man Special Operations Force, a 400-man Coastal Defense Force, and a 500-man Iraqi Air Force.

July 1

DIPLOMACY: In Baghdad, Iraq, the U.S. embassy formally opens for business for the first time since 1991.

July 4

POLITICS: In Baghdad, Iraq, Prime Minister Ayad Allawi says he will offer amnesty to all Shiite militias willing to surrender their weapons, particularly the Mahdi Army of cleric Moqtada al-Sadr.

July 5

AVIATION: U.S. warplanes bomb a safe house in Fallujah where wanted terrorist Abu Musab al-Zarqawi was reported to be hiding; 10 people are killed.

July 6

AVIATION: A military court finds air force Major Harry Schmidt guilty of dereliction of duty in the accidental deaths of four Canadian peacekeepers in Afghanistan in 2002. His wingman, Major William Umbach, is also reprimanded and forced to retire.

July 7

POLITICS: In Baghdad, the interim Iraqi government grants Prime Minister Ayad Allawi the power to impose martial law in regions where insurgents remain active.

TERRORISM: At Guantánamo, Cuba, the Pentagon establishes a military tribunal for captured terrorists, where nearly 600 prisoners can legally challenge their status as enemy combatants.

Insurgents kidnap a Filipino hostage and demand that his government pull out all 51 of its peacekeeping troops.

July 9

POLITICS: In Washington, D.C., a U.S. Senate committee unanimously declares that the Central Intelligence Agency and other intelligence agencies deliberately produced misleading intelligence about Iraq's prewar weapons programs. However, the report does not find that administration officials pressured analysts to produce conclusions that would support the move toward war.

In Afghanistan, elections scheduled for late 2004 are postponed until April 2005 owing to continuing political instability.

July 13

DIPLOMACY: In New York City, Pakistan's ambassador to the United States, Ashraf Jenangir Qazi, is appointed the new UN representative to Iraq.
TERRORISM: In Iraq, insurgents behead a Bulgarian hostage.

July 14

DIPLOMACY: In Manila, Philippines, the government announces it is pulling out all security forces from Iraq to meet the demands of kidnappers who had seized a Filipino truck driver.
POLITICS: In London, United Kingdom, a government committee concludes that British military intelligence was "seriously flawed" with respect to Iraqi weapons of mass destruction. However, there is no evidence that Prime Minister Tony Blair manipulated intelligence to push the case for invading Iraq. Blair, for his part, accepted responsibility for any mistakes that had been made.
TERRORISM: In Baghdad, Iraq, a car bomb explodes outside the American compound, killing 10 bystanders. The governor of Nineveh Province is also assassinated.

July 16

MILITARY: In Iraq, Australia deploys a 50-man Iraqi training team, which is tasked with speedily instructing an entire brigade of Iraqi soldiers.

July 18

AVIATION: U.S. warplanes bomb another terrorist safe house in Fallujah, Iraq, killing 12 people.
TERRORISM: In Iraq, insurgents assassinate a high-ranking Iraqi military official.

July 19–20

TERRORISM: The Philippine government pulls out all 51 of its peacekeeping troops from Iraq, per kidnappers' demands, and the next day the Filipino hostage is released unharmed.

July 20

MILITARY: In Iraq, insurgent activity takes the lives of three American soldiers, bringing the total number of combat deaths since March 2003 to 900.

July 21

TERRORISM: In Iraq, insurgents kidnap seven truck drivers from various nations and threaten to kill them if the Kuwaiti company they work for does not leave Iraq.

July 22

DIPLOMACY: In Canberra, Australia, the government releases the Flood Report, which finds little evidence to back up U.S. and British claims of Iraqi weapons of mass destruction. However, it does not accuse either administration of manipulating the evidence in favor of war.

MILITARY: In Washington, D.C., the U.S. Army inspector general concludes that the recent abuses at Abu Ghraib prison were a local problem and not a systematic problem.

July 23–26

TERRORISM: In Iraq, insurgents kidnap an Egyptian diplomat, then release him unharmed three days later.

July 28

MILITARY: In south Baghdad, Iraq, Iraqi security forces, assisted by coalition forces, attack a militant stronghold, killing 35.

POLITICS: The international organization Doctors Without Borders announces that it is finally withdrawing from Afghanistan after 24 years due to increasingly dangerous working conditions in the countryside.

TERRORISM: In Baquba, Iraq, a car bomb explodes outside a police station, killing 68 people and injuring 56.

July 29

DIPLOMACY: In Washington, D.C., President George W. Bush signs legislation to lift remaining sanctions against Iraq that were imposed by his father, George H. W. Bush.

August 1

TERRORISM: In Baghdad, Iraq, bombs set off outside four Christian churches kill 11 people and injure 47.

August 2

TERRORISM: An Internet videotape shows Iraqi insurgents killing and beheading their Turkish hostage.

August 3

TERRORISM: In Anbar Province, Iraq, insurgent activity takes the lives of three U.S. soldiers and three Iraqi national guardsmen.

August 5

TERRORISM: In Baghdad, Iraq, cleric Moqtada al-Sadr again orders his Mahdi Army to rise up against the American and coalition forces while he uses the sacred Imam Ali Shrine in Najaf as his headquarters.

August 7

TERRORISM: In Baghdad, Iraq, a car bomb outside the Jordanian embassy kills 11 people and wounds more than 50. To many observers, this act constitutes the start of a "real war."

August 7–17

MILITARY: Marines surround and attack supporters of Shiite leader Moqtada al-Sadr in the holy city of Najaf, Iraq, systematically killing nearly 600 fighters.

August 8
POLITICS: In Baghdad, Iraq, Prime Minister Ayad Allawi reinstates the death penalty for several crimes. Exiled leader Ahmad Chalabi is also wanted on counterfeiting charges.

August 16
POLITICS: In Iraq, more than 1,000 delegates choose a 100-member committee to oversee forthcoming national elections. This body also has the power to veto fiats decreed by the interim government.

August 18
POLITICS: In Baghdad, Iraq, the Iraqi National Congress appoints a 100-person national assembly to function as a parliament until national elections are held.

August 20
POLITICS: Throughout Afghanistan, 10.6 million Afghans are registered to vote in upcoming elections. The actual campaign begins September 7.
TERRORISM: In Iraq, two French journalists are kidnapped by insurgents demanding that the French government drop its ban on Islamic headscarves in schools. The French government refuses to comply.

August 24
MILITARY: In Washington, D.C., a panel headed by former defense secretary James Schlesinger states that failure to correctly monitor abuses at Abu Ghraib prison reached as high as the Pentagon. Defense Secretary Donald Rumsfeld and Lieutenant General Ricardo S. Sanchez are singled out in particular. It also says that interrogation techniques employed there violated existing military rules on the treatment of prisoners.

August 25
MILITARY: In Washington, D.C., an army investigative report concludes that military intelligence units are largely responsible for the abuses at Abu Ghraib prison and recommend disciplinary action against two officers. It also finds 54 individuals culpable in the abuses.
POLITICS: In Najaf, Iraq, Ayatollah Ali al-Sistani, who had been in the United Kingdom to undergo heart surgery, arrives back home and begins negotiating with cleric Moqtada al-Sadr for a truce with occupation forces.

August 26
TERRORISM: In Iraq, cleric Moqtada al-Sadr, having suffered heavy losses at the hands of American forces, signs a deal brokered by Ayatollah Ali al-Sistani and ends the siege of Najaf and Kufa.

August 27
TERRORISM: By the terms of a truce arranged by Ayatollah Ali al-Sistani, Shiite forces loyal to cleric Moqtada al-Sadr are withdrawn from the Imam Ali Shrine, while marines abandon their three-week siege of the city.

August 31
TERRORISM: Nepalese officials announce that insurgents in Iraq have massacred 12 Nepalese hostages they had captured a week earlier. The group Jaish Ansar al-Sunna posts videotapes of the killings on the Internet.

September 4
TERRORISM: In Kirkuk, Iraq, a suicide car bomber kills 14 police officers and three civilians. A further 12 police and five national guardsmen are killed fighting south of Baghdad.

September 6
TERRORISM: Outside Fallujah, Iraq, a car bomb explodes near a military convoy, killing seven marines and three Iraqi national guardsmen.

September 7
MILITARY: The American toll in Iraq reaches 1,000 dead and 7,000 wounded after fighting resumes with the Mahdi Army of cleric Muqtada al-Sadr.

September 10
MILITARY: In Fallujah, Iraq, the Fallujah Brigade disbands after failing to remove all foreign fighters from the city. During a riot outside a Shiite mosque, police also fire into a crowd of unarmed protestors, killing two and injuring five.

September 11
POLITICS: In Herat, Afghanistan, Governor Ismail Khan is dismissed from office by President Hamid Karzai; he is subsequently appointed minister of water and power.

September 12
AVIATION: In Baghdad, Iraq, U.S. helicopters strafe Iraqis gathered around a damaged American vehicle, killing 13 people including a journalist.
TERRORISM: Across Iraq, widespread terror attacks and bombings claim the lives of 60 people, including three Polish soldiers who died in an ambush.

September 13
AVIATION: U.S. warplanes bomb a terrorist safe house in Fallujah, Iraq, killing 20 suspected insurgents.

September 14
TERRORISM: In Baquba, Iraq, a suicide bomber kills 47 people lined up waiting to apply for jobs with the local police; an additional 114 are wounded. The terrorist group associated with Jordanian Abu Musab al-Zarqawi claims credit for the attack.

September 15
DIPLOMACY: In New York City, UN secretary-general Kofi Annan informs a BBC interviewer that the U.S.-led invasion of Iraq was illegal and violated the UN charter.
POLITICS: In Washington, D.C., the administration requests that the Senate shift $3.4 billion of the $18.4 billion allocated for the reconstruction of Iraq to improving security measures in that country.

Terrorism: In Washington, D.C., it is revealed that a highly classified National Intelligence Estimate prepared for President George W. Bush paints an especially grim picture of current Iraqi security.

September 16
Politics: In Washington, D.C., the Central Intelligence Agency releases a classified report first issued in July that predicts the possibility of wholesale civil war in Iraq along religious and ethnic lines.

Terrorism: The terror group al-Qaeda in Iraq demands that the United States release all Iraqi women it is holding in confinement or it will kill American hostages Eugene Armstrong and Jack Hensley.

September 16–17
Aviation: South of Fallujah, Iraq, U.S. warplanes continue hammering suspected insurgent safe houses, killing more than 50 suspected terrorists.

September 17
Military: In New York City, the UN Security Council votes to extend the International Security Assistance Force mandate, in Afghanistan through October 2005.

Terrorism: In Baghdad, Iraq, a suicide car bombing at a police checkpoint kills 13 people.

September 18
Diplomacy: The International Atomic Energy Agency passes a resolution demanding that Iran immediately halt its uranium-enrichment activities.

Terrorism: In Kirkuk, Iraq, a bomb explodes amid a group of Iraqi national guard recruits, killing 19 and wounding 67.

September 19
Diplomacy: In Tehran, Iran, the government rejects UN demands that it stop its uranium-enrichment program, insisting it enjoyed the right to do so under the Nuclear Non-proliferation Treaty.

Terrorism: Near Samarra, Iraq, a car bomb explodes near a joint U.S.-Iraqi military patrol, killing one Iraqi soldiers, and one civilian and wounding seven others.

September 20–21
Terrorism: Internet videos of American captives Eugene Armstrong and Jack Hensley being beheaded are believed to be the work of Jordanian terrorist Abu Musab al-Zarqawi.

September 21
Diplomacy: In Tehran, Iran, the government defiantly announces that it had begun the process of converting yellowcake uranium into a gas necessary for the enrichment process.

POLITICS: In Washington, D.C., President George W. Bush reacts to a recently declassified CIA evaluation of Iraq by insisting they were "just guessing" as to the chances of a civil war erupting there

TERRORISM: In Baghdad, Iraq, skirmishing resumes between U.S. forces and the Mahdi Army of cleric Moqtada al-Sadr. A car bomb also explodes near an Iraqi national guard recruiting center in the Jamiya district of Baghdad; no one is injured.

September 22

TERRORISM: In the Jamiya district of Baghdad, Iraq, a bomb explodes near the Iraqi national guard recruiting center, killing 11 people and wounding 54.

September 23

DIPLOMACY: In Washington, D.C., Iraqi prime minister Ayad Allawi addresses Congress and announces recent strides in security and stability, though he concedes work remains to be done.

September 25

MILITARY: In Iraq, a U.S. Army soldier is arrested and charged with the death of an Iraqi national guardsman in Adwar during the previous May; he faces 25 years in prison.

TERRORISM: In the Jamiya district of Baghdad, Iraq, a bomb kills seven Iraqis applying for the national guard; four marines and a soldier are also reported killed in skirmishes. A police captain is also gunned down by insurgents near Baquba

September 28

TERRORISM: In Baghdad, Iraq, insurgents release two Italian female captives amid reports that a ransom had been paid by the Italian government.

September 30

AVIATION: Over Fallujah, Iraq, U.S. warplanes strike at the suspected safehouse of wanted terrorist Abu Musab al-Zarqawi, killing 20 suspected insurgents and wounding 39.

DIPLOMACY: In Washington, D.C., Congress approves shifting $18.4 billion slated for Iraqi aid to reconstruction and job creation.

TERRORISM: In Iraq, several bombs explode during ceremonies inaugurating a new sewer plant, killing 41 people, including 34 children.

October

POLITICS: To enhance nation security, the 1,500-man Iraqi Highway Patrol and the 500-man Dignitary Protection Service are established.

October 1–3

MILITARY: In Samarra, Iraq, 3,000 U.S. troops, joined by 2,000 Iraqi security detachments, begin a gradual push into the city to ferret out insurgents operating there. They report killing more than 100 guerrillas once the operation concludes two days later. For the first time, Iraqi combat units distinguish themselves in fighting.

In Baghdad, government and U.S. authorities reason that Iraqi security forces will have to be expanded to 346,000 men to meet national needs; this is twice the figure first cited in October 2003.

October 4

DIPLOMACY: In Washington, D.C., Defense Secretary Donald Rumsfeld informs the Council on Foreign Relations that he does not see evidence of a "hard" connection between al-Qaeda and the regime of Saddam Hussein.

L. Paul Bremer III, a former high Iraq administrator, declares that President George W. Bush failed to deploy sufficient numbers of troops in Iraq to secure the entire country.

MILITARY: In Brussels, Belgium, NATO commander General James Jones says that 3,000 troops could be tapped to train Iraqi security forces.

TERRORISM: In Baghdad and Mosul, Iraq, three suicide car bombers kill 26 people and wound more than 100. Iraqi police and security forces engage in a firefight with insurgents in downtown Baghdad after the blasts there.

October 5

MILITARY: In Babil Province, Iraq, a force of 3,000 U.S. and Iraqi troops begin a sweep of the area to root out large numbers of insurgents operating there. This is also the first operation to feature Iraqi Special Forces in prominent roles.

October 6

DIPLOMACY: Chief UN weapons inspector Charles Duelfer issues a final report on Iraq, concluding that the regime had essentially destroyed all its illicit weapons of mass destruction in 1991 and had no significant programs under way to manufacture more. However, it acknowledges that Saddam Hussein could have easily resumed such programs if he wanted to.

MILITARY: In Samarra, Iraq, the government decides to maintain the 202nd Brigade, Iraqi national guard, and the First Ministry of Interior Commando Battalion in place as garrison forces.

TERRORISM: At Anah, 160 miles northwest of Baghdad, Iraq, a suicide car bomber strikes a checkpoint near an Iraqi national guard encampment; no casualties are mentioned.

October 7

DIPLOMACY: In New York City, the head of the UN arms inspection team releases his assessment of Iraqi weapons of mass destruction. It also states that Saddam Hussein made more than $11 billion in illicit revenues from questionable deals made during the UN-sponsored oil-for-food program up through March 2003.

October 8

TERRORISM: Abu Dhabi television airs a videotape that shows the beheading of British hostage Kenneth Bigley, who had been kidnapped the previous September.

October 9

POLITICS: Three years after tossing out the Taliban, national elections are held in Afghanistan to elect a new president. An estimated 8 million Afghans cast ballots for President Hamid Karzai and 17 other candidates.

MILITARY: In Brussels, Belgium, NATO headquarters announces that it is deploying 300 troops to Iraq as military trainers. The move was strongly opposed by France.

TERRORISM: In Iraq, the Mahdi Army of cleric Moqtada al-Sadr begins turning in its heavy weapons to the police. In return, U.S. forces suspend all military actions against the Sadr City section of Baghdad.

Near Karbabilah, Iraq, close to the Syrian border, insurgents attack an Iraqi national guard compound, killing 11 soldiers and injuring six.

October 10

TERRORISM: In Baghdad, Iraq, 10 Iraqis are killed by explosions at the oil ministry and the police academy.

October 12

POLITICS: In Ramadi, Iraq, U.S. and Iraqi security forces arrest Sunni cleric Sheik Abdul Aleem Saidy, along with his son.

October 12–13

MILITARY: Throughout Iraq, U.S. forces begin attacking known insurgent strong points to preclude any attacks during the holy month of Ramadan. Several mosques are raided in the process.

October 14

MILITARY: Fallujah, Iraq, is the object of several attacks by marines after peace talks between city representatives and government officials collapse.

TERRORISM: In Baghdad, Iraq, two bombs explode near the heavily guarded Green Zone occupied by Iraqi government officials and the U.S. embassy; five Iraqis are killed and 20 are wounded.

October 15

TERRORISM: In Baghdad, Iraq, a suicide bomber misses an Iraqi police patrol and kills 10 innocent bystanders.

October 16

POLITICS: In Fallujah, Iraq, peace talks between government officials and local insurgents break off due to the latter's intransigence.

TERRORISM: In Baghdad, Iraq, five Christian churches are bombed by insurgents.

October 19

TERRORISM: In an attack staged 80 miles north of Baghdad, Iraq, four Iraqi national guardsmen are killed and 80 are wounded after insurgents fire mortars into their camp.

October 20

MILITARY: In Baghdad, Iraq, army Staff Sergeant Ivan L. Frederick pleads guilty to mistreating Iraqi captives at Abu Ghraib prison; he receives eight years in prison.

October 23

TERRORISM: Outside Kirkish, Iraq, near the Iranian border, insurgents disguised as police halt three minibuses carrying 49 unarmed Iraqi national guard recruits and execute them and their three drivers. This is the deadliest insurgent ambush to date.

At Samarra, Iraq, four national guardsmen die in an attack upon their checkpoint. Meanwhile, in Anbar Province, a bomb explodes near an Iraqi military patrol, killing 16 policemen

October 24
POLITICS: In Afghanistan, Hamid Karzai receives 55.3 percent of votes cast, a simple majority of 4 million, thereby becoming the nation's first elected chief executive.
TERRORISM: Near Baghdad airport, Iraq, an insurgent rocket attack kills a U.S. State Department security officer.

October 25
MILITARY: In Iraq, a national security aide mentions that possibly 5 percent of all Iraqi security forces have been infiltrated by the insurgents.

October 26
POLITICS: In Baghdad, Iraq, Prime Minister Ayad Allawi blames the United States and its allies for the recent massacre of 49 Iraqi army recruits. Meanwhile, Falah al-Naqib, the interior minister, announces a new program to eliminate corruption in police forces.
TERRORISM: Insurgents abduct and murder 11 Iraqi army recruits between Hilla and Baghdad, Iraq, and the radical group Army of Ansar al-Sunna claims responsibility.

October 27
MILITARY: In southern Iraq, nearly 800 British troops are redeployed further north to free up U.S. soldiers scheduled for assaults on insurgent strongholds.

October 28
TERRORISM: The al-Jazeera network airs an undated videotape of Saudi terrorist Osama bin Laden in which he warns the United States of new attacks should it fail to amend its policies toward the Middle East.

Near Latifiya, south of Baghdad, Iraq, insurgents belonging to the Army of Ansar al-Sunna kill two senior Iraqi police officers.

October 29
MILITARY: In Washington, D.C., the Pentagon announces that it is extending the tours of 6,500 U.S. soldiers by up to two months.

October 30
TERRORISM: Outside Abu Ghraib, Iraq, a suicide car bomber attacks a marine convoy, killing nine Americans and wounding nine more. Iraqi police compound the problem by firing on several vans and minibuses, killing an additional 14 people and wounding 10.

October 31
TERRORISM: In Tikrit, Iraqi, an insurgent rocket attack against a hotel kills 15 Iraqis.

November 2
MILITARY: In Norway, NATO commences an eight-week training course for 19 mid- to high-level Iraqi security personnel.

TERRORISM: In Mosul, Iraq, a car bomb misses an Iraqi military convoy and kills four civilians instead.

POLITICS: President George W. Bush handily defeats Democrat challenger John F. Kerry to gain re-election. Kerry had largely based his campaign on mounting dissatisfaction over affairs in Iraq and the war against global terrorism.

November 3

POLITICS: In Afghanistan, the UN Afghan Electoral Commission declares that interim president Hamid Karzai has won the recent national election with 55 percent of votes cast, sufficient enough to avoid a runoff election. Despite threats from the Taliban, the process went relatively smoothly.

TERRORISM: In Baghdad, Iraq, police uncover the decapitated bodies of three Iraqi national guardsmen; a little-known group calling itself the Brigades of Iraqi Honorables claims credit for the act. Meanwhile, the violent group Army of Ansar al-Sunna posts a decapitation video on the Internet, claiming it is of Iraqi army major Hussein Shanoun.

November 4

TERRORISM: In southern Iraq, a suicide bomber kills three British soldiers.

November 5

AVIATION: U.S. warplanes begin a concentrated bombardment of insurgent positions throughout the city of Fallujah, Iraq, prompting an evacuation of 250,000 residents before a ground offensive begins. Only die-hard insurgents remain behind.

November 6

TERRORISM: In Samarra, Iraq, four car bombs explode as insurgents launch attacks against three police stations, killing 15 officers. Iraqi national guard commander Abdel Razeq Shaker Garmali is among those slain.

November 7

MILITARY: A force of 15,000 U.S. soldiers and marines begin surrounding the Sunni stronghold of Fallujah, Iraq, prior to attacking insurgent positions. In a preliminary move, men of the 36th Iraqi Commando Battalion seize Fallujah's main hospital to keep it from insurgent hands.

POLITICS: In Sulaymaniyah, Iraq, Brigadier General Sarkout Hassan declares that Islamic militants have been smuggling in new recruits from Iran to Fallujah and other hotbeds of insurgency.

In light of the forthcoming assault on Fallujah, the Iraqi government declares a state of national emergency for the next 60 days.

TERRORISM: In Haditha, Iraq, insurgents storm a police station, taking and killing 21 hostages, execution style. Another attack across town takes the life of Brigadier General Shaher al-Jughaifi, head of security for western Iraq.

November 8

MILITARY: In the biggest, conventional fight since the 2003 invasion, 10,000 U.S. soldiers and marines, backed by 2,000 Iraqi troops, engage in fierce house-to-house fighting in Fallujah, Iraq, with an estimated 3,000 to 5,000 Sunni insurgents. Two days into the battle, the Americans firmly control one-third of the city.

TERRORISM: In Mosul, Iraq, an insurgent mortar attack kills two American soldiers.

November 9

POLITICS: Outside Fallujah, Iraq, Prime Minister Ayad Allawi arrives to deliver a morale-boosting speech to his security forces; they cheer him in response.

TERRORISM: In Baquba, Iraq, insurgents attack two police stations, killing one officer and wounding eight.

North of Kirkuk, Iraq, a suicide car bomber attacks an Iraqi national guard camp, killing three soldiers.

November 10

MILITARY: Outside Fallujah, Iraq, Prime Minister Ayad Allawi appoints Major General Abdul Qadir Mohammed Jassim to head up security matters in western Anbar Province until civilian authority becomes possible.

TERRORISM: In Hammam al-Alil, Iraq, an Iraqi national guard battalion wilts in the face of an insurgent attack and abandons its base and armory to the attackers.

November 11

TERRORISM: Insurgents in Fallujah, Iraq, mount a last-ditch counterattack against U.S. forces, which only serves to weaken their already decimated ranks.

In Baghdad, Iraq, a car bomb explodes near a joint U.S.-Iraqi military convoy, killing 19 people.

In Mosul, Iraq, roving gangs of insurgents attack several police stations, looting several tons of arms, armor, and vehicles. A senior police officer is also shot dead. Task Force Olympia under Brigadier General Carter Ham is called in to restore order, and he concedes that insurgent command-and-control functions were exceptionally adroit.

November 12

MILITARY: In Fallujah, Iraq, fighting continues as the First Battalion of the Iraqi army presses further downtown.

In Maysan Province, Iraq, Brigadier General Adbul Hussein Mohammed Badar arrives to take charge of security matters; he flees later that day after being personally threatened by insurgents.

November 13

MILITARY: In Fallujah, Iraq, U.S. soldiers and marines attack and storm the final insurgent stronghold in the city, capturing it in heavy urban fighting.

In Ramadi, Iraq, U.S. forces occupy the largest mosque in the city and uncover several large arms caches stored inside.

POLITICS: In Baghdad, Iraq, a triumphant Prime Minister Ayad Allawi declares the city of Fallujah to be liberated from insurgent fighters.

TERRORISM: Near Mosul, Iraq, insurgents attack an Iraqi national guard base, killing two soldiers and wounding 21.

November 14

DIPLOMACY: In a surprising turnabout, the government of Iran pledges that it will suspend its uranium-enrichment program.

MILITARY: Fighting in Fallujah, Iraq, subsides after the Americans systematically eliminate between 1,200 and 1,600 Muslim terrorists at a cost of 95 dead and 560 wounded. Six Iraqis were also been killed and 40 wounded. This successful action breaks the back of the insurgency throughout the region.

As part of an effort to better screen army recruits, prospective Iraqis soldiers must be at least 20 years of age and possess a letter of recommendation from their local community council. Committees will also be sent into recruits' neighborhoods to assess and confirm the morality of each prospective soldier.

November 15

DIPLOMACY: The governments of the United Kingdom, France, and Germany announce an agreement with Iran to accelerate their program, of economic benefits once the latter's uranium-enrichment program ceases.

TERRORISM: In Baquba, Iraq, insurgents attack two police stations; it is by now believed that members of Saddam Hussein's former security service, backed by fighters from Syria, are behind recent attacks.

November 16

DIPLOMACY: In Washington, D.C., the Senate Subcommittee on Investigations concludes that Iraq under Saddam Hussein collected at least $21.3 billion by circumventing UN sanctions between 1991 and 2003. The former president is also accused of manipulating the oil-for-food program to his advantage.

MILITARY: In Brussels, Belgium, NATO headquarters agrees to expand the number of military trainers in Iraq from 65 to 400. These will be accompanied by 1,600 support staff who will not serve in combat situations.

TERRORISM: In northern Mosul, Iraq, fighters from the Patriotic Union of Kurdistan engage Iraqi national guardsmen in the al-Tamim neighborhood; two people are killed and three injured before order is restored.

In Baghdad, the Interior Ministry is investigating allegations that as many as 31 security recruits have been kidnapped by insurgents in Rutbah.

November 17

MILITARY: In Mosul, Iraq, Brigadier General Carter Ham declares the city back under U.S. and Iraqi control. However, insurgent mortar rounds still strike at the al-Ahrar police station downtown.

November 18

MILITARY: In Fallujah, Iraq, U.S. forces uncover a house used by Jordanian terrorist Abu Musab al-Zarqawi, along with buildings where Iraqi prisoners were tortured and executed by the insurgents.

TERRORISM: In Baghdad, Iraq, a car bomb explodes outside the Yarmouk police station, killing two Iraqis.

In Mosul, Iraq, an insurgent mortar attack wounds five Iraqi soldiers while two national guard officers are publicly beheaded by terrorists claiming an association with Jordanian terrorist Abu Musab al-Zarqawi.

November 19
MILITARY: In Baghdad, Iraq, Iraqi security forces raid a mosque associated with insurgents, killing three.
TERRORISM: In Baghdad, Iraq, a suicide car bomber strikes a police checkpoint in Maysalon Square, killing five officers and wounding four. Across town, a police convoy is attacked by another suicide car bomber, who kills one officer and wounds five.

November 20
TERRORISM: Near Baquba, Iraq, insurgents attack an Iraqi national guard training center, killing a recruit.

West of Mosul, Iraq, Iraqis find the bodies of eight policemen who had been executed. U.S. forces also detain three Iraqis national guardsmen for allegedly working with the insurgents.

November 21
DIPLOMACY: A group of leading creditor nations votes to cancel Iraq's $39 billion debt in order to boost the struggling economy and government.
TERRORISM: In Ramadi, Iraq, insurgents attack an Iraqi military convoy, killing nine national guardsmen and wounding 17.

In Mosul, Iraq, U.S. forces uncover the bodies of nine Iraqi soldiers who had been bound, gagged, and killed, execution style.

On the Internet, a group purporting to be allied to Abu Musab al-Zarqawi claims to have killed 17 Iraqi national guardsmen from Kisik.

November 22
TERRORISM: In Mosul, Iraq, insurgents gun down a leading Sunni cleric.

November 23
MILITARY: A force of 5,000 U.S., British, and Iraqi forces push into the so-called "Triangle of Death" south of Baghdad, Iraq, to root out large numbers of insurgents ensconced there.
POLITICS: In Washington, D.C., Defense Secretary Donald Rumsfeld says that Iraqi military units performed well during the battle of Fallujah, even though they were assigned supporting roles.
TERRORISM: In Baquba, Iraq, insurgents attack an Iraqi military convoy, killing three soldiers.

November 24
MILITARY: In Kut, southeast of Baghdad, Iraq, Prime Minister Ayad Allawi addresses 2,500 graduating troops from the Iraqi Intervention Force, slated to constitute a

new Second Brigade with that formation. These troops are especially trained in counterinsurgency techniques.

November 25
MILITARY: In Mosul, Iraq, U.S. and Iraqi security forces begin a sweep of troubled neighborhoods; they uncover the bodies of 11 Iraqis who had been bound, gagged, and executed.

TERRORISM: In Ramadi, police chief Colonel Fawas Armoot says that soldiers in Fallujah have uncovered rudimentary biological and chemical warfare laboratories operated by insurgents. He also says that security forces have detained five foreign fighters from Libya, Tunisia, and Syria who were attempting to cross into the country.

November 26
MILITARY: In Mosul, Iraq, U.S. and Iraqi security forces continue their sweep of the city, at one point arresting an imam suspected of being an insurgent leader.

POLITICS: In Iraq, Kurdish and Sunni politicians request a postponement of national elections in January over acute security concerns.

TERRORISM: In Mosul, Iraq, terrorists dump the bodies of two slain Iraqi soldiers at a busy downtown intersection.

November 28
MILITARY: South of Baghdad, Iraq, U.S. and Iraqi security forces perform land and amphibious raids against known insurgent hideouts, killing 17 terrorists and capturing 32.

In Basra, Iraq, British forces surround the headquarters of Brigadier General Diaa al-Kadhimi after he refuses to step down as national guard commander.

TERRORISM: In the al-Jadriya section of Baghdad, Iraq, police arrest two men driving a vehicle carrying explosives.

In Samarra, Iraq, insurgents attack the al-Wahda police station before capturing and sacking it. Local authorities decline to confront them.

November 29
TERRORISM: In Ramadi, Iraq, a car bomb explodes near an Iraqi security patrol, killing four police officers and wounding three others.

In Baghdadi, Iraq, 120 miles northwest of the capital, a suicide car bomber detonates himself at a police checkpoint, killing seven officers and a national guardsman.

In Mosul, Iraq, local authorities report that 50 police and security personnel have been killed over the last 10 days and that police patrols are nonexistent as the city is too dangerous.

In Najaf, Iraq, Governor Adnan al-Zurufi declares that he had his own security chief arrested for plotting to assassinate him and other regional officials.

November 30
MILITARY: In Babil Province, Iraq, a security sweep by U.S. and Iraqi forces nets 14 suspected terrorists and three arms depots. Meanwhile, the 11th Marine

Expeditionary Unit commander declares that Iraqi forces have assumed control of Najaf and are conducting limited operations there on their own.

December 1

MILITARY: In Washington, D.C., the Pentagon announces that U.S. manpower levels in Iraq will rise from 138,000 to 150,000 as of January. This increase will necessitate extending tours of duty for troops already deployed there.

December 2

POLITICS: In Baghdad, Iraq, National Security Minister Qassim Dawood says that Iraqi security forces are responsible for guarding the upcoming national elections and that U.S. forces will only be called in if the insurgents attack a major polling center.

December 3

TERRORISM: In Baghdad, Iraq, a suicide bomber explodes himself inside a Shiite mosque, killing 18 people, and an insurgent raid on a police station across town kills 12 police officers.

In Mosul, Iraq, insurgents attack three police stations, but no casualties are reported.

December 4

TERRORISM: In Mosul, Iraq, a suicide bomber rams his car into a bus carrying Kurdish militiamen, killing 18 and wounding 16.

In Baghdad, Iraq, a suicide bomber attacks a police station near the Green Zone, killing eight officers and wounding 38.

December 5

TERRORISM: In Tikrit, Iraq, insurgents attack a bus carrying Iraqi contractors, killing 17 of them.

Near Bayji, Iraq, a suicide car bomber rams into an Iraqi national guard checkpoint, killing three soldiers and wounding 128.

An insurgent attack upon an Iraqi military patrol near Latifiya, Iraq, results in two deaths and four wounded soldiers.

December 6

TERRORISM: In Baghdad, Iraq, U.S. Customs officials and their Iraqi counterparts announce that they have collared more than 40 terrorists attempting to smuggle arms to insurgents in Iraq.

December 7

MILITARY: General John P. Abizaid, head of the U.S. Central Command, says that the pace of training Iraqi security forces lags behind schedule and that they will not be able to provide adequate security for the upcoming national elections in January. He maintains that a temporary increase in U.S. military manpower may be necessary, along with additional embedded U.S. trainers and Special Forces.

POLITICS: In Kabul, Afghanistan, Hamid Karzai is inaugurated as the new president of Afghanistan; he will serve a five-year term.

TERRORISM: South of Baghdad, Iraq, a roadside bomb strikes an Iraqi military convoy, killing three national guardsmen and wounding 11.

December 8

MILITARY: In Kuwait, Defense Secretary Donald Rumsfeld is beset by complaints by army reservists destined to be deployed in Iraq.

TERRORISM: In Ramadi, Iraq, half of the city's police force fails to report for duty, apparently due to threats made against them by insurgents.

December 9

MILITARY: In Brussels, Belgium, NATO formally agrees with Iraq to increase its training staff from 60 to 300 officers drawn from Poland, Hungary, and the Netherlands. The governments of France, Germany, Belgium, Spain, Greece, and Luxembourg decline to participate.

POLITICS: In Iraq, the influential Ayatollah Ali al-Sistani throws his weight behind the new United Iraqi Alliance, an umbrella organization of several Shiite parties.

TERRORISM: In Mosul, Iraq, insurgents ambush a joint U.S.-Iraqi military patrol, killing one Iraqi national guardsman.

December 10

TERRORISM: In Samarra, Iraq, an Iraqi national guard patrol is ambushed by insurgents, killing two civilians in the process.

In Baquba, Iraq, four Iraqi national guardsmen are injured following an insurgent roadside bombing. The terrorists subsequently attack the survivors with gunfire.

Thirty-foot-tall sculptures of former Iraqi dictator Saddam Hussein were placed on the grounds of the Republican Palace in Baghdad. The sculptures once topped the towers of the palace but were removed following the overthrow of Hussein's regime. (*Defense Imagery*)

December 11

TERRORISM: On the road between Baiji and Tikrit, Iraq, insurgents ambush a police patrol car, killing two officers and wounding three. One of the slain is Brigadier General Razzaq Karim Mahmud, a senior commander.

In the town of Hit, Iraq, a minibus carrying Iraqi national guardsmen is ambushed by insurgents, killing seven soldiers.

December 12

MILITARY: South of Baghdad, Iraq, U.S. marines and Iraqi security forces apprehend 72 suspected terrorists near the Euphrates River.

TERRORISM: In Mosul, Iraq, reports surface that the bodies of at least 160 Iraqi national guardsmen have been uncovered around the city since November 12.

In Mahmudiya, Iraq, local security forces enjoy greater successes against the insurgents following the removal of a senior national guard officer who had been supplying the insurgents with information.

December 13–14

TERRORISM: Throughout Baghdad, Iraq, a string of car bombs at various checkpoints kill 20 people.

December 14

TERRORISM: In central Baghdad, Iraq, a suicide bomber detonates himself at the entrance to the heavily fortified Green Zone, killing three national guardsmen and wounding 12 people. The group al-Qaeda in Iraq claims responsibility for the attack.

In Samarra, Iraq, three children are killed in crossfire between insurgents and U.S. forces.

December 15

POLITICS: In Baghdad, Iraq, the Iraqi electoral commission declares that 230 parties and 3,500 candidates are running for office in the January national election. Meanwhile, Iraqi interim defense minister Hazim al-Shalaan complains that the slate of the United Iraqi Alliance is on "Iranian list" that will bring Iraq under that country's control.

December 16

TERRORISM: In western Baghdad, Iraq, a car bomb takes the lives of three Iraqi national guardsmen. As a precaution, Iraqi interim defense minister Hazim al-Shaalan orders Iraqi forces to guard churches and places of worship closely for the holidays.

December 17

DIPLOMACY: In Washington, D.C., Secretary of State Colin Powell and Iraqi finance minister Adil Abd al-Mahdi signs an agreement that cancels most of Iraq's $4.1 billion debt to the United States.

December 18

TERRORISM: In Samarra, Iraq, insurgents fire mortar rounds at an election office and a youth center; one civilian dies, and eight are wounded. Across town, Iraqi commandos storm a terrorist hideout and capture three insurgents and quantities of bomb-making materials.

In Mosul, Iraq, Iraqi national guardsmen engage insurgents in a firefight, killing three of them.

December 19

TERRORISM: In Najaf and Karbala, Iraq, car bombs aimed at Shiites kill 70 people and injure at least 175, while in Baghdad, gunmen drag three election officials from their car and shoot them to death.

December 20

MILITARY: In Washington, D.C., President George W. Bush concedes that the training of Iraqi troops is not proceeding as quickly as originally hoped for, but he remains effusive in his praise of Defense Secretary Donald Rumsfeld.

December 21

TERRORISM: In Mosul, Iraq, a suicide bomber detonates an explosive in a U.S. Army mess tent, killing 15 soldiers and four American contractors. A further 72 people, mostly Iraqi civilians, are injured. The shadowy group Ansar al-Sunna claims responsibility for the blast; the bomber was apparently a Saudi national wearing an Iraqi military uniform.

In Najaf, Iraq, police chief Ghalib al-Jazairi says that an insurgent in his custody has confessed to receiving terrorist training in Syria while supervised by a Syrian military officer.

December 23

MILITARY: In Baghdad, Iraq, 149 Iraqi police trainees graduate from six specialty training courses given at the Adnan training center. This curriculum imparts the basics of criminal investigation, leadership, and hostage rescue.

POLITICS: In Kabul, Afghanistan, President Hamid Karzai presents his new cabinet to parliament for approval.

December 25

TERRORISM: In Mosul, Iraq, a roadside bomb explodes next to a bus carrying Iraqi national guardsmen, killing five and wounding three.

December 26

MILITARY: In Baghdad, Iraq, General Babkir Shawat Zebari says that recent criticism of Iraqi security forces by President George W. Bush regarding recruits deserting and not willing to fight is unfounded.

TERRORISM: In southern Baghdad, Iraq, insurgent activity leads to the death of Colonel Yassin Ibrahim Jawad, a ranking police officer.

December 27

POLITICS: In Iraq, the Iraqi Islamic Party, the nation's largest Sunni organization, announces that it is sitting out upcoming national elections for fear of widespread violence. Head official Hussein Hindawi Mohsen Abdul Hamid says that the election should be postponed until the security situation has improved.

December 28

TERRORISM: In Baghdad, Iraq, shootouts with insurgents kill 23 Iraqi police and national guardsmen. In another instance, insurgents lure police into a booby-trapped house in the Ghazliya district, which explodes, killing seven officers and 25 civilians.

In Tikrit, Iraq, the Um Kashifa police station is attacked by heavily armed insurgents, and 12 officers are slain. Five additional police checkpoints are assaulted throughout the city, resulting in the deaths of five policemen and injuries to three more. An additional 12 police officers are captured and executed at one station.

South of Baquba, Iraq, insurgents stage a carefully orchestrated bombing with several improvised explosive devices going off at timed intervals. Several Iraqi national guardsmen are injured, especially after a suicide car bomber detonates himself in their midst.

December 29

MILITARY: In Baghdad, Iraq, interim defense minister Hazim al-Shalaan says that the Iraqi national guard will be directly incorporated into the regular Iraqi army as of January 6, 2005.

TERRORISM: In Mosul, Iraq, a top security official announces that Abu Marwan, a key member of the deadly al-Qaeda in Iraq group, has been captured. He had been responsible for training and arming terrorist cells.

December 31

MILITARY: By this date, 1,341 U.S. servicemen and servicewomen have been killed in Iraq since March 2003, with another 10,405 wounded in hostile actions. Of this total, 848 were killed in 2004, along with 7,997 wounded.

TERRORISM: Near Baiji, Iraq, a car bomb explodes near an Iraqi military patrol, killing two civilians and wounding five soldiers.

2005

January 1

TERRORISM: A videotape by terrorists allied with Abu Musab al-Zarqawi, aired on the Internet, shows the execution of five Iraqi soldiers.

January 2

TERRORISM: North of Baghdad, Iraq, a suicide car bomber strikes at a group of Iraqi national guardsmen, killing 18.

January 4

TERRORISM: In Baghdad Province, Iraq, Governor Ali al-Haidari is assassinated by insurgents determined to sidetrack upcoming national elections.

January 9

DIPLOMACY: In New York City, an independent agency concludes that the UN Food for Peace Program did not adequately monitor its dealings with Iraq, which spawned the rise of mammoth kickbacks and illicit revenues for Saddam Hussein's regime.

January 10
TERRORISM: In Baghdad, Iraq, insurgents attack and kill the city's deputy police chief and his son. Jordanian terrorist Abu Musab al-Zarqawi claims responsibility for the slaying.

January 11
POLITICS: In Baghdad, Iraq, Prime Minister Ayad Allawi candidly admits that some parts of the country and capital are simply too dangerous to hold elections with any assurance of safety.

January 12
DIPLOMACY: In Washington, D.C., the administration declares that the search for Iraqi weapons of mass destruction is over; none is found. Ironically, this was a major justification for the invasion of Iraq.

January 14
MILITARY: A court-martial at Fort Hood, Texas, finds U.S. Army Reserve Specialist Charles Graner guilty of abusing Iraqi captives at Abu Ghraib prison; he is sentenced to 10 years' imprisonment and receives a dishonorable discharge.

January 17
POLITICS: Around the globe, an estimated 250,000 Iraqi exiles and expatriates register to participate in forthcoming national elections.

In the last combat phase of the war, U.S. Marines moved on to Tikrit, where marines approached one of the lavish palaces maintained by Saddam Hussein. The contrast with the poverty of many Iraqis was striking. *(Defense Imagery)*

January 19
TERRORISM: Throughout Baghdad, Iraq, five car bombs explode, killing 26 people, including several Iraqi troops.

January 20
POLITICS: In Washington, D.C., George W. Bush is sworn in for his second term as president of the United States and commander in chief.

January 21
TERRORISM: In Baghdad, Iraq, a car bomb explodes outside a mosque, killing 14 people and injuring 40 more.

January 27
AVIATION: In Iraq, a Marine Corps CH-53 E helicopter crashes near the Jordanian border during a sandstorm, killing 31 marines. This is the deadliest single day in Iraq in nearly two years.

MILITARY: In Iraq, combat with insurgents takes the lives of four marines and two soldiers; the death toll since March 2003 now exceeds 1,400.

January 30
AVIATION: Over southern Iraq, a British C-130 Hercules transport plane crashes, killing 10 occupants. It is not clear if the crash was mechanically related or due to insurgent fire.

POLITICS: Despite the threat of terrorist attacks, an estimated 89.5 million Iraqis, representing 57 percent of the population, participate in the first democratic election in more than half a century. They choose 275 members for a Council of Representatives to finalize a new draft constitution, and members of 18 provincial assemblies.

TERRORISM: Across Iraq, terrorist attacks kill 40 people, including two Americans slain when a rocket strikes the American embassy in Baghdad.

January 31
MILITARY: The Afghan Secret Service unveils a program to purchase Stinger antiaircraft missiles still in the hands of numerous warlords.

POLITICS: In Baghdad, Iraq, Prime Minister Ayad Allawi touts the recent election as a "victory over terrorism" and the start of a long-awaited national dialogue.

February 3–7
DIPLOMACY: Secretary of State Condoleezza Rice arrives in Europe to mend relations damaged by the recent war in Iraq, with additional stops in Turkey and Israel.

In New York City, the United Nations issues a report that rebukes Benon Sevan of Cyprus, the former head of the Iraqi program, for helping a friend's company secure contracts to sell Iraqi oil.

February 6
DIPLOMACY: In New York City, the United Nations suspends Benon Sevan, a UN adviser, and Joseph Stephanides, of the Security Council staff, who illegally chose the Iraqi oil-for-food contractors.

POLITICS: In Afghanistan, Ayatollah Mohammad Asef Muhsini declares his retirement as the head of the Shiite Harrakat-i-Islami.

February 9–10
MILITARY: In Brussels, Belgium, NATO leaders announce the enlargement of their peacekeeping forces in Afghanistan.

February 13
POLITICS: In Iraq, results of the recent national election are announced, with the Shiite-dominated United Iraqi Alliance winning 48 percent of the vote and taking 140 seats in the National Assembly. The Alliance of Kurds take 75 seats while Prime Minister Ayad Allawi's party takes only 40 seats. The various Sunni parties largely boycotted the election.

February 14
DIPLOMACY: In Washington, D.C., a Senate subcommittee concludes that UN official Benon Sevan might have accepted up to $1.5 million in kickbacks from illegal shipments of Iraqi oil.

February 15
MILITARY: During a visit to Afghanistan, Senator John McCain calls for the creation of joint military permanent bases throughout the country.
POLITICS: In Bamiyan Province, Afghanistan, Habiba Sorabi is appointed to serve as the first female governor by President Hamid Karzai.

February 18–19
TERRORISM: Throughout this holy Shiite period in Iraq, insurgent attacks and bombings kill 70 people.

February 22
POLITICS: In Iraq, the victorious United Iraqi Alliance appoints Shiite politician Ibrahim al-Jaafari to succeed Ayad Allawi as the nation's prime minister. He is viewed as far more acceptable to Kurds and Shiites.

February 23
MILITARY: In the United Kingdom, two soldiers are convicted of abusing Iraqi prisoners in May 2003 at facilities in the southern city of Basra, Iraq.

February 25
TERRORISM: Throughout Iraq, a wave of car bombings kills another 25 people and injures dozens more.

February 27
DIPLOMACY: In Baghdad, Iraq, government officials state that the Syrian government has captured Sabawi Ibrahim al-Hassan, Saddam Hussein's half brother, along with 29 Baath Party members hiding in northeastern Syria.

February 28
TERRORISM: In Hilla, Iraq, a suicide car bomber kills 155 people and injures 175 more as they line up to apply for jobs with the Iraqi police. This is the deadliest single bombing since the U.S. invasion of March 2003.

March 1
MILITARY: In Kabul, Afghanistan, President Hamid Karzai appoints Uzbek warlord Abdul Rashid Dostum to serve as his military adviser.

March 4
MILITARY: At a U.S. military checkpoint in Baghdad, Iraq, U.S. soldiers shoot and wound Italian journalist Giuliana Sgrena, recently released from captivity by Iraqi militants, when her car fails to halt as ordered. However, government agent Nicola Calipari is killed, and the Italian government demands an explanation.

March 7
MILITARY: In Sophia, Bulgaria, Prime Minister Nikolai Svinarov attributes the March 4 death of a Bulgarian to friendly fire from U.S. troops.

March 10
DIPLOMACY: In Washington, D.C., the administration appoints Zalmay Khalilzad, the U.S. ambassador to Afghanistan, to act as American envoy in Iraq.
TERRORISM: In Mosul, Iraq, a suicide bomber kills 47 people and injures 100 while they pray at a Shiite mosque.

March 15
MILITARY: In Rome, Italy, Prime Minister Silvio Berlusconi says he is preparing to withdraw most of the 3,000 Italian troops from Iraq.

March 16
POLITICS: In Baghdad, Iraq, a large and diverse body of newly elected National Assembly members gathers for the first time in the heavily fortified International Zone. Recent elections favored the Shiites and Kurds, heretofore suppressed by the Sunni majority, and they are now beginning to appoint their own leaders. However, consensus is fleeting.

March 17
MILITARY: In Sofia, Bulgaria, Prime Minister Nikolai Svinarov announces that all 460 Bulgarian military personnel will be withdrawn from Iraq by the end of the year.

March 20
POLITICS: In Kabul, Afghanistan, upcoming parliamentary elections are again postponed by the election commission to September 18. They were originally to be held in June 2004.

March 25
AVIATION: President George W. Bush announces that his administration will sell highly advanced General Dynamics F-16 fighters to Pakistan, a valuable ally in the war against terror.

March 29

DIPLOMACY: In Baghdad, Iraq, UN secretary-general Kofi Annan declares that he will not resign after a second report on the UN oil-for-food program scandal criticizes his lack of oversight. The commission, chaired by Paul Volcker, criticized his aides for shredding potentially damaging documents.

POLITICS: In Baghdad, Iraq, members of the National Assembly meet again to chose their national leaders, but once again fail to agree on the composition of the new administration.

March 31

POLITICS: In Washington, D.C., a nine-member presidential commission on military intelligence concludes that the United States was "dead wrong" about the existence of Iraqi weapons of mass destruction. The same estimation also applies to weapons programs in North Korea, Iran, Russia, and China. President George W. Bush thanks the commission for its work and promises to "correct what needs to be fixed."

April 2

TERRORISM: In Baghdad, Iraq, insurgents attack Abu Ghraib prison, aiming to free some inmates, but they are repelled by U.S. forces; 23 soldiers and 13 prisoners are injured.

April 3–7

POLITICS: In Baghdad, Iraq, the new National Assembly makes halting moves toward finalizing a government by appointing Sunni Hajim al-Hassani as speaker and Shiite Hussain al-Shahristani and Kurdish Arif Taifour as his deputies.

April 6

POLITICS: In Baghdad, Iraq, the National Assembly chooses Kurdish leader Jalal Talabani to serve as president and Sunni Sheik Ghazi al-Yawar as second vice president.

April 7

POLITICS: In Baghdad, Iraq, the National Assembly officially sanctions Shiite Ibrahim al-Jaafari to serve as the nation's prime minister, at which point interim prime minister Ayad Allawi resigns. Jalal Talabani is also sworn in as the new Iraqi president. Significantly, al-Jaafari enjoys support from the Shiite-dominated United Iraqi Alliance, which controls a majority of seats in the assembly.

April 13

TERRORISM: In Kirkuk, Iraq, two bombs explode, killing nine policemen.

April 14

DIPLOMACY: In New York City, the Iraqi oil-for-food scandal continues as a U.S. attorney indicts David Chamblers of Houston-based Bayoil, U.S.A. for receiving kickbacks. Also, Tongsun Park, a South Korean businessman, is charged with attempting to bribe UN officials.

TERRORISM: In Baghdad, Iraq, two bombs take the lives of 19 Iraqis.

April 16
TERRORISM: In Baquba, Iraq, a bomb explodes in a popular restaurant, killing 13 people. Police also uncover the bodies of 19 people shot execution style at a stadium in Haditha.

April 20–21
TERRORISM: In Baghdad, Iraq, President Jalal Talabani says that the bodies of 50 recent kidnapping victims have been recovered from the Tigris River. Police authorities recovering the corpses are not sure if the victims were all executed at the same time or over a period of days.

April 21–23
AVIATION: Over Iraq, a civilian helicopter is shot down by insurgents, killing 11 passengers; six of these are members of the Blackwater U.S.A. security firm. Two days later, U.S. soldiers round up six individuals suspected of complicity in the attack.

April 24
TERRORISM: In Baghdad and Tikrit, Iraq, bombs take the lives of at least 21 Iraqis and wound scores more.

April 28
MILITARY: At Fort Bragg, North Carolina, a military jury sentences U.S. Army sergeant Hasan Akbar, a Muslim American, to death for the murder of two fellow soldiers at Camp Pennsylvania, Kuwait, in March 2003. He also wounded 14 more with grenades and a rifle.

POLITICS: In Baghdad, Iraq, the National Assembly approves a majority Shiite cabinet that also includes some Kurds and Sunnis. However, continued negotiations are required to fill a handful of portfolios still vacant.

TERRORISM: In Baghdad, Iraq, Sheika Lameah Khaddouri al-Sakri, a female member of the National Assembly, is gunned down by three assailants.

North of Baghdad, Iraq, a roadside bomb takes the lives of four American soldiers.

April 29
TERRORISM: In and around Baghdad, Iraq, a series of coordinated mortar attacks and car bombs claims the lives of 40 people, including three U.S. Army soldiers, and injures at least 90 more. A bombing in Mosul also kills three Iraqis and wounds nine, including an American soldier.

April 30
DIPLOMACY: In Rome, Italy, Prime Minister Silvio Berlusconi is outraged that troops charged in the death of Italian agent Nicola Calipari have been cleared.

May 1
POLITICS: In London, United Kingdom, the leaked "Downing Street Memo" dated July 23, 2002, causes an uproar when it indicates that the case for war against Iraq was decidedly unconvincing. However, it also maintains that President George W. Bush had resolved to take military action regardless.

TERRORISM: In Iraq, a bomb explodes during a funeral procession near the Syrian border; 25 people are killed.

May 2–4

MILITARY: At Fort Hood, Texas, Private Lynndie England pleads guilty to seven counts of abusing Iraqi prisoners at Abu Ghraib, although they are dismissed after the judge declares a mistrial.

May 3

DIPLOMACY: During a conference discussing the Nuclear Non-Proliferation Treaty, the Iranian government declares that it is resuming its nuclear activities.

MILITARY: In Kabul, Afghanistan, President Hamid Karzai convenes a meeting of 1,000 representatives to debate the question of foreign military forces in Afghanistan. They agree that assistance from the United States and NATO is important for the time being, but they cede a decision on permanent military bases to the parliament. They also call for an end to unilateral American military actions.

POLITICS: In Baghdad, Iraq, several government cabinet appointees are sworn into office, although five ministers and two deputy premiers remain unfilled because of disputes between Sunni and Shiite delegates. Vice President Ghazi al-Yawar boycotts the proceedings to protest the impasse.

May 4

TERRORISM: In Ebril, the capital of Kurdish Iraq, a massive bomb explodes, killing 60 people and injuring more than 150. The militant group Ansar al-Sunna claims responsibility for the act.

May 5

MILITARY: The U.S. Army announces that Brigadier General Janis Karpinski, 800th Military Police Brigade, has been demoted to colonel for dereliction of duty relative to abuses at the Abu Ghraib prison. It also says that Lieutenant General Ricardo S. Sanchez has been cleared of all charges stemming from the incident.

TERRORISM: In Baghdad, a bomb takes the lives of 22 people.

May 7

POLITICS: In Baghdad, Iraq, the final six cabinet appointees selected by Prime Minister Ibrahim Jaafar are approved by the National Assembly.

May 9

MILITARY: In western Iraq, marines make a concerted sweep of the area, killing 125 insurgents. This is the largest U.S. operation in several months, and it costs the lives of nine marines.

May 10

POLITICS: In Baghdad, Iraq, the National Assembly appoints a 53-member committee and tasks them with writing a permanent constitution.

May 11

MILITARY: The U.S. Army announces that Colonel Thomas Pappas has been fined and reprimanded for dereliction of duty stemming from abuses inflicted at Abu Ghraib prison.

POLITICS: After *Newsweek* magazine erroneously reports that U.S. troops in Guantánamo, Cuba, deliberately defaced a Qu'ran, riots and protests break out in Jalalabad, Afghanistan, and spread to 12 provinces; 14 people die, and 120 are injured.

TERRORISM: A string of coordinated bombings in three Iraqi cities takes the lives of 79 Iraqis.

May 12

TERRORISM: Riots in Afghanistan and Pakistan over alleged U.S. desecration of the Qu'ran take the lives of 17 people.

May 15

DIPLOMACY: In Washington, D.C., Secretary of State Condoleezza Rice urges the Iraqi government to appoint more Sunnis to positions of authority.

TERRORISM: In Baghdad, Iraq, police uncover the bodies of 49 Iraqi troops and civilians who had been executed. An aide to Grand Ayatollah Ali al-Sistani is also gunned down.

May 16

POLITICS: *Newsweek* magazine, feeling intense pressure from the Bush administration, apologizes for falsely reporting the desecration of the Qu'ran at Guantánamo, Cuba, and issues a retraction.

In Baghdad, Iraq, Sunnis agree to assist compiling a new national constitution after they receive 15 seats on the 55-member panel designated to write it; 10 other Sunnis will serve as advisers.

May 16–17

MILITARY: At Fort Hood, Texas, a military court finds Army Reserve Specialist Sabrina Harmon guilty of abusing prisoners at Abu Ghraib, Iraq. She receives a sentence of six months in prison and a dishonorable discharge.

May 17

DIPLOMACY: In Baghdad, Iraq, Iran's foreign minister, Kamal Kharrazi, arrives and indicates the possibility of closer ties between the two countries.

May 18

TERRORISM: In Iraq, U.S. officials concede that 450 Iraqis have been killed so far this month.

May 19

DIPLOMACY: In Baghdad, Iraq, the government accuses Saddam Hussein of being the aggressor behind the Iran-Iraq War in the 1980s and insists that he face a trial for war crimes.

May 20

POLITICS: The British newspaper the *Sun* and the American *New York Post* publish a photograph of former Iraqi president Saddam Hussein in his underwear, which many Muslim commentators find offensive.

May 21

POLITICS: In Iraq, a gathering of 2,000 Sunni Arabs form a political alliance to participate in the political process and ensure their voices are heard by the Shiite-dominated government.

May 23

DIPLOMACY: In Washington, D.C., President Hamid Karzai and George W. Bush gather to sign an agreement to allow continuing U.S. military operations in Afghanistan, along with access to Bagram Air Base. This Memorandum of Understanding does not address how long foreign troops are to be stationed there.

May 24

TERRORISM: Intelligence is received that wanted Jordanian terrorist Abu Musab al-Zarqawi has been wounded by U.S. forces.

May 25

MILITARY: In Hadithia, Iraq, 180 miles west of Baghdad, marines and Iraqi security forces sweep the area for insurgents and their supporters.

May 26

MILITARY: A U.S. Army investigation finds "no credible evidence" that soldiers had defaced the Qu'ran either at Guantánamo, Cuba, or elsewhere.

June 2

TERRORISM: In Baghdad, Iraq, the interior minister announces that 12,000 Iraqis have been killed in violence over the past 18 months. Bombs and insurgent attacks across the nation take at least 36 lives on this day alone.

June 3

POLITICS: In Washington, D.C., the Pentagon releases information on the 540 terrorist detainees and enemy combatants held at Guantánamo, Cuba.

June 9

TERRORISM: Outside Haditha, Iraq, a roadside bomb takes the lives of five marines.

June 12

POLITICS: In Washington, D.C., Republican congressman Walter Jones introduces legislation requiring President George W. Bush to establish a timetable for the withdrawal of U.S. forces from Iraq.

June 15

TERRORISM: In Khalia, Iraq, a suicide bomber attacks an Iraqi army mess camp, killing 26 soldiers.

June 16

POLITICS: In Baghdad, Iraq, Iraqi political leaders allow 16 Sunni politicians to join the committee that is writing the country's new constitution.

June 17

MILITARY: Marines and Iraqi security units begin a sweep near the Syrian border to stem the flow of insurgents and explosives into the country.

June 19

TERRORISM: In Baghdad, Iraq, a bomb inside a restaurant kills 23 Iraqis.

June 21

DIPLOMACY: In Baghdad, Iraq, Zalmay Khalilzad presents his credentials to President Jalal Talabani as the new U.S. ambassador.

June 22

AVIATION: Over Southwest Asia, a U-2 aircraft from the 9th Reconnaissance Squadron experiences a catastrophic failure and crashes, killing the pilot.

June 23

MILITARY: In Washington, D.C., General John P. Abizaid informs Congress that the strength of the ongoing Iraqi insurgency is about the same strength as it was six months earlier, but foreign fighters are entering the country. This contradicts an assertion by Vice President Dick Cheney that the uprising was in its "last throes."
TERRORISM: In Fallujah, Iraq, a suicide car bomber strikes a U.S. military convoy, killing six marines, including a woman, and wounding 13.

June 24

POLITICS: In Tehran, Iran, Mahmoud Ahmadinejad, the conservative mayor of the city, wins a surprising landslide election over former president Ali Akbar Hashemi Rafsanjani. His ascent places the country on a confrontational path with the rest of the world.

June 25

POLITICS: In Tehran, Iran, conservative president-elect Mahmoud Ahmadinejad declares his intention to make Iran into a stronger Islamic country.

June 26

DIPLOMACY: In Tehran, Iran, President-elect Mahmoud Ahmadinejad vows to press ahead with Iran's quest to obtain nuclear energy.

June 28

AVIATION: In Afghanistan, an army CH-47 Chinook helicopter attempting to rescue a stranded party of Navy SEALs is shot down and crashes, killing all 19 service members onboard, including eight additional SEALs and eight Special Forces troops. All were en route to rescue a four-man SEAL team cornered by Taliban units.
POLITICS: In Washington, D.C., President George W. Bush delivers a nationally televised speech marking the first anniversary of the transfer of national sovereignty back to the Iraqis. Despite current difficulties, he insists that the sacrifice "is worth it, and it is vital to the future security of our country."
TERRORISM: In Rashidya, Iraq, a suicide bomber kills an 87-year-old member of parliament and three others.

U.S. Navy SEALs such as these, members of one of the U.S. military's most highly trained and versatile Special Operations branches, conducted a variety of specialized operations in Afghanistan. On June 28, 2005, these men—except Hospital Corpsman 2nd Class Marcus Luttrell (third from right)—perished in Operation Red Wing, and group leader Lieutenant Michael P. Murphy (end right) was awarded the Medal of Honor posthumously. *(U.S. Navy)*

July 1
TERRORISM: In Baghdad, Iraq, a suicide car bomber detonates himself outside the party office of the prime minister, killing a guard.

July 2–7
TERRORISM: In Baghdad, Iraq, the group al-Qaeda in Iraq, kidnaps Egyptian envoy Ihab al-Sharif; five days later he is executed, and his body is dumped in the city streets.

July 3
MILITARY: In Afghanistan, army soldiers rescue the sole remaining member of a four-man SEAL team that had been overwhelmed by Taliban forces.

July 5
TERRORISM: In Baghdad, Iraq, a diplomat from Bahrain is shot in the hand, and gunfire is also leveled at the Pakistani ambassador's motorcade.

July 10
TERRORISM: In Baghdad, Iraq, a suicide bomber kills 25 army recruits; other attacks this day take a total of 40 lives.

July 13

TERRORISM: Air force general Randall Schmidt appears before the Senate Armed Services Committee and testifies that terrorist suspects ("detainees") at Guantánamo, Cuba, are being held under safe and humane conditions.

In Baghdad, Iraq, a car bomb explodes and kills 27 people, mostly children, who were gathered around a U.S. military vehicle; an army soldier is also killed.

July 15

TERRORISM: In Baghdad, a string of eight suicide bombings kills 22 people and wounds many others, including six U.S. soldiers.

July 17

POLITICS: In Baghdad, Iraq, a special tribunal files its first case against former president Saddam Hussein involving the murder of Shiite villagers following a failed assassination attempt.

TERRORISM: In Musayyib, Iraq, a suicide bomber detonates himself near a fuel truck, killing 70 people and injuring 150. Baghdad is also struck by four separate suicide bombings.

July 19

POLITICS: In London, United Kingdom, the group Iraqi Body Count issues its first report, stating that 25,000 civilians had been killed since the U.S. invasion of March 2003.

TERRORISM: In central Baghdad, Iraq, Sunnis Mejbil al-Sheik Isa and Damin al-Obeidi are gunned down by unknown assailants; they were involved in drafting the new constitution. The remaining Sunnis on the committee withdraw for fear of their lives.

July 20

MILITARY: A study released by the Pentagon concludes that Iraqi security forces are weak and only "partly capable" of fighting back the insurgency.

July 21

TERRORISM: In Baghdad, Iraq, two leading Algerian diplomats are kidnapped by gunmen.

July 24

TERRORISM: In Baghdad, Iraq, insurgents launch a series of coordinated attacks and bombings at Iraqi army checkpoints; six soldiers are killed. In addition, roadside bombs take the lives of two U.S. soldiers.

July 25

POLITICS: In Baghdad, Iraq, 12 of the surviving 14 Sunni politicians return to the committee drafting a new national constitution.

July 29

TERRORISM: At a town near the Syrian border, suicide bombers target an Iraqi army recruiting station, killing 26 people.

August 3
TERRORISM: In Haditha, Iraq, a huge roadside bomb kills 14 marines and their translator. In Basra, insurgents kill an American journalist and his translator after abducting them the evening previous.

August 4
DIPLOMACY: Diplomats from the United Kingdom, France, and Germany offer to allow Iran to legally obtain nuclear reactors, provided that it halt all uranium-enrichment programs.
MILITARY: Over the past four days, insurgent activity has taken the lives of 30 U.S. military members.

August 5
DIPLOMACY: In Tehran, the Iranian government rejects the latest European offer to curtail its uranium-enrichment program.
MILITARY: Beset by waves of terror attacks, U.S. and security forces begin repeated sweeps of Iraq's borders with Iran and Syria.

August 8
DIPLOMACY: In New York, the United Nations releases a third report concerning corruption arising from the Iraqi food-for-oil program. It paints Efraim Nadler and Alexander Yakovlev, officials associated with the program, as receiving illegal profits and kickbacks of $1 million.

August 9
TERRORISM: In Washington, D.C., Defense Secretary Donald Rumsfeld says that Iran is providing Iraqi insurgents with explosives and technical know-how.

August 10
DIPLOMACY: In Iran, the government removes all UN seals from a nuclear production facility and begins enriching uranium.

August 11
DIPLOMACY: In New York City, the United Nations passes a resolution demanding that Iran immediately suspend its uranium-enrichment programs.

August 15
POLITICS: In Baghdad, Iraq, the National Assembly votes to delay the final draft constitution to enable Sunni, Shiite, and Kurdish delegates to reach a compromise on hotly disputed issues, including women's rights, the distribution of oil, and the role that Islam will play in the government.

August 17
TERRORISM: In Baghdad, Iraq, a bomb explosion at a busy bus terminal kills 45 people and injures dozens more.

August 18
TERRORISM: In Samarra, Iraq, a roadside bomb takes the lives of four U.S. soldiers.

August 19
DIPLOMACY: The Danish oil concern Grundfos admits that it paid kickbacks to Iraqi authorities during the food-for-oil program.

August 22
POLITICS: In Baghdad, Iraq, the National Assembly receives a partially completed draft constitution with a promise that the finished document, with the remaining sticking points resolved, would be submitted in a few days.

August 26
POLITICS: In Baghdad, Iraq, Shiite and Kurdish delegates suspend negotiations with Sunnis in the National Assembly over what they perceive as intractable demands.

August 28
POLITICS: In Baghdad, Iraq, the finished draft constitution is submitted to the National Assembly; the document is subject to a national referendum on October 15, but Sunni politicians denounce it and urge its rejection.

August 31
TERRORISM: In Baghdad, Iraq, a Shiite religious procession is panicked by rumors of a suicide bomber, and the ensuing stampede on a bridge across the Tigris River kills nearly 1,000 people.

September 3
TERRORISM: Throughout northern Iraq, a string of bombings kills 17 Iraqi soldiers and four civilians.

September 5
TERRORISM: Near the Syrian border, the town of Qaim, Iraq, is seized by insurgents.

September 6
MILITARY: In Najaf, Iraq, U.S. troops turn over their base to Iraqi security forces.

September 7
TERRORISM: In Basra, Iraq, two bombings kill 20 people.

September 10–11
MILITARY: In Tal Afar, Iraq, a force of 11,000 U.S. troops and Iraqi security forces attacks a local militant stronghold; the insurgents are dislodged after 150 are killed and 48 captured.

September 14
TERRORISM: Throughout Baghdad, Iraq, a series of coordinated bombings kills 167 people and wounds 600; one suicide car bombing alone kills 112 people. The group al-Qaeda in Iraq takes credit for the attacks and states they are revenge for the recent U.S. attack at Tal Afar.

September 15
TERRORISM: In Iraq, a spate of suicide bombings kills 20 people, including 16 police officers.

September 17
MILITARY: As of this date, 1,895 military personnel of various nations have died in Iraq since March 2003; 1,472 are attributable to hostile action.

September 18
POLITICS: In Afghanistan, voters participate in the nation's first democratic parliamentary elections in more than 25 years. More than 5,800 candidates are fielded, but the turnout rate is only 50 percent.

September 26–28
MILITARY: At Fort Hood, Texas, a military court convicts Private Lynndie England of abusing prisoners at Abu Ghraib prison; she is sentenced to three years in prison.

September 28
TERRORISM: In Tal Afar, Iraq, one of the first few female suicide bombers strikes at army recruits near the Syrian border, killing six and wounding 35.

September 29
TERRORISM: The city of Balad, Iraq, a Shiite enclave, is struck by a wave of car bombings that kills 150 people.

An Afghan voter displays his finger, stained to show he has voted in the first post liberation parliamentary elections in Afghanistan on September 18, 2005. *(Department of Defense)*

October 1–7
MILITARY: A force of 1,000 U.S. Army troops begins Operation Iron Fist to root out Iraqi terrorists in the town of Sadah, near the Syrian border; fighting results in the deaths of 50 insurgents.

October 2
POLITICS: In Washington, D.C., General John P. Abizaid appears on a national news show to declare his optimism on security matters in Iraq.

October 5
MILITARY: The first day of the holy month of Ramadan is marred by an explosion outside a Shiite mosque in Hilla, Iraq, which kills 25 people.

October 6
TERRORISM: In Baghdad, Iraq, a bomb explodes on a crowded bus, killing 10 people.

October 7
MILITARY: In Iraq, two bombing attacks take the lives of seven marines.

October 11
POLITICS: In Iraq, Sunni politicians embrace compromises allowing revisions to the constitution and agree to support these changes in a public referendum.

October 11–12
TERRORISM: A string of bombings across Iraq kills 70 people, including 30 during an attack on an Iraqi army recruiting center.

October 12
POLITICS: In Baghdad, Iraq, the National Assembly agrees to consider changes to the constitution following an election slated for December 2005, at which point the Sunni-based Iraqi Islamic Party drops its opposition to its adoption.

October 15
POLITICS: Despite terrorist attacks, Iraqi voters turn out to approve a draft constitution for the country. This time voting is not marred by widespread violence.
TERRORISM: West of Baghdad, Iraq, a roadside bomb takes the lives of five U.S. soldiers.

October 15–18
AVIATION: At Langley Air Force Base, Virginia, the 27th Fighter Squadron flies F-22A Raptors to Hill Air Force Base, Utah, as part of Operation Combat Hammer in Iraq. There it drops its first JDAMs on a target range.

October 16
AVIATION: Near Baghdad, Iraq, a patrolling U.S. warplane observes Iraqi insurgents rolling artillery shells into a ditch and fires on them, killing 20 guerrillas.

October 19
POLITICS: In Baghdad, Iraq, the trial of former president Saddam Hussein opens under the aegis of five judges. Although implicated in many deaths, he will be charged with one specific incident, the massacre of Shiite villagers following a failed

assassination attempt in 1982. Seven other officials are on trial on the same charge; Hussein pleads not guilty.

October 21
TERRORISM: In Baghdad, Iraq, Sadoun al-Janabi, a defense attorney associated with the trial of Saddam Hussein, is kidnapped and subsequently murdered by unknown assailants.

October 22
POLITICS: In Washington, D.C., an administration spokesman is quoted by the news media as stating that the 170,000 U.S. and allied forces in Iraq cannot withdraw until Iraqi security forces are capable of standing on their own.

October 24
TERRORISM: In Baghdad, Iraq, a series of car bombings damages two large hotels; six people die, and a number are injured.

October 25
POLITICS: In Baghdad, Iraq, the government formally announces that voters have approved the new draft constitution by a wide margin, with 79 percent of Kurds and Shiites voting in favor. However, nearly two-thirds of all Sunni voters rejected the document. Parliamentary elections scheduled for December are the next step in the process.

October 26
POLITICS: At Bolling Air Force Base, Washington, D.C., President George W. Bush delivers an address in which he says the United States should never accept anything short of complete victory in Iraq.

October 27
POLITICS: In New York City, Paul Volcker issues the fifth and final investigative report into the Iraqi food-for-oil program under Saddam Hussein, finding it rife with corruption and fraud. Illegal kickbacks under this scheme totaled an estimated $1.8 billion.

October 30
TERRORISM: In Baghdad, Iraq, a string of insurgent attacks kills 11 people, including an adviser to Prime Minister Ibrahim al-Jaafari.

November 2
TERRORISM: South of Baghdad, Iraq, a car bomb outside a Shiite mosque and market kills 20 people.

November 5
MILITARY: In western Iraq near the Syrian border, U.S. troops and Iraqi security forces begin a concerted sweep through the region, encountering and killing 50 insurgents.

November 8
MILITARY: In Iraq, the state-run media run a report alleging that U.S. forces employed white phosphorous against civilians; the Americans subsequently acknowledge using the substance, but not against civilians.

TERRORISM: In Baghdad, Iraq, unknown gunmen target two attorneys representing former Baathist officials on trial with Saddam Hussein; one is killed and the other wounded.

November 10
TERRORISM: In Baghdad, Iraq, a bomb explodes at a popular restaurant, killing 34 people.

November 11
POLITICS: In a Veterans Day Speech, President George W. Bush condemns those accusing him of manipulating intelligence on Iraq as "irresponsible." He states that many of these same critics agreed with him that Iraq possessed weapons of mass destruction.

November 13
DIPLOMACY: In Cairo, Egypt, a gathering of Egyptian, Shiite, Sunni, and Kurdish leaders from Iraq unanimously condemns all attacks against civilians, religious services, and humanitarian organizations. It also calls for a timetable for the removal of foreign forces from the country.
MILITARY: In Baghdad, Iraq, U.S. forces uncover a detention facility operated by the Interior Ministry where 160 inmates were being illegally held and abused. The government promises to investigate matters.

November 14–16
MILITARY: In western Iraq, insurgent activity results in the deaths of seven marines.

November 15
POLITICS: In Washington, D.C., the Senate rejects a Democratic resolution requiring a timetable for the pullout of U.S. forces from Iraq by a vote of 58 to 40. However, the body subsequently approves a Republican resolution, 79-19, asking the president to report the situation to Congress every 90 days. A recent public opinion polls also shows for the first time that a slight majority of Americans wants U.S. troops removed from Iraq within 12 months.

November 16
POLITICS: In Washington, D.C., Vice President Richard Cheney accuses those who claim the administration falsified information during the buildup to the Iraqi invasion of making "one of the most dishonest and reprehensible charges ever aired in this city."

November 18
POLITICS: In Washington, D.C., the House of Representatives votes down a resolution sponsored by Congressman John D. Murtha that would have required the immediate withdrawal of all U.S. forces from Iraq.
TERRORISM: In Khanaqin, Iraq, suicide bombers posing as worshippers detonate themselves inside two mosques, killing 70 Kurds.

November 19
TERRORISM: In Baghdad, Iraq, car bombs explode during a funeral procession, killing 18 mourners.

November 21
POLITICS: In Baghdad, Iraq, a coalition of Shiite, Sunni, and Kurdish leaders requests a specific date for all U.S. forces to depart to be put in writing.

November 28
POLITICS: In Baghdad, Iraq, the trial of former president Saddam Hussein and his co-defendants resumes after a recess to allow defendants to meet with their attorneys.

November 30
POLITICS: In Annapolis, Maryland, President George W. Bush addresses Naval Academy midshipmen, defending the war in Iraq and categorically refusing to establish a timetable for the removal of American forces there. He also declares that, while the United States respects the country's new leadership, it will not allow a new dictatorship to seize power there.

The National Security Council issues a study called "National Strategy for Victory in Iraq," which outlines a program enabling U.S. forces to be withdrawn only after the insurgency has been squelched.

December 1
AVIATION: A missile launched from a Predator drone kills Hamza Rabia, a high-ranking al-Qaeda leader, and four others in northern Pakistan.
TERRORISM: Near Fallujah, Iraq, a marine steps on a cache of buried artillery shells, igniting them; 10 marines are killed, and 11 are wounded.

December 2
POLITICS: In Washington, D.C., the Pentagon admits that it hired the Lincoln Group, a private PR firm, to write pro-American articles for Iraqi newspapers. It also paid Iraqi journalists to compose similar pieces.
TERRORISM: A roadside bomb strike a marine convoy, killing 10 and wounding a dozen more.

December 3
TERRORISM: A suicide bomber strikes an Iraqi military convoy north of Baghdad, Iraq, killing three people and injuring 19.

December 5–7
POLITICS: In Baghdad, Iraq, the trial of former president Saddam Hussein resumes again, with nine witnesses appearing behind a screen to describe incidents of torture and beatings.

December 6
TERRORISM: In Baghdad, Iraq, two suicide bombers detonate themselves at the police academy building, killing 36 people and wounding 75.

December 8
DIPLOMACY: In Tehran, Iran, President Mahmoud Ahmadinejad casts doubt on the Holocaust in Nazi Germany and insists that the Jewish state be relocated to either Europe or the United States.

POLITICS: In Baghdad, Iraq, U.S. troops and Iraqi security forces uncover another prison secretly managed by the Interior Ministry; the 625 inmates show some signs of mistreatment, possibly torture.

December 9
DIPLOMACY: In New York City, UN secretary-general Kofi Annan roundly condemns Iranian president Mahmoud Ahmadinejad's denial of the Holocaust.

December 7–18
POLITICS: President George W. Bush makes appearances in Washington, D.C., Minneapolis, Minnesota, and Philadelphia, Pennsylvania, and then makes a nationally televised speech from the Oval Office, all in defense of the Iraq war. He reiterates he will not pull U.S. forces out until the government there can cope with the ongoing insurgency.

December 15
POLITICS: In Iraq, 11 million people—70 percent of Iraqi voters—turn out to elect 275 members to the first national parliament since the invasion of 2003. More than 300 diverse parties had registered for the contest.

December 18
POLITICS: In Washington, D.C., President George W. Bush gives a televised address and admits that Iraqi weapons of mass destruction have not been found. However, he insists that the nation now confronts two stark realities, victory or defeat.
TERRORISM: North of Baghdad, Iraq, insurgents block a highway and kill 20 truck drivers and civilians.

December 19–20
POLITICS: In Iraq, the national election commission states that the various Shiite parties have obtained a strong lead in national voting, but not an absolute majority. Sunni leaders make accusations of widespread fraud and call for new elections.

December 21
POLITICS: In Baghdad, Iraq, former president Saddam Hussein accuses his U.S. guards of torturing and beating him and his co-defendants.

December 29
POLITICS: In Iraq, the International Mission for Iraqi Elections pledges to investigate allegations of widespread irregularities during the recent parliamentary elections.

December 31
MILITARY: The recent death of a U.S. soldier in Iraq brings the death toll there up to 842 for the year 2005. Since 2003, a total of 1,694 have died in hostile actions with a further 13,943 wounded.
TERRORISM: Insurgent attacks across Iraq take the lives of 20 civilians. This is only one of the 34,1431 incidents reported in 2005, up from 2004's tally of 24,496.

2006

January 4

TERRORISM: North of Baghdad, Iraq, a Shiite funeral procession is struck by a suicide bomber, who kills 30 people and injures scores more.

January 5

MILITARY: Across Iraq, insurgent activity leads to the deaths of 11 American servicemen.
TERRORISM: In Karbala and Ramadi, Iraq, a coordinated series of bombings kills more than 100 people.

January 6

TERRORISM: A videotape of No. 2 al-Qaeda leader Ayman al-Zawahiri is aired by the al-Jazeera network, in which the terrorist declares that the recent talk of an American troop withdrawal from Iraq is a sign of defeat there.

January 7

AVIATION: A U.S. Army helicopter crashes in northern Iraq, killing eight U.S. service members and four American civilians.

January 8

MILITARY: The *New York Times* reports that 80 percent of marines killed by torso wounds in Iraq might have been saved had they been equipped with proper body armor.

January 9

TERRORISM: In Baghdad, Iraq, a suicide bomber enters the Interior Ministry compound and detonates himself, killing 18 people.

January 10

POLITICS: In Natanz, Iran, the Iranians resume their nuclear activities in defiance of the United Nations to produce nuclear fuel also capable of serving as weapons-grade uranium.

January 13

AVIATION: In Damadola, northwestern Pakistan, a U.S. missile strikes a house where the No. 2 al-Qaeda leader Ayman al-Zawahiri was believed to be having dinner; three houses are destroyed and 18 people are killed, but the terrorist apparently was not there. However, Pakistani authorities report that al-Zawahiri's son-in-law is among the dead.

January 17

TERRORISM: In Baghdad, Iraq, insurgents kidnap *Christian Science Monitor* journalist Jill Carroll, kill her interpreter, and subsequently threaten to kill her unless the United States releases all female captives in its possession.

January 19

DIPLOMACY: In Rome, Italy, the government announces that it is withdrawing all of its 2,600 troops from Iraq by the end of 2006.

POLITICS: In Iraq, the International Mission for Iraqi Elections concludes that there were indeed incidents of "fraud and other irregularities" in the December 15 parliamentary elections, but as a whole, the election was successful. It therefore rejects calls by Sunni and Shiite secular groups for new elections.

TERRORISM: The al-Jazeera network broadcasts a videotape of fugitive Saudi terrorist Osama bin Laden, in which he proposes a truce with U.S. forces in Iraq and Afghanistan, allowing them to withdraw completely from those Muslim lands.

January 20

POLITICS: In Iraq, the finalized results of the parliamentary elections are released. Not unexpectedly, the majority Shiites captured 128 seats, but they are 10 seats short of an absolute majority. The Sunnis captured 55 seats and the Kurds another 53; the remaining 25 seats are split among various minor parties.

January 23

POLITICS: In Washington, D.C., the special inspector general for Iraqi reconstruction issues a report that claims $9 billion is unaccounted for due to bad management practices by the U.S.-led Provisional Authority in Baghdad.

January 29

AVIATION: An all-Iraqi air force crew flies a C-130E while carrying Minister of the Interior Bayan Jabr to a summit in Tunisia. This is one of three C-130s operated by the 23rd Transport Squadron, based at Tallil Air Base, which is jointly staffed by American personnel.

TERRORISM: ABC co-anchor Bob Woodruff and cameraman Dick Vogel are injured when their vehicle is struck by a roadside bomb in northwest Baghdad; they are airlifted to a hospital in Germany for treatment.

January 30

DIPLOMACY: The governments of China and Russia join the United States, Britain, and France in requesting the International Atomic Energy Agency to take Iran before the UN Security Council, where sanctions may be imposed.

TERRORISM: The al-Jazeera network plays another videotape of al-Qaeda leader Ayman al-Zawahiri, in which he mocks President George W. Bush for failing to kill him in a recent attack.

February 3

MILITARY: At Al Kasik Training Station, Iraq, Captain LeeAnn Roberts becomes the first female instructor to perform firearms instruction for Iraqi trainees.

February 4

DIPLOMACY: In New York City, the International Atomic Energy Agency votes 27 to 3 to report Iran to the Security Council for its illicit nuclear activities. The Iranian government subsequently announces it is ceasing all cooperation with that agency.

February 14

DIPLOMACY: In Tehran, Iran, the government announces that it has resumed the production of enriched uranium, which can be used in either nuclear fuel or nuclear weapons.

February 15
POLITICS: In Washington, D.C., a report by the U.S. Senate finds Iraq's overall infrastructure still below prewar standards despite the $16 billion spent by the United States to improve it. It also highlights that insurgent activity rose 200 percent in terms of attacks between March 2004 and December 2005.

February 22
TERRORISM: In Samarra, Iraq, a suicide car bombing wrecks the famous Shiite Askariya Mosque, touching off a wave of sectarian violence between Shiites and Sunnis; at least 1,000 people are reported slain.

March 1
DIPLOMACY: In Kabul, Afghanistan, President George W. Bush makes an unannounced visit to discuss security issues with President Hamid Karzai. He subsequently ventures to Karachi, Pakistan, for talks with President Pervez Musharraf.

March 10
TERRORISM: In Iraq, the body of Tom Fox, an American member of Christian Peacemakers who was kidnapped in November, is found.

March 12
TERRORISM: In Afghanistan, a roadside bomb kills four U.S. soldiers.

March 13
DIPLOMACY: In London, United Kingdom, the government announces that it is reducing its troop strength in Iraq by 10 percent (800 men) beginning in May.

March 15
POLITICS: In Washington, D.C., Congress establishes the bipartisan Iraq Study Group to carry out an independent evaluation of conditions and progress in that nation. Assisting the effort are former secretary of state James A. Baker and former Illinois congressman Lee H. Hamilton.

In Baghdad, Iraq, former president Saddam Hussein testifies in his own defense for the first time. He also urges Iraqis to unite and oppose the U.S.-led occupation.

March 16
MILITARY: U.S. troops and Iraqi security forces commence Operation Swarmer by attacking insurgents near Samarra, in the largest air strike employed since the beginning of the war.
POLITICS: In Baghdad, Iraq, the new national legislature convenes for the first time but quickly adjourns.

March 21
POLITICS: In Washington, D.C., President George W. Bush announces that any decision on withdrawing troops from Iraq will "be decided by another president."
TERRORISM: Northeast of Baghdad, Iraq, a force estimated at 100 insurgents attacks a jail, kills 18 policemen, and releases 30 inmates.

March 23

MILITARY: In Iraq, a raid by U.S. and British Special Forces results in the freeing of three members of the Christian Peacemakers.

March 30

TERRORISM: In Baghdad, Iraq, insurgents release freelance journalist Jill Carroll. She subsequently states that she was abused in captivity and only made two anti-Western videotapes under coercion.

April 4

POLITICS: In Baghdad, Iraq, a special tribunal charges former president Saddam Hussein and six co-defendants with genocide following the deaths of 50,000 Kurds.

April 7

TERRORISM: In Baghdad, Iraq, a suicide bomber infiltrates the Shiite Baratha Mosque and then detonates himself, killing 90 people and wounding 175.

April 11

DIPLOMACY: In Tehran, Iran, President Mahmoud Ahmadinejad describes his country's uranium enrichment program, although he insists it will be used for peaceful purposes. Concurrently, Gholamreza Aghazadeh, the chief of Iran's Atomic Energy Organization, insists that the program is too small to be considered capable of manufacturing nuclear weapons.

April 12

TERRORISM: In Huwaider, north of Baghdad, Iraq, a car bomb explodes, killing 26 people.

April 13

DIPLOMACY: Mohammed ElBaradei, the head of the International Atomic Energy Agency, urges Iran to halt its uranium-enrichment program.

TERRORISM: Gunmen attack police north of Baghdad, Iraq, killing 17 officers with bullets and another 17 with bombs.

April 18–19

DIPLOMACY: In Moscow, Russia, a gathering of diplomats from Britain, China, France, Germany, the United States and Russia confer but are unable to agree on how to respond to Iran's nuclear enrichment program. The Chinese and Russians directly oppose the U.S. demand for sanctions.

April 20

POLITICS: In Baghdad, Iraq, Prime Minister Ibrahim al-Jaafari fails to cobble together a working coalition in parliament once Sunnis and Kurds refuse to support him.

In Pittsburgh, Pennsylvania, Democrat congressman John D. Murtha states to the World Affairs Council that the United States should remove all its troops from Iraq as soon as possible. He says many Iraqis continue to view the Americans as occupiers.

April 22

POLITICS: In Baghdad, Iraq, Shiite politician Nuri al-Maliki is declared the new prime minister and six new cabinet officials are named after months of political wrangling.

April 24

TERRORISM: In Baghdad, Iraq, a series of seven coordinated bombings kills 10 people and injures 76.

April 25

TERRORISM: A video posted on a Web site in Iraq shows Jordanian terrorist Abu Musab al-Zarqawi, head of al-Qaeda in Iraq, urging all insurgents to continue attacking U.S. forces.

April 26

DIPLOMACY: In Baghdad, Iraq, Secretary of State Condoleezza Rice and Defense Secretary Donald Rumsfeld arrive to urge Iraqi leaders to speed the process of forming a new government to win public confidence.

May 3

TERRORISM: In Iraq, gunmen attack recruits at a police station, killing 16; a total of 50 people die this day through various acts of violence.

May 5

AVIATION: Over Konar Province, Afghanistan, a U.S. Army CH-47 Chinook helicopter crashes, killing 10 soldiers on board.

May 6–7

TERRORISM: Throughout Baghdad, Iraq, the remains of 51 murder victims are uncovered by local authorities.

May 7

TERRORISM: In Baghdad and Karbala, Iraq, car bombs take the lives of 14 people.

May 9

TERRORISM: In Tal Afar, Iraq, 17 people are killed by a suicide bomber.

May 10

TERRORISM: In Baquba, Iraq, gunmen shoot and kill 12 employees of an electrical manufacturing plant as they sit on a bus; four more die when a bomb subsequently explodes in the vehicle.

May 12

MILITARY: In Balad, Iraq, a Shiite Iraqi army unit clashes with one composed primarily of Kurds; no casualties are reported.

May 14

MILITARY: U.S. Army units making a sweep north of Baghdad report encountering and killing 25 insurgents.

May 16
TERRORISM: In Baghdad, Iraq, roadside bombs and other violence claim the lives of 30 people.

May 18
MILITARY: Northwest of Baghdad, Iraq, a roadside bombing kills four U.S. soldiers.

May 20
POLITICS: In Baghdad, Iraq, enough politicians rally behind Prime Minister Nuri al-Maliki to formally approve his new government. However, ministers of defense, interior, and national security are still not named.

May 21–22
AVIATION: U.S. warplanes repeatedly strike a village near the Pakistani border where Taliban forces were massing for an offensive; an estimated 20 to 80 fighters are killed. Local authorities insist that 16 civilians also died.

May 22
POLITICS: In Chicago, Illinois, President George W. Bush gives a highly optimistic speech in which he portrays Iraq as an example that democracy is the Middle East's best hope.

May 24
MILITARY: In Afghanistan, Afghan security forces clash with Taliban insurgents, leaving five dead; they claim 24 guerrillas also died.

May 25
DIPLOMACY: In Washington, D.C., President George W. Bush and British prime minister Tony Blair hold a joint news conference in which they acknowledge misjudgements in the Iraqi conflict but refuse to consider a timetable for the withdrawal of troops.

May 29
MILITARY: In Kabul, Afghanistan, a U.S. Army cargo truck runs into an Afghan automobile and rioting ensues; 20 people are killed in the fighting.
TERRORISM: CBS reporters Paul Douglas and James Brolan are killed by a roadside bomb in Baghdad, Iraq, while reporter Kimberly Dozier is badly injured.

May 30
TERRORISM: In Baghdad and Hilla, Iraq, insurgent car bombs and mortars kill more than 40 people.

May 31
POLITICS: In Baghdad, Iraq, Prime Minister Nuri al-Maliki calls for a state of emergency in the southern city of Basra.

June 1
DIPLOMACY: In Washington, D.C., President George W. Bush warns Iran that it faces additional UN sanctions if it fails to halt production of enriched uranium and enter into negotiations to conclude such endeavors.

June 3

TERRORISM: In Basra, Iraq, a suicide bomber kills 27 people.

June 4

TERRORISM: North of Baghdad, Iraq, gunmen attack a crowded bus and kill at least 19 passengers.

June 6

DIPLOMACY: In New York City, five permanent members of the UN Security Council, joined by Germany, offer a package of incentives to Iran to stop enriched-uranium production. The deal includes a gift of light-water nuclear reactors for generating electricity.

June 7

TERRORISM: Near Baquba, Iraq, U.S. Special Forces direct an air strike by two air force F-16s that kills terrorist ring leader Abu Musab al-Zarqawi at his hiding place in Hibhib. This removes a senior al-Qaeda figure from the fighting. He had so earned the ire of senior leadership with his willingness to kill innocent civilians that they may have deliberately betrayed his location to the Americans to be rid of him.

June 8

POLITICS: In Baghdad, Iraq, parliament fills the cabinet positions of defense, interior, and national security, finally rounding out the administration of Prime Minister Nuri al-Maliki.

June 12

TERRORISM: An Islamist Web site declares that slain terrorism leader Abu Musab al-Zarqawi has been replaced by a new figure, Abu Hamza al-Muhajir, suspected to actually be Egyptian terrorist Abu Ayyub al-Masri.

June 13

DIPLOMACY: In Baghdad, Iraq, President George W. Bush arrives to confer with Prime Minister Nuri al-Maliki and show his support for the new government. Bush reiterates his stance that Americans forces will not depart until the Iraqi military is capable of standing on its own.
TERRORISM: In Kirkuk, Iraq, six bombs explode, killing at least 25 people.

June 15

MILITARY: In Iraq, the U.S. military announces that it has conducted 452 raids, killed 104 insurgents, arrested 759 terrorist suspects, and confiscated 28 caches of arms.
POLITICS: In Washington, D.C., a congressional committee notes that oil and electrical production in Iraq is still below prewar standards.

June 16

MILITARY: South of Baghdad, Iraq, insurgents attack a U.S. Army checkpoint, killing one soldier and capturing two others; both are subsequently found murdered.
POLITICS: In Washington, D.C., the House of Representatives votes 256 to 153 in favor of allowing the United States to fulfill its Iraqi mission without a timetable for withdrawal.

June 17
TERRORISM: In Baghdad, Iraq, several bombings and a mortar attack kill at least 35 people.

June 19
MILITARY: Three soldiers are accused of murdering three Iraqi detainees and of threatening a fourth soldier if he confessed to investigators.
TERRORISM: In Baghdad, Iraq, Khamis al-Obeidi is the third member of Saddam Hussein's defense team to be shot and killed.

June 20
DIPLOMACY: In Tokyo, Japan, Prime Minister Junichiro Koizumi announces that he is withdrawing all 550 Japanese troops from Iraq.

June 22
POLITICS: In Washington, D.C., the Senate votes 86 to 13 to defeat a Democrat resolution requiring the United States to withdraw from Iraq in July 2007. Another resolution, calling upon President George W. Bush to withdraw without a timetable, is also defeated, 60 to 39.

June 23
TERRORISM: In Hibhib, Iraq, a bomb explodes at a Sunni mosque, killing 12 people.

July 1
TERRORISM: In Baghdad, Iraq, a car bomb explodes in a predominately Shiite neighborhood, killing 62 people.

July 3
MILITARY: The U.S. Army accuses former soldier Steven D. Green, previously dismissed for a "personality disorder," with the rape and murder of an Iraqi girl and her family in March 2006.

July 7
POLITICS: In Baghdad, former president Saddam Hussein stages a hunger strike over the past week to demand better security for his defense team.

July 9
TERRORISM: In a Sunni neighborhood in Baghdad, Iraq, gunmen shoot and kill 42 people.

July 10
POLITICS: In Washington, D.C., the Government Accountability Office issues a report suggesting that the administration's Iraq postwar strategy was poorly planned.

July 11
POLITICS: In Washington, D.C., Democratic congressman John D. Murtha complains that the American occupation of Iraq is costing taxpayers $8 billion per month, which translates into $267 million a day or $11 million per hour.
TERRORISM: Ongoing sectarian violence between Sunnis and Shiites in Baghdad, Iraq, claims at least 50 lives.

July 12

TERRORISM: Northeast of Baghdad, Iraq, gunmen kidnap 24 people, killing the 20 Shiites among them.

July 13

MILITARY: An important sign of progress is reached when the U.S. military hands control of Muthanna Province, Iraq, over to local security forces. This is the first of 18 provinces returned to Iraqis since the 2003 invasion.

July 15

TERRORISM: In Baghdad, Iraq, insurgents capture the Iraqi Olympic Committee chairman and 30 other people during a raid upon a sports conference.

July 16

TERRORISM: In Mahmoudiya, Iraq, insurgents attack a crowded marketplace with automatic weapons and hand grenades, killing 50 people, including women and children. In the northern town of Tuz Khormata, a suicide bomber attacks a cafe frequented by Shiites, killing 26 people and injuring scores more.

July 17

TERRORISM: In south Baghdad, sectarian violence claims the lives of 40 people, mostly Shiites.

July 18

DIPLOMACY: In New York City, the United Nations releases a report stating that 14,338 Iraqis were slain in sectarian violence or terrorist acts from January to June 2006.
TERRORISM: In Kufa, Iraq, a suicide bomber targeting laborers waiting in line kills 53 people.

July 20

POLITICS: In Camp Fallujah, Iraq, General John P. Abizaid, the U.S. commander for the Middle East, says that sectarian fighting between Sunnis and Shiites is now a greater problem than the insurgency. He promises that additional forces will be deployed to Baghdad.

July 23

DIPLOMACY: In Iraq, Prime Minister Nuri al-Maliki flies to Washington, D.C., to discuss national security issues with President George W. Bush.
POLITICS: In Baghdad, Iraq, former president Saddam Hussein, who has been on a hunger strike for the past three weeks, is hospitalized and fed through a tube.
TERRORISM: In Baghdad, Iraq, a suicide bomber attacks a crowded market, killing 34 people and wounding 74 more. Meanwhile, in Kirkuk, a car bomb explodes near a courthouse, killing 20 people and injuring 159 bystanders.

July 25

DIPLOMACY: In Washington, D.C., President George W. Bush and Prime Minister Nuri al-Maliki meet to discuss security issues, and the president pledges to send additional thousands of troops to curtail escalating sectarian violence in Iraq. Such a maneuver casts doubt on projected troop withdrawals scheduled for the fall.

July 26
Diplomacy: In Washington, D.C., Iraqi prime minister Nuri al-Maliki addresses a joint session of Congress and appeals for additional money and troops as part of the war against global terrorism.

Politics: In Baghdad, Iraq, former president Saddam Hussein is released from the hospital and resumes his trial. He also states that, if convicted, he wishes to be executed by firing squad instead of being sent to the gallows like a common criminal.

July 27
Terrorism: In Baghdad, Iraq, a suicide car bomb explodes in an upscale Shiite neighborhood, killing 31 people and injuring more than 150. Parts of the city are also exposed to rocket and mortar fire.

July 29
Military: In Baghdad, Iraq, General John P. Abizaid announces the deployment of a 3,700-man brigade into the city to enhance security measures. This unit had been slated to return home, but continuing sectarian violence dictated its transfer from the northwestern part of the country.

July 30
Politics: In Baghdad, Iraq, several parliament members call for the dismissal of the interior minister due to his failure to suppress spiraling sectarian violence.

Terrorism: In Anbar Province, Iraq, incessant combat with insurgents takes the lives of four marines.

July 31
Military: The United States formally transfers military control of Afghanistan to NATO, which is now responsible for battling Taliban extremists and local drug lords.

August 1
Military: In Afghanistan, clashes with Taliban operatives result in the deaths of three British NATO soldiers.

Terrorism: A bombing and shooting spree across Iraq results in the deaths of at least 44 people.

August 2
Military: According to recent news reports, total U.S. military manpower in Iraq tops 133,000 troops. In light of escalating sectarian violence, it is painfully apparent they are not sufficient to stabilize the entire country.

Politics: In Baghdad, Iraq, President Jalal Talabani declares that the government is willing and able to take over security responsibilities for the entire country by year's end. Iraqi security forces have complete control of only one province, Muthanna, while the remaining 17 are in the hands of the Americans and their allies.

In Washington, D.C., Defense Secretary Donald Rumsfeld admits that while sectarian violence in Iraq appears to be on the increase, he refuses to state whether an all-out civil conflict is pending.

TERRORISM: In Anbar Province, Iraq, two American service members die in fighting with insurgents. Bombs and mortar shells also rock several soccer fields in Shiite parts of Baghdad, killing 53 people.

August 3

POLITICS: In Washington, D.C., General John P. Abizaid testifies before the Senate Armed Services Committee, in which he states that the levels of sectarian violence in Iraq are as bad as he has ever seen them. General Peter Pace, chairman of the Joint Chiefs of Staff, also declares that a religious-based civil war appears possible there.

TERRORISM: In the Panjwai district, Afghanistan, a suicide bomber kills 21 people.

August 4

POLITICS: In Iraq, large street protests take place around the country in support of Hezbollah militants in Palestine, then locked in deadly combat with Israel. Effigies of President George W. Bush and British prime minister Tony Blair are also burned.

TERRORISM: In Baghdad, Iraq, four roadside bombs kill seven Iraqis and wound five more.

August 9

POLITICS: In Washington, D.C., a CNN opinion poll finds that 60 percent of Americans question oppose continuing American involvement in Iraq; this is the highest percentage since Operation Iraqi Freedom began in March 2003.

August 10

TERRORISM: In Najaf, Iraq, a suicide bomber attacks a Shiite mosque, killing 35 people and wounding 122. An additional 37 Iraqis are killed in scattered fighting around the country.

August 11

DIPLOMACY: In New York City, the UN Security Council adopts Resolution 1700, which reaffirms the mandate of the UN Assistance Mission in Iraq for another year.

MILITARY: In Nurestan, Afghanistan, three U.S. soldiers die during clashes with supposed Taliban operatives.

August 12

MILITARY: In west Baghdad, Iraq, U.S. forces sweeping the neighborhood engage and kill 26 insurgents.

TERRORISM: Across the length of Iraq, scattered violence takes the lives of at least 50 Iraqis.

August 13

MILITARY: In Karbala, Iraq, Iraqi security forces engage a group of insurgents, killing 12.

TERRORISM: A Shiite neighborhood in Baghdad, Iraq, is hit by a string of bombings that kill at least 63 people and wound 143.

August 14

TERRORISM: In Baghdad, Iraq, a break in a gas pipeline leads to a tremendous explosion that injures 127 Iraqis. U.S. military authorities regard the matter as an unfortunate accident, but Prime Minister Nuri al-Maliki claims that the casualties are the result of a Sunni rocket and mortar attack on a Shiite area.

August 15

POLITICS: In Abu Ghraib, Iraq, the by-now infamous prison is emptied after 3,000 detainees are transferred to other locations, and the entire facility is handed back over to Iraqi security forces.

August 17

AVIATION: In Konar Province, Afghanistan, a U.S. air strike accidentally kills 12 Afghan policemen mistaken for insurgents.

TERRORISM: In Baghdad, Iraq, a car bomb explodes in Shiite neighborhood of Sadr City, killing 17 people.

August 19

POLITICS: In Washington, D.C., President George W. Bush's radio address reiterates his determination to stay the course in Iraq regardless of the sectarian violence occurring there. He maintains that such action is essential for defeating terrorists.

August 20

TERRORISM: In Baghdad, Iraq, snipers fire on Shiite religious processions, killing 20 people while 300 people are injured in the stampede that follows.

August 21

POLITICS: In Washington, D.C., President George W. Bush holds a televised news conference and declares that, while Iraq is "straining the psyche" of the nation, no American troops will be withdrawn "so long as I am president." He maintains that this is the only way to insure victory over the terrorists there.

In Tehran, Iran, Ayatollah Ali Khamenei declares that Iran will never forsake its nuclear technology despite the pressure being applied by foreign governments.

August 26

POLITICS: In Iraq, several hundred tribal chieftains sign a "pact of honor" to denounce sectarian violence and support national reconciliation.

In Iran, the government expands its nuclear program by starting up operations at a heavy-water nuclear plant.

August 27

POLITICS: In Baghdad, Iraq, Prime Minister Nuri al-Maliki appeals to his countrymen for an end to sectarian violence. He also denies that Iraqis would ever engage in a civil war.

TERRORISM: Across Iraq, an outbreak of random bombs and shooting takes the lives of 100 Iraqis. In the town of Khalis, an insurgent attack also kills two American soldiers.

August 28

MILITARY: Various military actions across Iraq take the lives of nine U.S. service personnel.

TERRORISM: In Helmand Province, Afghanistan, a suicide bomber kills 17 people.

August 29

POLITICS: In Salt Lake City, Utah, Defense Secretary Donald Rumsfeld addresses the American Legion convention and accuses opponents of the Iraq war of lacking the courage to fight terrorism and willing to engage in appeasement.

TERRORISM: In Baghdad, Iraq, government officials claim that, despite recent upswings in violence, new security measures by U.S. and Iraqi forces have resulted in a lower death toll for August than in the previous two months.

August 31

POLITICS: In Salt Lake City, Utah, President George W. Bush addresses the American Legion convention and calls the fight against Islamic extremism "the decisive ideological struggle of the 21st century."

TERRORISM: In Baghdad, Iraq, a coordinated series of bombing and attacks throughout Shiite neighborhoods kills 47 people and injures 200.

September 1

TERRORISM: In Washington, D.C., a Defense Department report indicates that Iraqi deaths rose 51 percent between May 20 and August 11 of this year. This translates into 120 deaths per day.

September 2

AVIATION: In Afghanistan, a British reconnaissance aircraft crashes, killing all 14 onboard.

MILITARY: In Kandahar Province, Afghanistan, Canadian NATO troops backed by Afghan security forces launch Operation Medusa to root out Taliban operatives there.

POLITICS: In New York City, the UN Office on Drugs and Crime states that opium production in Afghanistan has risen 50 percent over the previous year.

A CNN poll also released this day indicates that 58 percent of Americans surveyed oppose a continuing U.S. presence in Iraq, down two points from a month earlier.

September 3

MILITARY: U.S. forces capture Hamid Juma Faris, a senior al-Qaeda operative, in Iraq. He is best known for orchestrating the deadly attack against the Shiite Askariya Shrine last February.

September 4

TERRORISM: In Baghdad, Iraq, U.S. authorities announce that five servicemen were killed during insurgent attacks a day earlier. Iraqi police also discover the bodies of 33 victims of religious violence around the city, most of whom had been bound, gagged, and tortured before execution.

September 5

POLITICS: In Washington, D.C., President George W. Bush addresses a gathering of military veterans and likens the war against terrorism to that against Nazi Germany and the Soviet Union.

September 6

TERRORISM: President George W. Bush announces that 14 high-level terrorists have been transferred from abroad to detention pens at Guantánamo Bay, Cuba. He also awaits congressional authorization to conduct military tribunals for suspected terrorists.

September 7

POLITICS: In Atlanta, Georgia, President George W. Bush declares that America is safer five years after 9/11, due to action taken to protect the homeland.

In Iraq, coalition forces hand authority of all Iraqi armed forces over to Prime Minister Nuri al-Maliki.

September 8

POLITICS: In Washington, D.C., a report from the Senate Select Committee on Intelligence concludes that Saudi terrorist Osama bin Laden had no direct link to either Iraq or President Saddam Hussein. Democratic senator Jay Rockefeller IV also accuses President George W. Bush of misleading the nation in his pursuit of war with Iraq.

TERRORISM: A car bomb explodes outside the U.S. embassy in Kabul, Afghanistan, killing 16 people, including two American soldiers.

September 10

TERRORISM: In Gardez, Afghanistan, a suicide bomber kills the governor of Paktia Province and three other people.

September 11

POLITICS: On the fifth anniversary of the 9/11 terror attacks, President George W. Bush defends his decision to invade Iraq as part of the war against terror and insists "the worse mistake would be to think that if we pulled out, the terrorists would leave us alone."

TERRORISM: In Paktia Province, Afghanistan, the funeral procession for the late governor is attacked by a suicide bomber, who kills seven mourners and injures 40.

September 12

MILITARY: In Kandahar, Afghanistan, Canadian NATO forces conclude Operation Medusa, having killed between 250 and 500 Taliban operatives at a cost of four Canadians and one U.S. soldier dead.

September 16

POLITICS: In Baghdad, Iraq, Prime Minister Nuri al-Maliki again urges his countrymen to put aside traditional sectarian, ethnic, and political differences, and violence continues escalating in the capital. Since September 13 an additional 180 people have been killed in fighting.

September 18

TERRORISM: In a remote village in southern Afghanistan, a bomb kills four Canadians as they pass out gifts to Afghan children

September 19

DIPLOMACY: In New York City, President George W. Bush and Iranian president Mahmoud Ahmadinejad take turns addressing the UN General Assembly. Bush states that he has no objection to Iran pursuing peaceful nuclear power while Ahmadinejad rebukes the Security Council for demanding that his country stop its uranium-enrichment program.

MILITARY: In Washington, D.C., U.S. Middle East commander General John P. Abizaid gives a news conference in which he maintains the unlikelihood of American troop withdrawals from Iraq before the end of spring, 2007.

POLITICS: In Washington, D.C., former congressman Lee H. Hamilton and former secretary of state James A. Baker of the high-level Iraqi Study Group inform the news media that Iraq faces a critical need to justify the continuing presence of U.S. troops and support there.

September 21

POLITICS: In Baghdad, Iraq, the UN Assistance Mission records 6,599 Iraqi citizens killed during sectarian violence in July and August 2006.

In Washington, D.C., the 10-member, bipartisan Iraq Study Group has completed its six-month fact-finding tour, including interviews with high-level government officials; however, it sets no date for releasing its recommendations.

September 24

POLITICS: Several American newspapers report that a classified National Intelligence Estimate drafted in April concludes that the war in Iraq has actually worsened the terrorism threat by creating a new generation of Islamic radicals. The report concedes that the terrorist leadership in Iraq has been severely damaged, but also that the conflict there has strengthened the cause of radical Islam throughout the Middle East.

Former president Bill Clinton says in a televised interview that he had "worked hard" to try to kill or capture Saudi terrorist Osama bin Laden before leaving office in January 2001.

September 25

TERRORISM: In Kandahar Province, Afghanistan, terrorists shoot and kill Safia Amajan, who was the head of women's affairs in that province.

September 26

POLITICS: In Washington, D.C., President George W. Bush condemns the leaking of classified information concerning Iraq and maintains the recent war there has made it harder for terror organization to expand their numbers.

September 27

POLITICS: In Baghdad, Iraq, Saddam Hussein is ejected from court by the presiding judge for a third time after repeatedly shouting and gesticulating at him. He and his six co-defendants face the gallows if convicted of genocide.

October 3
MILITARY: Eight American soldiers die in Iraq, victims of roadside bombs and shooting incidents; this bring to 17 the total killed over the past four days.

October 4
MILITARY: In Baghdad, Iraq, a U.S. military spokesman announces that 21 servicemen have been killed over the previous five days and that in the past week the capital experienced the greatest number of bombings recorded in 2006.
POLITICS: In Iraq, the government suspended members of a police brigade after they were found to be assisting various death squads.

October 5
POLITICS: In Baghdad, Iraq, Secretary of State Condoleezza Rice warns Iraqi leaders that their time to settle political differences and learn to live amicably is limited. She also insists that current levels of violence throughout the country cannot be tolerated.

October 6
POLITICS: In Washington, D.C., former secretary of state James A. Baker, speaking as a member of the Iraq Study Group, mentions during a televised interview that his panel believes President George W. Bush should alter prevailing U.S. strategy in Iraq. It also suggests holding direct talks with the governments of Syria and Iran.

October 14
MILITARY: In Iraq, insurgent activity takes the lives of seven U.S. troops, bringing the total number of deaths for October to 28.

October 16
POLITICS: In Washington, D.C., President George W. Bush telephones Iraqi prime minister Nuri al-Maliki and assures him that he has no plans to pull U.S. forces out of Iraq.
TERRORISM: In Balad, Iraq, sectarian violence between Sunnis and Shiites continues as 91 Iraqis die in fighting. A further 76 civilians are reported to have been killed throughout the country over the past four days.

October 17
TERRORISM: In Washington, D.C., President George W. Bush signs legislation under which delineates rules for interrogating and prosecuting terrorists.

October 19
MILITARY: In Iraq, Major General William Caldwell admits that a recent, two-week campaign to eradicate insurgents and local militias had failed to reduce violence by an appreciable degree. Moreover, he intimates that a change in U.S. strategy is necessary.

In Washington, D.C., a Pentagon spokesman characterizes Caldwell's comments as candid and accurate.

October 20
TERRORISM: In an act of defiance, members of the Mahdi Army of cleric Moqtada al-Sadr seize the city of Amara, Iraq, then hand it back to Iraqi security forces.

October 23

TERRORISM: In Amarah, southern Iraq, news reports cite a new trend in the secular violence as extremist Shiites begin to attack and kill other Shiites.

October 24

MILITARY: In Baghdad, Iraq, American ambassador Zalmay Khalilzad and General George Casey declare that Iraqi security forces will be able to take over most security functions within the next 18 months.

October 25

MILITARY: In Washington, D.C., President George W. Bush says at a news conference that he is "not satisfied" with the situation in Iraq, but the United States is winning the war against terror and will adjust its tactics accordingly.

In Baghdad, Iraq, Prime Minister Nuri al-Maliki reacts negatively to the assertions of ambassador Zalmay Khalilzad and General George Casey, insisting that no country has the right to impose a timetable on Iraq or its security forces.

October 30

TERRORISM: In Baghdad, Iraq, and Anbar Province, sectarian and insurgent violence continues unabated, with the death toll of U.S. soldiers and marines exceeding 100 in the month of October.

November 2

TERRORISM: In Baghdad, Iraq, the Interior Ministry announces that 1,289 Iraqi civilians were killed in acts of violence in October.

November 5

POLITICS: In Baghdad, Iraq, a court unanimously sentences former Iraqi president Saddam Hussein to death by hanging for his role in the deaths of 148 men and boys in the Shiite town of Dujail in 1982. Hussein's brother-in-law, Barzan Ibrahim al-Hassan al-Tikriti, also draws a death sentence, while four other defendants will be imprisoned for life or up to 15 years. Throughout Iraq, Shiites and Kurds generally rejoice at the news while Sunnis react with outrage.

November 7

POLITICS: In the United States, midterm congressional elections are won by the Democratic Party, which campaigned strongly against the war in Iraq and promised to end U.S. involvement there.

November 8

POLITICS: In Washington, D.C., Secretary of Defense Donald Rumsfeld resigns from office in the wake of unfavorable midterm elections for the Republicans. He is succeeded by former CIA director Robert Gates, a university president and a member of the Iraq Study Group.

November 14–16

TERRORISM: In Baghdad, Iraq, a group of masked men invade the Ministry of Higher Education and kidnap several people in broad daylight. Nearby Iraqi security forces fail to intervene. However, the majority of those taken are released unharmed over the next two days.

November 15–17
MILITARY: In Washington, D.C., General John P. Abizaid of the U.S. Central Command testifies before the Senate Armed Services Committee. He argues for an increase in American troop strength in Iraq and against a timetable for an American withdrawal. He also flatly declares that the Bush administration failed to send adequate numbers of troops into the country following the fall of Saddam Hussein.

November 22
DIPLOMACY: In Baghdad, Iraq, a high-level Syrian diplomat visits Iraq for the first time in more than three years; he calls for a timetable for the withdrawal of all American forces.
TERRORISM: In New York City, the United Nations issues a report that estimates a total of 3,709 Iraqis were killed in sectarian violence in October. This averages out to 120 fatalities per day.

November 23
TERRORISM: In Baghdad, Iraq, car bombs and artillery fire resonate through the Shiite stronghold of Sadr City, killing more than 200 people and wounding scores more.

November 24
POLITICS: In Baghdad, Iraq, members of the National Assembly threaten to boycott the government if Prime Minister Nuri al-Maliki meets with President George W. Bush in Jordan.
TERRORISM: In Baquba, Iraq, armed Shiite militiamen storm into Sunni mosques in retaliation for attacks against them a day earlier; 200 people are killed.

November 25
DIPLOMACY: In London, United Kingdom, the government announces that it is withdrawing 6,000 troops by the end of 2007, leaving behind a force of only 1,000. In Warsaw, Poland, the government declares that its 900 soldiers in Iraq will be withdrawn by year's end.
MILITARY: North of Baghdad, Iraq, American troops, backed by Iraqi security forces, kill 22 insurgents.

November 29
DIPLOMACY: In Amman, Jordan, Iraqi prime minister Nuri al-Maliki declines to attend a meeting with President George W. Bush and King Abdullah II.
POLITICS: In Baghdad, Iraq, six cabinet members and 30 legislators resign from office to protest Prime Minister Nuri al-Maliki's proposed meeting with President George W. Bush in Amman, Jordan.

December 1
POLITICS: In Washington, D.C., a leaked classified memo mentions that former defense secretary Donald Rumsfeld has acknowledged the failure of the present "stay the course" strategy in Iraq, of which he was a major architect and proponent.

December 3
MILITARY: In Washington, D.C., the *Washington Post* publishes newly released Pentagon figures that American deaths in Iraq total 2,889; of these fatalities, 569 are due to "non-hostile action."

December 6
MILITARY: In Washington, D.C., Robert Gates is confirmed as secretary of defense by the U.S. Senate by a 95–2 vote. He had previously testified that, while the United States is not winning the struggle in Iraq, neither is it losing, and he urged patience. This same day the Iraqi Study Group, a bipartisan commission, releases a report that finds the situation in Iraq "grave and deteriorating." It also makes 79 recommendations, including withdrawing by 2008 all U.S. forces that are not essential for security.

December 9
POLITICS: In Baghdad, Iraq, Shiites and Kurds disagree with the findings of the Iraq Study Group report, while Sunni politicians also disagree with many of the proposed solutions for solving the nation's security problems.

December 10
POLITICS: In Baghdad, Iraq, President Jalal Talabani strongly takes issue with the conclusion of the Iraq Study Group findings and regards its findings as injurious to Iraqi sovereignty.
TERRORISM: In northern Iraq, a series of bombing and shootings takes the lives of 66 people, 46 of which were executed by sectarian death squads.

December 11
POLITICS: In Tehran, Iran, students at the University of Tehran heckle visiting President Mahmoud Ahmadinejad and throw firecrackers at his motorcade.
TERRORISM: North of Baghdad, Iraq, a roadside bombing kills three American soldiers, already making December one of the deadliest months of the Iraq occupation.

December 12
DIPLOMACY: In Washington, D.C., President George W. Bush confers with Iraqi vice president Tariq al-Hashemi in an attempt to smooth ruffled feathers arising from the Iraq Study Group recommendations.

December 14
POLITICS: In Baghdad, Iraq, Senator John McCain, a presumptive Republican presidential candidate, pays visits with Iraqi officials and says that the United States needs additional forces there. This assertion is the opposite reached by the bipartisan Iraq Study Group.

December 15
POLITICS: In Iran, national elections for local councils and the Assembly of Experts are won by reformers and opponents of hard-line conservative President Mahmoud Ahmadinejad.

December 16

POLITICS: In Baghdad, Iraq, Prime Minister Nuri al-Maliki announces that his government is now willing to accept the services of certain Baath Party members who were previously purged by the Americans in March 2003. This is viewed as an olive branch extended to the Sunnis, and President George W. Bush lauds the decision.

In Basra, Iraq, Senator John Kerry, an opponent of the war, says that the United States will face extreme challenges in obtaining whatever victory can be achieved in Iraq.

TERRORISM: In Iskandariyah, Iraq, sectarian violence takes the lives of 23 civilians, including two noted Sunni leaders. Meanwhile, in Baghdad, police uncover the bodies of 53 men who had been bound, gagged, then executed by death squads.

December 18

MILITARY: In Iraq, U.S. military authorities announce the death of three soldiers and marines, bringing the death toll for December up to 60.

POLITICS: In Washington, D.C., newly appointed defense secretary Robert Gates declares that American failure in Iraq would be disastrous.

December 20

POLITICS: In Washington, D.C., President George W. Bush informs a news conference that he has not yet decided whether he will dispatch reinforcements to Iraq. However, he insists that he will not open talks with the government of Iran or Syria, as recommended by the Iraq Study Group.

The Congressional Research Service notes that the war in Iraq has cost the American taxpayers $350 billion to date. The Pentagon also requests an additional $99.7 billion to fund its activities in both Iraq and Afghanistan.

December 21

MILITARY: Military prosecutors accuse four marines of committing atrocities against 24 Iraqi civilians at Haditha, Iraq; they are to face courts-martial for murder.

December 22

MILITARY: In Baghdad, Iraq, U.S. military authorities announce that five servicemen have been killed in action, bringing the cumulative death toll for December up to 76, the second highest monthly number for the year.

POLITICS: In Washington, D.C., Defense Secretary Robert Gates returns from a trip to Iraq, during which he weighed the possibility of increasing the 140,000 troops already there.

December 23

DIPLOMACY: In New York City, the UN Security Council approves a resolution banning the import or export of materials deemed useful to Iran's nuclear energy program. It also freezes the assets of a number of institutions and individuals thought involved in this matter.

December 26
POLITICS: In Baghdad, Iraq, an Iraqi appeals court upholds the death sentence of former president Saddam Hussein for crimes against humanity. The sentence is required by law to be carried out within 30 days, and, reportedly, throngs of Iraqis volunteer to pull the trap lever on the gallows.

December 28
POLITICS: In Crawford, Texas, President George W. Bush confers with his key senior advisers on a new policy for Iraq, which he promises to announce in the new year.

December 30
POLITICS: In a tightly guarded government security building north of Baghdad, Iraq, former president Saddam Hussein is sent to the gallows and hung.
MILITARY: Action against Iraqi insurgents takes the lives of six American servicemen, making December the deadliest month of the year for U.S. forces.
TERRORISM: In Baghdad, Iraq, loyal followers of Saddam Hussein set off four car bombs in predominately Shiite parts of the city, killing 70 people and injuring several more.

December 31
MILITARY: The government announces that the death toll for U.S. forces in Iraq for December is 115; the total since March 2003 is 3,000, with an additional 22,000 wounded. Estimates of the number of Iraqi civilians killed at the hands of numerous insurgent groups ranges from 30,000 to 650,000.

Two U.S. Explosive Ordnance Disposal technicians prepare to deploy their F-6 Andros robot to examine a suspected improvised explosive device while clearing a route for a convoy. *(Defense Imagery)*

2007

January 7
AVIATION: An Air Force AC-130H Spectre gunship attacks a suspected al-Qaeda training camp in Somalia.

January 10
MILITARY: In Washington, D.C., President George W. Bush announces the impending dispatch of 20,000 additional troops to Iraq in the hopes that this "surge" will lead to fewer outbreaks of violence there. Democrats who control Congress cannot muster sufficient votes to oppose him.

January 12
POLITICS: In Washington, D.C. Secretary of State Condoleezza Rice announces that President George W. Bush has authorized attacks on known Iranian agents operating in Iraq and training terrorist teams there.

January 16
TERRORISM: In New York City, the United Nations releases a report suggesting that 34,000 Iraqis were killed in sectarian violence in 2006.

In Iraq, two car bombs explode outside the entrance to Mustansiriya University as students departed classes; 70 people are killed.

January 17
TERRORISM: In Baghdad, Iraq, the government announces that it has arrested and detained several leaders associated with the Shiite Mahdi Army of cleric Moqtada al-Sadr.

January 20
AVIATION: Over northern Baghdad, Iraq, a UH-60 Black Hawk helicopter crashes, possibly from insurgent fire; all 13 passengers are killed.

January 22
TERRORISM: In Baghdad, Iraq, two car bombs explode in a crowded market, killing more than 80 people.

January 23
POLITICS: During his annual State of the Union address, President George W. Bush reiterates his plan to dispatch 20,000 additional troops to Iraq, confident that this "surge" will bring violence there to a halt.
MILITARY: In Washington, D.C., Lieutenant General David H. Petraeus testifies before Congress and admits that while the situation is "dire," it is certainly not "hopeless." He also strongly endorses the president's planned "surge."

January 24
AVIATION: Air-force gunships conduct a second round of strikes against suspected al-Qaeda terrorist training camps in Somalia.

POLITICS: In Washington, D.C., the Democratic-controlled Senate Foreign Relations Committee votes 12 to 9 to oppose President George W. Bush's intended "surge" in Iraq.

January 26
MILITARY: In Washington, D.C., the U.S. Senate unanimously approves Lieutenant General David H. Petraeus to serve as the new top commander of occupation forces in Iraq.

January 28
MILITARY: Near Najif, Iraq, U.S. troops and Iraqi ground forces battle a group of Sunni insurgents who are bent upon attacking and killing Shiite religious pilgrims celebrating the festival of Ashura; an estimated 250 terrorists are slain.

February 2
POLITICS: In Washington, D.C., a new National Intelligence Estimate is released by the 16 U.S. intelligence agencies, which states that Iraq, like it or not, is engulfed by a religious civil war between Sunnis and Shiites. It doubts there is much that the U.S. military or the Iraqi government can do about it but warns that a pullout of U.S. forces would certainly lead to escalating religious violence.

February 3
TERRORISM: In Baghdad, Iraq, a powerful truck bomb explodes in a predominately Shiite marketplace, killing 135 people and wounding more than 300.

February 7
AVIATION: Near Baghdad, Iraq, a Marine Corps helicopter crashes, apparently after taking ground fire.

February 10
MILITARY: In Iraq, Lieutenant General David H. Petraeus replaces Lieutenant General George W. Casey Jr. as head of coalition occupation forces.

February 11
MILITARY: In Baghdad, Iraq military authorities display evidence of Iranian involvement in terrorist activities throughout Iraq, mostly shaped "penetrator" charges that can destroy armored vehicles. They also says that recent raids by American forces in Baghdad have netted six members of the elite Iranian Revolutionary Guards. They have long been suspected of fomenting unrest among the sizable Shiite population.

February 12
TERRORISM: In Baghdad, Iraq, four car bombs explode in a Shiite marketplace, killing 70 people and wounding 120.

February 13
TERRORISM: In Washington, D.C., General Peter Pace, chairman of the Joint Chiefs of Staff, denies that there is a direct link between Iraqi terrorists and the Iranian

government, even though some bomb components aimed at American troops were manufactured in Iran.

February 18
TERRORISM: Two car bombs explode in a Shiite marketplace in Baghdad, Iraq, killing 60 people and injuring scores more.

February 19
MILITARY: North of Baghdad, Iraq, insurgents attack a U.S. Army patrol, killing two soldiers and wounding 17.

February 21
MILITARY: In London, United Kingdom, Prime Minister Tony Blair announces that he is withdrawing 1,600 British soldiers from Iraq within a few months. Roughly 6,000 will remain behind.

February 24
TERRORISM: In Ramadi, Iraq, a truck bomb explodes next to a Sunni mosque, killing 36 people.

February 25
TERRORISM: In Baghdad, Iraq, a suicide bomber kills 50 people outside a local university.

February 27
TERRORISM: Outside Bagram Air Base, Afghanistan, a suicide bomber kills 23 people and injures 24 during a visit by Vice President Richard Cheney.

March 4
MILITARY: In Baghdad, Iraq, 1,000 U.S. troops and Iraqi security forces sweep through the Shiite neighborhood of Sadr City, searching houses and establishing checkpoints. No casualties are reported.

March 4–7
TERRORISM: In Karbala, Iraq, Sunni insurgents commence a series of bombings against Shiite pilgrims in and around this holy city, killing 77 people and wounding 125 more. Attacks elsewhere result in another 40 deaths.

March 10
DIPLOMACY: In Baghdad, Iraq, U.S. and Iranian diplomats meet in an attempt to reduce the levels of sectarian violence in the country. The gathering includes representatives from the five permanent members of the UN Security Council and all six of Iraq's neighbors.

March 16
MILITARY: General John P. Abizaid is replaced by Admiral William J. Fallon as head of the U.S. Central Command.

March 19
POLITICS: In Washington, D.C., President George W. Bush gives a short speech marking the fourth anniversary of the war and declares that while the recent troop

"surge" has made some progress in bringing down levels of violence, more work remains to be done.

March 20

POLITICS: In Baghdad, Iraq, former vice president Taha Yassin Ramadan is hanged for his role in the deaths of 148 Shiites in Dujial in 1982.

March 23

MILITARY: In the Shatt al-Arab waterway, eight British sailors and seven Royal Marines in two inflatable boats are seized by Iranian Revolutionary Guards after they allegedly stray into Iranian territory. The British government strongly denies the allegation.

March 24

DIPLOMACY: In New York City, the UN Security Council votes unanimously to endorse tougher sanctions against Iran for failing to suspend its uranium-enrichment program. This action also strengthens financial sanctions approved in December 2006.

March 26

MILITARY: Four generals are rebuked by Pentagon officials for their role in covering up the friendly-fire death of former football hero Pat Tillman in Afghanistan.

March 27

TERRORISM: In the Shiite settlement of Tal Afar, Iraq, two car bombs explode, killing 83 people and wounding scores more; Shiite gunmen shoot 70 nearby Sunnis in retaliation.

March 28

DIPLOMACY: In Riyadh, Saudi Arabia, King Abdullah of Jordan declares that the U.S. occupation of Iraq is illegal.

March 29

TERRORISM: In Baghdad, Iraq, five suicide bombers attack heavily Shiite-populated districts, killing 125 people.

April 4

MILITARY: In Washington, D.C., the Defense Department issues a report suggesting that sectarian violence and attacks in Iraq have declined 26 percent since the recent "surge" was enacted. General David H. Petraeus, senior commander in Iraq, concedes that while security has improved in Baghdad, attacks still persist in other parts of the country.

April 5

DIPLOMACY: In Tehran, Iran, President Mahmoud Ahmadinejad orders 15 British personnel (including one woman) released after 13 days in captivity.

April 6

MILITARY: The 15 British service personnel freed by Iran hold a news conference to declare that they had been roughly treated and coerced into making televised statements that they deliberately entered Iranian territory.

TERRORISM: In Ramadi, Iraq, a truck loaded with chlorine gas explodes, killing 27 people, mostly children.

April 9
DIPLOMACY: In Tehran, Iran, President Mahmoud Ahmadinejad announces that Iran's nuclear program now has the capacity to produce its own uranium for nuclear power plants. He reiterates that UN sanctions will not deter the country from pursuing nuclear energy.

April 11
MILITARY: In Washington, D.C., Secretary of Defense Robert Gates announces that military tours in Iraq and Afghanistan will be extended three months to a total of 15 months. This step is undertaken to ensure that current manpower levels in Iraq can be maintained.

April 12
TERRORISM: In Baghdad, Iraq, a suicide bombing within the city's Green Zone occurs inside a cafeteria frequented by members of the national parliament; one member dies, and 22 are wounded.

April 18
TERRORISM: In Baghdad, Iraq, a car bomb explodes in a crowded market, killing 127 people and wounding 148.

April 23
MILITARY: In Diyala Province, Iraq, a suicide car bomber targets a patrol of the 82nd Airborne Division, killing nine soldiers and wounding 20.

May 2
MILITARY: In Shindand, Afghanistan, Afghan authorities claim that U.S. Marine Corps operations there resulted in the deaths of 42 civilians, prompting President Hamid Karzai to chide his allies for not doing more to reduce casualties among noncombatants.

May 8
MILITARY: In Afghanistan, marine colonel Jack Nicholson admits that recent operations in Shindand had accidentally taken the lives of 19 civilians, and that each of the victims' families were compensated $2,000 per Afghan law.

May 9
AVIATION: Afghan authorities claim that a U.S. air strike in Sarwan Qala, Afghanistan, killed 21 civilians a day earlier.

May 11
MILITARY: In Iraq, Major General Benjamin Mixon, commanding U.S. forces north of Baghdad, says that he needs additional troops and that the Iraqi government is both corrupt and dysfunctional.

May 13
MILITARY: In Helmand Province, Afghanistan, U.S., NATO, and Afghan security forces kill Mullah Dadullah. He is one of the highest-ranking Taliban leaders to die in combat.

May 15

MILITARY: In Washington, D.C., President George W. Bush nominates Lieutenant General Douglas Lute to serve as "war czar" for coordinating military matters in Iraq and Afghanistan.

POLITICS: In Iraq, the U.S. military states that 100,000 to 300,000 barrels of oil go unaccounted for every day. This represents a loss of $5 million and $15 million in revenues to the government.

May 24

MILITARY: In Washington, D.C., the Democratic-controlled Congress yields to the Republican administration of President George W. Bush by approving billions of dollars for the war in Iraq without attaching a timetable for withdrawal. Antiwar groups responsible for the recent Democratic victory cry foul.

May 25

POLITICS: In Kufa, Iraq, cleric Moqtada al-Sadr reappears after a long hiatus to denounce the continuing U.S. occupation.

June 13

MILITARY: In Washington, D.C., the Defense Department releases a report suggesting that while the level of violence in Baghdad and Anbar Province, Iraq, has declined dramatically since the troop "surge" began in February, attacks continue in other parts of the country.

June 15

MILITARY: In Washington, D.C., the Defense Department announces that the 28,500-person "surge" in Iraq is now complete, boosting American strength in that country to 160,000 men and women.

June 17

MILITARY: In Iraq, Lieutenant General Raymond Odierno says that attacks in Baghdad are way down and that 40 percent of the city is safe "on a routine basis."

June 19

MILITARY: In Baquba, Iraq, 10,000 U.S. troops, supported by 3,000 Iraqis, attack an insurgent stronghold. They are assisted by two Sunni organizations that had turned against the jihadist group al-Qaeda in Iraq. This is an early manifestation of what becomes generally known as the "Sunni awakening."

June 24

POLITICS: In Baghdad, Iraq, a court sentences former general Ali Hassan al-Majid, also known as "Chemical Ali," to death for crimes against humanity. His use of poison and nerve agents killed thousands of Kurds in 1987 and 1988.

June 28

MILITARY: In Washington, D.C., the Senate confirms Lieutenant General Douglas Lute as the new "war czar" for Iraq and Afghanistan.

July 2

TERRORISM: In Iraq, Brigadier General Kevin Bergner announces that the Quds (Jerusalem) Force of the Iranian Revolutionary Guards is training Iraqi Shiites in terrorist tactics at three camps outside Tehran, Iran. It is also supplying money and arms to the insurgents.

July 7
TERRORISM: In Amerli, Iraq, a truck bomb explodes among the Shiite Turkmen population, killing 150 people and injuring 240.

July 16
TERRORISM: In Kirkuk, Iraqi Kurdistan, a truck bomb explodes outside the headquarters of President Jalal Talabani's Patriotic Union of Kurdistan, killing more than 80 people and wounding 180.

July 24
DIPLOMACY: In Baghdad, Iraq, representatives from Iran, Iraq, and the United States gather to form a security subcommittee.

July 25
TERRORISM: In Baghdad, Iraq, celebrations of the Iraqi soccer team's victory over Saudi Arabia in Indonesia is marred by several explosions that kill 50 people.

July 26
DIPLOMACY: In Amman, Jordan, representatives from the United States, the United Nations, and the European Union gather to discuss ways of addressing the issue of the 1.5 million Iraqi refugees in Syria and 750,000 refugees in Jordan.

July 30
POLITICS: In Baghdad, Iraq, the national parliament declares a recess, even though much important legislation remains to be discussed.

August 1
POLITICS: In Baghdad, Iraq, six Sunni cabinet members complain that Prime Minister Nuri al-Maliki has restricted their participation in discussions on important issues.

August 14
TERRORISM: In Iraqi Kurdistan, four truck bombs explode in two remote villages, killing 250 people and wounding 350 more. A week later the Red Cross claims the toll was closer to 500 dead and 1,500 wounded.

August 21
DIPLOMACY: In Baghdad, Iraq, U.S. ambassador Ryan Crocker says that the government of Prime Minister Nuri al-Maliki has got "to do more" about national security and national reconciliation.

August 22
POLITICS: President George W. Bush addresses the Veterans of Foreign Wars, declaring that a premature pullout of U.S. forces from Iraq would lead to catastrophic loss of life there, as happened in South Vietnam.

August 23

MILITARY: In Washington, D.C., a National Intelligence Estimate issued by 16 intelligence agencies concludes that while the recent troop surge brought about improved security, it is unlikely that Iraqi leaders could effectively end sectarian violence by 2008, when U.S. troop levels are expected to decline. It warns that a premature pullout of forces would precipitate a religious war of catastrophic proportions.

August 28

POLITICS: In Reno, Nevada, President George W. Bush tells an American Legion convention that the establishment of a friendly government in Iraq is the best protection against Iran and a potential "nuclear holocaust" there.

September 2–3

MILITARY: In Basra, Iraq, the British army withdraws from its last base in the city. The 550-man garrison joins the 5,000 troops stationed at Basra airport outside of town.

September 3

DIPLOMACY: In Baghdad, Iraq, President George W. Bush makes a surprise visit to al-Asad Air Base to confer with Prime Minister Nuri al-Maliki and Sunni tribal leaders wishing to join coalition forces in the fight against insurgents.

September 11

MILITARY: In Washington, D.C., Lieutenant General David H. Petraeus testifies before a joint committee of Congress that the military "surge" has greatly reduced violence levels in Iraq. He therefore is in favor of a 30,000-troop drawdown in the region by 2008. Petraeus appears with U.S. ambassador Ryan Crocker, who also faces tough questioning.

September 13

POLITICS: In Washington, D.C., President George W. Bush makes a televised address to endorse General David H. Petraeus's recommendations regarding the gradual withdrawal of 30,000 U.S. combat troops from Iraq. He also maintains that the troop "surge" had successfully quelled violence there.

TERRORISM: In Iraq, Abdul Sattar Buzaigh al-Rishawi, a Sunni leader who recently conferred with President George W. Bush, is killed in a bomb attack.

September 16

MILITARY: In Baghdad, eight Iraqis are killed in a firefight involving armed employees of Blackwater USA, a private security firm. The Iraqi government denounces the killings and begins an investigation.

September 24

POLITICS: In New York City, Iranian president Mahmoud Ahmadinejad speaks at Columbia University after being accused by university president Lee Bollinger of acting like "a petty and cruel dictator."

September 25

DIPLOMACY: In New York City, Iranian president Mahmoud Ahmadinejad gets a chilly reception during his visit to the United Nations to address the General Assembly. At the podium he repeats that Iran will not abandon its nuclear power program despite the machinations of "arrogant powers."

TERRORISM: In Iraq, a terrorist group calling itself the Islamic State of Iraq claims responsibility for a bombing that killed 18 Sunni officials at a banquet marking local reconciliation efforts.

October 1

MILITARY: In Iraq, the U.S. military announces that 64 service members were killed in Iraq in September, down from 84 in August.

TERRORISM: In Baghdad, Iraq, a government official says that 884 civilians and 78 police were killed in September through sectarian violence, half the amount slain during the previous August.

October 5

AVIATION: A U.S. air strike near a largely Shiite-populated town kills 25 people, according to local authorities. A military spokesman says the strike came in response to an armed attack against army troops approaching the town.

October 6

POLITICS: In Iraq, a truce is arranged between Shiite forces under cleric Moqtada al-Sadr and a rival figure, Abdul Aziz Hakim.

October 7

POLITICS: In Baghdad, Iraq, the government condemns the actions of Blackwater U.S.A. on September 16, characterizing them as "deliberate murder."

October 8

DIPLOMACY: In London, United Kingdom, Prime Minister Gordon Brown announces that he will reduce the number of British troops in Iraq by half in the spring of 2008. He cites progress made by Iraqi security forces as the reason.

October 9

DIPLOMACY: In Ankara, Turkey, the parliament authorizes Turkish troops to invade northern Iraq and hunt down Kurdish guerrillas staging attacks from there. Recent clashes along the border region had cost the lives of two dozen Turkish troops.

October 10

DIPLOMACY: In Washington, D.C., the House Foreign Relations Committee passes a resolution condemning the massacre of Armenians by Turkey in 1915–23. In a heated response, the Turkish government warns that it will withdraw its support of U.S. actions in Iraq if the resolution is adopted by Congress.

October 11

AVIATION: A U.S. air strike on an insurgent position kills 19 militants and 15 civilians, according to Iraqi authorities.

October 12
POLITICS: In Arlington, Virginia, retired Lieutenant General Ricardo Sanchez admonishes the Bush administration for what he perceives as inadequate planning in the Iraq conflict. He also says that the celebrated troop "surge" is doomed to fail and that Iraq remains "a nightmare with no end in sight."

October 25
DIPLOMACY: In Washington, D.C., Secretary of State Condoleezza Rice and Treasury Secretary Henry Paulson introduce a new policy of heightened sanctions against Iran due to the Quds (Jerusalem) Force of the Revolutionary Guard's support of terrorism in the Middle East.

November
MILITARY: By midmonth, American combat fatalities in Afghanistan exceed 100, the highest annual total since the conflict began in October 2001. However, in Iraq, troop deaths will drop from a high of 126 in May to 37 in November.

November 6
MILITARY: The recent loss of six Americans makes 2007 the deadliest year for fighting in Iraq, bringing the total number of dead to 852.
TERRORISM: In northern Afghanistan, a parliamentary delegation touring educational facilities is struck by a suicide bomber, killing 77 people, including 67 children.

November 17
TERRORISM: In Afghanistan, a government investigation concludes that some of the casualties in the November 6 terrorist attack can be attributed to the parliamentary delegation's bodyguards.

November 18
TERRORISM: In Iraq, the monthly U.S. combat fatality total drops to 37, down from a high of 126 in May 2007. Thanks to the recent troop surge, the number of terrorist attacks against American troops has declined to its lowest level since January 2006.

November 24
MILITARY: In Diyala Province, Iraq, a brigade of 5,000 American soldiers is withdrawn and sent home, leaving overall troop strength at 157,000.

November 25
POLITICS: In Washington, D.C., the *Washington Post* reports that a recent National Security Council investigation of affairs in Afghanistan declared that the United States, NATO, and the Afghan government have failed to meet their strategic objectives.

December 3
DIPLOMACY: In Washington, D.C., a National Intelligence Estimate suggests that Iran has probably halted its work on nuclear weapons for the time being. The report is culled from the assessments of 16 U.S. intelligence agencies, which report their findings with "high confidence."

December 4
DIPLOMACY: In Washington, D.C., President George W. Bush plays down the recent intelligence report, noting that "Iran was dangerous, Iran is dangerous, and Iran will be dangerous, if they have the knowledge necessary to make a nuclear weapon."

December 10
MILITARY: U.S., NATO, and Afghan forces recapture the southern Taliban stronghold of Musa Qala in Helmand Province. This town is in one of the main poppy-growing regions in southern Afghanistan and is a major source of revenue from the drug trade.

December 16
DIPLOMACY: In Basra, Iraq, the British military formally turns control of the southern region over to Iraqi security forces. This constitutes the most significant turnover to the government since 2003, but 4,500 British troops remain in Iraq.

December 25
TERRORISM: In Baiji, Iraq, a suicide truck bomber strikes at a line of people waiting to receive rations of cooking gas; 25 are killed.

December 29
MILITARY: In Iraq, Lieutenant General David H. Petraeus reports that car bombings and other terrorist attacks have fallen by 60 percent since the start of the military "surge" in June 2007. However, 899 American troops have been killed, which, ironically, also makes this the deadliest year for American forces. Petraeus nonetheless considers al-Qaeda the greatest menace facing Iraqi stability and reconciliation.

December 31
MILITARY: The Associated Press reports that 110 American soldiers have died in Afghanistan this month, the highest number since Operation Enduring Freedom began in October 2001. The war also claimed an estimated 4,500 Taliban militants and 925 Afghan police.

2008

January 8
MILITARY: In Diyala Province, Iraq, U.S. and Iraqi forces conduct Operation Iron Harvest, which is aimed at eliminating final pockets of guerrillas from the region.
TERRORISM: In and around Mosul, northern Iraq, insurgents detonate a series of bombs aimed at U.S. troops; no casualties are reported.

January 9
POLITICS: The World Health Organization reports that an estimated 151,000 Iraqi civilians died between March 2003 and June 2006, mostly to acts of terrorism.

January 12
POLITICS: In Baghdad, Iraq, the national parliament passes a law allowing up to 27,000 members of the defunct Baathist Party to seek government jobs in the public sector, though they are barred from the Defense and Interior Ministries.

January 14

TERRORISM: In Kabul, Afghanistan, a bomb explodes in a luxury hotel, killing seven people. A shadowy terrorist known only as Homayoun claims responsibility.

January 15

MILITARY: In Washington, D.C., the Defense Department announces a one-time deployment of 3,200 marines to Afghanistan to thwart the possibility of a spring offensive by the Taliban. This step temporarily raises the total number of American troops there to 30,000; they are assisted by an additional 28,000 NATO troops.

January 18

MILITARY: During the Shiite Ashura festival, the militant Soldiers of Heaven give battle to Iraqi forces throughout southern Iraq, killing at least 66 people.

January 22

POLITICS: In Baghdad, Iraq, the government unveils the new national flag, which is identical to the old one save for the removal of the three Baath stars.

January 29

AVIATION: A missile strike launched by an unmanned Predator drone kills senior al-Qaeda leader Abu Laith al-Libi in the village of Khushali Torikel, North Waziristan, Pakistan. He is thought to be responsible for the failed suicide attack against Vice President Richard Cheney at Bagram Air Base, Afghanistan, in February 2007, which killed 23 people.

January 30

POLITICS: In Washington, D.C., retired general James L. Jones, chairman of the Atlantic Council, releases a report that maintains that NATO is not "winning" the war in Afghanistan because the country remains a "failing state." It cites poverty, a growing trade in opium, and resilient Taliban and al-Qaeda insurgents as the main causes.

February 1

TERRORISM: In Baghdad, Iraq, two suicide bombers attack a pet market, killing 99 people and injuring 123. The bombers were women with a history of psychiatric problems who had been recruited by the insurgents.

February 13

POLITICS: In Baghdad, Iraq, the national legislature authorizes a 2008 budget, an outline for provincial powers, and a sweeping amnesty for thousands of political prisoners. The last provision was a significant benchmark demanded by the U.S. government.

February 17

TERRORISM: In Kandahar, Afghanistan, a Taliban suicide bomber strikes an outdoor dogfighting competition, killing more than 100 people.

February 18

TERRORISM: In Spin Boldak, southern Afghanistan, a suicide bomber blows himself up near a Canadian military convoy, killing 38 people and injuring four Canadians.

February 24

POLITICS: In Iraq, cleric Moqtada al-Sadr announces he is extending his cease-fire for his Mahdi Army by another six months.

TERRORISM: In Iskandariyah, Iraq, a suicide bomber targeting Shiite pilgrims venturing to Karbala kills 56 people and injures 68.

February 28

MILITARY: The British government confirms that Prince Harry, third in line to the throne, had been serving in Helmand Province, Afghanistan, for the past 10 weeks. Once this becomes public knowledge, the prince receives orders to return home.

February 29

MILITARY: In northern Iraq, Turkish forces conclude an eight-day foray against Kurdish guerrillas and withdraw back to their homeland.

March 6

TERRORISM: In Baghdad, Iraq, two sequential bombs explode in a Shiite shopping district, killing at least 68 people.

March 11

MILITARY: In Tampa, Florida, Admiral William J. "Fox" Fallon unexpectedly announces his retirement as head of U.S. Central Command, concluding a distinguished career spanning four decades. Lately he had been less than enthusiastic about the turn of events in Iraq and favored a more rapid pullout of U.S. troops than General David H. Petraeus.

March 14

POLITICS: In Iran, conservative candidates allied with President Mahmoud Ahmadinejad win the first round of parliamentary elections by taking 163 of 260 seats in the Majlis. They also capture 19 of 35 seats in the Tehran City council.

March 17

DIPLOMACY: In Baghdad, Iraq, Vice President Richard Cheney arrives for talks with senior Iraqi officials.

TERRORISM: In the holy Shiite city of Karbala, Iraq, a bomb explodes, killing 43 people.

March 19

POLITICS: In Washington, D.C., President George W. Bush marks the fifth anniversary of Operation Iraqi Freedom by reiterating that the war was correct and that it will continue until absolute victory is attained.

March 23

MILITARY: In Baghdad, Iraq, an improvised explosive device kills four U.S. soldiers, raising the total number of American war-related fatalities to 4,000 and 29,600 wounded. Sectarian violence also takes the lives of 58 Iraqis.

March 25–30

MILITARY: In Baghdad, Iraq, President Nuri al-Maliki declares a military offensive against "rogue" Shiite militias in Basra who have been causing trouble; the operation ends five days later with 350 people killed, mostly from the Mahdi Army of cleric Moqtada al-Sadr.

March 30
POLITICS: In Baghdad, Iraq, cleric Moqtada al-Sadr orders his followers in Basra to stop fighting in return for certain concessions from the central government.

April 1
MILITARY: In London, United Kingdom, Defense Minister Desmond Browne says he is slowing down the scheduled drawdown of British forces in southern Iraq until the security situation there is better stabilized.
TERRORISM: In Baghdad, Iraq, the Interior Ministry announces that 2,012 Iraq civilians were killed in terrorist attacks in March.

April 6
MILITARY: In Afghanistan, a team under Captain Kyle Walton from the 3rd Battalion, 3rd Special Forces Group, engages 200 dug-in Taliban militants in the Shok Valley, a violent encounter that results in 10 Silver Stars being awarded.

April 8–9
POLITICS: In Washington, D.C., General David H. Petraeus testifies before Congress that significant progress continues to be made at reducing violence levels in Iraq but success remains fragile. He therefore recommends that after the troop presence drops to its pre-surge level of 140,000 men, all future withdrawals be suspended for an additional 45 days.

April 10
MILITARY: In Washington, D.C., President George W. Bush announces that he is accepting the recommendation of General David H. Petraeus regarding a suspension of troop pullouts.

April 23
MILITARY: In Washington, D.C., President George W. Bush announces that General David H. Petraeus is the new head of U.S. Central Command with responsibility for waging the war against terrorism throughout the Middle East and Central Asia. Lieutenant General Raymond Odierno will succeed him as top commander in Iraq.

April 27
TERRORISM: In Kabul, Afghanistan, President Hamid Karzai narrowly escapes an assassination attempt while observing a military parade. Three people are killed and 11 are wounded in the cross fire between the assassins and his bodyguards.

April 30
TERRORISM: In Kabul, Afghanistan, Afghan security forces kill wanted terrorist Hmayoun at his militant hideout.

May
MILITARY: In Iraq, American troop deaths for April are reported at 19, the lowest level since the war began in March 2003.

May 2
TERRORISM: The Associated Press reports that Iraqi civilian deaths for the month of April totaled 1,080.

May 5
DIPLOMACY: In Tehran, Iran, the government says it is suspending talks with the United States on Iraqi security.

May 10
POLITICS: In Baghdad, Iraq, negotiations between the national legislature and Shiite representatives of cleric Moqtada al-Sadr agree on a truce in the Sadr City region of the capital. This leads to a general drop in the number of U.S. and civilian deaths for the rest of the month.

June
MILITARY: The Associated Press reports that 45 coalition troops, including 27 Americans, were killed in Afghanistan in May; this is the highest one-month total since Operation Enduring Freedom began in October 2001. This number is higher than the number of troops killed in Iraq, which totals 31, including 29 Americans.

June 3
MILITARY: In Afghanistan, Lieutenant General David A. McKiernan is appointed commanding officer.

June 10
MILITARY: In Afghanistan, U.S. forces engage in a fight with Taliban militants just along the Pakistani border. This is followed by an air strike in the region that the Pakistani government claims killed 11 paramilitary soldiers.

June 12
DIPLOMACY: In Paris, France, representatives from several governments pledge $21 billion in aid for Afghanistan; the money will be spent to fight poverty, drugs, and violence.

TERRORISM: In Washington, D.C., a ruling by the Supreme Court invalidates the Military Commissions Act of 2006, thereby allowing detainees kept at Guantánamo Bay, Cuba, to challenge their detention in federal court.

June 13
TERRORISM: In Kandahar, Afghanistan, militants raid the Sarposa prison at night, freeing about 1,200 inmates, including 350 known Taliban.

July
MILITARY: In Iraq, the monthly death toll of American troops falls to 13, the lowest since Operation Iraqi Freedom commenced in March 2003.

July 6
AVIATION: In Nangarhar Province, Afghanistan, an American air strike kills several Taliban militants. However, Afghan government officials say that 47 civilians at a nearby wedding party also died.

July 7
TERRORISM: In Kabul, Afghanistan, a car bombing outside the Indian embassy kills 54 people.

July 13
MILITARY: A remote American outpost in southeast Afghanistan is attacked by an estimated 200 Taliban fighters.

July 19
DIPLOMACY: In Iraq, Prime Minister Nuri al-Maliki, in an interview in the German magazine *Der Spiegel,* appears to sanction a timetable for withdrawing U.S. forces from the country.

August 6
TERRORISM: At Guantánamo, Cuba, a military commission convicts Salim Ahmed Hamdan, a former driver of Osama bin Laden, of terrorist activities; he is sentenced to 66 months in jail, although 61 of these have already been served awaiting trial.

August 22
AVIATION: In northern Iraq, an army UH-60 Black Hawk helicopter crashes, killing all 14 soldiers onboard; the accident is ascribed to mechanical failure.

In western Herat Province, Afghanistan, an American air strike on the village of Azizabad kills several Taliban militants. However, Afghan government officials claim that 90 civilians also died in the attack.

A U.S. Army sergeant instructs an Iraqi Civilian Defense Force trainee in the proper way to clear his Tabuk assault rifle during marksmanship training. The Civilian Defense Force was designed to provide Iraqi recruits with soldier skills to work with and eventually replace coalition forces. *(Defense Imagery)*

August 25

DIPLOMACY: In Baghdad, Iraq, Prime Minister Nuri al-Maliki calls for the complete withdrawal of all occupation forces by 2011. Apparently, this deadline was agreed to in advance with American authorities.

September 1

MILITARY: In Anbar Province, Iraq, U.S. military authorities turn over control to Iraqi security forces. This area was formerly a center of the insurgency, but the so-called Sunni awakening induced many tribes and former insurgents to take up arms against al-Qaeda terrorists.

September 2

AVIATION: Investigators report that the August 22 air strike against Taliban forces in Azizabad, Herat Province, Afghanistan, apparently killed seven civilians. The Afghan government insists that the toll was much higher.

September 16

MILITARY: In Iraq, Lieutenant General David H. Petraeus turns command of the Multi-National Force-Iraq over to Lieutenant General Raymond T. Odierno.

September 24

POLITICS: In Baghdad, Iraq, the national parliament passes ground rules for forthcoming national elections to be held on January 29, 2009. This measure is viewed as a sign of growing stability in the country.

October 5

MILITARY: In Mosul, Iraq, a raid by American troops acting on a tip from the locals leads to the death of Abu Qaswarah, a Moroccan who was also the second most important al-Qaeda leader in that country; four other militants are also killed.

October 14

TERRORISM: In Baghdad, Iraq, Defense Minister Abdul Rahim Wardak declares that the improving security situation in the country has induced many foreign terrorists to leave the country and join the insurgency in Afghanistan.

October 21

MILITARY: In Baghdad, Iraq, the Iraqi cabinet calls for additional negotiations respecting the Status of Force Agreement allowing U.S. ground forces to remain in place after the UN mandate expires on December 31, 2008.

October 31

MILITARY: Lieutenant General David H. Petraeus is promoted to full general and formally assumes control of U.S. Central Command in Tampa, Florida. From there he will direct all military actions relative to Iraq, Afghanistan, and the Middle East.

December 20

MILITARY: The Associated Press reports that, since Operation Iraqi Freedom began in March 2003, 4,209 members of the U.S. military have been killed in combat. Of coalition forces, Britain has lost 176; Italy, 33; Ukraine, 18; Poland, 21; Bulgaria, 13;

Spain, 11, Denmark, seven; El Salvador, five; Latvia and Georgia, three apiece; Estonia, Netherlands, Thailand, and Romania, two each; and Austria, Hungary, Kazakhstan, and South Korea, one each.

2009

January 1
MILITARY: In Baghdad, Iraq, a propitious day arrives as U.S. forces turn security for the heavily defended Green Zone over to Iraqi security forces. In a separate ceremony, Saddam Hussein's former Republican Palace is also turned over to Iraq.

January 3
MILITARY: In Iraq, testing of the improved modular tactical vest begins with select marine forces. Apparently, the 84,000 standard, issue flak jackets in service, which cost more than $100 million to procure, are heavy, uncomfortable, and fail to stop bullets.

January 23
MILITARY: In Washington, D.C., James T. Conway, commandant of the Marine Corps, declares that, since the original combat mission in Iraq has given way to a nation-building mission, it is time to withdraw the 22,000 marines deployed there. He believes they could be better put to use fighting the Taliban in Afghanistan.

An Iraqi police officer shows his stained finger, demonstrating that he participated in the voting on January 31, 2009. *(Defense Imagery)*

January 26
AVIATION: Over Kirkuk, Iraq, a pair of OH-58D Kiowa helicopters collide in midair, killing the crew of four. The aircraft are attached to the 10th Mountain Division.

January 28
MILITARY: In Helmand Province, Afghanistan, Taliban gunfire kills two marines from the 2nd Combat Engineer Battalion, 2nd Marine Division, II Marine Expeditionary Force.

January 31
POLITICS: In Iraq, the latest round of elections for provincial officials proceeds with little interference. Initial results released on February 5 point to strong support for Prime Minister Nuri al-Maliki.

February
MILITARY: This month, fighting in Iraq takes the lives of 18 U.S. servicemen. The toll in Afghanistan stands at 24, double the number from a year ago.

February 17

POLITICS: In Washington, D.C., President Barack Obama announces that an additional 8,000 marines and 7,000 army troops will be deployed to Afghanistan by the summer of 2009.

In New York City, a UN report notes that 2,118 civilians were killed in Afghanistan in 2008, an increase over the 1,532 killed in 2007.

February 18

MILITARY: In Afghanistan, senior American commander General David A. McKiernan predicts that 2009 will be a rough year for coalition forces, despite the upcoming troop "surge."

February 27

AVIATION: At Fort Drum, New York, military authorities say that the January 26 collision between two U.S. Army OH-58D Kiowa helicopters occurred when they maneuvered while trying to avoid enemy ground fire.

POLITICS: At Camp Lejeune, North Carolina, President Barack Obama makes a policy speech in which he lays out a timetable for withdrawing all U.S. combat troops from Iraq. He maintains that the bulk of the 142,000 troops there will be gone by August 2010, although a small core of 35,000 to 50,000 will remain as late as 2011.

March

MILITARY: This month coalition casualties in Afghanistan number 28, while American losses in Iraq total nine. The latter is the lowest monthly figure since Operation Iraqi Freedom commenced in 2003.

March 10

MILITARY: In Washington, D.C., Lieutenant General George Flynn informs a congressional committee that forcing marines to wear too much body armor robs them of tactical mobility and speed. Current flak vets weigh 34 pounds, and troops tire much more quickly in consequence and have trouble moving in and out of combat vehicles.

March 19

DIPLOMACY: To Iran, President Barack Obama sends a videotaped message marking the spring holiday of Nowruz; this is seen as a conciliatory gesture toward the hard-line regime.

POLITICS: In New York City, a report in the *New York Times* states that the Obama administration seeks to double the size of the Afghan army and national police to 400,000 men, thereby placing a greater share of the defense burden on that nation.

March 23

MILITARY: In Kabul, Afghanistan, NATO leaders announce that Maulawi Hassan, a significant Taliban leader, had been killed by coalition forces two days earlier, along with nine of his allies.

March 27

POLITICS: In Washington, D.C., President Barack Obama announces a "retooled" strategy to defeat al-Qaeda in Pakistan and Afghanistan by sending billions in aid to the former and an additional 15,000 troops to the latter.

March 31

MILITARY: At Camp Pendleton, California, Sergeant Ryan Weemer, formerly of K Company, 1st Marines, is accused of killing an unarmed captive in Fallujah, Iraq. He is charged with premeditated murder.

April 9

POLITICS: In Washington, D.C., President Barack Obama requests a supplemental spending request from Congress totaling $83.4 billion. Of this amount, $75.8 billion is earmarked for the wars in Iraq and Afghanistan.

April 13

POLITICS: In Tehran, Iran, a closed court sentences Iranian-American journalist Roxana Saberi to eight years in prison for espionage on behalf of the United States.

April 20

MILITARY: In Iraq, preparations are made to ship 500 men of the 4th Engineer Battalion, who specialize in clearing roads of explosives, directly to Afghanistan. This is part of an overall strategy to relocate troops and resources to that new battlefield as the drawdown continues.

May

MILITARY: This month coalition forces sustain 27 fatalities in Afghanistan, while the United States suffers 25 combat deaths in Iraq.

May 6

DIPLOMACY: In Washington, D.C., President Barack Obama confers with President Asif Ali Zadari of Pakistan and President Hamid Karzai of Afghanistan. The United States wants both countries to adopt a more aggressive stance in fighting the Taliban.

May 11

AVIATION: In Washington, D.C., the Marine Corps announces that a squadron of its controversial MV-22 Osprey tilt-rotor transports is being deployed to Afghanistan. This computerized airplane/helicopter hybrid can carry 24 fully equipped combat troops at much higher speeds than conventional helicopters.

DIPLOMACY: In Tehran, Iran, President Mahmoud Ahmadinejad orders the release of Iranian-American journalist Roxana Saberi, who had been arrested in January and charged with spying for the United States.

MILITARY: In Washington, D.C., Secretary of Defense Robert Gates announces that he had "requested" the resignation of General David A. McKiernan, the senior American commander in Afghanistan. He then calls for a "new approach" to fighting the Taliban, which is why he is appointing Lieutenant General Stanley McChrystal, a former Green Beret with an exemplary background in unconventional warfare, to take charge.

May 17

POLITICS: In Washington, D.C., Defense Secretary Robert Gates concedes during a television interview that it may take years to get Afghanistan's military forces on a firmer footing so that they can assume a greater share of their nation's security.

May 20
AVIATION: In Tehran, Iran, President Mahmoud Ahmadinejad declares that a new Sajjil-2 missile, which has a range of 1,200 miles, has been successfully tested. This places both Israel and southeastern Europe within its range.

May 25
NAVAL: In the Gulf of Aden, six Iranian warships are deployed by President Mahmoud Ahmadinejad, apparently in a move calculated to intimidate Saudi Arabia.

May 28
MILITARY: In Kabul, Afghanistan, U.S. military authorities announce that coalition forces have killed 29 Taliban militants in eastern Paktika Province, near the border with Pakistan.

TERRORISM: In Zahedan, Iran, a bomb explodes in a Shiite mosque, killing 30 people and wounding 50. The Iranians blame local Baluchis of the militant Sunni group Jundallah, which resents Shiite oppression.

May 29
MILITARY: In Kabul, Afghanistan, U.S. military authorities announce another successful clash in Zabol Province, with 35 Taliban militants killed.

June
MILITARY: This month coalition casualties in Afghanistan amount to 38 dead while U.S. fatalities in Iraq total 15.

June 1
TERRORISM: In Wardak Province, Afghanistan, two improvised explosive devices tear into two American military vehicles, killing four soldiers.

June 2
AVIATION: In Helmand Province, Afghanistan, an attack by British helicopters apparently takes the life of Mullah Mansur, a noted Taliban leader.

June 7
MILITARY: In Zabol Province, Afghanistan, a coalition attack, backed by airpower, kills 20 Taliban militants.

June 8
MILITARY: In Helmand Province, Afghanistan, 7,000 marines from the 2nd Marine Expeditionary Brigade begin sweeping through Taliban-controlled areas. These troops are part of President Barack Obama's troop "surge."

June 12
POLITICS: In Iran, Iranians go the polls to elect a new president. The incumbent, Mahmoud Ahmadinejad, is expected to win handily, though he faces a strong challenge from former prime minister Mir Hossein Mousavi.

Ultimately, Ahmadinejad receives 62.6 percent of the votes cast, while Mousavi receives 33.8 percent. However, Mousavi claims widespread irregularities and asks the supreme leader, Ayatollah Ali Khamenei, for a new election.

June 15
MILITARY: In Kabul, Afghanistan, General Stanley McChrystal arrives to take charge of the war against the Taliban as head of U.S. and NATO forces. He relieves General David McKiernan in a low-key ceremony, promising to respect the traditions and religion of the Afghan people. "But while operating with care," he insists, "we will not be timid."

June 19
AVIATION: In western Farah Province, Afghanistan, a U.S. airstrike conducted by a B-1 bomber at dusk eliminates 78 Taliban fighters and may also have killed as many as 26 civilians nearby.

June 20
POLITICS: In Tehran, Iran, a political protest results in the shooting death of Neda Agha-Soltan, a 27-year-old woman who happened to be a bystander. Her death was captured on videotape and broadcast around the world on YouTube, making her the world's first Internet martyr.

Opposition leader Mir Hossein Mousavi demands that the recent national election be annulled due to widespread fraud.
TERRORISM: In Taza, northern Iraq, a truck bomb explodes outside a Shiite mosque, killing 82 people and wounding 250. Sunni extremists are blamed.

June 21
AVIATION: At Bagram Air Base, Afghanistan, Taliban missiles strike an American compound, killing two U.S. soldiers and wounding eight from the 82nd Airborne Division.

June 24
MILITARY: In south Oruzgan Province, Afghanistan, coalition and Afghan security forces kill 23 Taliban militants in a firefight near Tirin Kot, the local capital. Mullah Ismail, a noted local commander, is apparently among those slain.
TERRORISM: In Sadr City, Iraq, a bomb explodes in a crowded marketplace, killing 76 people and injuring 160.

June 25
POLITICS: In Iran, it is estimated that 17 people were killed by paramilitary forces as they protested the results of the recent national election.

June 28
MILITARY: In Iraq, top U.S. commander Lieutenant General Raymond T. Odierno declares that Iran is still interfering in Iraq, including arming and training Shiite insurgents. "I am not authorized to do anything outside the borders of Iraq," he insists.

June 29
POLITICS: In Tehran, Iran, the nation's powerful Guardian Council certifies the results of the national election. However, streets protests continue.

June 30
AVIATION: In eastern Khost Province, Afghanistan, a U.S.-led coalition airstrike kills 12 Taliban militants in the act of smuggling foreign fighters into the country. The fighters are linked to the wanted leader Siraj Haqqani.

MILITARY: In Iraq, all U.S. military personnel are withdrawn from Iraqi cities per the 2008 Status of Force Agreement between the United States and the Iraqi government, which declared the occasion a national holiday. Virtually all the 130,000 combat troops in the country are now deployed at forward-operating bases in the event that Iraqi security forces require their assistance.

July

MILITARY: This month coalition losses in Afghanistan number 76, including 45 U.S. fatalities. The Americans sustain eight deaths in Iraq.

July 1

MILITARY: Along the Lower Helmand River Valley, Afghanistan, 4,000 troops of the 2nd Marine Expeditionary Unit begin clearing out remaining Taliban operatives. This maneuver, code-named Operation Khanjar (Strike of the Sword), also involves 650 Afghan police and security personnel.

July 2

MILITARY: In southern Afghanistan, Operation Khanjar picks up speed as it engages Taliban fighters; one marine dies in combat. This is also the world's largest poppy-growing regions for the global heroin trade, and a major source of Taliban income. **POLITICS:** In Baghdad, Iraq, Vice President Joseph Biden makes a surprise visit to the troops; he will also meet with U.S. and Iraqi officials.

July 3

AVIATION: Over southern Afghanistan, a Marine Corps AV-8B Harrier jet drops a 500-pound bomb on a group of 20 to 40 Taliban militants seeking refuge in a walled compound, killing them all.

July 5

POLITICS: In Qom, Iran, the Association of Researchers and Teachers, an influential body of clerics, declares President Mahmoud Ahmadinejad's reelection to be illegitimate and calls on other clerics to oppose the government.

July 6

TERRORISM: In Kunduz Province, Afghanistan, a roadside bomb explodes near an American patrol, killing four soldiers.

July 8

MILITARY: In southern Afghanistan, Brigadier General Larry Nicholson states that additional Afghan police and security personnel are the key to containing and defeating the Taliban.

July 9

MILITARY: In Washington, D.C., Lieutenant General James Dubik of the Multi-National Security Transition Team tells Congress that Iraq's security forces have grown from 444,000 to 565,000 men since June 2007, but that their combat performance is hampered by a lack of experienced officers and sergeants. He maintains that the Iraqis will require additional help.

POLITICS: In Tehran, Iran, several hundred protestors defy authorities and clash with Basji militia while chanting "Death to the dictators"—a reference to President Mahmoud Ahmadinejad

TERRORISM: In Logar Province, Afghanistan, a massive truck bomb explodes, killing 25 people. The device detonated after the vehicle accidentally overturned on the road.

July 12

MILITARY: In Orzugan Province, Afghanistan, a joint coalition–Afghan attack kills 12 Taliban operatives in a major gun battle.

TERRORISM: In Helmand Province, Afghanistan, roadside bombs kill four marines as Operation Khanjar continues apace. Another roadside bomb in Thiqar Province narrowly misses Chris Hill, the U.S. ambassador.

July 13

TERRORISM: In Salaheddin Province, Iraq, seven U.S. troops are injured by a blast outside the Al Sharqat Qa'da council building. This is the first major attack on U.S. forces since they departed all urban centers on June 30.

July 14

TERRORISM: In Helmand Province, Afghanistan, Taliban gunfire takes the lives of two marines. The Taliban also release a video of captured Idaho National Guardsman Bowe R. Bergdahl, who appears shaken but in good health.

In Zahedan, Iran, authorities hang 13 suspected members of the Sunni extremist group Jandallah for their role in bombing a Shiite mosque.

July 15

AVIATION: Near the city of Qazvin, Iran, an Iranian airliner crashes in midflight, killing all 168 passengers on board. The three-engine Tupolev 154 was owned and operated by Caspian Airlines.

July 17

DIPLOMACY: In Baghdad, Iraq, the government suddenly announces new restrictions on the movement of American forces, above and beyond what was endorsed in the six-month-old security agreement. Henceforth, the Americans are to stop all joint patrols with Iraqi forces and conduct resupply convoys only at night. Privately, American military leaders are strongly contesting anything that hinders their right to self-defense.

POLITICS: In Tehran, Iran, former president Ali Akbar Hashemi Rafsanjani calls on the government to immediately release all people arrested and detained during last month's disputed presidential election. He speaks on the campus of the University of Tehran, surrounded by tens thousands of students and dissidents.

July 18

AVIATION: Over Afghanistan, an Air Force F-15 Strike Eagle crashes, killing both crew members. No reason is given for the accident, but hostile ground fire is ruled out as a probable cause.

July 19

Aviation: Over Kabul, Afghanistan, a Russian-owned Mi-8 civilian helicopter crashes shortly after takeoff, killing 16 people on board and injuring five.

July 21

Terrorism: In Gardez, Afghanistan, a pair of suicide bombers attack several government buildings, killing 14 people. Eight insurgents and six Afghan police officers also are killed in the incident.

July 22

Diplomacy: In Washington, D.C., President Barack Obama and Iraqi prime minister Nuri al-Maliki give a joint interview in which both are cautiously optimistic about Iraq's growing stability. The prime minister is insistent that Iraqi forces have proven more capable than their critics would have the American public believe.

July 24

Military: In Washington, D.C., White House spokesmen announce that Staff Sergeant Jared Monti, 10th Mountain Division, who died in Afghanistan on June 21, 2006, will be awarded a Congressional Medal of Honor.

July 30

Politics: In Tehran, Iran, police and Basji militia attack and beat thousands of anti-government protestors attending a memorial at the gravesite of 27-year old Neda Agha-Soltan, an innocent bystander who was cut down by a bullet during a political protest in June.

July 31

Politics: In New York City, the United Nations releases a report indicating that 1,013 Afghan civilians were killed between January and June 2009, 23 percent more than in the same period in 2008. Taliban attacks inflicted the bulk of these, but coalition airstrikes were also responsible for several deaths.

Terrorism: In Baghdad, Iraq, a string of explosions at five Shiite mosques kills 29 people and injures scores more. The Sunni-based al-Qaeda in Iraq is suspected of being behind the blasts.

August

Military: This month coalition fatalities in Afghanistan total 77, of which 51 are Americans. By contrast, there are seven U.S. combat deaths in Iraq, the lowest amount since the occupation began in 2003.

August 1

Diplomacy: In Tehran, Iran, the government announces that its security forces have apprehended three American backpackers who entered the country illegally from Iraqi Kurdistan. Apparently, they crossed the border from an unmarked area.

August 3

Politics: In Tehran, Iran, Ayatollah Ali Khamenei gives his official endorsement to Mahmoud Ahmadinejad's second term as president. In doing so he snubs scores of pro-reform lawmakers and clerics who are claiming that the June 12 election was wracked by fraud.

August 4
POLITICS: In Washington, D.C., several senators and military advisers write a letter to President Barack Obama, urging him to double the amount of Afghan security forces to police their own country, without further delay.

August 5
POLITICS: In Tehran, Iran, Mahmoud Ahmadinejad is sworn in for a second term as president. This comes at a time of increasing political unrest over what is popularly viewed as a rigged election.

August 6
TERRORISM: In western Afghanistan, a roadside bomb kills four marines after their vehicle is struck. As coalition forces push deeper into Taliban-controlled territory, casualties begin mounting.

August 9
POLITICS: In Tehran, Iran, Yadollah Javani, senior commander of the powerful Revolutionary Guards, calls for the arrest of opposition leader Mir Hossein Mousavi, former president Mohammad Khatami, and reformist candidate Mahdi Karroubi. All three have roundly denounced the reelection victory of President Mahmoud Ahmadinejad.

August 10
TERRORISM: In Baghdad, Iraq, a string of car bombings kills 42 people and injures scores more.

August 12–13
TERRORISM: In Helmand Province, Afghanistan, 500 men of the 2nd Battalion, 3rd Marines, are airlifted near the town of Dahaneh. Taliban operatives resist fiercely then withdraw, leaving eight dead behind.

August 13–15
TERRORISM: In Helmand Province, Afghanistan, Gulf Company, 2nd Battalion, 3rd Marines, eliminates any remaining resistance in Dahaneh. Taliban losses are 22 dead and five captured; marine losses are one killed.

August 15
TERRORISM: In Kabul, Afghanistan, a suicide car bomber strikes at NATO's Afghan headquarters, killing seven people and wounding 91; this daring attack comes only five days before the Afghan national election.

August 16
TERRORISM: In Helmand Province, Afghanistan, two British soldiers are killed by explosions, bringing the total number of fatalities there to more than 200.

August 17

DIPLOMACY: In Afghanistan, renegade warlord and Taliban ally Gulbuddin Hekmatyar declares that he is willing to help U.S. forces defeat the Taliban, contingent upon a time frame for the removal of all foreign troops. During the Soviet occupation, Hekmatyar received $600 million in American aid.

MILITARY: In Iraq, top U.S. commander Lieutenant General Raymond T. Odierno states that he wants to deploy more American forces in the northern areas to curtail terror campaign against civilians there.

TERRORISM: In southern Afghanistan, a roadside bomb kills another marine; the number of Americans fatalities this month stands at 22.

August 18

TERRORISM: Near Basra, Iraq, Iraqi security forces find a cache of Iranian-built rockets similar to those used to attack a nearby American base in July.

Outside Kabul, Afghanistan, a suicide bomber attacks a NATO convoy, killing seven and wounding 51 people. Among the slain are two Afghans who were working for the United Nations.

August 19

TERRORISM: In Baghdad, Iraq, two massive truck bombs explode outside the Foreign and Finance Ministries, killing 95 people and injuring almost 600. This incident is viewed as an indictment against Iraqi forces ability to provide adequate security in urban regions of the country.

August 20

MILITARY: By this date, the number of military deaths from Operation Iraqi Freedom stands at 4,332 dead, while 31,469 troops have been injured.

August 20–26

POLITICS: In Afghanistan, voters go to the polls as Prime Minister Hamid Karzai seeks a second term in office. However, preliminary results show that, while Karzai racked up a 45 to 17 percent lead over former foreign minister Abdullah Abdullah, reports of voting irregularities are widespread.

August 21

MILITARY: In Kabul, Afghanistan, a roadside bomb takes the life of First Sergeant Jose San Nicolas Cristomo, age 59. A Vietnam veteran, he is the oldest fatality of the war thus far.

August 25

TERRORISM: In Kandahar, Afghanistan, a car bomb explodes downtown, killing 43 people and injuring 65. Four U.S. troops are among those slain.

August 26

POLITICS: Noted Shiite cleric Abdul Aziz al-Hakim dies of lung cancer in Baghdad, Iraq. Hakim, a high-profile voice for moderation and reconciliation, was also a political kingmaker, working behind the scenes and managing to maintain close diplomatic ties with the United States and Iran.

August 29
TERRORISM: North of Baghdad, Iraq, two truck bombs explode outside a police station and a market, killing 16 people

August 31
MILITARY: In Kabul, Afghanistan, top U.S. commander General Stanley McChrystal declares the situation there "serious" and calls for a new strategy to defeat the Taliban. This is seen as a signal for additional U.S. and NATO troops to be deployed.

September 2
TERRORISM: In Kabul, Afghanistan, a suicide bomber strikes at a mosque, killing Abdullah Laghmani, deputy chief of the National Directorate for Security, and 22 others.

September 3
POLITICS: In Tehran, Iran, the Majlis approves General Ahmad Vahidi as the new defense minister, despite that fact that Vahidi is wanted in connection with the 1994 bombing of a Jewish cultural center in Argentina.

September 4
AVIATION: In Kunduz Province, Afghanistan, a NATO airstrike on two hijacked fuel tankers kills 90 people, including 40 civilians who were siphoning fuel for their own use. In response, President Hamid Karzai says he is forming a panel to investigate the incident.
MILITARY: In Washington, D.C., the Pentagon informs the 82nd Airborne Division that its tour of duty is being extended from 12 months to 14 months.

September 7
DIPLOMACY: In Tehran, Iran, President Mahmoud Ahmadinejad defiantly asserts that his country "will never negotiate" away its right to have nuclear power. However, he says he willing to discuss "global challenges" with Western leaders.

September 8
POLITICS: In Afghanistan, election totals show that President Hamid Karzai has received 50 percent of the vote, sufficient to avoid a runoff. However, the UN Electoral Complaints Commission says there is clear and compelling evidence of widespread voter fraud.

September 9
DIPLOMACY: In Brussels, Belgium, NATO secretary-general Anders Fogh Rasmussen warns that an early withdrawal from Afghanistan could have potentially disastrous consequences for the entire region. According to him, retreat is not an option despite signs that the Western alliance is tiring of the conflict.
POLITICS: In Washington, D.C., Secretary of Defense Robert M. Gates condemns the Associated Press for releasing a photo of mortally wounded marine corporal Joshua

M. Bernard, who died of wounds received in Helmand Province, Afghanistan, on April 14.

TERRORISM: In eastern Afghanistan, U.S. forces capture a cache of Iranian-made explosively formed penetrators, along with 104 BM-1 rockets and C-4 explosives. This is the latest proof that Iran is funneling aid and influence to the Taliban.

September 12
TERRORISM: In Afghanistan, a series of attacks takes the lives of 45 Afghan civilians and security forces.

September 14
DIPLOMACY: In Vienna, Austria, Ali Akbar Salehi, Iran's nuclear chief, says his country will hold discussions with world powers to reduce tensions arising from its nuclear program.

TERRORISM: An audiotape, purportedly made by fugitive Saudi terrorist Osama bin Laden, mocks President Barack Obama as powerless to stop the war in Afghanistan.

September 15
MILITARY: In Washington, D.C., Admiral Michael Mullen, chairman of the Joint Chiefs of Staff, says that he wants to see additional troops deployed to Afghanistan to defeat the Taliban insurgency there. He also notes that victory will require more time.

TERRORISM: In Baghdad, Iraq, militant rockets strike the Green Zone, where Vice President Joseph Biden is spending the night; two Iraqis are killed.

September 19
TERRORISM: In a statement released in time for the Muslim festival of Eid, Taliban leader Mullah Omar declares that all foreign forces in Afghanistan face defeat and urges them to learn the lessons of history.

September 20
AVIATION: Near Balad Air Base, north of Baghdad, Iraq, an army UH-60 Black Hawk helicopter crashes, killing one servicemen and injuring 12 others. The aircraft apparently went down in high winds and a sandstorm.

POLITICS: In Washington, D.C., President Barack Obama expresses his doubts that a troop "surge" in Afghanistan will help the situation. "Until I'm satisfied that we've got the right strategy," he declares, "I am not going to be sending some young men or women over there."

September 21
MILITARY: In Washington, D.C., General Stanley McChrystal, in a message on the *Washington Post's* Web site, declares that the United States will fail in Afghanistan without the addition of more combat troops.

September 22
AVIATION: South of Tehran, Iran, an Iranian military aircraft crashes, killing all seven occupants. President Mahmoud Ahmadinejad takes to the airwaves to warn that his nation is stronger than ever and will "cut off the hand" of any attacker.

September 25

DIPLOMACY: In Pittsburgh, Pennsylvania, President Barack Obama, British prime minister Gordon Brown, and French president Nicolas Sarkozy make a joint televised address in which they accuse Iran of constructing a secret uranium-enrichment facility near the holy city of Qom.

September 26

TERRORISM: In Helmand Province, Afghanistan, hostile gunfire takes the life of Lance Corporal Jordan L. Chrobat, 2nd Battalion, 8th Marines.

September 27

MILITARY: In Washington, D.C., Defense Secretary Robert Gates says that it would be a disastrous mistake for Congress to establish deadlines for an American withdrawal from Afghanistan. Both Admiral Mike Mullen, chairman of the Joint Chiefs of Staff, and General Stanley McChrystal, have endorsed the strategy of adding additional combat forces for an unspecified length of time.

September 28

MILITARY: In Farah Province, Afghanistan, U.S. forces battle Taliban militants, killing at least 30. No airstrikes were involved, in an attempt to cut down on civilian casualties.

September 29

MILITARY: In Iraq, top U.S. commander Lieutenant General Raymond T. Odierno announces that he is preparing to send thousands of troops home beginning with a brigade-size unit of 4,000 men.

TERRORISM: In Kandahar, Afghanistan, a roadside bomb explodes beneath a bus packed with riders, killing 30 and wounding 39.

September 30

DIPLOMACY: In Washington, D.C., Iranian foreign minister Manouchehr Mottaki arrives, apparently for discussions at the Pakistani embassy, which represents Iranian interests in the country. The United States and Iran have not had formal diplomatic relations since 1980.

MILITARY: In Washington, D.C., Lieutenant General Raymond T. Odierno warns Congress not to lose sight of Iraq, despite the impressive reductions in violence there. He hopes that the fledgling democracy emerges as a key U.S. ally in the Middle East.

In the fortified Green Zone of Baghdad, Iraq, the U.S. Army Emergency Room in the Iba Sina Hospital is turned over to Iraqi security forces.

October

MILITARY: This month's coalition fatalities in Afghanistan total 65, with 59 Americans. This is the deadliest month since Operation Enduring Freedom began in 2001. In Iraq, nine additional American servicemen are killed, bringing the total slain there since 2003 to more than 4,350.

October 1–25
DIPLOMACY: In Geneva, Switzerland, face-to-face nuclear talks between Western and Iranian leaders resume, and, under increasing pressure, the Iranians agree to allow International Atomic Energy Agency inspectors to monitor the newly revealed facility near the holy city of Qom. They also reach a tentative deal to enrich Iranian uranium in Russia and France, and in such a manner as to render it useless for potential nuclear weapons.

October 2
MILITARY: In Copenhagen, Denmark, President Barack Obama and General Stanley McChrystal confer aboard Air Force One to review their war strategy for Afghanistan. The administration cabinet is split over whether to increase the number of troops in that region, or to scale back and concentrate on defeating al-Qaeda in Pakistan.

October 3
TERRORISM: In Wardak Province, Afghanistan, an Afghan policeman, possibly a Taliban infiltrator, kills two U.S. servicemen, then flees.

October 4–6
MILITARY: In Nurestan Province, Afghanistan, U.S. forces engage in a protracted engagement with Taliban operatives, killing more than 100 foreign fighters; eight Americans are killed in a major attack on their remote outpost near the Pakistani border.

October 5
POLITICS: In Washington, D.C., President Barack Obama says that withdrawal from Afghanistan is not an option.

October 6
DIPLOMACY: In Tehran, Iran, the government announces that it is planning new centrifuges for a second uranium-enrichment site, although it insists all research there would be for peaceful purposes.
MILITARY: In Nurestan Province, Afghanistan, U.S. and Afghan security forces fight Taliban militants in mountainous terrain, killing at least 40.

October 8
TERRORISM: In Kabul, Afghanistan, a powerful car bomb explodes outside the Indian embassy, killing 17 people and injuring more than 80. This is the deadliest attack in the capital since September 17.

October 10
TERRORISM: In Kabul, Afghanistan, Defense Minister General Adbul Rahim Wardak declares that the Taliban insurgency, which started out as an Afghan-dominated movement, is being bolstered by the presence of thousands of foreign fighters from across the Muslim world.

October 14

DIPLOMACY: In Baghdad, Iraq, the government all but accuses Syria of aiding and abetting the series of large truck bombings in August and asks that the United Nations step in and help investigate. Former Baathist extremists are suspected in the blasts.

MILITARY: In London, United Kingdom, Prime Minister Gordon Brown announces his willingness to dispatch additional 500 British troops to Afghanistan, but only on the condition that NATO and the Afghan government also commit more resources to fighting the Taliban insurgency. Britain presently has 9,000 troops there.

In Washington, D.C., parts of General Stanley McChrystal's assessment of Afghanistan are released, in which he states that even the addition of as many as 80,000 additional troops many not win the war unless there is a major crackdown on government corruption. He believes that government indifference to its own populace is forcing many desperate citizens to assist the Taliban.

TERRORISM: In Baghdad, Iraq, the government human-rights agency releases a report that says 85,694 Iraqi citizens were killed in acts of terrorism between 2004 and 2008. The toll includes 263 college professors, 21 judges, 95 lawyers, and 269 journalists, all of whom appear to have been targeted.

October 16

MILITARY: In Washington, D.C., the Department of the Army cancels plans to deploy a brigade of 3,500 troops from the 10th Mountain Division to Iraq, citing the improved security situation there. This renders them available for deployment in Afghanistan, however.

TERRORISM: In Tal Afar, Iraq, a suicide gunman opens fire in a Sunni mosque before blowing himself up, killing 15 worshipers, including the imam.

October 17

TERRORISM: In Anbar Province, Iraq, a suicide bomber destroys a key Iraqi bridge near Ramadi that is heavily used by U.S. and Iraqi security forces.

October 18

TERRORISM: In the Pishtin district of Sistan-Baluchistan Province, Iran, a suicide bomber attacks a Shiite Mosque during a meeting of local tribal leaders and senior members of the Revolutionary Guard. The dead include the deputy commander of ground forces and the chief provincial guard commander. The blast is attributed to the Baluchi-dominated Sunni extremist group Jundallah, which is resisting religious oppression imposed on it by Iran's Shiite majority.

October 19

DIPLOMACY: In Tehran, Iran, government officials declare that they refuse to halt the enrichment of uranium in the country, even if the West provides them with sufficient fuel. The United States maintains that Iran is one to six years away from producing nuclear weapons.

MILITARY: In Tehran, Iran, the government warns the United States and Britain of retaliation following a terrorist attack against a Shiite mosque in eastern Iran. The blast killed five senior Revolutionary Guard commanders, including Deputy Commander Noor Ali Shooshtari, and 37 others.

POLITICS: In Afghanistan, the UN Independent Election Commission voids thousands of ballots from the August 20 national election, so a runoff election is inevitable. However, President Hamid Karzai rejects the assertion out of hand.

October 20

MILITARY: In Baghdad, Iraq, top U.S. commander Lieutenant General Raymond T. Odierno predicts a very rapid reduction of American forces in the country following the January 2010 elections. He intends to withdraw all combat forces by August of that year, with a complete withdrawal no later than 2011.

POLITICS: In Kabul, Afghanistan, Prime Minister Hamid Karzai is declared the winner of the recent national election with 49.7 percent of the vote, which will require a runoff election. Karzai, under pressure from the West, agrees to a new election slated for November 7.

In Tehran, Iran, Iranian-American Kian Tajbakhsh is sentenced to 15 years in prison for his alleged role in post-election unrest. His attorney is planning to appeal the verdict.

October 25

DIPLOMACY: In Iran, a team of UN inspectors arrives at the site of a once-secret Iranian enrichment facility. The government cites the inspection as proof of its willingness to work with concerned Western powers.

TERRORISM: In Baghdad, Iraq, a van and a minibus, packed with explosives, are detonated outside the Ministry of Justice and the Ministry of Municipalities. The blasts kill 155 people and injure 540.

October 26

AVIATION: In Badghis Province, Afghanistan, a U.S. Army UH-60 Black Hawk helicopter crashes, killing 14 Americans on board. To the south, two other helicopters collide in midair and crash, killing four troops and injuring two others. The cause of the accidents is not known.

October 27

AVIATION: In Nurestan Province, Afghanistan, NATO forces uncover the wreckage of a U.S. Army C-12 Huron transport aircraft that crashed two weeks earlier. Enemy action is ruled out, so the accident is attributed to the violent downdrafts common in mountain ranges.

TERRORISM: In Iraq, the militant Sunni group al-Qaeda in Iraq claims responsibility for the bombings in Baghdad two days earlier.

In Afghanistan, a rash of roadside bombings takes the lives of eight American servicemen.

October 28

TERRORISM: In Kabul, Afghanistan, militants storm into a UN guesthouse and detonate their explosive vests, killing 12 people, including six UN staff members.

October 29

AVIATION: In Berlin, Germany, General Wolfgang Schneiderhan, the inspector general, says that civilian casualties in the September 4 airstrike against two hijacked fuel trucks were unavoidable. He says that Colonel Georg Klein, who requested the strike, did so out of fear that the trucks might be used as suicide vehicles against his men.

October 31

DIPLOMACY: In Tehran, Iran, the government rejects a UN-backed offer to ship uranium out of the country and have it reprocessed abroad. It suspects that neither France nor Russia will honor the deal to return 20 percent enriched uranium back as promised.

November 1–2

POLITICS: In Kabul, Afghanistan, former foreign minister Abdullah Abdullah withdraws from the runoff election slated for November 7, because, in his own words, "a transparent election is not possible." Hamid Karzai is declared the winner by the UN Independent Election Commission on the following day.

November 3

POLITICS: In Kabul, Afghanistan, Hamid Karzai is sworn into office for a second term as prime minister and vows to help fight endemic corruption in government and politics.

November 4

TERRORISM: In Helmand Province, Afghanistan, an Afghan policeman, most likely a Taliban infiltrator, kills five British soldiers. Six other soldiers are wounded, along with two Afghan policemen.

November 6

MILITARY: In Ottawa, Canada, General Walter Natynczyk, chief of the defense staff announces that Canada will begin withdrawing its 2,800 troops from Afghanistan in the summer of 2011.

November 8

MILITARY: In Washington, army chief of staff General George Casey endorses President Barack Obama's plan to deploy additional forces in Afghanistan to combat the Taliban insurgency.
POLITICS: In Baghdad, Iraq, the national assembly passes a key law that will allow another round of national elections in January 2010. Of 196 ministers present, 141 vote for passage.

November 17

POLITICS: In Tehran, Iran, the government announces that it has sentenced five people to death for their role in post-election unrest. The Iranian Justice Department characterized them as members of "terrorist and armed opposition groups."

November 20

TERRORISM: In Farah Province, Afghanistan, a car bomb explodes in a crowded square only 55 yards from the governor's compound, killing 16 people.

November 22

TERRORISM: In Numaniyah, Iraq, insurgent gunfire takes the life of Sergeant Briand T. Williams of Sparks, Georgia. He has the distinction of being the last American fatality there during 2009.

November 29

DIPLOMACY: In Tehran, Iran, President Mahmoud Ahmadinejad announces that Iran is planning to build 10 new uranium-enrichment plants in defiance of the UN nuclear watchdog agency.

December 1

MILITARY: In Washington, D.C., Pentagon officials announce that marines will constitute the majority of 35,000 reinforcements to be sent to Afghanistan by the spring. This is part of President Barack Obama's "surge" for the region once American forces in Iraq begin withdrawing.

December 2

TERRORISM: In Cairo, Egypt, Ramin Pourandarjani, a 26-year-old Iranian expatriate who had exposed the torture of jailed prisoners in Iran, is mysteriously poisoned to death by an overdose of high-blood-pressure medicine in his salad.

December 4

AVIATION: In Helmand Province, Afghanistan, MV-22 transports drop the 3rd Battalion, 4th Marines, behind Taliban lines at Now Zad. A second column of marines simultaneously pushes northward from their Forward Operating Base at Now Zad, penetrating Taliban minefields with armored steamrollers. This is the first major Afghan operation undertaken since the "surge" was announced last spring.

December 7

POLITICS: In Tehran, Iran, President Mahmoud Ahmadinejad declares that the United States is blocking the return of Shiite Islam's Hidden Imam, who is the savior of all mankind.

December 8

TERRORISM: In Baghdad, Iraq, a series of coordinated car bombings takes the lives of 118 people and wounds 261 more. Officials begin to wonder if the Sunni-based al-Qaeda insurgency, largely dormant, is making a comeback.

December 9

DIPLOMACY: In London, United Kingdom, Amnesty International issues a report stating that human-rights violations in Iran are the worst in 20 years. The report includes allegations of rape, torture, and killings of dissidents in prison.

MILITARY: In Washington, D.C., General David H. Petraeus informs a congressional committee that progress against the Taliban in Afghanistan is likely to be slower than the military "surge" in Iraq was two years ago. He anticipates that at least 18 months will lapse before real progress can be measured in terms of reducing terror attacks against civilians and coalition personnel.

December 10

AVIATION: In Afghanistan, the first marine aviation unit fully equipped with MV-22 Osprey tilt-rotor transports deploys for active duty. This aircraft/helicopter hybrid carries 24 fully equipped troops at twice the speed and range of the CH-46E helicopter it replaces. Despite a checkered development program, the Osprey is popular with air crews and handles well.

December 14

AVIATION: In Wilmington, Delaware, Iranian agent Amir Hossein Ardebili, who was arrested in the country of Georgia after trying to smuggle U.S. helicopter technology to Iran, is sentenced to five years in prison following a guilty plea.

DIPLOMACY: In Tehran, Iran, the government announces its decision to try Shane Bauer, Sarah Shourd, and Josh Fattal for espionage after they inadvertently strayed into Iranian territory from Iraqi Kurdistan last July.

POLITICS: In Baghdad, Iraq, the government announces that Camp Ashraf, which houses 3,500 Iranian dissident refugees, is to be closed and its occupants relocated to a hotel in the northern part of the capital.

December 15

POLITICS: Across Iran, students mount large anti-government demonstrations. They claim that recent images of students burning pictures of Ayatollah Khomeini were staged by government officials.

TERRORISM: In Mosul, Iraq, car bombs explode across the city, killing nine people.

December 16

AVIATION: In Iran, the government test-fires its new Sajjil-2 missile. This is a two-stage weapon capable of hitting targets as far away as Israel and parts of Western Europe. Defense Minister Ahmad Vahidi goes on the record to state that the missile serves as a "strong deterrent" against any possible foreign attack—a euphemism for Israel and the United States.

December 17

DIPLOMACY: In Moscow, Russia, NATO secretary-general Anders Fogh Rasmussen appeals to the government to send a detachment of helicopters to Afghanistan, along with additional police to train Afghan security forces.

MILITARY: In Kandahar, Afghanistan, Admiral Michael Mullen, chairman of the Joint Chiefs of Staff, arrives at Camp Nathan Smith for a firsthand look at affairs. He plans to tour several other bases as well.

December 18

DIPLOMACY: In Oakland, California, Nora Shourd, mother of one of the three American hikers taken into Iranian custody, appeals for their immediate release to Ayatollah Ali Khamenei, the supreme religious leader.

December 19

MILITARY: In Maysan Province, Iraq, the government announces that Iranian forces have abandoned the al-Fakkah oil field in the face of Iraqi reinforcements, and that the Iraqis have hoisted the national flag over the well there. Iran and Iraq both claim that the al-Fakkah oil field lies in its territory.

POLITICS: In Tehran, Iran, police officials admit that three political prisoners seized during recent demonstrations have been beaten to death by their jailers at Kahrizak prison. Opposition leaders say that 72 people have died in political violence since the last national election.

In Tehran, Iran, a respected Shiite cleric and political dissident, Grand Ayatollah Hossein Ali Montazeri, dies peacefully in his sleep.

December 21

AVIATION: In Afghanistan, it is reported that the first MC-12W spyplanes, which are highly advanced and classified, are due to be deployed under the aegis of the U.S. Air Force. This four-man, twin-engined aircraft is equipped with videocameras and other sensors, and is capable of beaming real-time intelligence to troops on the ground.

December 23

POLITICS: In Isfahan, Iran, police clash violently with demonstrators mourning the death of reformist cleric Grand Ayatollah Hossein Ali Montazeri; four people are reported arrested.

December 25

TERRORISM: In Afghanistan, the Taliban release a videotape of captured Idaho National Guard private Bowe Bergdahl, who made anti-American statements, presumably under duress.

December 26

TERRORISM: In Baghdad, Iraq, a bomb explodes near the tent of Shiites making a pilgrimage to observe Ashoura festivals; three people are killed, and 16 are injured.

December 27

POLITICS: In Tehran, Iran at last 15 people are reported killed in clashes between political protestors and Basij militiamen. A further 300 demonstrators, who had taken to the streets chanting "Death to the dictator," are reported arrested. Significantly, today also marks the celebration of Ashoura, the most sacred holiday in the Shiite religious calendar.

December 30

POLITICS: In Tehran, Iran, the city's police chief threatens to show "no mercy" to demonstrators protesting a political crackdown against dissident figures. An estimated 500 people are arrested and detained.

TERRORISM: In Kandahar Province, Afghanistan, an improvised explosive device strikes a Canadian armored vehicle, killing four soldiers and a female journalist.

In Khost Province, Afghanistan, an apparent Taliban double agent recruited by the Central Intelligence Agency strolls into Forward Operating Base Chapman and detonates himself, killing seven agents and injuring six more.

In Anbar Province, Iraq, a bomb explodes in Ramadi, killing 23 people, 13 of them policemen.

December 31

MILITARY: For the first time since 2003, there are no recorded American fatalities in Iraq. "That is a very significant milestone for us as we continue to move forward," General Raymond T. Odierno declares. "And I think it also speaks to the level of violence and how it has decreased over time." Since the beginning of Operation Iraqi Freedom, 4,373 U.S. service personnel have been killed, including 898 in noncombat incidents. The story is reversed in Afghanistan, where 304 U.S. servicemen were killed this year, an increase of 151 fatalities over those sustained in 2008. This brings the death toll of Operation Enduring Freedom, launched in October 2001, to 933 service members. Among coalition partners, Canada is second with 32 deaths while 2,021 Afghan civilians were reported killed—465 of these by U.S. and coalition forces.

2010

January 1

DIPLOMACY: In Baghdad, an Iraqi government spokesman criticizes a U.S. judge for dismissing charges against guards working for the security firm Blackwater (later, Xe Services, LLC); they had been previously charged with the deaths of 17 Iraqi civilians.

January 3

DIPLOMACY: In Tehran, Iran, the government imposes a one-month deadline for Western leaders to accept its counterproposal to the reactor fuel deal. The Iranians are threatening to enrich their own uranium further and produce reactor fuel if it is not accepted.

January 12

TERRORISM: In Tehran, Iran, a motorcycle bomb kills Professor Masoud Ali Mohammadi, a prominent Tehran University nuclear physics professor. The government blames the United States and Israel for the incident, but Western analysts speculate that the professor's death is linked to his outspoken support for the dissident Green Movement.

January 14

POLITICS: The Iraqis Independent High Electoral Commission upholds a decision to ban 500 individuals from public office owing to their prior association with the Baath Party of Saddam Hussein. However, they maintain that the number is almost equally divided between Sunnis and Shiites.

TERRORISM: In Baghdad, Iraq, a court sentences 11 Iraqis to death for their role in the coordinated bombings of August 19, 2009. A triple bombing in Najaf this day also kills 25 Iraqis and injures 72 more.

January 16

DIPLOMACY: In New York City, representatives from the United States, China, Russia, France, Germany, and Britain gather to discuss possible avenues of action against Iran for its noncompliance toward the International Atomic Energy Agency.

January 17
TERRORISM: In Kabul, Afghanistan, a string of explosions near the presidential palace are suspected to be the work of Taliban operatives.

January 18
DIPLOMACY: In Baghdad, Iraq, UN Deputy Special Representative for the Secretary-General Christine McNab declares that Iraq is ready to transition to a longer-term developmental agenda. At the time she is addressing a multinational aid agency, the International Compact with Iraq.

January 23
DIPLOMACY: In Baghdad, Iraq, Vice President Joe Biden arrives to discuss the Independent High Electoral Commission's decision to ban several individuals, including some high-profile Sunnis, from running in the March 7 national election.

January 24
POLITICS: In Kabul, Afghanistan, the Independent Election Commission votes to delay national parliamentary elections from May 22 to September 18, citing a lack of funds and security considerations. The UN welcomes the move for the additional preparation time it grants to preparations.

January 25
DIPLOMACY: In Istanbul, Turkey, the fourth trilateral summit between Afghanistan, Turkey, and Pakistan takes place.
POLITICS: In Iraq, Ali Hassan al-Majid, cousin and former aid to Saddam Hussein, is executed. Known as "Chemical Ali" for his extensive use of nerve agents against Kurds during the Iran-Iraq War, he is responsible for the deaths of 5,000 people in the village of Halabja alone.

January 26
DIPLOMACY: In Afghanistan, a regional summit convenes with members from Turkey, Afghanistan, Turkmenistan, Tajikistan, Iran, Pakistan, and China.

January 28
DIPLOMACY: In eastern Afghanistan, chieftains from the Shinwari tribe, a large collection of Pashtun-speaking peoples, vows to assist the United States in fighting the Taliban in exchange for $1 million in local development projects. In doing so, they seek to bypass the Afghan national government, viewed by local tribal leaders as hopelessly corrupt.
MILITARY: In Paris, France, Defense Minister Bernard Kouchner announces that no new French combat troops will be sent to Afghanistan.

January 30
MILITARY: In Wardak Province, Afghanistan, fire is exchanged between a joint NATO-Afghan security force and a party of Afghan soldiers who mistake each other for the enemy.

January 31

MILITARY: In Washington, D.C., the government announces that it is deploying defensive missile batteries to several nations in the Persian Gulf, as well as maintaining a ship-based antimissile capability in that region.

February 1

TERRORISM: In Baghdad, Iraq, a female suicide bomber targets a gathering of Shiites then detonates herself, killing 41 people and injuring 106 others.

February 5

TERRORISM: In Karbala, Iraq, a string of car bombs aimed at Shiite religious pilgrims kills 32 people and injures 154 others.

February 6

MILITARY: In Helmand Province, Afghanistan, 16 Taliban fighters are killed by a joint NATO/Afghan security force during mine-clearing operations.

February 8

DIPLOMACY: In New York, Iran informs the International Atomic Energy Agency that it will begin producing enriched fuel for the Tehran Research Reactor, and revise design information for its Pilot Enrichment Plant at Natanz. The Iranians also blame the international community for failing to accept their earlier fuel deal counterproposal.

February 10

DIPLOMACY: In Washington, D.C., the government announces new domestic sanctions on Iranian Revolutionary Guard Corps companies and individuals. However, it offers to help purchase medical isotopes for the Iranians on the international market should they elect not enrich their own uranium.

February 12

POLITICS: In Tehran, President Mahmoud Ahmadinejad defiantly declares that Iran has produced 20 percent enriched uranium and will manufacture even more if it elects to do so.

February 13

DIPLOMACY: U.S. Secretary of State Hillary Clinton flies to Qatar and Saudi Arabia to discuss the present Iranian situation with Persian Gulf leaders.

MILITARY: In Helmand Province, Afghanistan, NATO and Afghan security forces commence Operation Moshtarak against Taliban insurgents based there. This involves a 6,000-troop assault on the city of Marjah, a known Taliban haven, which constitutes the largest single military action in Afghanistan since the American invasion of late 2001.

February 14

MILITARY: In Helmand Province, Afghanistan, an errant U.S. rocket accidentally kills 10 Afghan civilians in the face of stiffening Taliban resistance. Commanding general Stanley McChrystal immediately issues a statement deploring the deaths.

February 15

MILITARY: In Karachi, Pakistan, a joint sweep by American and Pakistani intelligence troops nets Mullah Abdul Ghani Baradar, a noted Taliban leader, along with several armed followers. The Americans claim his arrest represents the most significant human capture since Operation Enduring Freedom commenced in late 2001.

February 16

MILITARY: In Helmand Province, Afghanistan, U.S. Marines storm into a key police headquarters in Marjah. The building was previously used by Taliban forces as their headquarters.

February 17

DIPLOMACY: In Washington, D.C., Secretary of State Hillary Clinton informs reporters that should Iran develop its own nuclear weapons, it would lead to a regional arms race. She also asserts that Iranian actions do not support their claims of no interest in developing nuclear weapons.

February 18

DIPLOMACY: In New York City, the UN International Atomic Energy Agency complains that Iran has still not provided them with relevant technical data as to potential military dimensions of their ongoing nuclear program.

February 20

DIPLOMACY: In New York City, the UN International Atomic Energy Agency issues a report confirming that Iran has produced small quantities of 20 percent enriched uranium. It also calls upon the Iranians to clarify issues relative to possible nuclear weapons-related experiments.

February 21

AVIATION: Over Kabul, Afghanistan, an air strike called in by U.S. special forces accidentally kills 27 Afghan civilians. President Hamid Karzai immediately condemns the killings. Two U.S. helicopter pilots also die when their aircraft crashes inside Contingency Operating Base Speicher while landing. Mechanical failure, not enemy action, is suspected.

DIPLOMACY: In Tehran, Ali Akbar Salehi, head of the Iranian Atomic Energy Association, declares that he is forging ahead with plans to construct 10 more uranium enrichment sites, with work slated to begin within the next year. As a warning to the United States and Israel, he mentions that these sites will be made impervious to aerial attacks.

February 23

DIPLOMACY: The European Union announces that it is drafting new sanctions targeting Iran's energy and financial sectors in response to the failed Tehran Research Reactor deal.

February 25

MILITARY: In Helmand Province, Afghanistan, the Afghan national flag is raised over the town of Marjah, signaling its recapture from long-dominant Taliban forces.

February 26

TERRORISM: In Kabul, Afghanistan, a string of explosions and suicide car bombings kills 18 people, including French, Italian, and Indian nationals. The Taliban subsequently claim responsibility.

March 4

DIPLOMACY: Brazilian foreign minister Celso Amorim, having met with U.S. secretary of state Hillary Clinton, refuses to support new sanctions against Iran. Moreover, he vows that Brazil refuses to bow down to foreign pressure and favors diplomacy to confrontation.

TERRORISM: In Baghdad, Iraq, the first round of national elections is marred by several bombings, which kill 14 people.

March 6

TERRORISM: In Najaf, Iraq, a car bomb outside the Ali Holy Shrine takes the lives of three people; a further 54 are wounded.

March 7

TERRORISM: In Baghdad, Iraq, a string of al-Qaeda bombs kills 38 people during national elections. The national election commission also reports that 62 percent of eligible Iraqis voted, although that number declined to 53 percent in the capital.

March 13

TERRORISM: In Kandahar, Afghanistan, four Taliban suicide bombers kill 30 people and wound 40 more at a mosque and a road junction.

March 21

TERRORISM: In Helmand Province, Afghanistan, a Taliban suicide bomber targets an Afghan army vehicle but hits a market in the Gereshk district, killing 10 civilians.

March 22

DIPLOMACY: In New York City, the UN Security Council Approves Resolution 1917, which extends the UN Assistance Mission to Afghanistan until March 23, 2010.

March 26

DIPLOMACY: In New York City, the UN Security Council receives a letter from the Iranian government whereby it pledges to observe the Nuclear Non-proliferation Treaty and abide by the International Atomic Energy Agency.

TERRORISM: In the so-called Sunni Triangle near Khalis, Iraq, car and roadside explosions kill 32 people and wound 68.

March 28

DIPLOMACY: In Kabul, Afghanistan, President Barack Obama arrives for discussions with President Hamid Karzai before paying his respects to U.S. troops.

March 29

POLITICS: In Iraq, the recent round of national elections gives the Iraqi National Movement of former prime minister Ayad Allawi 91 parliamentary seats out of 325. Prime Minister Nuri al-Maliki's State of Law alliance comes in second with 89 seats, while the Shia religious movement of radical cleric Moqtada al-Sadr wins 70. The two main Kurdish parties win a further 43 sets. Because all parties fall short of the 163 seats necessary to form a government, intense negotiations commence. However, Prime Minister al-Maliki refuses to recognize the results and determines to challenge them in court.

March 31

DIPLOMACY: Reports surface that Dr. Shahram Amiri, a senior Iranian nuclear scientist who disappeared while making a pilgrimage to Mecca in 2009, has actually defected to the United States and is cooperating with the Central Intelligence Agency.
POLITICS: In Baghdad, Iraq, the Iraqi Council of Representatives accepts the provisional results of the recent election and proudly asserts how foreigners have affirmed the integrity of the process.

April 1

POLITICS: In Kabul, Afghanistan, President Hamid Karzai accuses foreign election observers of fraud during the 2009 national election.

April 2

DIPLOMACY: In Beijing, China, the government declares that it would support negotiations for new UN sanctions against Iran. In return, the Iranians dispatch Saeed Jalili, their top nuclear negotiator, to Beijing for talks with Chinese foreign minister Yang Jiechi.
TERRORISM: In Baghdad, Iraq, gunmen attack and kill 25 members of a Sunni militia known to oppose al-Qaeda.

April 3

MILITARY: In northern Afghanistan, German forces operating as part of the NATO-led command kill five Afghan soldiers in a friendly fire incident.

April 4

TERRORISM: In Baghdad, Iraq, a succession of three explosions kills 30 people and injures 200 more.

April 6

DIPLOMACY: In Washington, D.C., the United States releases its 2010 Nuclear Posture Review, which names Iran and North Korea as having breached their obligations toward nonproliferation.
TERRORISM: In various Shiite neighborhoods throughout Baghdad, Iraq, a string of seven explosions kill 34 people and injures 104 others.

April 8

TERRORISM: The Taliban release a video featuring captured American private Bowe Robert Bergdahl, who was seized in June 2009.

April 9

AVIATION: Over southern Afghanistan, a U.S. Air Force CV-22 Osprey, an aircraft usually associated with Special Operations, crashes with the loss of four crewmen and one civilian employee. Mechanical failure is suspected.

April 10

POLITICS: In Tehran, President Mahmoud Ahmadinejad declares that Iran has developed its own third-generation centrifuge, 10 times more effective than previous designs. The speech is delivered to commemorate Iranian Nuclear Day.

April 12

DIPLOMACY: In Washington, D.C., President Barack Obama and Chinese president Hu Jintao meet during a bilateral summit on global nuclear security. U.S. officials subsequently state that China has agreed to increased engagement on a tougher UN resolution against Iran, but the Chinese decline to mention any new sanctions.

April 13

DIPLOMACY: In New York City, the UN Security Council receives a letter from the Iranian government that denounces the U.S. nuclear posture as a threat to Iran.

April 17

POLITICS: In Kabul, Afghanistan, the Electoral Complaints Commission appoints two foreign commissioners to that body, over the objections of President Hamid Karzai. It also guarantees 68 seats in the lower house of parliament to women candidates.

April 17–18

DIPLOMACY: In Tehran, Iran, the government hosts a nuclear conference, attended by 60 nations, which focuses on the nuclear rights of Nuclear Non-Proliferation Treaty signatories.

April 19

POLITICS: The Iraqi Independent High Electoral Commission orders that votes cast on in the Baghdad region on March 7 be recounted.

April 23

TERRORISM: Shiite neighborhoods throughout Baghdad, Iraq, are struck by a wave of bombings that kill 61 people. No group claims responsibility for the act.

April 23–25

DIPLOMACY: In Vienna, Austria, Iranian foreign minister Manouchehr Mottaki meets with International Atomic Energy Agency (AEA) chief Yukiya Amano and Austrian foreign minister Michael Spindelegger. No word is mention of progress made or issues resolved, and the meeting is views as an attempt by President Mahmoud Ahmadinejad to head off a new UN sanctions resolution.

April 25

TERRORISM: The militant group al-Qaeda in Iraq releases an online report confirming that Abu Ayyub al-Masri and Abu Omar al-Baghdadi, two of its most senior leaders, have been killed by coalition forces.

April 26

AVIATION: A milestone is reached when the first commercial flight from Iraq lands at Gatwick International Airport, United Kingdom.

May 4

Politics: In Baghdad, Iraq, the president's council urges that a new government be constituted quickly, warning that delays could trigger a resurgence of sectarian violence.

May 5

Politics: In Iraq, the State of Law Coalition of Prime Minister Nuri al-Maliki and the Iraqi National Alliance of challenger Ayad Allawi agree to ally themselves in the national parliament.

May 10

Terrorism: A spate of new bombings across six Iraqi provinces results in the deaths of over 100 people.

May 10–13

Diplomacy: In Washington, D.C., Afghan president Hamid Karzai arrives for three days of discussion with President Barack Obama. The two men reaffirm their long-term strategic commitment between their nations.

May 16

Politics: In Baghdad, a recount of votes cast March 7 reaffirms a small plurality for the slate of candidates headed by former prime minister Ayad Allawi.

May 17

Diplomacy: An agreement is announced by President Luiz Inácio da Silva of Brazil, Prime Minister Tayyip Erdogan of Turkey, and President Mahmoud Ahmadinejad of Iran relative to a proposed nuclear fuel swap between the three.

May 18

Terrorism: At Bagram Air Base, Afghanistan, a Taliban suicide bomber kills 6 NATO soldiers and 12 civilians; five insurgents are also killed in a gun battle.

May 19

Diplomacy: In New York, the U.S. delegation announces that Russia and China have agreed to support a new round of sanctions against Iran for its illegal nuclear program.

May 20–21

Diplomacy: Brazilian president Luiz Inácio Lula da Silva declares that since Iran has been willing to engage in negotiations on its nuclear program with Brazil, the rest of the international community should likewise focus on negotiating a possible solution instead of pursuing sanctions.

May 21

Diplomacy: In Washington, D.C., the government reveals that it is removing domestic sanctions against several Russian agencies for past weapons and technology transfers to Iran. Russian officials are quick to point out that draft sanctions against Iran, presently under consideration, would not preclude the sale of antiaircraft missiles to that nation.

MILITARY: In Helmand Province, Afghanistan, 8,000 British troops come under the operational command of the United States.

TERRORISM: In al-Khalis, Iraq, a car bomb explodes outside a coffee shop, killing 22 people and wounding 53.

May 24

DIPLOMACY: In New York City, the International Atomic Energy Agency receives a letter from the Iranian government outlining its proposed nuclear fuel swap with Brazil and Turkey.

MILITARY: For the first time since 2003, U.S. forces in Afghanistan are more numerous than those deployed in Iraq.

May 25

DIPLOMACY: In Washington, D.C., Secretary of State Hillary Clinton states that the proposed nuclear fuel swap between Iran, Brazil, and Turkey is a transparent ploy to circumvent future action by the UN Security Council.

May 31

AVIATION: In Afghanistan, U.S. authorities that and American air strike near Kandahar has killed Mustafa Abu Yazid, a senior Taliban figure, along with several of his followers.

June 1–2

POLITICS: In Baghdad, Iraq, the supreme court certifies the results of the March 7 election. The Security Council subsequently congratulates the people of Iraq and calls upon all parties to respect the will of the voters.

June 7–8

DIPLOMACY: In Baghdad, a government official protests recent Iranian shelling of Kurdish rebels operating from northern Iraqi Kurdistan. They also claim that the Iranians are erecting a small base of operations on their soil to facilitate anti-guerrilla operations.

TERRORISM: A string of bombings in Baghdad and across Iraq targets police and members of the Sunni-based Awakening Movement; 11 people are killed and dozens more injured.

June 8

POLITICS: In Baghdad, Iraq, the parliament announces that it will convene soon to begin forming a new national government. However, negotiations are expected to take months as former prime minister Ayad Allawi's slate enjoys a two-seat advantage over the coalition led by Prime Minister Nuri al-Maliki.

June 9

DIPLOMACY: In New York City, the UN Security Council approves another set of sanctions against Iran's nuclear program; 12 vote for the measure, Brazil and Turkey oppose it, and Lebanon abstains.

June 12–14

POLITICS: In Baghdad, Iraq, Prime Minister Nuri al-Maliki and challenger Ayad Allawi confer over the political situation in the country. The national parliament also meets briefly, but then adjourns pending formation of a new national government.

June 13

POLITICS: The United States announces that it has uncovered vast mineral wealth in Afghanistan, including deposits of iron, copper, gold, and lithium. The estimated value of these materials is in excess of $1 trillion and could dramatically improve the bleak economic outlook for that poverty stricken nation.

June 20

TERRORISM: In Baghdad, Iraq, a bomb two car bombs explode in the Iraqi Commercial Bank, killing 27 people and injuring several dozen more.

June 23

MILITARY: In Paktia Province, Afghanistan, NATO forces surprise and kill a large number of Taliban insurgents lurking in Jani Khel near the Pakistani border. Among the dead is Qari Ismael, the district Taliban leader.

In Afghanistan, General Stanley McChrystal is relieved of command and replaced by General David H. Petraeus after making some ill-considered comments during an interview with *Rolling Stone* magazine. President Barack Obama subsequently claims that McChrystal was relieved, not because of inopportune remarks, but rather from a desire to unify the national security team.

July 1

MILITARY: In Helmand Province, Afghanistan, international and Afghan security forces make a sweep through the Baghran district, killing several Taliban insurgents in a four-hour firefight and capturing their district chief.

July 6

MILITARY: In Iraq, commanding general Raymond Odierno states that UN forces may have to replace withdrawing U.S. troops in Iraq's oil-rich northern region if feuding between Kurds and Arabs continues. The Kurds are pushing for a semiautonomous region, plus control of indigenous oil reserves. However, a compromise between the two groups remains fleeting.

At present, there are only 77,500 American troops remaining in Iraq, with the bulk slated for withdrawal in 2011.

In Ghazni Province, Afghanistan, members of a NATO patrol confront then kill five Afghan soldiers who apparently made threatening gestures toward them. The International Security Assistant Force promises to investigate the incident.

July 7

MILITARY: In Washington, D.C., Secretary of Defense Robert M. Gates recommends Marine Corps general James Mathis to succeed General David H. Petraeus as the new U.S. Central Command leader. General Mathis is best known for aggressive leadership at the Battle of Fallujah in 2004, but his penchant for blunt talk has raised some eyebrows.

In Kabul, Lieutenant General David Rodriguez, the nominal day-to-day commander of U.S. forces in Afghanistan, states that there might be some small adjustments to existing rules of engagement intended to reduce civilian casualties but no major changes.

In Helmand Province, Afghanistan, British coalition forces prepare to depart the Sangin district and hand control of this violent region over to the Americans. The British are currently redeploying their forces to the central area of the province.

July 8
MILITARY: In Washington, D.C., the government announces that it is delivering $3 billion in equipment aimed at countering the improvised exploding devies (IEDs) increasingly employed by the Taliban in Afghanistan. The equipment includes surveillance blimps, bomb-proof vehicles, manually controlled robots, and mine detectors.

TERRORISM: Insurgent activity in the Sangin District, Helmand Province, Afghanistan, kills three NATO service members, including one Briton.

July 10
MILITARY: In Paktia Province, Afghanistan, a combined U.S.-Afghan commando raid kills one Taliban guerrilla and takes eight captive.

TERRORISM: In eastern Afghanistan, four U.S. servicemen are killed by a roadside bomb, while two others meet a similar fate in the southern reaches of the country.

July 11
MILITARY: In Zabol Province, Afghanistan, a joint NATO-Afghan security sweep kills Malauwi Shahbuddin, a noted Taliban commander of the Shahjoy district, in addition to several followers.

The military death toll for June 2010 stands at 102 international service members killed, including 59 Americans. This is as much a reflection of expanded coalition operations against the Taliban as it is an increase in enemy activity.

TERRORISM: In Badakshan Province, Afghanistan, a remote-controlled Taliban bomb, coupled with a raid upon a checkpoint, kills 11 police officers and a governmental official.

BIOGRAPHIES

Abizaid, John P. (1951–)

U.S. Army general

John Philip Abizaid was born in Coleville, California, on April 1, 1951, and graduated from the U.S. Military Academy in 1973. He served as a second lieutenant in the 504th Parachute Infantry Regiment, rose to command a company, and distinguished himself during the U.S.-led invasion of Grenada in 1983. During the first Gulf War of 1991, Abizaid commanded a battalion in the 325th Airborne Regimental Combat Team stationed at Vicenza, Italy, and he subsequently served in northern Iraq while assisting the Kurds. Abizaid handled his affairs adroitly and commanded a brigade in the elite 82nd Airborne Division and also served as assistant commander of the 1st Armored Division in Bosnia-Herzegovina. In 1997, Abizaid returned to West Point as its 66th commandant, where he updated the curricula and clamped down on hazing abuses. He subsequently returned to Bosnia to command the famous 1st Infantry Division, parts of which deployed there as part of a UN-sponsored peacekeeping mission. At various times in his career, Abizaid studied at the Armed Forces Staff College and the U.S. Army War College, and he received a master's degree in Middle Eastern studies from Harvard University. Abizaid is also one of a handful of senior army officers fluent in Arabic, having studied at the University of Jordan in Amman.

During the initial phases of Operation Iraqi Freedom in spring 2003, Abizaid served with the Deputy Command (Forward), Combined Forces Command, U.S. Central Command. On July 7, 2003, he gained promotion to full general and succeeded departing general Tommy Franks as commander of the Central Command. This command organization oversees the activities of 250,000 U.S. troops across a 27-nation arc stretching from the Horn of Africa, through the Arabian Peninsula, to South and Central Asia. It figures prominently in military matters pertaining to the war on terror. No armchair general, Abizaid was a frequent visitor to Iraq and Afghanistan to help direct operations against Muslim extremists and terrorists operating in that region. For four years, he helped craft the strategy necessary to fight al-Qaeda in Iraq and the Taliban based in Pakistan with varying degrees of success. Like most senior American leaders, Abizaid was taken aback by the tenacity of the insurgents, who suffered heavy losses at the hands of coalition troops but were never quite eradicated. He expressed his unhappiness with the state of affairs before the Senate Armed Services Committee in August 2006, and he admitted that civil war in Iraq seemed very likely. Concurrently, Abizaid also contended with a rising tide of Muslim piracy in the Persian Gulf and Red Sea regions, which further threatened to undermine regional security and stability. On December 20, 2006, he announced his retirement from the Central Command and was replaced by Admiral William J. Fallon. Abizaid has been installed as a fellow at the Hoover Institute at Stanford University, in California.

Ahmadinejad, Mahmoud (1956–   )
president of Iran

Mahmoud Saborjhian was born in Garmsar, Iran, on October 28, 1956, the son of a blacksmith. His family relocated to the capital of Tehran while he was a child, and he adopted the religious surname Ahmadinejad. Growing up in a relatively poor and devoutly religious family imprinted him with qualities of Shiite piety that he displayed throughout adulthood. Ahmadinejad matured during a restive period in Iranian history when religious and conservative social circles resisted the reforms of Mohammad Reza Shah Pahlavi. In 1975, he entered the University of Science and Technology in Tehran in pursuit of several engineering degrees, but he also joined religious radical groups on campus. One of these, the Office for Strengthening Unity between Universities and Theological Seminaries, was responsible for seizing the American embassy in November 1979 and holding 52 hostages for 444 days. Ahmadinejad's role in these proceedings is not clear, but several former hostages claim he was one of the ringleaders responsible for interrogating them. After Iraq invaded Iran in 1980, Ahmadinejad joined the hard-line Revolutionary Guards, apparently as a Basij volunteer, and he spent the war years fighting Iraqis and Kurds in northwestern Iran. He handled himself capably and by 1988 was serving as a special adviser to the governor-general of Maku and Khoy in Iran's Kurdistan Province. Ahmadinejad subsequently returned to college and obtained his doctorate in transportation engineering in 1997 from the University of Science and Technology, where he also taught as a professor. Little known nationally, Ahmadinejad became a force in city politics, and in June 2003 he began his political career with a surprising victory as mayor. A staunch religious conservative, he appealed to the clergy and the underclass by crafting policies that addressed their needs, while also scaling back Western-style influences.

Ahmadinejad next parlayed his mounting popularity by running for the presidency of Iran. He campaigned on similar themes of religiosity, humbleness, and returning part of the nation's oil revenues back to the poor and won a startling 79 percent upset over Ali Akbar Hashemi Rafsanjani, a wealthy cleric and prior president. Ahmadinejad was sworn into office on August 3, 2005, as Iran's sixth president and the first chief executive who was not a cleric. In office, he continued elevating religion in public life and cracking down on vice and excesses, which had endeared him to the masses. On the diplomatic front, he has assumed a confrontational stance toward the United States and repeatedly called for the destruction of Israel. On September 24, 2007, he ventured to Columbia University in New York City to defend his position and was loudly condemned by protestors. Ahmadinejad also defied repeated calls by the United Nations to curtail Iran's quest for nuclear energy. On June 12, 2009, he was reelected by a questionable 62 percent of the vote, which led to widespread antigovernment protests and several deaths.

Allawi, Ayad (1945–   )
prime minister of Iraq

Ayad Allawi was born in Iraq in 1945, part of an affluent merchant family. He attended medical college in Baghdad and studied to be a neurologist and also joined the outlawed Baath Party. This was considered unusual, since the movement was dominated by Sunni Muslims and Allawi was a Shiite, and he gradually developed ties with Saddam Hussein. In 1971, he relocated to the United Kingdom to continue his medical training, although he resigned from the Baath Party four years later over dissatisfaction with the direction in which Saddam Hussein was taking the nation. Allawi became highly critical of Saddam Hussein and joined a network of former military exiles to oppose him, and in 1978 he was badly injured in an assassination attempt, presumably orchestrated from Baghdad. He spent nearly a year recuperating from his wounds and subsequently founded the Iraqi National Accord, an exile dissident group, which received funding and other forms of aid from British intelligence and the Central Intelligence Agency. He cultivated disenchanted military officers from the Baath Party, and in 1996, a coup was orchestrated against Saddam Hussein. The plot misfired and several individuals involved were executed, and all property belonging to the Allawi family, totaling $250 million, was confiscated. Despite this setback, Allawi continued receiving clandestine support and continued feeding Western agencies with intelligence regarding Iraqi internal affairs. In 2002, Allawi informed them that Saddam Hussein could deploy chemical weapons within 45 minutes of being ordered to do so, inducing President George W. Bush to topple him in April 2003.

No sooner had the Americans taken control of Iraq than the Coalition Provisional Authority established the Iraqi Governing Council to put a local face on transitional governance. Allawi was tapped to serve on the council and briefly held its rotating presidency in October 2003.

On May 28, 2004, he was unanimously elected to serve as interim prime minister in the period leading up to national elections. Despite his reputation as an outsider and a secular figure, Allawi was endorsed by Grand Ayatollah Ali Sistani, a respected Shiite leader. Once in power, Allawi reinstituted capital punishment and also created the General Security Directorate to suppress a raging Sunni insurgency in many provinces. For this reason, on June 28, 2004, a terror group offered a $285,000 reward for anyone who could assassinate him. Allawi remained uncowed, endorsed the American decision to reduce the terrorist stronghold at Fallujah, and also took measures to contain the Shiite militia of Moqtada al-Sadr. In January 2005, Allawi's party, Iraqi National Accord, fared poorly in elections due to his strident handling of

the insurgency. He resigned from power on April 7, 2005, and was replaced by Ibrahim al-Jaafari. A new coalition he started, the Iraqi National List, also performed poorly at the polls in December 2005. He ran again for prime minister on March 26, 2010, winning sufficient votes to deny Nuri al-Maliki a clear majority. An agreement to make Allawi the head of a new security council ended the political stalemate in November 2010.

Amin, Hafizullah (1929–1979)

president of Afghanistan

Hafizullah Amin was born in Paghman, Afghanistan, on August 1, 1929, the son of a civil servant and a member of the Pashtun tribe. He was educated locally and at Kabul University, then pursued graduate degrees at the University of Wisconsin and Columbia University. Returning to Afghanistan, Amin taught at various schools for several years and in 1964 was one of the founding members of the Marxist People's Democratic Party of Afghanistan (PDPA). He was elected to parliament in 1969 and became closely associated with the Khalq (People's) faction, as opposed to the doctrinaire, Soviet-oriented Parcham (Banner) faction. In April 1978, following the Saur Revolution, which installed Communists in power, Amin served as vice premier and minister of foreign affairs. However, he failed to coexist with President Nur Mohammad Taraki of the Parcham faction, whom he regarded as unfit to lead the country, and began plotting against him. The Soviets were aware of Amin's machinations and warned Taraki beforehand, after which the latter began plotting to assassinate Amin. Amin refused to meet with Taraki and subsequently demanded that the Soviet ambassador, Alexander Puzanov, guarantee his safety. A meeting was finally arranged between the two in September 1979, a shootout ensued, and Taraki was killed. On September 14, 1979, Amin took the reins of government after announcing that his adversary had died of an "unspecified illness." The Soviet Union, which had invested heavily in Afghanistan, was wary of Amin due to his independent nature and began looking for an excuse to depose him.

Once in power, Amin observed a strict Marxist line by introducing radical reforms intending to undercut the traditional religious and cultural power base in the conservative countryside. The result was massive unrest and open rebellion by several Islamic sects, all of which Amin ordered crushed with great brutality. Amin also turned his sights on the PDPA, purging it of Parchem members and executing several hundred dissidents. In November 1979, he ordered a large military operation in Paktia Province, which resulted in thousands of casualties and the birth of the mujahideen movement. With events spiraling out of control, Amin turned to the Soviet Union for military assistance, which proved his undoing. The Kremlin regarded his harsh regime as destabilizing to the country and was determined to halt his rather independent foreign policy, which included friendly overtures to Pakistan and the United States. On December 27, 1979, troops from the KGB Osnaz (Alpha Group) and GRU Spetsnaz forces stormed the Tajbeg presidential palace, killing Amin and several supporters. A radio broadcast from the Ministry of the Interior declared that the people had been freed from Amin, and that the Soviets were simply complying with terms of their 1978 Treaty of Friendship, Cooperation, and Good Neighborliness with Afghanistan. Amin was replaced by the far more tractable Babrak Karmal, now backed by thousands of Soviet troops.

Aziz, Tariq (1936–)

foreign minister of Iraq

Mikhail Yuhanna was born in Tell Kaif, northern Iraq, on April 28, 1936, the son of a waiter and member of the Chaldean (Nestorian) sect of the Catholic Church. Given the intense animosity of Muslims toward Christians, he changed his name to Tariq Aziz by the time he attended Baghdad University in the 1950s. Aziz graduated with a degree in English in 1958, trained as a journalist, and became politically active by joining the radical

Baath Party. In this capacity, he served as editor of the underground newspapers *al-Jumhurilya* and *al-Jamahir* while gradually working his way up the party ranks. When the Baath regime in Baghdad was overthrown in 1963, he fled to Syria to serve as editor of a Syrian Baathist paper. However, he was arrested for opposing the military faction of the Syrian Baathist party after it seized control in 1966, and Aziz returned to Iraq two years later following the Baathist coup there. By this time, Aziz had aligned himself with Saddam Hussein, a leading factional figure, and in 1972 he became the only Christian to serve on the Revolutionary Command Council running the country. He subsequently ran as a candidate for the Baath Command, and by 1977 he obtained full party membership. Saddam Hussein was particularly grateful for his services and appointed him minister of information in 1974 and deputy prime minister in 1979. His high profile in government circles made him a target of Muslim radicals, and he endured several failed assassination attempts during the 1980s. Iraq was then at war with revolutionary Iran, and Aziz distinguished himself as a diplomat by bringing several Arab and Western nations into a de facto alliance against Ayatollah Khomeini. His greatest triumph came in 1986 when he persuaded France to sell Iraq several Super Etendard jet fighters capable of launching Exocet antiship missiles at Iranian tankers. After the Iran-Iraq War ended in 1988, Aziz flew to Geneva for high-profile negotiations with Iranian foreign minister Ali Akbar Velayati, establishing an uneasy peace with his neighbor.

In 1990, Aziz found himself in the awkward position of defending Saddam Hussein's occupation and annexation of Kuwait. In January 1991, just days before Operation Desert Storm commenced, he returned to Geneva and negotiated inconclusively with U.S. secretary of state James A. Baker. Afterward, he was relieved as foreign minister but retained the title and post of deputy prime minister. In February 2003, Aziz arrived in Rome for an audience with the pope and pledged complete cooperation with disarmament measures. During Operation Iraqi Freedom, he was wanted by Coalition authorities and surrendered himself on April 24, 2003. On April 28, 2008, Aziz was tried for the deaths of 42 merchants accused of profiteering, and a jury convicted him of crimes against humanity on March 11, 2009. On October 26, 2010, the Iraqi High Tribunal sentenced Aziz to death for persecuting Shiite religious minorities. In November, Iraqi president Jalal Talibani refused to sign the order for Aziz's execution, signaling that Aziz would be spared.

Bani-Sadr, Abolhassan (1933–   )
president of Iran

Abolhassan Bani-Sadr was born in Hamadan, Iran, on March 22, 1933, into a wealthy and religious landowning family. After studying theology and law at Tehran University, he became politically active against the ruling shah, was arrested and wounded in several demonstrations, and finally fled to France in 1963. There, while pursing a degree in economics, he became radicalized by the ideas of the Marxist scholar Paul Vielle. Bani-Sadr, after encountering Ayatollah Ruhollah Khomeini in 1972, subscribed to the Ayatollah's idea of transforming Iran into an Islamic republic. He returned with Khomeini following the Islamic revolution of February 1979 and, as one of his closest aides, was appointed deputy economy and finance minister. On January 12, 1980, Bani-Sadr ran for the presidency and defeated a number of highly conservative and radical candidates by winning 78.9 percent of the popular vote. He inherited a country wracked by revolutionary fervor and simmering political discontent; consequently, his tenure in office was beset by conflict with two of the ruling Islamic Republican Party's (IRP) leading members, Ayatollah Mohammad Beheshti and Ali Akbar Hashemi Rafsanjani. Although Bani-Sadr enjoyed the favor of Ayatollah Khomeini, his confrontations with the IRP exploded following the seizure of the American embassy in Tehran in November 1979. His inability to obtain

the release of all hostages from radical students underscores how little control Bani-Sadr actually wielded over events. Nonetheless, in February 1980, Khomeini appointed him commander in chief and chairman of the Revolutionary Council, whereupon he attempted to stabilize the country and curb revolutionary excesses. His efforts were completely undermined that spring following the IRP's sweeping parliamentary victory, and he was forced to accept the radical Mohammad Ali Raja as his prime minister. Bani-Sadr's reputation tumbled further in July 1980 following a failed coup attempt by the armed forces, and several of his key appointees were tried and executed for treason.

The turning point in Bani-Sadr's political fortunes happened in September 1980, when Iraq invaded Iran to end simmering territorial disputes. He openly favored the armed forces over the Revolutionary Guards, in the struggle against Saddam Hussein, which did little to endear him to the ruling elite, and his inability to defeat the invaders led to his dismissal as commander in chief on June 10, 1981. Bani-Sadr was also accused of harboring anticlerical sentiments, especially against Ayatollah Beheshti, so Ayatollah Khomeini, his former ally, consented to his removal. He was impeached by the Majlis on June 21, 1981, and went underground for several weeks, during which time several of his closest associates were arrested and executed. Bani-Sadr fled the country for France with the help of the leftist mujahideen and subsequently settled in Paris. He remains an outspoken opponent of the Iranian theocracy.

Boomer, Walter E. (1938–   )
U.S. Marine Corps general

Walter E. Boomer was born in Rich Square, North Carolina, on September 22, 1938, and received a second lieutenant's commission in the U.S. Marine Corps while pursuing his bachelor's degree from Duke University in 1960. He rose to captain in 1965 and saw service in Vietnam from 1966 to 1967 as a company officer, winning a Silver Star for valor. After passing through the Amphibious

Warfare School at Quantico, Virginia, Boomer returned to Southeast Asia in 1971 as an adviser to South Vietnamese marines, and he was under fire throughout the communist Easter Offensive the following year. After additional study at American University, he taught management at the U.S. Naval Academy as the management department chairman and became a lieutenant colonel in 1976. Boomer served several years in various posts, rising to brigadier general in April 1986 and taking command of the 4th Marine Division, Fleet Marine Force, New Orleans. Boomer rose to major general on March 14, 1989, and lieutenant general on August 8, 1990, around the same time that Iraqi president Saddam Hussein launched his invasion of Kuwait. On August 15, 1990, Boomer arrived in Saudi Arabia as commanding general, U.S. Marine Forces Central Command and I Marine Expeditionary Force. In time, this consisted of the 1st and 2nd Marine Divisions, the 3rd Marine Air Wing, and the U.S. Army Tiger Brigade from the 2nd Armored Division. The unit gave marines the added punch of ultramodern Army M1 Abrams tanks to supplement their older M60 Pattons.

As Operation Desert Shield gave way to Desert Storm, Boomer favored a direct amphibious assault on the port of Ash-Shu'yabah, 20 miles south of Kuwait City, to provide the I Marine Expeditions Force with a supply base before pushing north. Such a move would also preempt any Iraqi counterattacks against the main overland thrust. However, he deferred to the coalition commanding general, H. Norman Schwarzkopf, to cancel any landings on the coast for fear that they would prove too costly and would delay the overland offensive. In return, Schwarzkopf approved Boomer's request to delay the attack from February 22, 1991, to February 24, to allow the marines more time to redeploy. Kuwait City was liberated during the so-called 100 hours campaign by marines, who had no trouble dealing with the Iraqi defenders. After the Gulf War, Boomer arrived at Camp Pendleton, California, as commanding general of the I Marine Expeditionary Force and commanding general of the Marine

Corps Base, where he remained until September 1991. He subsequently served as commanding general of the Marine Corps Combat Development Command, rose to full general on September 1, 1992, and performed his final duty as assistant commandant of the Marine Corps in Washington, D.C. Boomer retired from the marines on September 1, 1994, and presently serves as chairman and CEO of the Rogers Corporation.

Bremer, L. Paul, III (1941–   )
American diplomat

Lewis Paul Bremer III was born in Hartford, Connecticut, on September 30, 1941, the son of an affluent businessman. He graduated from Yale University in 1963 and earned a business degree from Harvard University in 1966 before obtaining his Certificate of Political Studies at the Institut d'Études Politiques de Paris. Bremer subsequently joined the Foreign Service and served in Kabul, Afghanistan, as a general officer, and as an economic officer in Blantyre, Malawi, from 1968 to 1971. Afterward, he held several posts in the State Department under Henry Kissinger from 1972 to 1976. Bremer then completed additional stints abroad as ambassador to the Netherlands in 1983 and ambassador-at-large for counterterrorism in 1986. He soon established himself as an authority on terrorism, and in 1999, Speaker of the House Dennis Hastert appointed him chairman of the National Commission on Terrorism. He also served in various positions throughout the corporate world as an adviser, CEO, and consultant with various large firms and won several awards from the State Department and the Secretary of State's Office. He was serving as chairman of Marsh Crisis Consulting, an insurance company, when terrorists struck the World Trade Center on September 11, 2001; his company lost 295 members in the attack. That fall, Bremer was appointed cochair of the Heritage Foundation's Homeland Security Task Force, which drew up the outlines for the nation's Department of Homeland Security. He burnished his conservative credentials impressively over the next two years, and in May 2003 President George W. Bush appointed him U.S. presidential envoy in Baghdad, Iraq, during a critical phase of the American occupation.

Once in Baghdad, Bremer assumed control of the Coalition Provisional Authority, a civilian governing agency tasked with helping Iraq reestablish sovereignty and day-to-day governance. However, one of his first acts was issuing Order Number 2 to dismantle the Baathist-dominated Iraqi army, for which he has been much criticized. Many unemployed soldiers subsequently joined the ranks of the insurgency, but, since the Iraqi army had already dissolved by the time the Americans occupied the country, Bremer's action appears moot. An important political landmark was reached on July 13, 2003, when he approved creation of the Iraqi Interim Governing Council while also developing guidelines for an interim constitution. This was signed into effect on March 5, 2004, following intense negotiations to placate competing religious and ethnic factions in Iraq, and on June 28, 2004, Bremer turned limited sovereignty back over to the Iraqi Interim Government. Iraq was then beset by a mounting Sunni-based insurgency, but Bremer remained confident that freedom and democracy would triumph over terrorism. He departed Baghdad shortly afterward and was replaced by John Negroponte. Bremer received the Presidential Medal of Freedom from President Bush on December 14, 2004, and he is active as a public speaker.

Casey, George W. (1948–   )

U.S. Army general

George William Casey, Jr., was born in Sendai, Japan, on July 22, 1948, during the U.S. military occupation of that country. His father, George W. Casey, Sr., was a West Point graduate who rose to major general and died in Vietnam when his helicopter crashed in July 1970. Casey grew up in South Boston, Massachusetts, and enrolled in the Reserve Officers' Training Corps while acquiring his bachelor's degree at Georgetown University.

As a second lieutenant, he served the first part of his career with the Mechanized Infantry, rising to brigadier general commanding the 3rd Brigade of the 1st Cavalry Division. Casey subsequently served as the assistant division commander of the 1st Armored Division in Germany, and he deployed with his men in Bosnia-Herzegovina between July 1996 and August 1997 for peacekeeping duties. He next rose to major general and assumed control of the 1st Armored Division in July 1999, performing competently for the next two years. In July 2001, Casey transferred to the Pentagon to serve as director of strategic plans and policy with the Joint Chiefs of Staff (JCS). In January 2003, he joined the JCS as its director, and he became the 30th vice chief of staff of the army in October 2003. He held that post until June 2004, when he received the challenging appointment to command the Multinational Force Iraq.

Casey replaced departing lieutenant general Ricardo S. Sanchez in Baghdad and was compelled to grapple with the same problems as his predecessor. Warring ethnic and religious factions within Iraqi society were attacking each other, while Sunni al-Qaeda terrorists attacked occupation troops and Shiite terrorists, armed and agitated by Iran, were also active. Casey sought to encourage Iraqis to shoulder increasing responsibility for their own security. To that end, he focused on training the demoralized Iraqi military, and he kept U.S. forces in the background. He also publicly stated that the national elections of December 2005 held the potential to unify Iraq and allow for an expedited withdrawal of American forces, but his expectations were dashed by increased sectarian violence. When President George W. Bush announced his plans for a troop "surge" to reinforce occupying forces in January 2007, Casey went on record opposing it, believing that a heightened American visibility might actually fuel the insurgency. He was replaced as coalition commander on February 10, 2007, by General David H. Petraeus. Two days earlier, however, the Senate approved his appointment as the new chief of staff of the army in Washington,

D.C., replacing General Peter Schoomaker. In September 2007, Casey raised political eyebrows again by stating that the concurrent deployments in Iraq and Afghanistan were wearing the army thin and taking a toll on military families who were enduring 15-month tours of duty. In November 2009, he also went on record as supporting General Stanley McChrystal's request to increase American troops in Afghanistan by 40,000 men.

Dostum, Abdul Rashid (1954–)
Afghan general

Abdul Rashid Dostum was born in Khvajeh Do Kuh, northern Afghanistan, into an Uzbek family. He began working for the state-run gas refinery in Sheberghan, Jowzjan Province, in 1970 and subsequently acquired military training in the Soviet Union. Dostum continued working for the gas industry, but he also was entrusted with local militia forces guarding these installations. During initial phases of the Communist-inspired Saur Revolution in 1978, he briefly abandoned military service, then rejoined following the Soviet invasion of December 1979. For several years thereafter, he and his Uzbek militia distinguished themselves in combat against Islamic-based mujahideen until Soviet troops finally withdrew in February 1989. Dostum fought well for the regime of President Mohammad Najibullah until April 18, 1992, after which he changed sides and supported mujahideen efforts to topple the Communists by seizing Kabul. He subsequently joined an alliance with Ahmad Shah Massoud and drove Islamic fighters under Gulbuddin Hekmatyar out of the city. Ensuing political arrangements did not suit Dostum, so in 1994 he switched sides again and supported Hekmatyar against Massoud and his ally, Burhanuddin Rabbani. This internecine squabble plunged Afghanistan back into the throes of civil war, through which the ultraconservative Taliban arose and conquered the country. Dostum patched up his relations with Rabbani and Massoud and, once Kabul fell in 1996, withdrew to his stronghold in Mazar-i-Sharif. His whereabouts were betrayed

to the Taliban by General Abdul Malik, a nominal associate, forcing Dostum to flee to Turkey. After Malik was himself ensnared by the Taliban, Dostum returned, assembled his forces, and drove his former ally's force back into Iran, although, in 1998, he again sought refuge in Turkey.

In fall 2001, U.S. forces began evicting the Taliban from power, and Dostum, in concert with General Mohammad Qassim Fahim and Ismail Khan, became one of three leaders of the Northern Alliance. He fought conspicuously at the battle of Qala-i-Jangi prison, helped crush a revolt by Taliban captives, and executed 3,000 of them in an unmarked grave. The new interim administration of President Hamid Karzai saw fit to appoint Dostum as deputy defense minister, and he continued running Mazar-i-Sharif as his personal fiefdom. Here, he has urged women to work outside the home and also encourages sports, music, and freedom of religion. Forces loyal to him also fought several pitched battles against Tajiki general Ustad Atta Mohammad Noor, but on March 1, 2005, Karzai elevated Dostum to the largely ceremonial post of chief of staff to the commander in chief. In February 2008, Afghan attorney general Abdul Jabar Sadit stripped him of his rank after he was charged with kidnapping a political rival, but the case was subsequently dropped. Recently, Dostum has criticized NATO's flagging campaign against the Taliban, boasting that 10,000 of his fighters could resolve the problem in six months.

Franks, Tommy (1941–)
U.S. Army general

Tommy Ray Franks was born in Wynneville, Oklahoma, and raised in Midland, Texas. He attended the University of Texas, Austin, for two years, then dropped out to join the U.S. Army in 1965 as a private. After passing through the Artillery and Missile Officer Candidate School at Fort Sill, Oklahoma, Franks was commissioned a second lieutenant and assigned to the 9th Infantry Division in South Vietnam. He performed well under fire, winning three Purple Hearts, and, in 1968, he returned to Fort Sill to command an artillery battery. Franks acquired a degree in business administration from the University of Texas in 1971 and, following a three-year tour in West Germany with the 2nd Armored Cavalry Regiment, attended the Armed Forces Staff College. In 1976, Franks served at the Pentagon as army inspector general, deployed again to Germany in 1981, and passed through the Army War College while receiving a master's degree in public administration from Shippensburg University, in Pennsylvania. In 1987, he was posted as chief of staff with the 1st Cavalry Division and subsequently accompanied his unit to Saudi Arabia in 1990, seeing active duty during Operations Desert Shield/Storm. In 1995, Franks received command of the 2nd Infantry Division in South Korea, and subsequently he became commander of the Third Army Forces Central Command in Atlanta, Georgia.

In June 2000, Franks's career took a dramatic turn when he was assigned as commander of U.S. Central Command, in Tampa Florida. Since the terrorist attack on the World Trade Center on September 11, 2001, he has played central and successful roles in the war on terrorism. Beginning in October 2001, he orchestrated Operation Enduring Freedom, which drove the Taliban regime from Afghanistan in less than 90 days with very few losses. In spring 2003, he was also called upon to direct Operation Iraqi Freedom to depose President Saddam Hussein. Franks, who had been limited to only 140,000 men, conducted a lightning-quick campaign that crushed Iraqi defenses and occupied a country the size of California in less than a month. A major challenge occurred when the government of Turkey would not allow the 4th Division to operate on its territory, and it was forced to be transported by boat to Kuwait after the fighting subsided. At that point, Franks sought to resign his command, but he was persuaded by Secretary of Defense Donald Rumsfeld to stay on. Iraqi was then convulsed by several sectarian-based insurgencies and al-Qaeda terrorists that the Coalition occupation troops had difficulty suppressing. The problem was continuing when Franks was replaced by Lieutenant General Ricardo Sanchez in June 2003. Reputedly, he had been offered the job of chief of staff of the U.S. Army, but Franks declined. He currently resides in Roosevelt, Oklahoma, and serves on the board of directors of Bank of America and several other institutions. In 2004, he published a best-selling memoir, *American Soldier*.

Gates, Robert (1943–)
secretary of defense

Robert Michael Gates was born in Wichita, Kansas, on September 25, 1943. He became an Eagle Scout, and after graduating from the College of William and Mary in 1965, he earned a master's degree in history from Indiana University in 1967, the same year he was recruited by the Central Intelligence Agency (CIA). Gates served a stint in the air force as a second lieutenant, from 1967 to 1969, before obtaining his doctorate in foreign policy from Georgetown University in 1974. He then left the CIA in 1974 to join the National Security Council, where he remained until 1979. Gates rejoined the CIA to serve as director of the Strategic Evaluation Center, and on April 18, 1986, he was appointed deputy director of the agency. Gates had a reputation as a crack analyst and intelligence briefer, and he performed those roles until March 1989. His career hit a bump in 1987, however, when he was revealed as very close to people involved in the Iran-Contra scandal, and, though nominated to serve as CIA director by President Ronald W. Reagan, he withdrew his nomination rather than have it rejected by the U.S. Senate. Nonetheless, President George H. W. Bush nominated him as CIA director, and he was confirmed on November 6, 1991, the first officer to rise from the very bottom ranks of the agency. His tenure was unremarkable, given that the Soviet Union collapsed that year, and he resigned from the CIA on January 20, 1993, to work on several corporate boards. His autobiography, *From the Shadows*, was published in 1996 and widely praised for its accuracy and impartiality. Gates next served as interim dean of the George Bush School of Government and Public Service at Texas A&M University, and on August 1, 2002, he was named the school's 22nd president. He developed the "Vision 2020" plan to make Texas A&M one of the top 10 public universities in the country, encouraged the hiring of 440 new faculty positions, sponsored a $300 million campus construction program, and increased minority enrollments. In February 2007, Gates was appointed president emeritus by the university board, and the following August he received an honorary doctorate from the school.

In the wake of the September 11, 2001, terror attacks, President George W. Bush offered Gates the position of head of homeland security, but he declined. However, on November 8, 2006, he was tapped to succeed departing secretary of defense Donald Rumsfeld, and he was unanimously confirmed on December 5, 2006. Once in office, Gates made his independence clear by sacking Secretary of the Army Francis J. Harvey and Army Surgeon General Kevin C. Kiley due to scandalous neglect at Walter Reed Army Hospital. He also declined to nominate General Peter Pace as chairman of the Joint Chiefs of Staff and instead selected Admiral Mike Mullen. On June 2008, he also relieved Secretary of the Air Force Michael Wynne and Air Force Chief of Staff Michael Mosley following the misshipment of nuclear weapons, and, in light of fiscal retrenchments, ended procurement of expensive weapons systems such as the F-22 Raptor. Gates enjoyed a pristine reputation seldom seen in Washington, D.C., so in January 2009, President-elect Barack Obama decided to retain him in office. Since then he has been the point man in the administration's plan to transfer military assets from Iraq to Afghanistan. On December 2, 2009, he testified before the Senate Armed Services Committee concerning Obama's combined troop "surge"/withdrawal from Afghanistan. While not agreeing with every aspect of the plan, Gates warned, in no uncertain terms, that a Taliban takeover of Afghanistan would "have severe consequences for the United States and the rest of the world."

Ghotbzadeh, Sadegh (ca. 1936–1982)
foreign minister of Iran

Sadegh Ghotbzadeh was born in Tehran, Iran, around 1936, as part of a religious, conservative merchant family. In the 1950s, he became politically active and openly opposed the regime of Mohammad Reza Shah Pahlavi, spending the next three decades working for his overthrow. He fled Iran due to his association with the religious wing of the National Front, and he enrolled in the Walsh School of Foreign Service at Georgetown University in 1959. Ghotbzadeh was eventually expelled because of his extreme political activism with the Islamic Student Association, and in 1963 his visa was cancelled. He subsequently ventured to France to join a large group of politically active Iranian expatriates. As a member of the National Front of Iran and the Freedom Movement of Iran, he became closely associated with dissident intellectuals headed by Abolhassan Bani-Sadr. In this capacity Ghotbzadeh subsequently became a disciple of Ayatollah Ruhollah Khomeini and joined his inner circle. In February 1979, he flew to Iran on the same airplane that carried the ayatollah back in triumph and was appointed managing director of National Iranian Radio and Television and tasked with bringing it in line with Islamic teachings. In this capacity, Ghotbzadeh orchestrated the firing of royalists, women, and leftists, which brought him intense condemnation from intellectuals and the interim government. In 1980, he was appointed the new foreign minister by now-president Bani-Sadr and became deeply embroiled in the American hostage situation in Tehran. Ghotbzadeh attempted to resolve the situation quietly with diplomacy but could made no headway in his dealings with the radical students who physically held the hostages. This failure prompted him to resign, but he informed the French press that presidential candidate Ronald W. Reagan was encouraging Iranian radicals to keep the hostages held until after the presidential election of November 1980.

Once out of office, Ghotbzadeh also fell from favor with the increasingly radical and theocratic government of Iran. He became an object of increasing suspicion once President Bani-Sadr was impeached and fled the county in June 1981, and Ghotbzadeh was detained several times then released on the orders of Ayatollah Khomeini. However, in April 1982, Ghotbzadeh was arrested along with a clique of army officers and clerics and accused of plotting to assassinate Khomeini and overthrow the government, then headed by the hard-line cleric Ayatollah Ali Khamenei. Ghotbzadeh denied any role in the plot, but a taped confession extracted while under torture led to his conviction. Hojatolislam Mohammad Reyshahri, chief judge of the new Military Revolutionary Tribunal, publicly outlined the plot with an elaborate chart linking Ghotbzadeh to royalist officers, "feudalists," leftists, and "phony clerics." He was sentenced to death following his 26-day trial before the Military Revolutionary Tribunal and executed by firing squad on September 15, 1982.

Gromov, Boris V. (1943–   )
Soviet general

Boris Vsevolodovich Gromov was born in Saratov, Soviet Union, on November 7, 1943, and began his lengthy army career in 1962 by attending the Suvorov Military Academy in Kalinin. In 1965, he attended the Higher Combined Arms Command School in Leningrad, and he was then groomed for command and staff work by graduating from the Frunze Military Academy in 1974. Gromov was next ordered to Afghanistan to lead a motorized rifle division, and he completed two tours of duty as a divisional commander in 1980. However, hidebound Soviet tactical dogma, far more suited to confronting a conventional adversary like NATO or the United States, proved unworkable in the sparse and mountainous Afghan countryside. The Soviets initially intended to establish garrisons and allow the Afghan national army to do most of the fighting. Nonetheless, the Red Army, bound to the few road systems available, lacked the mobility of its mujahideen adversaries and suffered heavy losses

from ambushes. Gromov left Afghanistan in 1982 to attend the Voroshilov Military Academy of the General Staff, from which he graduated in 1984. From 1985 to 1986, he fulfilled another tour in Afghanistan, at which point the mujahideen fighters, now armed with deadly American-supplied Stinger antiaircraft missiles, had driven off close air support for Red Army units, leaving them more vulnerable to ground attacks. Gromov nonetheless adjusted his tactics accordingly, enjoying considerable success against the guerrillas, and in 1987 was appointed commander of the Fortieth Army, the so-called "Limited Contingent of Soviet Forces," now numbering more than 100,000 men and backed by thousands of tanks, trucks, and artillery pieces.

As commander, Gromov's experience was roughly analogous to what the United States had endured in Vietnam: a hostile environment, difficult operating conditions, and a wily, intractable foe. Nonetheless, in January 1988, Gromov scored one of the biggest Soviet successes of the war when he took 10,000 men and lifted the siege of Khost, rescuing the garrison. By then the war had been lost, and, on February 14, 1989, he evacuated the final Soviet forces from Afghanistan, being the last Russian soldier to cross "Friendship Bridge" back to Soviet territory. In consequence of his actions at Khost, he received the Hero of the Soviet Union award, the military's highest honor. After the war, Gromov served as minister of the interior, and in 1992, he became commander of post-Soviet ground forces. He bluntly cautioned Defense Minister Pavel Grachev against intervening militarily in Chechnya while Russian forces were unprepared. In 1995, Gromov was elected to the Russian Duma, or lower house of parliament, as part of the My Fatherland Party, and in January 2000 he was elected governor of the Moscow oblast (region). A ruthless, capable administrator, he gained reelection as governor in December 2003.

Hakim, Mohamad Baqir al- (1939–2003)
Iraqi cleric

Mohamad Baqir al-Hakim was born in Naja, Iraq, in 1939, into a family of prominent Shiite scholars. He was the son of Grand Ayatollah Muhsin al Hakim Tabatabai, who for many years was the leading religious authority for the Iraqi Shia community. Hakim began his religious training in Najaf at an early age, and by the late 1950s, he had founded the Iraqi Islamic political movement. The government at that time was on a path toward secularism, a trend that increased following the Baathist coup of 1967, and he was increasingly viewed as an enemy of the state. Hakim was particularly vilified by the regime of Saddam Hussein, who arrested him in 1972 because of his religious activism. Protests by the Shiite majority population in Iraq resulted in his release a year later, but Hakim was rearrested in 1977 following an uprising in Najaf and sentenced to life in prison. He languished in prison until a popular outcry resulted in his release in July 1979. By this time, Hakim concluded it was unsafe for Shiite clergy to fulfill their religious duties in Iraq, so he fled to neighboring Iran just before the bloody Iran-Iraq War began in September 1980. While in exile, he helped found the Supreme Council of the Islamic Resistance in Iraq, which was dedicated to the overthrow of Saddam Hussein's regime. In 1982, he also helped create the armed Badr brigade, manned by exiled Iraqi Shiites, which made armed incursions into Iraq at the behest of Iran. In light of these actions, the Iraqi government arrested several members of his immediate family, executing five of his brothers and many other relatives.

Al-Hakim remained exiled in Iran over the next 23 years until the United States toppled Saddam Hussein in April 2003. As the nation's leading Shia theologian, he returned in triumph to Najaf on May 12, 2003, and began influencing political developments there. While al-Hakim was grateful that the Americans had overthrown the Baathists, he demanded that they leave Iraq as soon as possible. Coalition authorities feared he was going to demand the creation of an Iranian-style theocracy, but Hakim insisted on an Iraqi democracy that respected Islam. He also roundly condemned the Sunni-backed insurgency, especially its murderous campaign against Shia clerics, and he urged his followers to refrain from violence, regardless of

the provocation. The United States was fully aware of al-Hakim's influence in Iraq, so Washington invited him to help form an interim government. However, before his input could be fully measured, Hakim was killed in a car bomb explosion outside the holy Imam Shrine in Najaf on August 29, 2003, which also took the lives of 84 other people. At the time, both Sunni militants and Shiite followers of Moqtada al-Sadr were suspected of complicity in his murder. It has since been deduced that the al-Qaeda in Iraq terror network of Abu Musab al-Zarqawi planted the bomb. Such was Hakim's renown that his funeral procession from Baghdad to Najaf was accompanied by thousands of mourners.

Hekmatyar, Gulbuddin (1947–)
prime minister of Afghanistan

Gulbuddin Hekmatyar was born in Baghlan, northern Afghanistan, into a Kharoti Gilzai (Pashtun) family. He studied engineering at the University of Kabul from 1970 to 1972 but was arrested for antigovernment agitation. Released in July 1973, Hekmatyar fled to Pakistan and two years later joined the militant Jamiat-i-Islami (Islamic Party) as a mujahideen. As such, he conducted several guerrilla raids against the government. His religious views had also become increasingly radicalized, and by 1978, he emerged as the spiritual leader of his own militant group, Hezb-i-Islami. The Soviet invasion of Afghanistan in December 1979 served to heighten his political profile, and soon he emerged as the most powerful warlord among the Afghan resistance. This was principally because the Inter-Services Intelligence Service of Pakistan was responsible for funneling American military aid to the guerrillas, and, because they wanted influence over Pashtuns on both sides of the border, they made sure his group received more weapons than the rest. Hekmatyar's fighters were engaged in many battles against Soviet and Afghan army troops and acquitted themselves well in combat, but they gained a reputation for ruthlessness by killing civilians in terrorist attacks. Hekmatyar was also accused by other members of the seven-group mujahideen alliance of orchestrating attacks on their units in order to weaken them. After the Soviets departed in February 1989, Hekmatyar stepped up his attacks on the Communist regime of Mohammad Najibullah, and his fighters were among the first in Kabul following its collapse in 1992. Conflict immediately broke out with factions under Burhanuddin Rabbani and Ahmad Shah Massoud, so Hekmatyar forged an alliance with Uzbek militia under Abdul Rashid Dostum. Throughout this period of civil strife, Hekmatyar's fighters routinely bombarded residential areas of the capital, killing hundreds of civilians. However, on June 26, 1996, Rabbani and Hekmatyar concluded an alliance in which the latter also served as prime minister.

Once in power, Hekmatyar was quick to promulgate extreme Islamic prohibitions on women and Western influences, much as the Taliban would after they seized Kabul in the fall of 1996. His unpopularity forced him to flee to Iran and, at the commencement of Operation Enduring Freedom in October 2001, he called for a jihad against the United States. The American government branded him an international outlaw as of February 19, 2003, and two attempted assassinations of President Hamid Karzai are believed to be his handiwork. The government of Iran also officially expelled Hezb-i-Islami from the country and closed its offices in 2002, whereupon Hekmatyar returned to the border region between Afghanistan and Pakistan. In 2008, the Jamestown Foundation reported that Hezb-i-Islami is no longer marginalized in Afghan politics and is responsible for many terrorist attacks. Hekmatyar, long reviled at home as a self-serving extremist, remains one of the world's most wanted terrorists.

Horner, Charles A. (1936–   )

U.S. Air Force general

Charles A. Horner was born in Davenport, Iowa, on October 19, 1936, and graduated from the University of Iowa with a bachelor of arts degree. He was commissioned a second lieutenant through the ROTC program on campus and reported for flight training at Laredo Air Force Base, Texas. Horner earned his wings as an F-100 pilot in 1960 and flew three years with the 492nd Tactical Fighter Squadron at RAF Lakenheath, United Kingdom. In December 1963, he switched over to flying F-105s with the 4th Tactical Fighter Wing at Seymour Johnson Air Force Base, North Carolina, and two years later was deployed in Vietnam. Horner completed 41 combat missions over North Vietnam in fighter bombers. In 1966, he rotated back to Nellis Air Force Base, Nevada, to serve as an F-105 instructor, then he returned to the Vietnam War in May 1967 to fly an additional 70 combat missions as a Wild Weasel pilot, deliberately luring Communist air defenses so that they could be destroyed. In 1972, he attended William and Mary College to earn a master's in business administration. In July 1985, Horner became a major general and deputy chief of staff for plans, Headquarters, Tactical Air Command, Langley Air Force Base, Virginia. In March 1987, he served as commander of the Ninth U.S. Air Force and U.S. Central Command Air Forces based at Shaw Air Force Base, South Carolina.

Horner's greatest test came in August 1991, after Saddam Hussein invaded Kuwait with a massive army. He was appointed commander in chief–forward, U.S. Central Command, and directed the opening phases of Operation Desert Shield while General H. Norman Schwarzkopf was still stateside. This involved the buildup of several hundred aircraft and supporting units from the U.S. Air Force and its coalition partners. When Operation Desert Storm began the following January, Horner had at his disposal 2,700 warplanes from 14 nations, and they flew more than 100,000 missions prior to the ground phase of the campaign. They gutted Iraqi air defenses and armored formations, allowing the main attack to conclude after only 100 hours of fighting and extremely light losses. Horner was promoted to full general on July 1, 1992, and appointed to head up the North American Aerospace Defense Command, where he was responsible for the utilization of space for national purposes through a large network of satellites in orbit and ground stations around the globe. This assignment was followed by a stint as commander of the Air Force Space Command at Peterson Air Force Base, Colorado, and he then retired from active service on September 30, 1994. He currently resides in Fort Walton Beach, Florida, and serves on the board of directors of the U.S. Institute of Peace.

Hussein, Saddam (1937–2006)
president of Iraq
Saddam Hussein was born in Tikrit, Iraq, on April 28, 1937. He ran away from a cruel father at the age of 10 and was raised by a former military officer, who imbued him with a sense of duty and Pan-Arabism. Hussein relocated to Baghdad in 1957 and joined the shadowy Baath Party, in whose ranks he helped plot several insurrections against the government. After the party seized power in 1969, Hussein, who was both cunning and ruthless, was installed as chief of the state security apparatus. He slowly but steadily eliminated all his competitors and, on July 17, 1979, declared himself president of Iraq. Intent upon modernization, Hussein embarked on a crash program to develop the petroleum resources of Iraq and invested heavily in education, infrastructure, and arms purchases. Tensions rose with neighboring Iran after the Islamic revolution that toppled the shah, and simmering border disputes turned violent. Sensing weakness, Hussein ordered an invasion of Iran in the fall of 1980, which precipitated a bloody eight-year stalemate and thousands of casualties on both sides. Only through the illegal use of chemical weapons, which killed thousands of Iranians and Kurdish separatists, did his regime survive until a cease-fire was signed. Saddled by enormous war debts, Hussein began pressing the rich Arab Gulf States to cancel their loans and raise the price of oil to boost Iraq's annual income. When this failed, he ordered an invasion of Kuwait in August 1990, but an international coalition drove his troops out during Operation Desert Storm in February 1991. The Iraqis were humiliated while sustaining heavy casualties.

Bloodied but unbowed, Hussein embarked on a deliberate program to harass and obstruct UN arms inspectors in Iraq, who were searching for chemical, biological, or nuclear weapons programs. Economic sanctions brought Iraq to its knees economically but, buoyed by illegal funds from his oil-for-food program, he remained defiant. After the World Trade Center attack on September 11, 2001, President George W. Bush labeled Iraq as part of the "axis of evil" and threatened to topple him if he did not allow UN weapons inspectors in, but Hussein again obstructed their progress. The United States then called on the international community to rid itself of a potential nuclear threat, and, on March 20, 2003, Operation Iraqi Freedom began. The Iraqi army collapsed quickly, and Hussein went into hiding. Coalition authorities offered $200,000 for his capture, and his portrait was displayed on a pack of cards decorated with other fugitives. He was snared near Tikrit on December 13, 2003, and brought before Iraqi legal authorities, who charged him with committing atrocities. On November 5, 2006, he was found guilty of murdering 148 Iraqi Shiites following a failed coup against him and was sentenced to death. The sentence was carried out by hanging on December 30, 2006, bringing to justice one of the 20th century's most murderous dictators.

Karmal, Babrak (1929–1996)
president of Afghanistan
Babrak Karmal was born in Kamari, Afghanistan, on January 6, 1929, the son of an army general. He enrolled at the University of Kabul in 1949, dabbled in Marxism, and was subsequently jailed for political activism. Following his release in 1956, Karmal worked for the ministry of education before helping to found the Communist People's Democratic Party of Afghanistan (PDPA). Like most Afghan political organizations, it was deeply split by fac-

tions, in this instance by the Maoist-oriented Khalq (Masses) under Nur Mohammed Taraki and the Soviet-oriented Parcham (Banner) under Karmal, each of which regarded the other with contempt. On April 28, 1978, Prime Minister Mohammed Daoud was killed in a coup and the Democratic Republic of Afghanistan was proclaimed under Taraki. Karmal, then ambassador to Czechoslovakia, was ordered home to face trial but fled to Moscow for protection. In 1979, Taraki himself was overthrown by Hafizullah Amin, which prompted Soviet premier Leonid Brezhnev to invade Afghanistan on December 25, 1979. Amin was killed in the fighting, and Karmal was flown in from Moscow to serve as the new president while also holding the portfolios of prime minister, general secretary, and commander in chief. One of his first acts was to release 2,000 Parcham political prisoners and detain a like number of Khalq members. He also installed a Soviet-style secret police apparatus to enforce order and party rule.

For the next seven years, Karmal and his Soviet allies attempted to enforce a reformist, Communist agenda on the countryside, but this triggered a mass uprising by Islamic fundamentalist fighters, or mujahideen. In fact, the deeply traditionalist Muslim peasantry viewed him as an atheist and a Russian puppet. An intense guerrilla war erupted throughout Afghanistan, and the government enjoyed no real authority outside the capital of Kabul. Soviet forces responded to the unrest with a harsh brutality that drove nearly one-third of the population into neighboring Pakistan. The scope of resistance nonetheless intensified after 1980 when President Ronald W. Reagan ordered huge amounts of military assistance shipped to the mujahideen through Pakistan. By 1986, the Soviets were no closer to crushing organized resistance, and they blamed Karmal for the failure to implement meaningful reforms. Moreover, the occupation had proved to be a quagmire, and the present Afghan leadership was unable to help them extricate themselves. Unwilling to further subsidize Karmal's incompetence, the Soviets eased him from power on May 4, 1986, and replaced him

with the hard-line Mohammad Najibullah, his former security chief. Karmal was then sent to Moscow on the basis of "ill health" and kept there under wraps as Afghanistan continued unraveling. He briefly returned home in 1991 following the Soviet withdrawal, but he found life there untenable for former Communists and resettled in Moscow. Karmal died there on December 3, 1996.

Karzai, Hamid (1957–)
president of Afghanistan

Hamid Karzai was born in Kandahar, Afghanistan, on December 24, 1957, the son of a Popolazi tribal chief. He was educated in Kabul and subsequently studied in Simla, India, where he became fluent in English. Karzai was active in tribal affairs until 1979, when the Soviet Union invaded Afghanistan, and in 1983 he fled to Quetta, Pakistan, to raise money and weapons for the Afghan resistance. He gradually came to the attention of the United States, and, after the Soviets departed Afghanistan in 1989, Karzai served as deputy foreign minister under President Burhanuddin Rabbani. However, in 1992, an extreme Islamic movement called the Taliban arose in Kandahar and within four years controlled 90 percent of the country. Karzai again fled to Quetta in 1998, and two years later his aged father was assassinated outside a mosque by a Taliban operative. This killing prompted Karzai to strongly oppose the fanatical regime, and in fall 2000, he made a secret trip to the United States seeking military aid. A year later, this aid came in the form of Operation Enduring Freedom, which ousted the Taliban from Afghanistan after they refused to hand over terrorist Osama bin Laden. On December 23, 2001, a council of Afghan elders elevated the smooth-talking, urbane Karzai to the post of prime minister.

Karzai inherited a nation devastated by war and religious fanaticism. He immediately began soliciting foreign aid to assist reconstruction efforts and helped to solidify political support for his regime before the Taliban regrouped in Pakistan. Although accused by many Muslims of being an American puppet, his conduct of foreign policy proved quite independent, and in February 2002, he visited Iran to mend fences and encourage better relations between Washington, D.C., and Tehran. Relations with neighboring Pakistan had been somewhat more tense, given the reluctance of President Pervez Musharraf to crack down on Taliban strongholds along his northwestern border. However, Karzai's efforts at national dialogue and reconciliation at home also paid dividends on October 9, 2004, when he became the first democratically elected president of Afghanistan with 55.3 percent of the vote. Since then, Karzai has maintained a delicate balancing act of hosting several thousand U.S. and NATO troops on his soil to combat Taliban forces, while also urging restraint to reduce civilian casualties. He has also been reluctant to approve aerial spraying to eliminate poppy production in southern Afghanistan, a major source of the world's heroin supply, for fear of what it would do to the local economy. Karzai weathered four assassination attempts in 2002, 2004, 2007, and 2008, presumably by Taliban agents. In October 2009, Karzai defeated Foreign Minister Abdullah Abdullah to win a second term as president, although widespread allegations of fraud forced him into a runoff. Abdullah boycotted the proceedings, so Karzai won by default.

Khalilzad, Zalmay (1951–   )

Afghan-American diplomat

Zalmay Khalilzad was born in Mazar-i-Sharif, Afghanistan, on March 22, 1951, the son of a government official. Ethnically, he is considered a Pashtun Sunni Muslim, but his native language is Dari (Persian). After receiving his secondary education in Kabul, Khalilzad went to the United States as a high-school exchange student and then earned his bachelor's and master's degrees from American University in Beirut, in Lebanon. Khalilzad obtained his doctorate in political science from the University of Chicago as a disciple of noted conservative thinker Albert Wohlsetter, who imparted a pro-military slant to his think-

ing. He spent the decade of 1979–89 teaching at the university, where he also struck up cordial relations with Zbigniew Brzezinski, and he helped the administration of Jimmy Carter formulate its policy of supporting Afghan mujahideen in their struggle against invading Soviet forces. In 1984, President Ronald W. Reagan appointed Khalilzad to the Council on Foreign Relations, and from 1985 to 1989, he served as a senior adviser on the Afghan resistance and the Iran-Iraq War. Between 1993 and 2000, Khalilzad was director of the strategy, doctrine, and force structure at the influential RAND Corporation, where he contributed several significant monographs and other studies. Simultaneously, he advised Cambridge Energy Research Associates on a trans-Afghanistan gas pipeline project and, after 1996, functioned as an intermediary with the Taliban regime. In 1998, he also was a signatory of a letter to President Bill Clinton urging him to remove Saddam Hussein from power in Iraq.

Following the overthrow of the Taliban regime in the late fall of 2001, Khalilzad returned as a U.S. special envoy to the interim administration of Hamid Karzai, and in November 2003, he was appointed the U.S. ambassador to Afghanistan. As such, he advised Karzai on political matters and orchestrated establishment of the American University in Kabul, the nation's first Western-style institution of higher education. On June 21, 2005, Khalilzad was appointed ambassador to Iraq, where he helped the government establish free and fair elections. In February 2006, h e warned Bush that sectarian violence between Sunnis and Shiites was overtaking the armed insurgency as the number one threat to Iraqi security. Khalilzad was replaced by Ryan Crocker on March 26, 2007, whereupon he was confirmed as ambassador to the United Nations. There, he warned that Iran was helping insurgent groups in Afghanistan and Iraq, and he convinced the United Nations to impose additional sanctions after Iran refused to comply with resolutions respecting nuclear energy. He served until January 20, 2009, and returned to his native Afghanistan to possibly assume a significant post within the Afghan government. Khalilzad remains a stout defender and an articulate advocate of U.S. global leadership in the Muslim world.

Khalis, Yunnis (1919–2006)
Afghan mujahideen leader

Yunnis Khalis was born at Gandomak, Nangarhar Province, Afghanistan, in 1919, a member of the Khugiani tribe. After being thoroughly grounded in Islamic theology at the high school in Faizabad, he taught several years at a primary school. In time, Khalis emerged as a powerful religious figure in his native province, well-known for his conservative vision of Islamic society, and he acquired a reputation as the "godfather" of Nangarhar. In this capacity, he was a regular contributor to the conservative newspaper *Gahis* and also became a popular radio commentator. However, his beliefs set him on a collision course with the increasingly secularized Afghan government, especially after Mohammed Daoud overthrew King Mohammed Zahir Shah in 1973. That year Khalis sought refuge in Pakistan, where he encountered fellow fundamentalist Gulbuddin Hekmatyar in 1979 and joined his Hezb-i-Islami (Islamic Society) movement. The Soviet invasion of Afghanistan in December of that year also served as a clarion call to mujahideen across the Islamic spectrum, and Khalis became one of a few religious leaders to accompany fighters into the field. He garnered considerable attention fighting Soviet and Afghan army units in Badakhshan Province and broke with Hekmatyar to form his own movement, usually rendered as Hezb-e-Islami. Theologically, it differed little from Hekmatyar's group, but Khalis favored close cooperation with other Sunni-based resistance groups. He also counted many prominent mujahideen commanders, such as Abdul Haq, Amin Wardak, and Jalaluddin Haqqani, as fighters in his ranks.

With the fall of the Communist regime in Kabul in April 1992, Khalis was invited to serve on the Leadership Council (Shura-ye-Qiyaadi) within the Islamic interim government, but he sought no other public office. Instead of relocating to the capital, he returned to his native Nangarhar Province, where Hezb-e-Islami remained a force in local politics. Two of his former military commandeers, Haji Abdul Qadir and Haji Din Mohammad, served as provincial governors for several years. Khalis now embraced an extreme Islamic orthodoxy that opposed expanding the voting franchise, emancipating women, or allowing Shiite groups a voice in the national government. In September 1996, when the ultraconservative Taliban captured Nangarhar Province, Khalis quietly supported the regime, and his forces retained control of local affairs. He found it expedient in the late 1990s to relocate to Pakistan, where he remained until the United States vanquished the Taliban in the fall of 2001. Khalis and his supporters subsequently relocated to Jalalabad, and, while he still declined public office, the aged leader remained a powerful influence behind the scenes. Khalis died on July 19, 2006, and the movement he founded is carried on by his two surviving sons.

Khamenei, Ali (1939–   )
Iranian religious leader

Ali Sayyed Khamenei was born in Meshed, Iran, on July 17, 1939, into a family of religious scholars. In time he became fluent in Arabic and Turkish and gained critical renown as a religious writer. After completing his religious studies, Khamenei settled in the holy city of Qom in 1958, becoming a disciple of Ayatollah Ruhollah Khomeini, a leading cleric and harsh critic of Mohammad Reza Shah Pahlavi. He was arrested and exiled internally several times, but by 1979, with the Islamic revolution underway, he emerged at the forefront of events. Once the extremists seized power, Khamenei became closely associated with Ayatollah Khomeini's inner circle and embraced the notion of a formally empowered theocracy in all its forms. He was accordingly elected president of Iran on October 2, 1981, which confirmed his status as Khomeini's favorite. After surviving an assassination attempt that cost him the use of his right arm, Khamenei continued on as a reliable ally of all hard-line religious elements and doctrines, and, while he sought friendly relations with most nations, he continually lambasted the United States for being the "Great Satan." He also railed against Western influences such as blue jeans, movies, and rock music, which apparently did little to diminish his popularity with voters, and on August 16, 1985, he was reelected to the presidency.

Following the death of Ayatollah Khomeini, the Council of Experts appointed Khamenei the new Supreme Leader of Iran as of June 4, 1989. However, by 1997 the Iranian people wearied of Islamic extremism, and that year they defeated Khamenei's pick for the presidency, Ali Akbar Nateq-Noori, in favor of Mohammad Khatami, a noted reformer. A protracted cat-and-mouse game ensued between those wishing for greater liberty and conservative elements who resisted. Khatami, who was reelected in a landslide in June 2001, enjoyed minor success loosening up the intellectual arena, but he was perpetually thwarted by the all-powerful clergy. Khamenei continued attacking the United States and Israel, but he was also quick to condemn the World Trade Center attack on September 11, 2001. However, he put the brakes on Khatami's efforts to seek closer relations with the United States, and in June 2002, his ultraconservative Guardian Council rejected a bill that would have ended the use of torture in obtaining confessions as "un-Islamic." With the election of conservative Mahmoud Ahmadinejad as president on August 6, 2005, he changed his tack and frequently stepped in to moderate the confrontational nature of the new executive. He nonetheless embraced Ahmadinejad's determination to fully develop Iran's nuclear capabilities, even in the face of economic sanctions. In May 2009, he unequivocally endorsed the reelection of Ahmadinejad despite allegations of fraud and corruption. Khamenei remains a hard-line, anti-Western extremist.

Khan, Ismail (1946–)

Afghan politician

Ismail Khan was born in Shindand, western Afghanistan, in 1946 into a family of Tajiki ancestry. He attended the Kabul Military School and

Military Academy while a young man and by 1979 was serving as a lieutenant in the 17th Division. This unit was based in Herat, near the Iranian border, and growing dissatisfaction with the Communist-inspired rule of Nur Mohammad Taraki in Kabul prompted him to lead a rebellion in March 1979. This violent outbreak resulted in the deaths of several hundred Soviet advisers and was brutally crushed by government forces at a cost of 24,000 lives. Khan subsequently fled to Iran, and, throughout the decadelong struggle to evict Soviet forces from Afghanistan, he rose as a leading figure among resistance fighters associated with Burhanuddin Rabbani. In the course of many successful raids against Soviet troops, Khan acquired the nickname "Lion of Herat," and, along with Ahmad Shah Massoud, he was among the most respected of insurgent leaders. Such was Khan's renown among mujahideen and their patrons that he reputedly was the first to receive lethal Stinger missiles provided by the Central Intelligence Agency. His fighters were also among the best led among the Afghan resistance, and, following the Soviet withdrawal, Khan worked ceaselessly to help overthrow the Communist regime of Mohammad Najibullah in spring 1992. He was appointed governor of Herat for the next three years and distinguished himself in reconstruction efforts. However, in 1995, the Taliban threat arose, and Khan was forced to defend his province against their incursions. He did so successfully and at one point was able to attack their stronghold in Kandahar, but he was repelled by his former ally, Abdul Rashid Dostum. Khan fled to Iran again that year to organized armed resistance, but in 1997 he was betrayed to the Taliban by Abdul Malik, a former associate, and imprisoned under harsh conditions.

Khan and a handful of associates managed to escape captivity in Kandahar in March 1999, and he slipped back into Iran and continued his anti-Taliban insurgency. When the United States swept the Taliban from power in December 2001, he joined the Northern Alliance to help expel some remaining guerrillas, then resumed his position as self-appointed governor of Herat City. As before, he proved himself an adept, if autocratic, administrator and made great strides in reconstructing the war-torn city infrastructure. Buildings, roads, hospitals, and schools all began flourishing, and Khan was careful in cultivating close economic and trading ties with western Iran. Since Herat was traditionally a trading center, the merchant community flourished and remains one of Khan's strongest sources of political support. However, he has also been accused of running Herat like a personal fiefdom and for failing to pass on his fair share of revenues to the central government in Kabul. In September 2004, President Hamid Karzai removed Khan as governor, then subsequently reappointed him as minister of energy as a sinecure.

Khatami, Mohammad (1943–   )
president of Iran

Mohammad Khatami was born in Ardakan, Iran, on September 29, 1943, the son of a prominent Muslim cleric. After completing his religious studies in Qom in 1961, he graduated from the University of Tehran in 1970 with a degree in Western philosophy. Khatami is extremely worldly for a Shiite cleric, fluent in English and German, and he served as the chair of the Islamic Center in Hamburg until the Islamic revolution of 1979. He initially supported the uprising against Mohammad Reza Shah Pahlavi, but he gradually grew disenchanted with the extremism and intolerance of Ayatollah Khomeini's regime. In 1980, he was elected to the Majlis, or parliament, where he functioned as a moderate reformer. Two years later, he was appointed minister of culture and left his personal stamp on the revolution. Unlike many contemporaries, Khatami was very liberal in his cultural leanings and did much to encourage freedom of expression in film and media. This stance irritated many conservative clerics, who forced his resignation in 1992. Undaunted, Khatami next served as cultural adviser to President Ali Rafsanjani, another noted moderate, who also appointed him head of the national library.

On August 2, 1997, Khatami demonstrated the popularity of his ideas and ideals when he was elected president of Iran with 69 percent of the vote. He then championed political liberalization, women's rights, and freedom of expression, views that alienated the conservative clergy but gained him the continuing allegiance of the young, trade unionists, and disenchanted portions of the electorate. As a further indication of his appeal, legislative elections in May 2000 delivered 80 percent of the seats to reform-minded candidates. Meaningful change proved almost impossible in the face of entrenched opposition from the Islamic clergy, which had final say over all legislation. However, in June 2001, Khatami was reelected by an even bigger majority—77.4 percent. Armed with this mandate for change, he was empowered to make the first friendly overtures to Western Europe in nearly two decades. He was less successful in nudging the political establishment toward rapprochement with the United States, still derided as the "Great Satan," but Khatami roundly condemned the terrorist attack on the World Trade Center on September 11, 2001. On August 2, 2005, he stepped down from office after serving the maximum two terms allowed under the Iranian constitution and was succeeded by the religious hard-liner Mahmoud Ahmadinejad. Since leaving politics, Khatami has been highly visible on the world scene and has attended several world conferences promoting peace and understanding between nations. Undaunted by the confrontational tactics of his successor, he even lectured on political philosophy at the Washington National Cathedral in Washington, D.C. Consistent with his worldview, Khatami officially endorsed Reformist candidate Mir Hossein Mousavi in the highly contested 2009 Iranian presidential election.

Khomeini, Ruhollah (1900–1989)
Iranian religious leader

Ruhollah Hendi was born in Khomein, Markazi Province, Iran, on September 24, 1900, into a family of Shia Muslim clerics that traced their ancestry back to the prophet Muhammad. He received intense quranic instruction as a child and, in the course of his formal religious training, garnered attention as an original thinker of note. He also adopted the surname Khomeini to honor the town of his birth. As a theologian, Khomeini drew inspiration from Plato's *Republic* and envisioned a purely Islamic state headed by an all-powerful theocracy. In turn, the theocrats would draw their moral authority from the Qu'ran and all judgments were therefore infallible In the late 1950s, he began bitterly assailing Muhammad Reza Shah Pahlavi's modernization programs as anti-Islamic, and by 1963 riots were breaking out against the government. The following year, Khomeini was exiled, and he established a Shia theological school in neighboring Iraq. From there, he continued denouncing the shah's corruption and authoritarianism to such good effect that President Saddam Hussein of Iraq was pressured into deporting him. The fiery cleric subsequently relocated to Paris, France, where he enjoyed complete access to Western media and continued exhorting Iranians to overthrow the shah. In January 1979, the shah fled, and Khomeini returned to Iran in triumph to an adoring public. On April 1, 1979, he crowned his achievement by declaring the Islamic Republic of Iran with himself as ayatollah, a senior clerical rank within Shia Islam.

In practice, Khomeini ruled over a theocratic dictatorship based upon quranic principles and backed by armed fundamentalists and a secret religious police. In practice, media were heavily controlled and censored, non Islamic books and ideas were banned, and all forms of Western dress and entertainment outlawed. Consequently, women were stripped of political rights and forced to wear veils, religious attendance became compulsory, and non-Islamic minorities were harassed and discriminated against. His regime proved even more oppressive than its predecessor, and thousands of perceived opponents were summarily rounded up and executed. In fall 1979, to distract attention from a sagging economy, he encouraged radicals to seize the American embassy and take 63 hostages

while continually denouncing the United States as the "Great Satan." Khomeini remained a rallying point throughout the bloody Iran-Iraq War and for eight years refused all peace overtures from Iraq and the United Nations, preferring instead to try to overthrow Iraqi president Saddam Hussein and establish an Islamic state across the Middle East. The Iranians were finally forced into a cease-fire in 1988, which Khomeini accepted only with great reluctance and bitterness, and he continued blaming Iran's moribund, state-run economy on Americans and Zionists. He died in Tehran on June 3, 1989, widely mourned. Khomeini's tenure as a religious head of state was controversial, but he is regarded as the most influential Muslim cleric of the 20th century.

Maliki, Nuri al- (Nouri al- Maliki) (1947–)

prime minister of Iraq

Nuri al-Maliki was born in Abu Gharaq, Iraq, on June 20, 1947, into a prosperous Shia family. He attended Usul al-Din College in Baghdad and obtained a degree in Arabic literature. After graduating, he worked with the Education Department in al-Hillah and became politically active by joining the Shia Dawa Party, then outlawed by the secular Baathists of Saddam Hussein. Maliki fled Iraq in 1979 upon learning that the government intended to execute him, and he took refuge in Iran and Syria, while maintaining close ties to the Dawa Party. Maliki remained politically sidelined until Hussein was overthrown by the United States in 2003 and, relatively unknown to most Iraqis, finally returned home in 2005. A skillful politician, he quickly secured appointment as deputy leader of the Supreme National Debaathification Commission established by the Interim Government, which ruthlessly purged Hussein's Baathist associates from the government and military. The new Iraqi regime then faced the daunting task of bring Sunnis, Shiites, and Kurds together under one roof, despite centuries of distrust and animosity. This dissent prevented Ibrahim al-Jaafari, a Shiite and close associate of Maliki, from remaining in power as Iraq's first full-term, postwar prime minister. After al-Jaafari was ousted over charges of favoritism toward Shiites, Maliki became the de facto compromise candidate to succeed him on April 22, 2006.

At the time, Maliki freely admitted that he did not want the position, but he accepted out of an obligation to serve the nation. Iraq was then in the process of reconstruction but was still challenged by armed insurgencies fueled by Sunni terrorists and militant Shiite militias. As a Shiite, he walked a tightrope between convincing American occupation forces he could control the country and not appearing subordinate to them. However, spiraling civil violence finally prompted him to crack down on the Mahdi Army of Moqtada al-Sadr, which he forced from the streets of Baghdad and other cities. In June 2006, Maliki also introduced a bold national reconciliation plan that included former Baathists as well as Sunnis, confirming his ability to reach out and bargain with seemingly intractable minorities. The prime minister went to great lengths to demonstrate his independence from the United States by making friendly overtures to neighboring Iran, and, in September 2006, he arrived in Tehran on a goodwill visit. Maliki is also deeply engaged in talks with American authorities to resolve the critical issue of a joint U.S.-Iraqi security pact and the phased withdrawal of coalition forces from the region. In December 2008, he signed an agreement with President George W. Bush that mandated the removal of all U.S. troops from Iraq by 2011, a major breakthrough for both sides. Maliki ran again on March 26, 2010, but he failed to win a clear majority of seats against Ayad Allawi for the prime ministership. In November, an agreement was reached that allowed Maliki to stay in office, while Allawi was made head of a new security council.

McChrystal, Stanley A. (1954–   )

U.S. Army general

Stanley A. McChrystal was born on August 14, 1954, the son of a World War II army general. In 1976, he graduated from the U.S. Military Academy as a second lieutenant. After completing his parachute training at Fort Bragg, North Carolina, he served with the 82nd Airborne Division between 1976 and 1978, after which he returned to Fort Bragg to undergo Special Forces training. McChrystal has since acquired a long association with clandestine service, most of which remains highly classified, but he is known to have worked for the United Nations Command Support Group in South Korea, commanded a Ranger battalion in Saudi Arabia in 1990–91, and served as chief of staff with the elite XVIII Airborne Corps. He also earned degrees in national security and strategic studies at the U.S. Naval War College and a master's degree in international relations at Salve Regina University, and he received fellowships from Harvard University and the Council on Foreign Relations. McChrystal is renowned for his uncanny ability to successfully navigate the treacherous waters associated with Special Operations and the equally demanding task of dealing with politicians and diplomats. He rose to brigadier general on January 1, 2001, and served as assistant divisional commander with the 82nd Airborne Division, and in March 2003, at the commencement of Operation Iraqi Freedom, he served at the Pentagon as a member of the Joint Staff and vice director of operations. McChrystal assumed command of the elite Joint Special Operations Command in September 2003 and helped orchestrate the successful capture of Iraqi dictator Saddam Hussein in Tikrit, Iraq, that December. Iraq at the time was engulfed by a foreign-led insurgency, and McChrystal arrived to help direct highly secretive operations against them. He scored his biggest success in June 2003, when his operatives tracked, located, and directed the air strike that killed wanted Jordanian terrorist Abu Musab al-Zarqawi. Within minutes, McChrystal and his Special Forces team were on hand to identify al-Zarqawi's body. The general was responsible for similar operations during Operation Iraqi Freedom in Afghanistan, where he became temporarily mired in the controversy surrounding the friendly fire death of Captain Pat Tillman.

In light of his excellent performance and reputation, McChrystal advanced to lieutenant general in May 2008, and the following August, President George W. Bush appointed him director of the Joint Staff at the Pentagon. During the confirmation process, he was grilled by members of the Senate Armed Services Committee about allegations of prisoner abuse in Iraq and Afghanistan, but he was confirmed. In 2009, the new administration of President Barack Obama fulfilled a campaign pledge to place renewed emphasis on winning the war in Afghanistan, and McChrystal, given his unconventional background in Special Operations, was chosen to replace the more conventionally minded General David D. McKiernan as head of the International Security Assistance Force. One of his first deeds in this capacity was to declare the need for 30,000 to 40,000 additional American combat troops to halt the surging Taliban insurgency there. It took several months for Obama to review and evaluate his request, but on December 2, 2009, the administration agreed to deploy 30,000 troops over the next several months, coupled with increased emphasis on training for indigenous security forces. On June 23, 2010, McChrystal resigned his command owing to disparaging remarks concerning American diplomats in Afghanistan; he was replaced by General David H. Petraeus.

Mullen, Michael G. (1946–   )
chairman, Joint Chiefs of Staff

Michael George Mullen was born in Los Angeles, California, in 1946, and graduated from the U.S. Naval Academy in 1968. He completed tours in both the Atlantic and Pacific Fleets and successively commanded the tanker USS *Noxubee,* the guided missile destroyer USS *Goldsborough,* and the guided-missile cruiser USS *Yorktown.* An efficient officer, he received the Vice Admiral James Bonds Stockdale Award for Inspirational Leadership in 1987. His various assignments ashore included company officer and executive assistant to the commandant of midshipmen at the U.S.

Naval Academy, director of the Bureau of Naval Personnel, and chief of planning and provisions, surface officer distribution, Office of the Secretary of Defense. He graduated from the Naval Postgraduate School in 1985 with a master's in operations research and from the Harvard University Business School in 1991 with a master's in advanced management. Returning to sea as a rear admiral, Mullen commanded Cruiser-Destroyer Group Two and the *George Washington* Battle Group before serving as commander of the Second Fleet, NATO Striking Fleet Atlantic. He subsequently took the helm as commander of the Allied Joint Force Command, in Naples, Italy, with overarching responsibility for NATO affairs in the Balkans, Iraq, and the Mediterranean. On October 8, 2004, Mullen advanced to be commander of U.S. Naval Forces Europe, a post he held until he was appointed chief of naval operations at the Pentagon in 2007. Mullen had acquired an excellent reputation for efficiency and grasping the global complexities of naval strategy when, on June 8, 2007, Secretary of Defense Robert Gates nominated him to serve as chairman of the Joint Chiefs of Staff, the nation's highest military position. Easily confirmed, he was the first naval officer to occupy that seat since Admiral William Crowe in 1986. As chairman, Mullen was responsible for war planning on a worldwide basis, and he was called to testify before Congress on several occasions about the unstable conditions in Iraq. He responded bluntly to difficult inquiries and said he believed that, while the ongoing insurgency was difficult, progress had been made on the political front, and he did not envision permanent U.S. bases in that country.

Gates recommended on March 18, 2009, that Mullen serve a second term, newly elected president Barack Obama concurred, and the U.S. Senate unanimously reconfirmed him on September 25, 2009. As chairman, Mullen is tasked with articulating American defense needs for the 21st century, including the global war against terror. To that end he has openly supported Obama's plan to draw down American involvement in Iraq, while simultaneously enlarging the military commitment in Afghanistan, currently facing a resurgent Taliban movement. He has also lent conditional support to Obama's wish to begin removing American troops in 2011, while placing greater emphasis on preparing Afghan forces to secure their own country. An essential part of this strategy, from a regional standpoint, requires enlisting greater support from neighboring Pakistan. Testifying before Congress on December 3, 2009, Mullen said that "the outcome in Afghanistan bears directly on Pakistan's future."

Petraeus, David H. (1951–   )

U.S. Army general

David Howell Petraeus was born in Cornwall-on-Hudson, New York, and graduated from the U.S. Military Academy in 1974 in the top 5 percent of his class. His first assignment was with the 509th Airborne Battalion Combat Team in Vicenza, Italy, and he became closely identified with light infantry. Petraeus proved himself an adept officer, and, in 1981, he became aide-de-camp to the commanding general of the 24th Infantry Division (Mechanized). He also continued his education by attending the Command and General Staff College in 1983, graduating top in his class, and receiving a doctorate in international relations from Princeton University in 1987. In 1993, he served as the assistant chief of staff of the elite 101st Airborne Division, and he participated in several peacekeeping and nation-building ventures in Haiti and Bosnia in the 1990s. Petraeus commanded the 101st Airborne Division during Operation Iraqi Freedom, which overcame stiff enemy resistance and occupied the city of Mosul. He was successful at using both counterinsurgency warfare and civic relations to isolate the insurgents from the greater population. In February 2004, Petraeus accompanied his men back to the United States, and the following June, he was promoted to lieutenant general commanding the Multinational Security Transition Command Iraq.

Back in Iraq, Petraeus was tasked with rebuilding that nation's shattered military and security apparatus. His methodical methods made considerable progress, but at too slow a rate for many in Congress, who wanted to withdraw from Iraq. To this end, he testified before Congress several times and urged patience with the delicate task he was orchestrating. On January 27, 2007, Petraeus became a full general and replaced General George C. Casey as head of the Multinational Force Iraq. He employed an additional 20,000 soldiers sent to Iraq by President George W. Bush as a military "surge." Petraeus also placed greater responsibilities on the Iraqis for their own security while securing tribal alliances against the al-Qaeda terror network. The results were spectacular, and terrorist violence declined nearly 80 percent from the previous year. However, Petraeus was under no illusions. He insisted that more work needed to be done before the Americans could withdraw safely. On September 16, 2008, he handed over his responsibilities to General Raymond T. Odierno and returned home. The following month he accepted command of the U.S. Central Command, headquartered in Tampa, Florida, from where he directs military operations in 20 nations that stretch from Egypt to Pakistan, as well as Operation Enduring Freedom in Afghanistan and Operation Iraqi Freedom in Iraq. Following the resignation of General Stanley McChrystal on June 23, 2010, President Barack Obama appointed Petraeus commanding general of coalition forces in Afghanistan.

Powell, Colin L. (1937–   )

U.S. Army general, secretary of state

Colin Luther Powell was born in New York City on April 5, 1937, a son of Jamaican immigrants. He enrolled in the local ROTC program while attending the City College of New York and was commissioned a second lieutenant in the U.S. Army in 1958. Powell served actively over the next four decades, including two tours in Vietnam in which he was wounded and highly decorated. Back home, he accepted a number of high-profile political positions within the Office of Management and Budget and the Department of Energy. He rose to brigadier general in 1979, served as National Security Advisor under President Ronald W. Reagan, and in 1989 made history when President George H. W. Bush appointed him the nation's first African-American chairman of the Joint Chiefs of Staff, the nation's highest military post. He was responsible for helping to orchestrate Operations Desert Shield and Desert Storm in response to the 1991 Iraqi invasion of Kuwait and worked closely with General H. Norman Schwarzkopf during the run-up to the ensuing Gulf War. Powell became a familiar national fixture by appearing nightly on television, and his reassuring presence, smooth persona, and high popularity ratings prompted debate over his chances as a possible presidential candidate. Powell was reappointed in 1991 after Bush awarded him a Presidential Medal of Freedom for his services. However, he disagreed strongly with cuts in military spending proposed by President Bill Clinton and resigned from office in September 1993. The following year he served with an American delegation that went to Haiti and persuaded the ruling junta to restore the country to democracy without bloodshed.

Powell continued on as a private citizen for several years, and in 1995 he published his best-selling memoir, *My American Journey*. He also briefly considered running for president as a Republican but, as an exponent of affirmative action for minorities, felt his chances were unrealistic, and he withdrew from consideration in December 1995. However, in 2001, President George W. Bush appointed him the nation's first African-American secretary of state. This job grew increasingly complex in the wake of the September 11, 2001, attack upon the World Trade Center in New York, and Bush's intention to rid Iraq of President Saddam Hussein. It was Powell's task to lay out the American position to a skeptical United Nations, which he did with verve and style, although American claims of Iraqi weapons of mass destruction were never verified. Powell was stung by criticism that he failed to gather a large enough coalition for Operation Iraqi Freedom in 2003, and he concluded half a century of devoted service to the nation by retiring in January 2005. He was replaced by another African American, Condoleezza Rice.

Qadir, Haji Abdul (1951–2002)
vice president of Afghanistan

Haji Abdul Qadir was born in Jalalabad, Afghanistan, in 1951, part of a wealthy, landowning Pashtun family. As such he was well educated, multilingual, and seemingly destined to follow his father's trade of engineer until the Soviets invaded Afghanistan in December 1979. Qadir fled to Pakistan with several family members and joined the mujahideen faction under the conservative cleric Yunnis Khalis. He distinguished himself in combat against Soviet and Afghan army forces, gaining a measure of renown and political respectability. Toward the end of the war, he was invited to the Tora Bora cave complex of Saudi millionaire Osama bin Laden, and the two became formally acquainted. When the Kabul regime was finally overthrown in 1992, Qadir returned to his native province and became governor. At a time of extreme poverty and dislocation in Afghan history, he acquired a notorious reputation for lavish living, especially to impress foreign journalists paying their respects from abroad. Qadir and his family also were highly criticized for their clandestine links to the illicit opium trade, and during his tenure Nangarhar Province became the nation's second-largest opium-producing region. Upon further reflection, Qadir changed sides and supported UN efforts to help eradicate the drug trade from Afghanistan, a move that made him powerful enemies. However, the onset of civil war throughout Afghanistan enabled the ultraconservative Taliban movement to rise and gradually take control of the country by 1996, at which point Qadir again fled to Pakistan. His fiercely anti-Taliban viewpoints did not sit well with Pakistani authorities, and he was forced to relocate again, first to Germany and then to Dubai, where his brother, Abdul Haq, operated several businesses. It was not until the United States attacked the Taliban regime in the fall of 2001 that Qadir returned home and helped organize resistance as part of the Northern Alliance.

After the Taliban's fall in late 2001, Qadir was reappointed governor of Nangarhar Province by the Jalalabad consultive council, and he resumed his lavish lifestyle at the 125-year-old Kasr palace. He subsequently served as vice chairman of the Northern Alliance delegation that was dispatched to Bonn, Germany, to facilitate creation of a post-Taliban administration. However, insomuch as the Northern Alliance was dominated by ethnic Tajiks and Uzbeks, Qadir stormed out of the proceedings to protest inadequate Pashtun representation in the new government. The United Nations took his counsel to heart, and the following spring Hamid Karzai, a fellow Pashtun, was appointed the first interim president of Afghanistan. Qadir was named third vice president and urban development minister. However, he had made innumerable enemies in his 20 years as a warlord and for repressing the drug trade, and on July 6, 2002, Qadir was assassinated in Kabul. He was laid to rest in his native province, his passing indicative of Afghanistan's instability during the post-Taliban period.

Rabbani, Burhanuddin (1940–)

president of Afghanistan

Burhanuddin Rabbani was born in Badakhshan Province, Afghanistan, the son of Tajik parents. He attended a religious school in Kabul and received a bachelor's degree in Islamic law and theology from Kabul University in 1963. Rabbani subsequently earned a master's degree in Islamic philosophy from al-Azhar University, in Cairo, Egypt, in 1968. Back in Afghanistan, Rabbani taught at Kabul University and gained attention for organizing Islamic students against growing secular and Communist trends on campus. In 1971, he joined Jamiat-i-

Islami (Islamic Society of Afghanistan) and rose to prominence as a national Islamic leader, despite the fact that most of his followers were Tajiks and Uzbeks, not majority Pashtuns. Rabbani's protests brought him into direct conflict with government officials, and in 1974, he fled to Saudi Arabia and then Pakistan, where he began organizing Jamiat-i-Islami as an armed resistance movement to fight the regime in Kabul. His followers had conducted several guerrilla raids in concert with those of his rival, Gulbuddin Hekmatyar, and the Soviet invasion of Afghanistan in December 1979 only heightened his stature among fellow Afghans. Consequently, Rabbani's mujahideen, under the famous guerrilla leader Ahmad Shah Massoud, resisted the Soviets forcefully and helped lead to their eventual expulsion in February 1989. Following the collapse of Mohammad Najibullah's Communist regime in April 1992, Rabbani's forces were among the first to occupy Kabul. Once in control, their first action was to attack Hekmatyar's Hezb-i-Islami forces and drive them from the capital.

In the post-Soviet era, a political arrangement was made in March 1993 among the competing factions that allowed Rabbani to serve as president of Afghanistan following a brief interim administration under Sibghatullah Mojodiddi. His ensuing tenure in office was marked by escalating violence between former allies, and he could not wield real authority beyond the reaches of Kabul. However, when Rabbani refused to step down from power as promised, another round of internecine fighting, principally with Hekmatyar, commenced. The ensuing chaos enabled the extremist Taliban movement to take over the country, and Rabbani fled from Kabul to the Panjshir Valley with Massoud's forces. At the time, he was still internationally recognized as the legitimate president of Afghanistan, and he used his influence to help support the Tajik- and Uzbek-based United National and Islamic Front for the Salvation of Afghanistan (Northern Alliance) to resist the Taliban. Once the Taliban were deposed by the United States in the fall of 2001, Rabbani tried reasserting his authority as president, but that December the UN-sponsored Bonn Conference passed him over in favor of Hamid Karzai. He formally relinquished his power in July 2002 and has since served as head of the Afghan National Front in opposition to Karzai's administration.

Rafsanjani, Ali (1934–)
Iranian president

Ali Akbar Hashemi Rafsanjani was born into a family of prosperous farmers in Rafsanjan, Iran, on February 15, 1934. He underwent religious training at an early age and in 1948 arrived at the holy city of Qom for advanced theological training. There he met and befriended Ruhollah Khomeini, a noted cleric and sworn adversary of Mohammad Reza Shah Pahlavi. After Khomeini was exiled in 1961, Rafsanjani continued the struggle against the shah's so-called White Revolution, an attempt to introduce widespread Western-style reforms into Iran's deeply conservative Islamic culture. The shah's regime collapsed in January 1979, and the following month Rafsanjani became an influential member of the theocratic inner circle. Through astute political maneuvering, he also served as speaker of the Majlis, or parliament. Within a year, the nation's economy was on the brink of collapse, and Iraqi leader Saddam Hussein invaded Iran in an attempt to secure disputed border territories. By July 1988, the Iranians had suffered nearly half a million casualties, and Rafsanjani was called upon to serve as commander in chief of all armed forces. He was determined to pursue a final victory, but when it became apparent that Iraq, supported by the Russians and Gulf States, could not be beaten, he persuaded the ayatollah to conclude a cease fire.

Following Khomeini's death in June 1989, Rafsanjani was elected president to replace outgoing Ali Khamenei, now the new supreme spiritual leader. He quickly became identified with more moderate, reformist elements in the national leadership, especially in liberalizing the economy, additional rights for women, and higher education. And, speaking as a senior cleric, he did not hesitate to denounce more ideological members of the parliament for their resistance to reforms. Because the economy refused to improve, Rafsanjani was reelected in June 1993, but by a smaller margin than previously. In August 1997, he stepped down as president and was succeeded by another determined reformer, Mohammad Khatami, and went on to serve as chairman of the Expediency Council, which mediates problems between the Constitutional Council and parliament. On September 11, 2001, Rafsanjani roundly denounced the attack on the World Trade Center in New York, though he remained cool toward closer relations with Washington. He nonetheless maintained that better relations were possible should the Americans alter their behavior toward Iran. Rafsanjani ran again for the presidency in 2005 but lost in the runoff election to hard-liner Mahmoud Ahmadinejad. Two years later, he recouped his fortunes by gaining appointment as chairman of the Assembly of Experts, which selects Iran's next supreme leader, and that achievement was viewed as a victory of moderates over Ahmadinejad's reactionary allies. Rafsanjani cemented his influence on March 10, 2009, when he was reelected chairman, and he has denounced Ahmadinejad for fraudulently winning the presidential election.

Rumsfeld, Donald H. (1932–)
secretary of defense

Donald Harold Rumsfeld was born on July 9, 1932, in Chicago, Illinois, the son of a real-estate salesman. He graduated from Princeton University in 1954 with a bachelor's degree in political science, then joined the U.S. Navy as an aviator and flight instructor. In 1957, Rumsfeld relocated to Washington, D.C., to serve as a congressional aide, and in 1962, he began his own political career by winning a seat in the U.S. House of Representatives. He was reelected up through 1969, only to resign and serve as director of the Office of Economic Opportunity in the Nixon administration. Rumsfeld successively became director of the Economic Stabilization Program, U.S. ambassador to the North Atlantic Treaty

Organization, and White House chief of staff under President Gerald R. Ford. On November 11, 1975, Ford appointed him the 13th secretary of defense, becoming, at 43, the youngest individual to hold that office. He served until January 20, 1977, when Jimmy Carter replaced him with Harold Brown. Over the next 30 years, Rumsfeld distinguished himself in the private sector by serving as chief executive officer of several large corporations, but he also dabbled in politics by serving on Republican candidate Robert Dole's presidential campaign in 1996, and two years later he was chairman of the Commission to Assess the Ballistic Missile Threat to the United States. From 1999 to 2000, he lent his business expertise to the U.S. Trade Deficit Review Commission, and by 2000, he also served as chairman of the Commission to Assess United States National Security Space Management and Organization. Rumsfeld returned to military matters on January 20, 2001, when President George W. Bush appointed him to serve as secretary of defense for a second time. For several months into the new administration, Rumsfeld was at loggerheads with Pentagon officials in his drive to cut wasteful spending and increase efficiency, which senior officers felt he pursed to the point of actually hurting military preparedness. However, in the wake of the September 11, 2001, attacks, Rumsfeld was catapulted into the point man in the war against global terror. He was a major architect of Operation Enduring Freedom, which drove the Taliban regime from power in Afghanistan by December, but he basically allowed the military to fight the war as it saw fit.

Rumsfeld's next objective was helping to topple Iraqi president Saddam Hussein from power, which was effectively accomplished by Operation Iraqi Freedom in March 2003. This time, however, he was roundly criticized by political and military figures for winning the war with the barest minimum of troops but then failing to garrison the nation with adequate manpower. Consequently, the American military was able to contain, but not completely crush, an indigenous insurrection aided by outside terrorists. He was also criticized in 2004 for his handling of the Abu Ghraib prison scandal, which proved embarrassing to the United States. By 2006, dissatisfaction with affairs in Iraq helped the Democrats take control of Congress, and on November 8, 2006, Rumsfeld resigned from office and was replaced by Robert Gates, former head of the Central Intelligence Agency. He returned to his ranch in Taos, New Mexico, and also served on the boards of several corporations. On December 2, 2009, he appeared in Washington, D.C., at a dinner hosted by the Center for Security Policy and vehemently denied President Barack Obama's claim that he had refused to increase troop levels in Afghanistan when requested by the military.

Sadr, Moqtada al- (1973–)
Iraqi cleric

Moqtada al-Sadr was born in Baghdad, Iraq, on August 12, 1973, into a noted family of Shiite clerics. His father, Mohammad Sadeq al-Sadr, a leading religious scholar and vocal critic of Saddam Hussein, was assassinated on Hussein's orders in February 1999. Moqtada's father-in-law was also killed by government authorities in 1980. Moqtada al-Sadr studied theology at the Najif Hawza (seminary), but he was undistinguished as a student and became better known for his fixation with computer games. Thus, despite family ties, he cannot claim the religious title of *mujtahid* (ranking) cleric, due to his lack of advanced degrees and the years of theological study that accompany them. However, memory of the elder Sadr is strong among poorer members of the Iraqi Shiite community, and their loyalty is continually reinforced by a strong social network of charities and social services maintained by the family. Largely for this reason, following the ouster of Saddam Hussein by the United States in April 2003, Moqtada al-Sadr became the de facto spokesman and leader for millions of Iraqi Shiites, long oppressed by the Sunni minority. Sadr began jockeying for prominence on the Iraqi political landscape by condemning the American occupation and characterizing the Iraqi interim government as little more than puppets. Moreover, he continually whipped up his impoverished followers in Sadr City, a Baghdad suburb, in demonstrations against the government, coalition authorities, and anyone else thwarting his ambitions. Sadr is thought be behind the assassination of rival cleric Imam Abdul Majid al-Khoei on April 10, 2003, and a warrant for his arrest was issued by Judge Raed Juhi, but the sensitivity of the times required the Coalition Provisional Authority to place it under seal.

In April 2004, al-Sadr upped the political ante by ordering his personal militia, the Mahdi Army, to fight American forces in Najaf. The Americans responded with military force that overpowered the militia, inflicted hundreds of Shiite casualties, and forced al-Sadr to sign a truce with the government. Since then, he has limited his actions to vocal political opposition to the Iraqi government, and he has stridently denounced the new constitution as the product of foreign infidels. In 2007, the Iraqi government came close to ordering security forces to arrest al-Sadr and disarm his followers, at which point he fled to Iran He returned briefly on May 25, 2007, to ride in a long motorcade from Najaf to Kufa and condemn the continuing U.S. presence in Iraq, then returned to Iran. From there, he occasionally releases statements urging his followers to rise up against the occupiers. Outside his traditional base of supporters in Sadr City, this opportunistic and self-serving cleric does not command a wide following in Iraq, even among fellow Shiites. He was last reported studying religion in the holy city of Qom, Iran, through which he might gain the authority that only advanced degrees can confer.

Sanchez, Ricardo S. (1951–   )

U.S. Army general

Ricardo Sanchez was born in Fort Myers, Florida, in 1951 and raised in Rio Grande City, Texas. He enrolled in the Reserve Officers' Training Corps (ROTC) while attending the Texas A&M University at Kingsville, and he was commissioned a second lieutenant in 1973. While in school, Sanchez was named a Distinguished Military Graduate, an honor reserved for the top 10 percent of all ROTC graduates. He initially served as a platoon leader in the elite 82nd Airborne Division, but in 1977 he transferred to the armored branch. When Operation Desert Storm commenced in January 1991, Sanchez commanded the 197th Infantry Brigade (Mechanized), which assisted in the capture of the Iraqi port of Basra. Soon afterward, he advanced to colonel in charge of the 2nd Brigade, 1st Infantry Division. Sanchez left field operations to accept a position within the U.S. Southern Command as deputy chief of staff and director of operations. He then rose to major general and accepted command of the elite 1st Armored Division as part of the V Corps in Germany. He served there for two years before assuming command of the entire V Corps. In June 2003, he received the most daunting challenge of his career: commander of the Multi-National Force Iraq.

Iraq had been ruled by President Saddam Hussein, who quickly eliminated political or religious dissenters, whether they were Arab or Kurd, Shiite or Sunni. After he was deposed during Operation Iraqi Freedom, simmering resentments among these groups surfaced in an intractable insurgency aimed at occupying forces and one another. The Americans, previously greeted as liberators, now found themselves under increasing attack. As commander, it was Sanchez's responsibility to maintain order and facilitate reconstruction efforts, a task made doubly difficult by his strained relations with L. Paul Bremer III, head of the Coalition Provisional Authority. Worse, news of American misconduct toward Iraqi prisoners held at the Abu Ghraib prison came to light, and Sanchez, though he denied any culpability, was nonetheless in charge and held responsible for it. The Americans scored some notable successes against al-Qaeda operatives in Iraq and captured Saddam Hussein and killed his two sons, but Sanchez could not shake the stigma of Abu Ghraib. After relinquishing control of the multinational force to General George Casey in June 2004, he resumed command of the V Corps in Germany, a post he held longer than any other incumbent, but he was denied promotion to full general. On September 6, 2006, he turned over the V Corps to a superior officer, rather than to a successor, and ended a distinguished 33 years of military service by resigning. Sanchez presently resides in Texas and has lambasted the media for its "sensationalist tendencies." In 2008, he also published his memoir, *Wiser in Battle: A Soldier's Story,* which excoriates President George W. Bush's policies and handling of affairs in Iraq.

Sayyaf, Abdul Rasul (1946–)
Afghan politician

Abdul Rasul Sayyaf was born in the Paghman Valley, Afghanistan, in 1946 and studied religion at the Abu Hanifa Theological School and the Faculty of Theology at Kabul University. Sayyaf subsequently received an advanced degree from al-Azhar University in Egypt, and, after returning to Afghanistan in 1971, he functioned as a close aide to Burhanuddin Rabbani. He taught theology at the Shariat, a small Islamic university in Kabul, for two years, but in 1973 he became involved in a plot with Rabbani and Ahmad Shah Massoud to overthrow President Daoud Khan. The coup failed, and Sayyaf attempted to flee to Pakistan, but he was arrested and imprisoned. He remained jailed until a general amnesty was proclaimed by Communist president Hafizullah Amin in 1980. That same year, he migrated to Pakistan to join the mujahideen alliance, then embroiled in expelling Soviet occupation forces from Afghanistan. He founded the Ittihad-i-Islami Baraye Azadi Afghanistan (Islamic Union for the Liberation of Afghanistan), an umbrella group of several smaller organizations. In the course of combating the Soviets, Sayyaf made several fundraising trips to Saudi Arabia, where, because of his fluency in Arabic and very imposing presence, he raised millions of dollars for the resistance. He was also instrumental in convincing a wealthy Saudi, Osama bin Laden, to relocate to Jalalabad with

him and help arm and train fighters for the cause. Sayyaf's growing radicalization led him to establish a fundamentalist university near Peshawar, Pakistan, in 1985, called Dawa'a al-Jihad (Convert and Struggle), which enhanced his reputation among fellow fundamentalists.

After the Soviets departed Afghanistan in February 1989, Sayyad continued working to overthrow the regime of Mohammad Najibullah. This was accomplished in 1992, and he returned home to extract a measure of theological retribution. His Sunni fighters were soon implicated in a massacre of Hazara (Afghan Shiites) in the Afshar neighborhood of Kabul, and his rampages intensified during the new civil war that began in 1993. He also strongly opposed the theologically similar Taliban, which took control of Afghanistan in 1996, and committed atrocities against them. Sayyaf was known to operate terrorist training camps in the countryside, and one graduate, Khalid Sheik Mohammad, was the mastermind behind the destruction of the World Trade Center on September 11, 2001. Another alumnus, Abdurajak Janjalani, founded the Philippine terrorist organization Abu Sayyaf and named it in his honor. Critics further assert that he helped arrange the assassination of Ahmad Shah Massoud, a former compatriot and potential rival. The Taliban were swept from power by the United States in 2001, and Sayyaf transformed himself into a respected senior member of the *loya jirga* (tribal assembly). He has gone on record advocating a blanket amnesty bill for former mujahideen that would preclude any prosecution for war crimes.

Schwarzkopf, H. Norman (1934–)
U.S. Army general

Herbert Norman Schwarzkopf was born in Trenton, New Jersey, on August 22, 1934, the son of an army officer. He traveled abroad with his father on a yearlong visit to Iran in the 1940s and was indelibly impressed by this youthful encounter with Islamic religion and culture. Schwarzkopf subsequently attended the U.S. Military Academy, receiving his lieutenant's commission in 1956. After gaining his wings, he served with the 101st Airborne Division before becoming a member of the army's elite Berlin brigade. In 1964, he left the military briefly to obtain a master's degree in missile engineering from the University of Southern California. Schwarzkopf then fulfilled several tours of duty in Vietnam, where he was decorated for bravery with his third Silver Star before rising to brigadier general in 1978 and major general in 1982. The following year, he served as ground-force commander during Operation Urgent Fury, the U.S.-sponsored liberation of Grenada from Marxist revolutionaries. Afterward, he wrote a scathing critique of operations that generated badly needed reforms. Schwarzkopf received his fourth Silver Star in 1988 and spent a year at the Pentagon as deputy chief of staff. He then became head of the United States Central Command, headquartered in Tampa, Florida, charged with providing security for American interests throughout the Middle East. In spring 1990, mindful of the declining Soviet threat to the region, he conducted hypothetical war games that substituted Iraq's president Saddam Hussein as a potential aggressor. The following August, Iraq actually invaded neighboring Kuwait, and President George H. W. Bush authorized Schwarzkopf to lead the effort to oust it.

Using his existing Iraq plan, Schwarzkopf spent the ensuing six months assembling a 27-nation coalition to force the Iraqis from Kuwait. Many Arab nations proved willing to assist, and Schwarzkopf, because of his training in Middle Eastern affairs, melded this awkward assemblage of Western and Middle Eastern armies into a formidable military force of 500,000 people. Operation Desert Shield, the buildup of forces in the gulf region, succeeded without any serious problems. When Hussein then refused a United Nations order to leave Kuwait, Schwarzkopf commenced Operation Desert Storm to drive Iraq out in January 1991. He began the Gulf War with a monthlong aerial bombardment of Iraqi defenses and antiaircraft sites, which left Iraq's ground forces vulnerable to assault. When this failed to induce Iraq to depart, Schwarzkopf used a well-executed flanking movement that routed the Iraqis, inflicted 100,000 casualties in little more than 100 hours of fighting, and effectively liberated Kuwait. Schwarzkopf retired from the military in 1991 and published his memoir, *It Doesn't Take a Hero* (1992). He also received an honorary knighthood from Queen Elizabeth II. Today, Schwarzkopf lives in Florida, where he frequently appears as a TV military commentator and analyst.

Sistani, Ali Husaini al- (1930–)
Iraqi cleric

Ali Husaini al-Sistani was born in Mashhad, Iran, on August 4, 1930, into a family of distinguished theologians. Both his father and grandfather were noted Shiite clerics, so he began his religious instruction at the age of five, and by 1949 al-Sistani was allowed by clerics to study advanced Islamic law in the holy city of Qom. He proved himself adept as a religious scholar and in 1951 emigrated to the holy Shia city of Najaf in neighboring Iraq. There, al-Sistani studied at the Najaf Hawza (seminary) under the Grand Ayatollah Abu al-Qasim al-Khoei and served many years as his understudy. By 1961, his command of Islamic precepts was so advanced that he rose to the senior clerical level of *Ijtehad* at the age of 31, which enabled him to make judgments on theological questions. When Ayatollah al-Khoei died in 1992, al-Sistani, who was given the honor of leading the prayers at his funeral, was appointed grand ayatollah to succeed him. In this capacity, al-Sistani served as the leading religious figure for Iraqi Shiites and inherited an extensive network of charities, thousands of religious students in Iran and Iraq, and an active body of representatives constantly promoting his views in neighborhoods, mosques, and bazaars. Al-Sistani became a vocal opponent of Iraqi president Saddam Hussein, who, for the most part, brutally oppressed the Iraqi Shiite majority. In 1994, the government shut al-Sistani's mosque, and he was sentenced to a decade of house arrest in Najaf.

He nonetheless worked quietly, behind the scenes, shoring up the faith of his supporters at a time when many other senior clerics were being jailed or assassinated by the government.

After the United States toppled Saddam Hussein in April 2003, the quiet and unobtrusive al-Sistani found himself thrust into the public spotlight. With the mass of his followers unsure how to deal with the foreign occupation, he instructed fellow Shiites to welcome the Americans for the time being and not to contest them. His position contrasted sharply with the firebrand cleric Moqtada al-Sadr, who openly waged war against coalition forces in August 2004 and lost thousands of followers in combat. It was al-Sistani who arranged the truce in Najaf that allowing Sadr's Mahdi Army to leave the holy city and adopt a neutral stance. Politically, he criticized the Americans for slowness in allowing Iraqis to approve a new constitution, but he also instructed Iraqi Shiite women to vote, whether or not their husbands allowed it. Since then, al-Sistani has been a force for moderation in the Shia community, and he urges the faithful not to extract vengeance upon their Sunni neighbors for acts of terrorism against them, and blames the violence on foreign Wahabists. In 2005, al-Sistani openly embraced the nation's first democratic election and said it was obligatory for all Iraqis to both participate and respect the outcome. He also proved himself technologically savvy by becoming the first ayatollah to use the Internet and have his own Web site. This quiet cleric remains a force for stability during a turbulent time in Iraqi history.

Talabani, Jalal (1933–   )
president of Iraq

Jalal Talabani was born in Kelkan, Iraq, on November 12, 1933, into a Kurdish household. The Kurdish region, then dominated by Arabic-speaking Iraqis, has a long history of violence and activism in the cause of national independence. Talabani joined the process by organizing a secret student union at the age of 13. He entered Baghdad University to study law in 1953, but three years later he went into hiding after founding the outlawed Kurdistan Student Union. After the Hashemite dynasty was overthrown in 1958, Talabani served in the Iraqi army until 1961, when Kurds rebelled against the regime of Abdul Karim Qassem. He fought for independence over the next decade, but in 1975, after profound disagreements with the Kurdish Democratic Party of Massoud Barzani, he founded a breakaway faction, the Patriotic Union of Kurdistan (PUK). Iranian support for the Kurdish rebellion, so essential to its survival, ended after the shah reached a border agreement with Saddam Hussein in 1975, though Talabani continued waging a guerrilla war inside Iraq. Iranian aid to the Kurds resumed in 1980 following the Iraqi invasion of Iran, and Talabani and his PUK were conspicuous in their military action against Hussein's forces. Hussein responded by using chemical weapons against Kurdish civilians, killing thousands. Talabani and his followers resumed their low-level conflict until 1991, when Hussein's army was driven from Iraq by a U.S.-led coalition, and the Kurds again rose in revolt. The attempt was crushed, but Talabani gained international recognition as a Kurdish spokesman who arranged UN-sponsored safe zones for the Kurds in northern Iraq. A semiautonomous Kurdish Regional Government was then formed with Talabani as vice president, and, in 1998, he proved instrumental in securing an agreement with Barzani to outlaw fighting between Kurdish groups.

Talabani's fortunes advanced further in the spring of 2003 when his fighters openly assisted the U.S.-led coalition in overthrowing Hussein's regime during Operation Iraqi Freedom. As the nation's leading Kurdish political figure, he was invited to join the Iraqi Interim Governing Council, in which each member served as president for a month, and he helped draw up a new Iraqi constitution. Talabani then stopped agitating for Kurdish independence and sought to keep Iraq, with its disparate Sunni, Shiite, and Kurdish populations, functioning as a single entity. His moderate stance on many issues led to his election as president of

Iraq by parliament on April 6, 2005, which made him not only the first elected Iraqi head of state, but also the first Kurd in national history to hold executive powers. Since coming to power, Talabani has demonstrated consummate skill in coalition politics and helped create a measure of political stability among traditional ethnic rivals. His popularity was confirmed on April 22, 2006, when the parliament elected him to a second term as president.

Taraki, Nur Mohammad (1913–1979)
president of Afghanistan

Nur Mohammad Taraki was born in Ghazni, Afghanistan, on July 15, 1913, into a rural Pashtun family. He clerked for many years with a trading company in Bombay, India, and studied English at night school before attending Kabul University in the 1950s. He immersed himself in Marxist politics, and, on January 1, 1965, Taraki and Babrak Karmal founded the People's Democratic Party of Afghanistan (PDPA), a Communist organization with strong pro-Moscow leanings. Taraki served as general secretary while Karmal became secretary of the Central Committee. However, given the fractious nature of the Afghan polity, the PDPA quickly split into two distinct factions: the Moscow-oriented Parcham (Banner) under Karmal, and the Khalq (Masses) under Taraki, which was more militant and less orthodox. This deep ideological divide was never completely reconciled despite orders from Moscow to seek accommodation. On April 27, 1978, a Communist coup was orchestrated in Kabul that resulted in the death of President Mohammad Daoud Khan, and PDPA operatives swiftly seized control of the government. On May 1, 1978, Taraki was appointed president of the new Democratic Republic of Afghanistan, in addition to serving as prime minister and general secretary. In an attempt to promote party unity, Taraki appointed a cabinet consisting of both Khalq and Parcham factions under Karmal and Mohammad Najibullah, but

bitter personal and ideological rivalries precluded any peaceful settlement within the government.

Once in power, Taraki instituted far-sweeping changes to modernize Afghanistan's traditional methods of land ownership, forced marriages, sharia laws, and power structures in rural areas in the majority of the countryside. He was particularly adamant about providing equal rights and education for women, which went against ingrained Islamic beliefs in his conservative country. Consequently, Taraki's tenure in office was marked by political instability, protests, and violence against the government by religious extremists. Because of political resistance from Karmal and Najibullah, he finally stripped them of their official titles, and they fled to the Soviet Union. He also ordered the execution of thousands of religious and tribal elders who dared to oppose reform measures. Taraki was forced to appoint an archenemy, Hafizullah Amin, as his prime minister on March 28, 1979. Shortly afterward, in March 1979, he visited Moscow and requested that General Secretary Leonid Brezhnev deploy Soviet forces to support his regime, whereupon the Russians warned him that Amin was preparing a coup against him. Once back in Kabul, Taraki arranged several failed assassination attempts against Amin before being overthrown and murdered by his prime minister sometime in September 1979; his death was only reported to the public on October 10. This deed also provided the Soviets with a convenient pretext for direct intervention.

Zahir Shah, Mohammad (1914–2007)
king of Afghanistan

Mohammad Zahir Shah was born in Kabul, Afghanistan, on October 30, 1914, a Pashtun and son of high-ranking government minister Mohammad Nadir Shah. Educated in France, he was appointed assistant minister of defense and education at the age of 18, and, when his father was assassinated on November 8, 1933, Zahir Shah was proclaimed the new king. He was forced to share power with a regent, Sardar Hashim Khan, but, over the next four decades, he ruled capably, if cautiously. However, he had persistent problems with Prime Minister Sardar Mohammad Daud, his cousin, who precipitated a border crisis with Pakistan that took months to resolve. Zahir Shah was also committed to modernizing his backward nation, and in 1964 he promulgated a new constitution guaranteeing the separation of powers, civil rights, freedom of the press, and voting rights for women. However, when he went to Italy for eye surgery in July 1973, he was overthrown by his cousin Daud. This was the first of a series of coups and counter-coups that culminated in the Soviet invasion of Afghanistan in December 1979. The king, who was stripped of his citizenship by the Communist regime of Babrak Karmal, remained isolated in Rome for the next three decades, a helpless onlooker as his nation degenerated into a vicious cycle of violence and retribution.

After the Soviet invasion ended in February 1989, another round of internecine combat commenced between competing groups of mujahideen who struggled for supremacy. Destruction was rife and occasioned the rise of a fundamentalist movement, the Taliban, who proceeded to restore law and order through strictly enforced quranic rule. However, this policy was carried to such extremes that men were obliged to grow beards and women had to wear body-length burkas in public. However, when Mullah Mohammed Omar, the Taliban leader, refused to extradite Saudi terrorist Osama bin Laden to the United States following the World Trade Center attack on September 11, 2001, President George W. Bush commenced Operation Enduring Freedom to drive the Taliban from power. The Taliban were toppled by December, and the problem then became how to install a legitimate government acceptable to all the traditional warring factions in Afghanistan. In 2002, interim leader Hamid Karzai invited the aging monarch back to his former country, and he was greeted by thunderous applause. Zahir Shah opened a *loya jirga* (tribal assembly) on June 10, 2002, but declared from the onset his reluctance to return to the throne. Determined to serve as a symbol of national unity, he simply accepted the title "Father of the Nation." Once Karzai was elected to the Afghan presidency, several members of Zahir Shah's family and key supporters received sinecures in the new government. Zahir Shah died in Kabul on July 23, 2007, and the following day thousands of mourners paid their final respects to their aged monarch. He was the last of the 226-year Pashtun dynasty to rule Afghanistan.

APPENDIX I

PERSIAN GULF WAR: CASUALTY SUMMARY

Desert Shield/Storm as of January 29, 2010

CASUALTY TYPE	TOTAL	ARMY	AIR FORCE	MARINES	NAVY***
Killed in Action	144	96	20	22	6
Died of Wounds	4	2		2	
Missing in Action—Declared Dead	0				
Captured—Declared Dead	0				
TOTAL HOSTILE DEATHS	148	98	20	24	6
Missing—Presumed Dead	12		2	8	2
Other Deaths	223	126	13	36	48
TOTAL NONHOSTILE DEATHS	235	126	15	44	50
TOTAL IN-THEATER DEATHS*	383	224	35	68	56
TOTAL NON-THEATER DEATHS	1,565	608	299	171	487
TOTAL DEATHS	1,948	832	334	239	543
Killed in Action—No Remains	2				2
Missing in Action—No Remains					
Captured Declared Dead—No Remains					
Nonhostile Missing—Presumed Dead—No Remains	12	2	8	2	
Nonhostile Other Deaths—No Remains					
TOTAL—NO REMAINS	14	0	2	8	4
WOUNDED—NOT MORTAL	467	354	9	92	12
SERVING WORLDWIDE**	2,225,000	782,000	561,000	213,000	669,000
SERVING IN-THEATER—ACTIVE DUTY	584,342	271,654	70,741	90,866	151,081
SERVING IN-THEATER—RECALLED	110,208	78,512	11,666	12,660	7,370

*Inclusive dates are August 7, 1990, to September 14, 1991. Any casualty date in the detailed records after the end date represents a service member who was wounded during the period and subsequently died as a result of those wounds or a service member who was in a missing status during a part of the war period and was later declared dead.

**Estimated Figures ***Includes Coast Guard.

Prepared by: Defense Manpower Data Center

≈ APPENDIX II

OPERATION ENDURING FREEDOM: MILITARY DEATHS

October 7, 2001, Through March 6, 2010

		MILITARY SERVICE			
	Totals	Army	Navy	Marines	Air Force
CASUALTY TYPE					
Hostile	732	549	34	126	23
Nonhostile	273	190	20	40	23
Total	1,005	739	54	166	46
GENDER					
Male	985	728	51	165	41
Female	20	11	3	1	5
Total	1,005	739	54	166	46
OFFICER/ENLISTED					
Officer	136	98	9	19	10
E5-E9	413	321	25	42	25
E1-E4	456	320	20	105	11
Total	1,005	739	54	166	46
AGE					
> 35	158	129	10	7	12
Total	1,005	739	54	166	46

COMPONENT

Active	833	583	51	156	43
Reserve	47	33	3	10	1
National Guard	125	123			2
Total	1,005	739	54	166	46

RACE/ETHNICITY

American Indian or Alaska Native	15	7	4	3	1
Asian	13	9	4		
Black or African American	81	68	4	9	
Hispanic or Latino	77	50	4	18	5
Multiple races, pending, or unknown	10	7	1	1	1
Native Hawaiian or Pacific Islander	12	10	1		1
White	797	588	36	135	38
Total	1,005	739	54	166	46

Casualty areas include in/around Afghanistan, the Philippines, Southwest Asia, and other locations.

Appendix III

Operation Enduring Freedom: Military Wounded in Action

October 7, 2001, through March 6, 2010

| | MILITARY SERVICE | | | | |
	Totals	Army	Navy	Marines	Air Force
CASUALTY TYPE					
Hostile	5,190	3,916	98	1,037	139
Nonhostile					
Total	5,190	3,916	98	1,037	139
GENDER					
Male	5,136	3,872	96	1,034	134
Female	54	44	2	3	5
Total	5,190	3,916	98	1,037	139
OFFICER/ENLISTED					
Officer	393	321	7	44	21
E5-E9	1,916	1,508	40	273	95
E1-E4	2,881	2,087	51	720	23
Total	5,190	3,916	98	1,037	139
AGE					
> 35	485	432	7	12	34
Not Available	594	53	8	532	1
Total	5,190	3,916	98	1,037	139

COMPONENT

Active	4,397	3,159	97	1,014	127
Reserve	122	96	1	23	2
National Guard	671	661			10
Total	5,190	3,916	98	1,037	139

RACE/ETHNICITY

American Indian or Alaska Native	62	42	6	13	1
Asian	83	70	4	7	2
Black or African American	281	236	5	34	6
Hispanic or Latino	233	172	11	43	7
Multiple races, pending, or unknown	431	101	10	315	5
Native Hawaiian or Pacific Islander	20	13	3	3	1
White	4,080	3,282	59	622	117
Total	5,190	3,916	98	1,037	139

Casualty areas include in/around Afghanistan, the Philippines, Southwest Asia, and other locations.

APPENDIX IV

OPERATION IRAQI FREEDOM: MILITARY DEATHS

March 19, 2003, Through March 6, 2010*

	MILITARY SERVICE				
	Totals	Army	Navy*	Marines	Air Force
CASUALTY TYPE					
Hostile	3,469	2,524	65	851	29
Nonhostile	902	671	38	171	22
Total	4,371	3,195	103	1,022	51
GENDER					
Male	4,265	3,110	93	1,014	48
Female	106	85	10	8	3
Total	4,371	3,195	103	1,022	51
OFFICER/ENLISTED					
Officer	423	325	11	75	12
E5-E9	1,429	1,181	49	173	26
E1-E4	2,519	1,689	43	774	13
Total	4,371	3,195	103	1,022	51
AGE					
> 35	496	420	24	40	12
Total	4,371	3,195	103	1,022	51

COMPONENT

Active	3,558	2,550	79	883	46
Reserve	320	154	24	139	3
National Guard	493	491			2
Total	4,371	3,195	103	1,022	51

RACE/ETHNICITY

American Indian or Alaska Native	42	27	1	14	
Asian	81	53	5	23	
Black or African American	422	359	12	44	7
Hispanic or Latino	463	301	12	146	4
Multiple races, pending, or unknown	48	39	1	6	2
Native Hawaiian or Pacific Islander	50	41	1	8	
White	3,265	2,375	71	781	38
Total	4,371	3,195	103	1,022	51

*Data subject to change—Navy totals include one Coast Guard death

APPENDIX V

OPERATION IRAQI FREEDOM: MILITARY WOUNDED IN ACTION

March 19, 2003, Through March 6, 2010*

		MILITARY SERVICE			
	Totals	Army	Navy	Marines	Air Force
CASUALTY TYPE					
Hostile	31,716	22,033	634	8,624	425
Nonhostile					
Total	31,716	22,033	634	8,624	425
GENDER					
Male	31,099	21,491	629	8,583	396
Female	617	542	5	41	29
Total	31,716	22,033	634	8,624	425
OFFICER/ENLISTED					
Officer	1,865	1,381	36	411	37
E5-E9	10,297	8,251	241	1,577	228
Total	31,716	22,033	634	8,624	425
AGE					
> 35	2,819	2,405	90	234	90
Not Available	1,631	312	53	1,265	1
Total	31,716	22,033	634	8,624	425

COMPONENT

Active	25,120	16,664	531	7,574	351
Reserve	2,464	1,295	103	1,050	16
National Guard	4,132	4,074			58
Total	31,716	22,033	634	8,624	425

RACE/ETHNICITY

American Indian or Alaska Native	336	216	24	94	2
Asian	513	363	19	128	3
Black or African American	2,659	2,290	40	303	26
Hispanic or Latino	1,993	1,482	24	457	30
Multiple races, pending, or unknown	1,650	684	67	876	23
Native Hawaiian or Pacific Islander	187	147	5	31	4
White	24,378	16,851	455	6,735	337
Total	31,716	22,033	634	8,624	425

*Data subject to change

APPENDIX VI

MEDAL OF HONOR RECIPIENTS

(*-Posthumous Receipt)

Afghanistan

Giunta, Salvatore A.

Rank and Organization: Staff Sergeant, U.S. Army
For conspicuous gallantry and intrepidity at the risk of his life above and beyond the call of duty: Specialist Salvatore A. Giunta distinguished himself conspicuously by gallantry and intrepidity at the risk of his life above and beyond the call of duty in action with an armed enemy in the Korengal Valley, Afghanistan, on October 25, 2007. While conducting a patrol as team leader with Company B, 2d Battalion (Airborne), 503d Infantry Regiment, Specialist Giunta and his team were navigating through harsh terrain when they were ambushed by a well-armed and well-coordinated insurgent force. While under heavy enemy fire, Specialist Giunta immediately sprinted towards cover and engaged the enemy. Seeing that his squad leader had fallen and believing that he had been injured, Specialist Giunta exposed himself to withering enemy fire and raced towards his squad leader, helped him to cover, and administered medical aid. While administering first aid, enemy fire struck Specialist Giunta's body armor and his secondary weapon. Without regard to the ongoing fire, Specialist Giunta engaged the enemy before prepping and throwing grenades, using the explosions for cover in order to conceal his position. Attempting to reach additional wounded fellow soldiers who were separated from the squad, Specialist Giunta and his team encountered a barrage of enemy fire that forced them to the ground. The team continued forward and upon reaching the wounded soldiers, Specialist Giunta realized that another soldier was still separated from the element. Specialist Giunta then advanced forward on his own initiative. As he crested the top of a hill, he observed two insurgents carrying away an American soldier. He immediately engaged the enemy, killing one and wounding the other. Upon reaching the wounded soldier, he began to provide medical aid, as his squad caught up and provided security. Specialist Giunta's unwavering courage, selflessness, and decisive leadership while under extreme enemy fire were integral to his platoon's ability to defeat an enemy ambush and recover a fellow American soldier from the enemy. Specialist Salvatore A. Giunta's extraordinary heroism and selflessness above and beyond the call of duty are in keeping with the highest traditions of military service and reflect great credit upon himself, Company B, 2d Battalion (Airborne), 503d Infantry Regiment, and the United States Army.

*Monti, Jared C.

Rank and Organization: Sergeant First Class, U.S. Army.
For conspicuous gallantry and intrepidity at the risk of his life above and beyond the call of duty: Staff Sergeant Jared C. Monti distinguished himself by acts of gallantry and intrepidity above and beyond the call of duty while serving as a team leader with Headquarters and Headquarters troop, 3rd Squadron, 71st Cavalry Regiment, 3rd Brigade Combat Team, 10th Mountain Division, in connection with combat operations against an enemy in Nurestan Province, Afghanistan, on June 21st, 2006. While Staff Sergeant Monti was leading a mission aimed at gathering intelligence and directing fire against the enemy, his 16-man patrol was attacked by as many as 50 enemy fighters. On the verge of being overrun, Staff Sergeant Monti quickly directed his men to set up a defensive position behind a rock formation. He then called for indirect fire support, accurately tar-

geting the rounds upon the enemy who had closed to within 50 meters of his position. While still directing fire, Staff Sergeant Monti personally engaged the enemy with his rifle and a grenade, successfully disrupting an attempt to flank his patrol. Staff Sergeant Monti then realized that one of his soldiers was lying wounded in the open ground between the advancing enemy and the patrol's position. With complete disregard for his own safety, Staff Sergeant Monti twice attempted to move from behind the cover of the rocks into the face of relentless enemy fire to rescue his fallen comrade. Determined not to leave his soldier, Staff Sergeant Monti made a third attempt to cross open terrain through intense enemy fire. On this final attempt, he was mortally wounded, sacrificing his own life in an effort to save his fellow soldier. Staff Sergeant Monti's selfless acts of heroism inspired his patrol to fight off the larger enemy force. Staff Sergeant Monti's immeasurable courage and uncommon valor are in keeping with the highest traditions of military service and reflect great credit upon himself, Headquarters and Headquarters Troop, 3rd Squadron, 71st Cavalry Regiment, 3rd Brigade Combat Team, 10th Mountain Division, and the United States Army.

*Murphy, Michael P.

Rank and Organization: Lieutenant, U.S. Navy

For conspicuous gallantry and intrepidity at the risk of his life above and beyond the call of duty as the leader of a special reconnaissance element with Naval Special Warfare Task Unit Afghanistan on 27 and 28 June 2005. While leading a mission to locate a high-level anti-coalition militia leader, Lieutenant Murphy demonstrated extraordinary heroism in the face of grave danger in the vicinity of Asadabad, Kunar Province, Afghanistan. On 28 June 2005, operating in an extremely rugged enemy-controlled area, Lieutenant Murphy's team was discovered by anti-coalition militia sympathizers, who revealed their position to Taliban fighters. As a result, between 30 and 40 enemy fighters besieged his four-member team. Demonstrating exceptional resolve, Lieutenant Murphy valiantly led his men in engaging the large enemy force. The ensuing fierce firefight resulted in numerous enemy casualties, as well as the wounding of all four members of the team. Ignoring his own wounds and demonstrating exceptional composure, Lieutenant Murphy continued to lead and encourage his men. When the primary communicator fell mortally wounded, Lieutenant Murphy repeatedly attempted to call for assistance for his beleaguered teammates. Realizing the impossibility of communicating in the extreme terrain, and in the face of almost certain death, he fought his way into open terrain to gain a better position to transmit a call. This deliberate, heroic act deprived him of cover, exposing him to direct enemy fire. Finally achieving contact with his Headquarters, Lieutenant Murphy maintained his exposed position while he provided his location and requested immediate support for his team. In his final act of bravery, he continued to engage the enemy until he was mortally wounded, gallantly giving his life for his country and for the cause of freedom. By his selfless leadership, courageous actions, and extraordinary devotion to duty, Lieutenant Murphy reflected great credit upon himself and upheld the highest traditions of the United States Naval Service.

Iraq

*Dunham, Jason L.

Rank and Organization: Corporal, U.S. Marine Corps

For conspicuous gallantry and intrepidity at the risk of his life above and beyond the call of duty while serving as Rifle Squad Leader, 4th Platoon, Company K, Third Battalion, Seventh Marines (Reinforced), Regimental Combat Team 7, First Marine Division (Reinforced), on 14 April 2004. Corporal Dunham's squad was conducting a reconnaissance mission in the town of Karabilah, Iraq, when they heard rocket-propelled grenade and small arms fire erupt approximately two kilometers to the west. Corporal Dunham led his Combined Anti-Armor Team towards the engagement to provide fire support to their Battalion Commander's convoy, which had been ambushed as it was traveling to Camp Husaybah. As Corporal Dunham and his marines advanced, they quickly began to receive enemy fire. Corporal Dunham ordered his squad to dismount their vehicles and led one of his fire teams on foot several blocks south of the ambushed convoy. Discovering seven Iraqi vehicles in a column attempting to depart, Corporal Dunham and his team stopped the vehicles to search them for weapons. As they approached the vehicles, an insurgent leaped out and attacked Corporal Dunham. Corporal Dunham wrestled the insurgent to the ground and in the ensuing struggle saw the insurgent release a grenade. Corporal Dunham immediately alerted his fellow Marines to the threat. Aware of the imminent danger and without hesitation, Corporal Dunham covered the grenade with his helmet and body, bearing the brunt of the explosion and shielding his Marines from the blast. In an ultimate and selfless act of bravery in which he was mortally wounded, he saved the lives of at least two fellow marines. By his undaunted courage, intrepid fighting spirit, and unwavering devotion to duty, Corporal Dunham gallantly gave his life for his country, thereby reflecting great credit upon himself and upholding the highest traditions of the Marine Corps and the United States Naval Service.

*McGinnis, Ross A.

Rank and Organization: Private First Class, U.S. Army

For conspicuous gallantry and intrepidity at the risk of his life above and beyond the call of duty: Private First Class Ross A. McGinnis distinguished himself by acts of gallantry and intrepidity above and beyond the call of duty while serving as an M2 .50-caliber Machine Gunner, 1st Platoon, C Company, 1st Battalion, 26th Infantry Regiment, in connection with combat operations against an armed enemy in Adhamiyah, Northeast Baghdad, Iraq, on 4 December 2006.

That afternoon his platoon was conducting combat control operations in an effort to reduce and control sectarian violence in the area. While Private McGinnis was manning the M2 .50-caliber machine gun, a fragmentation grenade thrown by an insurgent fell through the gunner's hatch into the vehicle. Reacting quickly, he yelled "grenade," allowing all four members of his crew to prepare for the grenade's blast. Then, rather than leaping from the gunner's hatch to safety, Private McGinnis made the courageous decision to protect his crew. In a selfless act of bravery, in which he was mortally wounded, Private McGinnis covered the live grenade, pinning it between his body and the vehicle and absorbing most of the explosion.

Private McGinnis' gallant action directly saved four men from certain serious injury or death. Private First Class McGinnis' extraordinary heroism and selflessness at the cost of his own life, above and beyond the call of duty, are in keeping with the highest traditions of the military service and reflect great credit upon himself, his unit, and the United States Army.

*Miller, Robert J.

Rank and Organization: Staff Sergeant, U.S. Army.

For conspicuous gallantry and intrepidity at the risk of his life above and beyond the call of duty:

Staff Sergeant Robert J. Miller distinguished himself by extraordinary acts of heroism while serving as the Weapons Sergeant in Special Forces Operational Detachment Alpha 3312, Special Operations Task Force 33, Combined Joint Special Operations Task Force–Afghanistan during combat operations against an armed enemy in Kunar [Konar] Province, Afghanistan on January 25, 2008. While conducting a combat reconnaissance patrol through the Gowardesh Valley, Staff Sergeant Miller and his small element of U.S. and Afghan National Army soldiers engaged a force of 15 to 20 insurgents occupying prepared fighting positions. Staff Sergeant Miller initiated the assault by engaging the enemy positions with his vehicle's turret-mounted Mark 19 40 millimeter automatic grenade launcher while simultaneously providing detailed descriptions of the enemy positions to his command, enabling effective, accurate close air support.

Following the engagement, Staff Sergeant Miller led a small squad forward to conduct a battle damage assessment. As the group neared the small, steep, narrow valley that the enemy had inhabited, a large, well-coordinated insurgent force initiated a near ambush, assaulting from elevated positions with ample cover. Exposed and with little available cover, the patrol was totally vulnerable to enemy rocket propelled grenades and automatic weapon fire. As point man, Staff Sergeant Miller was at the front of the patrol, cut off from supporting elements, and less than 20 meters from enemy forces. Nonetheless, with total disregard for his own safety, he called for his men to quickly move back to covered positions as he charged the enemy over exposed ground and under overwhelming enemy fire in order to provide protective fire for his team.

While maneuvering to engage the enemy, Staff Sergeant Miller was shot in his upper torso. Ignoring the wound, he continued to push the fight, moving to draw fire from over one hundred enemy fighters upon himself. He then again charged forward through an open area in order to allow his teammates to safely reach cover. After killing at least 10 insurgents, wounding dozens more, and repeatedly exposing himself to withering enemy fire while moving from position to position, Staff Sergeant Miller was mortally wounded by enemy fire. His extraordinary valor ultimately saved the lives of seven members of his own team and 15 Afghanistan National Army soldiers. Staff Sergeant Miller's heroism and selflessness above and beyond the call of duty, and at the cost of his own life, are in keeping with the highest traditions of military service and reflect great credit upon himself and the United States Army.

*Monsoor, Michael A.

Rank and Organization: Master-at-Arms Second Class (Sea, Air And Land), U.S. Navy

For conspicuous gallantry and intrepidity at the risk of his life above and beyond the call of duty as automatic weapons gunner for Naval Special Warfare Task Group Arabian Peninsula, in support of Operation Iraqi Freedom on 29 September 2006. As a member of a combined SEAL and Iraqi Army Sniper Overwatch Element, tasked with providing early warning and stand-off protection from a rooftop in an insurgent held sector of Ar Ramadi, Iraq, Petty Officer Monsoor distinguished himself by his exceptional bravery in the face of grave danger. In the early morning, insurgents prepared to execute a coordinated attack by reconnoitering the area around the element's position. Element snipers thwarted the enemy's initial attempt by eliminating two insurgents. The enemy continued to assault the element, engaging them with a rocket-propelled grenade and small arms fire. As enemy activity increased, Petty Officer Monsoor took position with his machine gun between two teammates on an outcropping of the roof. While the SEALs vigilantly watched for enemy activity, an insurgent threw a hand grenade from an unseen location, which bounced off Petty Officer Monsoor's chest and landed in front of him. Although only he could have escaped the blast, Petty Officer Monsoor chose instead to protect his teammates. Instantly and without regard for his own safety, he threw himself onto the grenade to absorb the force of the explosion with his body, saving the lives of his two teammates. By his undaunted courage, fighting spirit, and unwavering devotion to duty in the face of certain death, Petty Officer Monsoor gallantly gave his life for his country, thereby reflecting great credit upon himself and upholding the highest traditions of the United States Naval Service.

*Smith, Paul R.

Rank and Organization: Sergeant First Class, U.S. Army

For conspicuous gallantry and intrepidity at the risk of his life above and beyond the call of duty: Sergeant First Class Paul R. Smith distinguished himself by acts of gallantry and intrepidity above and beyond the call of duty in action with an armed enemy near Baghdad International Airport, Baghdad, Iraq, on 4 April 2003. On that day, Sergeant First Class Smith was engaged in the construction of a prisoner of war holding area when his Task Force was violently attacked by a company-sized enemy force. Realizing the vulnerability of over 100 fellow soldiers, Sergeant First Class Smith quickly organized a hasty defense consisting of two platoons of soldiers, one Bradley Fighting Vehicle, and three armored personnel carriers. As the fight developed, Sergeant First Class Smith braved hostile enemy fire to personally engage the enemy with hand grenades and anti-tank weapons, and organized the evacuation of three wounded soldiers from an armored personnel carrier struck by a rocket propelled grenade and a 60mm mortar round. Fearing the enemy would overrun their defenses, Sergeant First Class Smith moved under withering enemy fire to man a .50 caliber machine gun mounted on a damaged armored personnel carrier. In total disregard for his own life, he maintained his exposed position in order to engage the attacking enemy force. During this action, he was mortally wounded. His courageous actions helped defeat the enemy attack, and resulted in as many as 50 enemy soldiers killed, while allowing the safe withdrawal of numerous wounded soldiers. Sergeant First Class Smith's extraordinary heroism and uncommon valor are in keeping with the highest traditions of the military service and reflect great credit upon himself, the Third Infantry Division "Rock of the Marne," and the United States Army.

Source: U.S. Army Center of Military History. "Medal of Honor," available online. http://www.history.army.mil/moh.html.

 # MAPS

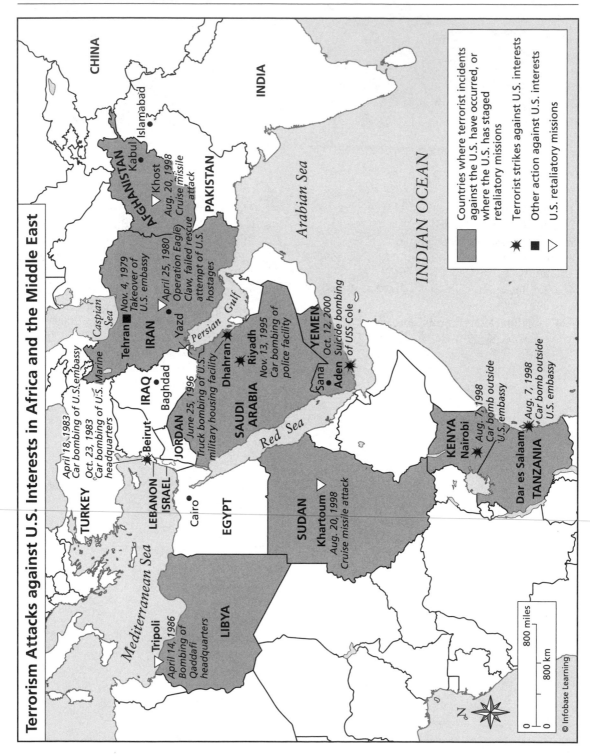

Terrorism Attacks against U.S. Interests in Africa and the Middle East

Legend:

Countries where terrorist incidents against the U.S. have occurred, or where the U.S. has staged retaliatory missions

✶ Terrorist strikes against U.S. interests

■ Other action against U.S. interests

▽ U.S. retaliatory missions

Map labels and annotations:

CHINA

INDIA

Arabian Sea

INDIAN OCEAN

Islamabad

PAKISTAN

AFGHANISTAN

Kabul

Khost
Aug. 20, 1998
Cruise missile attack

Nov. 4, 1979
Takeover of U.S. embassy

April 25, 1980
Operation Eagle Claw, failed rescue attempt of U.S. hostages

Caspian Sea

Tehran
IRAN
Yazd

Persian Gulf

YEMEN
Sana
Aden
Oct. 12, 2000
Suicide bombing of USS Cole

Dhahran
Nov. 13, 1995
Car bombing of police facility

Riyadh
June 25, 1996
Truck bombing of U.S. military housing facility

SAUDI ARABIA

Baghdad
IRAQ

JORDAN

Beirut
April 18, 1983
Car bombing of U.S. embassy

Oct. 23, 1983
Car bombing of U.S. Marine headquarters

LEBANON
ISRAEL

TURKEY

Cairo

EGYPT

Mediterranean Sea

Tripoli
April 14, 1986
Bombing of Qaddafi headquarters

LIBYA

SUDAN
Khartoum
Aug. 20, 1998
Cruise missile attack

Red Sea

KENYA
Nairobi
Aug. 7, 1998
Car bomb outside U.S. embassy

Dar es Salaam
Aug. 7, 1998
Car bomb outside U.S. embassy

TANZANIA

800 miles

800 km

N

© Infobase Learning

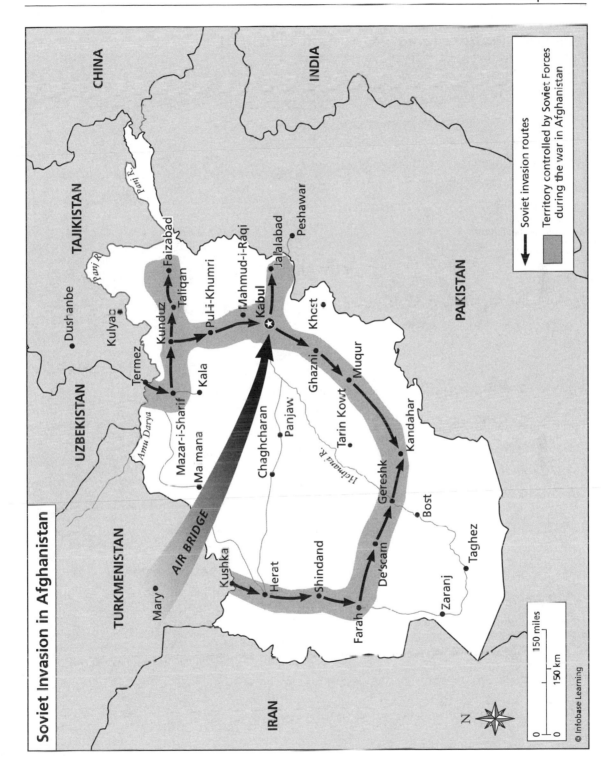

Soviet Invasion in Afghanistan

CHINA

INDIA

TAJIKISTAN

PAKISTAN

Peshawar

Faizabad

Jalalabad

Mahmud-i-Raqi

Dushanbe

Puli-Khumri

Taliqan

Kabul

Kulyab

Kunduz

Khcst

Termez

UZBEKISTAN

Kala

Muqur

Ghazni

Mazar-i-Sharif

Tarin Kovt

Kandahar

Mamana

Panjaw

Chaghcharan

Gereshk

Bost

AIR BRIDGE

Taghez

TURKMENISTAN

Descam

Kushka

Mary

Herat

Shindand

Zaranj

Farah

IRAN

N

150 miles

150 km

© Infobase Learning

Amu Darya

Panj R.

Panj R.

Helmand R.

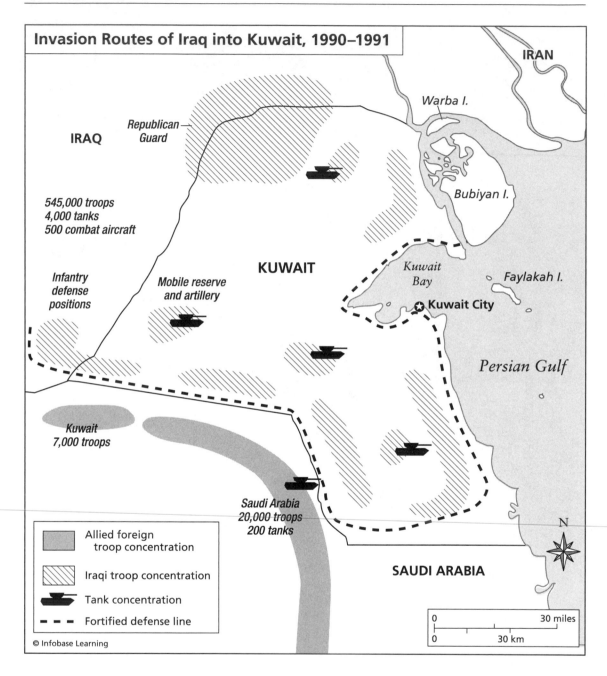

Invasion Routes of Iraq into Kuwait, 1990–1991

IRAN

IRAQ

Republican Guard

545,000 troops
4,000 tanks
500 combat aircraft

Infantry defense positions

Mobile reserve and artillery

KUWAIT

Warba I.

Bubiyan I.

Kuwait Bay

Faylakah I.

Kuwait City

Persian Gulf

Kuwait
7,000 troops

Saudi Arabia
20,000 troops
200 tanks

SAUDI ARABIA

N

Allied foreign troop concentration

Iraqi troop concentration

Tank concentration

Fortified defense line

0   30 miles

0   30 km

© Infobase Learning

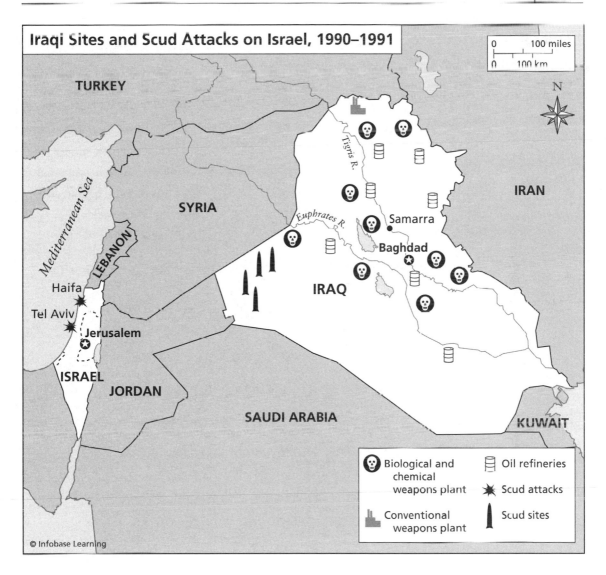

Iraqi Sites and Scud Attacks on Israel, 1990–1991

0   100 miles
0   100 km

N

TURKEY

SYRIA

IRAN

LEBANON

Mediterranean Sea

Tigris R.

Euphrates R.

Samarra

Baghdad

IRAQ

Haifa

Tel Aviv

Jerusalem

ISRAEL

JORDAN

SAUDI ARABIA

KUWAIT

Biological and
chemical
weapons plant

Conventional
weapons plant

Oil refineries

Scud attacks

Scud sites

© Infobase Learning

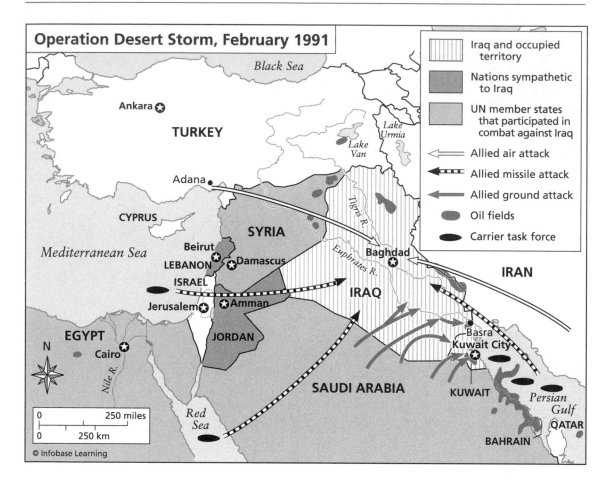

Operation Desert Storm, February 1991

Legend:
- Iraq and occupied territory
- Nations sympathetic to Iraq
- UN member states that participated in combat against Iraq
- Allied air attack
- Allied missile attack
- Allied ground attack
- Oil fields
- Carrier task force

Black Sea

Ankara

TURKEY

Lake Urmia

Lake Van

Adana

CYPRUS

SYRIA

Tigris R.

Baghdad

IRAN

Mediterranean Sea

Beirut
LEBANON Damascus

Euphrates R.

ISRAEL

Jerusalem Amman

IRAQ

EGYPT

JORDAN

Basra
Kuwait City

Cairo

Nile R.

SAUDI ARABIA

KUWAIT

N

Persian Gulf

QATAR

0   250 miles

Red Sea

0   250 km

BAHRAIN

© Infobase Learning

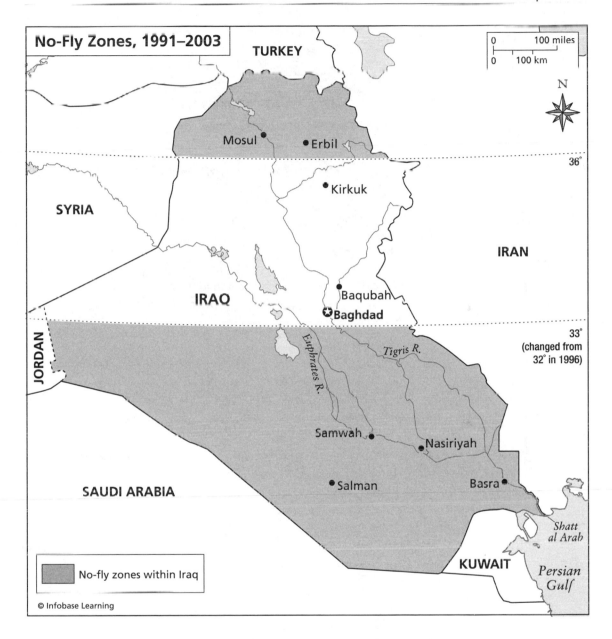

No-Fly Zones, 1991–2003

TURKEY

0   100 miles
0   100 km

N

SYRIA

Mosul   ● Erbil

36°

● Kirkuk

IRAN

IRAQ

● Baqubah
✪ Baghdad

33°
(changed from
32° in 1996)

JORDAN

Euphrates R.   *Tigris R.*

Samwah   ●
Nasiriyah

SAUDI ARABIA

● Salman   Basra ●

Shatt al Arab

KUWAIT   *Persian Gulf*

No-fly zones within Iraq

© Infobase Learning

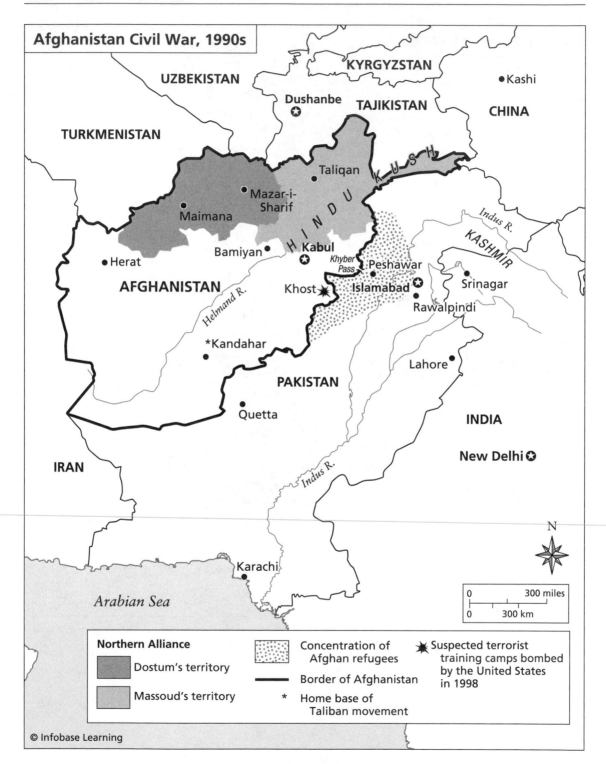

Afghanistan Civil War, 1990s

KYRGYZSTAN

UZBEKISTAN

•Kashi

Dushanbe ✪   TAJIKISTAN

CHINA

TURKMENISTAN

•Taliqan

Mazar-i-
•Sharif

•Maimana

Indus R.

KASHMIR

•Herat

Bamiyan •

Kabul ✪

AFGHANISTAN

Khyber
Pass

•Peshawar

Khost ✸   Islamabad ✪

•Srinagar

Rawalpindi

Khost

•Kandahar

•Lahore

PAKISTAN

INDIA

•Quetta

New Delhi ✪

IRAN

Indus R.

N

Karachi •

Arabian Sea

| 0 | 300 miles |
| 0 | 300 km |

Northern Alliance

Dostum's territory

Massoud's territory

Concentration of
Afghan refugees

Border of Afghanistan

* Home base of
   Taliban movement

✸ Suspected terrorist
   training camps bombed
   by the United States
   in 1998

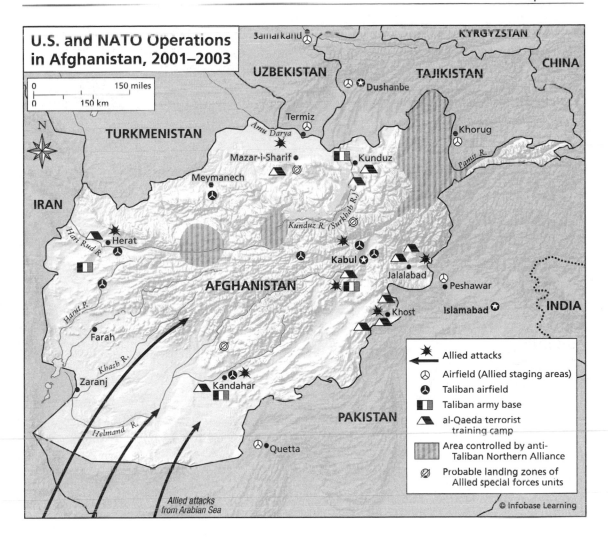

U.S. and NATO Operations in Afghanistan, 2001–2003

0   150 miles
0   150 km

N

KYRGYZSTAN

CHINA

UZBEKISTAN

TAJIKISTAN

Samarkand

Dushanbe

TURKMENISTAN

Termiz

Amu Darya

Khorug

Pamir R.

Mazar-i-Sharif

Kunduz

Meymanech

Kunduz R.   *Surkhab R.*

IRAN

Hari Rud R.

Herat

AFGHANISTAN

Kabul

Jalalabad

Peshawar

Harut R.

Farah

Khost

Islamabad

INDIA

Khash R.

Zaranj

Helmand R.

Kandahar

PAKISTAN

Quetta

*Allied attacks
from Arabian Sea*

Legend

✺ Allied attacks

⊘ Airfield (Allied staging areas)

☁ Taliban airfield

▮▮ Taliban army base

◣ al-Qaeda terrorist
    training camp

▓ Area controlled by anti-
    Taliban Northern Alliance

⊘ Probable landing zones of
    Allied special forces units

© Infobase Learning

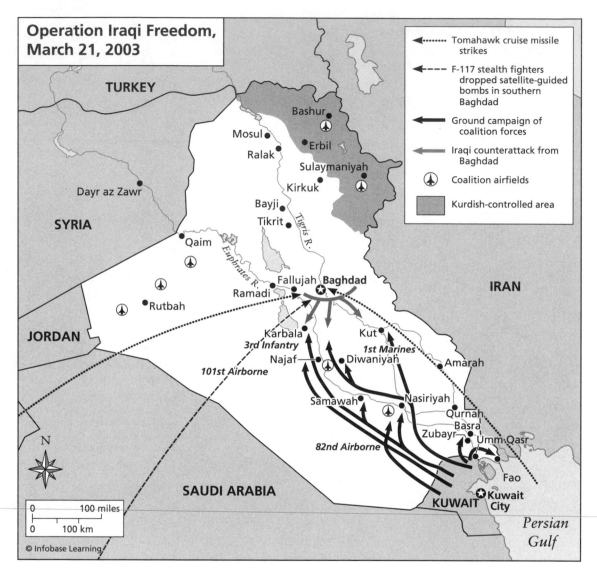

Operation Iraqi Freedom, March 21, 2003

TURKEY

Bashur

Mosul
Ralak
Erbil
Sulaymaniyah
Kirkuk

Dayr az Zawr

SYRIA

Bayji
Tikrit

Qaim

Rutbah

JORDAN

Fallujah   Baghdad
Ramadi

Karbala
3rd Infantry
101st Airborne

Najaf

Kut
1st Marines
Diwaniyah
Amarah

Samawah
Nasiriyah
Qurnah
Basra
Zubayr   Umm Qasr

82nd Airborne

N

Fao

KUWAIT   Kuwait City

SAUDI ARABIA

IRAN

Persian Gulf

0   100 miles
0   100 km

© Infobase Learning

Legend:
- Tomahawk cruise missile strikes
- F-117 stealth fighters dropped satellite-guided bombs in southern Baghdad
- Ground campaign of coalition forces
- Iraqi counterattack from Baghdad
- Coalition airfields
- Kurdish-controlled area

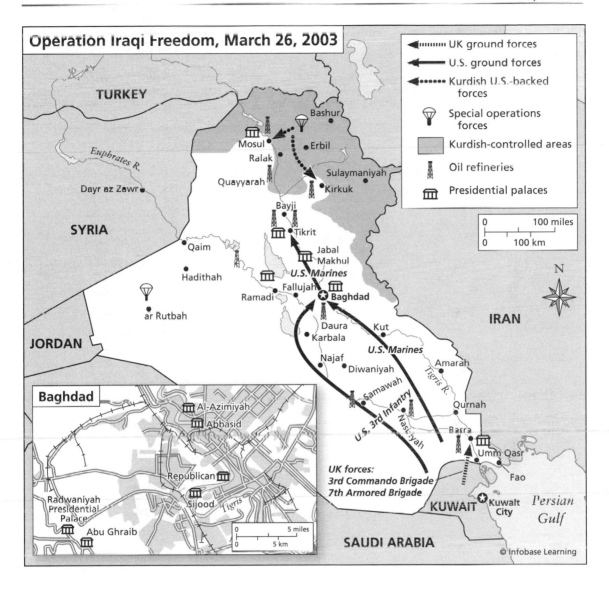

Operation Iraqi Freedom, March 26, 2003

UK ground forces
U.S. ground forces
Kurdish U.S.-backed forces
Special operations forces
Kurdish-controlled areas
Oil refineries
Presidential palaces

TURKEY

Bashur

Mosul
Erbil
Ralak
Quayyarah
Sulaymaniyah
Kirkuk

Euphrates R.

Dayr az Zawr

Bayji

SYRIA

Qaim
Tikrit

Jabal
Makhul

Hadithah

U.S. Marines
Fallujah

Ramadi
Baghdad

ar Rutbah

JORDAN

Daura
Karbala
Kut

IRAN

Najaf
U.S. Marines
Diwaniyah
Amarah

Samawah
Qurnah

U.S. 3rd Infantry
Basra

Nasiriyah

UK forces:
3rd Commando Brigade
7th Armored Brigade

Umm Qasr
Fao

KUWAIT   Kuwait
City

Persian
Gulf

SAUDI ARABIA

0   100 miles
0   100 km

N

Baghdad

Al-Azimiyah
Abbasid

Republican

Radwaniyah
Presidential
Palace
Sijood

Abu Ghraib

Tigris

0   5 miles
0   5 km

© Infobase Learning

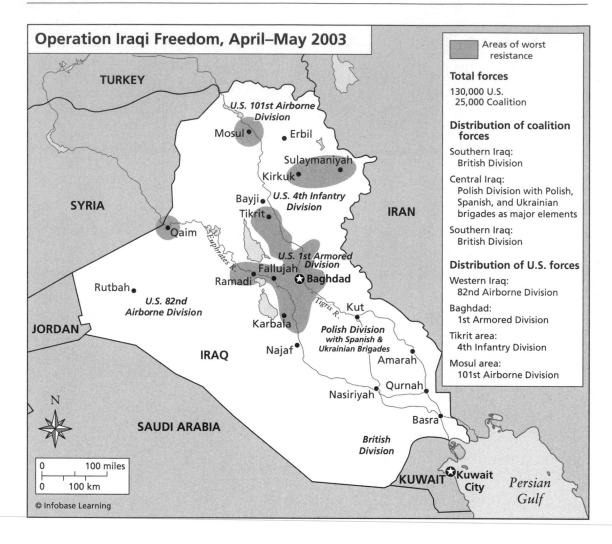

Operation Iraqi Freedom, April–May 2003

TURKEY

U.S. 101st Airborne Division

Mosul

Erbil

Sulaymaniyah

Kirkuk

SYRIA

Bayji

U.S. 4th Infantry Division

Tikrit

IRAN

Qaim

Euphrates R.

U.S. 1st Armored Division

Fallujah

Baghdad

Rutbah

Ramadi

U.S. 82nd Airborne Division

Tigris R.

Kut

Karbala

JORDAN

Polish Division with Spanish & Ukrainian Brigades

IRAQ

Najaf

Amarah

Qurnah

Nasiriyah

N

SAUDI ARABIA

Basra

British Division

0   100 miles

0   100 km

KUWAIT   Kuwait City   Persian Gulf

© Infobase Learning

Areas of worst resistance

Total forces

130,000 U.S.
25,000 Coalition

Distribution of coalition forces

Southern Iraq:
British Division

Central Iraq:
Polish Division with Polish, Spanish, and Ukrainian brigades as major elements

Southern Iraq:
British Division

Distribution of U.S. forces

Western Iraq:
82nd Airborne Division

Baghdad:
1st Armored Division

Tikrit area:
4th Infantry Division

Mosul area:
101st Airborne Division

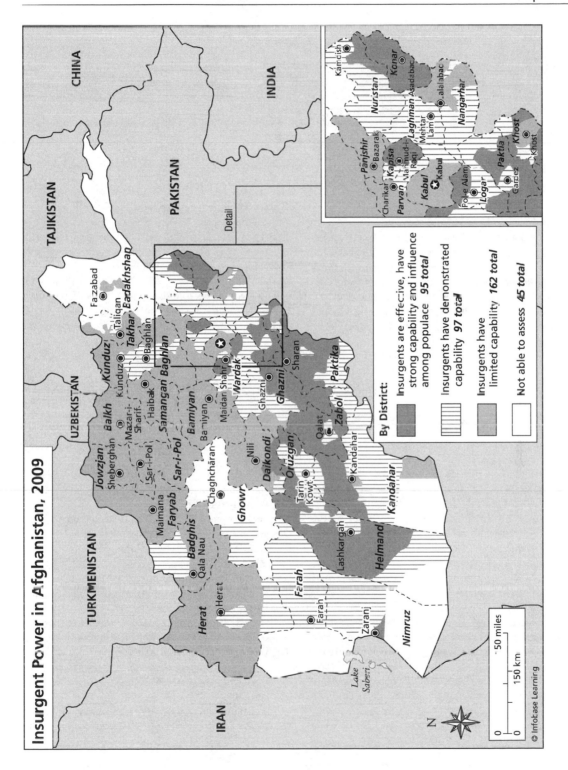

Insurgent Power in Afghanistan, 2009

CHINA

INDIA

PAKISTAN

Detail

TAJIKISTAN

UZBEKISTAN

TURKMENISTAN

IRAN

Fazabad

Taliqan
Takhar   *Badakhshan*

Kunduz
Kunduz   Baghlan
Balkh   *Baghlan*
Mazar-i-Sharif   Haibak
Samangan
Sheberghan   *Samangan*   *Bamiyan*
Jowzjan   Sar-i-Pol   Ba*miyan*
Sar-i-Pol   *Bamiyan*   Maidari Shahr
Faryab   *Sar-i-Pol*   *Wardak*
Maimana   Chaghcharan   Nili   Ghazni
Ghazni
Badghis   *Ghowr*   *Daikondi*   *Ghazni*
Qala Nau   *Daikondi*   Qalat   Sharan
Herat   Tarin   *Oruzgan*   *Zabol*   *Paktika*
Herat   Kowt   *Paktika*
Lashkargah   *Kandahar*
Farah   *Helmand*   Kandahar
Faran   *Helmand*
Zaranj
Nimruz
Lake
Saberi

By District:

Insurgents are effective, have strong capability and influence among populace **95 total**

Insurgents have demonstrated capability **97 total**

Insurgents have limited capability **162 total**

Not able to assess **45 total**

(Detail inset:)

Kamdish
Nuristan   *Konar*
Laghman   Asadabad
Panjshir   Mehtar   Jalalabad
Bazarak   Lam   *Nangarhar*
Charikar   *Kapisa*   Mahmud-i-   *Paktia*   *Khost*
Parvan   Raqi   Gardez   Khost
Kabul   Pol-e Alam   *Khost*
Kabul   *Logar*

N

0   50 miles
0   150 km

© Infobase Learning

BIBLIOGRAPHY

✳ AFGHANISTAN ✳

Barakat, Sultan, ed. *Reconstructing War-Torn Societies: Afghanistan.* New York: Palgrave Macmillan, 2004.

Block, Jeremy S. *Embracing the Occupiers: Conversations with the Future Leaders of Afghanistan and Iraq.* Westport, Conn.: Praeger Security International, 2009.

Crews, Robert D., and Amin Tarzi, eds. *The Taliban and the Crisis of Afghanistan.* Cambridge, Mass.: Harvard University Press, 2008.

Docherty, Paddy. *The Khyber Pass: A History of Empire and Invasion.* New York: Union Square Press, 2008.

Downing, David. *Afghanistan.* New York: Marshall Cavendish, 2009.

Ewans, Martin. *Conflict in Afghanistan: Studies in Asymmetric Warfare.* New York: Routledge, 2005.

Giustozzi, Antonio. *Koran, Kalashnikov, and Laptop: The Neo-Taliban Insurgency in Afghanistan, 2002–7.* New York: Columbia University Press, 2007.

Malik, Hafeez. *U.S. Relations with Afghanistan and Pakistan: The Imperial Dimension.* Karachi, Pakistan: Oxford University Press, 2008.

Misdaq, Nabi. *Afghanistan: Political Frailty and External Interference.* New York: Routledge, 2006.

Montgomery, John D., and Dennis A. Rondinelli, eds. *Beyond Reconstruction in Afghanistan: Lessons from Development Experience.* New York: Palgrave Macmillan, 2004.

Morgan, Matthew J. *A Democracy Is Born: An Insider's Account of the Battle against Terrorism in Afghanistan.* Westport, Conn.: Praeger Security International, 2007.

Nojumi, Neamatollah. *The Rise of the Taliban in Afghanistan: Mass Mobilization, Civil War, and the Future of the Region.* New York: Palgrave, 2002.

Peimani, Hooman. *Falling Terrorism and Rising Conflicts: The Afghan "Contribution" to Polarization and Confrontation in West and South Asia.* Westport, Conn.: Praeger, 2003.

Pratrap, Anita. *Island of Blood: Frontline Reports from Sri Lanka, Afghanistan, and Other South Asian Flashpoints.* New York: Penguin Books, 2003.

Rashid, Ahmed. *Descent into Chaos: The U.S. and the Failure of Nation Building in Pakistan, Afghanistan, and Central Asia.* New York: Viking, 2008.

Roberts, Jeffrey J. *The Origins of Conflict in Afghanistan.* Westport, Conn.: Praeger, 2003.

Runion, Meredith L. *The History of Afghanistan.* Westport, Conn.: Greenwood Press, 2007.

Sinno, Abdulkader H. *Organizations at War in Afghanistan and Beyond.* Ithaca, N.Y.: Cornell University Press, 2008.

✳ IRAN ✳

Aghaie, Kamran C. *The Martyrs of Karbala: Shi'i Symbols and Rituals in Modern Iran.* Seattle: University of Washington Press, 2004.

Alexander, Yonah. *The New Iranian Leadership: Ahmadinejad, Terrorism, Nuclear Ambition, and the Middle East.* Westport, Conn.: Praeger Security International, 2008.

Ansari, Ali M. *Confronting Iran: The Failure of American Foreign Policy and the Next Great Crisis in the Middle East.* New York: Basic Books, 2007.

Artjomand, Said A. *After Khomeini: Iran under His Successors.* New York: Oxford University Press, 2009.

Asgharzadeh, Alireza. *Iran and the Challenge of Diversity: Islamic Fundamentalism, Aryanist Racism, and Democratic Struggles.* New York: Palgrave Macmillan, 2007.

Azimi, Fakhreddin. *The Quest for Democracy in Iran: A Century of Struggle against Authoritarian Rule.* Cambridge, Mass: Harvard University Press, 2008.

Baer, Robert. *The Devil We Know: Dealing with the New Iranian Superpower.* New York: Crown Publishers, 2008.

Bayandor, Darioush. *Iran and the CIA: The Fall of Mosaddeq Revisited.* New York: Palgrave Macmillan, 2010.

Bergman, Ronen. *The Secret War with Iran: The 30-Year Clandestine Struggle against the World's Most Dangerous Terrorist Power.* New York: Free Press, 2008.

Bowden, Mark. *Guests of the Ayatollah: The First Battle in America's War with Militant Islam.* New York: Atlantic Monthly Press, 2006.

Cook, Alethia. *U.S.-Iran Relations: Policy Challenges and Opportunities.* New York: Palgrave Macmillan, 2009.

Cordesman, Anthony H. *Iran's Developing Military Capabilities.* Washington, D.C.: CSIS Press, 2005.

Cordesman, Anthony H. *Iran's Military Forces and Warfighting Capabilities: The Threat in the Northern Gulf.* Washington, D.C.: CSIS Press, 2007.

Crane, Keith, Rollie Lai, and Jeffrey Martini. *Iran's Political, Demographic, and Economic Vulnerabilities.* Santa Monica, Calif.: Rand Corp., 2008.

Dabashi, Hamid. *Theology of Discontent: The Ideological Foundation of the Islamic Revolution of Iran.* New Brunswick, N.J.: Transaction Publishers, 2006.

Davaran, Fereshteh. *Continuity in Iranian Identity: Resilience of a Cultural Heritage.* New York: Routledge, 2010.

De Bellaigue, Christopher. *The Struggle for Iran.* New York: New York Review Books, 2007.

Ehteshami, Anoishiravan, and Mahjoob Zweiri, eds. *Iran's Foreign Policy: From Khatami to Ahmadinejad.* Reading, U.K.: Ithaca Press, 2008.

Fitzpatrick, Mark. *The Iranian Nuclear Crisis: Avoiding Worse-Case Outcomes.* Oxford, U.K.: Routledge for the International Institute for Strategic Studies, 2008.

Freedman, Lawrence. *A Choice of Enemies: America Confronts the Middle East.* New York: Public Affairs, 2008.

Furtig, Henner. *Iran's Rivalry with Saudi Arabia Before the Gulf War.* Reading, U.K.: Ithaca, 2002.

Ganji, Babak. *Politics of Confrontation: The Foreign Policy of the USA and Revolutionary Iran.* New York: Tauris Academic Studies, 2006.

Ghamari-Tabrizi, Behrooz. *Islam and Dissent in Postrevolutionary Iran: Abdolkarim Soroush, Religious Politics, and Democratic Reform.* New York: I. B. Tauris, 2008.

Gheissari, Ali, ed. *Contemporary Iran: Economy, Society, Politics.* New York: Oxford University Press, 2009.

Gonzalez, Nathan. *Engaging Iran: The Rise of a Middle East Powerhouse and America's Strategic Choice.* Westport, Conn.: Praeger Security International, 2007.

Goodarzi, Jubin M. *Syria and Iran: Diplomatic Alliance and Power Politics in the Middle East.* New York: Tauris Academic Studies, 2006.

Jafarzadeh, Alireza. *The Iran Threat: President Ahmadinejad and the Coming Nuclear Crisis.* New York: Palgrave, 2007.

Jervis, Robert. *Why Intelligence Fails: Lessons from the Iranian Revolution and the Iraq War.* Ithaca, N.Y.: Cornell University Press, 2010.

Kairouz, Anthony. *Nuclear Iran: A Prelude to WW III.* Bloomington, Ind.: AuthorHouse, 2007.

Katouzian, Homa. *Iran in the 21st Century: Politics, Economics, and Confrontation.* New York: Routledge, 2007.

Katzman, Kenneth, ed. *Iran: U.S. Concerns and Policy Responses.* Hauppauge, N.Y.: Nova Science Publishers, 2008.

Langewiesche, William. *The Atomic Bazaar: The Rise of the Nuclear Poor.* New York: Farrar, Straus and Giroux, 2007.

Ledeen, Michael A. *The Iranian Time Bomb: The Mullah Zealot's Quest for Destruction.* New York: St. Martin's Press, 2007.

Mafinezam, Alidad. *Iran and Its Place among Nations.* Westport, Conn.: Praeger, 2008.

Mattair, Thomas R. *Global Security Watch—Iran: A Reference Handbook.* Westport, Conn.: Praeger Security International, 2008.

Melman, Yossi. *The Nuclear Sphinx of Tehran: Mahmoud Ahmadinejad and the State of Iran.* New York: Carroll and Graf Publishers, 2007.

Mir-Hosseini, Ziba, and Richard Tapper, eds. *Islam and Democracy in Iran: Eshkevari and the Quest for Reform.* New York: I.B. Tauris, 2006.

Murray, Donette. *U.S. Foreign Policy and Iran: American-Iranian Relations Since the Islamic Revolution.* New York: Routledge, 2010.

Parsi, Trita. *Treacherous Alliance: The Secret Dealings of Israel, Iran, and the United States.* New Haven, Conn.: Yale University Press, 2008.

Rakel, Eva P. *Power, Islam, and Political Elite in Iran: A Study on the Iranian Political Elite from Khomeini to Ahmadinejad.* Boston: Brill, 2008.

Slavin, Barbara. *Bitter Friends, Bosom Enemies: Iran, the U.S., and the Twisted Path to Confrontation.* New York: St. Martin's Press, 2007.

Smith, Benjamin D. *Hard Times in the Lands of Plenty: Oil Politics in Iran and Indonesia.* Ithaca, N.Y.: Cornell University Press, 2007.

Taheri, Amir. *The Persian Night: Iran under the Khomeinist Revolution.* New York: Encounter Books, 2008.

Takeyh, Ray. *Hidden Iran: Paradox and Power in the Islamic Republic.* New York: Times Books, 2006.

Varzi, Roxanne. *Warring Souls: Youth, Media, and Martyrdom in Post-Revolution Iran.* Durham, N.C.: Duke University Press, 2006.

Wehrey, Frederic, et al. *Dangerous But Not Omnipotent: Exploring the Reach and Limitations of Iranian Power in the Middle East.* Santa Monica, Calif.: Rand Corp., 2009.

✳ IRAQ ✳

Alfonsi, Christian. *Circle in the Sand: The Bush Dynasty in Iraq.* New York: Vintage Books, 2007.

Anderson, Liam D. *The Future of Iraq: Dictatorship, Democracy, or Division.* New York: Palgrave Macmillan, 2008.

Armstrong, David, Theo Farrell, and Bice Maiguashca, eds. *Force and Legitimacy in World Politics.* Cambridge: Cambridge University Press, 2005.

Arnold, James. *Saddam Hussein's Iraq.* Minneapolis: Twenty-First Century Books, 2008.

Balaghi, Shiva. *Saddam Hussein: A Biography.* Westport, Conn.: Greenwood Press, 2006.

Borden, Arthur M. *A Better Country: Why America Was Right to Confront Iraq.* Lanham, Md.: Hamilton Books, 2008.

Cockburn, Patrick. *Muqtada al-Sadr and the Battle for the Future of Iraq.* New York: Scribner, 2008.

Cordesman, Anthony H. *Iraq's Insurgency and the Road to Civil Conflict.* Westport, Conn.: Praeger Security International, 2008.

Cordesman, Anthony H. *Gulf Military Forces in an Era of Asymmetric War.* Westport, Conn.: Praeger Security International, 2007.

Coughlin, Con. *Saddam: His Rise and Fall.* New York: Harper Perennial, 2005.

Danchev, Alex, and John MacMillan, eds. *The Iraq War and Democratic Politics.* New York: Routledge, 2005.

Davis, Eric. *Memories of State: Politics, History, and Collective Identity in Modern Iraq.* Berkeley: University of California Press, 2005.

Fayazmanesh, Sasan. *The United States and Iran: Sanctions, Wars, and the Policy of Dual Containment.* New York: Routledge, 2008.

Gardner, Lloyd C. *The Long Road to Baghdad: A History of U.S. Foreign Policy from the 1970s to the Present.* New York: New Press, 2008.

Gunter, Michael M. *The Kurds Ascending: The Evolving Solution to the Kurdish Problem in Iraq and Turkey.* New York: Palgrave Macmillan, 2007.

Hiltermann, Joost R. *A Poisonous Affair: America, Iraq, and the Gassing of Halabja.* New York: Cambridge University Press, 2007.

Hybel, Alex R. *The Bush Administrations and Saddam Hussein: Deciding on Conflict.* New York: Palgrave Macmillan, 2006.

Ismael, Tareq Y. *The Rise and Fall of the Communist Party of Iraq.* New York: Cambridge University Press, 2008.

Jacobson, Sidney. *After 9/11: America's War on Terror.* New York: Hill and Wang, 2008.

Johnson, James T. *The War to Oust Saddam: Just War and the New Face of Conflict.* Lanham, Md.: Rowman & Littlefield, 2005.

Kaplan, Lawrence. *The War Over Iraq: Saddam's Tyranny and America's Mission.* San Francisco: Encounter Books, 2003.

Katzman, Kenneth. *Iraq: Post-Saddam Governance and Security.* Hauppauge, N.Y.: Nova Science Publishers, 2009.

Kaufman, Robert G. *In Defense of the Bush Doctrine.* Lexington: University of Kentucky Press, 2008.

Kelly, Michael J. *Ghosts of Halabja: Saddam Hussein and the Kurdish Genocide.* Westport, Conn.: Praeger Security International, 2008.

Kinzer, Stephen. *Overthrow: America's Century of Regime Change from Hawaii to Iraq.* New York: Henry Holt Books, 2006.

Knights, Michael, ed. *Operation Iraqi Freedom and the New Iraq: Insights and Forecasts.* Washington, D.C.: Washington Institute for Near East Policy, 2004.

Knights, Michael. *Troubled Waters: Future U.S. Security Assistance in the Persian Gulf.* Washington, D.C.: Washington Institute for Near East Policy, 2006.

Long, Jerry M. *Saddam's War of Words: Politics, Religion, and the Iraqi Invasion of Kuwait.* Austin: University of Texas Press, 2004.

Lusane, Clarence. *Colin Powell and Condoleezza Rice: Foreign Policy, Race, and the New American Century.* Westport, Conn.: Praeger Publishers, 2006.

Malone, David. *The International Struggle Over Iraq: Politics in the UN Security Council, 1980–2005.* New York: Oxford University Press, 2006.

Moore, Robin. *Hunting Down Saddam: The Inside Story of the Search and Capture.* New York: St. Martin's Press, 2004.

Munson, Peter J. *Iraq in Transition: The Legacy of Dictatorship and the Prospects for Democracy.* Washington, D.C.: Potomac Books, 2009.

Natali, Denise, ed. *The Kurds and the State: Evolving National Identity in Iraq, Turkey, and Iran.* Syracuse, N.Y.: Syracuse University Press, 2005.

Newton, Michael A. *Enemy of the State: The Trial and Execution of Saddam Hussein.* New York: St. Martin's Press, 2008.

O'Keary, Brendan, John McGarry, and Khaled Salih, eds. *The Future of Kurdistan in Iraq.* Philadelphia: University of Pennsylvania Press, 2005.

Olson, Robert W. *The Goat and the Butcher: Nationalism and State Formation in Kurdistan-Iraq since the Iraqi War.* Costa Mesa, Calif.: Mazda Publishers, 2005.

Pfiffner, James P., and Mark Pythian, eds. *Intelligence and National Security Policymaking on Iraq: British and American Perspectives.* College Station: Texas A&M University Press, 2008.

Ritchie, Nick. *The Political Road to War with Iraq: Bush, 9/11, and the Drive to Overthrow Saddam Hussein.* New York: Routledge, 2006.

Rohde, Achim. *State-Society Relations in Ba'thist Iraq: Facing Dictatorship.* New York: Routledge, 2010.

Rosen, Gary, ed. *The Right War?: The Conservative Debate on Iraq.* New York: Cambridge University Press, 2005.

Schwab, Orrin. *The Gulf Wars and the United States: Shaping the Twenty-first Century.* Westport, Conn.: Praeger Security International, 2008.

Shiner, Phil, and Andrew Williams, eds. *The Iraq War and International Law.* Portland, Oreg.: Hart Publishing, 2008.

Simpson, John. *The Wars against Saddam: Taking the Hard Road to Baghdad.* London: Macmillan, 2003.

Solomon, Louis D. *Paul D. Wolfowitz: Visionary Intellectual, Policymaker, and Strategist.* Westport, Conn.: Praeger Security International, 2007.

Sponeck, Hans-Christof, Graf. *A Different Kind of War: The UN Sanctions Regime in Iraq.* New York: Berghahn Books, 2006.

Steavenson, Wendell. *The Weight of a Mustard Seed: An Iraqi General's Moral Journey during the Time of Saddam.* New York: Collins Publishing Group, 2009.

Swansborough, Robert H. *Test by Fire: The War Presidency of George W. Bush.* New York: Palgrave Macmillan, 2008.

Traub, James. *The Best Intentions: Kofi Annan and the UN in the Era of American World Power.* New York: Farrar, Straus and Giroux, 2006.

Weiss, Thomas G., Margaret E. Crahan, and John Goering, eds. *War on Terrorism: Human Rights, Unilateralism, and U.S. Foreign Policy.* New York: Routledge, 2004.

Widmer, Edward L. *Ark of the Liberties: America and the World.* New York: Hill and Wang, 2008.

Wright, Robin G. *Dreams and Shadows: The Future of the Middle East.* New York: Penguin Press, 2008.

Yetiv, Steven A. *In Absence of Grand Strategy: The United States in the Persian Gulf, 1972–2005.* Baltimore: Johns Hopkins University Press, 2008.

✳ SOVIET INVASION OF AFGHANISTAN ✳

Adamec, Ludwig S. *Historical Dictionary of Afghan Wars.* Lanham, Md.: Scarecrow Press, 2005.

Afghanistan's Unknown War: Memoirs of the Russian Writers-War Veterans of Special Forces, Army, and Air Forces on Soviet-Afghan War and the Afghan Terrorism. Toronto: Megapolis, 2001.

Bonosky, Phillip. *Afghanistan: Washington's Secret War.* New York: International Publishers, 2001.

Carew, Tom. *Jihad! The SAS Secret War in Afghanistan.* Edinburgh: Mainstream, 2000.

Coll, Steve. *Ghost Wars: The Secret History of the CIA, Afghanistan, and bin Laden from the Soviet Invasion to September 10, 2001.* New York: Penguin Books, 2005.

Davies, L. Will. *Fighting Masoud's War.* South Melbourne, Australia: Lothian Books, 2003.

Edwards, David B. *Before the Taliban: Genealogies of the Afghan Jihad.* Berkeley: University of California Press, 2002.

Ellis, Deborah. *Women of the Afghan War.* Westport, Conn.: Praeger, 2000.

Ewans, Martin, Sir. *Conflict in Afghanistan: Studies in Asymmetric Warfare.* New York: Routledge, 2005.

Feifer, Gregory. *The Great Gamble: The Soviet War in Afghanistan*. New York: Harper, 2009.

Grare, Frederic. *Pakistan and the Afghan Conflict, 1979–1985: With an Afterword Covering Events from 1985–2001*. Karachi, Pakistan: Oxford University Press, 2003.

Grau, Lester W., and Michael A. Gress, eds. *The Soviet-Afghan War: How a Superpower Fought and Lost*. Lawrence: University Press of Kansas, 2002.

Jalali, Ali Ahmad. *Afghan Guerrilla Warfare: In the Words of the Mujahideen Fighters*. London: Compendium, 2001.

Kaplan, Robert D. *Soldiers of God: With Islamic Warriors in Afghanistan and Pakistan*. New York: Vintage Books, 2001.

Klaits, Alex. *Love and War in Afghanistan*. New York: Seven Stories Press, 2005.

Lesch, David W. *1979: The Year That Shaped the Modern Middle East*. Boulder, Colo.: Westview Press, 2001.

Loyn, David. *In Afghanistan: 200 Years of British, Russian, and American Occupation*. New York: Palgrave Macmillan, 2009.

Maley, William. *The Afghanistan Wars*. New York: Palgrave, 2002.

Nasir, B. K. Zahrah. *The Gun Tree: One Woman's War*. Karachi, Pakistan: Oxford University Press, 2001.

Pazira, Nelofer. *A Bed of Flowers: In Search of My Afghanistan*. New York: Free Press, 2005.

Roselle, Laura. *Media and the Politics of Failure: Great Powers, Communication Strategies, and Military Defeats*. New York: Palgrave Macmillan, 2006.

Rubin, Barnett R. *The Fragmentation of Afghanistan: State Formation and Collapse in the International System*. New Haven, Conn.: Yale University Press, 2002.

Tamarov, Vladislav. *Afghanistan: A Russian Soldier's Story*. Berkeley, Calif.: Ten Speed Press, 2001.

Tanner, Stephen. *Afghanistan: A Military History from Alexander the Great to the Fall of the Taliban*. Karachi, Pakistan: Oxford University Press, 2003.

White, Terence. *Hot Steel: from Soviet-Era Afghanistan to Post 9/11: Frontline Encounters of the Longest-Serving Foreign Correspondent in Kabul*. New York: Penguin Books, 2006.

Yetiv, Steven A. *The Absence of Grand Strategy: The United States in the Persian Gulf, 1972–2005*. Baltimore: Johns Hopkins University Press, 2008.

Yousef, Mohammad. *The Battle for Afghanistan: The Soviets versus the Mujahideen during the 1980s*. Barnsley, U.K.: Pen & Sword Military, 2007.

Zoya. *Zoya's Story: An Afghan Woman's Battle for Freedom*. New York: William Morrow, 2002.

❋ IRAN-IRAQ WAR ❋

Al-Marashi, Ibrahim. *Iraq's Armed Forces: An Analytical History*. New York: Routledge, 2008.

Karsh, Efraim. *The Iran-Iraq War, 1980–1988*. Oxford, U.K.: Osprey Publishing, 2002.

Mottale, Morris M. *The Origins of the Gulf Wars*. Lanham, Md.: University Press of America, 2001.

Potter, Lawrence G., and Gary G. Sick. *Iran, Iraq, and the Legacies of War*. New York: Palgrave Macmillan, 2004.

Ward, Steven R. *Immortal: A Military History of Iran and Its Armed Forces*. Washington, D.C.: Georgetown University Press, 2009.

❋ TANKER WAR ❋

El-Shazy, Nadia El-Sayed. *The Gulf Tanker War: Iran and Iraq's Maritime Swordplay*. New York: St. Martin's Press, 1998.

Walker, George K. *The Tanker War, 1980–88: Law and Policy*. Newport, R.I.: Naval War College, 2000.

Wise, Harold L. *Inside the Danger Zone: The U.S. Military in the Persian Gulf, 1987–88*. Annapolis, Md.: Naval Institute Press, 2007.

Zatarain, Lee A. *Tanker War: America's First Conflict with Iran, 1987–88*. Philadelphia: Casemate, 2008.

❋ THE GULF WAR ❋

Acree, Cynthia B. *The Gulf Between Us: A Story of Love and Survival in Desert Storm*. Washington, D.C.: Brassey's, 2003.

Alfonsi, Christian. *Circle in the Sand: The Bush Dynasty in Iraq*. New York: Vintage Books, 2007.

Bacevich, Andrew J., and Efraim Inbar, eds. *The Gulf War of 1991 Reconsidered*. Portland, Oreg.: Frank Cass, 2003.

Bourque, Stephen A. *Jayhawk! The VII Corps in the Persian Gulf War*. Washington, D.C.: Department of the Army, 2002.

Carlisle, Rodney P. *Persian Gulf War*. New York: Facts On File, 2003.

Crawford, Steve. *The First Gulf War*. Redding, Conn.: Brown Bear Books, 2009.

Dastrup, Boyd L. *Operation Desert Storm and Beyond: Modernizing the Field Artillery in the 1980s.* Fort Sill, Okla.: Command Historian's Office, United States Field Artillery Center and School, 2005.

Davis, Richard G. *On Target: Organizing and Executing the Strategic Air Campaign against Iraq.* Washington, D.C.: Air Force History and Museums Program, 2002.

Delong, Michael. *A General Speaks Out: The Truth about the Wars in Afghanistan and Iraq.* St. Paul, Minn.: Zenith Press, 2007.

Emering, Edward J. *The Campaign Decorations and Medals of the Persian Gulf War (1990–1991).* San Ramon, Calif.: Orders and Medals Society of America, 2005.

Evans, Anthony A. *Gulf War: Desert Shield and Desert Storm, 1990–1991.* London: Greenhill Books, 2003.

Finlan, Alastair. *The Gulf War 1991.* Oxford, U.K.: Osprey Pub., 2003.

Finlan, Alastair. *The Royal Navy in the Falklands Conflict and the Gulf War: Culture and Strategy.* Portland, Oreg.: Frank Cass, 2004.

Hayden, H. T. *Marine Corps Aviation in the Gulf War.* Charleston, S.C.: Nautical & Aviation Publishing Co., 2000.

Jamieson, Perry D. *Lucrative Targets: The U.S. Air Force in the Kuwait Theater of Operations.* Washington, D.C.: Air Force History and Museums Program, 2001.

Kagan, Frederick W., and Christian Kubick, eds. *Leaders in War: West Point Remembers the 1991 Gulf War.* New York: Frank Cass, 2005.

Knights, Michael. *Cradle of Conflict: Iraq and the Birth of Modern U.S. Military Power.* Annapolis, Md.: Naval Institute Press, 2005.

Lehrack, Otto J. *America's Battalion: Marines in the First Gulf War.* Tuscaloosa: University of Alabama Press, 2005.

Long, Jerry M. *Saddam's War of Words: Politics, Religion, and the Iraqi Invasion of Kuwait.* Austin: University of Texas Press, 2004.

MacArthur, John R. *Second Front: Censorship and Propaganda in the 1991 Gulf War.* Berkeley: University of California Press, 2004.

Marolda, Edward J. *Shield and Sword: The United States Navy and the Persian Gulf War.* Annapolis, Md.: Naval Institute Press, 2001.

Olsen, John A. *Strategic Air Power in Desert Storm.* Portland, Oreg.: Frank Cass, 2003.

Pelletiere, Stephen C. *Iraq and the International Oil System: Why America Went to War in the Gulf.* Westport, Conn.: Praeger, 2001.

Peters, John S. *Infidels in the Holy Land: A Mechanized Infantryman's Personal Account of the 1990–91 Gulf War.* Tarentum, Pa.: Word Association Publishers, 2003.

Putney, Diane T. *Airpower Advantage: Planning the Gulf Air War Campaign, 1989–1991.* Washington, D.C.: Air Force History and Museums Program, 2004.

Schwab, Orrin. *The Gulf Wars and the United States: Shaping the Twenty first Century.* Westport, Conn.: Praeger Security International, 2008.

Stanton, Martin. *Road to Baghdad: Behind Enemy Lines.* New York: Presidio Press, 2003.

Swofford, Anthony. *Jarhead: A Marine's Chronicle of the Gulf War and Other Battles.* New York: Scribner, 2003.

Thompson, Alexander. *Channels of Power: The UN Security Council and U.S. Statecraft in Iraq.* Ithaca, N.Y.: Cornell University Press, 2009.

Toomey, Charles J. *XVIII Airborne Corps in Desert Storm: From Planning to Victory.* Central Point, Oreg.: Hellgate Press, 2004.

Whitcomb, Darrel D. *Combat Search and Rescue in Desert Storm.* Maxwell Air Force Base, Ala.: Air University Press, 2006.

Wiener, Robert. *Live from Baghdad: Making Journalism History Behind the Lines.* New York: St. Martin's Griffin, 2002.

Woods, Kevin M. *The Mother of All Battles: Saddam Hussein's Strategic Plan for the Persian Gulf War.* Annapolis, Md.: Naval Institute Press, 2008.

❋ OSAMA BIN LADEN ❋

Bergen, Peter L. *Holy War, Inc.: Inside the Secret World of Osama bin Laden.* New York: Free Press, 2001.

Bergen, Peter L. *The Osama bin Laden I Know: An Oral History of Al-Qaeda's Leader.* New York: Free Press, 2006.

Corbin, Jane. *Al-Qaeda: In Search of the Terror Network That Threatens the World.* New York: Thunder Mouth Press/Nation Books, 2003.

Fury, Dalton. *Kill Bin Laden: A Delta Force Commander's Account of the Hunt for the World's Most Wanted Man.* New York: St. Martin's Press, 2008.

Jacquard, Roland. *In the Name of Bin Laden: Global Terrorism & the Bin Laden Brotherhood.* Durham, N.C.: Duke University Press, 2002.

Landau, Elaine. *Osama bin Laden: A War against the West.* Brookfield, Conn.: Twenty-First Century Books, 2002.

Randall, Jonathan C. *Osama: The Making of a Terrorist.* New York: Vintage Books, 2005.

Rawshandil, Jal-il. *Jihad and International Security.* New York: Palgrave Macmillan, 2006.

Robinson, Adam. *Bin Laden: Behind the Mask of the Terrorist.* New York: Arcade, 2002.

Smucker, Philip. *Al Qaeda's Great Escape: The Military and the Media on Terror's Trail.* Washington, D.C.: Brassey's, 2004.

✳ OPERATION ENDURING ✳ FREEDOM

Brooks, Michael G., ed. *U.S. Army Advisors in Afghanistan.* Fort Leavenworth, Kans.: Combat Studies Institute Press, 2009.

Carroll, Andrew. *Operation Homecoming: Iraq, Afghanistan, and the Home Front, in the Words of U.S. Troops and Their Families.* Chicago: University of Chicago Press, 2008.

Chayes, Sarah. *The Punishment of Virtue: Inside Afghanistan after the Taliban.* New York: Penguin Press, 2006.

Cordesman, Anthony H. *The Lessons of Afghanistan: War Fighting, Intelligence, and Force Transformation.* Washington, D.C.: CSIS Press, 2002.

Cordesman, Anthony H. *Winning in Afghanistan: Creating Effective Afghan Security Forces.* Washington, D.C.: CSIS Press, 2009.

Darack, Ed. *Victory Point: Operations Red Wings and Whalers: Marine Corps' Battle for Freedom in Afghanistan.* New York: Berkley Caliber, 2009.

Dilworth, Robert L. *Fogs of War and Peace: A Midstream Analysis of World War III.* Westport, Conn.: Praeger Security International, 2008.

Drendel, Lou. *Operation Enduring Freedom: U.S. Military Operations in Afghanistan, 2001–2002.* Carrollton, Tex.: Squadron/Signal Publications, 2002.

Exum, Andrew. *This Man's Army: A Soldier's Story from the Front Lines of the War on Terrorism.* New York: Gotham Books, 2004.

Fick, Nathaniel. *One Bullet Away: The Making of a Marine Officer.* Boston: Houghton Mifflin, 2005.

Friedman, Brandon. *The War I Always Wanted: The Illusion of Glory and the Reality of War: A Screaming Eagle in Afghanistan and Iraq.* St. Paul, Minn.: Zenith Press, 2007.

Garcia, J. Malcolm. *The Khaarijee: A Chronicle of Friendship and War in Kabul.* Boston: Beacon Press, 2009.

Grant, Rebecca. *The First 600 Days of Combat.* Washington, D.C.: Iris Press, 2004.

Holmes, Tony. *F-14 Tomcat Units of Operation Enduring Freedom.* New York: Osprey Publishing, 2008.

Jacobson, Sidney. *After 9/11: America's War on Terror (2001–).* New York: Hill and Wang, 2008.

Jobson, Robert. *Harry's War: The True Story of the Soldier Prince.* London: John Blake, 2008.

Jones, Seth G. *Counterinsurgency in Afghanistan.* Santa Monica, Calif.: Rand National Defense Research Institute, 2008.

Kilcullen, David. *The Accidental Guerrilla: Fighting Small Wars in the Midst of a Big One.* New York: Oxford University Press, 2009.

Koontz, Christopher N., ed. *Enduring Voices: Oral Histories of the U.S. Army Experience in Afghanistan, 2003–2005.* Washington, D.C.: Center of Military History, United States Army, 2008.

Lambeth, Benjamin S. *Air Power against Terror: America's Conduct of Operation Enduring Freedom.* Santa Monica, Calif.: Rand Corp., 2005.

LeBleu, Joe. *Long Rifle: A Sniper's Story in Iraq and Afghanistan.* Guilford, Conn.: Lyons Press, 2009.

Lewis, Damien. *Apache Dawn: Always Outnumbered, Never Outgunned.* London: Sphere, 2008.

Loyn, David. *In Afghanistan: 200 Years of British, Russian, and American Occupation.* New York: Palgrave Macmillan, 2009.

Luttrell, Marcus. *Lone Survivor: The Eyewitness Account of Operation Redwing and the Lost Heroes of SEAL Team 10.* New York: Little, Brown, 2007.

Mackey, Chris. *The Interrogators: Task Force 500 and America's Secret War against Al Qaeda.* New York: Back Bay Books, 2005.

Maloney, Sean M. *Confronting the Chaos: A Rogue Military Historian Returns to Afghanistan.* Annapolis, Md.: Naval Institute Press, 2009.

Mills, Greg. *From Africa to Afghanistan: With Richards and NATO to Kabul.* Johannesburg, South Africa: Wits University, 2007.

Moorcraft, Paul, ed. *The New Wars of the West: Anglo-American Voices on the War on Terror.* Havertown, Pa.: Casemate, 2005.

Morgan, Matthew J. *A Democracy Is Born: An Insider Account of the Battle against Terrorism in Afghanistan.*

Westport, Conn.: Praeger Security International, 2007.

Peabody, Lawrence B. *Afghanistan Security.* Hauppauge, N.Y.: Nova Science Publishers, 2009.

Robertson, William G. *In Contact!: Case Studies from the Long War.* Fort Leavenworth, Kans.: Combat Studies Institute Press, 2006.

Schaeffer, Frank, ed. *Voices from the Front: Letters Home from America's Military Family.* New York: Carroll & Graf, 2004.

Terrill, Christopher. *Commando.* London: Century, 2007.

Ussery, Easton H., ed. *War in Afghanistan: Strategy, Military Operations, and Congressional Issues.* Hauppauge, N.Y.: Nova Science Publishers, 2009.

Wrage, Stephen D. *Immaculate Warfare: Participants Reflect on the Air Campaigns over Kosovo, Afghanistan, and Iraq.* Westport, Conn.: Praeger, 2003.

Wright, Donald R., ed. *A Different Kind of War: The United States Army in Operation Enduring Freedom, October 2001 September 2005.* Fort Leavenworth, Kans.: Combat Studies Institute, 2009.

✳ OPERATION IRAQI ✳ FREEDOM

Anderson, Jon Lee. *The Fall of Baghdad.* New York: Penguin Press, 2004.

Benedict, Helen. *The Lonely Soldier: The Private War of Women Serving in Iraq.* Boston: Beacon Press, 2009.

Berinsky, Adam J. *In Time of War: Understanding American Public Opinion from World War II to Iraq.* Chicago: University of Chicago Press, 2009.

Borden, Arthur M. *A Better Country: Why America Was Right to Confront Iraq.* Lanham, Md.: Hamilton Books, 2008.

Burden, Matthew C. *The Blog of War: Front-Line Dispatches from Soldiers in Iraq and Afghanistan.* New York: Simon & Schuster Paperbacks, 2006.

Campbell, Donovan. *Joker One: A Marine Platoon's Story of Courage, Sacrifice, and Brotherhood.* New York: Random House, 2009.

Carafano, James J. *Private Sector, Public Wars: Contractors in Combat: Afghanistan, Iraq, and Future Conflicts.* Westport, Conn.: Praeger Security International, 2008.

Cerf, Christopher. *Mission Accomplished! Or How We Won the War in Iraq: The Experts Speak.* New York: Simon & Schuster Paperbacks, 2008.

Collins, Joseph J. *Choosing War: The Decision to Invade Iraq and Its Aftermath.* Washington, D.C.: National Defense University Press, 2008.

Cordesman, Anthony H. *Iraq's Insurgency and the Road to Civil Conflict.* Westport, Conn.: Praeger Security International, 2008.

DeLong, Michael. *A General Speaks Out: The Truth about the Wars in Afghanistan and Iraq.* St. Paul, Minn.: Zenith Press, 2007.

Earle, Robert. *Nights in the Pink Motel: A Strategist's Pursuits of Peace in Iraq.* Annapolis, Md.: Naval Institute Press, 2008.

Egnell, Robert. *Complex Peace Operations and Civil-Military Relations: Winning the Peace.* New York: Routledge, 2009.

Ehrenberg, John, ed. *The Iraq Papers.* New York: Oxford University Press, 2010.

Gallagher, Matt. *Embracing the Suck in a Savage Little War.* Cambridge, Mass.: Da Capo Press, 2010.

Goldstein, Barry M. *Gray Land: Soldiers on War.* New York: W. W. Norton, 2010.

Gray, Wesley R. *Embedded: A Marine Corps Advisor Inside the Iraqi Army.* Annapolis, Md.: Naval Institute Press, 2009.

Groen, Michael S. *With the 1st Marine Division in Iraq, 2003: No Greater Friend, No Worse Enemy.* Quantico, Va.: History Division, Marine Corps University, 2006.

Holmstedt, Kirster A. *The Girls Come Marching Home: The Saga of American Women Returning from the War in Iraq.* Mechanicsburg, Pa.: Stackpole Books, 2009.

Hosmer, Stephen W. *Why the Iraqi Resistance to the Coalition Invasion Was So Weak.* Santa Monica, Calif.: Rand Corp., 2007.

Hussain, Imtiaz, ed. *Afghanistan, Iraq, and Post-Conflict Governance: Damoclean Democracy.* Boston: Brill, 2010.

Johnson, Shoshana. *I'm Still Standing: Memoirs of a Woman Soldier Held Captive in Iraq.* New York: Simon and Schuster, 2010.

Katzman, Kenneth. *Iraq: Post-Saddam Governance and Security.* Hauppauge, N.Y.: Nova Science Publishers, 2009.

Kays, D. Christopher. *Leadership, Loyalty, and Deception: Lessons Learned from the Race to Find Weapons of Mass Destruction.* New York: Palgrave Macmillan, 2009.

Kennedy, Kelly. *They Fought for Each Other: The Triumph and Tragedy of the Hardest Hit Unit in Iraq.* New York: St. Martin's Press, 2010.

Kinsey, Christopher. *Private Contractors and the Reconstruction of Iraq: Transforming Military Logistics.* New York: Routledge, 2009.

Knights, Michael. *Cradle of Conflict: Iraq and the Birth of Modern U.S. Military Power.* Annapolis, Md.: Naval Institute Press, 2005.

Knights, Michael, ed. *Operation Iraqi Freedom and the New Iraq: Insights and Forecasts.* Washington, D.C.: Washington Institute for Near East Policy, 2004.

Kozlowski, Francis X. *The Battle of An-Najaf.* Washington, D.C.: U.S. Marine Corps History Division, 2005.

Lebovic, James H. *The Limits of Military Capability: Lessons from Vietnam and Iraq.* Baltimore: Johns Hopkins University Press, 2010.

Lee, Lavina. *U.S. Hegemony and International Legitimacy: Norms, Power, and Followership in the Wars of Iraq.* New York: Routledge, 2010.

Mansoor, Peter R. *Baghdad at Sunrise: A Brigade Commander's War in Iraq.* New Haven, Conn.: Yale University Press, 2008.

Mills, Dan. *Sniper One: On Scope and Under Siege with a Sniper Team in Iraq.* New York: St. Martin's Press, 2008.

Mockaitis, Thomas R. *Iraq and the Challenge of Counterinsurgency.* Westport, Conn.: Praeger Security International, 2008.

Moore, Robin. *Hunting Down Saddam: The Inside Story of the Search and Capture.* New York: St. Martin's Press, 2004.

Munson, Peter J. *Iraq in Transition: The Legacy of Dictatorship and the Prospects of Democracy.* Washington, D.C.: Potomac Books, 2009.

Myers, Richard B. *Eyes on the Horizon: Serving the Frontlines of National Security.* New York: Threshold, 2009.

O'Donnell, Patrick K. *We Were One: Shoulder to Shoulder with the Marines Who Took Fallujah.* Cambridge, Mass.: DaCapo, 2006.

Ricks, Thomas E. *The Gamble: General David Petraeus and the American Military Adventure in Iraq, 2006–2008.* New York: Penguin Press, 2009.

Rogers, Paul. *Iraq and the War of Terror: Twelve Months of Insurgency, 2004/2005.* New York: Palgrave Macmillan, 2006.

Rosen, Mir. *The Triumph of the Martyrs: A Reporter's Journey into Occupied Iraq.* Washington, D.C.: Potomac Books, 2008.

Ryan, David, and Patrick M. Kiely, eds. *American and Iraq: Policy-Making, Intervention, and Regional Politics.* New York: Routledge, 2009.

Samuel-Azran, Tal. *Al Jazeera and U.S. War Coverage.* New York: Peter Lang, 2010.

Scheuer, Michael. *Marching towards Hell: America and Islam after Iraq.* New York: Free Press, 2008.

Schumacher, Gerald. *A Bloody Business: America's War Zone Contractors and the Occupation of Iraq.* St. Paul, Minn.: Zenith Press, 2006.

Schwab, Orrin. *The Gulf Wars and the United States: Shaping the Twenty-first Century.* Westport, Conn.: Praeger Security International, 2008.

Swansborough, Robert H. *Test by Fire: The War Presidency of George W. Bush.* New York: Palgrave Macmillan, 2008.

Thompson, Alexander. *Channels of Power: The UN Security Council and U.S. Statecraft in Iraq.* Ithaca, N.Y.: Cornell University Press, 2009.

Tucker, Mike. *Ronin: A Marine Scout/Sniper Platoon in Iraq.* Mechanicsburg, Pa.: Stackpole Books, 2008.

Tucker, Mike. *Operation Hotel California: The Clandestine War Inside Iraq.* Guilford, Conn.: Lyons Press, 2009.

Ucko, David H. *The New Counterinsurgency Era: Transforming the U.S. Military for Modern Wars.* Washington, D.C.: Georgetown University Press, 2009.

Weinberger, Caspar W. *Home of the Brave: Honoring the Unsung Heroes in the War on Terror.* New York: Forge, 2006.

INDEX

Note: **Boldface** page numbers indicate biographical entries. *Italic* page numbers indicate photographs.